War and Law Since 1945

War and Law Since 1945

GEOFFREY BEST

CLARENDON PRESS · OXFORD

*This book has been printed digitally and produced in a standard specification
in order to ensure its continuing availability*

OXFORD
UNIVERSITY PRESS

Great Clarendon Street, Oxford OX2 6DP

Oxford University Press is a department of the University of Oxford.
It furthers the University's objective of excellence in research, scholarship,
and education by publishing worldwide in

Oxford New York

Auckland Bangkok Buenos Aires Cape Town Chennai
Dar es Salaam Delhi Hong Kong Istanbul Karachi Kolkata
Kuala Lumpur Madrid Melbourne Mexico City Mumbai Nairobi
São Paulo Shanghai Singapore Taipei Tokyo Toronto

with an associated company in Berlin

Oxford is a registered trade mark of Oxford University Press
in the UK and in certain other countries

Published in the United States
by Oxford University Press Inc., New York

© Geoffrey Best 1994

ISBN 0-19-820699-2

Cover illustration: remains of German tanks at Sidi Rezegh in Libya, Imperial War Museum.

'In memory of Pierre Boissier and of Hedley Bull'

Preface

This book is the outcome of many years' thinking and writing about certain questions arising from the relationship between what we call civilization and war. For instance, why do different societies have different ideas about right and wrong behaviour in war? How did the system of international law which the European society of States evolved for itself and then disseminated all round the globe come to have at its heart a body of rules and principles for the proper conduct of wars, and why were they formulated just so? And, irrespective of whether it may have worked well or badly in times past, does this body of rules and principles in our own time successfully moderate the conduct of wars (armed conflicts, as many nowadays prefer to call them) as the theory of our civilization expects it to do?

It is with the third of these questions—not 'why do wars happen?' but 'what happens in wars?'—that this book is mainly concerned. War, in one form or another, is something of which many States, societies, and persons in our contemporary world have direct and, very often, unhappy experience. To all the others who are spared direct experience of it, war remains a subject of intense anxiety and interest because of the sympathy and indignation felt for its victims by onlookers, who moreover must often reflect that their own immunity might not last for ever. War and the risk of war are universally acknowledged to be, if not the outstanding shame and horror of our age, at least top-equal with the outstanding ones. It is precisely on that account that the parts of international law supposed to control and moderate it, the Laws of War as they were formerly known, have become, in our age, more highly developed than ever before and popularly known as International Humanitarian Law.

Law is not the only means by which the nastiness of war-conduct can be moderated, but it is a prominent one, deep-rooted in the history of our civilization and, it can be argued, rather an admirable one. The present generation has witnessed two big bursts of activity to enlarge and refine it: the first, directly after the Second World War; the second, in the 1970s, with debate about its merits still going on. Almost all armed forces profess to incorporate elements of it in their basic instruction, and some of them are known effectively to do so. So much attention is being paid to it in contemporary debate and reportage about the causes and conduct of wars that one may reasonably guess that more people are now aware of it (or, more likely, bits of it) than in any previous period of human history.

Certainly more lawyers—some of the ablest of them, civilians based in non-military institutions—are engaged in teaching it and in talking and writing about it than ever before. This expansion of the law of war's substance and personnel has included unprecedented efforts to extend general knowledge and appreciation of it; above all, the International Red Cross's programme of virtually unlimited 'dissemination'. Its popular title brings it automatically within the attention-range of everyone interested in what are known as humanitarian and human rights issues and events. The question whether, for all its contemporary sophistication and apparent high repute, it actually works well or not, is therefore one which may be expected to interest a large number and wide range of people.

So much of a lifetime's experience has gone into this book that I wish it were possible to mention all the many persons who have signally helped, guided, and supported me. I beg readers however to believe that while responsibility is emphatically mine alone for whatever may be found wrong in these pages, many others are entitled to share the credit for whatever may be right. Some, to whom I feel more than ordinarily indebted, will be named at the end. But first, I must mention certain institutions which have done much to make the work possible.

The International Committee of the Red Cross, through various of its dignitaries and officials, has been generously supportive and encouraging ever since I had the privilege of introduction to it twenty-three years ago by Pierre Boissier. My admiration for the work of the ICRC is as warm as my regard for those members of its staff whom I have seen most of; and if in recent years I have called upon them less than formerly, it is in large part because I began to fear that over-dependence on them and their great institution might constrain my independence of judgment, or conduce to a misleading impression that I have written a Genevan sort of book. Not everything I write conforms to what, rightly or wrongly, I perceive as ICRC orthodoxy; but nothing that I write is meant to diminish, or indeed is capable of diminishing, the ICRC's uniquely valuable place in the global order of humanitarian things. I trust that readers will have no difficulty in realizing that my long studies of IHL have only fortified my sense of its extreme importance, and my respect for that unique organization which is, so to speak, its curator.

To the Joseph Rowntree Charitable Trust, I am hugely indebted for the means to write Part II of the book. Its generous research grant enabled me to make such use of public archives in the USA, Canada, Australia, France, Ireland, and Sweden as time and authority permitted. There was enough left over to buy a few extremely expensive law books and to pay for secretarial help of the sort which is so helpful to writers whose retirement precedes their mastery of the word processor. Besides gratitude, I owe to these benefactors an apology for having taken so much longer over the work than was at first expected. Illness through much of the 1980s was not the only cause of that delay. The more I thought about my project, and the more I looked at the ordinary run of writing about contemporary humanitarian law, the more did I realize that the most useful book I could write was not the comprehensive description I had originally thought of but an analytical critique; a look from the outside rather than from inside; a critique which moreover would place IHL in among the other great international institutions which have a part in the endeavour to promote peace and to prevent or at least to limit wars. Because I very much dislike war, it is with regret that I have been driven to the conclusion that this branch of international law seems unable to do as much to prevent war as many of us had hoped, or to make its conduct less atrocious. If my explanation of the law's practical shortcomings lends strength to the movement to correct them, I shall feel well rewarded.

Retirement (rather too early, in my case) is a mixed blessing. Time on one's hands is good; but on the other side of that attractive medal loom losses of administrative support and scholarly comradeship. Severe deprivation of those kinds has been kept from me by the generosity of the following institutions, to which I am heartily grateful: the Research School of Social Sciences at the Australian National University, for a three months' fellowship in 1984; the Woodrow Wilson International Center in Washington, DC, for a guest scholarship in 1985; the London School of Economics and Political Science, for three years' fellowship in its Centre of International Studies, 1982–5, followed by academic membership of its International Relations department through 1985–8; and the Warden and Fellows of St Antony's College, for the senior associate membership with which they honoured me when I moved to Oxford and began to help with the work of its IR group in 1988. I am obliged to the Nuffield Foundation for the 'small research grant' which enabled me to have a second bite at the National Archives in Washington in October 1990. And I can hardly find words adequate to say how grateful I am to Ivon Asquith, Anne Gelling, Tony Morris, and others at the Oxford University Press for having remained so patient and considerate throughout so many years of waiting.

For permission to use, to varying extents, books and papers in their keeping, and for assistance in the use of them (almost everywhere I have been impressed by the helpfulness of librarians and archivists), I thank the authorities in charge of the British Library, the Bodleian Library, the Public

Record Office, and the British Red Cross; in the USA, the Library of Congress, the National Archives, and the American Red Cross; the Australian Red Cross and the Australian Archives; the Archives of the Departments of External Affairs in Ottawa, Dublin, and Stockholm; and those of the Ministère des Affaires étrangères at the Quai d'Orsay in Paris.

Two groups of people I must thank by name for their helpfulness. One group is those benevolent persons, experienced in this or that part of the IHL story, who let me talk with them about it and in one way or another sought to advance my understanding of it. All those occasions were informal. None of them took the form of an 'interview'. I was not 'muckraking'. Sometimes I heard nothing I did not know or intuit already. But encounters with persons who have participated in parts of the history one is writing about leave their mark in various ways, and I am sure that the texture of my book would be thinner without them. May I therefore—with profound apologies for omitting such titles as I am aware of, for fear of omitting those I am not—mention as supportive interlocutors at one time or another: Adelouahib Abada, Georges Abi-Saab, George Aldrich, Maggie Black, Melchior Borzinger, Peter Cameron, Daniel Dufour, Brian Hodgson, Jean Hoefliger, Sylvie-Stoyanka Junod, Charles Lysaght, James Makin, Ian Marriott, Toby Nichols, John de Salis, Frank Sieverts, and Waldemar Solf.

And finally there are some individuals I must mention, because of their unfailing helpfulness on many occasions when I have most needed them. Everyone else who has been helpful will, I'm sure, not think me ungrateful to them if I say how particularly grateful I am to (alphabetically, and again omitting titles) Sydney Bailey, François Bédarida, Marigold Best, the late Hedley Bull, Owen Chadwick, Wilhelm Deist, Michael Dockrill, Michael Donelan, Brian Elliot, Hans-Peter Gasser, Françoise Hampson, Michael Howard, Andrew Hurrell, Christiane Johannot (as she then was), Frits Kalshoven, George Kateb, Michael Meyer, Tony Morris (my patient and resourceful editor at the OUP), William V. O'Brien, W. Hays Parks, Adam Roberts, Brian Roberts, the late Christopher Thorne, Michel Veuthey, and Andrew Wheatcroft. Some of them may be surprised to see what they have helped me to write. The responsibility for the book is, of course, and I repeat, entirely mine.

G.B.

Contents

Abbreviations, Short Titles, and Archive References

1. Abbreviations

AEC	Atomic Energy Commission
AmJIL	*American Journal of International Law*
AP1, AP2	Additional Protocols 1 and 2 (1977)
BYIL	*British Yearbook of International Law*
CBW	Chemical and Biological Warfare
CDDH	Conférence Diplomatique sur le Droit Humanitaire (1974–7)
GA	General Assembly (of the United Nations)
GC	Geneva Convention
HCP	High Contracting Party
ICJ	International Court of Justice
ICLQ	*International and Comparative Law Quarterly*
IGO	Inter-Governmental Organization
IHL	International Humanitarian Law
IMT	International Military Tribunal
ILC	International Law Commission
ICRC	International Committee of the Red Cross
IRRC	*International Review of the Red Cross*
NGO	Non-Governmental Organization
OAS	Organization of American States
PASIL	*Proceedings of the American Society of International Law*
POW	Prisoner of War
PP	Protecting Power
PR	Public Relations
UDHR	Universal Declaration of Human Rights (1948)

Short Titles (*of books often referred to*)

Bothe, Partsch, and Solf	Michael Bothe, Karl Josef Partsch, and Waldemar Solf, *New Rules for Victims of Armed Conflicts* (Nijhoff, The Hague, etc., 1982).
Final Record	*Final Record of the Diplomatic Conference of Geneva of 1949*, 3 vols., the 2nd in two parts A and B (Federal Political Dept., Berne, n.d.)
Official Commentary	the ICRCs *Commentary on the Additional Protocols of 8 June 1977* ... (Nijhoff and the ICRC, Geneva, 1987). Yves Sandoz, Christophe Swinarski, and Bruno Zimmerman are listed as editors, but so many other names appear with equal prominence on the title-page, it is not clear which of them would head the poll in a library catalogue.

Oppenheim   L. Oppenheim, *International Law, 2: Disputes, War and Neutrality*, 7th edn. edited by Hersch Lauterpacht (Longmans, London, 1952)

Pictet's *Commentary*   the ICRC's (Official) *Commentary on the Geneva Conventions of 12 August 1949*, 4 vols., one for each of the four Conventions, published in Geneva respectively in 1952, 1960, 1960, and 1958. They are separately edited by a variety of hands, but Jean S. Pictet is described as the 'general editor', and they are always referred to by his distinguished name.

Roberts and Guelff   Adam Roberts and Richard Guelff (eds.), *Documents on the Laws of War* (2nd edn., Clarendon Press, Oxford, 1989).

Schindler and Toman   Dietrich Schindler and Jiri Toman, *The Laws of Armed Conflicts . . .* (2nd edn., Sijthoff, Alphen aan den Rijn, and the Henry Dunant Institute, Geneva, 1981).

Schwarzenberger   Georg Schwarzenberger, *International Law as Applied by International Courts and Tribunals*; ii, *The Law of Armed Conflict* (Stevens, London, 1968).

Archive References

Am RC   The Archives of the American Red Cross, Washington, DC.

AUST   Records of the Department of External Affairs, The Australian Archives, Canberra.

AUST RC Archives and Registry of the Australian Red Cross Society, East Melbourne.

CAN   Records of the Department of External Affairs, Ottawa.

FR   Ministère des Affaires étrangères. Archives et Documentations, Centre des Archives Diplomatiques de Nantes.

IR   Archives of the Irish Department of External Affairs, held in the National Archives, Dublin.

SW   Archives of the Ministry for Foreign Affairs, Stockholm.

UK   Archives of the Foreign Office (FO), Home Office (HO), and War Office (WO) held in the Public Record Office (PRO), Kew, near London.

US   State Department papers held in the Diplomatic Branch of the National Archives, Washington, DC.

If international law is, in some ways, at the vanishing-point of law, the law of war is, perhaps even more conspicuously, at the vanishing-point of international law.

Hersch Lauterpacht, in *British Yearbook of International Law* (1952), 382

PART I

The Background to the
Laws of War

1 | Introduction

War, Law, and the Laws of War

This book's premiss is that there is more armed conflict in the world than is good for its inhabitants and the reputation of their species as one characterized by the faculty of reason and a sense of morality. War always has been and still remains a problem and puzzle from many points of view. The author does not believe that war must in all circumstances be a bad thing or the worst of all conceivable things, but he is among those who believe that there has often been and that there continues to be more war and armed struggle than there should be, and that much of it is more deadly, destructive, and cruel than it need be. Law is far from being the only means by which humankind and its civilizations have sought to reduce the incidence and to mitigate the effects of public and political violence, but it is—not least because of its ties to religion and ethics—one of the most interesting of them; one moreover which contemporary preoccupations with humanitarianism and human rights have made rather fashionable. The purpose of this book is to examine its place and usefulness in this global context.

What, then, has law to do with war? The question is all the more worth putting because at first sight law and war appear to be opposites. The Romans, who knew a lot about both, left a broad hint that indeed they were so: *inter arma silent leges*. If law signifies the calm hearing of ordered arguments and the settlement of disputes not by violence but by lights of justice and reason, how can it be consistent with an institution which represents the turning from rational discourse in order to settle disputes by a trial of armed strength? Resort to the violence of armed conflict, with all its usual chances and accidents, its frequent furies and inhumanities, its lists of casualties, trails of desolation, and legacies of hatred, looks like the antithesis of everything comprised in that ark of civilization's covenant, the rule of law. War unquestionably has those unruly, disreputable, and horrid attributes. They are a truth-telling and legitimate way of representing it. They are among the reasons why pacifists decide to have nothing to do with it and why conscientious non-pacifists hesitate before resorting to war or (supposing that they have any choice) letting it be forced upon them. But they are not the whole of the story. There is a more acceptable version of it; the other side of the coin, bearing another dimension of its paradoxical meaning.

What happens in war is one thing; why war happens is another. Considered as a political institution, as 'organized violence carried on by political units against each other' and as 'an inherently normative phenomenon' distinct from mere violence, war can look less formless.[1] This is war's less unacceptable aspect, which lends a degree of respectability to its title to a central place in international history and in the study of international relations. Seen in this light, war (which for the political scientist includes the threat and capability of it) is simply an irreducible matter of historical and political fact of which it is sensible to make the best rather than the worst because it can be seen as indispensable to the making of necessary change in the relations of States and the maintenance of desirable order among them. No wonder, then, that international law from its earliest days—when of course it went under other names, e.g. in Romano-Europe, *jus gentium*, more or less translatable as the law of nations—had close to its heart the laws and customs of war.

Part I of this book offers a sketch of the essentials of the history of that branch of international law from those earliest days until the first half of the present century. Readers who are inclined to be sceptical about the possibility of law restraining war will there find evidence of its having sometimes and to some extent done so; certain periods of history and certain circumstances having been more propitious for it than others. The historical record of the law of war does not support the proposition, beloved of some men (I am not sure whether I ought to say 'men and women') of violence and self-styled 'realists', that the very idea of it is absurd or delusory; although, as shall be shown in Part III, contemporary history and circumstances have in many respects proved so unpropitious as to give the cynics and sceptics a good deal of encouragement. That apart, the idea of an international law of war, paradoxical though it must at all times seem and peculiarly difficult for it though present times are, is as valid and valuable as ever it has been. The evidence presented in these pages speaks for itself.

---

[1] Hedley Bull, from whom these quotations are taken (*The Anarchical Society: A Study of Order in World Politics* (London, 1977), 184 and his review of Walzer in *World Politics*, 31 (1979), 588–99), thus (in the former work) elaborates this crucial definition: 'Violence is not war unless it is carried out in the name of a political unit; what distinguishes killing in war from murder is its vicarious and official character, the symbolic responsibility of the unit whose agent the killer is. Equally, violence carried out in the name of a political unit is not war unless it is directed against another political unit.'

Public International Law, and the Law of War as Part of It

But, some readers may be asking themselves, what of international law itself? Our war-laden branch of the legal tree cannot be isolated from the trunk that bears it. The part should be considered in the context of the whole, and one does not have to go far along any channel of international studies nowadays before bumping into questions about the nature and status of international law; meaning in this context, of course, *public* international law, as distinct from the overlapping more private sort which is indispensable for most of the conduct of trade, finance, personal disputes, property dealings, and so on. This is no place, nor am I a properly qualified person, for comprehensively making the case for international law's reality and importance. But something of the sort must be attempted, lest the sceptic, recovered from the rebuff he received in the last stage of the argument, find an opening for the renewal of his criticisms in this one.

The prima-facie complaint about international law is simply this: that it holds together better on paper than in practice, and that States determined to ignore it can do so more or less with impunity; and can find, it must be added, international lawyers to produce a reading of the law in their favour. The Kaiser and his ministers have for many decades been held up to obloquy for calling a treaty 'a scrap of paper', but that is because of the power of British and French propaganda and because Britain and France won the war; not because Germany was by any means the only country to have treated instruments of international law as so much waste paper.

This weakness of the law is a consequence of the fact that international law is first and foremost inter-State law, made by States for their own purposes and advantages; which have not so far been perceived to demand, on occasions when their 'vital interests' are dramatically at stake, submission of their independent freedom of action ('sovereignty') to effective supranational institutions. In other words, and arguing from the national analogy which comes naturally to all of us, if States wish to break or bend the law, there is no force corresponding to the policeman, the bailiff, and the court officer to stop them doing so; not to mention superior enforcement by the judge, the prison governor, and the commander of troops called out to aid the civil power.

The weakness cannot be denied, but it is not nearly so damaging as is easily suggested by surveying the workings of international society from the outside. The showy, notorious breaches are relatively rare. States observe all of the law most of the time and most of it all the time because they find it convenient, profitable, and helpful. It is the normal and regular guide to the conduct of relations between States when they are 'at peace' with one another; the practice of States is one of its main sources, and not surprisingly therefore one of its main functions is to assist the practice of States.

Rules and practices like this in a numerous and mixed society demand a certain amount of give and take from the members. States do not always relish the immediate consequences of their obligations but by and large they honour them. States that pick and choose which rules to keep and which to break risk getting a bad name and sooner or later suffering in consequence. They may, if they are superpowerful or especially egoistic, desperate or ideologically obsessed, decide on particular occasions not to mind the name-calling and to bear with the consequences. Instances from events of the past few decades flock at once to mind, not to mention the lamentably special case of the breaches of human rights law which are standard practice in many countries, and to a smaller extent persistent in most. The heavens have not fallen upon the doers of these calculated illegalities and (placing on some of them the most favourable interpretation) extralegalities. The lawbreakers and law-benders have, in popular parlance, got away with it. But the efforts that have in almost all instances been made to produce legal (at any rate, legal-sounding) justifications, and to excuse the denounced deeds as exceptional, speak volumes. No State denies the virtue of the idea of international law, and the particular breaches of the present system of it which States may exceptionally engage in are not necessarily to be read as gestures towards the invalidation of the system as a whole. States which take liberties with the system nevertheless assume that the system survives and will continue to survive despite them: an assumption which evidently has some rude truth in it, although one may well ask whether the system can forever stand such strains.

The sceptic's second line of attack proceeds directly from this latter point. Still inclining to brand as bogus a legal system which lacks a sovereign power of enforcement, he returns to the charge by comparing this international system, so-called, with what he holds up by contrast as a *real* legal system: a national one. It is real and respectable, he says, because it is unitary and coherent, a pyramid or scaffolding of authorities crowned by a sovereign power able to make the law work and to guarantee that lawbreakers suffer. Anything less, he likes to maintain, is not worth the great name of law.

This argument sounds impressive but its premises are faulty. Its description of a national system of law is an ideal one, not overly recognizable in reality. This is what political and legal theorists want us to believe national systems are like, not what they actually are like. Are there many countries in which every subject or citizen obeys every law and every disobedient act is infallibly detected and punished? There are not; and the very idea of such countries, incidentally, is apt to make one wonder whether they would be pleasant to live in. On the other hand, there are plenty of countries, both pleasant and unpleasant to live in, where many laws are repeatedly broken, where the rule of law is just a sinister bad joke, and where lawbreakers are rarely brought to book. If the argument is pursued to the point of observing that desuetude and neglect of law, carried beyond a certain just-bearable point which will vary from place to place, undoes a State's claims to respect (because it is failing to do what States exist to do), the answer can only be that States of such disreputable character nevertheless usually continue to be accepted as members of international society, albeit subject to various degrees of cold-shouldering. Whether international law is less observed in its proper sphere than is the national law of some of the disreputable States that will by now be in the reader's mind, must be difficult to determine.

Differences between the legal systems of States and the inter-State legal system are of course much more significant than likenesses; their juxta-position in the previous paragraph was simply to help make the point that, whatever the latter's defects, they cannot be called into evidence to damn it without implicitly damning many of the former too. But one of the apparent differences between the systems invites reflective comment, because it constitutes one of international law's more peculiar characteristics. Much international law of the contemporary age, not least in the humanitarian and human rights fields, and especially where the General Assembly of the UN is involved, is 'normative'. Normative means standard-setting; adding to established State practice, the aspirational concept of State practice as it is expected, intended, or hoped to become at some future date. The common man may find it bothersome that the great word Law can now be used in two such different senses: what is to be observed and enforced here and now, and what is aimed at as observable and enforceable later on. The international affairs community has sought to make the best of this split by inventing a distinction between two sorts of law: 'hard' and 'soft', the difference being that whereas there is some possibility of retribution being presently visited upon breaches of the first, no such possibility is attached to the second. If the sceptic, persistently returning to the fray, eggs on the common man to note that 'soft law' is not what he is used to in his own country, the answer to both of them is, again, that national law may actually not be of such uniformly 'hard' consistency as its political theorists and propagandists like to claim. A Briton, for example, finds it difficult to find much hardness in the laws supposed to regulate the speed and sobriety of drivers of vehicles on his country's roads, the fouling by dogs of his country's pavements and public parks, and such public use of radio and cassette head-sets as may annoy fellow passengers in trains and buses. It is not only in the international field that the power to set standards may turn legislators into visionaries.

International law and national law are least alike in their sources. Here at any rate, in national systems of law, the theorists' sovereign stands more or less unchallenged, allowing a clear view of where law comes from and how it is made. The legislature or legislative branch is a familiar facet of every constitution. But the sources of international law are more complicated and confusing, largely because there is so much overlapping between them. State practice, already mentioned, is one of them. Practices and standard observances which States generally find so helpful to their intercourse that they become formalized and habitual tend to turn into Customary Law. Somewhere beneath customary law's foundations are certain general or fundamental principles, e.g. 'elementary considerations of humanity'.[2] Some of the most fundamental of these are said by some experts to be *jus cogens*, i.e. to be 'peremptory norms', which there can be no argument about. (Nevertheless there is!) Formal arrangements and contracts between States (on matters which, by the way, may already be lodged in customary law) are registered in Treaties, Conventions, and Covenants; also, as has within the last generation become increasingly apparent, under such less impressive titles as Agreements and Accords. International law thus originated is generally called 'conventional law', which is confusing to the common man, whose natural inclination is to think that conventional means customary. He must become even more bewildered when informed that (parts of) 'conventional law', when accepted by almost all States for some consider- able length of time, can actually become 'customary law', as for example the International and other Military Tribunals after the Second World War considered to have happened to parts, at least, of the fourth Hague Convention's Land-Warfare Regulations, and the 1929 POW Convention.[3]

---

[2] The Corfu Channel case: International Court of Justice, Judgment on the merits, 9 Apr. 1949, p. 22 of the official report (Leyden, Sijthoff, n.d.)

[3] I cautiously say 'parts, at least' because of the caution expressed by Theodor Meron, 'The Geneva Conventions as Customary Law' in *AmJIL* 81 (1987), 348–70 at 359, and because of the way it was put by Lauterpacht in his magisterial article in the 1952 *BYIL* 373 n.: 'The IMT at Nuremberg and various other war crimes tribunals affirmed expressly, in relation to the treatment of POWs, that numerous provisions of the Hague and Geneva Conventions were merely declaratory of existing international law.' Even Kalshoven, as authoritative as any contemporary writer can be, seems to tread a bit warily when he refers to this matter in *Constraints on the Waging of War* (Geneva, 1987) at 18: 'It remains for us to mention here that

Such are the several springs from which public international law—otherwise and more comprehensively known as the international law of peace, war, and neutrality—originates and the channels through which it flows: 'A mighty maze, but not without a plan.' The plan is the wish and will of States that this body of law which they have caused or permitted to come into being shall do what it is meant to do: ease and sweeten their relations not only in peace (supposedly their usual relationship) but also in war, which political theory generally has viewed as the less usual state of affairs and which therefore, if moderated by law, may be hoped not to mark more than a passing storm in States' normal relations.

The idea of the rule of law in international relations has reference to war no less than to peace, and in the international law of war that idea becomes flesh. Our sceptic may here insist on making another intervention. He will argue that *this* branch of international law, whatever its occasional limited successes, is in the final account nothing more than camouflage and fraud; not the astonishing paradoxical achievement of civilization that it is sometimes represented to be, but rather a convenient means by which some theorists of civilization cast a comforting veil over the frightening features of the juggernaut from whose progress its own seems inseparable. On this occasion, the sceptic may be more difficult to silence. The law of war has never functioned as well as has, for much of the time, the law of peace. The reasonable civilized man, knowing what war means, could never have expected it to; he would be content with it as the lesser of a choice of evils; as, at least, better than nothing. Its history contains ups as well as downs. In course of the ups—in certain relatively happy times, places, and episodes—it has achieved more than the sceptic allows. It has shown that it can approximate to the civilized idea of it. But whether or not the ups can be judged collectively to outweigh the downs, and whether the downs can be so prolonged and terrible as effectually to discredit the whole idea and to signify that belief in the law of war is *not* better than nothing—these are questions the sceptic remains free to pose because neither the historian nor

according to a widely held view, the principles and rules embodied in [the Hague Regulations] had, by the time of the outbreak of World War II, been so widely accepted by States that they had become part of international customary law. After the war, this view was endorsed in so many words by the IMT at Nuremberg.' The IMT's endorsement appears in its much-reproduced judgment; section headed 'The Law relating to War Crimes and Crimes against Humanity', fifth paragraph. It comes on p. 65 of the British HMSO's official publication of it (London, 1946, Cmd. 6964). Intertwining with conventional and customary law is the other, slighter, contributive source of case law, as determined in the variety of courts (many of them national, like maritime prize courts and military tribunals) where international law may be administered.

any other scholar can pretend to answer them. The best that any of us can do is to learn from the historians and social scientists who study the causes of armed conflicts and what goes on in them; attempt to distinguish the cultural and political circumstances which minimize rather than maximize the risks and evils of armed conflicts; consequently to promote and support such policies in our own and other reachable States as are calculated to create those circumstances; and to be ready to bear the unpopularity of them, for they are likely to be strong-minded and forceful.

Objectives, Methods, and Limitations of This Book

My aim and hope in writing this book have been that it will interest readers in realms as different as politics, history, ethics, military studies, and law. Let me explain to these different interest-groups and the more general readers ranged behind them, what they may respectively get out of it—and what they may not.

In a world where news of armed conflicts comes before us every day and comment on them is often in terms of their lawlessness, there is no need to point out the relevance of a book about those parts of international law which purport to moderate the violence of wars and to protect and succour their victims. It cannot be said that books in this field are lacking. The international law of war, alias humanitarian law, has become something of a boom industry in the legal realm and raises a regiment of professional experts. The way in which those experts write about it and debate it among themselves, however, is not often directly communicable to all the others who also have pressing interests of their own in the subject and who, some of them, also write and confer increasingly about it, conscious that, beyond the legal experts with whom they may happily have contact, are many from whom they are cut off.

I began my professional career as a historian mainly of British religious and cultural matters. Becoming interested in the ethics and sociology of war, I moved from insular to international and from civil towards military subjects in mid-career; applied myself to the history and present state of the law of war and the working of its institutions; and concluded at last that the best base from which to conclude my work and to write this book is the branch of studies loosely known as International Relations, with whose representatives at the London School of Economics and the University of Oxford I have happily been associated over the past ten years. If the book is a mixture of bits of all the so-called academic disciplines with which I have had dealings over the past forty years, that is the inevitable outcome of the way my mind has moved. I have had to follow where the argument has led, and I truly believe that an adequate appreciation of the importance to the world of international humanitarian law—an appreciation, that is, of how it has become part of what we think of as civilization, and of how much civilization depends upon it—does in principle require the fraternizing of all the disciplines and interests involved in it. The subject has too much of humanity's blood and future in it to be safely confided to the care of any one of the several parties with claims on it. But whether my own attempt to bring them together turns out to be successful, only my critics (I hope they will not be too sectarian in spirit) will be able to judge.[4]

To one group of readers however I must issue the warning that this book, if taken in the wrong way, could seriously endanger their professional health. I refer to law students. I hope many of them *will* read it, and enjoy my explanations of how this great subject of their studies has come to be as it is, how much besides law has gone into the making of it, and how it functions within the politics of international society. But I am not a lawyer, I am under no obligation to think about law as lawyers have to, nor do I try to write about it as they do, e.g. when I write of a practice being conventional, I mean conventional in the sense of customary, habitual, not in the international-legal sense of deriving from a convention alias treaty. The aspects of it which seem important to the conduct of my analysis and the telling of my story are not necessarily coextensive with those which must be important in legal exegesis and disputation; nor do I, writing with such purposes and within such limits, pretend to cover the ground as comprehensively as a professional expert has to do. Anyone who uses this book in preparation for an academic examination in the international law of war is asking for trouble!

---

[4] There is one area of IHL to which I may not have given, within my chosen frame, sufficient space, and that is the law of war at sea. The reader will indeed find pages on submarines, hospital ships, mines, and blockade; he will not find much on the matters of which so much was heard during the Iran–Iraq war of the 1980s: rules of engagement, reflagging, territorial waters, and war zones. For this lack I have no better excuse to offer than that the law of war at sea has always been something of a subject apart (which is how naval authorities like to have it!) and that the current efforts of the ICRC and other bodies to promote a clarification and modernization of it have not yet come to anything. There is a good survey of the present situation by Ross Lebow. 'The Iran–Iraq Conflict in the Gulf: The Law of War Zones', in *ICLQ* 37 (1988), 629–44. See further, Dieter Fleck, 'Rules of Engagement for Maritime Forces and the Limitation of the Use of Force under the UN Charter', in *German Yearbook of IL*, 31 (1988), 166–86, and W. J. Fenrick, 'Legal Aspects of Targeting in the Law of Naval Warfare', in *Canadian Yearbook of IL*, 29 (1991), 238–81.

Terminology and Abbreviations

I have not striven for overall consistency in my references to the principal subject of the book, because styles of referring to it have changed over the years and I have allowed the form of my reference to change with them. By the later nineteenth century, this subject was known in the English-speaking world as 'the law of war' or some close variant thereof, e.g. 'laws and customs of war' or 'international law of war and peace'. In Germany and France, where most of the scholarly writing then came from, it was respectively *Kriegsrecht* and *Droit de la guerre*. Within the past generation, for reasons explained in due course, it has become fashionable to give it softer-sounding titles, substituting 'armed conflict' for 'war' and introducing the word 'humanitarian'. My admired colleague Adam Roberts, Professor of International Relations at Oxford and a noted expert on my subject, is of sterner stuff and continues in the second edition of his (co-edited) collection of documents to call them the *laws of war*. The other standard collection, by the Swiss experts Schindler and Toman, calls them the *laws of armed conflict*. In the voluminous collections of essays (a.k.a. Festschriften) recently presented to two of its most distinguished dignitaries, Jean Pictet and Frits Kalshoven, it is called (*international*) *humanitarian law of armed conflicts*. Many people nowadays shorten it for convenience into simply 'humanitarian law'. I am not myself much attracted by this fashion, for reasons which will appear below, but I understand why it has happened and I am very anxious not to deter its followers from reading what I have to say, because they cannot care more about the subject than I do. Therefore I have let the law(s) of war of the earlier part of the book become international humanitarian law in the later. But with so much cross-referencing, some inconsistencies are bound to occur, for which I apologize to those whom they offend.

International humanitarian law being something of a mouthful, I shall consistently abbreviate it into IHL. There will be other space-saving abbreviations, which it is convenient to introduce here as part of a thumbnail sketch of the main lines of the subject's history. The legal instruments at the heart of it have since 1864 been the Geneva Conventions, the GCs; the latest and current GCs date from 1949, and the third of them deals with POWs, prisoners of war. There are also the Hague Conventions of 1899 and 1907 and the Land War Regulations annexed to the 4th Convention of 1907 (not abbreviated); and since 1977 the two Protocols Additional to the Geneva Conventions, AP1 and AP2. These Protocols themselves are the product of a great 1974–7 conference which will appear under the initials CDDH, the accepted shortening for the Geneva Conférence Diplomatique sur la Réaffirmation et le Développement du Droit International Humanitaire applicable dans les Conflits Armés. The institutions most important to IHL are the various elements of what is now properly known as the International Red Cross and Red Crescent movement; the reader will often meet the International Committee of the Red Cross as the ICRC and sometimes simply the RC, the Red Cross, to indicate the movement at large. When explaining the treaties and their supposed operation, I shall shorten High Contracting Parties to HCPs and Protecting Powers to PPs. No need, I'm sure, to explain what is meant by the UN. PR must also be familiar to the contemporary reader. Its occurrence here may surprise him; but the fact is that it is impossible realistically to discuss the uses of humanitarian and human rights law without taking note of the part they are made to play in the booming political business of public relations; something which includes the age-old concern of propaganda but nowadays has much more to it. Human rights law has come to matter more and more in this field; UDHR is how its book of Genesis, the 1948 Universal Declaration of Human Rights, will be referred to.

2 | The Laws of War from Early Modern Times to the Second World War

An Essay on the Essentials

No one can tell how war began among men but there is evidence of it from earliest times; evidence not just in the form of weapons meant for fighting and of human remains broken by weapons, which cannot of themselves signify anything as serious as war, but of fighting by organized groups for collective purposes. Protection or seizure of territory and/or property is the most likely purpose, but it is not difficult to suppose that the causes may also have included affronted pride and honour, shortage of women and other essential breeding stock, or simply the indulgence of the lust, greed, and megalomania of despotic rulers.

States have been known throughout history to engage in armed hostilities for such base purposes; but so also, and more frequently, have gangs of bandits, outlaws, freebooters, and criminals, who for that matter are well capable of fighting for horses, women, and territory too. The distinctions between States and other collectivities, between public war and other forms of armed conflict, are in many respects crucial, and the critical reader may be assured that they will be properly observed when the context so requires. In one respect, however, the distinction is immaterial. All collectivities, whatever their political character and whether they have any political character or not, generate their own codes of conflict behaviour. What at some levels are the rules of chivalry between knights, the mutual respect of gentlemen, and fair play among sportsmen, at other levels are honour among thieves and the rules of vendetta. The codes which become the social ethics and laws of States (and from thence, ultimately, the public law of inter-State relations) find their largest practical significance in historical and political terms, but their working can never be properly understood without bearing in mind the wide spread of their social and psychological roots.

From the times of the earliest oral and written testimony there is evidence that those who planned and conducted public war could admire and recommend practices designed to control its course and moderate its nastiness. Rulers might display, and like to be seen to display, humane dispositions; or, in shaping their war aims, to reckon it profitable not to be more destructive than was unavoidable. Priests and prophets (besides perhaps having a part in shaping the minds of rulers) might deprecate excessive slaughter or plead the cause of 'the innocent'. Warrior castes would enforce among themselves codes of conduct determining their methods of combat, and these might tend to the sparing of life—the lives, at least, of their own kind. Military organizers might wish to limit the loss of expensively trained soldiers, difficult to replace. Generals could have little difficulty recognizing the good sense of not wasting lands off which their armies, now or later, would have to feed. And so on. An inclination towards restraints and prohibitions in war is perceptible among enough of our species' earlier civilizations and/or cultures for the historian of humankind to regard it as essentially a normal aspiration, more or less as old as war itself; and to that extent, encouraging to the belief that our own generation's attempts to pursue it in the later twentieth century have the weight of history behind them.

They do. But they have also behind them as a matter of historical record repeated disappointments of those aspirations and failures of those attempts, which are in many respects deceptive and illusory. Too much can be made of them, especially by those who wish to persuade us that the failures of conflict-restraint in our own time stand in shameful contrast with what they believe to be its earlier successes. Failures were no less in earlier times than in our own, and from similar causes. What rulers or priesthoods enjoin as best-case behaviour can have little relation to what armed forces actually do in worst-case situations; and it is into such situations, as a matter of course, that the natural hazards and hardships of war and the frequent bunglings of military planners often throw them. The application of those admired humanitarian injunctions in any case has to be critically appraised. We have to inquire in each instance: What kind and what level of war was in view when those injunctions were issued? Restraints enjoined, and even enforced, in dealing with a respected and culturally related foe have usually had nothing to do with what is expected in conflict with those perceived as barbarians, savages, infidels, subhumans, and so on.

Then there are circumstances to be brought into account. High standards of humanity and restraint observed in fair and easy campaigning times can crack and crumble, even *vis-à-vis* respected enemies, once the going gets rough. As for religion: no major religion's claim to wartime humanitarianism is to be taken at face value. Setting aside the historical facts that wars have often had religious causes and that wars perceived as crusades or holy wars have always been among the most savage, it is not denied that every major faith can produce selections of texts purporting to moderate its believers' demeanour in war. It would be presumptuous to doubt the earnestness with which those believers may desire to behave so; but consider from how many wartime sources dross pours upon purely religious ideals! Apart from the normal mix-up with competing or parallel affiliations (tribal, racial, national, cultural, etc.) which spiritual leaders are sometimes reluctant to recognize or admit, there are in armed forces and above all when on active service the close and urgent pressures of peer-group, patriotism, brutalization, hardship, temptation, fear, and frenzy. It is a commonplace that under the hammers of war the best of men can be driven to behave in the worst of ways.

That cautionary commentary on the conditions of observance of the laws of war, ancient and modern alike, is offered in no cynical or destructive spirit but as introduction to a realistic scene-setting for my study of its most recent and contemporary phases. It is at any rate obvious that the historical record of the antiquity, ubiquity, and persistence of proposals for limiting the conduct of war proves the undying attraction to at least some sectors of most societies known to us, of the idea that war, so long as it cannot be done away with or done without, must be subjected to ethical and legal controls. In principle applicable equally to conflicts within States and to conflicts between them, this idea naturally had its part in the primitive codes for the conduct of inter-State relations which can be made out in the regions of some of the more sophisticated early civilizations: in India, for example, and in what we now call Indonesia and the Middle East; in Greece and Rome and in the realms of Islam. The ever more elaborate code which evolved in western Europe from the fifteenth century *pari passu* with its commercial, maritime, and military expansion could be conscious of none other than Mediterranean and European sources; but the relative ease with which that regionally developed model entered into universal service as the public international law the world knows today is largely because the ideas behind it might be not unfamiliar to other regions and because some of those regions already had experience of something similar.[1]

Of the branch of that public international law which has to do particularly with war, I published a general modern history in 1980, titled *Humanity in Warfare*. It was well received, but if I could start all over again I

[1] This gigantic theme, for long unaccountably neglected by International Relations writers, was at last opened up by Hedley Bull and Adam Watson (eds.), *The Expansion of International Society* (Oxford, 1984). I should like to think that my book adds to that one a facet which it happens to lack.

would write it differently. In the present book, which is to some extent the earlier one's sequel, I take opportunity *en passant* to remedy what I now see to have been its defects. Some of these were noticed by reviewers, some were not, and not every reviewer's criticisms were sensible. One popular historical writer, of so choleric a disposition that he had evidently not been able to bear to read (or skip) beyond the first chapter, complained about my having chosen to begin my story so late in time as the eighteenth century. The reason I did so still seems to me good. Chivalry, honour, discipline, and self-restraint had been common enough concepts among the military-minded time out of mind, and the ancient world was still a major repository of admired exemplars whom the publicists liked to cite. But it was only during the maturity of the Enlightenment that something recognizably like our modern international law of war achieved full form, that it found in the philosophers and publicists commensurate literary expression, and entered into the common discourse of the ruling élites of the whole European States-system.

More just was the criticism that the book was Eurocentric. It certainly was more so than I now think reasonable. There is no dodging the fact that the great body of law already assembled by the time of the Second World War was entirely of European or (which in a matter like this was culturally much the same thing) American composition. But when it came to the ways that law was used, I focused too much on the wars which Europeans and North Americans fought among themselves, and attended hardly at all to the wars accompanying their imperial and colonial expansions. Perhaps also I was misguided not to look at all at the wars in Africa and Asia fought entirely beyond the Europeans' ken. That lack, if lack it was, is amply remedied here. The armed conflicts that appear in the second half of this book are almost all located in the 'less developed' parts of the world. The international law of war, whose very mixed experiences in those regions it is this book's aim to describe, is no longer exclusively of European and American making. This aspires to be a properly international study of an entirely international subject.

More regrettable, though not inexplicable, was the skimpiness of my treatment in that 1980 book of the years since 1945. Still at that date engaged as a teacher with history rather than international relations, I had as yet no special concern with the contemporary period. To the three world wars (counting that of 1792–1815 as the first, which it effectively was) I extended an indulgence which I denied to the world-wide conflicts of our own time and the extraordinary political circumstances that have accompanied them. In common with most writers of that time, I neglected to notice the growing relevance of the new international law of human rights and I placed too much confidence in the beneficent prospects of the 1977 Additional Protocols. When in doubt, I clung loyally to—as one might put it—the Geneva version of the story instead of pausing to wonder whether there might not be something more or something else to say. About some parts of the contemporary scene unreasonably optimistic, about others unnecessarily pessimistic, I just began at the time of writing to sense what I became well aware of soon after, that I was losing the sense of perspective and direction that had carried me through the earlier chapters. What I wrote in them has quite well stood the test of time. Nevertheless I have changed my mind about a few matters, e.g. the place of Rousseau in the story and the significance of the St Petersburg Declaration, and I believe I can now better identify the things that matter most. This part of the present book is therefore to some extent a revision, at the same time as it is a distillation, of what I wrote fourteen years ago.

Jus ad bellum and *jus in bello* since the Seventeenth Century

The law of war, as a development within European history and Atlantic civilization from the later seventeenth to the turn of the twentieth century, has every appearance of a success story. War remained a respected and, by most informed judgments, necessary element of international relations, but its risks were increasingly well realized and attempts to avoid it (by Great Power pressure or, what was not always quite the same thing, submission to arbitration) often succeeded. When war did happen, battles indeed tended to be more concentratedly murderous for the armed forces engaged in them, but the progress of medical science on the one hand, the vogue for humanitarian activity on the other, did something at last to redress that balance. Civilian populations, for their part, seemed to be suffering proportionately less than previously. Political science recognizes the International Committee of the Red Cross (established, though not at first under that name, in 1863) as the grandest of the pioneer NGOs. In the war department of the history of international law, a new chapter was opened by the Geneva Convention of 1864 (the first multilateral humanitarian treaty) and the St Petersburg Declaration of 1868 (the first treaty for weapons-limitation). The great Peace and Disarmament Conference which convened at The Hague in 1899 was a portent of an altogether unprecedented kind. Progress, which the men (I am not so sure about the women) of the nineteenth century were quick to sense in the changes going on all around them, was sensed in this field too. Wars might become nastier but, it was commonly argued, they would be fewer and shorter. It seemed not impossible, even in as momentous a respect as this, for bourgeois civilization to have its cake and eat it too.

That was soon to be proved a delusion, and it is not difficult to see why. The eighteenth- and nineteenth-century development of the international law of war—remarkable and admirable so far as it went—had grown lopsided. In its preceding major phase, the phase which carried it from cloister and college to court and counting-house and whose crowning text was Grotius's 1625 *De Jure Belli ac Pacis*, it still travelled on tracks laid down in its earliest origins. Its concerns were as much with the causes as the conduct of war; in the convenient technical language of the science, *jus ad bellum* as well as *jus in bello*. By Grotius's time, it was dealing copiously with the question of how men should behave when they were fighting, but it also still dealt seriously with the question whether they should be fighting at all. The rights and wrongs of engaging in war at all were as much part of it as the rights and wrongs of how war was conducted.

But lopsidedness was beginning to show. There had been some point in harping on the *jus ad bellum* through the long run of centuries when the political authorities of Europe were contained within the body of a single Christendom and while there was in the papacy a capacity for universal jurisdiction. The harping became of more nearly theoretical character once that unity had been broken around the turn of the sixteenth century and, moreover, the heads of those States, no matter whether they were resistant to Rome or still faithful to it, were deploying the new political language of sovereignty: independent, autonomous, and almost always, to begin with, of divine right. This did not necessarily also mean unaccountable. Political theorists soon began to debate whether rulers were accountable to God alone or rather to the people—from which latter position it would be no great step to the modern doctrine of popular sovereignty. But no matter whither the political argument about the head of State went, the nation-State itself was on its own, and whether it chose to go to war or not was held to be its own affair, for decision in the light of its own perception of national interest and the extent of its regard—which might of course be very considerable—for the standards of its civilization.

The fact of this development was for long obscured by the continued use of the old *jus ad bellum* language. This was still found useful for presenting the tougher aspects of State policy in a favourable light, but it no longer had any hard attachment in the real world. The idea of a superior authority by which the doings of national governors or governments could be judged had lost the institutional connection which formerly lent it credibility. It lingered longest in the legal and political texts, but finally disappeared from them too. After a phantasmal sort of half-life, it went into the long hibernation which only ended when universal jurisdiction again became something that statesmen could discuss without being thought eccentric or absurd, this side of 1900.

The story however was not all one of loss. While the *jus ad bellum* withered on the bough, the *jus in bello* flourished like the green bay-tree. One might almost believe that some mysterious law of compensation was at work, but the explanation is more commonplace. Europe's political system and standards were changing, but its common culture was undamaged: culture in the broad sense that matters here, the culture of the élites which governed its States, maintained its social standards and ran its armed forces. Through those élites there percolated shared beliefs and a capacity for mutual recognition which moderated the natural force of national and regional attachments. This was no doubt particularly true of the titled aristocracy, whose more cultivated members could be quite cosmopolitan. But in varying measure it applied to the professional classes too, who took a good deal of their social style from the aristocracy, who if they were religious at all could scarcely be anything but Christian, and whose education so far as they had much was rooted in the same Latin and Greek classics. It applied most of all to the profession of arms, whose members were bound also by the extra-strong bond of the code of military honour. Among them above all others there circulated a sense of shared values and mutual respect, particularly favourable to the observation of unwritten rules of honourable and decent behaviour.

That the *jus in bello* should have flourished in eighteenth- and nineteenth-century Europe, to the extent that it was generally known about and considered a good thing, was therefore not surprising. To the officers upon whom almost exclusively lay responsibility for its observance, it was simply part of their professional ethic and way of life. Outlines of it might be learned from simple manuals of military science, weightier studies were increasingly provided by those men of learning who by the early nineteenth century were close to being called international lawyers, but for the most part the laws and customs of war were something the young officer picked up on the job, part of the way his elders thought and talked.

It must not be imagined that those laws and customs made more than an occasional and limited difference to what actually happened in war. The Enlightenment's self-congratulations in particular have to be cautiously appraised. War did not for some golden interlude become a humane activity.[2] The common soldiery, most of it drawn from cultures very different from the officers', went on behaving as it always had done towards enemies and the civilians close to its marches and camps. Deliberate atrocities and avoidable horrors happened as they always had done and always will. But they were publicized and deplored as they had generally not been in earlier times. The desire to reduce the quantity of them was real and by the later eighteenth century convincingly growing. There was an interested public for discussion and argument about the application of the principles of the law in particular cases, those principles were taken for granted, and their base was in the main body of the culture, not merely in its legal superstructure. Never until the later nineteenth century, and not much even then, needed reference be made to treaties of the kind which now fill the contemporary textbooks on the subject. As an English expert wrote, not without a touch of foreboding, in the year when the first of those treaties was signed, 'It is always to be borne in mind that the positive laws of war, like the laws of honour or of etiquette, are creatures of use, though founded in reason and convenience—they are kept alive by tradition, and perish when they become obsolete.'[3]

But within this green garden, the worm was at work. Time would show that the *jus in bello* on its own, with or without treaties, was not going to be muscular and versatile enough to keep war within what decent men might consider acceptable bounds. The officers and gentlemen who took the laws of war in general seriously and valued the idea of minimizing war's nastiness, were in fact restrained by a hand they could not see as clearly as the one they could. The hand they felt rather strongly upon them was that of principle. The hand of which they were hardly yet aware was that of technology. The means at their disposal for injuring, damaging, and killing, however formidable they might seem at the time, were by later standards feeble, short-range, and inaccurate. What they might have done if they had means to do it (weapons, manpower, mobility) is made apparent in the rows about legality and decency which punctuated the military history of the eighteenth and nineteenth centuries. The number and frequency of those rows indicated not weakness in the law of war but vigour, not ignorance but familiarity. The principles of the law and customs of war commanded universal admiration, but their application on particular occasions was something about which men might differ. Apparent breaches of it upset people because they valued it so much. No established military hero or

---

[2] Its horrid realities have recently been powerfully depicted by Christopher Duffy, *The Military Experience in the Age of Reason* (London, 1987).

[3] Montague Bernard, in *Oxford Essays* (Oxford, 1856), 88–136 at 120.

pundit spoke dismissively of it. Revolutionary voices now and then did so but the French armies of the 1790s in practice settled down to behave much like all the others. Napoleon was a stickler for it. Clausewitz's strong language about war's explosive unpredictability and drastic tendencies was aimed not at the principles of chivalry and humanity—he was himself a model of those virtues—but at the wishful-thinkers who wanted to take war out of history: fogies and pedants who said it could be fought according to rule-book and sentimentalists who thought it could be fought with kid gloves. 'War and its forms', he reminded them, 'result from ideas, emotions and conditions prevailing at the time.'[4]

In fact everyone with strong experience of the active conduct of war understood two things very well: first, that its laws and customs could only be observed in relation to circumstances and, second, that in any ordinary tussle between law and military necessity, law would have to be accommodating. To accommodate was not to collapse. Every time something notably nasty happened or was threatened to happen, men's feelings were affronted and principle was promptly invoked; but beyond the sanctuary of absolute prohibitions or inhibitions (relatively few, and in any case experienced by individuals rather than groups), principle was not always easy to tie exclusively to one side of an argument. Men of honour regarded their rules of personal conduct as inflexible, but strategy and tactics and the group behaviour which went with them were something different, to which the inelastic concepts of honour and decency were not directly transferable. A principle which, looked at from one angle seemed to discourage an act of war otherwise feasible and advantageous, might be less forbidding when looked at from another. Some examples will illustrate what I mean.

Even the principle of honour, the self-respecting officer's quasi-religion, was not immune from the force of circumstance. For one thing, national prejudice got in the way; prejudice which itself was graded. Xenophobes like Nelson and snobs like Wellington, however punctilious in proper demeanour towards captured French officers, were reluctant to admit that they were gentlemen. Wellington once remarked, 'A French officer will cut your throat if you tell him he is not a gentleman, but that does not make him one.'[5] Yet so much lower down the scale did British officers place Spaniards, supposed to be their allies, that after the battle of Vitoria in 1813 they walked arm-in-arm around the town with the French prisoners who shared

---

[4] Cited from Bk. 8, ch. 2 of *On War* by Michael Howard and Peter Paret in their edn. of that famous book (Princeton, NJ, 1976), 580.
[5] David Howarth, *A Near Run Thing* (London, 1968), 26.

their mess and snubbed the Spanish officers together. As for inflexibility, it is a nice point whether honour survived intact such a timeless episode as figured in Jean Renoir's 1937 film about the First World War, *La Grande Illusion*. The aristocratic German commandant of the French officers' prison tells the senior French officer (another aristocrat) that he will call off his search of the room if given an assurance that no escape equipment is concealed in it. The French officer gives such an assurance, but the escape proceeds none the less, the escape rope having been concealed not in the room but hanging from its window, outside.

New weapons, at their first introduction, usually cause a furore because the people they are used against allege they are needlessly nasty. It is more often their unaccustomedness and immediate effectiveness that draws obloquy rather than objectively measureable nastiness. They break the bond which will naturally have developed in the victims' minds between the weapons they are used to (together with the tactics they are wont to employ) and the norms of decent, law-abiding warfare which they will have convinced themselves they observe.

Crossbows, gunpowder, red-hot shot and dumdum bullets are well-known cases in point. All except the last-named entered into common usage as soon as technology and finance permitted; dumdums (in the broad meaning of soft-nosed and knife-notched bullets that spread out on entering flesh) however stayed under the ban placed by popular military culture on weapons too horrible (in imagination, at least) to bear thinking of. Some new weapons may, indeed, in those days never even have got off the drawing-board because of ethical objections. A recurrent theme of the more fastidious law-of-war writers over the centuries is of the decent-minded monarch who, approached by an inventor with the offer of a brilliant new way of killing off the enemy, tells the inventor he should be ashamed of himself and sends him packing. Pierre Boissier, the first serious historian of the ICRC, told a version which went further. Louis XV, according to him, not only declined to let his military men make use of just such an invention but incarcerated the inventor for the remainder of his days, so that no other power could be tempted to use it either.[6] Napoleon's men are said to have indignantly turned down an offer by the American engineer Robert Fulton to make some sort of submarine or torpedo that would destroy the British fleet blockading Brest.

---

[6] I heard this from him about 1972. Louis XV appears in a good humanitarian light in his *Histoire du Comité Internationale de la Croix-Rouge: De Solférino à Tsoushima* (Paris, 1963), 172–6. A similar story, with a Doge as hero, appears in James Morris's *Venice* (2nd edn., London, 1983). I cited the next sentence's story in my *War and Society in Revolutionary Europe* (London, 1982), 143 and 312.

It is not easy to establish the extent to which these stories are true. They contain elements of undoubted truths: that the idea of multiplying the horrors of war does not of itself attract reflective warriors, that the killing power alone of new weapons proposals need not be the only criterion applied to them, that the civilian mind may be much more bloodthirsty than the soldierly one, and so on. The history of that part of the law of war dealing with weapons-limitation tells the same story. From the first essay in that vein in 1868 there has been a steady interest in the prohibition of weapons 'of a nature to cause superfluous injury or unnecessary suffering', the latest (1977), English-language version of the ancient formula.[7] But it is an interest that has far outrun achievement. The whole truth about the history of weapons innovations is that almost all of them, whatever the nature and strength of the objections at first encountered, slip into common use as soon as the objectors can acquire them for themselves, whereupon the law adapts accordingly. Just as one generation's luxuries become another's necessities, so weapons or war practices deplored by one age have tended to become accepted by the next. The history of war shows how very difficult it is to stop competitions in armaments between States rich enough to afford them, and how the only weapons States will readily commit themselves to forgo are those of little prospective use to themselves. The period of recent history covered in this book is historically unprecedented in its discovery of weapons which even States able to afford them seem inclined to ban.

Another ancient principle with a wobbly history is that concerned to restrict the effects of fighting to the fighting men themselves. From as far back as there is written evidence of the laws of peoples and the decrees of kings come examples of injunctions to distinguish in combat between warriors and the rest: between the arms-bearing, 'combatant' part of society, the part which alone made it able to conduct war, and the other 'non-combatant' parts whose contribution to war-making could be at most indirect and, in the case of those old men, women, and children who have always figured as the essential non-combatants, probably not even that.

This faint green line of continuity between early human behaviour and modern humanitarianism should not be made to carry more weight than it can bear. Injunctions of more bloodthirsty character could be just as easily collected by anyone minded to do so, and, what matters more, relevant variables are rarely specified—whether the war in question was defensive or offensive, against kinfolk or strangers, of acquisitive or destructive purpose, and so on. Humanitarian commentators in our own time too easily fall into

---

[7] AP1, Article 35(2); the second of the three 'Basic Rules' of Methods and Means of Warfare.

the good-natured error of transferring their universalist principles on to ages and peoples whose views of their own species were strictly discriminatory. The fact nevertheless is that the principle we now know as that of non-combatant immunity had a long history of diffused recognition before the European writers of the nineteenth century incorporated it in their blue-prints for global international law, with a bonus (wondrously characteristic of their epoch) giving protection also to private property.

But another fact has equally to be borne in mind, a fact not from the military but from the political side of the story. Through most of history and, to the best of my knowledge, throughout the world, subjects were expected to share the rough and the smooth of war along with their fighting men, for all, without distinction, were perceived to be in the same political boat. Subjects experienced with their rulers, or as the will of their rulers determined, the consequences of the conflicts in which those rulers became engaged. The humane heart which was capable of perceiving individuals and groups as war-victims had no organic link with the political head. Subjects were in principle committed wholesale to war by their rulers and it was their fate and duty to accept its outcome, however those rulers might shape it.

The harsher logical aspects of that outcome, death and enslavement, were in practice rarely enforced. A *tour d'horizon* of the world history of inter-national warfare suggests that belligerent practice and political theory were generally out of step. A rapid sketch like this can do no more than lightly allude to the sorts of circumstances, the mixtures of motives, which moved rulers to milder conclusions, made wars less wholly destructive and deadly than the political theory of them authorized, and in so doing produced—as an acceptable by-product, if not as an original element—the all-important concept of the non-combatant. Humane disposition, perhaps religiously prompted but not necessarily so, was self-evidently one of those motives. Respect for women in particular and for the helpless in general struck an ancient chivalric chord. So far as the *jus in bello* came from Christian just-war doctrine, that too enjoined respect for 'innocent' persons. Self-interest, less self-evidently, was another. Groups with status, wealth, bargaining power, and contacts beyond their own borders (e.g. monarchs, 'feudal' nobilities, priestly and warrior castes) would evolve arrangements of mutual advantage.

With regard to lower social levels, and wherever settled civilizations had become established, it would become obvious to all but the ideologically demented that living subjects—productive, taxable, serviceable—were preferable to dead ones, especially wherever it could be believed that the region they inhabited was underpeopled. Nothing did more to crystallize and launch the concept of the 'non-combatant' than the perception that besides being harmless he was also useful; a perception ever more widely held wherever and whenever the restrictive principles of mercantilism gave way to the progressive idea that populations were the human capital from which the wealth of nations sprang. That consideration apart, there could be technical problems too. Large masses of human beings, even though they may be unwanted by those with power over them, are actually quite difficult to dispose of without problems and publicity, as Turkey found out when, in the First World War, it decided to get rid of its Armenians, and Germany when, in the Second, it set about the extermination of Europe's Jews and gypsies. It is significant that where only small and compact masses were involved, and massacre consequently was technically feasible, as in the classic case of besieged towns which refused summonses to surrender, the ancient logic continued to colour military practice until quite recent times, and the non-combatant remained exceptionally at risk.

Grotius, Rousseau, and the Non-Combatant

No writing has been more determinant of the consideration given to the non-combatant in the modern history of the law of war than Grotius's early seventeenth-century masterwork already referred to, *De Jure Belli ac Pacis*. Grotius is worth lingering on because in his pages appears, more plainly than ever before, the non-combatant in all his possible roles and situations. Grotius makes an eloquent and sophisticated presentation of the grounds on which non-combatants may be regarded as excludable from the operations and consequences of war. His argument runs more or less on these lines. The non-combatant is almost certainly 'innocent' regarding the issues of the conflict. Involving him in it cannot bring advantage to the combatants, excluding him cannot damage their chances. In any case, what he does is useful not only to society here and now but perhaps also to posterity. Hurting him not only does no good but displays a discreditably vicious temperament; sparing him on the other hand testifies to a decent and compassionate spirit and honourably commands gratitude, affection, and admiration. Rulers and commanders may respect the non-combatant because there are no practical military reasons why they should not do so and because there are good religious and ethical reasons why they should. Their military efficiency will not usually be diminished; and even if in some circumstances it should minimally be so, Christian teaching and chivalric example offer plenty of precedent and justification for taking risks and accepting losses in a virtuous cause.

Grotius's seminal passages about the non-combatant are of course only a part of the broad-branching whole of his considerations on the law of war and peace; just as the book which is of such lasting interest to students of law and war is itself only part of the whole of an extensive and varied *œuvre*, all of it interesting to students of religion and politics.[8] Everything he wrote should, ideally, be read within that over-arching context and with an eye for the characteristics of mind and personality which pervade the whole of it. Characteristics of particular relevance here are his spirit of moderation and his acceptance (whether conscious or not, is immaterial) of ambiguity in the aspects of human affairs and the attitudes of sensible men towards them. He seems to have sought calmly and kindly to stand above the mêlées of a Europe oversupplied with men of superheated temper and dogmatic certainty, men intolerant of questioning and 'incorrectness'. The great treatise with which we are most concerned was prompted in part by his conviction, expressed in paragraph 29 of its lengthy preface, that 'A remedy must be found for those who believe that in war nothing is lawful, and for those for whom all things in war are lawful.'[9] The same concern with both sides of a significant question colours his political writing. Richard Tuck, in whose monograph *Natural Rights Theories, their Origin and Development* Grotius has a prominent place, characterizes his political thought as in some essential respects 'Janus-faced', 'its two mouths speak[ing] the language of both absolutism and liberty'.[10] Humanitarianism (and, for that matter, human rights), we are thus early reminded, has no necessary connection with representative government and democracy. The relevance of these political ideas to his law-of-war doctrine not seeming to be widely understood, it is the aim of the next few pages to explain them.

The core of Grotius's argument for moderation in the conduct of war, and for relief consequently for the non-combatants who were its principal victims, was that, after all, and despite the great weight of popular belief and constant practice to the contrary, moderation was possible. Possible in two essential respects: material and psychological. In the material aspect, war could still be engaged in (it is essential to remember that Grotius had no

---

[8] The quatercentenary of his 1583 birth produced several survey-evaluations of his achievement. Very good, and most relevant to the present book, is Bull, Kingsbury, and Roberts (eds.), *Hugo Grotius and International Relations* (Oxford, 1990).

[9] Often cited; my first sight of it was in H. Butterfield and M. Wight, *Diplomatic Investigations* (London, 1966), 91.

[10] R. Tuck, *Natural Rights Theories, their Origin and Development* (Cambridge, 1979), 79.

doubt that the waging of war *could* be necessary and virtuous) and brought by the fighting-men, whose proper business it was, to its military conclusion without the habitual accompaniment of nastiness to non-combatants. As for the psychological aspect: far from finding such moderated war-practice difficult and unnatural (as militarism and machismo would suggest), men ought to be able to realize it as congenial and even 'natural'. A crucial element of the philosophical tradition within which Grotius was working was the conviction that man was naturally a social animal and that his capacity for sociability was not confined within the borders of his own immediate community. Grotius did not find it, in the philosophic sense, 'natural' to wish to hurt other people and to hate foreigners. Christians misunderstood their faith in their all-too-common failure to understand this. The mind of Grotius, we are thus reminded, was enlightened by a liberal modernist vision of Christianity which did not come naturally to many of his co-religionists.

Grotius was a passionate exponent of the Christian virtue of 'charity'. He believed that it should incline Christian warriors especially to observe all the restraints and compassions which, as his chapters on non-combatants and associated matters were meant to show, were practically possible. Inter-Christian wars, then, whether they were internal or external, were in principle the category of wars most susceptible of the moderations he preached. (It is essential to remember about Grotius that his prescriptions for war-conduct were directed at civil and 'private' wars as well as interna-tional, 'public' ones.) They ought not to be needlessly or thoughtlessly engaged in, and the fact of the common culture shared by both parties would enable them to understand and support each other's efforts at preservation and compassion. But it was not within the Christian world alone that he supposed moderation in warfare to be possible. The natural-law tributary source of his thinking gave him to believe that recognition of common humanity and practice of common kindness were in principle within reach of all religions and cultures, although it is evident that he knew little about the non-Christian ones and that he believed 'barbarians' as such might be morally inaccessible. We are reminded by these intimations of universalism that Grotius has a title to be listed among the founding forefathers of our modern doctrine of human rights.

Grotius is of special importance in the story of humankind's endeavour to restrain warfare, because his contribution to it was set in rock as solid as the idea of civilization itself. The 'restraints' section of the great treatise on the law of war and peace has to be read within its proper context. The work as a whole is often regarded as a landmark not simply in the development of the law of war but, beyond that, of public international law in general and of the idea of a society of States which sustains it.[11]

Grotius's concern to keep warfare within civilized bounds was contained within his concerns to enable States (a concept which for him had fuzzier edges than it has acquired for us) to coexist on reasonably good terms with one another, and to encourage the subjects of States to think of the subjects of other States, even unfamiliar ones, as human kith and kin. It is partly because his expositions of these great matters are done with such compassion and sensitivity that he gives, here as elsewhere, an impression of 'ambiguity', making possible his appeal to parties of differing tendencies. Adopting the terminology of contemporary international relations theory, one may say that analysts on the realist side of its spectrum admire Grotius because he understood that, although States may be said to inhabit a sort of international society, their often separate interests are liable to come into conflict and war is a normal means of resolving it; whereas analysts on the idealist side admire him because his sense of the cultural affinities of States and peoples enables him to envisage them in a relationship better describable as an international community, and because he thought it therefore reasonable that they should be very cautious about getting into conflict with one another and very self-controlled if nevertheless they did so.

The Grotian system of moderate allowances of moderated warfare and of non-combatant immunity within it is so attractive that it is easy to neglect the terms and conditions upon which it rests. To recall them in the light of experience is to be reminded that such a system is far from easy to achieve and to maintain. These are the terms and conditions that matter most. First, Grotius placed much confidence in the 'humanizing' powers of cultural closeness and Christian charity; more confidence than history shows to have been justifiable. Second, as a faithful inheritor of the Christian 'just-war' tradition, he listed the good causes which alone could justify recourse to war: which meant that the gains in banning wars for 'bad' causes had to be set against the losses of allowing, or commanding wars for 'good' ones, which necessarily included wars of self-defence and retribution against 'bad' aggressions. Third, his attractively long list of non-combatants rests on two assumptions: that war-makers are in principle willing and able to divorce military from economic and political considerations, and that the persons whom it is wished to distinguish as non-combatants do objectively appear to be such to sceptical enemy combatants and dispassionate third parties.

[11] Modern analysts of international relations regularly refer to 'the Grotian system' and 'Grotian theory', whether they believe its value is exceptional (as did e.g. Hedley Bull) or simply substantial.

That third condition, which demands reference to Grotius's political theory, is important chiefly as a sort of time bomb which went off under Rousseau, and helps to account for his extraordinary contribution to the non-combatant question, a century and a half later. Grotius's war-makers themselves—sovereign princes, for the most part—might well be absolute to an extent that freed them from any sort of external check on what they did in either the approach to war or the bringing of it to a close. This is significant, not because representative and democratic forms of government are known to be more moderate and law-abiding than absolute ones, and certainly not because Grotius was himself unambiguously absolutist in tendency, but because it was an important element of his logical and systematic political philosophy, rooted as it was in 'rights' and constructed by 'contract', that the (putative) original transfer of rights and liberties to the sovereign could go so far as to include even the rights of self-defence and personal liberty themselves. Which was to say, as Grotius's logic led him to do, that a people could legitimately be in a condition of unfreedom, even slavery (not an unimportant topic at that time), because its ancestors had 'contracted' to be so, and that a sovereign could conclude a war with the surrender of his subjects's liberties.

This grim theoretical possibility is not irrelevant to the law of war, to which we now return. There is a sterner side to Grotius than humanitarian writers notice when they pick out of Book III of his best-known book the chapters about protecting non-combatants. Haunted by that side, I am inclined to take with fewer qualifications than Grotius's more sympathetic expositors urge us to attach to it, the appearance at the head of the contents-analysis of Book III's first chapter the classic basic maxim: 'In war things which are necessary to attain the end in view are permissible.'[12]

That maxim, in one form or another, i.e. either in Grotius's positive form or in the negative form, 'nothing is allowed which is unnecessary to . . .', recurs in the works of all of Grotius's successors; not surprisingly, since it must be the first article of belief of everyone whose thinking about war has enough ethical sophistication to include the idea of restraint. Of course its contexts changed with time. The terms and conditions that were in his successors' minds tended to be tougher and less ambiguous. Grotius was of the last generation of *jus gentium* theorists to be concerned with private as well as with public war and to use the term in its old sense to cover the

---

[12] Having entered the unfamiliar field of early modern scholarship wherein I am little more than an amateur, I wish to acknowledge the force of Peter Haggenmacher's exegesis of that passage in his contribution to Dufour, Haggenmacher, and Toman (eds.), *Grotius et l'Ordre Juridique International* (Lausanne, 1985), 115–43 at 129, and to say that I have not failed to understand what he says about the translation's misplacement of the chapter headings.

relations of individuals within the whole community of humankind as well as the relations of (rulers of) States with one another. An important part of the development in the direction of modern international law (which writers with insight into what was happening significantly preferred to call *jus inter gentes*)[13] was to restrict its field of application exclusively to the relations of sovereign States, and to claim for sovereign princes themselves an exclusive monopoly of the right to use armed force. With the cult of the sovereign ruler and the progressive desuetude of just-war, *jus-ad-bellum* criteria (which, for Grotius, retained all their traditional moral importance), the interests of the State trumped those old criteria: 'national interest' became the sole and ordinary ground which sovereign rulers and the lawyers who served them would think it necessary to advance to justify recourse to arms. With these narrowings of perspective and concentrations of interest there filtered through the war-making establishments also a rougher, secularized reading of that classic maxim. By the time it went through the complicated mind of Clausewitz, little trace remained of its original religious provenance and authority.

No matter what the changes in its contexts—military, political, intellectual, and so on—the idea of the non-combatant remained through the eighteenth and nineteenth centuries very much where Grotius had established it. It continued to receive such observance as the mentalities and dispositions of belligerents suggested and circumstances permitted. Grotius, it may be remarked *en passant*, does not appear to have been for the internationally minded of those centuries the pre-eminent founding father-figure he has become in the twentieth. Perhaps as time went by he came to look a bit old-fashioned, less in tune with the developing interests of the Ages of Enlightenment and Progress than, to mention three authorities who were at least as much looked up to, Pufendorf, Wolff, and Vattel. Vattel, moreover, in *Le Droit des gens* (for which *The Law of Nations* is the most nearly suitable translation), his *magnum opus* of 1758, was so copious and emphatic about non-combatant immunity and other primary points of restraint in warfare that he at once became the most attractive and accessible writer for humanitarians to refer to.[14]

Since Vattel, an experienced diplomat, was well informed about the conduct of international relations, and since his law-of-war passages were

---

[13] For this significant shift, I am grateful to the valuable article of J. L. Holzgrefe, 'The Origins of Modern International Relations Theory', in *Review of International Studies*, 15 (1989), 11–26 at 21–2.

[14] I might here sceptically note that Vattel was also, with the necessary ambiguity of the genre, emphatic about military necessity and State interests; his essential idea being that it is for each nation to decide what its conscience demands of it.

presented within the controlling frame of a treatise on public international law generally, what he wrote about it could justifiably be regarded as weighty. That is more than could as confidently be said of a more celebrated intellectual who, in a much more famous book published only four years later, included in the course of a political argument some remarks about civilian populations in wartime which, lifted out of context, have ever since been cited as the non-combatant's supreme talisman:

La guerre n'est donc point une rélation d'homme à homme, mais une rélation d'État à État, dans laquelle les particuliers ne sont ennemis qu'accidentellement, non point comme hommes, ni même comme citoyens, mais comme soldats; non point comme membres de la patrie, mais comme ses défenseurs. Enfin chaque État ne peut avoir pour ennemis que d'autres États, et non pas des hommes, attendu qu'entre choses de diverses natures on ne peut fixer aucun vrai rapport.

The writer was Rousseau, the book *Du contrat social* (1762), and one of the things he was up to when he penned those pregnant lines was, oddly enough, laying the ghost of Grotius. Grotius the political theorist, not Grotius the jurist. Grotius, as we have already seen, had made himself conspicuous among the natural-rights writers by carrying to their logical hypothetical extreme the liberty-losing consequences of original contracts between peoples and princes. To the libertarian side of Rousseau, the absolutist aspect of Grotius was odious. It was one of his many concerns to combat the idea that men ever could or should make over or sacrifice to any 'other' power the liberty that was theirs by nature; nothing upset him more than the idea that they could do it to the extent that Grotius had suggested. Rousseau therefore took the opportunity, when expounding his political theory, to remark in the course of his chapter 'On Slavery' (where this celebrated passage appears) that when princes chose to go to war with one another, their subjects should in no wise be thought of as totally committed too. Wars between States in the Grotian system were, from Rousseau's angle, not what we would call national or peoples' wars. They were wars between rulers and the State-apparatuses which they controlled, and subjects should therefore, so Rousseau argued, be left out of them, except in so far and for so long as they were actively involved in fighting. Men of one nation did not have to hate men of another just because their rulers chose to quarrel. Men were not subjects (or, rarely, citizens) simply of the country—they were also members of the enveloping community of human-kind; to outweigh the rights of rulers, Rousseau threw into the other side of the scales the rights of men.

Another way of expressing the matter appears in other of Rousseau's writings; his plentiful and perceptive writings about international relations and the place of war within them.[15] War, argued Rousseau in those other places, was not, as Hobbes had maintained, the *natural* state of mankind but an aspect of his *social* state: 'the necessary result of the creation of separate States and concomitant creation of the international anarchy between them'.[16] The hostile relationships existing between subjects of States at war with one another were therefore in some sense *accidental*. They were the product not of natural human antipathies but of State-engendered ones. Subjects enlisted by States to fight under those rival banners could thus reasonably be expected to recognize and respect the fellow human-being beneath, or beyond, the enemy uniform.

This is an attractive way to ground the combatant–non-combatant distinction in political reality but whether it fairly represents the total tendency of Rousseau's complicated thinking about the matter is open to question. He remains of all great political theorists the most difficult to pin down. His allusions in that *Social Contract* chapter to the (customary) legal distinction were deployed in service of a political distinction which mattered very much to him: the distinction between, on the one hand, States and rulers and, on the other, the people whom rulers called subjects but whom Rousseau wanted to call citizens. But in other places, when fired by his beloved idea of correctly principled republics whose citizens on entering into political communities abandoned none of their freedom, he displayed quite a different attitude to popular involvement in war. He did not then or consistently maintain the distinction between State and people. The citizens of his free republics were at the same time to be their valiant defenders. He admired members of nations who struggled to be free or to defend their freedom. Rousseau was an ardent advocate of the citizen-soldier, predicating of him and, by extension, his family an intensity of patriotic virtue that was as unlikely to promote moderation in war as it was to keep separate the combatants' and non-combatants' interests. Not surprisingly, and also because national self-determination was another of the causes he espoused, his were among the ideas most influential in creating the French revolutionary 'nation-in-arms' and launching it into total war. None of Rousseau's sentences was to become more generally misleading—whether

---

[15] My principal guides (between whose differing interpretations I have sought to find the most plausible path) have been F. H. Hinsley in *Power and the Pursuit of Peace* (Cambridge, 1967), ch. 3, Grace Roosevelt's *Reading Rousseau in the Nuclear Age* (Philadelphia, Pa, 1990), and Stanley Hoffmann and David P. Fidler, *Rousseau on International Relations* (Oxford, 1991). I take this opportunity to express grateful appreciation of the considerable pains to which David Fidler put himself, several years ago, to help me view this part of my book in a lawyer's light.

[16] Andrew Hurrell's summary of it, in a private communication.

actually 'untrue', is left to others to determine—than that in which he stated
that private persons 'are only enemies accidentally . . . in their capacities
as soldiers . . . defending their *patrie*'. Patriotic and *a fortiori* national
sentiment is not thus to be put on and taken off with the soldier's uniform;
and Rousseau, in part at least of his capacious mind, knew it.[17]

These principles regarding civilian persons seemed to be about as immu-
table as any in such a field could be. The idea of non-combatant immunity
appealed to every strand which had become wound into the European and
North American law of war. Respect for women in particular and for
the helpless in general struck an ancient chivalric chord. So far as the *jus in
bello* came from Christian just-war doctrine, that too enjoined respect of
'innocent' persons. Enlightenment philanthropy, sometimes Christian-based
but just as likely to be deist or secularist, besides deploring war's waste and
cruelty and beginning systematically to succour its victims, went further
than most Christians were yet able to do in envisaging a world-wide human
community. Dedication to commerce and belief in progress bred a sense of
relief that religious wars, notoriously given to massacre and mayhem,
seemed to be things of the past, and rejoiced—as was possible to do from
1714 to 1793 and again through much of the nineteenth century—that
'limited war' had become the fashion. Military professionals welcomed
every development that improved discipline and kept soldiers' eyes on their
main business, the mastering of their armed opponents.

And yet non-combatants proved not to be so immune after all; and not
just because of those unavoidable accidents which make civilians' lives in
wartime more or less hazardous. The principle asserting their protection stayed central in the law books, unchallenged in the etiquette of
civilized warfare, but in practice it was bent whenever the conduct of war
required it to be. This requirement was most likely to make itself felt in two
areas, which will suitably be labelled 'Economic Necessity' and 'Popular
Engagement'.

Invasion and Occupation, Blockade and Bombardment

The economic necessities of war-making on land consisted mainly in solving
the problems of subsistence. There was a limit to the amount of food and
forage an army could carry with it or arrange in advance to be brought to

---

[17] The exact extent and texture of Rousseau's influence on the French Revolution remains
controversial but no one doubts that it was in one way or the other considerable. The spirit of
the text of *La Marseillaise* and the 1792–3 rhetoric of total social mobilization for national war
do not fit easily with the pacifistic *Social Contract* sentences.

wherever it intended to go. The normal thing was to extract supplies from
the land and the people around the camps and along the lines of march.
With the increasing professionalization and material sophistication of the
eighteenth and nineteenth centuries, experience showed that the best results
could be got by payment or promise of payment, even if the transactions
were forced ones. The law books and military manuals accordingly developed thick sections headed 'Requisitions' and 'Contributions': requisitions
being what was taken in kind and, at least in theory, paid for; contributions
being the money that might be levied, perhaps in lieu of requisitions. To
these arrangements the commercial obsession of the nineteenth century
added the hopeful gloss that the population of the losing side, when the
war was over, could recover the value of what it had been required to hand
over to the armies of the winner by presenting the receipts to its own
government.

Needless to say, this scheme never worked anything like as smoothly in
practice as in the textbooks. (It was of course the German armies who tried
hardest to make it work; the lists of requisitions they were ready to give
receipts for in occupied France in 1870–1 are wondrous to behold.) Unless
an occupying army was exceptionally businesslike and well disciplined
and the population of the occupied territory exceptionally docile, food and
fuel and forage would be seized to the extent that it was needed, and if
the occupation moreover turned out to be lengthy enough, the economic
resources of that territory would be exploited for the benefit of the
occupier's homeland. Personal privation, damage to property, and domestic
disruption were the least of the afflictions which the civil population of
countries thus invaded and occupied would suffer. But by the military
authorities responsible for it, no breach or bending of legal principle would
be admitted. None of this constituted the technical offence of direct attack
on civilians. It was simply doing what the continental necessities of war
required to be done. How naïve to suppose that non-combatant immunity
could mean that armies should go without victuals or shelter, or that losers
should not contribute handsomely to winners' costs in beating them!

From across the seas, however, these matters appeared in another light.
The necessities of war at sea were different from those of war on land. In
the course of the nineteenth century an interesting argument developed
between, on the one side, the lawyers and generals of the European continental States and, on the other, their counterparts in Britain and the
USA, known collectively to the Continentals as the Anglo-Saxon school, an
argument which by the last decade of the twentieth century is by no means
over, although its geographical base has shifted. The economic purpose of

war, ultimately fundamental to all war-makers, was more obvious to the maritime powers and more openly admitted by them. How naïve to imagine that war for them could mean anything else! Their fleets might just occasionally fight each other in battles inviting comparisons with those of land armies, but whereas armies victorious in battle then went on to occupy and exploit territory, victorious fleets blockaded ports and seized merchant shipping. The real war at sea was commercial: choking the enemy's trade channels until he surrendered and then appropriating his trade to oneself. Enemy civilian property (as commercial traffic was classified in the law-of-war lexicon) thus stood at risk for a different reason; not just because it kept armies going until one side or the other had surrendered, but because it was in itself what war was chiefly about. So dominant an issue was this indeed for the great powers by the middle of the nineteenth century that they appended to the Treaty of Paris in 1856 concluding the Crimean War a Declaration of ground rules for maritime economic warfare which became (as it remains in the documents books) the first law-of-war multilateral treaty.

Not what it did to civilian property but what it tended to do to civilian persons was the aspect of the 'Anglo-Saxon' style of warfare which 'Continental' writers, when they were so minded, excoriated as a betrayal of the principle of non-combatant immunity. Anglo-Saxon writers for their part responded that their countries were unfairly picked upon for doing no more than any country would do in war when opportunity offered. The points brought into issue then are at issue still. No matter how much the capabilities of war-making have changed, the terms under which this debate is conducted in the twentieth century remain the same as in the eighteenth: blockade, contraband, and bombardment. The blockade of enemy ports and the seizure, anywhere on the high seas, of contraband of war (i.e. in its strict and particular original sense, munitions and implements necessary for war-making) of course were the most obvious ways for a naval power to bring an enemy to heel. It had early become an accepted part of the customary law of war at sea that once a close blockade was established, neutrals' rights were suspended. If they ran blockades or carried contraband, they did so at their peril. That was an intelligible and reasonably limited definition of maritime belligerent rights, which neutrals could live with; not that they usually had any choice in the matter.

Anguish and controversy only began when a dominant naval power sought to push its advantage beyond those limits: to exercise the right of total blockade beyond the close limits of cannon-shot or daylight visibility and to interpret as contraband not just military materials but the total sum of everything that could keep a nation's war effort going, which in the end meant to starve it out.[18] Logically, and given the identity of interests between armed forces and civil population which nation-States liked to proclaim, there were no obstacles or limits to this extension of the doctrine. Civilians inevitably would suffer but (it could be argued by analogy) a State at total war was no more entitled to use them to shield its soldiers' stomachs than soldiers in action were entitled to use them to shield their persons. Historically, there were the objections which neutrals would of course raise as their traditional rights were eroded. Britain duly encountered those objections and perforce had to take account of them as its rise to global naval dominance made it the first to bend the law in this direction. But it was not the last.

War at sea brought with it a variety of complications in the relationship between belligerent and neutral generally lacking in war on land. The Declaration of Paris in 1856, the Hague Peace Conference of 1907, and the London Naval Conference of 1908–9 successively reshaped rules which subsequently withered under the blasts of war. Britain (in 1780–2, 1793–1814, and 1914–18), the USA (in 1862–4 and 1941–5), and Germany (in both world wars), their navies by the early twentieth century additionally armed with submarine and mine, in turn found themselves calculating how far the patience of neutrals could be pushed before it broke, and what were the pros and cons of turning neutrals into enemies. When the context of the debate was grand strategy and the value in view was national survival, the principle of non-combatant immunity was worn to a ravelling. By the end of the Second World War, it was clear that non-combatants in an all-out war could expect immunity neither on the high seas nor in a blockaded land. Whether and to what extent endeavours since then to reinstate the principle have succeeded, we shall see in due course.

Even more debilitating to the ancient customary principle of non-combatant immunity, because linked in this century to an invention even more death-spreading than the submarine and the mine, was the ancient tactic of bombardment. Fortified towns had been subject to bombardment in war ever since military technology first provided means to do it, and from the very beginning the practice has provoked controversy. No element of law-of-war history better illustrates the continuity of its problems. Bombardment when it was done by primitive mortars and siege-guns

---

[18] As to limits and distances, there has always been argument both between would-be enforcers of blockade and its victims, and between the enforcers themselves; for glimpses whereof, see Hall's *International Law* (8th edn., Oxford, 1924), 857 n. 1 and 923, where successive entries in the index are: 'English and American theory', 'French theory', 'English and American practice', 'English practice preferred'.

evoked exactly the same arguments, some minor and some major, as when done hundreds of years later by Heinkels, B-52s, and ICBMs. Bombardment, then as now, tended to be inaccurate. No one challenged the right of besiegers to bombard fortifications and the men-at-arms manning them. But their shot and shell often missed the mark, injuring townsfolk and damaging non-military buildings, and very likely setting the whole place on fire. Some inaccuracy was inevitable. No jurist or general was so unrealistic as to complain about it. Beyond a certain point, however, the damage unintentionally done might appear to be, in modern terminology, disproportionate. That was the minor ground of criticism. The major one began with the suspicion or, worse, certainty that such (another modern term) collateral damage was not unintentional after all. The bombarder and, as he more usually is in our own century, bomber might deliberately be hitting civilian persons and premises. Many of his motives could carry no legal justification—they might for instance simply be racial or religious hatred, or the showing of a terrible example to places not yet attacked—but two of them might carry some.

The first plausible excuse might be that the legitimate targets in the place under attack, the properly military objectives, were so mixed up with their non-military or not-so-military surroundings that, given the acknowledged impossibility of absolute accuracy, nothing less than what we have come to call area or blanket bombardment would satisfy military necessity. The primary intention, after all, was not to hit civilians; but how could they not be hit unless their presence were allowed to serve as a shield for the military? Dirty tricks of that sort were incompatible with the legal conduct of war. The principle of non-combatant immunity certainly is bypassed, but it has always seemed difficult to sustain it in such cases, which by their nature, are rare.

The second justification sometimes brought forward for the bombardment of civilians on the other hand, although by no means so rare, remains beyond the legal pale. This is when a civilian population is characterized by the hostile belligerent as being so much at one in mind and spirit with the military that its morale becomes a sort of military target itself. The same excuse was offered for the indiscriminate bombardment of besieged towns in the years of gunpowder as for the indiscriminate bombing of cities in the days of air forces; that the military enemy would have to stop fighting if the civilian enemy's war-supporting will were broken. This is the practice of terror; and one of its logical extensions is genocide. By it, the principle of non-combatant immunity is not just bypassed, it is jettisoned. It has often been so in our terrible century, but we should be aware that the modern novelty lies in the scale of the monstrosity, not in the mere fact of it.

Expansion and Codification of the Law

The point of my pages so far has been to determine the status, and to indicate the strengths and weaknesses, of the laws and customs of war as they were understood in the European and Atlantic worlds through the centuries before they began to be codified into modern international law of global, no longer merely regional application. Those strengths and weaknesses may be summed up under three heads.

In the first place, they were of more than regional interest and potential appeal. Their Europeanness was not inevitably going to be an obstacle to their extension beyond. The idea of restraint in war could make political sense in every continent. The major religions in at least some part of their doctrine and practice cultivated love and mercy, and some spoke of brotherhood. Royal families and titled aristocracies, the natural leaders of armies and arbiters of manners in predemocratic times, were typically committed to principles of honour, generosity, and fidelity. On the other hand, the road towards universality was potholed with regional, cultural, and class exclusiveness. The senses of human affinity and recognition upon which restraint of violence towards armed enemies most confidently rests stopped short of so many divides: racial, religious, national, caste, and so on. Reciprocity, another precondition, in such circumstances was so much the more difficult to establish—and quite impossible whenever it was absorbed by all-mastering compulsions to revenge.

In the second place, and so far as European regional practice went, the laws and customs of war were by the eighteenth century well embedded in every country's military tradition, helping to form the attitudes of all ranks and conditions of men from noblemen and generals down through the lesser gentry and professionals of the officer corps (for whom before the nineteenth century it was nothing unusual to move from one national army's service to another's) to some indistinct petering out among the more civilized of the common soldiery. On the other hand, one cannot doubt that for most of the common soldiery, then as in many countries now, consideration and generosity towards enemies, whether military or civilian, came as an unnatural idea which conflicted, moreover, with much of the tough, xenophobic mentality that basic military training sometimes aimed (now, as then) to create. It must also be remembered that common soldiery's perceptions of the enemy can differ from those of their commanders.

In the third place, the weight attached to those laws and customs by those who took them to heart owed nothing to the letter of treaty law, everything to the spirit of culture. Versions of them were indeed available in print, at all levels from scholarly tomes to handy manuals, but officers and gentlemen stuck to them because their religion and *mores* impelled them to, not because their government had signed treaties guaranteeing that they would. Unwritten law can be more binding than written. On the other hand, its principles were in two respects less fixed and predictable than might be thought convenient or desirable. First, ideas varied from army to army about how to implement principles in particular circumstances, for example exchange of prisoners or care of wounded; and second, the principles were always liable to be bent to meet the demands of military necessity, as commanders subjectively perceived it. These uncertainties and flexibilities engendered a continuous background noise of complaints, misunderstandings, and allegations of bad faith. The process of codification into full-fledged treaty-registered international law has its proximate origins in the desire to silence them.

The codification of the laws and customs of war, as they were understood by the European empires and most of the States of the Americas, began with the regulation of maritime commerce in wartime, a branch of law which, the Declaration of Paris (1856) noted, had 'long been the subject of deplorable disputes'. Uncertainty about rights and duties 'gives rise to differences of opinion between neutrals and belligerents which may occasion serious difficulties, and even conflicts'; therefore it was 'advantageous to establish a uniform doctrine' about blockades, contraband, and (what the larger naval powers by then could dispense with, and therefore wished to deny to the smaller ones) privateering. Nothing further of comparable public importance was done about war at sea until a comprehensive codification was attempted by the Hague Peace Conferences and the London Naval Conference which rapidly followed them. So awkward an element had the sea by then become for restrained warfare, that scarcely one of the legal principles endorsed by those conferences survived the 1914–18 War intact.

The other main branches of the law of war all began to be codified in the 1860s. Why they should have come together with a rush is a question which invites enquiry. It must have been more than a happy coincidence that this should have happened in the same decade as witnessed, by much good historical judgment, the birth of modern warfare.

The US government (i.e. the Union or 'the North') engaged an eminent immigrant German jurist, Franz Lieber, to produce for its armies a codification of basic principles and accepted rules of war on land.[19] It could not yet be clear, when he did so, that the war would be a long one and that unprecedented masses of men would have to be raised to fight it, but from the start it was clear that most of the American professional officers were going to be on the Confederate side and that the generally less experienced men in charge of the Union's militias and volunteers would need all the instruction they could get about how to fight *comme il faut*. What could be got away with in wars against 'Red Indians' and Mexicans would not wash in a contest with Southern gentlemen. The President was determined that hostilities should be conducted with all possible propriety, in order to raise no avoidable obstacles to the restoration of peace and amity.

What was useful for the Union armies proved useful also for the international lawyers—just then establishing themselves as a distinct profession— and philosophical soldiers all over Europe who were thinking that a codification on Lieber's lines could be of great advantage in their continent too. The Brussels Project of an International Declaration concerning the Laws and Customs of War, 1874, and *The Laws of War on Land*, a manual of the Institute of International Law, made at its Oxford meeting, 1880, were only the best known of a flourishing kind.[20] Lieber's invention, a good deal simplified, became part of international law in 1899 when a set of Regulations respecting the Laws and Customs of War on Land was annexed to one of that year's Hague Conventions (confirmed with insignificant changes in 1907). 'The Hague Regulations' or 'Rules', as they are commonly known, have provided the basis for lawful land warfare ever since, and are reproduced in all collections of its documents.

Franz Lieber was at work on the first codification of the rules on combat through the same months as a small committee of citizens of Geneva—only one of them a military man—was at work on what would produce in 1863 the International Red Cross movement and in 1864 the first codification of law regarding care of the sick and wounded. Official military provisions for them were notoriously defective. Florence Nightingale was only the first of a famous band of caring women seeking to improve hospital conditions from the later 1840s. The shocks George Russell transmitted from Balaclava anticipated by ten years those transmitted by Henry Dunant from Solferino. But whereas *The Times* war correspondent's object was to move British public opinion to exert pressure on its government, the Genevan philanthropist's was to persuade European public opinion to a bold inno-

[19] It appears as Numero Uno in the most comprehensive collection of IHL documents, Schindler and Toman.
[20] They too are reproduced by Schindler and Toman, as numbers two and three.

vation in international law. Improvement of military hospitals was by then in capable hands. It was what happened to the wounded on the way there—supposing that they made it—that concerned Dunant. There was a diffused understanding that battling armies would respect the immunity of each other's ambulance teams, and opposing generals would sometimes sign local agreements ('conventions') before battles, determining among other humanitarian things the signs by which those teams and their field hospitals should be identifiable. But such *ad hoc* arrangements were laborious, confusing, and unpredictable. What was needed, as Dunant so remarkably perceived, was an international agreement establishing simple humanitarian arrangements that could be understood by everyone and that would work anywhere. In other words—the Geneva Convention of 1864.[21]

The third of the codifying innovations of the 1860s was the St Petersburg Declaration of 1868. Its significance went far beyond its proclaimed purpose, which was the small one of banning the use, as between the 'contracting parties', of a new and nasty invention—explosive and/or incendiary bullets. Not only is it a famous landmark in the long history of 'forbidden weapons', its preamble (which was longer than the instrumental bit of the text) included a summary of the law-of-war philosophy, the like of which was not to recur in any such place and the pithy excellence of which would never be equalled. Even though it must appear in any good documents book, it deserves to be quoted here *verbatim*, partly because it is such an expressive period piece, and partly because around each of its expressions of principle may be sensed hovering those attendant spirits of qualification and adaptation which are part and parcel of the law of war's mixed history.[22]

On the proposition of the Imperial Cabinet of Russia, an International Military Commission having assembled at St Petersburgh [29 November/11 December 1868] in order to examine into the expediency of forbidding the use of certain projectiles in times of war between civilized nations, and that Commission, having by common agreement fixed the technical limits at which the necessities of war should yield to the requirements of humanity, the Undersigned are authorized by the orders of their Governments to declare as follows:

Considering that the progress of civilization should have the effect of alleviating as much as possible the calamities of war;

That the only legitimate object which States should endeavour to accomplish during war is to weaken the military forces of the enemy;

That for this purpose it is sufficient to disable the greatest possible number of men;

---

[21] In Schindler and Toman, 214–15. Immediately preceding it are the 1863 Conference resolutions which launched the Red Cross.

[22] It says much of the way that the law of war is normally read by IHL experts that the commentaries in the two best English-language documents books, the Swiss one just cited, and the Oxford one by Roberts and Guelff, say nothing at all about the Preamble.

That this object would be exceeded by the employment of arms which uselessly aggravate the sufferings of disabled men, or render their death inevitable;

That the employment of such arms would, therefore, be contrary to the laws of humanity;

[Then four paragraphs about the projectiles, and an invitation to other States to accede to the agreement.]

The Contracting or Acceding Parties reserve to themselves to come hereafter to an understanding whenever a precise proposition shall be drawn up in view of future improvements which science may effect in the armament of troops, in order to maintain the principles which they have established, and to conciliate the necessities of war with the laws of humanity.

Particularly to be noted is it that this Declaration, often cited in IHL circles as the premier proof-text of civilian immunity, says nothing explicitly about the non-combatant. Its oblique implications concerning him may be paraphrased thus. There was affirmation that 'the necessities of war' must of course, in as many respects as possible, 'yield to the requirements of humanity'; which, so far as civilian populations were concerned, was the easier for warring civilized States to do because they had come to accept that war's 'only legitimate object' should be 'to weaken the military forces of the enemy', and to leave one another's civilian populations as far out of it as possible. Non-combatants were not expressly mentioned. It was evidently believed that they ought not to be involved, and no doubt hoped that they need not be involved; but no less evidently was it implied that, to the extent that they did become involved and that their involvement obstructed the achievement of the war's main object, they were put (or they put themselves) at risk.

Readers who, because they think I overdo the elastic aspect of the principle, object to that paraphrase of the St Petersburg Declaration's preamble (and perhaps object also to what I earlier said of the incessant debate about non-combatants) are invited to reflect upon these three facts. First, not one war in which any of that Declaration's signatories subsequently became engaged was unaccompanied by allegations that non-combatants had had an excessively bad time of it. Secondly, exactly the same anxious, flexible, and ultimately non-committal approach to the problem of the non-combatant (who in this case *is* named as such) was taken and was moreover spelled out in considerable detail in the USA's universally admired 'Lieber Code' of only six years earlier. Thirdly, the much sparser European equivalent, the Brussels Draft Declaration of 1874, by contrast appropriates the term non-combatant to the non-fighting members of armed forces and says hardly anything at all about the problem of the non-combatant in the civilian sense of the Lieber Code and subsequent usage.

From the 1860s, concern about civilian immunity seems to have been steadily on course towards its pre-eminence in our own age. What had for long been of no more than occasional though recurrently intense interest to 'the public' (i.e. such portions of populations as had access to information about public affairs and liked to form views about them) now became one of its permanent fixed interests. Since the nature and tendencies of this fixation are of crucial relevance to the argument of this book, some explanation of it is required.

Non-Combatants and Civilians: Dawn of the Modern Dilemma

The particular problem of the non-combatant, as it has taken shape since the 1860s, can be properly understood only as part of the whole massive question of the social experience and perception of war. A western European like myself living through the last years of the twentieth century does well to remark how relatively limited and insubstantial, by historical and global standards, has become his society's idea of war. Broadly speaking and by what must be a conservative reckoning, war has through much of known history and in much of the world formed part of the living-room furniture of most persons' minds. It has been usual for most societies to be instructed by their political and religious authorities that war was sometimes unavoidable and that engagement in officially supervised, collectively approved wars was admirable. War and fighting had a place, sometimes an all-devouring one, in peoples' folklore and mythology; in their culture whether popular, bourgeois, or 'high'; in their community and family histories, scales of human and moral values, lifestyles and expectations; in their interfaces with the apparatus of the State whose subjects they were; in their status in the community where they most belonged; in their patriotism (whatever might be its stretch of attachment); in their ideas about foreigners (whom they might perceive to lie as close as in the next valley or village); and in their images of security and their apprehensions of danger. All that, without taking into consideration also the actual impacts of hostilities when they happened, and the mingling of fresh experiences with all the memories and beliefs already accreted. Acceptance of war with whatever mixture of excitement and terror, joy, and grief, was an ordinary part of the mentality of ordinary people, just as war itself was part of the accepted data of social and national existence.

Until the Napoleonic years, in the Christian quarters of the globe, only tiny minority religious sects like Mennonites, Brethren, and Quakers subjected this common acceptance to principled critical scrutiny—a scrutiny which led them to reject it as misguided and dangerous. But things changed as those momentous years came to an end, their gains and losses were totted up, and civilized lessons were attempted to be drawn. The pacifist sects for the first time found themselves in a more numerous company with allies who, if not properly pacifist, were at any rate pacifistic.[23] The international peace movement thenceforward held up the institutions, habits, and consequences of war to continuous criticism. Its rival and opposite the 'war movement', as one might call it, no longer had it all its own way.[24] But reinforcements arrived from an unexpected quarter. The war movement was saved from the strain of having to meet the arguments of the peace movement head on by the encouragement that could be drawn from what was described above: the codification and on a broader plane the popularization, from the 1860s onwards, of the newly christened international law of war with its intimations that war need not be as nasty as the anti-war party said it was, and that in any case non-combatants and their private property could largely be kept out of it.

Thus was generated the germ of the tragic illusion that has boomed *pari passu* with the 'progressive development' of international humanitarian law: the two-faced illusion whose active aspect invites civilian war-lovers to imagine that they can have their belligerent cake and eat it, whose passive aspect encourages war-haters to hope that when war happens, civilians will not be hurt. From that time on, public opinion and political pressure ever more became part of the process by which the substance of the law was determined and its codification advanced. No wonder that Rousseau's optimistic sentences and the 1868 Declaration's ideal definition of war's 'sole legitimate object' became repeated *ad nauseam*! The irony was that, through those very same decades when the first recognizably modern international lawyers were writing the first editions of the great textbooks on the law of war (some of them have continued to serve well into our own time), developments in military science and mass politics were making more difficult the achievement of that law's traditional purposes.

Such was the spirit in which the codification of the laws and customs of war proceeded through the later decades of the nineteenth century and into the beginning of the twentieth, reaching its climax in those great

[23] I adopt the terminology, not indeed invented by Martin Ceadel but effectively used, explained, and made widely known in his book *Thinking about Peace and War* (Oxford, 1987).

[24] I have been able to find no more apt term to characterize the socio-political tendency of that undiscriminating majority of Europeans who appear to have been war-lovers or war-accepters. See my *Humanity in Warfare*, ch. 3, pt. 1.

international conferences at The Hague in 1899 and 1907 and, with much
less éclat and success, in London in 1908–9. The Hague conferences and
their legislative products remain central to IHL debate. Improved regulation
of the means of fighting wars was not everyone's idea of a proper achievement for conferences summoned (as the Hague ones were) to advance the
cause of peace, but to the optimists of the civilized world, more numerous
and vocal than the pessimists, it appeared as a part of that progressive
development of more or less everything in which they liked to believe—and
which indeed in those years before the deluge, was not too difficult to
believe in. The sceptics however had the greater insight, and among
them must be placed the military experts who doubted whether law
codified would bend any less before the blasts of military necessity than law
customary had always done. The question cries out for investigation: what
sort and how much of an impact did the Hague Conventions make on the
armed forces of the soi-disant civilized powers, their planning and training,
before 1914? When I first wrote about their historical context ten years ago,
my assumption was that the impact must have been instant and enormous.
Better informed by now about the causes and characteristics of international
conferences, about military organization and the *mores* of the military
profession, customary law, and the levels of impact made by comparable
Conventions on contemporary armed forces, I wonder whether it amounted
to much more than paperwork.[25]

There are always difficulties in discovering what military men really think
about this question of the binding force of treaty law. It is one of the last
topics on which even so honour-conscious and honesty-admiring a set of
men (I speak only of the officer corps of which I know something, the ones
close to home) are likely to give illuminating answers. Many factors get in
the way of their doing so. Officers no doubt mean it when they affirm that
the law of war commands respect, offering as it does some reduction of the
nastiness of war affecting themselves and non-combatants and perhaps (this
may be culturally variable) enemy combatants too. Ordinary decency and
self-respect must be found among them at least as often as anywhere else,
self-sacrifice and chivalry probably more often. Courage is not the only
human quality their kind may carry beyond the call of duty. But duty does
not demand to be carried beyond the call of common sense as commanders
exercise it in connection with their sense of responsibility towards their
men, and as they assess their options in the field. It required an extraordinarily well-disciplined and politically instructed navy to be able to

---

[25] This question is suggestively touched on by Draper in 'Implementation of International
Law in Armed Conflicts', in *International Affairs*, 48 (1972), 46–59 at 55–6.

live with the idea that one of its ships might now and then have to become 'HMS *Initial Sacrifice*' in order that its country may enjoy the diplomatic advantage of conspicuously obeying the law.[26] The formal addition of a legal element to all the others which operational decision-makers have to take into consideration—something which the lavishly lawyered US army has specialized in—may illuminate the difficulty but doesn't get round it; it may mean no more than that, when there has to be a law-bending, the excuses and justifications will be thought out at an early stage that will better protect the benders.

Good soldiers moreover cannot willingly emerge from their share in lawmaking at diplomatic conferences, openly saying that some restriction their government has just undertaken to place on their war operations is impractical or absurd. But they may think it, knowing that when it comes to the crunch in battle, victory and survival cannot help being stronger motives than strict legality (I say strict, because the military perception of the matter may be that that law is not broken when it is necessarily adapted); and that, in any case, there will always be plausible excuses for what they do: reprisals, retaliation, absence of reciprocity, mistakes, misinformation, and so on. There will always be ways round. Legislation that demands the impossible (which is especially how politically pressured humanitarian legislation can appear) need not be talked about, but the history of warfare shows that it will, in the urgent event and the last resort, be ignored.

The War of 1914–1918 and its Aftermath

The great codifications of the later nineteenth century were soon put to the test. It did not take long after the first of August 1914 for wisdom to appear to have been on the sceptics' side. Complaints and charges arose from all quarters, and every party laid the blame fair and square on the other side. Allegations of atrocity and lawless doings had long been part of the common stuff of wartime politics and propaganda, but the variety and mass of them that now filled paragraph, print, and (brilliant new device) screen had no precedent in the most developed countries, any more than did the intensity of the popular hatreds they fomented. The recent codifications of the laws of war were a handy aid to vilification. Never before had belligerents been able to roast enemies for breaking promises they had only

[26] See Daniel O'Connell, *The Influence of Law on Sea Power* (Manchester, 1975), 82–4. Dr Vaughan Lowe has pointed out to me that O'Connell's idea would not helpfully apply to a situation where the said sacrificial ship might be the *only* ship around.

recently, and so publicly, made. In such respects, as in so many others, the 1914–18 experience was novel. But the root causes of the alleged and apparent atrocities etc., the tendencies and the inclinations, were the same as they always had been. Opportunity and expansion came from novelties of scale and science.

By novelty of scale I simply mean that the war went on for so long despite the speed with which so much of its apparatus was capable of working: railway trains, internal combustion engines and steam turbines, telegraph, telephone, and wireless, and finally aeroplanes. These, it had been widely supposed—and notwithstanding the continuing omnipresence of horse and mule—would contribute to make it a sharp war perhaps, but a short one. Nor could the other and more momentous effects of science and technology have been anticipated except (as indeed they were) by a few seers and fantasists. Science put hitherto unimagined weapons and capabilities into the hands of war-makers, and the scale of the war presented them with hitherto unimagined needs or opportunities for their use.

So it was that Germany, reckoning that its chances of victory were greater in proportion as the war was short, staked everything on a plan which required the violation of Belgium's treaty-guaranteed neutrality, and in its anxiety and haste responded savagely to Belgian non-cooperation. The occupation of Belgium then continued for much longer than expected. Because the Hague Regulations' section on 'Military Authority over the Territory of the Hostile State' (poor little would-be-neutral Belgium, 'hostile'!) was concerned mainly with old-fashioned matters of property, taxation, and reparations, Germany had to invent an occupation policy which as time went on included forced deportation of labour to Germany and such exploitation of Belgium's scanty resources that mass starvation was averted only by a neutral-run famine relief scheme. Whether German occupation practices departed much from the vague but unquestioned customary legal obligation to go as humanely as circumstances allowed with subjected civilian populations, was angrily disputed and may still be so. The German answer to this, as to so many other criticisms of its war conduct, was that other countries in the same circumstances would have done much the same. To which other countries' most obvious answer, appealing as it were from the *jus in bello* to the *jus ad bellum*, was that they might not have invaded Belgium in the first place.

So again Britain, for whom economic pressure on Germany by classic naval means offered the best chance of victory—one that however might take a long time to work, and had to take account of neutral susceptibilities—left behind the traditional idea of close and particular blockade in favour of distant and general blockade, at the same time advancing from the time-honoured, strictly military definition of contraband to a total one including civilian victuals—a deadly pressure sustained after the armistice to make sure that the Germans would sign on the dotted line at Versailles. To this strategy of strangle-and-starve, Germany responded in kind, matching British blockade methods mine for mine and, much more momentous, developing for the purpose unprecedented new techniques of submarine warfare. In the course of their maritime ju-jitsu and its accompanying slanging-match, both parties declared great stretches of the high seas to be 'war zones' which passenger ships and neutrals entered at their peril. Almost all of the law which until 1914 had seemed to govern the relations of belligerents with each other and with neutrals in wartime went by the board; as it was bound to have done, given its assumptions of limited war and its inevitable failure to allow for the invention of revolutionary new weapons which States at total war would insist on using. Fisher and Tirpitz at last could do what Nelson and Napoleon would have liked to do, had they been able.

A momentous function of new weaponry was thus to enable a belligerent to keep operating in a medium otherwise inaccessible to him, as the ocean threatened to be to Germany; U-boats remained a fearful menace to Britain long after Tirpitz's battleships ceased to matter. But there were other functions too, not less impressive. Poison gas held out the prospect of breakthrough in a medium that was becoming impassable: flat land itself. The prospect of a breakthrough was what led the German army so ill-advisedly to initiate the use of gas on the Western front in the spring of 1915; ill-advised, partly because of the singular odium it would bring upon the first users but more because Germany's enemies were better positioned to exploit the invention, once its use had been initiated. Whether it was 'illegal' or not was a question fiercely disputed. Germany argued that, by the strictest literal reading of the 1899 Hague Declaration concerning Asphyxiating Gases, it was not. No one could deny that it was open to the charge of being 'contrary to the usages of war'; but so is every innovation, and not many have remained contrary for long.

A third radical function of new weaponry was to enable belligerents to enter a medium hitherto inaccessible: the air. There now appeared the possibility of using the air for bombardment. It came within belligerents' reach to achieve, in one and the same swift, selective operation, what had until then been perhaps possible only slowly by means of effective blockade (plus interception of contraband) and accurate bombardment (where the location of arsenals, shipyards, and so on permitted): the destruction of an enemy's war industries and the whole economic system sustaining them. Such was the law-regarding aspect of the matter. Other aspects of it, brought into debate from its very earliest uses, were more questionable, and remain so still. The risks to which bombardment, blockade, and its land-bred brother siege exposed civilians were now vastly extended. Artillery bombardment had never been wholly accurate, even when bombarders sought to make it so; bombing from aeroplanes was much more inaccurate, even when bombers sought not to be so. Questions of distinction and proportionality became more relevant that ever before, but most pressing of all questions now was the question of intent. What parts of enemy economy and population were being attacked?

In no other area of hostilities was the central legal principle of civilian immunity enveloped by more dangerous a cloud. Belligerents who actually wished to menace and terrorize enemy civilians but did not relish being seen as lawbreakers found here their ideal let-out. What was actually intentional could be excused as accidental. Bombardment's 'collateral' effects on civilian persons and objects had not always been deplored, and had sometimes been deliberate. Blockade and siege, nominally to hurt combatants and their means of fighting, incidentally also hurt civilians and their means of subsistence; as might precisely be intended by a belligerent believing that a socially solid enemy's will for fighting had its sources no less in his civilian that his military sectors. History had not often provided opportunities for getting at civilian sectors and industrial centres remote from coasts and war zones. Sherman's destructive and purposefully intimidating march through Georgia and South Carolina in 1864 was most unusual, a land-locked time-warped prefiguring of what would become the daily business of strategic bomber forces before the end of the 1914–18 War, and remain with them ever thereafter.

The Hague conferences produced some codifications of the law regarding bombardment. They confirmed the long-standing principles that deliberate attacks on civilians (not mentioned as such but frequently intended or implied) and on 'undefended' places were unlawful, and they incorporated the more recently solidified principle of respect for civilian and 'cultural' property, i.e. whatever was not evidently of primary value to armed forces or public administration. But perforce they left untouched the sources of the law's deficiencies in this respect, which lay in obscurities of definition, subjectiveness of perception, and opportunity for fraud, deficiencies that would by no means be remedied when the word 'civilian' formally entered into the language of the treaty-texts, two generations later.

Assessment of the legality of bombardment (the word usually reserved for what was done by land or sea) and bombing (usually meaning the aerial sort) can be a delicate undertaking. It requires in effect that each particular event be placed on a graduated scale, of which only the opposite extremities are free from a permanent affliction of fog. The extreme point at the lawful end is, of course, where the object of attack is beyond reach of dispute military. But not all objectives in battle, and rather few in economic warfare, are as simple as that. Arguments begin almost at once as we move along the scale. The business of 'targeting' which precedes all serious and lawful bombing operations can be replete with nice distinctions. If civilians are conspicuous within the target area, what precautions will be taken to warn or avoid them? If any are hit, was there military justification? If the object of attack is not soldiers in the battle zone but the factories, railways, mines, and farms which keep soldiers going, an almost infinite range of questions may be put. Are not those factories chosen because they are easy to get at rather than because it is essential to destroy them? Why not bomb the railway bridge outside the town instead of the station in the middle of it? Why bomb those coal-mines at all if you can wreck the roads around them? Who will go hungrier in consequence of the wasting of fields and destruction of their irrigation system—soldiers or civilians?

The questioning takes on a different tone when the civilian population is that of a nation which puts itself into a state of 'national defence', mobilizing (as has often been done) the whole national teenage and adult workforce to serve the war effort, and arming all adult males from 16 to 60. Wherever this happened (as it did for a spectacular first modern time in revolutionary France), the civilian's probable participation in the workings of an economy perhaps totally mobilized for national struggle made it difficult to distinguish him as clearly as the principle of non-combatant immunity required. The difficulty moreover was twofold. It lay not just in distinction, it lay also in perception. The onset of mass politics raised awkward questions about the reality of civilian separateness from hostile involvement. The committed humanitarian answer to these questions—insistence that the civilian as legally defined should be given the benefit of every doubt—might be considered unacceptable on grounds not merely of military necessity (with its shady stepbrother, military convenience) but also of morality. Why, to put the question to which even so conscientious and humane a man as Abraham Lincoln found no soft answer, should the 'civilian population' of a productive region of a total-war-waging nation-State be spared a share of the dangers and sufferings which it wished on to its soldiery? The problem has been growing, and nothing has been done about it, for more than a hundred years. There is no simple or unambiguous legal answer . . . until one reaches the indisputably illegal end of the scale, where the unarmed civilian population is the sole and unmixed object of attack. By no conceivable means can the arguments sometimes advanced in supposed justification of such attacks stand up within the classic 'European' law-of-war framework of ideas, but a European must admit that such arguments have been heard, and acted on, in his cultural region, before remarking that they continue to be heard and acted upon outside it.

The fundamental humanitarian principles of protecting the sick and wounded, and of treating prisoners decently, survived the war intact, strengthened, indeed, by so many millions of people's becoming acquainted, in the course of so prolonged a war, with the work of ambulances and hospitals on the one hand, the predicaments of POWs and their families on the other. The ICRC and the national Red Cross societies came out of the war raised in reputation and regard, and the least controversial item of the post-war codification agenda was the forging, in 1929, of a further Geneva Convention to improve the protection of prisoners of war beyond the relatively brief specifications in chapter 2 of the Hague Regulations.

The implementation of these acclaimed 'Geneva' principles however remained subject to the same hazards and pressures as before, actually heightened now by the effects of new revolutionary ideologies and—one of our constant themes—military technology. Marxism-Leninism on the one side, the Fascism which at once rose to fight it on the other, included in their rejection of so much of their European cultural heritage a rejection of various of the bases of international law, the law of war of course included. The immediate necessity of dealing with the real world modified their impacts in practice. Lenin's first impression, that his newly established USSR would have no need of a foreign policy, was early disabused. Public international lawyers were needed by the new Russia no less than the old to work the levers of the system their ideology condemned. The new Russia also found that it had to have an army, in which military experience even of prerevolutionary wars was useful. Fascist ideology was less bent on total innovation. Gladly accepting from its European inheritance the ideas of nation-States and of war between them, it was, in its early days anyway, committed to a working alliance with the traditional military professionals brought up to fight those wars. Not until the later 1930s did the fundamentally anti-human tendencies of these new ideologies, already evident in domestic policy pursued in time of peace, begin to make a characteristic mark on the conduct of war. Nowhere were the Geneva principles more disregarded than where the new revolutionary ideology was locked in mortal combat with its counter-revolutionary opposite, all over eastern Europe.

The effect of new military technology on humanitarian observance was felt and seen much sooner. Red crosses can rarely have been painted more largely than they were on the roofs of military hospital marquees and on the flanks of hospital ships, but pilots of aeroplanes that bombed the former and captains of submarines that torpedoed the latter always said afterwards that they had not been able clearly to distinguish the protective emblem, and no doubt, in that war when honour and chivalry were still forcible words, those pilots and captains were usually telling the truth. (Comparable markings and guarantees were never agreed on for ships carrying POWs; not much of a problem in the First World War, but a big and tragic one in the Second.)

That however was not the only, and not even the main, way the ever-stretching distance between weapon and target began to make its distinctive twentieth-century mark. The laws of war had historically been developed on the assumption that the man trying to injure or kill an enemy could see what he was doing. Nor was this an unreasonable assumption. Until about the dawn of the twentieth century it was generally true in respect of all major weapons except long-range artillery, and (as we have seen) it was precisely on the occasions when artillery was used in sieges against invisible targets that basic law-of-war principles were most likely to be thought at risk. But within our own century, attack from great distances on invisible objectives has become increasingly possible, with the inevitable consequence, that the personnel involved can find it difficult to realize what they are doing. This, once thought of, may appear to be so obvious as to be scarcely worth remarking on; but it was not obvious as recently as three generations ago, and it demands notice in any explanation of how the ancient fundamental principles of the law of war have been affected by the sometimes revolutionary modern developments of the means, methods, and purposes of warfare to which they have had to relate. It may be difficult to experience feelings of common humanity with people fifteen miles beyond or five miles beneath. It might be difficult to aim accurately at such distances. It can be difficult, when someone apparently has aimed at military objectives over such distances, has hit the neighbouring civilians instead, and has said he is sorry, to know whether he means it or not.

The First World War very much changed the total context in which the law of war operated and in which alone it can be properly understood. 1919 marks as much of a shock in its history as 1945. This was concealed from contemporaries, as it may still be concealed from the enquirer who goes not beyond the documents books, by the fact that codification continued along the same lines as theretofore, with an eye particularly to what had so to speak 'gone wrong' between 1914 and 1918. The new weapon which had been pronounced the most objectionable, gas, was prohibited by the Geneva Gas Protocol of 1925. The two new weapons-delivery systems which had caused the most controversy, the submarine and the bomber, were repeatedly debated and were made the subject of several attempts to control their use, the practicality and authority of which it is not necessary to discuss here.[27] A move was made towards the better protection of 'cultural property'.[28] Weightiest of this flimsy bunch were the 1929 Geneva Conventions, one of them simply a further improvement of the already well-established rules for the protection of the sick and wounded. The other greatly enlarged The Hague's minimal rules for the humane treatment of prisoners of war and institutionalized many of the supportive practices that had been evolved (to a considerable extent, at the initiative and by the agency of the ICRC) in the course of the First World War. Another novel Convention was in preparation for the protection of civilians in occupied territory, a category of war-victims which that same war had high-lighted; but the Second World War broke out before it could be enacted.

So profound and unsettling, however, was the impression made upon that generation of survivors by, as they called it, the Great War, that their consequent responses went far beyond such patching of the *jus in bello*. It was no doubt desirable that war should never again be fought in ways as beastly as those in which the Great War had specialized. But how much more desirable that great wars should never happen again, and that the use of armed force among States, so far as it could not be absolutely prevented, should be controlled to serve their common good! The attempt to ensure this was in effect to resurrect and adapt, in forms appropriate to the age, some of the ideas of the *jus ad bellum*. The Covenant of the League of Nations asserted its members' acceptance of the obligation 'not to resort to war'. It went on to catalogue means by which war-causing pressures could be lightened (principally, by disarmament) and inter-State disputes resolved without resort to violence, by submission to judicial arbitration and/or to the wisdom of the League's Council. The Covenant hopefully expressed confidence that members, the justice of whose cause the Council could not unanimously establish, would nevertheless have 'the maintenance of right

---

[27] The 1923 Hague Rules of Aerial Warfare are given, with explanatory commentary, in Roberts and Guelff, 121–35. Their pp. 147–51 say all that needs to be said about 'the 1936 Proces-Verbal relating to the Rules of Submarine Warfare set forth in Part IV of the Treaty of London of 22 Apr. 1930'.

[28] The 'Roerich Pact', given in Schindler and Toman, 653–5; one of the several humanitarian and human-rights 'first steps' taken by the (previous incarnations of) the Organization of American States.

and justice' on their banners when reluctant resort to violence was forced upon them; the Covenant threatened States which were so antisocial as to choose to resort directly to it with the imposition of sanctions (in the first instance economic, but ultimately military ones) so effective that they would be made to cease fire.

The League of Nations may be criticized in retrospect for not having done more to reaffirm and reinforce the law of war. It is not fair to go into that question without taking into consideration the reasonableness of the League's endeavours to make that law redundant. Many of them were reasonable enough, as far as they went; which was as far as the currently prevalent account of the causes of the 1914–18 War permitted.

Great significance being attached to armaments build-ups and the 'arms races' that achieved them, the League encouraged and promoted measures of disarmament and arms control. The results were in the short run disappointing, as all the world well knows, but they were pioneers nevertheless of the series of conferences and treaties which has become a fixed part of the international politics of our own times. The Covenant's obstacles to the initiation of aggressive war (using that term loosely to mean resort to arms except for self-defence) were supplemented by the Geneva Protocol of 1924 and the Pact of Paris in 1928; thus establishing, well before the Second World War, the line which the United Nations was to pursue directly after it, and ever since.

Another of the UN's main lines which in fact began with the League is deep-rooted in the belief—never more ringingly proclaimed than by the League's founder-in-chief Woodrow Wilson—that wars would be much less likely to occur if all governments were democratic and if all nations had governments of their own choice. The peace settlement policy set great store on democratic elections and parliamentary governments wherever it could launch them. It boosted the already well-established idea that national self-determination was a sort of natural right (the next generation would call it a human right) and sought to avert some of the damage likely to follow the literal pursuit of so purist a doctrine, by committing certain new States and States with enlarged borders to respect the civil, political, and cultural rights of their ethnic minorities. In these so-called minority treaties, as in other of the League's works as well, are seen piecemeal anticipations of the worldwide human rights programme which, not many years later, would inspire so many of the works of the UN. For League and UN alike, the underlying philosophy was that respect for the justice implicit in the idea of rights was a necessary precondition of the peace that alone enabled them to be fully enjoyed.

The technical defects, the idealistic impracticalities of the League of Nations' blueprint for a less warring world are clear enough. Not so clear is it that the League was wrong to try. That blueprint, after all, had neither more nor less success than any ordinary national government has when, for example, it declares the imposition of a speed limit on road traffic; a familiarly imperfect piece of legislation already brought into evidence. The League's means for catching its speeders were defective too, and the individual egoism, aggressiveness, and folly which make most of the problem on the roads pose problems many times worse in their collective embodiments. But none of that need be taken to mean that the idea of the League of Nations was a bad one. Although historically war has been the staple means of registering the ebbs and flows of relative wealth and power among peoples, it is demonstrably an unreliable device for settling international disputes, besides being all too attractive a device for satisfying collective greed, pride, panic, and lust. The League's offer of alternative and un-bloody means of resolving such disputes was sensible and attractive; coming when it did, on the morning after Europe's terrible night before, it was at least as sensible as ever is an appeal from man drunk to man sober.

So much may plausibly be said for the Covenant of the League of Nations and the League's consequent endeavours to reduce the likelihood of war. But all the same, there were grievous gaps and flaws in its guiding ideas about the sources and causes of armed conflicts. Like the ideas which underpinned the patchy codifications of the law of war going on through the same years, they were retrospective. Founded in a concern to establish what had gone wrong with civilization that brought down upon it the deluge of 1914–18, they could scarcely by expected to see or, except for the rare few with exceptional insight, imagine what new sources and causes were about to engulf them. One such new source indeed was already vividly present to them: Bolshevism. The League Covenanters saw at first no possibility of accommodating at their table the revolutionary new communist State which ridiculed their principles and announced its wish to overthrow their constitutions. Far from it! The principal Covenanters, at the very same time as they were consolidating peace in western and central Europe, were in fact sending expeditionary forces into Russia to fuel the civil war and to bring it, if they could, to a counter-revolutionary conclusion. Not for the first time, the red spectre made restless the nights of the propertied classes of the Western world, with the difference this time, that the Russian Revolution and the world-revolutionary network sustained by its example added a troublesome new item to the classic list of causes of serious armed struggle.

What those ruling classes could not see was that another and, so far as international security was concerned, an even more dangerous item was about to be added by Bolshevism's opposite number, fascism. This was quite difficult for anyone of non-communist disposition to realize for several years, and was impossible for fanatical anti-communists ever to realize, because the loudest instrument in the fascist brass band was anti-communism. Because of this, fascism in general, and its extraordinary Germanic National Socialist version in particular, were able for a long while to sail under conveniently false colours. Because communists liked to denounce traditional Christianity and liberal values, fascists could pose as their protectors. Because communists made no secret of their ambition to overthrow the 'bourgeois' social order, fascists let themselves appear as its defenders. Because communists talked and sang so much about internationalism and the supremacy of class over national allegiance, fascists were ideally placed to champion patriotism. And because (as there has already been cause to remark) the party line issuing from the Soviet academies was that international law was a self-serving bourgeois invention, fascists could be supposed to believe in it.

All of these constructions put upon fascism were in fact mistaken, as by the middle of the 1930s was becoming clear to all but prejudiced observers. Fascism's militarist ultranationalism bred admiration of war and rejection of the restrictions that international organization was inclined to place upon it. Nazi fantasies about world empire were every bit as inimical to the freedom and independence of peoples as Comintern fantasies about world revolution. In years when connections were beginning to be traced between the degree of social harmony within States and their behaviour as neighbours in international society, it quickly became apparent that fascism was just as antipathetic to pluralism as communism, was capable of being just as beastly to groups designated as internal enemies, and would in fact go so far as to seek to exterminate them when it got the chance.

These were not matters to which international law, as generally understood through the three centuries or so preceding the First World War, was thought to be applicable. Of course notoriously beastly conduct of governments towards their own subjects was always liable to excite shocked comment among educated élites of other countries. Maltreatments of particular groups towards whom an élite or, as time went by, a mass public could racially, religiously, or ideologically empathize indeed sometimes prompted measures of forceful intervention which might—as they did in several phases of the Christian European States' relations with the Ottoman Empire, and as in the United States' and British imperialist wars of

1898–9—turn into full-scale open war. The developing science of international law retained a small vague space for these activities, casting an aura of possible legitimacy around them under the title of humanitarian intervention, but the balance of opinion strained against them, on the grounds that what was humanitarian on the surface was all too likely self-interested beneath, and that in any case what States did to their own subjects was their own affair and no one else's. None of international law's axioms was held to be more fundamental than that of the sovereign sanctity of 'domestic jurisdiction', and until after the First World War it was inviolate. According to Article 2(7) of the Charter of the United Nations, it still is. But also according to the Charter, and the developing practice of the UN, other principles of international law appear to have become of ostensibly equal importance—observation of human rights, for one. Torrential complications consequently have arisen since the Second World War; but it was the Covenant and practice of the League of Nations which first poked a tentative finger through the dyke of domestic jurisdiction that used absolutely to inhibit them.

Criticism of the policy and conduct of States towards their own populations in time of peace was therefore a matter to which fascist and communist governments 'between the wars' (as Europeans self-revealingly put it!) could object with as much apparent legitimacy as those of other ideologies. How States parties to the Geneva and Hague Conventions conducted themselves in time of war was of course a matter of legitimate concern to the other parties, provided the 'war' recognizably came into one of the two categories of armed conflict to which alone the principles and rules of international law applied: war between sovereign States, or rebellions so substantial in scale and so 'civilized' in style that third parties might find it prudent or proper to accord them 'recognition of belligerency'. Internal conflicts of that order were the only ones that international law was at that epoch allowed to be concerned with.

The Spanish Civil War, 1936–9, did not in the event technically answer to that description, because most of the parties interested or involved in it—intervenors both open and 'covert', neutrals and would-be neutrals whether sympathetic or the opposite—showed more than the usual resourcefulness in parting from precedent when it suited them. Nevertheless it offered one of the three opportunities before 1939 to see whether fascist and communist influences in war resulted in the doing of anything different from what modern industrial States would do anyway. This interesting question is not easy to answer; least of all in the tragic Spanish case, where established customs of civil war were savage anyway and where the insurgents' crack

Moorish troops continued to do in Spain what they were accustomed to do in North Africa. Perhaps the imperatives of class war on the one side, of crusading anti-communism on the other, did further reduce the likelihood of prisoners being taken alive and worsen the conditions of those who nevertheless were so taken. More certainly they combined easily with the totalitarian tendencies on both sides of the shifting front to enforce a degree of control of the civilian population indistinguishable sometimes from a reign of terror.

'Terror' being systematically employed in those years by both communists and fascists, it is necessary in this context to remark that their uses of it were not identical, and that fascism's speciality was its use of terror in war. Whatever beginnings had been made by both sides in the First World War of what in the Second would, sometimes carelessly, be called 'terror bombing', it seems indisputable that fascism bore particular responsibility for its hothouse cultivation in the years leading up to 1939. To be feared, to inspire terror, and to do so in the course of spectacular destruction was delightful to the fascist mind. My conclusion is that Guernica, Madrid, and Barcelona and (on the other side of the world, where an ideology close to Europe's fascism possessed the minds of many of the militarists) Nanking would not have been bombed the way they were if fascism had not had a hand in it. A Briton would like to think that only fascism could have devised the ingenious spraying of liquid mustard gas over the semi-naked tribal warriors of Abyssinia, but there is plenty of evidence that some British imperial minds were attracted by the idea of doing something similar to troublesome Afghans and Somalis.[29]

Fascism's innovations were the most notable turns for the worse in the conduct of war between 1919 and 1939. There appear to have been no turns for the better. All potential belligerents, as the prospects of war drew closer, prepared for the worst; to suffer what might be unavoidable and, if they were strong enough to take initiatives, to do as much damage as they could. Among the major military powers, professions of legal good intention were not lacking. They were however chiefly designed to serve the ends of political and public relations; they coexisted in at least some of the most influential minds, civilian and military alike, with a readiness to get away with whatever could be got away with and with predictable *arrières-pensées* that reciprocity was after all the master-rule—that arguments of necessity and reprisals could be relied on to excuse almost any excess—and in any case that, in desperate last resorts, anything was permissible.

[29] See Edward M. Spiers, *Chemical Warfare* (London, 1986), 37, and David Omissi, *Air Power and Colonial Control: The Royal Air Force 1919–1939* (Manchester, 1990).

The War of 1939–1945

The Second World War, considered as an episode in the history of the
law of war, ran true to form established during previous centuries. The
core principles of restraint and discrimination for the sake of humanity
were observed not badly when men had will and space to observe them;
observance of them shrank towards vanishing-point where will and space
were lacking.

By 'space' I mean no more than absence of pressures and inducements
(whether of mental, technical, or circumstantial character) to bend or break
the principles in order to achieve victory or avoid defeat. Space in this sense
was at its most plentiful in 'the desert war' of 1940–2; small in scale but
strategically momentous. The Axis generals, at that distance from home and
in that milieu, were fairly free from ideological interference, and the chief
of them, Rommel, was an un-Nazi type with an exceptional reputation for
old-fashioned professional virtues of decency and chivalry. No startling new
weapons or methods were there to complicate matters, and the commonest
of all circumstantial complications, the presence of civilians, was conspicuous by its absence.

At the opposite pole were the wars on the Soviet Union's European side
and around Japan's side of the Pacific. In the former, the circumstances
included huge civilian populations and Russian weather; technology provided continuously improved methods of slaughter; ideology was at its most
powerfully and viciously demanding; neither side saw any advantage in
reciprocity. The ICRC, the extent of whose freedom to implement the
Geneva Conventions and supportively to improvise beyond them is not a
bad rule-of-thumb test of the relative decency of armed conflict, found itself
almost wholly excluded and impotent. The war between the Japanese and
the 'white' empires was for somewhat different reasons nearly as awful,
with the ICRC not much less incapacitated. Radically new weapons and
methods made possible by 1945 such devastating bombings of cities as had
not been experienced even in Europe; civilians were again inextricably
involved and only came out of it less badly to the extent that there was no
policy of deliberate extermination; and ideology in the form of the Japanese
military ethic of never surrendering and utterly despising enemies who did
was compounded on both sides by dehumanization and contempt.

The war as it was fought between the European Axis powers and the
United Nations (as they began to call themselves in 1942) in, mainly,
western Europe and the oceans adjacent, particularly illustrated the law

of war's continuing strengths and growing weaknesses: its unavoidable vulnerability to the passions and lusts of combatants inflamed by war at its most total and absolute. Religious, cultural, and (loosely) racial affinities made possible some survivals of chivalry and common human feeling. The prohibition on battlefield use of chemical weapons was observed, more from calculation, it must be said, than principle. The Red Cross emblem and the white flag retained some authority. Although an unknown and in the nature of things unknowable proportion of would-be surrenderers was killed, large numbers of prisoners were taken and on the whole were not badly treated; the ICRC was able to do much of what the Geneva Conventions expected of it, and the Protecting Power system still had some life in it. Critically situated neutrals facilitated humanitarian relief work so far as belligerents allowed. But they did not allow much; pre-eminent in their minds were distrust of the enemy and a ruthless desire to pile pressures upon him, too many rather than too few. The civilian populations of occupied and fought-over countries were victimized equally with those of enemy nationality. As well as being an international war, nominally subject to its corresponding branch of international law, it was also in many places a civil conflict, technically beyond the scope of that law and with its ordinary horrors magnified by *odium ideologicum*. The Gestapo etc. on the one side, the NKVD etc. on the other, added their own inimitable terrors. (Inimitable until then, anyway; many States would quickly become adept in the same black arts.)

The temptation or tyranny—I really do not know which word better characterizes it—of technology, its power to bend legal principle close to breaking-point or even beyond it whenever military advantage could be made out and military necessity pleaded, was peculiarly exemplified by some of the uses made of air power, the area (setting aside the novel nuclear one) in which material development was most dramatic. Every major bomber force, as it acquired the means and the excuses, ran the gamut from bona fide precision-bombing of military targets through area-bombing of mixed military and civilian targets to *mala fide* deliberate bombing of civilians; the means including, by the last year of the war, history's first ballistic missiles. Each army, as and when circumstances permitted, called on its related air force for tactical bombing support which became ever more excessively destructive and murderous in proportion as means were available. Towards the end of the war, the vast size of bombing operations often partly resulted from the need to keep such an accumulation of bombers and aircrews occupied and from air barons' determination to keep their forces in full view. Ground troops, for their part, were more and more encouraged to embrace the sometimes self-deluding idea (as e.g. at Monte Cassino) that the enemy defensive positions would surely be weakened by a soaking in bombs, and to leave out of account (as e.g. at Caen) the civilians who were going to be soaked too. A new random element of indiscriminateness came from the frequent inability of low-and-fast-flying pilots to resist the temptation to shoot up trains, vehicles, boats, groups of people, and so on when they were unable to see or know exactly whom or what they were hitting.

The conduct of war in the air showed up as in a brilliant X-ray picture what happened to the classic law of war when it was subjected to the batterings and debilitations of total war waged with radically progressive technology. In that unrestrictive medium, where so much injury could be inflicted so fast and from such distances, more legal bruises were suffered and bones broken than in the war on land or at sea; while those countervailing opportunities which land and sea war more obviously afforded for at least partial observance of the law, and for personal adherence to its underlying principles, were relatively lacking. But the record was mixed over the whole spectrum. It may be summed up thus. There was a good deal of observance of the law when governments and commanders judged it to serve their own interest; interest which might be reckoned in quite an enlightened, generous, and long-term way but which equally might amount to no more than convenience. When such a judgment was not reached, the law and the humanitarian impulse of the principles behind it had no power over or (except as elements of propagandistic explanation) place in the larger matters of policy and strategy, though they might still affect small-scale tactical and personal decision-making.

From these accumulated modern experiences, it seems possible to draw two lessons relative to observance and implementation of the law of war. The first lesson is that its most perfect and bona fide observance depends above all on an essential and chivalrous predisposition: a willingness to take risks and to accept losses for the sake of legal correctness or humanitarian principle. Sacrificial observance of this kind is, for obvious human reasons, not often to be met with, and for practical reasons already explained is in any case likeliest to occur when small groups and individuals can get a direct moral sense of what they are doing and to whom, at the opposite end of the decision-making scale from such politically popular dispositions as to 'do anything that saves the life of one of our boys'.[30] Not many commanders of

---

[30] Françoise Hampson's comparisons of US and British understandings of the law in the UN-authorized action against Iraq in early 1991 led her to admit to a suspicion 'that the RAF and British Army, although not prepared to take unnecessary risks, are prepared to take greater

costly assaults on heavily defended cities have for the sake of the civilians refrained from aerial bombardment, as did MacArthur at Manila in early 1945. (Such other-regarding readiness must not be confused with the self-regarding readiness to take suicidal losses even on a grand collective scale for the sake of religious and/or political principle, as exemplified especially in the Japanese imperial warrior ethic.)

The second lesson is that not much effect is to be expected from the prospect of trial and punishment, which the aftermath of the Second World War suddenly made to loom so large. Whatever motives there may be for conscious decisions to do the lawful and humane thing rather than the easy and ruthless thing—and those motives can vary from anguished conscience to rule-book pedantry—they seem in the 1939–45 war hardly at all to have included fear of subsequent punishment for failure to do so. The United Nations from 1943 made increasing play of their resolve to bring (the popular new phrase for such) 'war criminals' to trial. Axis officers and officials who knew anything about the aftermath of the 1914–18 war, and who were in a position to compare their countries' situations then and now, cannot have doubted that something of this sort would be attempted. But professional warriors, tending from instinct or principle to suppose that when they found themselves doing hard things because of military necessity or political orders (as they would naturally represent it to themselves) they were only doing what any professional would do in similar circumstances, could not bring themselves to believe that much would come of it. Wehrmacht officers who after the close of hostilities were charged with criminal offences seem often to have been genuinely surprised. The law of war had not, they believed, contained that possibility; and their faith was not wholly groundless. The victorious allies' military tribunals applying that law in fact acquitted many of them.

More justifiably apprehensive about their post-war prospects were the Axis officers and officials whose activities appeared to be simply criminal and atrocious, inviting retribution whether in legal form or not. It was these officials and understrappers of the Nazi party, these officers and other ranks of the SS, SD, Gestapo, collaborator policemen, etc. whose attempts in the closing weeks of the war to cover their tracks, to hide, and to escape showed well-merited apprehension. Their trials after the war attracted

risks in order to reduce the danger to civilians'. See her contribution to the 1992 *Proceedings of the American Society of International Law*, 45–54 at 53. I note that the 'Rules for Leaders' section of the generally admirable 'Rules of Engagement issued to soldiers who fought in Operation Just Cause' (the USA's intervention in Panama in Dec. 1989) includes this: 'Without endangering your unit or risking the success of the mission, take measures to minimize risk to civilians.' See the US *Army Times*, 13 Aug. 1990, 11–12.

much attention, and their punishments evoked the most unqualified applause. But the popular use of the term 'war crimes' to describe these cases along with those sketched in the preceding paragraph was in varying measures mistaken and misleading. Some of those deeds were war crimes in the proper meaning of the term but the greater part were simply crimes; crimes however of such a nature as to demand special definition. The proceedings with regard to them did not so much vindicate the law of war as demonstrate its inadequacy.

The reassertion of the law of war, even had it been in such an improved and updated form as was available by 1950, would not on its own and in these circumstances have stretched far enough to restore reality to the idea of a legal community of States. What gradually became clear to the planners of post-war international law enforcement was that the activation of the existing law of war would have to be accompanied by the formulation of a new branch of international law to deal with cognate matters not so clearly under the law of war's purview or clearly not under it at all. Not all of these latter categories of dreadful things that had been done took place in war-time, and of those that did, e.g. as incidents of the long military occupation of overrun territories and the exploitation and oppression of their populations, the connection with what might be called war crimes proper, i.e. acts done by combatants in direct course of their pursuit of military success, could seem tenuous. International law at that date held it no crime for a government to murder its own subjects. Civilians had, within the past decade, been killed on so many occasions, in such varied circumstances, and under so many pretexts, that there could be real difficulty in distinguishing the more justiceable instances from the less. The worst instance of all, the Nazi drive to exterminate Jews and gypsies, was only the most conspicuous of those instances. From the resources of jurisprudence accordingly were crystallized, first, for immediate application in the post-war trials, a new category of international offences, 'crimes against humanity'; and, second, for incorporation in the new international legal order to be inaugurated by the United Nations, a universal law of human rights, within which those crimes would be subsumed.

PART II

Reconstruction of the Laws of War, 1945–1950

3 | The United Nations and the New Legal Order of the World

The establishment of the United Nations Organization in 1945 was the central act of recognition by the war-surviving generation that something striking had to be done to avoid the recurrence of such disasters. It at once became the popular sign and symbol, for such people as could raise their vision and ideas above merely local considerations, that something actually was being done, whether within the UN or, as was the case with much of what follows below, at one or two removes from it.

The law of the Charter was the hub of the international community's post-war reconstruction of its legal apparatus. Whether in restatements of classic principles (e.g. States' sovereignty in domestic jurisdiction) or assertions of new ones (e.g. prohibition of all but defensive self-help by States), the UN Charter at once became the authoritative statement of law for the conduct of international relations, at the same time as it authorized the establishment of all the new organs which were to assist them.

At a certain remove from it was the law of war. Already centuries-old, it would have continued to serve the community whether the UN had been born or not. Optimists about the new order tended not to like the thought pressed on them by the more pessimistic that the new order was unlikely to make so clean a break with the past as to rob this branch of international law of its traditional usefulness. They made no difficulty, however, about using it to support the prosecution of the men who had brought the old order to its terrible close. Old-style 'war crimes' figured in the Nuremberg and Tokyo indictments equally with new-style 'crimes against peace' and 'crimes against humanity'.

'Crimes against humanity' were a canny, cautious half-way house to human rights. They were so to speak invented (in fact distilled, like human rights proper, from a confluence of cultural streams) in order to make possible the prosecution of Axis leaders for the dreadful things they had done distant from battle-fronts and in time of peace as well as war; crimes which the traditional law of war could by no means be stretched to cover. So far, the description would just as well fit crimes against human rights, plans for the protection of which were beginning to be canvassed during the same years as witnessed the drafting of the Nuremberg indictment. Human rights were moreover expressly mentioned in the Charter as something to which the new world organization was committed. But warning lights flashed. The State whose contempt for human rights had been so conspicuous as to determine the UN to protect them had vanished in the completeness of its defeat. For four years after the war, there was no German State. There was therefore, in the case of Germany, no sovereign power to be directly affronted. But UN members were States with the jealous concern for sovereignty common to their kind. The wartime rhetoric which rushed them into commitment to post-war protection of human rights was tacked on to their political theory, not integrated into it. In short; the matter had not been properly thought out, and its consequences had not been adequately considered.[1]

Whatever rash suggestions they may have allowed to slip into the UN Charter, the four great powers involved in shaping the Nuremberg indictments were not about to set a precedent that could immediately be used to their own disadvantage. To 'crimes against humanity' was therefore tacked the qualification that such crimes had to have been committed during the war or as part of the alleged criminal conspiracy to launch the war.[2] They could therefore be viewed less as harbingers of new-style crimes against human rights than as extensions of old-style war crimes; the view of them which the victors preferred and which plainly appeared in the Tokyo indictment, where the headings of the indictment were 'Crimes against peace', 'Murder', and 'Other conventional war crimes and crimes against humanity'. But the other view was possible, for those who understood what was meant by the then rather novel expression 'human rights' (in English at any rate it had quite a different ring from the familiar 'rights of man') and who looked forward to the development of law regarding them.

The new law and doctrine of human rights persistently influenced the old law of armed conflict in two ways. First, they shared a concern about human beings *in extremis*. However much further afield human rights doctrine might go in claiming for all persons equally, everywhere, 'liberty rights' and 'benefit rights' in abundance, the heart of its matter was the

---

[1] My justification for putting the matter that rather unsympathetic way is the less than wholly happy stories of human rights since their début in the Charter and their canonization in the UDHR. Only a minority of States to begin with professed themselves willing to be committed by binding instruments, e.g. covenants or conventions, to observe and implement these rights themselves. The majority, led in the deliberations of both the UN and the OAS by the USA, were determined to go no further than declaratory exhortation.

[2] For a glimpse of the delicacy of the task of wording *and punctuating* this part of the indictment, see Oppenheim, 575 n. 5, and Bradley F. Smith, *Reaching Judgment at Nuremberg* (London, 1977), 60.

protection of human beings from abuses and misuses of armed power; to put it another way, from violent excesses of otherwise legitimate controlled force. The four major human rights instruments (the European Convention of 1950, the American one of 1969, and the two International Covenants of 1966) do not say this in so many words, but this is what they have clearly meant in their intersecting short-lists of rights so absolutely fundamental that in no circumstances—no war, no public emergency, no national crisis, not one of those occasions when armed forces normally appear as primary props of authority or simply as authority itself—may they be abrogated. The short-list at its shortest, where all four instruments intersect and overlap, is very short indeed; protecting no more than the right to life, the right not to be tortured or otherwise inhumanely treated, the right to trial before sentence, and the right not to be punished for what was not an offence at the time of commission. Experience since the 1960s, when, so to speak, human rights came fully on stream, has sadly suggested that this list of life-saving minima must be somewhat lengthened if it is to do much good; in particular, by the addition of judicial and procedural guarantees capable of preventing murder, torture, and so on during the interval between arrest and trial. At these crucial junctions of life and death, human rights law runs over the same tracks as humanitarian law, seeking the protection of the same people at the same time from the same sort of armed abuse. Because the two legal streams had such different sources, protagonists, and preoccupations, their community of interest took some years to be realized and generally admitted; but by the turn of the 1980s it was becoming popularly admitted to such effect that careful people found it desirable to recall the differences as well as the similarities, lest the specificities of each be lost sight of in a cloud of universalized goodwill.

If there was positive overlap only in their shared concern for the protection of human beings *in extremis*, there was another more unspecific, yet in its implications perhaps more important, way in which human rights law, once it was fairly launched upon the world, impinged on the law of armed conflict. Together they offered a comprehensive course of treatment for the pains of humankind suffered from the too ready, too restrictionless use of armed violence to which it had, in war and in peace alike, become accustomed. The law of armed conflict had the purpose of restricting the uses of violence between States and (in the case of civil wars) between governments and rebels. Human rights law had (among other things) the purpose of averting and restricting the uses of violence by governments towards their subjects whether formally in rebellion or not; a field of conflict for which international law by definition brought no remedies.

The complementarity between the two law-streams was not as much emphasized in the years of their first convergence as it might have been. The optimistic ethos within and around the UN discouraged anything that might look like an admission that the law of armed conflict could retain importance and usefulness in the world. Perhaps there was also, among the more dedicated and reflective human rights experts, a certain feeling that there was no need to point out anything obvious. It was there for all to see, after all, in the preamble to the Universal Declarations: 'it is essential, if man is not to be compelled to have recourse, as a last resort, to rebellion against tyranny and oppression, that human rights should be protected by the rule of law.' Of the main text, many parts implied and some asserted that full and proper observance of its human rights would not only maximize social harmony within States but also promote friendly relations between them. The more successful the human rights programme, therefore, the less need should there be to fall back on that body of law which was civilization's last resort when other means of avoiding and limiting violence failed.

The relationship between the two bodies of the law, although rarely emphasized, was nevertheless too obvious to escape notice. The occasion when it attracted attention was the debate about a preamble to the Geneva Conventions. This was part of the baggage brought to the diplomatic conference from the last of the conferences preliminary to it, the International Red Cross one at Stockholm. Preambles were familiar enough features of international instruments. They could contain vital matter, as did the preamble to the fourth Hague Convention of 1907. They were not indispensable but they were recognized to be a good way of making general statements about principle and purpose. It had therefore seemed good to the promoters of the most innovatory part of the new legislation, the Civilians Convention, to attach to it a preamble which would solemnize and strengthen it by explicitly proclaiming it to be a human rights instrument and in particular a protection of basic, minimal human rights: 'the safeguard of civilization', 'the basis of universal human law'.[3] Upon this enterprise the ICRC made what it believed to be an improvement in its preparation of the Stockholm texts for their diplomatic finalization. It proposed that a preamble—the same preamble—be attached to each of the four Conventions, affirming the protective principle common to them all and remaking the human rights point in more general terms: 'Respect for the personality and dignity of human beings constitutes a universal principle

---

[3] Pictet's *Commentary*, i. 20.

which is binding even in the absence of any contractual undertaking.'[4]

What happened in Geneva to this draft for a common preamble is instructive; indispensable, in fact, to an understanding of the negotiating history of the Conventions and the meanings between their lines. No one objected to the human rights reference, which might indeed have been difficult to do for delegates of States which had more or less gone along with the UDHR six months or so before. A few States, with Australia at their head, wondered why a preamble was needed at all, but would have accepted the ICRC's version or either of the American suggestions, which kept close to it.[5] Other States however wanted something more ambitious; and here appeared difficulties which could never be resolved. One group of them, including those obviously in close liaison with the Holy See, considered it appropriate and desirable to include an acknowledgement of the sovereignty of God: 'the divine source of the human charity' whose activity, along with the workings of the human conscience, were relied on to add spirit to the Conventions' legal letter.[6] Much discussion was devoted to the questions of how this religious deference was to be expressed. Sir Robert Craigie, for example, told the UK delegation that it 'should not object to a suitable reference to the Supreme Being', which, if only he could have achieved it, would have satisfied Mgr. Bertoli.[7] But there was a rival concept.

Another group of States, with the USSR at its head, sought to use the preamble to advertise their own idea of what mattered most in the Conventions (e.g. the Nuremberg Principles rather than the Supreme Being) and what they were meant to achieve (e.g. diffusion of the belief that non-socialist States were not seriously interested in preventing or limiting war).[8] Earnest and laborious efforts at compromise satisfied nobody. There was also—which was unusual in a conference which in most respects ran with smooth efficiency—a good deal of confusion as to what was being voted for and who was voting for what. Chagrin and disappointment were widespread when the confusion and cross-purposes culminated in an abrupt vote which determined that there should be no preamble at all.[9] This was certainly not consistent with the wishes of the majority of delegations. It remains a matter for speculation, whether a preamble acceptable to a religion-acknowledging majority would have damaged the standing of Con-

---

[4] Ibid. 21.

[5] *Final Record* III, 96.

[6] Paul de la Pradelle, *La conférence diplomatique et les nouvelles conventions de Genève* (Paris, 1951), 286.

[7] UK: FO, 369/4153 K. 5652, delegation's meeting on 3 June 1949. *Final Record*, IIA, 69.

[8] US: 514.2 Geneva/6-2749, telegram of 27 June 1949.

[9] Pictet's *Commentary*, I. 22–3. *Final Record* IIB. 522–3, III. 99.

ventions in the eyes of the religion-rejecting remainder. What seems beyond doubt is that the human rights affiliation expressly claimed by the original, minimal preambles was in itself accepted by all parties to the 1949 diplomatic conference to the point even of being taken for granted.[10]

Equally clear to participants who sympathetically recognized the rising sun of human rights was the extent to which the new Conventions reflected it; 'human rights operating on the wartime scene', as an American army lawyer rather surprisingly remarked at the American Society of International Lawyers' annual meeting on IHL in 1949.[11] Prominent from the start in this respect was G. I. A. D. Draper, whose 1958 book on *The Red Cross Conventions* made him the leading authority on the subject which he remained throughout the rest of his life. A Catholic scholar's familiarity with natural law shows in his conclusion that the Conventions 'confirmed, if confirmation were needed, that international law confers rights and duties upon individuals as well as upon States'. He went on to specify what they had done 'in the field of human rights' and pointed out that 'in respect of both legal definition and enforcement' they went 'considerably further than the European Convention of Human Rights of 1950'.[12] The Civilians Convention he described as 'truly a legal charter of fundamental and detailed human rights in time of armed conflict'.[13] It seems probable from what he says about Common Article 3 in chapter 1 of that book, and in the 'second thoughts' of several years later, that he held the opinion that has since become commonplace, that it is a declaration of human rights in miniature.[14] Another juridical veteran, R. Quentin-Baxter of New Zealand, who had represented his country in Geneva when the Conventions were made, later looked back on that Article's unique significance as having marked how, 'for the first time since the founding of the UN, States had acknowledged in a treaty instrument a degree of international accountability for their dealings with their own citizens'.[15]

Adopting Quentin-Baxter's perspective upon forty troubled years of human rights history, we can see that the law regarding human rights was not for many years the help to humanitarian law that Draper and others appeared at first to think it could be. States at once discovered that they

---

[10] The preamble's brief life and regretted death is well told by the Holy See's delegate Mgr. Bertoli in *Final Record* IIB. 522–3.

[11] Willard B. Cowles, in *PASIL*, 43 (1949), 121.

[12] Draper, *Red Cross Conventions*, 24.

[13] Ibid. 48. See also what he says on 45.

[14] The later work is *The Geneva Conventions of 1949* in The Hague Academy series, *Recueil des Cours*, 1965 (I), 61 ff.

[15] His article 'Human Rights and Humanitarian Law; Confluence or Conflict?' in *Australian Yearbook of International Law*, 1985, 94–111 at 102.

could ignore the Universal Declaration with even more impunity than they could assert (in the face of all evidence) that their internal troubles did not merit the application of Common Article 3. The only binding human rights instrument to follow close in the wake of the Universal Declaration, the one adopted in 1950 by the Council of Europe, applied to the very family of States which was least likely to find it embarrassing or inconvenient. Other regions and States were slow to follow. Long before the 1966 International Covenant on Civil and Political Rights could attract enough signatories to enter into force, the horrors of internal wars through the 1950s and 1960s brought realization that human rights law was, for the time being anyway, even less use than the converging laws of Geneva and The Hague.

Frustration at the apparent impotence of *both* legal systems, humanitarian and human rights law alike, contributed to bring about a new initiative in 1968. A UN-mounted conference in Tehran on Human Rights passed unanimously a resolution on 'Human Rights in Armed Conflict' which requested the General Assembly to ask the Secretary-General to institute a searching inquiry into the defects and weaknesses of the law and to make proposals for its improvement. The outcome of that inquiry and the very impressive expert reports that came out of it was the process of legal 'reaffirmation and development' which issued at last in the Additional Protocols of 1977.[16]

'Human rights' as such were less in evidence at the end of the process than they had been at its beginning. Perhaps because management of the process moved early from the UN, where human rights was a catch-all lingua franca, to the ICRC, where it wasn't—perhaps because human rights through those years was becoming a political battle-cry that embarrassed prudent practitioners of neutral humanitarianism—these two branches of law remained at the close of the process no closer in form than they had been when it began. Their affiliations in principle, on the other hand, became only more marked as time went by.

So far as concern about 'human rights in armed conflict' was aroused by what happened in internal wars, it received little comfort from the 1977 Protocols. The ICRC and, one may reasonably surmise, the majority of those whose interest in the process was humanitarian rather than political, began the work that led up to them in the expectation that IHL would be

---

[16] Resolution XXIII of the 'International Conference on Human Rights' is reproduced in Schindler and Toman, 197–8. The GA's Resolution 2444 of 19 Dec. 1968 follows it on 199–200. The two main Secretary-General's Reports on 'Respect for Human Rights in Armed Conflicts' are UN Papers A/7720 dated 20 Nov. 1969 and A/8052 dated 18 Sept. 1970. Parts 9 and 10 of the latter may be found in Leon Friedman (ed.), *The Laws of War* (2 vols., New York, 1972). These papers are so good, it is a pity they are not easier to get hold of.

given much the same weight and relevance in respect of internal as of international wars. Their expectations were dashed. By the time they finished, they were wondering whether the victims of civil wars would be any better off than they had been before they began.

'Non-international armed conflicts' as covered by the Second Protocol were so restrictively defined that most such would have to continue under cover (such as it was) of Common Article 3; nor was there any likelihood that the new instrument, so far as it went, would be any better observed than the old one. The later 1970s and 1980s therefore witnessed the growth of interest in the direct application of human rights law to every sort of conflict that was not simply, solely, and unarguably 'international'. Human rights law of course did not cease to obtain within States engaged in such wars, but its relevance to the protection of war-victims and sufferers became of less interest, for two reasons; first, there could be no question but that the whole body of IHL in such cases was applicable; and second, that IHL actually offered larger protection to most categories of war-victims than human rights law did.

International wars of that clear-cut classic kind however remained exceptional. Most of the armed conflicts that attracted humanitarian attention were either civil wars or wars of 'mixed status'; as to which the relevance of humanitarian law could be either flatly denied or, if the parties to them chose, endlessly argued about. That the ICRC had nevertheless effected humanitarian interventions in many such situations rested on its preference for avoiding public legal argument (there is no means of judging what arguments went on behind the scenes) and its talent for skirting legal questions altogether by simply 'offering its services', as Geneva law gave it a right to do, and getting at least some of them accepted by governments which knew from experience that its neutrality and discretion could be trusted. What the ICRC thus did was magnificent but it was unique to that body and, when all was said and done, the ICRC was dependent on the grace of the governments with which it was accustomed to deal. It was not the vindication of law and assertion of rights that 'human rights in armed conflicts' activists looked for. IHL continued to be, in various respects, disappointingly ineffective. The question therefore arose: whether and to what extent could human rights law be brought to fill the gap?

The later pages of this book, calling on organizations concerned mainly with human rights law as well as those primarily concerned with humanitarian law for evidence of beastly and unlawful conduct in armed conflicts, will show how the interests of the two legal branches have converged. They have discovered many interests in common. The judgment of persons who from the beginning understood their shared sources and discerned the extent of their overlap has been more vindicated than that of persons who strove to deny their affinity and to keep them apart. Interests however are not the only thing they have learned to share. Experience has also taught them that they run into the same ubiquitous obstacle: the doctrine and passion of national sovereignty.

Humanitarian and human rights IGOs and NGOs found themselves on the same side of one of the most momentous public arguments of our time. It is not an argument with any possible end in sight; not least, because its subject is to some extent imaginary. 'Sovereignty' speaks on different levels to different publics; some of which read more into it than others do. What it means in the realms of politics and international relations, where it originated, is simply that effective authority exists within such-and-such a State, that what goes on within the borders is primarily its own affair, and that the supreme representative of that authority alone represents its inhabitants *vis-à-vis* other States and *their* inhabitants. It is a term of political and legal art, and a centrally important one; but it does not, as such, say anything about the stature of a State or the quality of its international relations. In popular political usage, however, and in patriotic/nationalist rhetoric, it is made to say a great deal.

At those less discriminating popular levels, the main use of 'sovereignty' is to gild the gingerbread of 'independence' and 'autonomy'. It boosts the national ego. It does for the collectivity what is done for the macho male individual by big phrases like 'Walk Tall!', 'Nobody talks to me like that . . .', and so on. But it is at least in part fanciful. It is as much the expression of feelings as the measurement of situations. The idea that States are absolutely free to act in any way they choose, as individual human beings can existentially feel themselves to be, is an illusion. It can nevertheless be a pleasing one, especially at times of national danger (real or imagined), because of the attractions and reassurances that come with sentiments of group solidarity and uniqueness. Patriotic and populist politicians and publicists have always easily exploited it and may be expected to go on doing so, for as long as a 'nation-State' remains the basic unit of political thought and experience.

The facts of life in the society of States are however not as sovereignty-bravado portrays them. Its rhetoric does not fit their reality. Tom Thumb standing on his dignity cuts little ice among the Titans. Even Titans can find their range of options to be disagreeably restricted. The sovereign right of States to pursue and secure their own interests as to their own judgments seems best can be exercised only in reasonable proportion with their re-

spective wealth and importance and within the web of international connections and commitments in which every State, even the most powerful, must
find itself at any time situated. The more powerful the State, the more likely
of course that the web will have been partly of its own devising. But whether
States are powerful or feeble, deep or shallow-rooted, the web is there all
the same, constraining States with its guidelines and restraints, prohibitions and contractual obligations; and international law is one of its
tougher fibres.

These checks and controls, familiar enough features of international
relations in times of peace, appear in the guise of the law of war to do
something of the same sort when times are not so peaceful. Some elements
of the law of war in fact offer striking early examples of such self-imposed
limitations on sovereign autonomy. The Fourth Hague Convention (which
has the Land-War Regulations annexed to it), for example, contains in its
preamble the famous recognition that, whatever those Regulations specifically say or do not say, civilians and combatants alike 'remain under the
protection and the rule of the principles of the law of nations, as they result
from the usages established among civilized peoples, from the laws of
humanity, and the dictates of the public conscience'.[17] Articles 22 and 23 of
the Regulations list a series of express absolute prohibitions following an
affirmation of the ancient principle that 'the right of belligerents to adopt
means of injuring the enemy is not unlimited'.

Thus far, by the early years of our century, had already in fact progressed
the self-limitation of States' sovereignty. The fact was not, to the best of my
knowledge, commented on in such terms. The nationalistic political climate
did not favour such admissions. The pride and honour of States required
them to appear to be absolutely independent of one another. It was moreover undoubtedly the fact that, no matter what bilateral or multilateral
commitments they undertook, States obviously retain the power to scrap
them in a crisis, on condition that they were willing to accept the consequences (i.e. to commit what is well known in sporting circles as a
'professional foul'). Decision-makers among whom reason has a place
would of course seek to reckon what the consequences of such scrappings
might be, but history shows them to lie largely beyond rational assessment.
The German government's decision (taken, be it noted, not in the extremity
of imminent defeat but to pin down elusive victory) to scrap what little
remained of submarine-warfare rules in early 1917 is an example of how

---

[17] Always since then referred to as the Martens Clause, its apparent originator having been
Feodor de Martens the Russian delegations's legal expert.

mistaken such assessment could be. In almost direct consequence, the USA entered the war and Germany lost it. The great self-help gesture turned out to be not so cleverly calculated a risk after all. Neither did the more complicated risk which Japan took a quarter of a century later when, without a declaration of war or anything like it, it destroyed the greater part of the United States' fleets and air forces in Hawaii and Luzon. Japan's calculations of American responses turned out to be extraordinarily wrong. Superior wisdom however prevailed when the United Kingdom and Germany, at their respective defeat-facing crises during the Second World War, considered whether or not to dishonour their undertakings regarding chemical warfare. They decided not to.[18]

The rhetoric of sovereignty resounds as loudly as ever it did, but since the Second World War it has been increasingly at odds with both the practical arrangements and the moral professions of the international order. The practical arrangements—financial and commercial institutions, regional organizations, defensive alliances, the UN and all its agencies, and so on— are not our business; the moral professions and their legal outcomes are. The victors of 1945 were on the least shaky plank of continuing solidarity in their shared moral outrage at what Nazi Germany had done to the peoples in its power; not just enemy peoples (though that was bad enough), but its own people too. Enthusiasm for the punishment of wickedness and for the creation of a better world led them (the victors) into virgin legal territory. They ran into the problems which were briefly noticed at the beginning of this chapter. The existing international law might provide broad enough ground for indicting crimes against the subjects of enemy States and the populations of occupied territories. It provided hardly any ground for indicting or even for stigmatizing what a government or any of its servants did to its own people. Governments since the beginning of time of course had been free to stigmatize shocking goings-on in other countries, but always as a political act carrying its own risks with it, never with any weightier legal justification than the alleged right of humanitarian intervention could give it; a right alleged by all parties except one exercising it to be no more than a nice-looking cover for self-interested *realpolitik*, and deemed by historians to have usually been precisely that. The several moves made in and after 1945 to regulate what States did to their own people came therefore as a striking innovation, an inroad without precedent into State sovereignty as it had always been understood and until very recently prac-tised; a control of States' freedom to mishandle human beings in peacetime

---

[18] See Edward M. Spiers, *Chemical Warfare* (London, 1986), ch. 4.

strikingly analagous to the law of war's control of how they handled them (those, that is, on the enemy side) in time of war.

It had to be admitted that this ambitious programme ran well beyond what could actually be achieved. To prevent States conducting their internal affairs as Hitler's Germany had done was obviously a good thing, but was there no way to achieve it other than by authorizing States to interfere with each other's conduct of what they would persistently regard as their own business? The virtue-conscious victors here encountered one of the many facets of their constant dilemma. How far dared they go in detection of wickedness among the vanquished without inviting embarrassing *tu quoque* responses or establishing interference precedents that could prove awkward later? A pointed fragment of *tu quoque* argument in fact did get through the organizers' filters at the Nuremberg IMT, and remarkably helpful was it to the defence of the commander of Germany's U-boats, Admiral Dönitz. That there was no more of it did not on its own invalidate the IMT's sentences on defendants found guilty of war crimes and crimes against humanity. But the possibilities of *tu quoque* argument went far beyond specific forensic application. The whole of the Nuremberg proceedings lacked virtue for those who, contemplating the two Russian judges sitting alongside the two each from the UK, the USA, and France, already knew or were beginning to realize just how atrociously the internal affairs of Stalin's Russia were conducted; and no State was more sensitively jealous of its sovereign prerogatives than the USSR.

Other and more simply political factors contributed to water the new human rights wine. The victors fell out among themselves, as heterogeneous coalition partners always do. Their early agreement on the principles and plan of the UNO concealed rich possibilities of disagreement on how those principles were to be interpreted and how the details of the plan should be worked out. Some of the major premises on which the UN was founded at once turned out to be mistakes; e.g. that the immediate and greatest dangers to peace would come from resurgent Germany and Japan, and that there was no such thing as atomic energy, let alone that one major power would possess an effective monopoly of it. The more it became clear, from 1947, that the Security Council after all was not going to be able to relieve States of their classic preoccupations with security, the less were States inclined to relinquish much of the sovereignty that classically went with it. The USSR and its socialist allies moreover, although second to none in loathing of fascism and determination to suppress it, maintained that the best way to prevent it was to foster socialism instead, and the only way to foster socialism was for socialist governments to assert sovereignty to the full.

How 'internationalism' nevertheless went hand-in-hand with socialism, as socialists and communists swore it did, was more intelligible to them than it ever was to human rights activists of the liberal tradition.

Enough of the human rights programme was nevertheless achieved in the immediate post-war years to mark a revolution in international law and organization. It did not go so far as to overthrow the classic doctrine of the sovereignty of States. That doctrine stood intact in the UN Charter (Article 2, paragraphs 1, 4, and above all 7) and has been faithfully repeated ever since in all major UN legislation. But from 24 October 1945, the day the Charter entered into effect, it has had competition. Alongside it, and prefigured in the Charter itself, there ran a parallel legislative stream of humanitarian and human rights rules and standards which States undertook at least to take note of and which, if words mean anything, they should in some last resort be required to observe. Human rights were the first to begin to crystallize. Promotion and encouragement of 'respect for human rights and for fundamental freedoms for all without distinction as to race, sex, language or religion' appeared in the first article of the Charter as one of the purposes of the UN. Chapters 9 and 10 spelled out States' obligations in more detail. Greater detail still appears in the UDHR. Its historic function was to provide, earlier than might otherwise have happened, an agenda of what precisely States should do, and to give human rights a sort of charter and an impressive moral authority of their own, pending the enactment of the legally binding conventions which were always intended to follow it. Members of the UN insist that they retain full sovereign rights, and nominally indeed they do so, yet they stand committed at the same time to a variety of human rights observances which in principle entitle their neighbours to complain in case of neglect. As signatories of the Geneva Conventions, which were being forged through the same months and which were ready for signature only nine months later than the UDHR, they stood committed more firmly still to the detailed series of humanitarian observances which it is the business of the remainder of this book to examine.

4 | The Geneva Conventions of 1949

Through the same months and years that the war-crimes trials were struggling towards their conclusions, a systematic review of the Geneva side of the law was quietly in progress; a review which issued in the four Geneva Conventions of the summer of 1949. Discreetly orchestrated by the International Committee of the Red Cross and confined within what that body understood to be its prudent limits, this review was so long-drawn-out and, relatively speaking, so undramatic that it attracted hardly any public attention. Yet some of its debates and achievements would have profoundly interested the more reflective members of the public. The 'Nuremberg' and 'Tokyo' stories from the outset attracted great publicity, and have not ceased to engage historians' attention. This 'Geneva' story, though thematically connected with those others and like them part of the general history of the law of war, has scarcely so far been told except by lawyers to lawyers for their own professional interest and purposes.[1] It can be told (and it richly merits being told) more amply and historically.

Approaches to the Diplomatic Conference

The formal beginning of the Conventions-making process was a letter sent by the ICRC's President on 15 February 1945 to governments and national societies, outlining a provisional programme and inviting their help in assembling documentation. Governments' reactions varied in proportion with their sense of priorities—for almost all of them, after all, there was still a war on!—and with their perceptions of Geneva. Max Huber's letter, for example, came as no surprise to Washington. American Red Cross officials' customary close collaboration with the administration already included preparation of a revision agenda. In Washington, Geneva's initiative was expected and seemed only natural. To Whitehall on the other hand, it appeared strange and bothersome. Already in the preceding autumn the

---

[1] The great exception is Paul de la Pradelle, *La conférence diplomatique et les nouvelles conventions de Genève du 12 août 1949* (Paris, 1951). One of a distinguished dynasty of international lawyers (to an earlier member of which, Albert Geouffre de Lapradelle [*sic*], is owed a superb history of *La conférence de la paix, La Haye* (Paris, 1990), he was a professor at the University of Aix-en-Provence and Monaco's delegate at the Diplomatic Conference. He evidently wrote for many besides his fellow professionals.

Canadian High Commissioner in London, who had heard about the ICRC's plans and obviously approved of them, found 'Mr Roberts, head of the POW Department of the Foreign Office' quite abruptly dismissive of the notion that the UK would or should find time for them, 'anyway for five years'.[2] Not all British officials were of the same uncooperative mind. Through the later months of 1945 the men of Whitehall for the most part proved willing enough to add this to their other burdens, and there was no lack of understanding among those who had actually been (to use their habitual expression) 'working the Conventions' as to the extent to which they were susceptible of improvement. But whether the ICRC was the proper body to guide the process, and (if so) in what terms the UK should recognize and deal with it, were questions which gave Whitehall a degree of trouble unmatched in any other capital whose official papers I have been able to penetrate. The UK took a long while to make up its mind to go to the party.[3]

The nature of the party became a little clearer with Huber's letter to the 'Big Five' (USA, USSR, UK, France, and China) on 5 September 1945, formally proposing a meeting of 'government experts' at the earliest opportunity. The USSR in the end declined to participate, on the ground that its 'preliminary studies' were still going on. The other four States sooner or later replied affirmatively but too slowly for the 'experts' to meet as soon as the ICRC had hoped.[4] The Conference of Government Experts for the Study of the Conventions for the Protection of War Victims, all-important as a baptism of governments into measure of responsibility for the process, did not meet until April 1947.

At this juncture it will be convenient to sketch certain political and behavioural elements of the story without which some of its events are incomprehensible: the attitudes, the 'states of mind' if one may so characterize them, of the more important actors—all of them, necessarily, States, except for the ICRC itself. That States therefore would approach the business with at least some political purposes, was obvious enough. What is not so obvious is that there was politics in it for the Red Cross too.

It is no part of this book's purpose to contribute to the internal history of the international Red Cross movement, but one aspect of it cannot be

---

[2] CAN 619-40c. Letter signed S. Morley Scott to Ministry of External Affairs, 15 Sept. 1944.
[3] I have sketched the British officials' states of mind in 'Making the Geneva Conventions of 1949: The View from Whitehall', my contribution to the Jean Pictet *Festschrift* (ed. C. Swinarski, Geneva and The Hague, 1984), 5–15.
[4] These events are chronicled and characteristically glossed in UK: FO 369/3592, K. 17349, 17350, 17355-6, and 17358.

avoided: the relations between its two international networks, the ICRC and the League of Red Cross Societies. The issues that divided them were operational, financial, and constitutional. Each was ambitious to promote the international activities of the movement and to extend Red Cross work into new fields of post-war and peacetime usefulness; all of which meant engaging the sympathies and tapping the resources of National Red Cross Societies. How was the work to be divided, and who was to be boss? From the ICRC's point of view, the League could all too easily have the appearance of a pushy, Americanized, cuckoo in the Red Cross nest. National Societies, however, found it in some ways attractive. It understood their keenness to expand peacetime work and, being for all its American preponderance an international organization after the model of the League of Nations, it offered more regard for national susceptibilities and more scope for power-sharing than the exclusively Swiss-run, self-recruiting, ICRC— not to mention more scope for the power-wielding in which some Societies and individuals were keenly interested.

The constitution of the international Red Cross movement became enormously complicated as it went through successive adjustments to try to keep its act together. The difficulty was successfully enough overcome for the duration of the war by the movement of the League headquarters from Paris to Geneva and the formation of a 'mixed commission' in which League and ICRC shared such work as was not statutorily limited to the latter. Once hostilities were over, the mixed commission was gradually wound up, and Red Cross politics took up again from where they had left off in 1939, with the difference that the war had given some National Societies new ideas of how they wanted the movement as a whole to develop, and that some of them had become accustomed to work in such close alliance with their governments that they contributed to the membership of their States' official delegations, and in debate might show themselves more on their States' side than on the ICRC's.

The ICRC itself had, of course, a comprehensive agenda of things that needed to be done to the 'Red Cross' and 'POW' Conventions, to make them work better in time of total war. Most of those items were easily enough understood and sympathetically received by States, whose own lists more or less matched them. Nor was there any objection in principle to the innovation of a Civilians Convention, something which the Red Cross movement had long pressed for. The States' discussion of it was to prune the ICRC's original concept of certain details thought to be incompatible with vital military and security interests; but more than enough would remain to make prospective military occupiers wonder whether they had not given away too much. More disappointing to the ICRC and its constituency was the fate of its attempt to get the whole contents of the Conventions extended from their well-established international field of application to cover civil wars as well. The ICRC knew from the outset that this would prove more controversial than rank-and-file Red Cross enthusiasts could guess; and indeed it would be the cause of many of the conferences' liveliest disputes. The final issue of the attempt (Common Article 3) was a lot less extensive than had been hoped.

Throughout these endeavours, the ICRC lay open to suspicions of 'empire-building'. Especially among National Societies on the League rather than the ICRC side of their constitutional rivalry were such suspicions prone to sprout; but States as well, even those normally most supportive of the ICRC, could be quick to rush to conclusions that the Genevan body was aspiring too high. This was as unfair as it was unavoidable. The ICRC, through these events as so often since, was thrust into a role which invited misunderstandings. Not a 'State' or anything like one, it had to play a quasi-political part and to deal with diplomats in a properly diplomatic way. Legally separate from the government of its own country, it nevertheless had to work closely with it in all matters connected with the diplomatic conference that would conclude the revision process and the final form of the instruments there formulated; for only a State could presume to convene such a conference, and according to established practice Switzerland would act as the repository of ratifications and accessions. Suspicions that the ICRC in Geneva and the Federal Foreign Office in Bern worked hand in glove for their mutual advantage no doubt had some justification, but the fact was that they could hardly avoid doing so, if the Geneva Conventions were to be what the international community wished. If the ICRC thereby became committed to ascending a path of seemingly endless operational expansion and international political significance, that was because the States of the world could use it and the state of the world demanded it, not because of any lust for self-aggrandizement. The bed it allowed to be made for itself was a big one, but it was also in some respects a bed of nails.

The USSR was the State most profoundly hostile to the ICRC—but not the most dangerous—its hostility being so great that it refused to communicate. Ideologically and perhaps also temperamentally wedded to the principle that 'he who is not with me is against me', the Soviet regime had acquired by 1939 an impression that the ICRC's attempt to practise an even-handed humanitarianism during the Spanish Civil War showed it to be soft on fascism; just as various Red Cross endeavours to relieve sufferings caused by the post-revolutionary civil war tinted Bolsheviks' feelings about the Red Cross with a suspicion that National Societies of 'bourgeois' provenance were disproportionately concerned about the sufferings of the revolution's enemies. That the Red Cross generally was of 'bourgeois' or (even worse from the Soviet angle) aristocratic composition was in any case undeniable. It was a sociological fact of life which Red Cross members in 'bourgeois' States have, rightly or wrongly, refused to believe to be any distraction from their commitments to impartiality and neutrality in humanitarian practice. Soviet communists embattled in a dangerous world would be likely to perceive things differently.

Relations between the ICRC and Moscow however were not bad, so a Geneva veteran privately told the senior French negotiator, until the end of 1939. He characterized them as 'tout à fait reguliers et corrects'. The USSR actually contributed to the ICRC's funds double the amount that the USA gave it; and this annual subsidy continued to arrive even after 1 September 1939. But when the ICRC offered its services in the usual form at the outbreak of the winter war between the USSR and Finland, it received no reply.[5] Thereafter, things went from bad to worse. The USSR's suspicion gave way to conviction that the ICRC was soft on fascism—the fascism which, in the Second World War, nearly destroyed it. Fascist States maintained national Red Cross Societies and bent them to suit their own purposes. The ICRC, asserted the Soviets and their allies, should have excommunicated those fascist-linked Societies. It had even shown itself willing to act on the German Red Cross's request in April 1943 to conduct an inquiry into the circumstances of the Katyn Forest massacre, and had withdrawn only when it became clear that there would be no co-operation from the Soviet side. Then there was the matter of the Russian POWs. With a degree of hypocrisy that must remain unmeasurable, the USSR was to blame the ICRC for having done nothing during the war to protect those Soviet prisoners in German hands from whose grim fates Moscow had actually, at the time, entirely dissociated itself. Hostilities were barely over before the USSR added another complaint to its list. The ICRC, in collusion with the 'bourgeois' States and their National Societies, was now being accused of being so interested in the plight of war victims that it was encouraging Russian citizens in POW and internment and 'displaced persons' camps to entertain wicked thoughts about not returning to Russia at all, despite the warmth of the welcome Mother Russia stood waiting to give them. Moscow therefore was not going to have any more to do with Geneva

---

[5] Notes by Lamarle on conversation with Jacques Chenevière in FR: Direction des Unions Internationales, Inv. 84-40.

than it could avoid. Its Red Cross and Red Crescent spokesmen would (sometimes) attend international Red Cross conferences convened under League auspices. At the meeting of the Board of Governors of the League in Oxford in July 1946, they joined with a will in the harrying of the ICRC that first came into the open there. They might attend regional conferences like the one in Belgrade in late September 1947. They would not attend occasions organized by the ICRC, nor did they ever in those years reply directly to such communications as the 'monarcho-fascists' of the ICRC addressed to them.[6]

Moscow was scarcely any more genially disposed towards Bern. Diplomatic relations between them, for long broken, were restored with difficulty in March 1946. Soviet touchiness about receptions given to Russian expatriates whether voluntary or involuntary, extended to the Swiss also. In the middle of 1945 the USSR even for a while seemed to hold certain Swiss citizens hostage until it could convince itself that Soviet POWs who had escaped from Germany into Switzerland were not being obstructed on their homeward path. No doubt a country so very 'bourgeois' as Switzerland seemed a particularly implausible base for a species of impartial and neutral philanthropy which in any case communists believed to be as impossible as it was, politically speaking, undesirable.

Soviet refusal to engage in dealings with the ICRC of course included refusal to participate in the mainstream of preparations for the 1949 diplomatic conference. Until Soviet delegates actually and unexpectedly turned up at that conference, the USSR's intentions regarding the new Conventions could only be guessed. Guessing about it occupied a good deal of the other States' correspondence, for it appeared desirable to all, and supremely important to some, to involve the USSR in this legislative process and to get it committed to the instruments that would crown it. Until Soviet delegates were present to make their country's views directly known, the other States had to infer what they could from what was said by Russia's eastern European allies and clients, some of whom sometimes attended the preparatory meetings or other occasions when their state of mind might be revealed. Yugoslavia was from the start the most aggressive of the Soviet Union's allies, voicing exactly the same litany of grievances against the ICRC for pre-war and wartime moral delinquencies and adding to them a local quarrel of its own about the Red Cross's handling of Yugoslavs in camps in Italy and Austria. At the main preparatory occasion in 1947, the

---

[6] 'Monarcho-fascistes' from report by Prince Frédéric de Mérode on the Stockholm Conference in *Mieux Vivre* (the Belgian Red Cross's monthly review), Sept. 1948.

Government Experts' Conference in April, it was Poland that was presumed to be putting the Soviet case. There was no one officially to put the Soviet case at the Stockholm Conference in the following year although the confirmation of Soviet hostility was made plain by characteristic public rudenesses.[7]

Sweden, which provided the venue for that important conference, stood very tall in the Red Cross world in those years, and had a particular interest in its proceedings. Sweden had managed to remain neutral throughout the war but had engaged in so much humanitarian activity as to win it universal respect and admiration. The Swedish Red Cross had figured prominently in many notable relief operations, and the dashing Count Bernadotte, its president, was by the end of the war a world figure taken to be representative of the liberal and humane values for which the war had been fought, zealous now for relief, reconciliation, and recovery. Bernadotte himself lived up to the idea popularly held of him. He evidently felt he was a man with a mission (indeed, many missions) and he was impressive enough a character (besides having good connections with the élites of the victorious powers) to be able to throw his weight around. The strengths and weaknesses of the man were illustrated in the controversy that raged over his uniform and aeroplane. Uncritically devoted to what he like many others simply called 'the Red Cross idea', he invented for himself a unique sort of Red Cross uniform, of military cap and greatcoat with red crosses on hatband and lapels; and he used the emblem also to signalize the ultra-important work he ultimately undertook for the UN as its mediator in Palestine; most conspicuously, on the aeroplane the UN provided for him! Whether or not the Secretary-General liked that, I do not know. The ICRC certainly did not like it, and strove to persuade him to drop it. Bernadotte could not understand why he should, but agreed to let the issue be decided by the Stockholm Conference. There, the decision went politely but firmly against him—only a few weeks before he was assassinated by an Israeli extremist in Jerusalem.[8]

Within the Red Cross movement itself, Bernadotte's idea of it tended to put him on the side of the Leaguers against the ICRC. He was early in the field, pressing from 1946 his plan 'to force the International Committee to become international in composition as well as function', and as primary

---

[7] Rudenesses reported in despatches from Stockholm and Prague in UK: FO 360/3969, K. 9831 and 9878.

[8] Partly based on an elaborate Memorandum by the Direction des Unions Internationales about the Stockholm Conference, dated 3 Sept. 1948, in FR: S.3.15, Croix-Rouge International: Dossier General, Relations avec l'ONU.

host at Stockholm in 1948 benevolently presiding over the continuing campaign against the ICRC, led on that occasion by the Americans and Belgians.[9] Red Cross politics may not however have explained the whole of his and his country's interest in these matters. A very grand design was suspected by at least two Foreign Offices. The political director of the Swiss Foreign Office on 2 August 1948 told the British representative in Geneva 'that the Swiss government were very much concerned by the Swedish proposal that the Committee should be internationalized . . . First, because the Swedes were anxious to establish their claim to a position of neutrality comparable to that of Switzerland, and secondly, because of the personal ambition of Count Bernadotte.' None of this was news to Whitehall. 'We have known for some time', recorded a senior FO official on 9 August, 'that Count Bernadotte has had ambitions that Sweden should become a Northern Switzerland, permanently neutral, with himself as head of the Swedish Red Cross, either rivalling or taking the place of the IRCC [*sic*]. The Soviet government dislike the Swiss government and the ICRC, and they may have encouraged Count Bernadotte.'[10] Similar beliefs about Sweden's hopes and Bernadotte's ambitions were held by the dominant figure of the British Red Cross Society, Sir John Kennedy. In an April 1948 conversation with a War Office official, he remarked that since Sweden was not succeeding in becoming 'identified with Switzerland as a neutral' and because the Count had not got himself on to the Committee, 'the Swedes now seem to be swinging into support of the Slav point of view, and this tendency may be encouraged by a growing sense of fear of their great neighbour'.[11] Their great neighbour was certainly difficult to get on with, even for those with most desire to do so.

Fear of the USSR was firmly believed by the American and British diplomats involved in this business to be a major force in the minds of all the continental European participants, and to explain part of their extreme anxiety to enact as comprehensive a Civilians Convention as could be achieved. If this was the case, no explicit evidence of it has come to my eye; but then, it might not be something that people would freely talk about. More obvious and freely admitted as motive for interest in such a Convention was what had happened to militarily occupied countries during the war just over. Of those which were active in the preparatory work, by far the most significant was France.

---

[9] James T. Nicholson's report, 4 Sept. 1946, on the Preliminary Conference of Red Cross Societies in Geneva, 26 July–3 Aug. 1946, p. 7; in AM RC: 041.IRC, Prelim. Conf. 1946.
[10] UK: FO 369/3969, K. 8961 and 9000.
[11] UK: FO 369/3968, K. 5429.

France seems to have been in every respect the State whose approach to the revision process was the most complicated. This was the consequence partly of the country's recent unpleasant experiences, partly (so the Americans and British surmised) of political confusion and constitutional weakness.

Two major features of French politics could not fail to strike Western observers. First, they were continuously in a 'provisional' period from the liberation in later 1944 until the autumn of 1946; second, the Communist Party was very active, not only as a participant in those early politics but also after the November 1946 elections, as the largest party, as one of the parties of coalition government until the following spring, and as the most obvious anti-American, Soviet-sympathizing party in western Europe thereafter. France looked a mess to condescending Anglo-American eyes, which missed the early strength and determination of its drive for economic recovery and failed to sense the latent national power that de Gaulle would later unloose. The occasional indecisiveness of its delegation at the 1947 and 1949 conferences was set down to divisions within the French cabinet and to fluctuations of pressure from the lobbies of former servicemen, prisoners of war, and deportees.

The French approach was moreover marked by the singular complexity of the nation's recent experience. On the one hand, they knew all about being invaded, occupied, exploited, imprisoned, interned, and deported. On the other, they had learned much of the difficulties of achieving lawful-belligerent recognition for respectable resistance fighters. Behind those current preoccupations was a more ancient one which appeared when the Interministerial Committee charged with preparing for the Diplomatic Conference got on to the question of work levels appropriate for POWs. France in those years needed all the labour it could get for material reconstruction, and was getting as much as it could from German POWs, whom it was accordingly loath to repatriate as speedily as the ICRC thought proper. Those POWs also worked more than eight hours a day—the limit which, if only other things had been equal, they would have liked to prescribe for the protection of French POWs in any future conflict. Albert Lamarle, who would in due course head the delegation to the Government Experts' Conference in 1947, settled the question thus. 'France must', he said, 'give priority to its demographic and biological interests . . . The physical protection of Frenchmen who might become POWs represents an essential and permanent interest which must outweigh a merely temporary one.'[12]

[12] 9th meeting of the Commission Interministérielle, 17 Jan. 1947, in FR: Série Union, CI. My translation.

One more hallmark of the French approach needs to be mentioned. France showed much anxiety to get the USSR involved, and some ruthlessness in pursuit of that elusive goal. Whitehall and Washington wondered to what extent this could be attributed to communist influence or simply to fear of the Soviet Union. Concern about Moscow's participation was certainly, among the 'Western States', a French speciality; and it seems to have been this, rather than complicity in League politicking against the ICRC, that moved it in the end to suggest that if selling the ICRC down the river was the only way to lure the USSR to the conference table, that was where the ICRC would have to go.[13] Nothing, fortunately, came of this desperate expedient, and at the Diplomatic Conference France actually supported the ICRC better than some other States.

The United Kingdom's relatively straightforward and simple approach was belied by its cantankerous conference behaviour. Revision of the Red Cross and, more, the POW Conventions was from the start accepted in Whitehall as desirable and necessary. The UK had acquired rich experience of POW law and administration and it shared with the Commonwealth States and the USA a constructive ability to see both sides of the question: that of the captured, as well as the captor. Despite inevitable hiccoughs in their wartime relationship, the UK came out of the war with admiration for the ICRC and gratitude to it. The ICRC for its part seems to have found the UK's POW administration co-operative and businesslike. The UK thus willingly took to the conferences a well-digested plan for the improvement of the Conventions in which it was really interested, and found that most of its proposals were generally acceptable.

With those traditional Red Cross concerns, however, the UK's serious interest ended, and its sympathy with ICRC evaporated. It had little enthusiasm for the idea of extending the Conventions to cover internal as well as international conflicts. The UK's opposition became so obsessive and niggling as to make it the most unpopular of the delegations in 1949 and to attract the criticisms even of its closest allies. Two general explanations may be offered over and above its principled critique of the draft texts. First, Whitehall had a different relationship with its National Red Cross Society

---

[13] UK: FO 369/4144, K. 2447; copy of correspondence between the French Embassy in Washington and the State Department, Jan. 1949, and FO minute by John Alexander. The chairman of the US delegation to the 1947 Government Experts' Conference, Albert E. Clattenburg, in the 'secret' part of his Report (dated 26 Aug. 1947) remarked that 'Behind what they [the European 'technical experts'] said openly could be sensed the apprehension that a new occupation of their countries might occur at any time. This scarcely concealed fear was as strong in the presumably Soviet-orientated delegations of Poland and Czechoslovakia as in the Netherlands, Norwegian, and Belgian delegations and in the at least partly Communist-influenced French delegation.' US: Diplomatic Papers, 514.2 Geneva/8-2647.

from that felt to be normal in other countries, and was in consequence completely out of touch with what went on in the international Red Cross movement. Where other national administrations (most notably, the USA, but in varying degrees all of those involved in this business) took their National Societies into their confidence, Whitehall would not do this, and the power-holders within the British Red Cross—itself, at that time, a markedly hierarchical body—did not press them. The Foreign Office was thereby saved from worry about dealing with any part of the international Red Cross movement other than the ICRC itself; which, again, showed Whitehall in a peculiar light. The USA and the others about which something is known were relatively untroubled by worries about the *status* of the ICRC. The ICRC was—as it remains—anomalous and unique; a Swiss-based, Swiss-run NGO to which have accrued, with the (often tacit) concurrence of States and for the general advantage, quasi-political and diplomatic functions. Most Western States, it seems, witnessed this pragmatic, piecemeal development without jealousy or concern. Whitehall however was extraordinarily uptight about it, and the UK's interests cannot be considered to have been advanced throughout these negotiations and conferences either by its caginess towards the ICRC or by its refusal to soil its sovereign hands by sending official delegates to the IRC Conference in 1948.

The USA's approach was relatively relaxed. Wartime experience of the operation of the 1929 Conventions gave it an agenda for revisions and improvements sufficiently similar to the UK's for them to be able to work together on most Red Cross and POW problems; their points of difference were interesting but infrequent. From the USA's initial experience of the war as a neutral—a neutral moreover whose citizens still circulated freely around the warring lands—sprang its sturdier backing of the objects of the proposed Civilians Convention; from its own historic experience of civil war, perhaps, its greater sympathy for the proposal to carry the Conventions into the field of internal conflicts.

Its military men however saw eye to eye with those of the UK (and in the final event with the USSR's too) whenever military and humanitarian considerations conflicted. The grit which sometimes got into the British and American delegations' relations with each other at the 1947 and 1949 conferences was less from substantive than from procedural, stylistic differences; British negotiating behaviour often seemed tiresome, and Britain's conviction of its superior wisdom and equal importance just a bit hard to take.

The USA was also relaxed about the USSR. There was little concern in

Washington about the question of Soviet participation. The French especially could not understand this and sought by every means, to the last minute, to stir the State Department to see things their way; but to no avail. By the winter of 1948–9, Washington seems not to have given a damn whether the Russians came to the party or not; a strong-minded indifference which, observation of Russian diplomatic conduct may lead one to surmise, actually did more to persuade them to turn up than French fussing.

Although there was close and easy collaboration between government departments and the American Red Cross, and intimate sharing between them of both preparatory and conference work (to the extent, it is worth noticing, that the Society's man there, Harold Starr, shared his nation's representation on Committee I alongside Mr McCahon of the State Department and Cmdr. Hunsicker of the US Navy), the State Department appears not to have become embroiled in Red Cross politics. It did not crusade for the ICRC against the League, nor did it encourage the League against the ICRC. The US administration seems to have assumed that it could deal with whatever international Red Cross central body might exist, but with a presumption in favour of the ICRC, whose work during the war it, like Whitehall, openly respected and admired. The American Red Cross, however, was deeply immersed in the political affairs to which we have already referred. How could it not be, when the League had begun and grown up as its protégé—when North America was providing the greater part of the money for Red Cross relief and rehabilitation work, to which in those immediately post-war years there seemed no end—and when the Chairman of the American Red Cross was also Chairman of the League?[14]

The long delay between the ICRC's formal invitation and the Government Experts' Conference gave the League ample opportunities to get into the act. It could not have been wholly left out anyway—the constitution of the IRC and interwar precedent ensured that—but now that crusading Leaguers were advancing on a broad front to force the ICRC, if they could, to surrender or at any rate to share its prerogatives, its special interest in the Conventions was bound to be counted among them. The campaign began with a brisk engagement at the Oxford meeting of the Board of Governors of the League through the middle days of July 1946 and was carried on

[14] The European leaders of the campaign against the ICRC were certainly caballing with the American Red Cross through these years. Out of their plottings, meetings, and conferences came satisfaction on some of the financial and administrative matters which vexed them. But they failed to budge the ICRC from what it regarded as its prerogative with regard to the GCs in wartime; and however much the American Red Cross may have been willing to go along with the would-be internationalizers from 1946 through 1948, no evidence appears of its doing so in 1949.

directly thereafter in Geneva, where a Preliminary Conference of National Societies met to review 'various questions which had arisen during the war' and which would have to be dealt with in 1948.[15] One outcome of this Preliminary Conference was the establishment by the League's Executive Committee of a Special Commission to scrutinize the papers the ICRC was preparing for that 1948 Conference, the movement's seventeenth, scheduled to take place in Stockholm.

From mid-1946, the ICRC, then, was not in as complete control of the process as it would presumably have wished. The League was in no position to interfere with its management of the Government Experts' Conference in April 1947. But apart from that, the ICRC had to manage a three-ring circus from a wobbly position which some of the performers were actually seeking to overturn. On the one hand, the USSR and the States which already were, or soon would be, its satellites, were hostile for many reasons, and pleased to fish for their own long-term purposes in these troubled waters; the UK was supportive of the ICRC's work but had a chronic blockage about its status; and France was obsessed with the need to bring the USSR into the process at no matter what cost to the ICRC. On the other hand, the activists of the League were resuming their congenital campaign against the primacy of Geneva and exploiting all the National Societies' wartime difficulties and frustrations as means of eroding it. In these circumstances, it was not surprising that there was a certain confusion about who was preparing what for Stockholm, and, subsequently, through what Red Cross organ(s) its draft texts should receive their last trimming before going into the agenda of the diplomatic conference.

Governments could be confused too about what might happen at Stockholm, and how much it mattered. They were under little legal obligation to take its proceedings seriously. States which were parties to the GCs could send delegates to the movement's quadrennial conferences and could share, if they wished, in the framing of its resolutions; but in no way could that authority extend to determining the final outcome of a treaty-making process in which a diplomatic conference would hold all the trumps. But the Stockholm Conference could not be completely ignored, even by States as detached from the IRC and its statutes as the UK. There was even in Whitehall, once it was all over, something of a wish that the UK should

---

[15] AUST RC: copy of report for his own Red Cross Society by C. G. White of New Zealand. He notes the ganging-up of the American Red Cross with the League's European militants and most interestingly summarizes some of what was admitted about unauthorized (and in some instances improper) uses of the emblem during the war—and Germany's permission of some of them.

have taken the conference more seriously, because, whatever its international legal status, and apart from political considerations like protecting the ICRC against its underminers and deciding what to do about the USSR (by now, for the West, a matter of growing concern), the conference was a stage through which the draft texts of the agenda for the diplomatic conference had to go. The shape there given them would make the work of the Diplomatic Conference, according to how you looked at it, rougher or smoother. From the UK's point of view, it was made rougher. W. H. Gardner, one of the UK's two official observers (the UK would not let any officials go as delegates), reported when he got home that the texts had been made worse and that the draft Civilians Convention in particular was now 'in a form which could not, I think, possibly be accepted by the UK government unless it was drastically altered'. The US representative, however, he had to admit, was of the opinion that the texts were good enough to go on to the agenda for Geneva and moreover that governments refraining from full participation in Stockholm had only themselves to blame if they didn't like its products.[16]

The draft texts that issued from the 1948 conference were not quite the same as those on which the 1949 conference went to work. The ICRC tinkered with them *en route*, as it had tinkered also with the drafts that issued from the 1947 conference *en route* to Stockholm. The professional draft-scanners in government departments were quick to notice the changes thus made and to adjust their action-plans accordingly. Some of those changes stuck, others didn't. Their varied fortunes calibrate the degree to which the ICRC, whether despite or because of the pressures it was under from the rest of the movement, retained practical control over the shaping process through the new Conventions' three years' development. It persisted in using its own judgment and pressing for its own ideas, without necessarily consulting States beforehand. Most remarkable of the ICRC's ventures in this line was the appearance in the 1949 agenda of four new common articles (i.e. common to each Convention) to meet the Stockholm *voeu* that something strong should be done to 'repress violations of the Humanitarian Conventions'. What it had done was to convene in Geneva in December 1948 a little committee of experts: Hersch Lauterpacht, the UK's most

---

[16] UK: FO 369/3969 K. 10003. Gardner, a War Office official, in 1949 became one of the most effective members of the British delegation to the Diplomatic Conference. Most people found him abrasive. The mildest reference I have found is in the Swedish delegation's report of 20 May 1949. Complaining that the slow progress was due largely to the British, it said that 'the spirit of the estimable but pompous Mr Gardner hovers over the whole', SW: HP/30/B, File XXII; like most of the Swedish records I have used, kindly translated for me by Gill Rydin.

distinguished international law professor; Jean Graven, one of Switzerland's; Capt. Martinus Mouton of the Netherlands navy and a judge in its
supreme court of appeal; and the respected British lawyer Col. Henry
Phillimore, bringing like Mouton fresh experience of the war-crimes business from his membership of the Nuremberg prosecuting team.[17] Under the
chairmanship of Max Huber, himself a most distinguished international
lawyer, and judge for many years on the Permanent Court of International
Justice, this group produced draft articles from which in the end, after much
wrangling and a lot of watering-down, came the 'grave breaches' common
articles which were among the 1949 Conventions' more startling novelties.

It was not for several months certain when the diplomatic conference
would at last meet. What procedure was least likely to ruffle Russian
feathers? Should there be a second Government Experts' meeting, to restore
order to the texts after Stockholm's humanitarian changes and additions
(which appalled Whitehall, and did not much appeal to Washington and
Canberra either), or would it suffice to set a gap in the middle of the
diplomatic conference, during which governments could review progress?[18]
This latter proposal was quite unacceptable to States whose delegates had to
travel from great distances; they insisted that the conference, once it met,
should get on with the job and finish it without intermission. The Swiss
government was of the same mind. By the end of September 1948 it sent to
governments its invitation to start on 25 March 1949. But the diplomatic
conference did not actually begin until 21 April, nearly a month later,
France having discovered that its delegation's effective leader, Albert
Lamarle, and certain others were inconveniently committed to other conferences at the same time.

The delegations geared up for a conference about which much seemed
unpredictable. Their respective concerns and sensitivities are of more than
merely local interest; the Cold War, after all, was breaking out all round
them. Whether the USSR would participate or not was of course the
principal question continuously discussed through the winter months. How
far the 'Stockholm texts' would and could serve as a satisfactory basis for
serious diplomatic business, was another, towards which the ICRC's hopeful booklet of *Remarks and Proposals* of February 1949 and the British
Government's cautionary *Memorandum [on the] Conventions for Protec-*

---

[17] For sources and further details, see where this episode is more fully dealt with below.
[18] For British and US reactions to the Stockholm version, see Gardner's Report in UK: WO
32/14872 and his covering letter cited in n. 16 above. What he says there about some
Americans' *privately* expressed amazement is confirmed with regard to 'the majority of
countries' by the Australian representative J. D. McAteer in AUST: A. 1838, 1481/1 part 1(A)
no. 95 and by the Australian Red Cross man's later letter in A. 462, 846/11(1).

tion of War Victims (sent to Berne with a request that copies should be sent to all likely participants) offered different answers. Then there were questions about the invitations list. What about Japan and Germany? Whitehall thought both should be there in some modest capacity, and Japan did in the end send observers, but Washington firmly banned any sort of representation from Germany.[19] Berne's disappointment at the non-participation of Ceylon and (which was all the stranger for its having sent delegates to the 1947 conference) South Africa was duly conveyed to Whitehall.[20] There was communication of views between States hopeful of mutual support or seeking to make friends and exercise influence. What of that kind went on between Moscow and the satellite capitals cannot be known; it was however to be observed at the conference that the satellites always voted the way the USSR did, and that there was evidently preplanned division of debating labour between them. Canada in its preparations showed more care to consult the USA than the UK. Australia and New Zealand communicated with each other more often than Australia did with any other State. Denmark sought to get the Scandinavians together in advance of the conference but didn't quite succeed. In Geneva however they all, Finland included, 'collaborated harmoniously'.[21]

The USA did little advance consultation about the business of the conference with any States except Canada and the UK; its extensive exchanges with France were all to do with the Russian problem in every ramification the French gave it. Certain differences from the UK's positions were early identified and attempts were made to resolve them; above all when the British head-of-delegation-designate, Sir Robert Craigie, was able to stop off in Washington in late February 1949 in course of an American holiday. He recorded that he got on well personally with the men he met and was glad in particular that Leland Harrison—like himself, an experienced former ambassador—was going to be his American counterpart. But substantial differences remained, now and then to ruffle relations between the two powers throughout the conference, each delegation repeatedly recording its regrets that the two were not more wholly in harmony with each other. To be out of step with their major wartime allies of 'the special relationship' did not seem to the Americans quite right. Equally removed

[19] UK: FO 369/4146 K. 3023, 3145, 3258, and 4147 K. 3449.
[20] UK: FO 369/4147 K. 3637.
[21] SW: HP/30/B, Files XXI–XXIII *passim*. The Swedish chief delegate's official report took special note that this was the first time since the war that Finland had appeared at an international conference. Admittedly, he wrote, it had behaved cautiously but, 'as far as I could find, the Soviet delegation has not on any occasion attempted to influence the Finns' point of view'.

from the ideal and more surprising to the men from Washington, because apparently unanticipated, was the development of some unreliability, amounting to a sort of indiscipline, among the South Americans. To what extent their delegates were instructed to vote on this occasion with the USA is not known (Brazil for one said it had been so instructed at the 1947 conference); certain it is that the US delegation, which devoted one of its two big receptions exclusively to the South Americans, felt some indignation when they were not with it at important junctures.[22]

The UK's mixed relations with what might have been expected to prove natural allies, the Commonwealth States and the USA, have already been noticed. With none of the Commonwealth briefs and preoccupations did the UK's entirely match but tactful preliminary discussions and predictable fellow-feeling made sure that no abrasions turned septic. Co-operation between them all grew as the 1949 conference went on and about half-way through it they began 'periodical meetings for tactical co-ordination'. Canada's leaning US-wards on occasions of UK–US differences seems not to have been found upsetting. India, besides being 'too much tarred with the "humanitarian" brush', was thought to be reluctant to join line-ups against the Soviet Union. Pakistan by way of contrast was found very helpful, not least because it could often bring the other Muslim delegations along with it.[23]

Both UK and US delegations found it desirable to add to their burdens (already onerous, since they were not numerically large, and they came with exacting briefs) some systematic lobbying and nobbling. While, to quote the decorous terms of Leland Harrison's official report, 'the various members of the [US] Delegation entertained at lunch small groups of delegates with whom they desired to become better acquainted', the UK delegation sought to redress the unpopularity of its negotiating tactics by systematic social-izing. At its twelfth daily meeting on 5 May, the British situation was reviewed and a plan made. Sir Robert Craigie reported that he had 'a fairly satisfactory talk with Mr Harrison'. John Alexander, the delegation's strategist, 'said that it seemed to him that the two people who were out to disagree with the UK, if they could find any excuse to do so, were Mr Castberg of the Norwegian delegation and General Dillon of the US.' What to do about them? Could they be softened? 'Mr Gardner [the War Office's warhorse] said that although he thought Mr Castberg was a fanatic in his

---

[22] The 1947 Brazilian, on p. 8 of Clattenburg's Report cited in n. 13. For the other Latin Americans, US Dip: 514.2 Geneva, 7-649 and 7-1149.

[23] UK: FO 369/4164 K. 10540. Craigie's draft for his final conference Report, dated 4 Nov. 1949, paras. 25-32.

views, he was more open to reason than General Dillon.' Craigie then undertook to have a go at Castberg, while Alexander, it was agreed, 'should try his skill on General Dillon'.[24]

But that was not all. The UK had made a bad start and was not easily going to overcome it. Alexander undertook to 'circulate a tentative proposal for consideration on a possible disposition of forces'. Mr W. V. S. Sinclair of the Treasury Solicitor's Office, concurring, said that he had 'already started work on the Mexicans'. A week or so later, the scheme was ready; Alexander's twenty-fourth circular, headed 'Liaison with other Delegations', proposed 'a sort of duty list showing who would undertake what and with whom . . . Omitted are the Great Powers (including Monaco), the Commonwealth of course, and those it would be difficult if not profitless to court.'[25] How useful all this planned socializing actually was cannot be reckoned. The papers of the UK delegation record its continuance to the very end, together with anxious assessments of the voting prospects, like this of 11 July, when the thirtieth circular contained a memo by Alexander about them. Normally with the UK, he judged, and always persuadable, were ten: Canada, Australia, New Zealand, Greece, Luxemburg, France, Italy, Belgium, the Netherlands, and Ireland. Perhaps persuadable, about a dozen, headed by the USA, 'the free Scandinavians', and the Holy See. The Central and South Americans plus Finland, he characterized as unpredictable floaters. Against the UK, nine, i.e. the Soviet bloc plus Israel.[26]

Israel, Monaco, and the Holy See together constituted a trio of oddities illustrating the degree of influence that can be wielded by small, even micro-States, given favourable place and circumstance. Britain's social strategist Alexander was not being entirely satirical in his reference to 'the Great Powers (including Monaco)'. Monaco's chief delegate was the vigorous and influential French law professor from Aix-en-Provence, Paul de Geouffre de La Pradelle.

Monaco mattered partly because *he* mattered. He was one of the most thoughtful contributors to the debates (two years later publishing a uniquely valuable book about the 1949 conference) and he was a weighty spokesman for that most persistent of pressure-groups, the International Committee of Military Medicine and Pharmacy, from which, based in Monaco before the war, had flowed a stream of humanitarian proposals.

---

[24] UK: FO 360/4148 K. 3792 and 4151 K. 5008. Craigie in para. 20 of the report cited added that Dillon 'frequently gave such violent expression to his views as to arouse general comment in Conference circles'.

[25] Beyond the documents cited in n. 24, also 4150 K. 4903.

[26] UK: FO 369/4157 K. 6842. But the USSR joined the UK on some practical issues, as Craigie's reports from time to time acknowledged.

Monaco's vote of course was always with France. It was also, whenever possible, on the side preferred by the Holy See. The Vatican may be presumed to have been as active behind the conference scenes as it was in them. Canada, for example, although only in part a Roman Catholic State, was made party to Rome's conference hopes, fears, and displeasures.[27] The UK can by no means have been high on Rome's list of diplomatic allies, but quite early in the 1949 conference Mgr. Bernardini, Papal Nuncio in Switzerland and head of the Holy See's delegation, arranged a meeting with one of the the British delegation, to communicate to it also his special concerns: the status of captured medical and religious personnel, the state of the law regarding repatriation of POWs, and certain grievances. The Holy See, he said, had not been asked to help in the opening ritual of selecting vice-presidents; it felt that 'in a humanitarian convention there should be at least one reference to God, even if it annoyed the Russians', and there was opposition to its desire to be among the potential substitutes for a protecting power.[28] The British papers do not show how these disclosures were received. They (the papers) are more revealing of British reactions to Israel's lively entry upon the international conference scene.

Israel had only been an independent State for a few weeks (since 14 May 1948) when Uruguay enquired of the Swiss government, on the government of Israel's behalf, whether it could at once proceed to accede to the 1929 Conventions. The Swiss Minister in London enquired what the UK and the Commonwealth countries thought about this.[29] By the time the Stockholm Conference opened, ten days or so later, Egypt—the only open objector—could be told that Israel, having duly acceded, had been thought by the Swiss government and the ICRC fit to attend as an observer.[30] Mr Gardner afterwards told how he had sought (unsuccessfully) to soothe Egyptian feelings by pointing out that being an observer did not necessarily mean much; the list of observers including, for example, the Girl Guides and Boy Scouts. But Israel was no silent observer after their fashion (or, on that occasion, the Russian). It made a defiant speech (heard in stony silence) defending its humanitarian record and intentions, insisting only that Red Cross relief work in Israel must be equally for Jews as well as Arabs.[31] By the time the diplomatic conference met, eight months later, relations between Israel and the Arab Muslim States were set in the familiar mould. Syria lost

---

[27] CAN: 619-B-40 vols. 3 and 5 *passim*.
[28] UK: FO 369/4151 K. 5011. As described by Col. Sayers.
[29] UK: FO 369/3969 K. 9347, letter of 11 Aug. 1948.
[30] UK: FO 369/3969 K. 9522.
[31] Gardner's Report on the Stockholm Conference, cited in n. 16 above.

no time in challenging Israel's presence. Nothing came of that, but a great deal came from Israel's insistence that, if Muslim States would not forgo their use of the Red Crescent emblem in lieu of everyone else's Red Cross (to which, if it could again become the sole, universal symbol, Israel for its part could willingly conform), Israel would have to ask to be allowed to use the Red Shield of David. The issue at once became politicized. For the first time in such Red Cross gatherings, high international politics drove humanitarianism (albeit only momentarily) into the ditch. Long and heated were the debates over this, and considerable the irritation of feelings. At the first vote, Israel was defeated by 21 to 10, with 8 abstentions and 19 absentees. Because it had been a roll-call vote, intense political lobbying ensued; to an extent which the senior Australian delegate alleged to have been a real nuisance. It was agreed the vote should be by secret ballot. So it was, again to Israel's discomfiture, this time, by 22 to 21.[32]

The Diplomatic Conference: What Happened, and What did not Happen

The course of the conference was chiefly determined by three factors: the texts of the agenda before it, the relative strengths of the States' delegations attending it, and the instructions given them by their respective governments. (It should be remembered that ICRC experts participated only as 'observers'.) What went on at the conference was by no means coextensive with what came out of it. The four new Conventions, its famous fruits, will be analysed in the next section. This section will recall the fruits which withered on the bough. For persons concerned with history, politics, and international relations as well as (or rather than) law and practice, what did not get into the Conventions can be at least as significant as what did.

The extent to which delegations' negotiating behaviour was determined by control from their capital was a matter often discussed. Clearly, it was more satisfactory for a party engaged in the making of bargains and compromises to know whether the other party could reliably deliver. Did its instructions give it power to commit the State that sent it? How many matters had to be referred back? Was there at any rate a fixed State policy, or were domestic politics liable to break in? The UK and US believed this to be the case with the French, and there was evidence of it in the fact that the nominal head of the French delegation, Robert Betolaud, was not, as were his counterparts, a professional diplomat or lawyer but Minister for Ex-

---

[32] *Final Record* IIA, 18 and 91; IIB, 231–2.

Service Men and War Victims, occupationally embroiled with one of the touchiest topics of French post-war politics.

The US and UK delegations for their parts knew no such embarrassments, but themselves related differently to their capitals. The US delegation enjoyed larger freedom of manœuvre than the British and its communications with Washington were a lot simpler. The UK delegation arrived at Geneva with a very detailed brief and almost no discretion to depart from it without reference back to base. When the brief proved unrealizable, the British officials therefore had to add to their already heavy labours a running correspondence with Whitehall, not to mention a growing amount of making and receiving visits, which was of course something only the European participants could much engage in. The three 'white' Commonwealth delegations had clear and full instructions, which enabled them to restrict their homeward references to the few big novelties or dilemmas which had lain beyond imagination.

The texts were basically those evolved in Stockholm the previous year. The ICRC's intermediate processing of them introduced few changes of substance. All the more serious Geneva participants had reservations about this or that aspect of the Stockholm texts, but only the UK openly professed to find them intolerable. Since the UK had chosen to stand aloof from the debates which forged them, it was not perhaps well placed to demand their wholesale reconstruction. That, however, was what it did, first by means of the circular letter already referred to, sent to Berne for distribution early in 1949; also by intensive lobbying around the Commonwealth countries and, to a lesser (because warier) extent, the USA; and by its delegation's issuing, during the conference itself, 'an enormous number of amendments, some of which bore no resemblance to the articles in their original text'.[33] Some of this activity achieved what the British meant it to achieve but at a price of popularity and influence which persuaded Britain's natural friends that it would have been better avoided, not least because of the handles it gave to States less naturally friendly.

The delegations varied enormously in size, experience, and talent. At the heads of at any rate the larger ones stood professional diplomats, brought in for the occasion; the mastery of the business which such men quickly

---

[33] Circular letter referred to in n. 19 above. 'Enormous number of amendments' criticized by Col. Hodgson in pts. 1 and 6 of his final Report; AUST: A. 1838, IC 1481/1 pt. 3. The Americans also found them tiresome; see Airgrams 514.2 Geneva/5-249 and 5-949. The latter said, 'Hope for modification British tactics has not materialized despite close liaison. This regrettable situation since we forced into position opposing them on nearly all procedural issues. . . . Apparent British losing votes thus reducing their potential to help us on some major points we were relying on.'

acquired was impressive. The bodies of the delegations of the larger powers were normally filled by the same or some of the same expert officials who had been working on the draft texts through the past two or three years, and who, in many cases, already knew one another, from the Government Experts' and Stockholm meetings. They were likely to know the texts backwards, to understand exactly what it was all about, and to be quick to spot signs of ignorance and unfamiliarity in delegations less well prepared, so the others thought, because of inexperience, insulation, unimportance, unintelligence, inattention, or (as was sometimes alleged) irresponsibility.[34]

Delegates of States which were taking the process very seriously could not but be irritated when delegates of the less serious orated at length, made impractical proposals, and cut committee meetings (which was happening increasingly as the weeks wore on), without ceasing to matter equally with all other parties when it came to the votes which in the end decided everything. There were no necessary correlations between size of State, size of delegation, and quality of contribution to the work of the conference. Monaco, for instance (delegation of three), carried weight, as has already been said, and Burma's solitary delegate, General Oung, who came to Geneva from his usual post as military attaché in London, was a host in himself. Denmark was a small State by world standards but its delegation of seven was larger than China's or India's, its members knew what they were talking about, and its leader's personality gave it a cutting-edge that could scarcely have been predicted.[35]

The very first thing the Soviet delegate did at the first business meeting was to move the addition to next day's agenda of the item, 'Invitation of Byelorussia and of the Ukraine to the Conference'; no one objecting, on either occasion, the USSR's own conference strength was brought up to the norm it had enjoyed from the beginning in the UN. No delegation intervened in debate more often or more purposefully. Whether it was as well prepared (by the standards the 'Western' powers set themselves) as it could have been, was a question not easy to decide. Notoriously, the USSR had taken no part in the past three years' preparatory labours. Now it suddenly plunged into the work of the final stage, espousing the Stockholm texts with an enthusiasm which could only arouse suspicion. Sir Robert Craigie got the impression that the Russians were technically well prepared as well as

---

[34] e.g. the US delegation's complaint in its airgram to Washington, 17 May 1949: 'Many delegates on Committee III [for the Civilians Convention] absolutely unqualified deal with subject, lack instructions on military and security aspects, or lack instructions entirely.' US: 514.2 Geneva/5-1749, para. 11.

[35] The official list in *Final Record* I describes him as: 'HE Georg Cohn, Doctor of Laws, Envoy Extraordinary and Minister Plenipotentiary'.

tactically adroit; a senior member of his team, Arthur Strutt of the Home Office, thought otherwise, and claimed that the Russians' legal chief, Morosov, actually admitted he had not till then studied the draft of the Civilians Convention.[36]

The enthusiasm shown by the Soviet Union and its satellites for the Stockholm texts aroused surprise and suspicion on other grounds than their having had no share in the making of them. It seemed odd, at any rate to the British, Commonwealth, and American delegations, that the USSR, so experienced and formidable in military respects, so 'realistic' and ruthless in political ones, should espouse the draft texts which the rest of the major military powers considered to have been stretched by humanitarian enthusiasm to unacceptably 'idealistic' lengths. Scrutiny of the Soviet and East European attachment to them, as part of those States' overall behaviour at Geneva, must be preceded by examination of the generally 'humanitarian' mood which pervaded the conference and provided one of its characteristic flavours. The ways in which delegates experienced it and reacted to it explain much of their behaviour there, besides adding a chapter to the history of an age-old debate.

To maintain some humane limitations on the conduct of warfare was every party's purpose, as it had been the purpose of every endeavour through the previous eighty years. The problem facing them now was— subject to an all-important *mutatis mutandis*—the same classic problem it always had been: to what limitations in the nature and use of weaponry was war-making in its present phase susceptible? The just-finished war displayed such devastating developments in both nature and use that reflective and sensitive people everywhere seem to have shared a common concern to subject them to legal control. What would have been the views of the German and Japanese delegations, had such been able to participate in the debates, we can only guess; but it is reasonable to deduce from the com- plaints issuing from Berlin and Tokyo from time to time during the war that, even there, enough of the idea of war-limitation existed for German and Japanese voices to have been able to join in the post-war chorus. They might not have introduced any more false notes and indiscipline than were already in it.

There is less doubt as to where a survey of the humanitarian spectrum would end than of where it would begin. It came to its end-stop with the inability of some of the most powerful victors honestly to commit them-

---

[36] UK: FO 369/4164 K. 10667, 7 Nov. 1949, commenting on Craigie's draft. His HO colleague Speake had already complained about this in early June; 4154 K. 5919.

selves to certain limitations possessing, as even spokesmen of their military establishments would admit, much humanitarian attractiveness. It might well begin with the variety of ambitious ideas showing throughout the Red Cross movement as soon as the war was over, and finding formal expression in reports and resolutions of its international meetings.[37] The 'Preliminary Conference of the National Red Cross Societies' in Geneva 26 July–3 August 1946 expressed a hope that even the National Societies of warring States might hold together in wartime. As for IHL, besides demands for maximal extension of protection to civilians suffering under enemy occupation or as aliens in enemy territory, there was a firm resumption of the pre-war demand for the prohibition of aerial bombardment of civilians, plus a recommendation to extend the prohibition also to 'the use of all means of chemical and bacteriological warfare, as well as the employment of atomic energy for purposes of war.' A much-acclaimed expression of the mood of that conference was given by a Greek delegate, Professor Michel Pesmazoglu. International law, he insisted, remained what it had been before the law-breaking horrors of 'total war' broke loose.

War has been transformed into butchery and belligerents strike army and civilian population alike without any distinction between the two. However, all abuses lead to a reaction. . . . International conscience demands the condemnation of all these barbarous proceedings. The world is amazed and stunned before these rivers of blood, these hillocks of bones, these mountains of ruins. . . . A new crusade is being gathered together against these abuses. . . . We have been convened here to accomplish this universal desire. . . . We are conscious of the will of all those whose lives, either as hostages, deportees, or on the field of battle, were sacrificed to the madness of men who believed that the protection of human beings was merely a figment of the brains of intellectuals. . . .
  All these martyrs do not demand revenge but they cry out that their sacrifice shall not have been in vain. They ask to be the last victims of these theories according to which man exists only for the State and not the State for the happiness of its citizens.[38]

The ICRC (whose place in the implementation of such ambitious schemes was contentiously disputed by the League's proponents) could never, of course, express its humanitarian aims in such enthusiastic terms. Yet, in all essentials of IHL, its own hopes and plans were similar to those of the movement at large as represented at this 1946 conference, and in referring to (preatomic) bombing the conference needed only to refer to pre-war

[37] Copies of reports on these immediately post-war meetings were kindly provided from the archives of the Australian Red Cross Society by its then Secretary-General, Ms Noreen Minogue, when I visited her HQ early in 1984.
[38] AM RC: 041.IRC, Prelim. Conf. 1946.

ICRC resolutions and to the ICRC's wartime series of circulars to the belligerents, deploring the rising scale of indiscriminateness and the consequent civilian sufferings; a series summed up in that dated 5 September 1945 (and not failing to note the atomic culmination of horrors), whose penultimate paragraph read thus:

Totalitarian war has bred new techniques. Has it therefore to be admitted that the individual must cease to be legally protected and must be considered as simply an element of warring collectivities? That would be a crumbling of the fundamental principles of the international law caring for the physical and spiritual protection of the human being. . . . If war denies [his] worth and dignity, it will proceed irresistibly to destruction unlimited, because the intelligence of man, as it progressively seizes the forces of the universe to make use of them, seems only to accelerate along this fatal road. . . . But the Red Cross ideal remains an incarnation of the ideas of the intrinsic worth and dignity of people.[39]

A means of protecting civilians and other non-combatants to which the ICRC was significantly devoted, and of which in these years it made much in the course of its endeavours to pack one of the sinister jinn of total war back in its bottle, was the creation of 'safety zones', guaranteed to be innocent of combatant character and therefore, by the ICRC's hopeful thinking, excludable by belligerents from their military operations. Much discussed (not in Geneva circles alone) during the years before the war, and to some small extent already experimented with in China and Spain, it formed the basis of the attempts the ICRC made towards the end of the war to persuade belligerents to recognize this and that city or district as such a zone, for the benefit of the war-victims, who were there or who could be assembled there.[40] The uniform unsuccess of those attempts prompted the ICRC, throughout its planning for the Diplomatic Conference, to argue that such zones should be delineated and agreed upon well in advance of the conflicts in which they could be life-saving. This was one of the most consistent planks of the humanitarian platform from which it orchestrated, as best it could, the much larger programme of demands coming up from the Red Cross movement generally.

Only parts of this programme got into the 1947–9 conference texts. Those items had to go which military and political critics would find most impractical, but enough remained to make the *soi-disant* realists of the

[39] 'La fin des hostilités et les taches futures de la Croix-Rouge', 370th circular from the ICRC to Central Committees of National Red Cross Societies. The passage I have translated comes near the end.
[40] Pictet's *Commentary*, IV. 123. The pre-war movement in this direction was spelled out in an ICRC Memorandum to Belligerents' Governments, 15 May 1944: 'Localités et zones sanitaires, localités et zones de sécurité.'

delegations marvel at the 'idealism' disclosing itself in some of the others. One of the forms it took was astutely described thus by the head of the US delegation to the first of the official series of conferences, that of Government Experts in Geneva in 1947:

The attitude of the technical experts from the liberated European countries, while perfectly understandable as a reaction to the horrible experiences which they had for the most part undergone personally, revealed a lack of balance, perspective and administrative experience ... which sometimes made it hard to keep the meeting on a realistic plane. These delegates exhibited to a surprising degree reliance upon international legislation as a means of eliminating evil from the minds of men.[41]

Perhaps it was still possible, in early 1947, to hold such hopes of the power of international law in the new era believed to be opening. By 1949 the dream had rather faded. A rougher-tongued but not necessarily harder-hearted head of delegation, Australia's Col. W. R. Hodgson, in his official report thus summarized what had happened to 1947's draft texts during their 1948 detour through Stockholm. The ICRC's draft as there amended, he wrote,

aimed, as one might expect, at humanitarian guarantees on the broadest possible scale, and laid down stipulations regarding the liberty of action of contracting parties within limits which might have appeared at Stockholm to be acceptable by the various States. However, at this diplomatic conference where only Governments were represented it was attended by many delegates who had experience of the administrative difficulties which arose during the world war, and they brought to the discussions their own preoccupations and those of their Governments concerning collective defence, war necessities, and the needs of security. Consequently the discussions gravitated between the two poles of realism and idealism. Many delegates ... who had experienced the horrors of enemy occupation or who for one reason or another feared it in future were always to be found on the side of the widest and most complete protection for all protected persons, especially civilians, while at the same time they sought to deny any rights to the protecting or detaining power. The Soviet Union constantly voted with this group, [and so did Latin Americans] who had no practical experience and were guided by what can only be termed sickly sentimentality.[42]

Hodgson thought of himself, as did other experienced delegates, as seeking to achieve as many humanitarian goals as military and political realism permitted, an all too easily misunderstood attitude which came out crisply in an early exchange with Mlle Andrée Jacob of the French delegation. It must have been a tense moment. The UK delegation thought it worth noticing.

---

[41] Document cited (p. 1) in n. 13 above.
[42] Document cited (para. 8) in n. 33 above.

The French delegate asked Col. Hodgson if in his view the object of the conference was to protect the interest of civilians or of the State. Col. Hodgson replied that both State and civilians had obligations and rights and that we must see that there was a fair balance between the two.[43]

If the missing preamble was one of the two big events of the Convention-making process to which the Conventions themselves offer no clue, the other was the failure to ban indiscriminate bombing. This was almost entirely an enterprise of the USSR and its satellites, and its steady unfolding through the conference weeks became a matter of much excitement for the American and British Commonwealth delegations. Nothing in the conference's closing stages more divided them from the Soviet bloc or disclosed the difference of purposes which had brought them to Geneva.

Concern about total war's practice of indiscriminate bombing was not, of course, a communist monopoly. Concern and anguish were widespread throughout all the countries that emerged from the war, whichever side they had been on. The Red Cross movement, as has already been noticed, was only one of the many channels through which this great fear made itself apparent and sought for solace. Indiscriminate bombing was—how indeed should it not have been?—regularly part of thoughtful people's picture of the inhuman excesses into which war had wandered, high on the list of war practices that clamoured to be brought under control.

Where and how that control was to be discussed and determined were however matters upon which opinions would be influenced by political considerations and the course of events. In 1945 and 1946, when wounds and remorse from the preatomic bombing era were still raw and no clear way to handle the worse troubles of its atomic successor was yet visible, it was reasonable that the agenda for Geneva should include bombing. By 1947 it was not so clear that it had to. The ICRC had never concealed its conviction that indiscriminate and terror bombing as increasingly practised in the war was lawless, at least in the sense that it contradicted the fundamental principles of IHL to which the signatories of its treaties were committed. It can, however, hardly have wished further to complicate an already complicated task by adding to its Geneva agenda an item which could, given the then rules of the legislative game, be plausibly represented as belonging more to The Hague.[44] (Or perhaps, hopefully, the UN.)

---

[43] UK: FO 369/4149 K. 4768, notes of the UK delegation's 6th meeting. This exchange is reported in very similar words in the *Final Record* IIA, 622.

[44] Nothing came of the Netherlands Government's discreet enquiry, about the time of the beginning of the Diplomatic Conference, whether it would be a good idea for it to initiate a revision of Hague law to match what was being done in Geneva. Little more seems to be known of this episode than Kalshoven has written in his contribution to van Panhuys *et al.* (eds.), *International Law in The Netherlands* 3 (Alphen a.d. Rijn and New York, 1980), 289–

So much was true of bombing in general. But if atomic bombing was something special and different and much more urgent, was it to be dealt with on its own? Through 1946, an affirmative answer became increasingly credible. At the very beginning of that year, the General Assembly established *nem. con.* its Atomic Energy Commission to produce plans for, *inter alia*, the prohibition of atomic weapons. From the middle of that year, the AEC was discussing the USA's plan for that end and the USSR's alternatives. Progress was scarcely encouraging, but the business seemed to be continuing and while that could *bona fide* be believed, it would not be unreasonable to argue that no other body should tinker with the new, dread and specialized business of control of atomic weapons and energy so long as the AEC had it in hand.

It was therefore not surprising that aerial bombardment, not even in its dramatic and dreadful latest form, no more figured in the agenda for the 1947 Government Experts' Conference than did any other method of prosecuting war. Even those who had it at the forefront of their minds could persuade themselves that it would be better dealt with elsewhere. But it turned up at the conference nevertheless, and as part of a 'peace' package which was soon to become familiar to international conference *aficionados*. The conference was not a long one, lasting only from 14 to 26 April. The proceedings, when they opened, could be expected to be politically uncontentious by persons for whom contention came chiefly in communist dress: no Soviet presence, neither Yugoslavs nor any other central or eastern European delegations except one from Czechoslovakia, which at that date, it must not be forgotten, was still apparently an independent Western-style parliamentary democracy. What happened next was admirably described by Clattenburg in the 'secret' annexe to his 'unrestricted' report.

The Polish delegation arrived quite late and attended regularly only the meetings of Committee 3 on the problems of civilians. Almost immediately after arrival their spokesman began lobbying among the delegations of the liberated nations for the adoption at the final plenary sessions of the meeting of a resolution against further use of war as a means of settling disputes and against the use of weapons of mass destruction in war, the text of which they had evidently brought with them from Warsaw.

The intention was to introduce the proposal as a surprise move.

The Polish intention was first brought to the attention of the American delegation in strict confidence by a member of one of the delegations from the liberated countries,

335 at 293–4. The only mention of it I have noted is a copy of an *aide-mémoire* from Berne to London, seemingly dated 10 July 1947, in AUST: IC 46/81/7; its purpose is to apprise the British government that the Netherlands one has no objection to the Swiss/ICRC project.

who had obtained a copy and an outline of the Polish plan of strategy. A check several days later revealed that the British Empire delegation had not yet been informed of the project.

Careful study led the US delegation to conclude that besides being 'political rather than technical or humanitarian', the Polish resolution was also dangerous; 'it embodied language which might in certain circumstances permit a signatory to renounce obligations thereunder on the ground that the ICRC or the UN had joined forces with "fascism".' It therefore had to be thwarted but with enough tact and indirection to protect them from too easy a charge of 'voting for the continuance of war as a political weapon', something that Moscow and its allies were perceived by Western diplomats as very ready to do, even though some months still had to pass before it would become familiar as an element of their great peace offensive which would provide political 'noises off' for the 1948 and 1949 conferences.

Agreement was easily reached with the UK delegation on a procedural device to smoke the Poles out. Circulation of copies of their resolution soon made it clear that most heads of delegations were worried about it. 'The ICRC also confidentially expressed concern through its officers.' Simply to reject it on grounds of incompetence and irrelevance would however look like

a sterile way in which to deal with a dynamic subject of vital concern, since most of the delegates would have preferred success of the United Nations' efforts to prevent war to success of their own effort merely to mitigate the effects of war. . . . With all this in mind, the American delegation collaborated in the development of a substitute recommendation (rather than resolution) covering the main points of the Polish project but eliminating all political cant and all phraseology that has so far been depreciated into international double talk. . . . The Brazilian delegate, having stated that he was under orders to give the American delegation full support, was asked if he would like to present the project and readily assented.

The introduction of the Polish resolution at the final session then met the following situation: A Brazilian counter-proposal was introduced, to the complete surprise of all delegations except the American. The liberated countries' delegations (except Czechoslovakia which seconded the Polish proposal) expressed a carefully prepared and concerted position that the Polish proposal exceeded their competence. The British Empire delegations had no prepared position discernible to any observer. It was clear even in this confusion that the Polish project had no chance, that there had been no 'ganging up' on the Poles, and that all the delegates sympathized with the professed objectives of the Polish delegation. Detailed discussion of the Brazilian proposal was prevented by the oversight of the Brazilian delegate in not preparing copies for distribution. In the circumstances, the British delegate proposed in a single sentence a simply worded recommendation against the further use of war as a political weapon which he made up on the spur of the moment.[45]

---

[45] Document cited (pp. 6–8 *passim*) in n. 13 above.

Sir Harold Satow's happy inspiration, 'apparently to the general relief, was unanimously agreed and accepted'.[46] The USSR and its satellites having absented themselves from the Stockholm Conference in 1948 (the year when their peace offensive really got going), there was no political pressure to include peace and bombing matters in the draft texts. The preservation of peace was in that darkening year of course on most people's minds, and 1947's promises of progress towards the control of atomic energy had so far proved false. These and related matters often came up in discussion. But the governments that were represented at Stockholm were in agreement with the ICRC and the League of Red Cross Societies (then at the zenith of its bid for equality of international status) that there were already enough difficult and contentious matters in the draft texts, without hazarding their prospects even further. The Stockholm texts went to Geneva with much in them that might be controversial because it was alleged to be impractical, but nothing that would be controversial because it was, in the cold-war climate of 1949, political. Moreover, the Swiss Government had assured several anxious enquirers that 'the Conference would make no departure from the humanitarian field to embark upon questions of a political nature'.[47]

From the moment that Soviet participation became known, however, an infusion of politics was to be expected. Its delegation's arrival created quite a sensation. So far as I can make out, none of the authorities involved had any advance notice of it. The USSR had of course been invited to participate at the same time as all the other States, but it sent no reply. The behaviour of Moscow's allies was therefore scrutinized for clues as to what Moscow itself might intend. At the end of March, the British Legation in Berne sent word that Czechoslovakia, the first satellite to reply (to the invitation of 20 September 1948) had just said it would not go. But two weeks later, and only one week before the opening, the wind changed. From Berne now came word that Hungary had accepted. A senior Swiss foreign ministry man told the British minister there 'that this change of policy, presumably on instructions from the Kremlin, might well herald similar changes by other satellites and might also be connected with the Soviet peace offensive'. Meanwhile, the British minister further informed his headquarters, 'a Soviet delegation appeared unexpectedly at last week's meetings in Geneva of the Executive Committee of the League of Red Cross Societies. Similarly a Czech delegate is taking part in tariff talks at Annecy.'[48] What might these things portend? Only on opening day itself was the mystery resolved—to be telegrammed at

[46] UK: FO 369/3794 K. 8146; Satow's own account of the affair.
[47] *Final Record* IIB, 504.
[48] UK: FO 369/4147 K. 3637 and 4148 K. 3947.

once to London by Sir Robert Craigie. The USSR had arrived, and seven satellites with it![49]

So the Soviet Union was going to participate after all. (There must have been dancing in the corridors of the Quai d'Orsay.) But what the character of its participation would be remained puzzling. No clue was available from the records of previous conferences. Was the USSR going to be serious about the Conventions or was it there simply for political and propaganda purposes? The Western delegations' close and suspicious scrutiny of the Soviet bloc's conference behaviour proved for many days unrewarding. That behaviour appeared to be so normal, even exemplary (the US delegation reported on 2 May that the USSR was even working in committees with Spaniards), that there was no choice but to conclude that the USSR was in some way serious about the Conventions as well as pursuing predictable political objectives.[50]

Absence from Stockholm in 1948 did not prevent the USSR in 1949 becoming an enthusiastic advocate of the Stockholm texts. 'One can only guess at their underlying purposes,' the Canadian deputy head told Ottawa on 19 May. 'It is certainly strange to see the Soviet government in the role of upholder of the Stockholm draft with all its drastic limitations on the rights of sovereign governments in time of war.'[51] This did not remain a problem. As the weeks went by, the Soviet delegation was seen increasingly to share the opinions of the 'realists' on issues of State security, and actually to out-do them on issues of international supervision. To the ardent humanitarian tone of the Stockholm texts however the USSR and its bloc remained ostentatiously faithful. It very soon became clear that one of their political objects was to depict States which scrutinized those texts critically as the enemies of humanity, and States which enthused about them as its friends.

As friends of humanity, and also, by natural association of ideas, of peace. The Soviet bloc's principal tactic, as it was gradually disclosed, was to emphasize its own attachment to peace by proposing such ostensibly war-limiting amendments to the texts as the Western 'realists' would have to oppose. Until the atomic finale, which formed (as Col. Hodgson put it) 'the highlight of the conference', the main line of advance towards this goal was to urge, with regard to the Civilians Convention, that its list of prohibited

[49] UK: FO 369/4148 K. 4555.
[50] US: 514.2 Geneva, 5-249, airgram of 2 May 1949. Craigie's 4 May report on the first week's work opined that 'this "honeymoon" cannot last, for the Russian delegation are clearly out for the Stockholm draft in its most extreme form' which not only 'the Slavs but also the so-called "humanitarians"' will support. FO 369/4149 K. 4590.
[51] CAN: 619-B-40, vol. 5.

and punishable offences against civilians (murder, torture, medical experimentation, etc.—a list upon which there was general agreement) should have added to it some such phrases as, 'also all other means of exterminating the civilian population' and of causing 'extensive destruction of [civilian] property'.[52]

Alarm bells rang throughout the Western corridors. It was obvious enough whither all this was tending. Unless the definition of civilians was tightly pinned to those who were in an enemy's hand either as aliens in his territory, or because he was occupying their territory, it could extend to cover the civilian population of an enemy country. And what besides genocide could the other phrases be pointing to but the sorts of area and indiscriminate bombing which had become American, British, and Commonwealth specialities? Meeting the Soviet bloc's well-contrived humanitarian offensive put the US and UK on the defensive and in a dilemma. 'Clearly nothing must be included . . . which would restrict freedom to carry out operations, particularly bombing,' wrote Sir David Roseway, the War Office dignitary who channelled the armed services' view to their man in Geneva, Mr Gardner. 'We consider that "extensive destruction of property" should be qualified by some such phrase as "except as may occur or be required in the course of accepted acts of warfare".[53] Again it would be necessary to qualify the phrase "the extermination of protected persons" in the same way. In both cases,' he naughtily added, 'it might be as well to introduce the word "deliberate" or even "cold-blooded" if there is a Russian word for this!'

But flatly to stand out for civilian bombing would look so bad! A long airgram from the US delegation to the State Department, despatched within a few hours of the USSR's launching this phase of its offensive, reviewed the prospects in all their awkwardness. For the moment, the danger had been averted by a procedural move. But:

3. Obvious emotional appeal Soviet draft such that if vote had been taken, USDel would have lost regardless of merits. . . . 7. On proposed Article 19A, USDel had direct support Canada only. United Kingdom, Denmark, France, Netherlands remained silent. Norway, Belgium, Mexico indicated inability perceive USDel point [the procedural one], considering question purely one of drafting. France known to share this view. . . . 9. Canada has stressed conference called to protect war-victims, not rewrite Hague Rules of Land warfare. . . . 10. USDel has received compliments from delegates who apparently fear express any views, for opposing Soviets without support and for withstanding liberal abuse and misrepresentation. 11. Many

[52] e.g. Morosov and other speakers in Committee 3 on 6 and 10 May; *Final Record* IIA, 645–51.
[53] UK: FO 369/4153 K. 5618, letter of 9 June.

delegates on Committee III absolutely unqualified deal with subject, lack instructions on military and security aspects or lack instructions entirely. In many circumstances, impossible predict outcome voting on foregoing amendments. Indications, for example, that Mexico and Guatemala may be misled by any seeming humanitarian plea into following Soviet lead.[54]

Blocking the Soviet bloc's moves was made the more difficult and nerve-wracking by fear that, if it were done too openly and bluntly, the USSR would find a congenial pretext for walking out. No one wanted that to happen. So the Western delegations soldiered on into the early days of July. Committee III's meeting on 15 June witnessed a widening of the offensive. The British delegation reported that the head of the French delegation cut through the fog of verbal war by asking the Soviet delegate to

state plainly what methods of exterminating the civilian population they had in mind ... The lady delegate from Romania for the first time made it clear that the Soviet amendment was in fact intended to apply not only to occupied territory but to all civilian populations ... In her view the Conference was not concerned to defend the laws of war but to defend the civilian populations ... The Russian delegate had nothing to say beyond the constant propaganda which we are encountering to the effect that the UK and US are always opposing the noble and humanitarian aims of the USSR. No answers were given to the questions put by the French delegate and by Sir Robert Craigie.[55]

The curtain went up on the final act of this political drama on 6 July, and even after so many weeks of warning, the form of it came as a surprise. Swift through the wires to headquarters sped the astounding message. The USSR, in defiance of the agreed rules of procedure and all norms of conference behaviour, had tabled in Committee III a draft resolution to ban atomic weapons. How should this be handled? Like all the Soviet bloc's earlier ventures in the same direction, it put the Anglo-American allies in the 'no-win' situation of being able to oppose it only at the cost of appearing, to those who wished to see them so, bellicose and ruthless. London early made up its mind to play it cool. As the Australian ambassador, who was made of sterner stuff, put it in his report: 'Right up to the last, the UK, Swiss, and French delegates felt it was imperative for publicity and propaganda reasons that a counter-resolution should be presented to and passed by the conference.'[56] Washington for long remained indecisive but in the end spoke with a voice of thunder. This was no hour for softness. Sir Robert's eirenical

[54] US: 514.2 Geneva, 5-1749, airgram dated 17 May.
[55] UK: FO 369/4154 K. 5952, enclosed with Craigie's 8th despatch dated 21 June. These exchanges appear in *Final Record* IIA, 716–19.
[56] AUST: A. 1838, IC 1481/1, pt. 3, para. 11.

counter-resolution, if passed, 'might prove an embarrassing precedent . . . It might give the Russians an opening for pushing their policy with regard to atomic energy matters in international bodies other than the AEC of the UN.' If the UK persisted, the US delegation would abstain or even oppose.[57] London came to heel, reconciling itself with the reflection that the Russians had already clocked up such a run of seeming moral victories, another could not hurt.[58] Ottawa had sought a tough line from the start.[59] Canberra was willing to go along with it. No surprise, therefore, that once the tough line had been agreed on, Col. Hodgson's considerable experience in standing up to the Soviet Union in Security Council and General Assembly should get him the job of spokesman. His speech at the 34th plenary meeting on 9 August seemed to his backers 'very effective'.[60] They were content to leave it at that. But the USSR had the last words. The Soviet bloc made *nine speeches*, more or less identical, and *Pravda* was to note how 'the Soviet representative Morosov unmasked Hodson [*sic*] as the advocate of the Anglo-Americans who . . . preferred to remain in the background.'[61] About that, at least, Moscow was right.

That high drama concluded with the rejection of the Soviet Union's draft resolution as 'inadmissible' by 35 votes to 9, with 5 abstentions. One of the abstainers, Col. Rao of India, promptly expressed feelings which no doubt were shared by many of those who had voted with the majority. The UN, he said, was just now the proper place for debating this problem of ABC weapons. India could therefore not vote for the USSR's resolution. But neither could it bring itself to such a 'sterile attitude' as to vote against it. The resolution 'presented a problem which ought to have been tackled positively and constructively'.[62] Further evidence of the tragic ambivalence of feelings among the majority was provided in the speech made by Switzerland's head of delegation, Mr Plinio Bolla, a speech aptly described by La Pradelle as 'une intervention nuancée'.[63] In remarking that his government would have to vote against the Soviet resolution (because the conference's terms of reference did not cover it), he expressed his assurance that such votes would not be read as votes of indifference to the acute and growing needs to prevent war and to find a solution to the particular war-

---

[57] UK: FO 369/7425, a telegram to the FO from the British Embassy in Washington.
[58] Ibid., Craigie's instructions from the FO.
[59] CAN: 7949-AK-40, vol. 1; a batch of letters, etc. 7 July–12 Aug.
[60] So judged by the Canadian delegation, as conveyed to Ottawa on 12 Aug., in ibid.
[61] A Tass report from Geneva, in *Pravda* 12 Aug. under the heading 'In defence of the loftiest principles of humanism'; complete translation in CAN: 619-B-40, vol. 5.
[62] *Final Record* IIB, 508.
[63] La Pradelle, *La conférence diplomatique*, 40.

making question the USSR had pressed upon them. The UN and its AEC were at the present time seeking a solution.

It is not for us to judge the activities of these organizations, and still less to give them advice, but we may perhaps express a wish and a hope that these international organizations will succeed in the task they have undertaken, for the greater benefit of all nations. The wish of a small country which possesses no material power is of little import, as we are perfectly aware, but according to the wisdom of all times and all places, it is better to light one small candle than to curse darkness.[64]

One year later, ICRC was to take a big risk by lighting another.

The Diplomatic Conference closed three days later on 12 August. After the straight West–East confrontation about atomic weapons which filled the greater part of the 9th, the recurrent political and national point-making which went on through the discussion of all the other resolutions that had been tabled, and the expressions of reservations (principally the Soviet bloc, the USA, the UK, and Israel) and regrets (principally the Holy See and ICRC) and self-importance (Mexico and Monaco) which followed the formal voting on the Conventions on the 11th, the closing ceremony was— once it had got over the USSR's last trump relative to 'mass extermination'—all sweetness and light.[65] Only three persons spoke. The president of the Conference, M. Max Petitpierre, concluded his much-admired term of office with a soberly moving review of the conference achievements and a reminder that they must all nevertheless profoundly wish that the Conventions they had made would never be needed. Then came the 'Auld Lang Syne' part of the occasion, genially managed by Col. Hodgson, once again the West's readiest spokesman, and the affable head of the Soviet delegation, General Slavin. Moved by the former and seconded by the latter, 'The delegates rose and the vote of thanks [to Switzerland and Geneva] was carried by acclamation.' M. Petitpierre briefly returned thanks, wished them all a safe journey home, and declared the Diplomatic Conference closed. Some of the business, not necessarily the least important bits of it, was now part of history. The history of the rest was only just beginning.

[64] *Final Record* IIB, 504. De la Pradelle acutely noted its policy implications. Craigie remarked in his 12th despatch, 12 Aug., that Bolla's short speech 'undoubtedly impressed some of the waverers'.
[65] *Final Record* IIB, 527–31.

5 | Making the Geneva Conventions

The Protection of Civilians

This was a long-standing Red Cross project to which the experiences of 1939–45 gave urgency and direction. By the end of the Second World War it had become a matter of major international concern. Nothing was—and nothing is—more crucial to IHL than the distinction between combatant and non-combatant, which, being translated into popular terms, approximates to the difference between the military and the civilian population. Setting aside as best it can the modern world's many tendencies to blur or even to abolish that difference, the humanitarian community tenaciously argues that civilians must be spared so far as the necessities of modern war permit. Between 1939 and 1945 their sufferings had been great and had been experienced under three principal heads: (*a*) civilians residing or travelling in a foreign country at the time of its becoming a formal enemy of their own State, and on that account subjected, as enemy aliens, to detention and other forms of maltreatment; (*b*) civilians of a country subjected by an enemy to military occupation; (*c*) civilians of belligerent States suffering in consequence of enemy attacks, whether directly aimed at them or incidentally hitting them, as was especially felt to be the effect of much aerial bombardment.

From a general humanitarian point of view, no one of these three categories of civilian suffering could be said to need attention more or less urgently than the others. Political circumstances however directed that only the first two—'enemy aliens' and 'civilians under enemy military occupation'—should be given much of the new Convention's protection. It was, above all, as sufferers from enemy military occupation that the majority of the European States represented at the 1947–9 conferences felt an urge to make new law for the protection of civilians. The most conspicuous sufferers from bombing, Germany and Japan, were unable to put their case, while the bombing specialists, the USA and the UK, had every reason for preventing the case being put. As we have seen, the case *was* put, to the small extent that terms of reference and rules of procedure permitted, by the USSR and its allies; but with a mixture of political and humanitarian motives that was impossible to unravel and that was in any case so obvious as to enable 'the bombers' to discredit them and to swing majorities (among whom must have been mixed feelings) against them.

The ICRC had a different approach to the same problem which could certainly not be morally discredited but which was open to so many objections on grounds of military realism that it too got virtually nowhere. This approach was by way of what were familiarly known as 'Geneva Zones', i.e. clearly designated areas of exclusively non-military and Red Cross interest which warring parties could agree to respect and avoid. Having for many years cherished this idea, the ICRC put it to the Government Experts in 1947. Disappointed but not disheartened by their refusal to accept commitments stronger than the merely permissive, it took the idea to Stockholm in more mandatory form: 'In time of peace already, [the parties] shall endeavour to set up ...'. The Stockholm Conference of course accepted that, with respect to 'hospital and safety zones and localities' (for the wounded and sick and specially vulnerable), and added to it a permissive draft article for the larger idea of wartime-arranged 'neutralized zones' for the sanctuary of civilians in general.[1] Both articles made it into the final text of 1949 but the former was made to revert to the merely permissive mode. A telegram from the Home Office on 30 May 1949 to its senior man in Geneva conveyed to him the British (which was more or less identical with the American and Canadian) Chiefs of Staff view:

They could never accept from the operational point of view any obligation to declare [beforehand] safety zones or to recognize willy-nilly those declared by an enemy. [A compromise proposal by the Netherlands was deemed to be] open to serious practical difficulties. From an operational point of view could only be accepted if we were assured that operational requirements would be decisive when it came to consider whether or not we could recognize such a zone.[2]

Equally reluctant was the UK to advertise in advance the geography of its plans (such plans as it had, anyway) for the evacuation of civilians from 'vulnerable' to 'safe' areas.[3] Such arguments were, as the US delegation put it in a worried telegram to Washington, doubly difficult for the 'Anglo-Saxon delegations' to deploy against a proposal with great 'emotional appeal', because they seemed to belong to the realm of war contingency

[1] These appeared as Articles 12 and 12(b) in the Stockholm text.
[2] UK: FO 369/4151 K. 5299.
[3] The telegram just mentioned was accompanied by a 'secret and immediate' one, as from one HO man to another, about Britain's emergency plans for the evacuation of civilians and how slight was their correspondence with the proposed Hospital and Safety Zones. But in any case, 'We do not want our evacuation plans discussed in public and must rely on argument already submitted that in a small country like UK it would be uneconomic to organize safety zones on basis contemplated. Even if our reception areas fall within the definition of safety zones we do not want to have to disclose to other powers in peacetime their location.'

plans—a provenance the USSR would not fail to point out.⁴ In the end however this turned out to be one of the many disputes which the process of give and take could resolve. Two species of optional Geneva Zones remained in the Civilians Convention, among it a few provisions applying to *all* civilians in wartime, *anywhere*: civilians *tout court*. The Canadians, when it was all over, had mixed feelings about it. The human rights aspect of it had no appeal for at least some of them.

There is an interesting and very controversial part of the Civilians Convention which is not limited in its application to protected persons but which applies to the whole of the population of countries in conflict. This part deals with respect for and protection of hospitals; special guarantees for children, especially those separated from their families; the possibility of passing medical supplies through the blockade to an enemy population; the right to send and receive family news. This part of the Convention created more controversy than any other at Geneva. It had a great appeal to delegates whose chief interest is in theoretical humanitarian ideas. Other delegates, including the Canadian, were inclined to doubt the wisdom or necessity of putting into an international treaty rules for the behaviour of a government towards its own citizens in its own country. It is true that there are precedents for dealing in an international instrument with the duties of a government towards its own population; notable examples are the International Labour Organization Conventions, the Convention on Genocide, the Universal Declaration of Human Rights and the Draft International Covenant on Human Rights. Nevertheless it is arguable that the Civilians Convention would be a good deal better if it were limited to the protection of aliens and did not undertake to tell governments how to respect their own hospitals and their own sick and wounded.⁵

The part of the Civilians Convention dealing with undifferentiated civilians is a relatively small one. What fills the bulk of the Convention is its main business, the protection of civilians in the hands of the enemy. This necessarily meant setting limits to what States and their armed forces could do to the enemy civilians upon whom their hands lay. The long section of Regulations for the Treatment of Internees (section IV, containing fifty-seven of the 159 articles) requires no notice here. Its purpose was to oblige States to provide for enemy civilian detainees a decent regime generally similar, *mutatis mutandis*, to that already existing for the benefit of POWs. Any sketch of the latter would serve well enough for both. More relevant to our inquiry are the limits and obligations which States signatories of the

---

⁴ US: 514.2 Geneva/6-749, 7 June 1949, airgram from Harrison to State Department.

⁵ CAN: p. 15 of Memorandum (mimeographed), dated 20 Sept. 1949, by the more senior of the Dept. of National Defense's two representatives at the conference, Col. John Crawford of the Directorate of Medical Services. Mr Dacre Cole of the Department of External Affairs' Historical Division, most helpful during my visit to Ottawa in early 1985 but unable at that time to locate any of his country's official reports on the 1947-9 conferences, subsequently discovered this one and kindly mailed it to me. Its location is unstated.

Convention bound themselves to observe in their handling of undetained enemy civilians, i.e. for the most part the civilian populations of occupied territory.

The achievement of these sections of the Convention turned out to be more controversial and troublesome than had been expected by the parties keenest on them: accredited spokesmen of the populations which had recently suffered so much under enemy military occupation, and humanitarians from all over who sympathized with them. That the Germans and the Japanese and their respective allies and/or subordinates had variously twisted, perverted, or simply ignored the law on belligerent occupation, no one denied. Such excesses had to be stigmatized, punished, and prevented. The post-war series of war-crimes trials had already, by mid-1949, administered much punishment to guilty individuals and groups (e.g. the German SD and SS). Now, in this extension of Geneva Law, was the time and place to arrange for prevention. This proved to be less simple a matter than outsiders might have expected, because of the wide divergence of views among the insiders themselves. The USA's admirable Albert Clattenburg commented on it more than once in his 1947 Report.

The state of mind of the delegates of the liberated countries described above led in the first place to the making of wholly impractical suggestions almost as though it were believed that legislation could make the lot of conquered peoples and other war victims pleasant . . . ; as a Chinese Red Cross delegate is reputed to have said the preceding summer, the cure for all China's problems would be to have new conventions along these lines and then to persuade some other power to occupy the entire country.[6]

On the other side, it had to be pointed out, however unpopularly, that not every tough measure the Germans had taken to maintain their authority as belligerent occupiers was illegal. It had furthermore to be said that no law of belligerent occupation could be rational and credible which did not legitimize measures of a certain toughness. International law expects of decent occupiers a sort of juggling act. They are expected to maintain as much as they can of the normal character and amenities of life in occupied territories, at the same time as they must be allowed to maintain their own presence and security there, pending the determination of those territories' fate in a war-closing peace treaty. The compromise that has to be reached is also one between two sets of rights: human rights, as they were coming to be expressed in the very earliest of the years covered by this part of the

---

[6] Document cited (p. 4) in Ch. 4 n. 13.

book, and belligerent rights, dating from time out of mind and not indefinitely malleable. By no stretch of rational imagination can civilians in occupied territories be expected to observe towards their temporary masters the same love, honour, and obedience as they are expected to observe towards their normal national rulers. They may wish, they may even be instructed, to offer resistance. But international law, having a care equally for the interests of each party, must prescribe proper forms for that resistance if the invader/occupier is to regard it as anything but criminal.[7]

Of this inescapable requirement to juxtapose and compromise, the humanitarian interest in 1949 had to be reminded by those who regarded themselves as more realistic. It was made easier for them by their own contemporary experience. They were the occupiers now (as often they had been in the past), and throughout this argument were now and then moved privately to uneasy thoughts by noticing that some of the things which people complained of Germans having done were things they themselves had done when playing the same occupying role. Clattenburg had mildly complained in 1947 that

The French delegation in particular seemed to have no concept of the problems facing their own General Koenig [commanding in the French zone of occupation in Germany]. Each effort to raise these points brought the response, 'Germany is a special case without parallel in which a criminal situation existed; we are discussing the general case.' And none of those making this argument seemed.able to realize that in recognizing the existence of a special case, they were establishing a precedent which would give their future mistrusted adversary perfect justification to determine the existence of a 'criminal situation' in their own respective countries whenever they might come under foreign domination again.[8]

But if some members of the French delegation at that conference did take a one-sided view of the question, it was not because they had not had both sides put to them at their interdepartmental committee meeting a few months before. M. Duhamel must have seen, and may indeed have come to the meeting armed with, an excellent memorandum from the Fédération Nationale des Déportés et Internés de la Résistance, which included this adjuration:

It is a matter of forgetting, so far as may be necessary, the unequal and atrocious struggle in which we were engaged against the Germans, and of not viewing the problem under this double hypothesis: seeing the problem of the individ-

---

[7] This matter is dealt with below.　　[8] As in n. 6 above.

ual 'Resistant' as quite a different thing from that of occupied countries in general. It must not be forgotten either that France today is itself an occupying power.[9]

In Sweden also could both sides of the question be understood. Sweden was not, nor was ever likely to find itself, an occupying power; but its peculiar neutral status enabled it to see the two sides of the question with a clarity denied to its recently occupied Scandinavian neighbours. One of the things being discussed in the Swedish Foreign Ministry through the early months of 1949 was whether they should go along with the extreme anti-occupier line proposed by Dr Georg Cohn, Denmark's head of delegation, or 'agree with the greater military powers such as the USA which would probably favour many limitations on the rights granted civilians in occupied countries'.[10]

Our review of a belligerent's relations with such enemy civilians as may lie under his hand may now proceed by examining, first, his obligations towards them; concentrating again on the obligations attached by the Civilians Convention to him as military occupier. The Hague Regulations, it will be remembered, laid down little law about this, partly because by the 'standard of civilization' then believed to prevail, little was thought enough. That little now became supplemented in these particular respects, which may be summarized thus:

Article 49: The occupier may not forcibly transfer or deport civilians, either individually or *en masse* from occupied to his own or any other territory, except, temporarily and not normally to anywhere outside their own territory, in the event that 'the security of the population or imperative military reasons so demand'; in which event they must be 'transferred back to their homes as soon as hostilities in the area in question have ceased'. Nor may population transfers be effected in the other direction, from the occupier's own territory into that he occupies.

Article 50: The interests of children, especially those 'orphaned or separated from their parents', are to be respected.

Article 51: Civilians may not be compelled to do any work—particularly not any work that implicates them in military operations—except what is 'necessary either for the needs of the army of occupation' or for their own

---

[9] FR: undated and anonymous Memorandum, typed on yellow paper, listed simply under title, Fédération Nationale des Déportés et Internés de la Résistance. It seems highly likely that this was Duhamel's brief for the meeting of Lamarle's committee on 10 Jan. 1947. The original reads, not 'hypothesis' but 'hypnosis'; but I assume that to be an error.

[10] SW: HP/30/B, File XXI, a 4-page typed Memorandum by Professor Torsten Gihl, legal adviser to the Swedish Foreign Ministry, dated 21 March 1949; kindly translated for me by Ulla Monberg. He displays extreme wariness of Denmark's Dr Cohn.

population's good; nor (Article 52) may the occupier drive them to work for him by artificially creating unemployment.

Article 53: No destruction of property, public or private, 'except where . . . rendered absolutely necessary by military operation'.[11]

Article 55: The civilian population must possess adequate food and medical supplies. If local resources prove inadequate, the occupier must 'bring in' whatever is needed, and if he cannot do that from resources at his own disposal, he must (Articles 59–63) 'agree to relief schemes on behalf of the said population' and facilitate their execution by such neutral States or 'impartial humanitarian organizations' (ICRC, National Red Cross Societies, etc.) as may volunteer to institute and administer such schemes. An obligation to facilitate them, it must be added, is placed by Article 23 (in the 'undifferentiated civilians' part of the Convention) on the adversary State, at least so far as regards the essential relief of under-15s, 'expectant mothers and maternity cases'.

A civilian population so well cared for by a military occupier, the reader may reflect along with the Chinese delegate cited above, would be in clover. The clover would have been even lusher had not most of these articles already been trimmed into a nearer relation to likely reality by the representatives of the occupying interest. The form in which these (and, *a fortiori*, the order-maintaining articles twinned with them) came to Geneva from Stockholm appalled the 'occupiers'. Some of these civilian-sustaining articles gave them a lot of trouble. Those to do with food supply, for instance. The likely cost of maintaining the levels set in the Stockholm texts was one thing, sure to strike in particular the two major Western military powers which had recently been put to huge expense to sustain the civilian populations of occupied Germany and Austria. But the military and political implications were another thing, more worrying in the long run. The more the US Army looked at these requirements, the less did it like them. It badgered the US delegation through the early weeks of the conference either to reject them or, when the State Department remonstrated that the Army should have thought more seriously about the matter months ago, to water them down with such expressions as 'as soon as military operations permit' and 'subject to its military necessities and logistic ability'.[12]

---

[11] Draper notes on p. 41 of his *Red Cross Conventions*: 'This is a matter of objective determination and is not decided by the opinion of the military commander at the time of the destruction.' How that opinion might relate to the Rendulic judgment (dealt with in Part III), I leave for legal experts to determine.

[12] US: 514.2 Geneva/4-2249, 2549, and 2949, and 5-249. These papers show the head of the delegation strenuously objecting to being pressed by the army to withdraw from positions the US accepted at Stockholm, and the army somewhat modifying its demands accordingly.

More serious still in strategic perspective was the obligation to import food from outside and to facilitate its being brought by others (Stockholm text, draft Articles 20 and 49). The UK had been the more uneasy of the two great naval powers about this, having relied for so long on blockade in war-making and having been spared the USA's recent bitter experience of an enemy's refusal to allow relief shipping through his maritime defences.[13] To what had been provisionally worked out at the Government Experts' Conference in the spring of 1947, the UK felt no profound commitment. To the Stockholm Conference's endorsements and elaborations, it paid (for reasons already indicated) no attention whatever. The UK went to Geneva in the spring of 1949 hoping to get draft Article 20 deleted. It prudently refused to put any trust in the guarantees supposed to be given by the Protecting Power that only civilians—and those, moreover, 'performing no work of a military character'—would benefit from supplies thus let through the net. Moreover, the UK would be obliged to set aside for relief purposes a specified quantity of shipping that could ill be spared. By the middle of June it was clear that although the USA and Canada supported the British position, no hope remained either of deleting the article or of turning it from the mandatory into the permissive mode. The best that could be got, then, was a giant boosting of the safeguards, which, with somewhat unexpected help from Norway's Professor Castberg, was duly accomplished.[14]

The other blockade-bending proposal, the Stockholm text's Article 49, was especially embarrassing to the USA on two counts. First, the Americans had themselves invented it in 1947. Based largely on their own wartime practice in the 'Greek Relief Program', it had been devised to avert such undesirable proposals as the total outlawing of food-blockades, and the army had at that epoch agreed to it. The second prospective embarrassment was entirely political and related more to the future than the past. The head of the US delegation put it as heavily as he could in a telegram to Washington on 25 April.

[13] It was an American grievance that the American Red Cross had not been allowed during the Second World War to take relief ships into Japanese-held areas for the benefit of (needy categories) of civilians detained there; State Department and American Red Cross officials were ready now to back the preparation of 'relief ships' and the fixing of 'safe conduct' sea-routes in advance. Britain's Second World War experiences led its officials to see the matter in a different light. The memory of shipping shortages and the Admiralty's refusal to contemplate more than *ad hoc* arrangements together caused an Anglo-American difference of opinion which may be glimpsed in US: 514.2 Geneva/2-2548 and 7-1648, and UK: FO 369/3968 K. 5862, paras. 126–36.

[14] The conclusion of this difficult matter was Article 23 of the Civilians Convention. Thierry Hentsch, *Face au Blocus* (Geneva, 1973), 226–8 felt it had not worked fairly during the Nigerian Civil War, 1967–70.

In view US achievement feeding Germany and Japan, US proposal delete or seriously weaken Article 49 would be construed as intention change policy with clear political implication, in view present world situation, that territory occupied in future would not be fed. With press and public admitted to sessions, wide exploitation such implication likely.[15]

In the end, changes were made and bargains struck that enabled the US Army and Navy Departments to accept these Articles as they eventually came out of the Geneva wash as Articles 23, 55, and 59. But it cost their delegation in Geneva a quantity of work and embarrassment it could well have done without. Foreign policy considerations had to be pressed against military ones:

Governments most interested in these Articles are Atlantic Pact signatories and others who fear imminent invasion. Possible effect on morale and policy such governments of apparent reversal US policy because of army dissent position so far held should be carefully considered high level.[16]

And, as always, a subtle antagonist was forever fishing in such troubled waters: 'Swiss press has already contrasted Soviet support humanitarian provisions Stockholm draft with British and US efforts define more clearly Common Article 2.'[17]

The Security of Belligerents

The other side of the coin from protection of civilians was protection of combatants. What powers did the Civilians Convention leave with or give to States to maintain their security and that of their armed forces against challenges from civilian, or seeming-civilian, sources? At first sight this may appear a contradiction in terms or a self-evident absurdity. It must have appeared so to many of the participants in the 1948 Stockholm conference, and no doubt it appeared so to some of those who turned up in Geneva for the Diplomatic Conference in the following year. By the time the Diplomatic Conference had finished dealing with it, however, the majority of the States represented there had come to recognize that it really was a problem, though much dissatisfaction remained with the compromise solutions eventually formed.

The problem had two principal aspects, approximating roughly to the two modes in which such a challenge might present itself: the more, and the less, violent. The more violent will be dealt with later under the heading of

[15] US: 514.2 Geneva/4-2549.
[16] US: 514.2 Geneva/5-249, telegram of 2 May 1949.   [17] Ibid.

guerrilla and resistance fighters. The less violent is better dealt with here, as a follow-on from the section on the provisions made for the better protection of civilians. But the reader must be warned that there is much overlap between them.

Such unrealism as may be detected in those provisions has its roots chiefly, of course, in their unspoken assumption—an assumption which moreover runs through all IHL, and must do so—that some degree of law-respecting goodwill pervades both parties to the belligerent relationship. Its absence perhaps matters less when those parties are armed forces than when one is an army and the other a civilian population. Even if the members of opposed armed forces have a dislike, or are taught to have a dislike, for each other, the discipline to which they are normally subject may ensure some respect for law; besides which, the law-protected enemies they are most likely to encounter person-to-person are by definition the least likely to continue to threaten or bother them: surrenderers, prisoners, and the disabled. An army however stands in a different relationship towards an enemy civilian population. Instead of recognizable categories of fellow fighters, once seen never, probably, to be seen again, there is a mass of people alien in more than one sense to the soldiers who have to live among them. A perfectly docile occupied population is scarcely conceivable; and so far as it might exist, it would by most conventional canons of judgment (e.g. nationalist, patriotic, collectivist, tribal) be contemptible. There can hardly not be some hostility and resistance shown to the uninvited, forceful, menacing stranger. The awkward questions were therefore inescapably posed: how much trouble should the occupier be prepared to put up with, and how tough was he allowed to get when the amount of trouble became unbearable? From some of the major war-crimes trials—the 'High Command' and 'Hostages' trials above all—came clearly the warning that the toughness could not lawfully go beyond a certain point; but in none of them was it suggested that he must passively submit to whatever indignities and injuries the occupied population chose to inflict upon him.

The security- and order-maintaining parts of the Civilians Convention show how the Diplomatic Conference trod this tightrope. They were the necessary counterpart to the civilian-protecting parts, which otherwise and on their own must be considered pure fantasy. Much argument and a certain amount of unpleasantness had to be gone through before they were reached. The recently occupied countries found them bitter pills to swallow. The countries with experience as occupiers feared lest they were giving away too much. On only one item of their security agendas did they achieve total satisfaction, a satisfaction proportionate to the dissatisfaction and disappointment it caused to the others and to the ICRC. This was Article 5, empowering States, whether in their own territory or in territories they might be occupying, to arrest and, if absolute military security required it, hold *incommunicado* civilians suspected of spying, sabotage, or other activities 'hostile to its security'. This was too much like recent Axis practice to escape anguished criticism. The ICRC spokesman singled it out for comment in his contribution to the discussion on the final vote. The ICRC, he said, although pleased to assist in an expert capacity in the conference's committee work, had felt it proper to leave discussion of 'the Articles themselves' to governments alone.

But you can scarcely be surprised that the ICRC, which is and should remain exclusively concerned with humanitarian questions, cannot forget the tragic occasions when thousands of human beings were imprisoned and cut off from the world, simply because they were regarded [by States' subjective judgments, he might have added] as constituting a danger to the security of the State, and were therefore denied the right of being visited by the Committee.[18]

Nothing of this sort had been in the draft texts of 1947 and 1948. But the US, UK, and Commonwealth diplomatic papers show how pressure in this direction built up through those years to such an extent that their departments of internal affairs on the one hand, their army departments on the other, were refusing to agree to signature unless their security demands were met. The US delegation's annoyance at the persistence of second thoughts about security was somewhat soothed by its conclusion that most other delegations seemed to find themselves in the same boat.[19]

For the maintenance of its security and of general order in occupied territory, the Civilians Convention prescribed, first, the continuance of the normal operations of the ordinary penal law of the land; and, second, to the extent that the functioning of that law should be undermined by its officials' non-cooperation or should be in any case inadequate to meet the occupier's security and military requirements, the enforcement of his own penal laws by his own military courts. A vast disagreement developed with regard to the nature and scale of punishments that the occupier might inflict. Once again, as always throughout this legislative process, the problem was that of

[18] *Final Record* IIB, 526. Carry's misgivings on that occasion were elaborated, together with an instructive scrutiny of the many and awkward differences between the French and English texts, in Pictet's *Commentary* on the Civilians Convention. Its sombre conclusion, on p. 58, is that the article is 'an important and regrettable concession to State expediency. What is most to be feared is that widespread application of the Article may eventually lead to the existence of a category of civilian internees who do not receive the normal treatment laid down by the Convention but are detained under conditions which are almost impossible to check.'

[19] UK: FO 369/4155 K. 6165, 4156 K. 6272 and 6382. US: 514.2 Geneva/3-1449, 4-149, and 5-949.

reconciling the views of those who had experienced the nastiest sort of military occupation with the views of those who resignedly assumed that military occupation could never be nice. The latter went a surprisingly long way to satisfy the former's feelings. They allowed Articles 33 and 34 of the Civilians Convention to reassert in more peremptory terms the illegality of collective punishments and 'all measures of intimidation or of terrorism'; they clarified what the major war-crimes trials left unclear: that not only the execution but also the mere taking of hostages was illegal. They further distanced themselves from excessive Second World War practices by accepting a total ban on reprisals against civilians (as distinguished from other categories of persons protected by the Convention). They agreed to a variety of prohibitions of physical and moral maltreatment of civilians (Articles 27, 31, and 32). They even agreed, some of them after much heart-searching, not to use the death penalty in punishment of offences 'solely intended to harm the Occupying Power, but which [do] not constitute an attempt on the life or limb of members of the occupying forces or adminis-tration, nor a grave collective danger, nor seriously damage the property of the occupying forces or administration or the installations used by them' (Article 68).

But at one distant point they stuck. They would not yield to the popular demand to do without the death penalty also in respect of the most serious offences ('espionage, serious acts of sabotage against the military instal-lations of the Occupying Power or of intentional offences' causing fatalities) in countries where the death penalty had been in use before the occupation began. That appeared to mean that a capital-punishment State could protect its occupation-resisting civilians—even those who killed any number of occupying troops, etc.—by the neat expedient of declaring the death penalty abolished just before the occupying forces arrived. To the British and Americans and their usual allies, this seemed lunacy. The Americans, although they had not so far been without set-backs, considered their loss by 17:15:11 of a vital amendment to Article 68, just before its passage on 3 August by 33:5:5, the 'first important point we have lost in conference. Defeat accomplished by Soviet bloc, French, Scandinavia, and scattered votes in Assembly.'[20] This part of this Article was the only bit of the Conventions to which the UK and USA and a few others objected so gravely that they made formal reservations to it at the time of signature.

The scale of violence of likely resistance to an enemy occupier, already

---

[20] US: 514.2 Geneva/8-449, telegram of 4 Aug. The debate is in *Final Record* IIB, 424–31. At that stage it was still 'Article 59' of the Stockholm text, but in the final reckoning it became the Article 68 of the 4th GC which it remains.

matched to a high level by the severest of the Civilians Convention's prescribed penalties, reaches its natural climax in armed struggle of the kind commonly known as guerrilla or partisan war. European experience between 1939 and 1945 again was decisive in shaping the post-1945 legislation. (South-East Asian experience would have been no less relevant, but as a matter of fact it was rarely cited; on this area of IHL, as on most others, it was European experience that filled the minds and speeches of the legislators.) In almost every country that had been invaded and/or occupied during the recent war, there had been guerrilla warfare. For some of them, it was one of their wartime experiences of which they were proudest, e.g. the USSR, Greece, Yugoslavia, Poland, and France. Invaders and occupiers—which is to say, Germany and its allies—had reacted with savagery and indignation: savagery, because they knew of or could imagine no other way of beating it and the civilian populations enveloping it; indignation, because they believed or persuaded themselves to believe that it was unethical and illegal. Not now to vindicate and legitimize it was unthinkable for those veterans of it who had survived and for the regimes who owed at least some (in the Yugoslav case, the whole) of their liberated existence to it.

The question was therefore on the legislative agendas of most European countries as they entered the revision process. It was on the ICRC's agenda too. Almost wholly fruitless had been their attempts during the second half of the war to persuade the German authorities that, setting aside the legalistic and diplomatic objections of which they made so much, and looking simply at what was going on in the field, resistance fighters who more or less succeeded in fulfilling the conditions laid down in Article 1 of the Hague Regulations (as many did) should be recognized as lawful combatants. The UK and USA, for their parts, were certainly not as enthusiastic about this business as their late allies. They had no quarrel with the political aspect of the question, the easing of that narrowly State-tied strait-jacket which the 1899 and 1907 conferences had wrapped round them. The military operational aspects however were a different matter. They had gone along with so much of it during the war that they now risked looking ungrateful, hypocritical, and Germanic when they said, as they often felt they had to, that the safer you made things for the partisan, the riskier you made them for the civilian.

The Civilians Convention, in any case, was not where any improved legislation regarding guerrillas would appear. The whole point about the lawful guerrilla fighter, so far as he could be identified and described, was that he was not a civilian. The Civilians Convention was for protecting civilians who remained civilians and whose gestures of resistance, therefore, would be punished as crimes, just as would any acts of guerrilla warfare which lay outside whatever lawful scope could be defined. Guerrilla operations within that scope would entitle the guerrilla fighter to be regarded as a lawful or (to use the terminology usefully publicized at that epoch by Professor Richard Baxter) a 'privileged combatant'; to be distinguished, by the same terminology, from the 'unprivileged combatant', a category including the spy and the saboteur as well as the partisan operating outside IHL's scope. It was therefore not in the Civilians Convention that the new definition was placed but in the Prisoners of War Convention, the one where, in Geneva law, lawful combatant status was defined.

Discussions about this definition were lengthy and contentious, because besides opening up the usual division between the occupied and the occupier points of view, they bumped into two of the most awkward questions that can arise in connection with IHL—both of them intimately to do with the status and protection of civilians.

The first of these awkward questions came up in the course of attempts to establish the limits within which guerrilla operations could be recognized as lawful. The tragic fact was, is, and always will be, that what is good for the guerrilla tends to be bad for the civilian.[21] The Western cultural tradition within which both Geneva and Hague law developed knew no principle more important than the distinction between the soldier and the civilian. Through the centuries of the law's fundamental development, 'the soldier' meant the uniformed regular soldier, fighting under his country's flag against other similar soldiers fighting under theirs. He never liked guerrillas, partly because they made campaigning and occupation more risky and uncomfortable than they might otherwise be, partly (if he was a decent sort of fellow) because the activities of guerrillas made it difficult for him to handle civilians as he otherwise might. If guerrillas were mixed up with civilians (as was their usual style), how could you be sure a civilian *was* a civilian? The British regular army, perfectly representative of its kind in this respect, accepted international law's division of enemy populations into two classes: 'the armed forces' and 'the peaceful populations'; the *Manual of Military Law* which guided it through the 1940s went on to observe:

It is one of the purposes of the laws of war to ensure that an individual must definitely choose to belong to one class or the other, and shall not be allowed to

---

[21] To put it thus is, of course, to adopt the classic law-of-war view of the civilian as distinct from the soldier, and of the civilian interest as one that can be clearly separated from his. This is not how the matter will usually appear to persons viewing armed conflicts from within the tradition of peoples' and revolutionary wars.

enjoy the privileges of both; in particular, that an individual shall not be allowed to kill or wound members of the Army of the opposed nation and subsequently, if captured or in danger of life, to pretend to be a peaceful citizen.[22]

But that was precisely what a guerrilla, unless hedged about with tight controls, would like to do: and, moreover, very much what the theory of revolutionary warfare required him to do.

The other awkward question was one of feeling and principle, related to that *jus ad bellum* half of the old law of war, which, as has already been observed, was coming back into mid-twentieth century people's minds as they sought to rid the world of the bane of wanton aggression. Put in crude and simple terms, the question was: should not the *jus in bello* go easy on irregular combatants fighting for a cause which the *jus ad bellum* pronounced to be just? And what could be more just, more indisputably justifiable than to fight in patriotic defence of one's homeland against a flagrant aggressor? Guerrillas of national resistance movements were of course very likely to feel thus about their desperate work and to resent the law's lack of sympathy for what they had to do in their 'irregular' predicament; but so also might civilians feel as they sought, by whatever other means came their way, to discharge what they felt to be their patriotic duties.

The civilian side of this case was interestingly pressed at the 1949 conference by Dr Georg Cohn, head of the Danish delegation. Increasingly to the vexation of the traditionalists and regulars, repeatedly he argued that civilians using violence to defend themselves and/or their country against what he would persist in calling illegal aggressions should not be submitted to the full rigour of the law as it traditionally stood. The way he put it embarrassed the traditionalists, first, because what he said about illegal aggressions was true (the UN Charter and the IMT judgments, so fresh in mind, prevented any forgetting of the fact); second, because they had to tell him that although it was true, it was irrelevant. In so doing they had to expose in all its disturbing nakedness the fact which can embarrass well-wishers of IHL: that it applies impartially and indifferently to both or all sides in an armed conflict without regard to the merits of the conflict's causes. The doctrine of belligerent equality is how lawyers know it. Embarrassing though it may be, it is ethically defensible. The rights and wrongs of wars can be difficult to establish. So far as it is in the interests of the society of States to establish national guilt or innocence, the task of doing so

---

[22] Cited in course of the exhaustive consideration given to this matter by the Interdepartmental Committee on the Geneva Conventions chaired by W. H. Gardner; para. 40 of its May 1948 report, in UK: FO 369/3968 K. 5862. (Two copies of this very long and revealing document are to be found in AUST: A 4311/152/2.)

lies with other branches of international law and organization than IHL and
its organs. To deal with infractions of *jus in bello* is as much as they can,
perhaps, handle. In any case, history and experience prove to anyone
capable of persuasion that belief in the exclusive justice of one's cause does
not necessarily promote humanitarian observances. Dr Cohn's last shot was
in the plenary meeting of 26 July, when they were going, for the last time,
through the articles of the new POW Convention. Sir Robert Craigie gave
him the 'official' answer.

[In] international law it is clear, firstly, that States which deliberately order the
commencement of hostilities without a previous declaration of war or a qualifying
ultimatum commit an intentional delinquency but they are nevertheless engaged in
war. Secondly, that States which allow themselves to be dragged into a condition of
war through unauthorized hostile acts of their armed forces commit an international
delinquency but they are nevertheless engaged in war. Thirdly, that in all these and
similar cases all the laws of warfare must find application, for a war is still a war in
the eyes of international law even though it has been illegally commenced.[23]

Civilians, then, were to be given (in, be it always remembered, *international* armed conflicts) no protection or privileges other than those prescribed in the Civilians Convention's definition of the rights and obligations
of occupying powers. An unwilling subject of a military occupation who
offered resistance to it would be classified as either a civilian offending
against the occupiers' penal laws or a lawful combatant qualifying under
the new rules defining combatant status. Those rules were to be found, not
in the Civilians Convention, but in the POW Convention, Article 4. Some of
the more significant novelties were as much political as military. The biggest
change was the legitimization of armed resistance *in occupied territory*. The
Hague Regulations' phraseology had implied, and all regular military doctrine had asserted, that once an occupation existed *de facto*, guerrilla
resistance to it was impermissible *de jure*. There was indeed room for
argument about what constituted an occupation but no benefit of the doubt
was allowed to the resister. Now, the question was definitively settled. So
long as a properly 'organized resistance movement' could fulfil the military
conditions (described below), it could lawfully operate in no matter how
thoroughly occupied a territory. Two other innovations freed such movements from the stigma of illegitimacy fastened in the late wars by the
German government on all armed forces and groups owning allegiance to
other national authorities than the one Germany chose to recognize, e.g. to

---

[23] *Final Record* IIB, 268. Craigie found Cohn very difficult to take, describing him in his final
report as 'narrow and obstinate', 'impervious either to reason or argument', and so on; UK: FO
369/4164 K. 10540, para. 38.

name the most obvious case, the Free French government-in-exile as opposed to the government allowed to sit in Vichy. Now room was made not only for 'members of regular armed forces who profess allegiance to a government or an authority not recognized by the Detaining Power' (which had been exactly the case of the *Forces Françaises de l'Intérieur* in so far as they operated in occupied territory) but also for 'members of . . . organized resistance movements belonging to a Party to the conflict'. This 'belonging', says the ICRC's official Commentary, was intended to be understood largely and liberally enough to include the variety of cases encountered in the Second World War.[24]

All such guerrilla fighters who wished to be regarded as lawful combatants had to meet also these conditions: '(*a*) that of being commanded by a person responsible for his subordinates; (*b*) that of having a fixed distinctive sign recognizable at a distance; (*c*) that of carrying arms openly; (*d*) that of conducting their operations in accordance with the laws and customs of war.'

This was the same list as in the Hague Regulations, unchanged despite everything that had happened since. Its reiteration in the 1949 Conventions can only not be presented as a victory for the 'occupiers' over the 'occupied' because the former, if they had had their own way, would have made the conditions even more exacting. The same arguments were gone through again in 1949 as had already consumed time and patience in 1947 and 1948. The 'occupiers' sought in particular to add the condition of control of territory, even if its borders and extent changed from time to time. It did not seem to them an unreasonable condition. How, wondered Mr Clattenburg in his 1947 Report, could partisans 'conform to the requirements of Article 1 of the Hague Regulations . . . without having effective control of some area, no matter how small'?[25] The UK delegation in 1949 sought to tighten the screw, its particular concern being 'that partisans could not be recognized unless they had established headquarters to which communications could be sent in order that the Protecting Powers should be able to visit prisoners taken by partisans'.[26]

This was asking more than partisans worthy of the name could grant. A partisan force broadly and confidently enough established to hold prisoners in a style which the ICRC could respect and to receive visits of inspection is

[24] The Second World War sources of these innovations are quite extensively described in Pictet's *Commentary*, iii. 52–64.
[25] Report cited (p. 5) in Ch. 4 n. 13.
[26] UK: FO 369/4150 K. 4769; report of the Committee II meeting on 27 Apr., in *Final Record* II A, 241–3.

no longer a partisan force but something more public and formal; in a word, more 'regular'. And, historically, this is how successful partisan forces have sometimes developed. From whatever small, obscure, arguably 'criminal', and 'terroristic' beginnings they can evolve in size, presence, and standards until they are difficult to distinguish in basic practical and operational terms from the regular armed forces pitted against them (which themselves, of course, are likely to have acquired 'irregular' skills in order to beat the partisans at their own game). The regular 'occupier' interest at Geneva in 1947 and 1949 therefore was not demanding the intrinsically impossible or the simply unreasonable. It was however pushing the partisan, 'occupied' interest into the corner most conducive to its own convenience and least suitable for true partisan purposes. Nothing in the end came of these extremer attempts to restrict partisans, but the Hague Regulations' conditions themselves were already restrictive enough. The 1949 solution of this problem was, in truth, no solution at all but (as, given the actually insoluble nature of the problem it had to be) a goodwill-requiring compromise weighted on the side of the political interest then in the ascendant. We shall see in Part III how things changed when that political interest went into decline.

Wounded, Sick, and Shipwrecked

The first and second Geneva Conventions, the Red Cross Conventions *par excellence*, need not keep us long. So self-evidently great was the importance of what they stood for and so universally valuable their aim, that their contents excited relatively little argument at any of the conferences which culminated in the finalization of the 1949 versions. Their principal purpose was to reaffirm the principles which had been at the heart of Geneva law since its pioneering codification in the early 1860s: the protection and care of soldiers and sailors rendered *hors de combat* by wounds, sickness, and/or shipwreck; similarly, the protection and support of the men and women who undertake that care, and of the distinctive sign they carry. These concerns having already been embodied in long-established and carefully devised Conventions, little more needed to be done after the Second World War than to correct the few things that had gone badly wrong and to add a few things made desirable by changes in the nature of war and innovations in its techniques.

The most interesting piece of reaffirmation came in GCI's Article 18, on the Role of the Population. It had been one of the main points of the first Geneva Convention, product of an epoch when military medical services were generally inadequate, that it encouraged the civilian population to come to the aid of the military sick and wounded and protected them while they did so; 'generals of the belligerent powers' were not to think ill of them for having cared impartially for the wounded of each and every nationality. Article 18 now reaffirmed and elaborated this noble idea. Specific reference to 'invaded and occupied' areas indicated where it had most been battered during the Second World War. Alien military authorities during occupation, and restored national authorities after liberation, had then been quick to interpret humanitarian aid to suffering soldiers etc. of 'enemy' provenance as, in the first case, acts of resistance and, in the second, acts of treason. There was the further and contradictory problem, that civilians in some circumstances had shown not too much but too little compassion for enemy combatants in distress: airmen from crashed planes had sometimes been set upon by angry (and perhaps officially encouraged) civilians; injured members of occupying armies had been left to die by those who might have succoured them.

On all these possible aspects of the matter, Article 18 was fairly straight-forward. But about the most awkward—and indeed, in strictly legal and military terms, insoluble—aspect, it kept mum. Where, for instance, did the humanitarian obligation to succour an ailing resistance fighter or parachuted airman end and the arguably patriotic duty of concealing him begin? Pictet, summarizing the opposite tendencies of the 1947 and 1949 conferences, adopts the sense of the latter in pointing out 'that the absence from the Convention of any allusion to control [by the occupying authorities] did not necessarily mean that control was pro-hibited', and that they would undoubtedly make such rules as they should think fit. Draper, taking that for granted, can do no better than to 'suggest that [the civilian] may be prosecuted for the concealment but not for the tending'.[27]

Unmistakably of Second World War origin are the legal gaps attempted to be filled in the course of the crucial Article 12. It begins with a reaffir-mation of the original basic principles of Geneva law—in effect, rendering in statutory form the Red Cross's primary principles of humanity, neutral-ity, and impartiality—but whereas the 1929 Convention did not find it necessary to define impartiality any more closely than by the expression, in its first Article, 'without distinction of nationality', it is now spelled out as

---

[27] Pictet's *Commentary*, i. 190. Draper's *Red Cross Conventions*, 78–9. Draper discloses some quirkiness here. He analyses the Article in such terms as to suggest that Solferino-like situations are what really matter, takes examples solely from the Anglo-American side of the Second World War, and evades the 'resistance' difficulty.

'without any adverse distinction founded on sex, race, nationality, religion, political opinions, or any other similar criteria'. The protection of the wounded and sick from 'attempts upon their lives or violence to their persons' is at once weighted with a particular prohibition of their being 'murdered or exterminated, subjected to torture or to biological experiments'. To Draper is owed illumination of the significance of the final sentence of the central paragraph: the wounded and sick 'shall not wilfully be left without medical assistance and care, nor shall conditions exposing them to contagion and disease be created'. Pictet passes over this with Red Cross commonplaces but, wrote Second World War and war-crimes-trials-experienced Draper: 'Interrogating staffs find that wounded aircrew suffering from shock, burns and wounds tend to be profitable subjects for interrogation purposes'; recalling also 'the German practice in the recent war of sealing off camps of Russian prisoners of war when typhus or tuberculosis was discovered'.[28]

It remains only to remark briefly on the way these two Conventions attempt to keep up with technological progress. Aerial warfare had so enormously developed that hardly any area of IHL was untouched by it. In *this* area, the necessary thing was to bring aircrews who ended up in the sea within the general category of 'shipwrecked' and to rework the rules supposedly securing the identification of medical aircraft; rules which, as may easily be imagined, must be technically sophisticated if they are to keep up with the speeds at which aircraft can now move and radar etc. can now locate them. The particular problem of aircrews suddenly became pressing in 1940, when so many landed in the English Channel. David Howarth, who was himself involved in rescue operations, summed it up neatly: 'the Germans tried seaplanes marked with the Red Cross and our fighters (since Red Cross aircraft were not foreseen by the Geneva Conventions) shot them down; and the RAF used motor launches of their own, and the Germans shot them up.'[29] Hospital ships in a lesser degree present similar difficulties (other than those made by medical aircraft going to and from them). The 1949 GCs perhaps succeeded in catching up with the state of the art as it had been in 1945, but already by the time they came into force the Sisyphean cycle was turning again. How the problem was handled next time round, may be glimpsed in Section Two of API: eleven Articles on medical transportation in all its aspects; to which the specializing reader may add the

---

[28] Pictet's *Commentary*, i. 139, and Draper, *Red Cross Conventions*, 76–7 and n.
[29] *Pursued by a Bear: An Autobiography* (London, 1986), 108.

chapter on distinctive signals in its Annexe of Regulations concerning Identification.[30]

Prisoners of War

Prisoners of war took a giant stride along the road to becoming the most favoured category of war victim: more popularly favoured by far than the wounded and sick, on whose account the series of Geneva Conventions began. The 1949 POW Convention, so much enlarged beyond the 1929 bridgehead, was made up of 143 articles and five annexes. Apart from the articles that were common to all the Conventions, the POW Convention was simply a comprehensive code for the humane treatment of prisoners from the moments of capture and interrogation through all the facets of the internment (not a detail escaped the expert legislators' notice) up to their return to normalcy through the gates of release, repatriation, or death. None of the three other Conventions possessed as concentrated a character or invited such concentrated attention. Its spotlight focused on just one actor, the POW, and one crowded stage, the POW camp.

This Convention's concentration of attention on the situation of the POW matched and reflected the intense interest in him shown by Western publics. What happens to their warriors when taken prisoner has a capacity to worry them even more than what happens to those of their menfolk whom war disables for life or removes from life altogether. This must be because, while the dead can be commemorated and the disabled can to a great extent be forgotten (as it is all too convenient and comfortable for governments that they should be), thought and memory of the POW are both naturally and artificially kept alive by the fact that whatever happens to him can be called the enemy's fault. The cult of the POW becomes an extension of the national conflict. IHL here finds, however unsolicited and unwelcome, one of its major uses as a seed-bed of popular national sentiment and emotion.

In not every country is it so. Those cultures, for example, are immune to the cult of the POW which believe that good warriors should not become POWs in the first place. The use of prisoners as bargaining counters in post-war negotiations (as e.g. after the 1971 India–Pakistan conflict, and after

---

[30] This Annexe, not given in Roberts and Guelff, is in Schindler and Toman, 609–16. The specialist should consult Philippe Eberlin 'La modernisation de la signalisation protectrice et les communications des unités et moyens de transport sanitaires', in the Pictet *Festschrift*, 47–75, and his articles 'The Protection of Rescue Craft' and 'Underwater Acoustic Identification of Hospital Ships', in the IRRC nos. 246 (1985) and 267 (1989) respectively.

the Iran–Iraq war of the 1980s) has been a distressing throw-back towards bad old times when prisoners could count themselves lucky if they were only enslaved. There is in any case no limit to the suspicions and hatreds that malignant ideologies and religions can breed in the skulls of subjects who might otherwise not have bad ideas about foreigners. Against all such denials of common humanity, the principles of IHL are firmly opposed; drawing hope and strength from the altruistic and charitable elements to be found somewhere in every major world religion and philosophy. By two hundred years or so ago the laws and customs of war observed by Western States (at least in wars between themselves) had evolved so far as to enjoin decent handling of prisoners and to deprecate neglect of the helpless wounded and sick. The beginnings of the Red Cross movement a hundred years or so ago were primarily to do with the wounded and sick. Prisoners gradually came within its purview as the ICRC found ways of meeting the demands of governments and peoples alike—demands barely heard before the age of mass and mainly conscript armies—for communication with prisoners and relief of their more urgent needs. There developed a strong demand for it, which the ICRC met. But there never was any objective ground for judging POWs to be the most tragic and/or deserving of the several main categories of war-victims with whose protection and relief the Red Cross and IHL busied themselves. They simply happened to be one on which converged the emotions of mass politics, the self-interest of the military, and the ICRC's generous willingness to enlarge its field of usefulness.

The POW Convention crowned this convergence by offering POWs what only recollection of their extraordinary sufferings in the Second World War can keep one from considering a rather extraordinary amount of comfort, protection, and privilege. The last of those words is brought to mind by Article 85: 'Prisoners of War prosecuted under the laws of the detaining Power for acts committed prior to capture shall retain, even if convicted, the benefits of the present Convention.'

The effect of that is that even the most awful of (war) criminals, fallen as a prisoner into the hands of an enemy State, brought to trial, found guilty, and sentenced to long imprisonment, must throughout the whole experience be treated to the standards of food, accommodation, visits by representatives of the Protecting Power and the ICRC etc., prescribed for POWs instead of the (almost certainly lower) standards applied to the Detaining Power's own nationals. The USSR and its allies in due course entered a reservation to this article, making clear their intention to adhere to 'Nuremberg' practice and to subject 'persons convicted of [war crimes and crimes against humanity] to the conditions obtaining in [their respective] countries for those who undergo their punishment'. Why, they demanded, should a war criminal get off more lightly simply because he subsequently qualified to be a POW?[31]

The majority and Western view at the Diplomatic Conference was the more remarkable for being a reversal of the Western States' earlier view as well as for welshing on their own war-crimes-trials precedents. From the trial of General Yamashita in late 1944 through all the war-crimes trials that followed, the victor-judges had insisted that the then current Geneva Convention's articles concerning the trial of POWs did not apply to trials for offences committed before capture. Indeed it was generally doubtful whether any fixed legal standards did apply to those trials, most of them having been 'based on special *ad hoc* legislation and not on the regular penal legislation of the countries accused'.[32] No sign appeared at the Government Experts' meeting in 1947 that the Western States were going to depart from these by then well-trodden ways. Quite the opposite! The ICRC was disappointed when its modest proposal 'that prisoners of war accused of war crimes should continue to receive all the benefits of the Convention *until their guilt was definitively proved*' was turned down as too soft.[33] With the UK and US representatives at their head, the majority favoured the withdrawal of Convention protection as soon as 'a prima-facie case was made out against them'.

In not much over a year, all was changed. The ICRC, having stuck to its modest guns, was amazed to find the 'Anglo-Saxon' delegations now swimming with the humanitarian tide so far as to demand protection (in the form of continued POW benefits) after sentence even for war-crime-convicted prisoners or those convicted of crimes against humanity. With this great leap forward, the ICRC for its part was not going to quarrel. The quarrelling was done by the USSR and its allies. With each side reversing its usual stance *vis-à-vis* the Stockholm texts, a series of heated debates reached their climax in the 16th plenary on 27 July.[34] It is difficult not to feel that the

---

[31] This reservation may be read in Roberts and Guelff, 332, under the heading 'Albania'. As will be seen on p. 333, under the heading 'Bulgaria', it was shared also by that State and by USSR, Byelorussia, Ukraine, Czechoslovakia, Poland, East Germany, China, North Korea, and North Vietnam.

[32] Pictet's *Commentary*, iii. 414.   [33] Ibid. 415 (my emphasis).

[34] *Final Record* IIB, 303–12, from which all cited passages come. Within not much more than a year, North Korean predilection for calling American prisoners 'war criminals' was showing that Western worries had not been unreasonable.

honours went to the Soviet bloc. Not only had they consistency on their side, they could also plausibly claim to represent the general opinion of mankind. That POWs accused of perhaps terrible crimes should enjoy the benefits of the Convention through the period of arrest and trial, was not unreasonable, and the USSR was not proposing anything else; but that such lavish benefits should continue after conviction was incredible!

No one will ever understand such a decision. It is proposed to punish persons for breaches of the Convention by raising the left hand, and to ensure, by raising the right hand, that the same persons shall be entitled to the benefits of the Convention the provisions of which they have violated.

Thus Mr Morosov. His Bulgarian colleague Mr Mevorah turned the knife in the wound by comparing the Anglo-American attitude on this point with the line they had taken about enemy civilians 'suspected of activities directed against the security of the State'. Nothing had been considered too bad for them! Even though 'nothing but more or less indefinite suspicions' might exist with regard to them,

Yet we would be ready to decree the complete forfeiture of the rights and privileges granted by the Convention. . . . If you are prepared to deprive [such] persons of their civil rights (although this has not yet been proved and they have not yet been tried), surely you ought *a fortiori* to have the courage to sentence war criminals guilty of crimes against humanity to the loss of their civil rights, particularly if these criminals have been tried in accordance with the principles of the Convention.

British, Dutch, and American spokesmen did their best on the other side of the argument. Only one of them got anywhere near revealing what had been the main determinant of the Anglo-American volte-face, about which those countries' diplomatic papers for 1948–9 offer hardly any clue. The USA's General Dillon said that since there was so much difference between different countries' prison regimes—under which, by the USSR's amendment, the war-crime-convicted POW would serve his sentence—you could never be sure that it would not actually be more severe than you would like. You could not, in fact, be sure it would not be as bad as what he had seen in Dachau and Buchenwald. To this broad hint can be added, from evidence elsewhere, the Western powers' growing fear that in any conflict that might develop between them and the Eastern bloc, the latter, by making out that Western soldiers etc. were generally implicated in the crime of aggressive war, could thus conveniently free itself to handle POWs roughly.

Another issue that was resolved signally to the POW's advantage—and by necessary implication to the civilian's disadvantage—was whether the work that could legitimately be required of POWs should include the clearance of minefields, i.e. mines previously laid by their own side. It became revealed as a British speciality to demand that this was reasonable and proper. It was not all that dangerous a job; appropriate training could be given in advance; if they knew that their own men might have to remove the mines, belligerents would perhaps keep better records of where they laid the beastly things, and besides, what were the alternatives? Either the Detaining Power's own troops or the POW's civilian compatriots. The question was answered as soon as it was put. The employment of POWs for mine-clearance was a point about which the British War Office felt passionately, and it nearly became one of the many points on which the UK found itself at odds with its natural friends. The Canadian subcommittee working on the POW Convention draft in preparation for Stockholm went so far as to call the British proposal 'iniquitous'.[35] At the Diplomatic Conference, the UK with the help of the USSR and Denmark won the battle in committee but lost the campaign when Canada, Australia, and the USA, after what Col. Hodgson described as 'a long and bitter debate', got that decision reversed in the 15th plenary on 27 July; the UK having gracefully under-taken to join the abstainers.[36]

Unanimous in resolve to provide against any recurrence of the awful experiences of the Second World War, and relatively little disturbed by the political point-making which repeatedly disturbed their work on the Civilians Convention, the delegations in 1949 produced a POW Convention which in every respect appeared to protect the prisoner better than he had been protected in 1929. Compare the 1929 article about food (Article 11: 'shall be equivalent in quantity and quality to that of the depot troops') with its 1949 counterpart (Article 26: 'shall be sufficient in quantity, quality and variety to keep POWs in good health and to prevent loss of weight or development of nutritional deficiencies. Account shall be taken also of the habitual diet of the prisoners', etc.). Not at first sight an obvious improve-ment, given that the feeding of depot troops has usually been pretty good. Such a high standard had it set, indeed, that the US authorities had been gravely embarrassed in 1944–6 by complaints at every level from the local press up to Congress that German prisoners held in American camps were eating better than many American citizens.

The 1929 rule however worked to a different effect on prisoners in

[35] CAN: 619-B-40, vol. 2; report dated 2 May 1948.
[36] Hodgson's Report (p. 105) cited in Ch. 4 n. 33. *Final Record* IIB, 298 shows the vote as 23:19:4. Hodgson says 'A number of delegates did not attend at the meeting.'

Japanese camps. Just as no army in the Second World War fed its own men as richly as did that of the USA, so no army fed its own men more frugally than that of Japan. Even when the diet it provided was consistent with that 1929 rule, it could not satisfy prisoners accustomed to other more varied and substantial foods. Parity with civilian diet was considered as a possible standard, only to be rejected as running into the same difficulties. The 1949 rule was therefore supposed to steer between them, and to protect the prisoner at all events from sickness and malnutrition. But of course comparisons between the diet of prisoners and that available to the detainer's soldiers and civilians would continue to be made, and it has to be remembered that soldiers and civilians often experience sickness and malnutrition themselves. The plain meaning of the POW Convention, as usual, is that the prisoner must be the last to suffer.

Repatriation and the status of captured medical personnel were (apart from 'offences committed before capture') the only questions specific to the POW Convention that excited much passion. The matter of the status of captured medical personnel, for all that it occupied a vast amount of negotiators' time and emotion, may be rapidly dealt with. It was the chosen battleground of that effective pressure group already mentioned, the International Committee for Military Medicine and Pharmacy, which had allies in many continental military and political establishments, though not those of the UK, the Commonwealth, or the USA. The noble side of the medics' case was that their humanitarian and in a sense 'neutral' calling required and justified the exemption from POW-style capture to which the Geneva Conventions so far had entitled them. The not-so-noble side was the touchy *amour propre* which impelled them to claim a degree of separateness and privilege that was, within the frame of the Conventions, unique. They did not wish to lose that special status now. A battle went on behind the scenes, the conclusion of which appeared in Article 33.[37] Medics were 'not [to] be considered as prisoners of war', but were to be called 'retained personnel' instead. Since this difference of nomenclature mattered so much to them, they may be thought to have won a sort of victory.

Repatriation was a more momentous affair. Repatriation concerned the whole body of POWs whom a Detaining Power would be sending home, according to Article 29 of the 1929 Convention, 'as soon as possible after the conclusion of peace', if not sooner. Never had numbers been greater than at the close of the Second World War. Besides all those who had surrendered while the war was still going on, there was the much greater

---

[37] UK: FO 369/4149 K. 4765 and 4152 K. 5509 offer a glimpse behind the scenes.

number of those taken into custody when the war ended in the 'mass capitulation' of the armed forces of a totally dissolved State. The victorious allies, desperate to avoid the burden of providing full POW treatment for such millions, argued not unreasonably that the 1907 and 1929 legislation had not envisaged such occurrences.[38] The ICRC for its part stoutly maintained that the allies should approximate to POW standards to the maximum extent possible, and that any shortfall from them only strengthened the case for rapid repatriation.

But here came another and greater difficulty, which made the ICRC's relations with some of the victors even more delicate. The USA was pleased to get rid of its prisoners without delay (except those wanted for criminal investigation or for intelligence purposes), but the USSR, France, Belgium, and the UK wanted to get some work out of them before letting them go. Whether the terms of any ultimate peace treaty would include Versailles-style reparations was extremely doubtful. Meanwhile, with so much of their countries in ruins from German devastation, what was more reasonable than to have the Germans who had fallen into their power (or who had been transferred into it, as by the USA to France and by the UK to Belgium) help to repair some of the damage they had done? The argument, again, was not unreasonable, but the ICRC had to reject it, so far as it could with the tact and prudence demanded by circumstances so extraordinary. What, if anything, passed between Geneva and Moscow on this score, I know not. What passed in Paris and London as a result of the ICRC's polite, persistent remonstrances is however clear enough. However much France and the UK needed this labour, there was not the slightest legal warrant for enforcing it; it was not a comfortable precedent for a victor who might not be victorious next time; and, what weighed more heavily with every passing month after 1948, it inhibited them from criticizing, as freely as they would have wished, the USSR's interpretation of its generous moral entitlement.

Nineteen forty-eight was the year when France and Britain put themselves in the right on this matter: Britain, by completing its repatriation, and France, by retaining only those (there turned out to be a satisfactorily large number) who were willing to work for pay and who could thus be described as 'free workers'.[39] At the Diplomatic Conference, only the UK sought to qualify the proposed new rule that 'Prisoners of war shall be released and repatriated without delay after the cessation of active hostilities.'

---

[38] References to this matter recur throughout the British diplomatic archives; good points of entry are FO 369/3593 K. 17428–9 and 3795 K. 8957 and the whole file 371/64259.

[39] C. 14952 in the file mentioned in n. 34.

Sweetening self-interest with altruism, the UK sought to the last to persuade other likely repatriators that not only would strict observance of this rule be difficult or risky for them, it could also be against the best interests of the repatriated.[40] Besides which, it left unresolved the very awkward question of compulsory repatriation. Large numbers of prisoners who had willingly or reluctantly been connected with the USSR did not wish to be sent there when the time came for their release. Some preferred suicide. The ICRC early became anxious to make the new rule conditional on the consent of the presumed beneficiary, and with the aid of certain sympathetic States persisted in the search for means to save him from a fate he might think worse than death; but to no avail. Its last shot was when Austria on 23 June having proposed such an amendment had it rejected by a large majority.

General Sklyarov (USSR) feared that a prisoner of war might not be able to express himself with complete freedom when he was in captivity. Furthermore, this new provision might give rise to the exercise of undue pressure on the part of the Detaining Power. General Parker (USA) shared that opinion.[41]

It would take a few more years' consciousness of human rights and certain vexatious experiences during the Korean War to persuade the Western powers to reopen their ears to what the ICRC had been trying to tell them.

Application and Enforcement

Application is about where, when, to whom, and in what manner the Conventions become applicable. Enforcement is about how they are applied or supposed to be applied, and what provisions are made for their execution.

The 1949 Conventions, except for what was envisaged in their Common Article 3, were to apply 'in all cases of declared war or of any other armed conflict which may arise between two or more of the High Contracting Parties, even if the state of war is not recognized by one of them . . . also [in] all cases of partial or total application of the territory of a HCP, even if the said occupation meets with no armed resistance.'

What is *not* there said about 'war' is more significant than what *is* said. Whether 'a state of war' in the classic formal sense is admitted or not, the Conventions apply as soon as an 'armed conflict' exists. Thus they are made much more widely applicable than the 1929 Conventions and The Hague

---

[40] *Final Record* IIA, 449–50.   [41] Ibid. 462.

Conventions before them, whose obligations States might be able or forced to avoid on legalistic grounds, just as from now on they would be able to avoid the obligations of Article 3. Thus the USA and the UK had declined to recognize that there was a war going on between China and Japan from 1937. Thus, between 1939 and 1945, 'the aggressors eluded [their obligations] by refusing to recognize the existence of a state of war. At other times, the setting up of puppet governments served to disguise a *de facto* state of war under apparently legal conditions of peace. In yet other instances, a legal state of war subsisted, since hostilities had not been brought to a conclusion by recognized legal procedure, although existing conditions were no longer, in reality, conditions of war.'[42] The emphatic addition of the phrase 'armed conflict' (which the ICRC had sensibly sought since before the war) was designed to avert evasive casuistries of these kinds. The field of application was widened further still by the sentence about 'occupation'. It was not going to be possible to deny the existence of a hostile relationship because a big State's invasion of a little one's territory encountered no opposition.

A third paragraph of Article 2 blocks off another potential evasion of IHL responsibilities: the argument invited by the 'general participation clause' in the Hague Conventions and other pre-1929 instruments, that if one party to a conflict has not obliged itself to observe them, those that have done so need not stay obliged either.[43] Now the latter stood obliged to honour their obligations so long as the former undertook to 'accept and apply the provisions' of the Convention(s)—and, it must be presumed, so long as it proceeded convincingly to do so.

When we turn from occasions and circumstances to enquire how the Conventions were designed to apply to people, we find first that the Conventions have in view the protection of persons in certain clearly defined situations. Each Convention cares for its own kind. The definitions are exact and searching; the summaries given here must of course *not* be used as substitutes for the real thing by anyone to whom the real thing legally matters. The categories of protected persons are: in GC1, lawful combatants who are wounded or sick on land; in GC2, the same (plus crews of merchant ships and civil aircraft) who are wounded, sick, or shipwrecked at sea; in GC3, unwounded lawful combatants and all wounded, sick, or shipwrecked

---

[42] From the preamble to the report of the third commission (on 'Condition and Protection of Civilians in Time of War') of the Government Experts' Conference, Apr. 1947 (Geneva, ICRC), 270.

[43] Draper usefully summarizes the prehistory of this matter in his *Red Cross Conventions*, 11–12.

ones who have fallen into the hands of the enemy and thus become POWs;
in GC4, civilians, meaning for the most part (i.e. except for those limited
'own country' applications glanced at above) persons not defined in and
protected by Conventions 1, 2, and 3 who belong to a Convention-
observing State and find themselves, in case of a conflict or occupation, in
the hands of an enemy power. Since the definitions of protected persons in
Conventions 1, 2, and 3 are, in Baxter's terms, of 'privileged combatants',
it follows that 'unprivileged' ones engaging in a conflict or fighting against
an occupation cannot, in IHL terms, be anything but civilians. The Conventions' universe is a curious one, utterly unlike the human rights one. People
become real in it only in certain situations or when they are doing certain
things; on which occasions they become very real indeed, and can find
themselves protected from the blasts of armed conflict better than the less
choosy-looking human rights instruments can protect them.

Human rights, it must again be said, are not entirely out of sight in the
1949 Geneva Conventions. It has already been shown how some of the
Convention-makers were well aware of what was going on at the UN and
of its relevance especially to the Civilians Convention and to whatever
extensions of the Conventions were made from international into internal
armed conflicts. The Canadian delegations's 1949 report already referred to
clearly implied that interferences between governments and their own subjects were more of a human rights than an IHL business. A senior British
Home Office man had no doubt about it. 'The place for a provision
designed to protect civilians from their own government is the Charter [sic]
of Human Rights', noted Arthur Strutt in November 1948 as he prepared
his section of the draft instructions for the UK delegation to the 1949
conference. As for the 'wars of religion' instanced at Stockholm as a type of
non-international war in special need of humanitarian regulation, 'This is
not appropriate for the Civilian Convention but will be covered by the
Genocide Convention currently being considered by the UN.'[44]

Four months later, a Foreign Office official sent to the Home Office his
subtle thoughts on the policy aspects of the human rights question as it now
stood after the Universal Declaration. There was to be a Convention in due
course but, he reckoned, not for years. The UK therefore was in

a fortunate position. (*a*) We can safely cut out of the preamble or other inoperative
parts of the draft Conventions any words which tend to say less well, or with less
authority, what has already been said in the Declaration of Human Rights. (*b*) When
it comes to the binding and operative clauses of the individual Conventions, we can,

[44] UK: FO 369/3970 K. 12091.

if we are careful, . . . make use of the following arguments to suit our convenience: (i) Where we wish a particular clause or phrase to be *included* . . . we can claim that since a Convention on Human Rights has not yet been agreed and since the Declaration is not binding, it is important and justifiable to include the particular aspect of the case in the Convention we are considering; (ii) where we wish a particular phrase or clause to be *excluded* we can vary the argument slightly by saying that the more general and all-embracing clauses on Human Rights have no place in particular Conventions dealing with limited aspects of the problem and should more properly be left for inclusion in the eventual Convention on Human Rights. . . . This is a little tricky but I think quite tenable if used with care.[45]

In the event, human rights were hardly at all mentioned at the Diplomatic Conference, not, at any rate, in its debates as officially reported. Dr Cohn, the Danish champion of civilian self-defence, was probably the delegate who most often referred to them. They served his purpose, which by the standards of the weightier delegations was novel and eccentric. The military men and diplomatic officials of those delegations found no need to complicate discussion of the rugged issues before them by opening doors to a conference chamber where war and its problems were only reluctantly admitted to exist. But rights were in the air, and the 1949 Conventions to some extent embrace them. Human rights are not mentioned as such in Common Article 3's statement of minimum humanitarian rules to be observed in internal conflicts, but human rights is exactly what that Article is about, as has since then become universally recognized. Apart from that, as Draper put it in his classic 1958 commentary: 'the guiding principle underlying all the articles [of the POW Convention] is that humane and decent treatment is a right and not a favour.'[46] Many after 1945 may have felt that the time was more than ripe for advance to this position, which appears to be a better one for the beneficiary of the Conventions' protections, protections so comprehensive as to include provisions for supervision and enforcement. But how reliable would they be? How surely would they operate? Reflection on the risks that could follow overemphasis on rights prompted the British War Office's Mr Davidson to these thoughts in the spring of 1948:

In the 1929 Convention there is no reference anywhere to any form of sanctions and this, no doubt, was quite deliberate. A prisoner, in time of war, is completely at the mercy of the DP and it is a doubtful policy to put into documents threats which can only be carried out by the Power which is victorious . . . [Prisoners, in their own interests, ought not to be encouraged] to say to Camp Commandants that they will have them punished at the end of the war.[47]

[45] UK: FO 369/4144 K. 2680.   [46] Draper, *Red Cross Conventions*, 51.
[47] UK: FO 369/3966 K. 2487. Also in WO 32/13094.

How, apart from 'punishment at the end of the war' (for which hopeful provision was made), was observance and execution of the Conventions to be enforced?. Much time was given in the conferences, much space in the Conventions, to these important matters. Consideration of them may be divided into three parts: the lengths to which a State was expected to go to honour its undertakings; the arrangements made for outside bodies to assist, inspect, and supervise; and the provisions for punishment of neglect and infractions.

The seriousness of States' undertakings was emphasized in the Common Article which stood at the head of each Convention. It is a very short article but it speaks volumes: 'The HCPs undertake to respect and to ensure respect for the present Convention in all circumstances.' Those three closing words announce the legal death of reciprocity. HCPs bind themselves to stick to the Conventions whether an enemy is a party to them or not, and whether an enemy, although nominally a party, bothers to observe them or not. This of course does not mean, in the former case, that such a party should not hasten to 'accept and apply' them, or, in the latter, that a party should not rapidly mend his ways. To keep your promise while an enemy gives himself advantages by breaking his promise may become more than flesh and blood can stand. For better or for worse, reciprocity and reprisals can hardly be kept from asserting themselves sooner or later. But this article is calculated to delay that time by enjoining faithful observance of the law even in the face of disappointments and rebuffs, in the twin hopes, first, that one good example would encourage another, and, second, that it might be possible at least to delay the start of those indignant retaliatory tit-for-tats which almost always spiral beyond proportionality.

The other newly meaningful words in Common Article 1 are: 'and to ensure respect'. States' undertakings to respect the Conventions are thereby understood to include all national instruction and education that may be necessary, in peacetime as well as in time of war. It is a commonplace wherever IHL is taken seriously that by the time an armed conflict gets going, it is far too late to begin instruction in IHL. Its complexity has become considerable, its principles take time to sink in. Armed forces have discovered within the past ten years or so that the Hague side of IHL is most effectively taught as part and parcel of normal operational training. That may be thought a somewhat tardy discovery but governments generally have been more tardy still in honouring the other half of this obligation, spelt out in the 'dissemination' Articles: 47/48/127/144. Not only military but 'civil instruction' is specified. The most overt aim is the instruction of entire populations in the principles and the principal rules of IHL, in order that there should be no ignorance or misunderstandings about them when and if they have to be implemented. Another, less apparent aim is to assist the moral education of peoples by ensuring that it does not ignore these branches of ethics and international relations.

'Respect and ensure respect' has within this decade had yet the third meaning put upon it: that HCPs should therefore feel entitled to express concern to one another about failures in this respect without necessarily inviting the charge of improper interference in a State's own affairs. To what extent States have in fact discreetly done this in the past remains unknown. The large extent to which States, even the usually most discreet of them, have since the early 1950s been in the way of using human rights as a public bludgeon suggests that to remind one another about IHL should mark no bothersome departure from established practice. It was however thought something of a novelty when the ICRC, in May 1983, circulated to all 151 HCPs an appeal that they should use all their efforts to see that in the Iran–Iraq war:

IHL should be observed and that a stop should be put to those violations of it which were affecting the lives, the physical or mental integrity and the treatment of tens of thousands of POWs and civilian victims;

The ICRC should be allowed to fulfil in every respect the humanitarian tasks of protection and assistance which the society of States has entrusted to it;

The machineries established by the Convention to ensure their observance should be allowed to work, in particular the designation of Protecting Powers.[48]

To what extent States thus circularized made representations to Iran and Iraq is unknown. If any did, they and the ICRC must have been disappointed by the results.

This exceptional endeavour to bring outside pressure to bear on defaulting HCPs was prompted by the failure of the Conventions' provisions for their, so to speak, inside supervision, i.e. by machineries operating within the territories of the belligerents or controlled by them.[49] This question of supervision or scrutiny, which is the ICRC's preferred translation of the French word *controle*, occupied much of the attention of the conferences of the later 1940s. Just as the 1929 Diplomatic Conference had sought to

---

[48] My translation from Yves Sandoz 'Appel du CICR dans le cadre du conflit entre l'Irak et l'Iran', in *Annuaire française de droit international*, 29 (1983), 161–73 at 170.

[49] The most intelligible and (within a modest length) thorough survey of this tangled topic known to me is: François Bugnion, 'Le droit humanitaire applicable aux conflits armés internationaux: Le problème du contrôle', in *Annales d'Études Internationales*, 8 (1977), 29–61. I take this opportunity to say how much I appreciated M. Bugnion's generosity and patience on the three occasions when he helped me to understand certain ICRC matters of which he has profound experience.

provide means of supervision, so much need for which had been demonstrated in 1914–18, so now the need for still better means of supervision had been demonstrated by 1939–45 experiences. But supervision and enforcement could not be guaranteed except by neutral presences from outside. Enforcement, if it was seriously intended to go that far, would require the acceptance by States of some degree of what they would call interference with their sovereignty; perhaps also some degree of threat to their security. In no other part of the debates did the claims of humanity and sovereignty more directly confront one another. In the end, sovereignty won.

Everything turned on the degrees of authority to be given to 'the Protecting Power' (or its substitute) and to the ICRC (or an equivalent). Protecting Powers were the standard device by which States had learned how to secure, so far as circumstances permitted, their interests in States with whom their relations had become hostile. The practice was for a belligerent to find a neutral willing to offer to act as 'protector of its interests' (people, property, etc.) in its enemy's territory, and for that enemy to accept the offer, if it valued the reputation of a civilized State. Among functions picked up by the PP had been, during the First World War, a variety of activities aimed to implement the POW parts of the Hague Regulations. Together with the ICRC, which, given the same inducements, greatly enlarged its own usefulness in the same field, PPs showed that the purposes of international humanitarian legislation could not be realized unless room was made by it for the action of neutral and impartial supervisors and go-betweens. It was an open question whether the ICRC or the PP should be given the larger supervisory responsibility, and how large exactly it should be. The Diplomatic Conference that made the 1929 POW Convention came down on the side of the PP. While it left plenty of room for the ICRC to do and even to enlarge its customary activities, only the PP was given any measure of statutory authority to do its work. The willingness of belligerents to accept and permit the ICRC's activities, and to agree upon the installation of PPs was taken for granted.

The 1939–45 War showed that things were not quite so simple. Where goodwill or self-interest oiled the wheels, the system worked well enough. In particular it was discovered that a PP gained in authority and leverage by representing *both* opposing parties. Switzerland and Sweden performed prodigies of diplomatic and humanitarian operations as PPs respectively for thirty-five and twenty-eight belligerent States. So far, so good. But where those oils were lacking the 1929 system seized up. Nothing in it obliged belligerents to let PPs do anything on behalf of enemy civilians or to admit them to occupied territories; nor did it anticipate in any way the event of a belligerent's refusal to accept an enemy's nominated PP on the ground that it did not recognize the existence of the nominator, as Germany, notably, persisted in not recognizing governments-in-exile. The moment the war was over, another great crack appeared in the fabric; the dissolution of the German State brought directly in its wake the demission of the PPs that had been acting on its people's behalf, leaving those people diplomatically unprotected. Correction of these defects in the machinery of supervision, together with the enlargement of the number of things that needed to be supervised, presented the Convention-makers with a complicated task. None of the States which were normally in the majority in 1949 seems to have wished to reduce the role of the PP (which would have been difficult anyway, given all the non-IHL things it might be expected to do). But how much the ICRC was to do in support of the PP or independently of it, or perhaps even as a substitute for it, and whether any other body could be established that might do the same things better—these were questions of the most searching and awkward kind.

What was done about the PPs is rapidly told. They (or their substitutes, whose tale is *not* so rapidly told) were given wide and heavy responsibilities; mostly to do with POWs and civilians as defined and protected in Conventions 3 and 4, but also to do with notification of wounded, sick, and dead 'person[s] of the adverse Party falling into [a belligerent's] hands' in Conventions 1 and 2, and with 'scrutiny' of the application of all four Conventions. Exactly how big its list of tasks should be, and whether the tasks should be spelled out in detail, excited little controversy. The muscle of the stronger military powers was used to substitute for the Stockholm texts' words 'supervise' and 'control', the weaker word 'scrutinize'.[50] The UK, which for a long while pursued an *idée fixe* that the list should be a short one (lest the PP find the burdens unbearable), changed its tune when

Switzerland (echoed mildly by Sweden) said that while they might have some objections to make on individual points, they did not feel that the role of PP should be limited solely to that of a pillar-box. If supervision . . . did not mean giving orders to the belligerents, it certainly involved a measure of responsibility for ensuring, by such means as were open that the terms of the Convention were complied with.[51]

So the PP was left with a lot of things to do and to ensure that others did, but no larger power than to 'scrutinize' what went on in some sort of 'co-

---

[50] *Final Record* IIB, 18–20, 57–8, and 110 show 'scrutinize' emerging from the debates as the nearest the heavyweights could get to a word which would mean nothing at all; 'watch over', 'examine', and 'observe' ran it close. Unwilling to give the game away completely, however, they consistently voted down the USSR's attempts to have a sovereignty-saving clause added.

[51] UK: FO 369/4150 K. 4975; notes on the UK delegation's 10th meeting, 3 May.

operation' with the host belligerent. That was one of the several climb-downs towards national sovereignty from the high, even supranational humanitarian ground taken in Stockholm. Another was the addition to the common article in question (8/8/8/9) of this monitory third paragraph:

The representatives or delegates of the PPs shall not in any case exceed their mission under the present Convention. They shall, in particular, take account of the imperative necessities of security of the State wherein they carry out their duties. Their activities shall only be restricted as an exceptional and temporary measure when this is rendered necessary by imperative military necessities.[52]

The handle thus given to States to control the activities of PPs would have been heavier still if the Diplomatic Conference had accepted the USSR's proposal that

With regard to their co-operation in the application of the Conventions, and the supervision of this application, the activity of the Protecting Powers or of their delegates may not infringe the sovereignty of the State or be in opposition to State security or military requirements.[53]

The host State, of course, judging for itself when its sovereignty, security, or military requirements were involved! The UK delegation, itself prominent in the opposition to giving the PP anything like *carte blanche*, found the USSR's amendment unacceptable. It pursued as usual an emollient line rather than the confrontational one sometimes preferred by Canada, Australia, and the USA. 'No useful purpose would be served by concealing our opposition to the Soviet proposal,' recorded its circular memorandum early in June, 'but we might indicate that our fear was that a "fascist" power could use this provision to prevent the PP operating at all.'[54]

But the strong-sovereignty States had another card up their sleeve. Were they obliged to agree to the appointment of a PP at all? The Conventions assume that PPs will be appointed and use quite imperative language about them: 'The present convention *shall* be applied', 'The Parties to the conflict *shall* facilitate', and so on (my italics). But what if a belligerent State should decide that acceptance of a PP might bring more trouble than it was worth? About simple failure to agree to the appointment of a PP, by whatever process of prevarication, pedantry, or fault-finding, the Conventions have nothing to say.

Nor have they any more to say about failure to accept, in lieu of a PP, the

---

[52] This was how it reads in GC3 and GC4; the last sentence was removed from its appearances in GC1 and GC2. *Final Record* IIB, 344–6 shows the thwarting of the USSR's attempts to keep it in them.
[53] *Final Record* IIB, 59.
[54] UK: FO 369/4153 K. 5652; notes of the UK delegation's meeting on 3 June.

substitute for it specified in Common Articles 10/10/10/11. There was enough of the mandatory in this ('the DP *shall* request . . . or *shall* accept') for the Soviet bloc to make it, at the time of signature, the subject of a reservation, giving notice that their consent would be a precondition for any search for a substitute where the protection of their own nationals was involved. The point was an obvious one, but they presumably wanted to make doubly sure that no possibly seductive influence would be brought to bear on their nationals while they were beyond their grasp.

'Neutral States' are mentioned as possible substitute-PPs, but what the substitutes Article is really about is the ICRC or (supposing it could be found) some other similarly neutral and impartial humanitarian organization. Determining what kinds of organizations might qualify, and how much recognition or superiority should be accorded to the ICRC itself, proved difficult and exciting. You did not have to be a partisan of the League in its campaign to prise open the prerogatives of the ICRC to understand that Switzerland, hemmed in as it had been by the armed power of *one* belligerent, was not in 1939–45 as suitable a base for the ICRC's work as it had been in 1914–18. What if the worst should happen and Switzerland should be invaded? That had nearly happened more than once in the recent war. M. Lamarle took the opportunity to discuss the matter frankly with the ICRC's Claude Pilloud and Jean Pictet when he was in Geneva for an ECOSOC meeting not long before the Stockholm 1948 Conference. They opined that belligerents would surely be anxious not to seem to attack the ICRC, but admitted that Switzerland, if invaded, would fight and that their organization would lose its essential neutrality. Lamarle concluded his account of the interview by wondering whether many ICRC dignitaries would think the same way as Pictet who, he observed, belonged to 'one of those patrician families in whom still lived the traditions of their struggles for independence'.[55] He (Lamarle) tactfully left the subject by inviting the Genevans to ask themselves: What would Henry Dunant have decided to do?

Did the world's humanitarian headquarters have to be land-locked in the heart of Europe? Australia and New Zealand had no animus against the ICRC, but nevertheless admitted to having found Geneva's remoteness a problem. The ICRC's prospects were not bright in 1947. Clattenburg's report on that year's conference said that

the delegates by tacit agreement did not really come to grips with the problem of establishing the identity and character of the agency which would observe the

[55] FR: S.3.15 (as in Ch. 4 n. 8), dated 2 Aug. 1948.

execution of the new conventions. . . . It was clear that those powers whose international activities most plainly reflect the possibility of new wars were unwilling to accept the ICRC as a trusted neutral agency in its traditional field. [And so] it was clear enough that a new agency had to be formed which would not embody the same objections or pretexts.[56]

The Government Experts accordingly embraced the French suggestion that they should refer simply to 'the competent international organization'. 'Wherever this expression appears in the documentation of the meeting,' reported Clattenburg, 'it represents the need of a satisfactory agency and the avoidance of detailed discussion on the subject.'[57]

The British Home Office representative gave quite an optimistic assessment of its prospects: 'The vagueness of the expression . . . is in the circumstances unavoidable, it has the merit however that in practice the solution may be found in *ad hoc* reliance on a broadened field of activity for the IRC' (*sic*). No one, he insisted, wanted to 'endow the IRCC [*sic*] with any kind of political significance' (which the ICRC for its part did not seek, though touchy diplomatic purists like Whitehall's supposed it did). There was however room for argument about how best to secure the ICRC—if that was what the 'competent international organization' was going to boil down to—in the desired plenitude of functions.

Some of the delegations at times gave the impression that the conventions would gain in value if specific powers in certain respects were conferred therein upon the IRC . . . The UK view, on the other hand, was that the functions of the IRC were established by tradition, and capable within their own humanitarian sphere of indefinite expansion in practice provided they were not interfered with. We preferred to prescribe that their historical functions should not be hampered by the convention, rather than that they should be defined, since the definition in question might well result in some countries in their only being allowed to carry out the duties prescribed in the conventions within their sphere. . . . Unfortunately, when we accepted the French suggestion . . . it was mistakenly concluded [by the IRCC] that some governments were in favour of supplanting the IRCC by some international political body. It took an inordinately long time to correct this misapprehension.[58]

By the time the next conference of the series took place in Stockholm, fifteen months later, the 'competent international organization' had disappeared. The ICRC, for obvious reasons, was not going to develop the idea,

[56] Clattenburg's Report (pp. 11–12) cited in Ch. 4 n. 13.

[57] Clattenburg's Report, 12. He continued: 'In the introduction to the report of the 3rd Committee . . . will be found a happy cobweb of words spun by Ambassador Desy (Canada) to provide a reassuring explanation for the expression in question. The Ambassador could not be more explicit without injuring the feelings of his hosts.' It appears on pp. 270–1 of the 1947 Report, cited in n. 38 above.

[58] UK: FO 369/3795, K. 8345.

and apparently no one else had done so. The draft prepared for Stockholm by the ICRC, after vaguely referring to the possibility of some unspecified 'impartial and efficacious' PP-substitute, returned to *terra firma* with the specification of itself as a prime example of the sort of 'impartial humanitarian agency' which, along with any obliging neutral State, should be invited to undertake the required protective duties.[59] This was in essence the same formula as would appear, with a good many conditions and qualifications, in the 1949 texts as they finally emerged. A hierarchy of protective bodies is to be discerned. At the top, the Protecting Power, which 'shall' be there. If it isn't, 'an organization which offers all guarantees of impartiality and efficacy' *may* be agreed on to do the PP's work. If that fails, a neutral State 'shall' be requested to stand in. And if *that* fails, the Detaining Power 'shall request or shall accept . . . the offer of the services of a humanitarian organization such as the ICRC to assume the humanitarian functions performed by PPs.' Taken along with the common article just preceding it, which protects and affirms the legitimacy of the ICRC's offer of services, everything points to the ICRC as being, at the end of the day, the body upon whom care of the Conventions' designated categories of protected persons will fall. The humanitarian buck stops there.

The interesting idea of some superior international, even sovereignty-overriding supranational, organization that should stand above *mêlées* and mitigate their horrors did not however completely disappear. It survives in the second of the Resolutions passed at the end of the Diplomatic Conference, and once again it came from France. It is interesting not least because it bore witness to the earnestness with which some parties pursued the ideal of authoritative supervision and enforcement of IHL within sovereign territories; and also because the country of its origin has not always been noted for practical internationalism. But surviving French official papers from these years, 1946–9, show persistent and inventive interest in this matter. For instance, at their interministerial committee meeting as early as 6 February 1947, there was a thoughtful exchange of ideas about it between Lamarle and Georges Cahen-Salvador (Section head at the Conseil d'État and also listed as the French Red Cross Society's representative). Would humanitarian purposes be better or worse served, they wondered, if a supervisory body could be set up under UN auspices? Could the ICRC's statutes be modified to allow it to become such a body without damaging it in essential respects?[60]

[59] *Draft Revised or New Conventions for the Protection of War Victims*, for the 17th International Red Cross Conference (Geneva, ICRC, May 1948), 57.
[60] FR: Série Union, C.I.

Their aspirations found sufficient satisfaction that year in the idea of a 'competent international organization'. Perhaps because it was so vague, it attracted little support through the months that followed. Lamarle by August 1948 was beginning to canvass 'a high commission (*un aréopage*) of persons chosen from a variety of countries on account of their international standing and their reputation for impartiality'.[61] He failed, that month, to gain the support of the ICRC's new president, Paul Ruegger, who didn't believe such people as Lamarle had in mind could do a job which must require 'long training in a delicate sort of administrative work and profound familiarity with diplomatic practices'.[62] Undeterred, Lamarle brought a full-fledged version of it before the Diplomatic Conference. He must have been disappointed by its reception there. The UK delegations's fifty-second meeting noted that 'Denmark, the USSR, the US, and Australia all paid tribute to the noble intentions of the French delegate and promptly added that the proposal was both impractical and useless.'[63] Col. Hodgson called his government's attention to it 'as a good example of some of the amazing proposals, completely impracticable, placed before the Conference'.[64] Amazing or not, it obviously seemed practical enough to the French and—though he can hardly be considered an impartial and independent judge of such a matter—to Professor La Pradelle, who soon afterwards was describing it with enthusiasm as 'alone going to the roots of the problem' and as 'a body of international functionaries wholly detached from any political allegiance', rather like (so he suggested) what was to be found in some of the UN's special agencies.[65] In 1949 it was still possible to believe in neutrals. But the Soviet bloc didn't.[66] The final form of the French proposal, worked out in the Mixed/Joint Committee with the help of the

---

[61] FR: S.3.15.

[62] FR: Box labelled: Affaires Étrangères, Croix-Rouge Conférences Internationales, Stockholm 1948, Toronto, 1952 (my translation).

[63] UK: FO 369/4157 K. 6836.

[64] AUST: A. 1838/I. C. 1481/1, pt. 3, p. 112.

[65] La Pradelle, 'La conférence diplomatique', 231-2.

[66] Nor did the American Clattenburg, though he would not have admitted it so openly. The 'secret' part of his 1947 Report (see Ch. 4 n. 13 above) contains these thoughts, which can hardly have been his alone. How, he wonders, can governments possibly 'find a large enough group of "political eunuchs" (to use the expression of Senator McKellar) properly qualified to carry out impartially and with the full confidence of belligerents' all the various functions which delegates have been specifying? 'For just as it has been becoming increasingly impossible for governments to remain neutral, so has increased the difficulty of remaining neutral personally. War is no longer a hot-headed dispute between equals; it is the contest between St George and the Dragon. The dispute is over the identity of the characters. Despite their utmost attempts to blind themselves to the fact or to conceal it if they could not, the majority of the neutral nationals engaged in the field of political and humanitarian mediation during the past war looked upon the Allies as St George, not the Dragon.'

always eirenic British, had to survive Morosov's battering and an adverse vote of 32 : 8 : 4 on its way to being ceremonially embalmed among the conference Resolutions.[67]

That interesting suggestion for the scrutiny of observance of the Conventions being thus shunted into a siding, the responsibility devolved upon Protecting Powers and the 'impartial humanitarian organizations' that might be able to operate instead of, or alongside, them. One point indeed was fixed. The ICRC would be there by right whenever an international armed conflict existed and had claimed victims as defined in the four Conventions. Those Conventions obliged Detaining Powers, at the very least, to admit the ICRC to places where it was holding POWs and civilian internees and to facilitate its work of liaison between them and the societies from which they were cut off. But the ICRC had a second title to admission and support. This title, to which the Conventions obliquely refer in one of their Common Articles, was what the Statutes of the International Red Cross and Red Crescent Movement and the ICRC's own vocabulary call its 'right of initiative'. By virtue of this reasonable deduction from decades of valued practice, the ICRC is free to offer its services whenever it believes they can be useful, including in internal conflicts.[68] States are no less free to refuse them, but they have no right to resent the offer as customarily they tend to resent such offers from other States. To those two titles for presence in a situation of conflict might also be added that of a PP-substitute! The variety of functions thus brought within the ICRC's reach is potentially vast, functions conceivably going beyond the simply humanitarian, in proportion as host States might permit them to do so. But nowhere in this potential panoply of powers is there any trace of enforcement authority. If a PP's authority is no more than to 'scrutinize', the ICRC's can in no way be stronger. Observance of the Conventions cannot be enforced within the territories of HCPs by any authority from without.

Nor can judgment be given by any external and presumably impartial authority in matters of dispute over interpretation, application, and observance of the Conventions. Here was another issue where sovereignty

[67] *Final Record* IIB, 487–9.
[68] Common Articles 9/9/9/10, titled 'Activities of the ICRC', read (with appropriate changes in the description of war victims in view): 'The provisions of the present Convention constitute no obstacle to the humanitarian activities which the ICRC or any other impartial humanitarian organization may, subject to the consent of the Parties to the conflict concerned, undertake for the protection of wounded and sick, medical personnel and chaplains, and for their relief.' Art. 81 of API puts the same points rather more strongly: 'The Parties to the conflict shall grant to the ICRC all facilities within their power so as to enable it to carry out the humanitarian functions assigned to it by the Conventions and this Protocol' etc., and 'the ICRC may also carry out any other humanitarian activities . . . subject to the consent', etc.

asserted sway over supranationality, to even greater effect than with regard to supervision; and again the result was the same: embalmment among the Resolutions. Resolution I reads thus:

The Conference recommends that, in the case of a dispute relating to the interpretation or application of the present Conventions which cannot be settled by any other means, the HCPs concerned endeavour to agree between themselves to refer such dispute to the International Court of Justice.

It is all that remains of an endeavour to give the Conventions a set of judicial teeth (even if in the nature of things they were likely to be false ones). The extent of the distaste in which sovereignty-obsessed States held it may be judged from the fact that it is the only one of the twenty-seven draft common articles that disappeared completely from the final text.

The other items of the series remain in unburdensome form in Common Articles 11/11/11/12, 'Conciliation Procedure', and 52/53/132/149, 'Enquiry Procedure'. They make no advance on the comparable articles in the 1929 Conventions and it could well be argued that they mark a relative regression from what was thought proper then. The Conciliation procedure prescribed for 'cases of disagreement ... as to the application or interpretation' of the Conventions amounts to no more than that PPs 'shall lend their good offices' towards reaching all-round acceptable conclusions and that, once such have been reached, belligerents 'shall be bound to give effect to the proposals made to them'. The enquiry procedure prescribed for the more serious business of 'alleged violations' is even less onerous to the alleged violators. Not PPs but belligerents only may request that 'an enquiry shall be instituted, in a manner to be decided between the interested parties'; beyond which, they 'should agree on the choice of an umpire' to settle questions of procedure, if they could not manage to settle such among themselves.

The feebleness of these gestures in the direction of supervision and enforcement is no fair measure of the amount of time devoted to their consideration from 1946 through 1949. No doubt their history reflects the change of mood through those years, from immediate post-war optimism about the prospects for international goodwill and justice to Cold-War cautiousness and disillusion. The optimistic phase began with the IRC carrying over from before the war its conviction that the 1929 provisions relied too much on goodwill and on an enlightened reading of national self-interest. The Government Experts had before them in 1947 the recommendation that there should be 'a single central and permanent agency' to investigate alleged violations of the Conventions at any HCP's instance, and that belligerents should positively facilitate its operations. Such radical notions could not but excite argument. The ICRC's report says that while 'all the Delegations agreed on the principle of investigation and procedure', the liveliest debates were about 'the constitution of the commission of enquiry', and how far international courts should be involved.[69] This meant referral to two bodies: the already existing ICJ, whose President, some delegates thought, was ideally suited to be a sort of 'supreme arbitrator' (an exposed position *not* coveted by the President of the ICRC, upon whom other delegates sought to press it), or an international criminal court, the idea of which was beginning to fascinate and tantalize the minds of the optimistic.

The watering-down began at once. What went to Stockholm for the 1948 Conference was a weakened version of those bold notions: no 'central and permanent' agency poised to spring into investigative action, but a commission appointed *ad hoc* from standing panels; no stated obligation of parties to do what the commission said, but simply an assumption or hope that they would do something about its 'recommendations' when they received them. The President of the ICRC was after all brought in as nominator of the third member of the commission in the event that the President of the ICJ should be 'a national of a belligerent State'. The text however retained some promising teeth, which came out of Stockholm more or less intact. The inquiry procedure did not require the agreement of both or all parties to set it going; any HCP alleging a violation could demand it, and since panels of names were to be compiled in advance, its operation so far could be regarded as automatic. But how much further would States, when they came into their own at the following year's Diplomatic Conference, let the inquirers go into what they (States) would sensitively regard as their own affairs? In 1949 it was unsurprisingly discovered that they would not let them go anything like so far. Out came the teeth, leaving only the relatively unthreatening Common Article 52/53/132/149 mentioned above. Out went also every reference to the ICJ. Professor La Pradelle and Dr Cohn headed the group which sought to make the best of it. Morosov and his Bulgarian colleague Mevorah joined Col. Hodgson in making the worst; the bluff Australian adding that

it seems unlawful and, above all, it is impracticable. In a dispute arising out of the interpretation or application of a Convention, expedition is the whole essence of the settlement of such a dispute and the International Court is the very last tribunal in the world from which to get a decision expeditiously.[70]

---

[69] As pp. 65–7 in n. 42 above.   [70] *Final Record* IIB, 367.

Expedition was actually no more the essence of the issue than principle. It is impossible to judge the extent to which States were moved by one or the other, or were sincere in what they said about either. France's suggestion that reference to the ICJ should be removed from the main texts and gone over by another working party before embalmment among the Resolutions got over a many-sided difficulty. The Soviet bloc and a few others abstained, only Australia voted against. La Pradelle wrote its obituary:

Thus, by a radical deformation which robbed it of all strength even in the merely directive sense, ended the career of the Danish amendment which had at least the virtue of reminding the Diplomatic Conference that it is not possible to dissociate the works of Charity and Justice.[71]

Repression of Violations

Along with the ideas of supervision and enforcement of the Conventions went naturally the idea of punishing violations of them. A twofold problem appeared: first, to distinguish the offences to be singled out for 'repression' (the technical word for it), and, second, to find suitably fool-and-knave-proof means of repressing them.

Distinguishing the offences at once became a thick and thorny problem because of its unavoidable overlap with the war crimes then so much in the news. Violations of the Geneva Conventions would appear to be war crimes too. But war crimes as a genre went far beyond Geneva law's limits. If violations of Geneva Conventions were to be formally stigmatized as war crimes, they would have to be distinguished as war crimes of a particular sort. Without the great and telling words 'war crimes' attached to them, would they be taken seriously enough? So far, the question was one of legal judgment and institutional policy. But politics came into it too. War crimes were coming to mean different things on opposite sides of the opening Cold-War divide. The prospect dawned that the UN's International Law Commission, which was just beginning its work near the end of 1947, would take up the prevention and punishment of war crimes. There was talk of the establishment of a permanent international criminal court, perhaps in the form of a department of the already well-established ICJ. The door thus suddenly opened to a several-sided contest. Just while the American and British administrations were losing enthusiasm for the prosecution of war crimes (an enthusiasm their military, moreover, had never shared), the

---

[71] His book, p. 284. He had made this cause his own, and deplored the French delegation's pursuit of unanimity as 'weak'.

Soviet Union was about to bring to Geneva a new enthusiasm for it. The ILC's announced work on it could be used to support opposite policies. Parties concerned to minimize the extent of the new Conventions' approach to war crimes could point to the ILC as a better forum for dealing with an issue stretching far beyond Geneva's peculiar province. Parties concerned to make sure that at least something got done before the international community lost its post-war sense of urgency could point, as the Dutch for example did from early days of the Diplomatic Conference, to the agonizing slowness of the ILC's progress.[72]

If the USSR's intrusion in 1949 of its own enthusiasm pressed the debate in one direction, the USA's loss of enthusiasm since 1947 pressed it in the other. The USA in 1947, strongly supported by Belgium and the Netherlands, wanted a general statement to appear in each new Convention, to the effect that infractions constituted war crimes; and such an article indeed appeared in the ICRC's draft for improved Conventions. The UK showed so much anxiety and caginess about this that one is driven to surmise that only desire to minimize disagreements with its great ally and to avoid the embarrassment of seeming to backtrack on Nuremberg kept it from explicit remonstration. The British FO papers show the matter being carefully examined from every aspect. Its German departments liked the proposed innovation, which would rule out the sort of complaints about retrospective legislation which had given German criticism of Nuremberg some colour of justice. Its UN department joined its legal advisers in branding as simply silly the idea of referring alleged breaches to the Security Council. As to the substance of the draft war-crimes article, several difficulties had to be faced. Apart from the unwisdom of encouraging POWs to overact the part of the barrack-room lawyer, there were real risks that its effects could be ethically counter-productive. 'War crimes' just then carried 'an idea of grave moral guilt', which one would not wish to be adulterated by attaching them to any but major breaches of the Conventions; yet any listing of breaches which *were* war crimes could lead to the supposition that non-listed breaches were *not*. The UK's conclusion, after much consultation between the Foreign and War Offices, was that 'war crimes' would be better not mentioned at all.[73]

So many new ideas being thus floated at a time and in an atmosphere which discouraged sceptics and conservatives from admitting disquiet, the

[72] UK: FO 369/4149 K. 4721.
[73] Summary of the contents of FO 369/3966 K. 2487, registered on 16 Feb. 1948. It contains a lot of FO and WO minutes and notes on this matter and copies of relevant documents from the Government Experts' Conference. The long memorandum on 'War Crimes in connection with the POW and Allied Conventions' with which it concludes apparently became the basis for UK policy thereafter.

ICRC ventured to amalgamate its own hopes with the Government Experts' wishes. It put before the Stockholm Conference a draft article which identified breaches of the Convention as war crimes, subject to universal jurisdiction and on condition that HCPs, if they would not institute trials in their own national courts, should extradite accused persons to HCPs who would.

This draft came through Stockholm more or less unchanged. What made it the object of continuing anxiety in official circles—its continuing equation of violations with war crimes and the strength of its demand that States should actively repress them—endeared it to the Red Cross rank and file. But the ICRC, prudently concerned to save the substance in a form which governments could swallow, then set in train a process of further consideration which was to produce one of 1949's biggest bombshells. Whitehall was early made privy to the plan, the ICRC no doubt hoping thus to engage its sympathetic interest. M. Pilloud, chief of its legal division, drew back a corner of the curtain in a letter to Mr Gardner. The Stockholm Conference, he recalled, had asked the ICRC to pursue further studies of this complex question of the repression of breaches. War crimes not being one of the branches of international law in which they felt most at home, they needed expert advice. Col. Phillimore and Capt. Mouton, respectively the British and Dutch legal experts at the 1947 conference, were two specialists and practitioners whose names came at once to mind. But much bigger game was in their sights. They thought it desirable also to have

a person versed in international law, who would be able to represent in some measure the doctrinal point of view. The works published by Professor Lauterpacht, who is a professor, if I am well informed, at Cambridge University, have specially interested us and we would be happy to learn if you think it would be possible for him to be consulted.[74]

The hesitant reference to Cambridge can have been no more than what Pilloud thought was required by courtesy and diplomatic style. Hersch Lauterpacht was the most famous international law professor in the UK and one of the most eminent in the world. To engage his advice and support would be a colossal *coup*. One wonders why the ICRC felt it necessary to approach the great man thus obliquely. Was it because he was thought less likely to help if approached directly, or because the British Government was so touchy about the ICRC's status? Whatever the explanation, Lauterpacht was written to by one of the Foreign Office's lawyers, Joyce Gutteridge (a Cambridge graduate and herself daughter of a law professor there) and

[74] UK: FO 369/3970 K. 11153, letter dated 24 Sept. 1948.

on 3 November he rather grandly replied that, although he was extremely busy, 'This is not a matter with regard to which I would feel inclined to refuse co-operation.' From then on he dealt directly with Geneva, and the ICRC's powerful little working-party of war-crimes experts—Lauterpacht, Mouton, Phillimore, and Professor Jean Graven of Geneva University, chaired by Max Huber—did its work in December, the Foreign Office showing no interest in it other than to decline to pay the two Britons' travel expenses which, it argued, fell to the ICRC.[75]

The draft new articles that came of all this were quite revolutionary. In the place of the relatively brief and simple sentences that had served so far, four Common Articles now appeared, the main purport of which was: (i) to bind HCPs 'to incorporate the present Convention as part of their national law' and to ensure that the whole of it was respected and acted upon; (ii) beyond that, to classify 'as crimes against the law of nations', and to undertake to extradite for trial elsewhere if they would not bring to trial themselves, 'grave breaches of the Convention'; grave breaches being defined as including 'in particular those which cause death, great human suffering, or serious injury to body or health, those which constitute a grave denial of personal liberty or a derogation from the dignity due to the person, or involve extensive destruction of property, also breaches which show by reason of their nature or persistence a deliberate disregard of this Convention'; (iii) a ban on the 'superior orders' defence, coupled with attachment of 'full responsibility . . . to the person giving the order, even if in giving it he was acting in his official capacity as a servant of the State'; and (iv) a set of safeguards of fair trial consistent with, *inter alia*, the general principles of law and humanity.

The virtues of these proposals are striking and obvious. The alarming expression 'war crimes' had been removed without any sacrifice of principle; 'crimes against the law of nations' was in fact a broader and more elevated way of achieving the same goal. IHL's affinity to the human rights law of which Hersh Lauterpacht was a prominent apostle was made crystal clear in the descriptions of grave breaches. And in what was provided relative to the plea of superior orders, the personal responsibility of officials, and the guarantee of fair trial, there were incorporated three of what would soon be universally known as the 'Nuremberg Principles'.

It proved to be all too much for the nationally mind-set lawyers and soldiers whose judgments were going to be crucial. Their unease was aggravated by the fact that these novelties did not come before them until the very

---

[75] Ibid., K. 12137, 13141.

eve of the conference. The ICRC's *Remarks and Proposals*, in which they were revealed, is dated (in its English translation) February 1949, but there is no trace of them being known in Whitehall before the last week of March, and as for the Americans, their delegation's first sight of 'these unprecedented recommendations' was not until it got to Geneva.[76] One may presume that delegations which had travelled from even further were in the same boat.[77]

Within the English-speaking delegations, reactions were mixed. Some development beyond the Stockholm draft had been expected, but not as much as this. There was an immediate inclination to find grounds for turning it down. For the US delegation and others, the lateness of its delivery was the preferred excuse; for the British (characteristically, given Whitehall's neurotic objection to the ICRC's doing anything that, by Whitehall's reckoning, only States could do) the further fact that it was from the ICRC that first news of the development came, not the Swiss Government.[78] On the other hand there was much public enthusiasm for a development of this kind and no one could deny, while the star of Nuremberg stood so bright in the sky, that it was a good idea to make sure that international law meant what it said. Nor was it possible to pass off these radical proposals as 'unrealistic'. The hand that presented them was the hand of the ICRC, but the voices were those of men profoundly versed in the conjunction of the military and the legal. Mouton was both a Dutch naval captain and a judge in his country's supreme court of appeal; Phillimore had been one of the British prosecuting team at Nuremberg; and Lauterpacht, in his capacities as editor of Oppenheim's classic treatise on international law and as the War Office's chosen expert on revising the law-of-war part of its *Manual of Military Law*, was by no means the kind of international lawyer of whom generals tended to be suspicious. The Dutch adoption of them undoubtedly helped to keep them alive. But it did not save them from drastic surgery. Whose hands were upon the knife, and why, awaits discovery. Most of the surgery was accomplished out of sight, between early May and the middle of July, by a Western group among whom the UK was later said (privately) by Hodgson and (publicly) by Mouton to have played the most active

[76] First appearance in Whitehall is in a long letter (secret) from the War Minister's private secretary, 25 Mar., to his counterparts in the FO, HO, and Lord Chancellor's and Attorney-General's Offices, briefing them for the Cabinet working party which would be monitoring the progress of the Conference. American surprise is expressed in US: 514.2 Geneva/5-249.

[77] Ottawa cannot have known about it before receiving Wershof's communication from London, dated 12 Apr.; CAN: 619-B-40, vol. 5.

[78] The lateness is noted in Pictet's *Commentary*, i. 360, and the minor row about it appears in *Final Record* IIB, 24–5. Whitehall's characteristic objection to the diplomatic incorrectness is in the letter cited in n. 76 above. UK: FO 369/4147 K. 3539.

part.[79] When the subject resurfaced, the proposals were shorn of the elements that had made them so interesting to the progressive legislator.

Their new form, later wrote Hodgson, 'was carefully framed to avoid any reference to crimes or to make any particular reference to any international tribunal or to create a precedent which would conflict with existing international law'.[80] Beyond that, the 'superior orders' bit had sunk without trace. From the hostility which military men generally felt towards it, one may feel justified in surmising that they had been particularly glad to see it go.

It is a measure of the boldness of what the ICRC and its legal consultants had proposed that even after so many of their proposals had been abandoned, enough remained to rank the Penal Sanctions and Grave Breaches common articles among the Conventions' most striking innovations; innovations which, although accepted without much further debate in 1949, were to cause Western governments many headaches through the years immediately following, as they faced up to the problems of implementation. Such debate as there was, was mainly about the Grave Breaches. This debate resolved itself into two parts. First, were these Grave Breaches to be described as crimes? Nobody doubted that they *were* crimes and that the common man would certainly reckon that their specification in the Conventions would suppose them to be describable as international crimes. The Stockholm text had equated them with war crimes; the ICRC and its midwinter consultants had called them crimes against the law of nations. But now, at the Diplomatic Conference, a tense struggle broke out between (to name just the leaders on each side) the USSR, passionately desirous to keep crimes in the text, and the USA, determined at all costs to get them out.[81] Why? The ostensible reasons were not quite the whole explanation. Reasons given in debate for opposition to the word 'crimes' were, 'firstly because this word had a diferent meaning in the national laws of different

---

[79] Hodgson mentions these goings-on behind the scenes in his Report, pt. 3, 114–15 (see Ch. 4 n. 33). Mouton's passing allusion to the British role is in *Final Record* IIB, 31.

[80] Hodgson's Report, pt. 3, 114 (see Ch. 4 n. 33).

[81] UK: FO 369/4148 K. 3905 (opinion of Attorney-General, 11 Apr. 1949) and 4150 K. 4975; notes of the 10th meeting of the UK delegation, 3 May, appendix on top-level meeting of UK and US heads of delegations and legal advisers to seek common ground on the war crimes question. The papers in CAB. 130/46, Gen. 281(0)7, besides revealing the great interdepartmental row referred to above, contain a letter from Craigie to Sir Eric Beckett (senior legal adviser at the FO) containing this interesting passage: 'On our side, we were a little shy of specifically mentioning any violation which, in some unforeseen or exceptional case, might become genuinely inevitable. On the other hand, most other delegations here (and particularly the Americans) seem to rely on the theory of "impossibility" as a defence in such cases and to feel more confident than we do that this doctrine would succeed before an International Court in a genuine case.'

countries and secondly because an act only becomes a crime when this act is made punishable by penal law. This conference is not making international penal law but is undertaking to insert in the national penal laws certain acts . . . which become crimes when they have been inserted in the national penal laws.'[82]

Lightly veiled behind the first sentence cited above was the Western States' fearful conviction that the Soviet Union and its allies would stretch the meaning of 'crimes' to cover whatever *they* believed to be crimes. As has already been remarked, this seemed very likely to include the planning of, and the participation in, whatever they classified as aggressive war, and the conduct of whatever they chose to call mass extermination. The USSR carried on the battle to the last possible moment but lost it. Grave Breaches appear in Common Articles 49/50/129/146 and 50/51/130/147 as Grave Breaches and nothing else.

This concept was undoubtedly born of the desire to distinguish really serious infractions—the sort which were worthy of the alternative 'war crimes' description—from run-of-the-mill infractions. These latter would have been equally punishable if some humanitarian enthusiasts had had their own way. Indeed they had been equally punishable under Article 29 of the 1929 Wounded and Sick Convention, which was one of the reasons why that article had remained almost a dead letter. To specify *grave* breaches now was a way of keeping things serious. The Lauterpacht group's proposals could easily seem rather too general. The British War Office, which was by no means hostile to the principle, for example offered these thoughtful and moderate criticisms:

The inclusion as war crimes of (*a*) 'a grave denial of personal liberty', (*b*) 'a derogation from the dignity due to the person' or (*c*) 'extensive destruction of property' would be to attack the inevitable results of war itself. Every person conscripted into the Army is subjected to 'a grave denial of personal liberty' and probably in some instances 'a derogation from the dignity due to his person'. Many acts of war involve extensive destruction of property.[83]

The lists of more particular Grave Breaches as they were finally specified seem to have been universally accepted as a minimum; some States, the USSR among them, of course remaining disappointed that the lists were not longer. The lists varied slightly from Convention to Convention to meet what were thought to be the needs of each category of 'protected persons or

---

[82] *Final Record* IIB, 116; summary of argument put by delegates of USA, UK, France, Australia, and the Netherlands.
[83] UK: FO 369/4147 K. 3539.

property'.[84] Common to all was 'wilful killing, torture or inhuman treatment, including biological experiments, [and] wilfully causing great suffering
or serious injury to body or health'. The POW and Civilians Conventions
added compulsion to serve 'in the forces of the hostile power' and wilful
denial of 'the rights of fair and regular trial' as those Conventions had just
prescribed them. The Civilians Convention and the Wounded and Sick (and
Shipwrecked) Conventions added 'extensive destruction and appropriation
of property, not justified by military necessity and carried out unlawfully
and wantonly'; for civilians alone was added 'unlawful deportation or
transfer or unlawful confinement' and the taking of hostages.

Such were the Grave Breaches of the Conventions, to which HCPs bound
themselves by the preceding common article to apply certain penal sanctions. Here again the Diplomatic Conference, although going by no means
so far as some desired, was reckoned by others to be startlingly innovative.
There being no international criminal court, and reference to Nuremberg-
and Tokyo-style international tribunals being excluded, the place of trial
and judgment could only be national. But national courts were given, with
regard to these particular offences, universal jurisdiction, i.e. power to try
foreigners as well as the persons normally within their jurisdiction, and
HCPs were committed to making sure that 'persons alleged to have committed such grave breaches' were brought to justice; if not in their own
courts, then by process of extradition in another's.

The principal difficulty and headache which this Common Article
brought to Western States which conscientiously desired to fulfil their
responsibilities under the Conventions was, how to legislate so as to catch
alleged criminals and then to extradite those whom they chose not to bring
to justice themselves, if they were not to choose—as for political reasons
they very well might—simply to let them slip away. Such matters caused no
headaches in one-party States and/or dictatorships, where law, whatever
was said of it in the constitution, was understood to be in the service of the
regime, to be run hot or cold according to need from the political mixer-tap.
Very different were the prospects facing, for example, the British and US
governments when they contemplated the varieties of opposition predict-

[84] UK: FO 369/4163 K. 10039, written during the post-conference months when the officials
in Whitehall were wondering how to handle the new Conventions, contains rich minutes about
this. How on earth, enquired the Treasury Solicitor on 6 Oct., did the words 'or property' get
past the War Office's watch-dog Mr Gardner? But after all it was harmless enough, 'as not only
does it quite exceed any imagination of which I am capable to see how "great suffering or
serious injury to body or health" can be inflicted on property, but there are, so far as I am
aware, no buildings protected by the POW Convention.' Miss Gutteridge agreed that such
nonsense only got into the final version because of 'Vaillancourt [the Canadian head delegate]
wanting his lunch and not allowing the drafting committee enough time' to look at it properly.

able in Parliament and Congress! It might take years and it could by no
means be relied on to get through without modifications. The USSR scored
another of its several 'moral victories' at that conference by arguing that
States should complete the appropriate legislation within two years, and by
hinting that only lack of seriousness about it could explain their refusal to
accept such a time-limit. In the event, the USSR did not find itself in a
position to ratify the Conventions much sooner than the USA and the UK,
for whom the enactment of appropriate legislation was certainly the major
brake on their doing so. They ratified, at last, in 1955 and 1957 respectively;
the USSR in 1954.

These undertakings for the pursuit, arrest, trial, and punishment of grave
violators of the Conventions constituted one of their more remarkable
and, by all humanitarian, liberal, and non-militarist criteria, progressive
elements. Not as firmly wedded to the Nuremberg Principles as they might
have been and deliberately lifted out of the mainsteam of international
criminal jurisdiction that was expected to flow from Nuremberg (but was
about that time running into the sands at the UN), the Penal Sanctions and
Grave Breaches common articles nevertheless marked a significant step along
the international legal road.[85] The minimizing description of it given by
Mouton when presenting the report of the subcommittee which did the
watering-down was exaggerated.[86] It was his business—his unhappy business, one can confidently reckon—on that occasion to allay nationally
fixated fears by emphasizing the extent to which the internationalist intentions of the original proposal had been eliminated. Any lingering traces of
them might spell death to the Convention's chances of ratification in some
States. But to harp as he did on the national aspects was to give a false
impression. What national courts were to do was to 'apply sanctions for the
enforcement of international rules and for that purpose [they] must have
and exercise an effective universal jurisdiction'.[87] The law they were enforcing was international penal law no less. It was immaterial that 'grave
breaches are punishable because they are breaches of international law (i.e.
treaty provisions) and not because these acts are in themselves breaches of
international law which all States are free to punish'.[88]

---

[85] Hodgson's Report, 114–15: 'the amendment [in *Final Record* III, 42] was carefully
framed to avoid any reference to crimes or to make any particular reference to any particular
international tribunal or to create a precedent which would conflict with existing international
law.'
[86] As in n. 82 above.
[87] Draper, *Red Cross Conventions*, 106.
[88] Michael Meyer, 'Liability of POWs for Offences Committed Prior to Capture: The Astiz
Affair', in *ICLQ* 32 (1983), 948–80 at n. 95.

This section on application and enforcement of the Conventions may close with a juxtaposition of two common articles which illustrate respectively the truths that some articles are more weighty than they actually seem, while others seem more weighty than they actually are. One of these latter (Common Articles 52/53/132/149) sets up a procedure for inquiry into alleged violations, which could of course open the door to embarrassing disclosures. The procedure however requiring agreement 'between the interested Parties', and, failing that, their agreement on the choice of an 'umpire', its chances of getting off the paper must have seemed so slim that delegates could pass it on the nod. The final records of the Conference thus record its progress; '35 votes to nil, with one abstention', 'no opposition to this Article', and simply 'adopted'.[89] The other Common Article (51, 52, 131, 148) received a bit more attention at the Diplomatic Conference and several times survived only by modest majority votes. Nowhere in the reported discussions do the minority's deeper feelings and suspicions about it come to the surface.[90] Its ostensible object, as described in the report of the Joint/Mixed Committee on all the common articles it had worked on, was 'to render null and void, in advance, any contractual exemption by which a victor State could prevail upon the conquered State to cease to hold the victor responsible for any violations of the Conventions committed by the organs of the latter'.[91]

Nothing could seem more virtuous or reasonable. Superior strength was to be prevented from amnestying its own malefactors. But there were hidden aspects which Col. Hodgson early spotted and, with the UK delegation's sympathetic support, resisted to the end.[92] Most serious was the military question, which Hodgson thus expressed in his final report:

The intention of the Italian delegation was clear, though it was not forthcoming in public. As it stands, this article will provoke a conflict between Government and Commander-in-Chief. The Commander-in-Chief will naturally insist all destruction by bombing is a military necessity, but the Government is responsible for all destruction not of imperative military need. Who is to judge? It is recognized as one of the stupid decisions of the Conference, but the UK, USA, Australian, Canadian,

---

[89] *Final Record* IIB, 37, 131, 364.

[90] The final version seems innocuous enough: 'No HCP shall be allowed to absolve itself or any other HCP of any liability incurred by itself or by any other HCP in respect of breaches referred to in the preceding Article.'

[91] *Final Record* IIB, 133.

[92] One such aspect was financial; it appeared to prevent even an omnipotent victor from excluding from the terms of peace a loser's claims for compensatory payments. Whatever might be the ideal morality of such a prohibition, Hodgson thought it practically absurd.

and all practical-minded delegations were outvoted by the Soviet Group European States and by weak-kneed sentimentalists.[93]

Non-International Armed Conflicts

At no point was the 'humanitarian' approach more at odds with that of the 'realist' than with reference to internal wars. Such a description of the two approaches does little justice to the variety of motives and concerns actually present on each side. Their interactions form one of the liveliest sub-plots of the Geneva drama of 1949, just as its denouement, Common Article 3, was (against all expectations) quickly to become the most significant and arguably the most useful article of all.

The idea of extending Conventional protection to victims of internal wars was not new. Its Red Cross history goes back at least to 1912, when at the Washington International Red Cross Conference of that year an attempt at such an extension had been summarily squashed by the Russian delegation. In practice its sources are more to be found in the history of civil wars, wherein it is shown how international law's content of moral sensibility and humanitarian principle could be made available for the regulation of hostilities whenever the warring parties were capable of wishing them to do so. Something of this sort, for example, happened by gentlemen's agreement in the English Civil War in the middle of the seventeenth century. Something much more formal and substantial happened in the American Civil War in the middle of the nineteenth, when the normal direction of the flow of influence (from international to national) was reversed to give the international law of war its first formal code: the Instructions issued by the Union government to its armies in the field, 'Lieber's Code', often mentioned in Part I above.

By that time it was universally accepted that recognition of a *de facto* non-State belligerent by the State against which it was warring or by neutral States would bring the rules and sanctions of international law into force. Nothing surprising, therefore, that early twentieth-century promoters of the law of war should wish to get its non-international applications formally registered, and to spread its softening influences over as many more fields of fire as they could. Their record by 1939 showed a few successes, of which the more enthusiastic of them (Col. Hodgson and his like would have said, the softer-headed!) naturally made the most. Mixed experiences in Russia and Hungary in 1918–19 stimulated the production of a comprehensive

[93] Hodgson's Report, 116.

programme of legal development by the 1921 Geneva IRC Conference, which seemed at once to be vindicated by the ICRC's considerable success in the Upper Silesian troubles of that same year.[94] The ICRC was much less successful in its attempt to be neutrally helpful in Ireland in 1921–2; and despite some notable humanitarian *coups* and much brave endeavour, its attempts to be so again in Spain in 1936–9 cannot be counted as encouraging. The Spanish Civil War demonstrated, as civil wars so often do, that ideologically divided fellow nationals can hate and distrust one another more even than they may hate enemies who are foreign.

The goal however remained a worthy one; all the more so after the experiences of 1939–45 had shown how easily an ill-disposed HCP could evade its legal responsibilities by arguing that the war it was fighting was not the international one to which alone the law was relevant. The Red Cross movement therefore, as after the war it focused on the question of revising and improving the Geneva Conventions, had their extension to civil wars in the centre of its sights. The ICRC, by no means unwillingly, made the movement's cause its own, and included the matter in the Government Experts' agenda for 1947.

Startling innovation though it was, it occupied relatively little time or attention either then or through the twenty-four months that were to pass before the Diplomatic Conference at last grappled with it decisively. How to explain this? One element of explanation lay in the form of its presentation. In Geneva in 1947 and at Stockholm in 1948, it appeared as part of the first two common articles on the new Conventions' application. In those early stages of their development they were intended to apply equally 'to all cases of declared war' etc. between HCPs, 'all cases of partial or total occupation', and 'in all cases of armed conflict not of an international character' occurring within an HCP's territory. This prominent placing, which might have been expected to focus attention on it, seems rather to have had the opposite effect so long as the substance of the Conventions was still undecided.[95] The extent of application, it was thought, could wait to be settled until there was a clearer view of what exactly was to be applied. Governments could also reflect, through the 1947 and 1948 conferences, that the settlement of major political accounts was not due until the Diplomatic Conference with which the series must close. The British government,

---

[94] This little-known latter episode is well reported in André Durand, *Histoire du CICR, 2: De Sarajevo à Hiroshima* (Geneva, 1978), 164–5. The tangled Irish episode next mentioned is quite extensively covered in ibid. 185–9.

[95] For coming to that conclusion on so important a matter, I must admit that I have only the British, US, and French diplomatic sources to go on.

consistently rigid in its diplomatic deportment, tended to refer to what the ICRC called (and most governments were content enough to call) a 'Conference of Government Experts' by such terms as 'the unofficial meeting convened by the ICRC', the 'unofficial meeting for the exchange of information, opinions and criticisms', and so on.⁹⁶ As for the Stockholm conference, the UK (as has already been shown) refused to take it seriously. No other State of whose policy-making I know anything treated Stockholm so lightly; but it remained the fact that, when it came to political issues, States did not actually have to take it too seriously. Of all the government delegates present, none but the Greek ones (at that date, embroiled in vicious civil war) said anything flatly in opposition to this part of the drafts, and the only other governmental comment came from the USA, demanding that reciprocity should be required.⁹⁷ The draft common article on Applications with the civil war extension in it could therefore be left as an unsolved, though admittedly a perplexing problem until the closing round.

For the UK and Commonwealth bloc, moreover, the problem possessed dimensions of danger not so apparent to most other States and not apparent at all to the simply humanitarian. The danger lay in the word 'colonial' which, until the ICRC prudently removed it after Stockholm, accompanied the word 'civil' in descriptions of the sorts of non-international war to which the Conventions were to be applicable.⁹⁸ Its disappearance from the Stockholm texts of course did not mean that it was no longer implied, and in fact it buoyantly resurfaced at Geneva in 1949. Meanwhile it gave Whitehall food for solemn thought, whenever Whitehall's preparations for Geneva went beyond the relation of the Conventions to international and (as it must have been in the minds of those involved) mainly European wars.

The form in which the innovation came before the Diplomatic Conference, then, was that each of the new Conventions was to be as equally applicable to non-international as to (in the cases of the POW and Civilians Conventions) international armed conflicts, subject to reciprocity. This, as the Canadian delegation's final report bluntly put it,

was, of course, a very novel and difficult proposition. It would mean that a contracting government would be under treaty obligation *vis-à-vis* a rebel organization.

⁹⁶ Remarks taken from UK FO 369/3793 K. 1822 and 3794 K. 5778.
⁹⁷ ID: External Affairs Department Archives, File 341/137/1; Memorandum dated 23 Mar. 1949. The lively report on the Stockholm goings-on, sent to the dept. four months earlier by Cashman of Defence, is in File 341/137, 'Preparatory Work 1939–49'.
⁹⁸ See the *Revised and New Draft Conventions for the Protection of War Victims: Texts Approved and Amended by the 17th International Red Cross Conference* (Geneva 1948), 10. Common Art. 2 has the vital new phrase about 'all cases of armed conflict not of an international character'; a small-print footnote says: 'The words "especially cases of civil war, colonial conflicts or wars of religion" have been deleted.'

Many delegations, including those of the United States, the United Kingdom, France, and Canada were opposed to this sweeping provision, feeling that it is both unreasonable and unworkable. The Soviet government was strongly in favour of retaining this clause or something close to it.[99]

Thus came to the surface in the 1949 debates two big and serious arguments: one rooted in political philosophy, and relating to the rights and duties of States and subjects; the other entangled with the ideological argument about the rights and wrongs of empires and colonialism.

If the draft texts of the new Conventions had not proposed their application to the less determinate condition of 'armed conflict' as well as the more determinate one of 'war', the difficulty would scarcely have existed. From the standpoint of international law, it mattered not at all whether warring parties were, to begin with, States or not. What mattered was whether there was 'recognition of belligerency'. Once a State, whether itself belligerent or neutral, had recognized a party's belligerency, everyone knew where they stood, and the relevant legal wheels could begin to turn. A war which was enough of a war to cause that to happen was by definition one which affected external interests and relationships. International law therefore was appropriately applied. But who could tell what was an 'armed conflict'? It was a phrase, remarked the British government in the memorandum circulated to prospective participants before the 1949 conference,

which goes much beyond a state of war as recognized in international law and which might cover a riot in which arms are used. It is thought that no government will be prepared to agree to the inclusion in an international Convention of a provision to deal with an international question of this nature and it is suggested that persons involved in a riot are not war victims and should be excluded from the scope of the Conventions.[100]

Ascertaining the threshold of applicability was one aspect of this problem. Assessing its implications for governments was another, admirably summarized in the Home Office's contribution to the formation of the UK delegation's brief for the Diplomatic Conference. Strutt put it to his War Office colleague Davidson that the whole thing was a mess and a muddle.

The place for a provision designed to protect civilians from their own government is [he wrote] the Charter of Human Rights; but the draft Charter now in preparation expressly avoids the imposition of obligations during 'a period of emergency'. Until the 'lawful' Government has been overthrown, the nationals of a country owe allegiance to that Government and no other. The concept which underlies the

---

[99] CAN: the Defence Dept's. Report on the Diplomatic Conference, dated 20 Sept. 1949, para. 26 on pp. 9–10. See n. 5 above.
[100] UK: FO 369/3970 K. 11941, para. 3.

Civilians Convention—that another Government has an interest in and claim on the civilians classified as enemy—does not apply in the case of civil war. It would be impracticable therefore either (*a*) to bind a lawful Government to treat one of its own civilian subjects, who owe it an unqualified allegiance, as 'enemy aliens', and hold them less answerable for breaches of its laws than the remainder of the population simply because they favoured the rebels, or (*b*) to attempt to 'protect' the lawful Government's loyal civilian subjects against the rebels by international convention instead of by the law of the land. The proposals on civil war, notwithstanding the attempted safeguards in the last sentence, seem to be inconsistent with the fundamental right of the lawful Government—well-recognized in international law—to treat the insurgents' armed forces, and *a fortiori* their civilian co-operators, as traitors.[101]

From the British War Office, as indeed from the perspective of any professionally thoughtful army department, the judgment was likely to be the same. Some parts of the law of war could easily enough be transferred from its usual international setting to the civil one, e.g. rules about weapons and the methods of using them, the general principles of discrimination and proportionality, and standard humanitarian observances like respect for the Red Cross emblem, the white flag, and the dignity of the surrendered person. Fundamentals of the law and customs of war on one side, fundamentals of human rights on the other (as the Home Office writer wisely noted) should be universally respected. But that the great new corpus of privileges and protections and immunities thought to be desirable for foreign enemy POWs should be transferred to prisoners who in the ordinary senses of the word were rebels and criminals (and perhaps traitors too) was bound to seem an unreasonable and ill-considered invasion of the political space seemingly essential to sovereign States' survival.

'Rebels' and 'traitors' was how insurgents were likely to be perceived in colonial wars as well. The more ideological argument which arose from this proposal was between the Western imperial powers, which admitted to having empires, and the USSR, which did not. By 1949, the UK was deeply embroiled with the (mainly communist) insurgency in Malaya. The Netherlands had just about lost the battle for what the world was learning to call Indonesia. The French were locked in combat with the Viet-Minh nationalists (also communists) in what the world called Indo-China, and were beginning to consider how to avoid running into similar trouble in North Africa. These armed conflicts would clearly classify as non-international— no imperial power was likely to dignify them as anything more!—and the proposal before the Diplomatic Conference therefore meant that imperial

---

[101] UK: FO 369/3970 K. 12091; a long letter, this part of it dated 3 Nov. 1948.

HCPs would be accepting unprecedented restrictions on their freedom in dealing with them.

The word 'colonial' had gone from the draft text before it got to Geneva but its spirit hovered between the lines and the professional anti-colonialists gleefully shone spotlights upon it. They bracketed together 'civil and colonial' whenever they could. The British, to name but one of the delegations with overseas colonies to think about, knew exactly what was at stake; specifically mentioned at one time or another in the UK's diplomatic papers were Indo-China, the Netherlands East Indies, Northern Ireland, Aden, and, most frequently, Malaya; also, 'there was always the danger of communist risings in various European countries'.[102] The more Whitehall contemplated the 'non-international' extension, the less did it like it and the more vexing did it find the Soviet bloc's exploitation of its embarrassment. The Attorney-General's opinion was early sought. He minuted his strong opposition 'to our entering into any Convention which would prevent our treating insurgents as traitors', and advised the delegation not to be surprised at finding themselves in a minority and an unpopular position. The UK could not dodge the issue. We are a colonial power, he wrote; 'It is charming to find the USSR, Hungary, Romania, and Bulgaria advocating the application of the Conventions to civil war. They have taken pretty good care in those countries that civil war could never occur.'[103]

These skirmishes were uncomfortable—once again, the Western States found themselves put unfairly (as they thought) on the defensive—but they were not really dangerous. It early became clear that the UK and France and their usual fellow voters were not going to accept the proposal in anything like the form in which it first came before them. At the same time, none of them wished to incur the odium of rejecting it altogether. The UK from the start was in the most unconcealed opposition to it. Sir Robert Craigie reported that his delegation 'therefore settled down to a war of attrition in which the anomalies and difficulties inherent in the various drafts . . . were successively exposed'.[104] In this respect, at least, the Britons' inimitable tactics must have found some admirers. The more that item of the Stockholm text was worked over, the more complicated did it become, without however increasing its promise of becoming at last more acceptable. A magical resolution of the problem was then produced by the French.

---

[102] e.g. UK: FO 369/3970 K. 12091 (in Mr Davidson's reply, dated 17 Nov.) and 4155 K. 6033 (a note to the FO from Trafford Smith of the Colonial Office dated 25 June 1949); also CAB. 130/46 Gen. 281, meeting of ministers at 10 Downing Street, 28 Mar. 1949.

[103] UK: FO 369/4150 K. 4885.

[104] Craigie's Draft Report, para. 42 (see Ch. 4 n. 23).

Common Article 3, as it then and finally became, must be judged the most notable of France's several major contributions to the fruitful success of the 1949 conference. The genius of the French invention lay in its removing at a stroke all grounds of objection on high political principle (States' rights, subjects' duties, etc.) while at the same time introducing into the Conventions their most striking and unequivocal human rights element; and perhaps, in its antepenultimate sentence concerning the ICRC, the most striking and useful of all their humanitarian provisions.

The political difficulty so far had been that States would not indiscriminately concede to rebels, revolutionaries, secessionists, and so on the rights of belligerent equality. So long as the proposed extension into 'non-international' armed conflicts involved the whole of the Conventions, with all their manifold directions as to how belligerents should handle people in their power, so long would anxious governments fuss about the identification of such conflicts. They had known what an international war was, but how were they to know a non-international armed conflict when they saw one? How were they to tell it from mob violence, riots, and banditry? Could any external body—the General Assembly or the Security Council, perhaps, or the ICJ—be looked to for advice or adjudication? These were not silly or necessarily non-humanitarian questions. The ICRC in promoting this revolutionary extension of the law, and the International Red Cross at its Stockholm Conference, had not given enough thought to its political and practical aspects; aspects which now engaged the attentions of successive subcommittees. Their labours and everyone's anxieties were therefore cathartically eased when the French delegation radically simplified the issue by proposing, instead of so unwieldy and ill-fitting an application of the whole of the new conventions, the simple application by one common article of the humanitarian gist of them. Whatever difficulties might subsequently be discovered as to its interpretation and application, no one was anxious to discover them now. At the same time, it was all but impossible for governments to refuse to observe towards non-combatants and those who were *hors de combat* the human rights here specified. The words 'human rights' are not used, but that was what they were.

The only quasi-respectable ground on which objection could be made to such exemplary undertakings was that their presence in the Conventions in this form was an affront to the sovereign independence of States: 'the right to do what they would with their own', etc. Only one delegate pressed this point or made much of it: General Oung of Burma (Myanmar); but he was joined by eleven others against the article when it came to the final vote

(34 : 12 : 1).[105] The vote having been by secret ballot, one cannot from the published records alone tell who they all were, let alone why they voted that way. Some, perhaps, voted against it because they had preferred the original proposal and disliked this one for not going far enough.[106] The Burmese delegate however made no bones about his motives. What he disclosed of them, along with his remarkable criticism of the article in general, is well worth attending to, for it was the momentous first sounding of a theme to be heard more and more often as the coming years unrolled.

General Oung presented himself as, and was apparently accepted as, spokesman of 'the Asiatic countries'.[107] His own country had just recovered its independence, along with India, Pakistan, and Ceylon (Sri Lanka), in the first batch of sheddings from Britain's imperial load. India and Pakistan (together with Sri Lanka, not present) had stayed within the Commonwealth. Burma at once signalled its political line by *not* joining the Commonwealth. The line its delegate now took about Common Article 3 expressed what soon became recognizable as that of newly independent States in the less developed parts of the world. He maintained that the Article was both dangerous and offensive to countries like his. It was dangerous because, in spite of all that could optimistically and/or disingenuously be argued to the contrary, it was bound to 'incite and encourage insurgency' and to slow down its suppression. The bigger, older States had taken great pains, he said, to exclude from the Conventions all human rights recognitions that might endanger their security during international wars. Why, he asked, should smaller, newer States be put to security risks during internal wars? No government, least of all a newly independent one, needed to have gratuitous spanners thrown into 'its own legal machinery to maintain the security of its population and the prosperity of its States'.[108]

But there was an earlier stage of violence or potential violence to be considered. General Oung continued:

Some of you, especially the delegations of colonial powers, have been remarkably broadminded to support the Article, though it is going to encourage colonial wars. We, the smaller nations, naturally feel much enthusiasm for colonial wars, we like to help them, but . . . there is every hope . . . that in this highly enlightened age the remaining conquered countries of the world will also receive their independence without the loss of a single drop of blood. So the only help that the Article will give,

---

[105] *Final Record* IIB, 338–9.
[106] See e.g. ibid. 79 and 83.
[107] Ibid. 78 and 102. Corroborated by La Pradelle, 'La conférence diplomatique', 213 n.
[108] *Final Record* IIB, 337, 329.

if you adopt it, will be to those who desire loot, pillage, political power by un-democratic means, or those foreign ideologies seeking their own advancement by inciting the population of another country.

He had other unpleasantnesses to lay on 'the colonial powers' while he was about it. In words which to the humanitarian ear forty years later have a tragic hollowness in them, he maintained that their attitude, if they really were keen on this Article, was offensive because it was interfering and patronizing.

I do not understand why foreign governments would like to come and protect our people. Internal matters cannot be ruled by international law or Conventions . . . No government of an independent country can, or ever will be, inhuman or cruel in its actions towards its own nationals . . . When we talk about the humane treatment of persons taking no part in hostilities, there is surely no need to treat persons who take no part in the hostilities otherwise than humanely. In our country we give such persons every encouragement, and even rewards.[109]

His objections to interference did not end with States. They extended also to the ICRC itself, to which that vital antepenultimate sentence of Common Article 3 gave *carte blanche* to 'offer its services'. Exaggerating, it would appear, the extent of the authority the ICRC or any similarly 'impartial humanitarian body' would derive from this permission, and underestimat-ing the degree of tact it would actually exercise in making use of it, he said that such non-governmental interventions were no less offensive and dis-turbing than those by governments.

Acceptance of outside intervention, even if it be from a humanitarian organization, would certainly confuse the issue, create further misunderstanding, prolong the dispute or even involve a State in an international dispute of serious dimensions. I again appeal to your sense of justice, to the declaration in the Charter of the United Nations, that you do not intervene in matters essentially within the domestic jurisdiction of any State nor aggravate the situation, especially that of a domestic nature.[110]

Everything—indeed, rather more than everything—that could be said in fair criticism of Article 3 was said by the delegate for Burma. He also acutely anticipated many of the difficulties that were to be encountered in its application. Considering how much good sense and political prudence there was in his remarks besides their evident extravagance, prejudice, and

---

[109] Ibid. 327–30.

[110] Ibid. 337. His closing words speak volumes about conference conduct: 'Since I have always happened to speak on delicate subjects I have always been defeated by abstentions. I am afraid I have been placing some of my friends in an embarrassing position, that of either voting for me or of not voting for me.' Therefore he requested that the final vote on this article be taken by secret ballot; as indeed, after much wrangling and unpleasantness, it was.

touchiness, it might be thought surprising that his was the only voice raised thus stridently against Common Article 3, and that he did not receive more support in public. The USA and USSR delegations did not conceal that they did not like it as much as (their differing amended versions of) the original Stockholm text. Col. Hodgson remained grumpy about it. Dr Cohn characteristically discovered problems in it that no one else could understand. Quite a lot of amendments were tabled and voted on between its first public appearance on 24 June, and the last debate about it on 29 July.[111] There was never any sort of consensus about it. It was at the best, as most of IHL has to be, a compromise, a compromise moreover which the great majority of delegates wanted to reach without too much fuss. After all, it was unthinkable after so many years of seeking and so much humanitarian expectation to fail to do something about civil wars; the new article had enough virtue and novelty in it to constitute a radical breakthrough; and, as has already been observed, the difficulties and problems that could still be found in the French version were nothing compared with those that had absolutely obstructed the road to compromise earlier on. But certain difficulties and problems remained, and although nobody besides General Oung seems to have wished to dwell on them, they did not wholly escape notice.

What was an 'armed conflict not of an international character'? The question remained unanswered. Everyone agreed that it could not mean 'the exploits of bandits or riots of any kind', just as everyone agreed that it must mean 'civil war' and (although the admittedly imperial powers would not admit this publicly) colonial rebellion.[112] But where the one sort of conflict began and the other ended, no one sought to enquire. It seemed to satisfy delegates to observe that the question hardly mattered, since no more was being asked of governments than elementary decencies they would (supposedly) be observing anyway. Henceforth, the argument ran, all States were going to respect basic human rights; no State would contemplate the torture or serious maltreatment or execution without fair trial even of criminals, bandits, and so on. Why then fuss about whether a non-international armed conflict existed or not?

A possible ground for fussing, upon which delegates did not linger, lay in the article's equal application to 'each Party to the conflict'. That it could bind an insurgent body big enough to be acknowledged as a belligerent recognizable in international law was of course admitted. But such legal

---

[111] It seems unnecessary to footnote all these appearances. They may easily be located in the excellent index in *Final Record* III, 203 ff. Note that what became Common Article 3 was known throughout the conference successively as Article 2/4 and 2A.

[112] The Venezuelan Col. Falcon Briceno, in *Final Record* IIB, 333.

niceties had been left behind once M. Lamarle had effected his French revolution. The question was now one of scarcely definable parties to wholly undefined conflicts. Whatever those parties might turn out to be, they were certainly not going to be among the signatories in 1949. How then could the Conventions be said to bind them? No better explanation could be given than that States, in committing themselves to the Conventions, committed not simply the institutions and officials under their direct management but also the whole of their populations, whom, by the common articles on Dissemination, they undertook to instruct about the Conventions. That was the meaning particularly attached to Common Article 1's undertaking 'to ensure respect' for the Conventions 'in all circumstances'.[113] Rebels and secessionists were therefore to find themselves committed to Common Article 3's human rights requirements by an act of the regime they were fighting against. It was, from a humanitarian point of view, magnificent, but it was distinctly odd as law. The comfortable way round this problem was to assert with Sir Robert Craigie that even though (as he had to believe) 'insurgents could not be bound by an agreement to which they were not a party . . . any civilized government should feel bound to apply the principles of the Convention *even if the insurgents failed to apply them*'.[114] In other words, it was a human rights matter.

There was little comment because there was universal agreement on the last sentence of the new article, affirming that its application 'shall not affect the legal status of the Parties to the conflict', i.e. rebels who observed the rules were not going to get any political advantages from it; least of all, enhanced legal status. General Oung of course did not fail to observe that in fact they would do so, and experience was to prove him right. The theory of Common Article 3, however, as the delegates in 1949 read it, was satisfactorily explicit; insurgents who abided by its rules could look for no rewards other than, first, decent treatment by the regime in the event of their falling into their hands, and, second, the satisfaction of a clear conscience.

It remains only to comment on the provision which has already commanded attention: 'An impartial humanitarian body, such as the ICRC, may offer its services to the Parties to the conflict.' The delegates at Geneva in 1949 can have had no idea of the significance which was going to attach to it in the coming time, and the ICRC itself, one imagines, can hardly have foreseen the extent and variety of uses that would be made of it. In the latter stages of the Diplomatic Conference, it passed without much comment. No doubt this was largely because, like other potentially objectionable features

---

[113] e.g. *Final Record* IIB, 53, 79, 94.   [114] Ibid. 94 (my emphasis).

of the final version of the 'non-international' extension it was a lot less objectionable than the earlier versions had been. In them had loomed, beside the ICRC and its like (so far as there were any such) the spectre of the Protecting Power; bad enough to sovereignty-obsessed minds in the context of international war, quite intolerable in the context of civil. Now, in this final version, there was no longer any question of Protecting Powers. All that remained of external intervention was this permission for the ICRC to *offer* its services for humanitarian purposes and those alone; with the strong meaning hidden between the lines that such an offer was not to be regarded by its recipients as an impertinence. General Oung, as we saw, did not conceal his belief that it might be. If other delegates thought the same, they are not reported to have said so.

The USSR and its bloc presumably had no intention of admitting any other external body to operate independently in its territory. Mr Morosov opined at one stage that 'it did not seem necessary to mention the ICRC, since the Committee or any other body would always be free to offer their services'. But faced with the USA's and others' preference for stronger wording that would positively require civil-war-stricken States to accept such offers—to make of them, in fact, offers they could not refuse—the Soviet Union accepted the sentence as it stood, and so did every other speaker. The ICRC consequently could feel free to exercise what it would soon be calling its 'right of initiative', with some assurance that governments would not take offence at its doing so and some hope that the humanitarian services it offered might be accepted.[115] But whether they actually would be, and whether the ICRC's judgment that a Common Article 3 type of non-international armed conflict was going on would prove universally acceptable, remained to be seen.

---

[115] The Swiss delegate Plinio Bolla, in *Final Record* IIB, 335.

6 | The Contribution of the Courts
Nuremberg, Tokyo, and the Rest

All of the trials conducted by the victorious UN powers after the Second World War are popularly known as 'war-crimes trials' and, strictly speaking, most of them were so. The persons in the dock were usually there because they were accused expressly of offences against the laws and customs of war as codified in the 1899 and 1907 Hague Regulations and the 1929 Geneva Conventions. The judgments given in some of those courts were, as shall soon appear, of importance in relation to the clarification and development of the law of war, and (with the possible exception of the Nuremberg Principles) to that alone. The Nuremberg Principles are so called because they originated in a Resolution of the General Assembly (Resolution 95, adopted on 11 November 1946) headed: Affirmation of the Principles of International Law recognized by the Charter of the Nuremberg Tribunal. They were in some fashion reaffirmed by the UN's International Law Commission (established by GA Resolution 174 on 21 November 1947) in mid-1950.[1] Jurists tend to be evasive and non-committal about the extent of their significance, but at least it can be said that the GA's unanimous vote 'indicated subscription by a large number of States to the substantive law of war crimes, including the principle of individual criminal responsibility, and to the lawful exercise of criminal jurisdiction over such individuals'.[2] Only at the two most conspicuous of these post-war trials (which are to be numbered in hundreds), the International Military Tribunals known to history as the Nuremberg and Tokyo trials, were defendants tried also for other alleged offences. It is important to bear in mind what was the relationship of those other offences with the law of war, and what it was not.

Crimes against humanity, which figured equally with crimes against peace and war crimes in the Nuremberg Indictment, were thus carefully defined: 'murder, extermination, enslavement, deportation and other inhumane acts

---

[1] They are reproduced in Schindler and Toman, 883 and 835–6 respectively. Roberts and Guelff, always cautious, leave them out.

[2] Draper in *US Naval War College International War Studies* 62 (1980), 247–62 at 259–60. He might have added the law on crimes against humanity, which Principle VI equally lists. Lay-folk who have taken at face value the phrases about the supremacy of international over national law, and have accordingly perceived opportunity to initiate actions against members or officials of their own governments, have to the best of my knowledge been consistently disappointed.

committed against any civilian population, before or during the war, or persecutions on political, racial or religious grounds in execution of or in connection with any crime within the jurisdiction of the Tribunal', i.e. the planning and waging of the Axis's aggressive war. A narrow door was thus opened to enable the prosecution of German ministers and officials for some of the worst things that had been done to German nationals and other German-controlled persons before the war. The Nuremberg Principles kept the same door open with potential regard to committers of crimes against humanity in other countries and on subsequent occasions, provided only that the acts in question were 'carried on in execution of or in connection with any crime against peace or any war crime'. As one result of this, France has been able to continue prosecution of alleged war criminals after the lapse of the number of years within which war crimes remained punishable.[3] What future there may be for this concept of crimes against humanity, born of the Second World War, only time will tell. The case for keeping it warm and using it remains, alas!, apparently as convincing as was the case for formulating it in the first place; but it continues to suffer from this difficulty among others, that, with so much of its substance covered by the law on war crimes on one side and with as much again covered by the laws on human rights and genocide on the other, it retains little distinct meaning of its own.

The indictment of crimes against peace made more of a mark, but of an indistinct and questionable kind. The Nuremberg and Tokyo judgments could only add to what had already been done by the Pact of Paris and, much more impressively, the Charter of the United Nations to make criminal the planning and conduct of aggressive war. No part of the IMT proceedings, probably, was more popular than this with the victorious powers' general publics, which had been accustomed to justify their sacrifices as those of peace-lovers dealing with double-dyed aggressors. In the USA above all this was passionately believed, making that country the mainspring for the inclusion of this category of crimes in the indictments. The USSR proved ready enough to go along with this, provided the indictments were so drawn as to exclude any of its own recent actions (e.g. to go no further back than 1939–40, its occupation of eastern Poland, its war against Finland, and its ingestions of the little Baltic States) which the

---

[3] For a lively presentation of the French experience by the chief prosecutor in the case of Klaus Barbie, see Pierre Truche, 'La notion de crime contre l'humanité . . .' in *Esprit*, 181 (May 1992), 67–87. States have had to decide for themselves whether to take notice of the GA's Resolution 2391 of 26 Nov. 1968, 'Convention concerning non-applicability of statutory limitations to war crimes and crimes against humanity'.

uninformed and unfriendly might misunderstand. The UK and France were from the outset sceptical, reckoning that misunderstandings—not of Soviet foreign policy alone!—were indeed all too likely, and despairing of ever attaining a universally acceptable definition of 'aggression'. Aggression, however, was exactly what Marxism-Leninism knew how to define. It was something to which capitalist imperialism and fascism by their very nature were committed, something they could not forswear or do without. Communism on the other hand by its own account of itself was a peaceable creed, warlike only when justly defensive. The USSR and its allies therefore at once became the liveliest upholders of this part of the indictment, their enthusiasm for it waxing as the enthusiasm of its chief begetter, the USA, waned. The Soviet bloc's devotion to the Nuremberg Principles, thus early manifested and undiminished thereafter, was and remains attributable, first, to their particular emphasis on crime against peace, and their consequent relish for the prospect of bringing its perpetrators to properly publicized trial; second, to the air of authority this could give to their qualifications of military actions against them as aggressive and 'unjust' and of such actions undertaken by themselves as necessarily defensive and 'just'. Discourse about the proper interpretation and applications of the law of war has since the turn of the 1950s been confused by one set of States' use of this terminology and another set's avoidance of it.

War crimes was the sector of post-war criminal proceedings that most contributed to legal development. Reconstruction of the law of armed conflict seemed necessary and desirable to forward-looking minds as the war's unfolding course daily disclosed the law's existing weaknesses. By the time the war ended, the ICRC and the various government departments with which it had been collaborating all had ideas about how the Geneva side of the law needed to be strengthened and improved, an aspect of the legal and humanitarianism business of which the world knew little. What the United Nations (as from 1943 the anti-Axis allies were calling themselves) knew very much of in this respect was the war crimes committed or alleged to have been committed by German authorities and armed forces, by their European allies and underlings, and on the other side of the world by the Japanese and their collaborators. The concept and expression could of course in principle have invited application on *both* sides of the conflict, but in the circumstances of the time it inevitably became attached by the victors to the losers. 'War crimes' summed up, without exhausting, what was most vile and barbaric in the way the vanquished regimes had conducted hostilities and the prolonged occupations that went with them; and, the call of principle duly acknowledged, it must be said that the quantity and character of what now came to light was far worse than what could have been charged (or what indeed subsequently *has* been charged) to the account of the victors.

War crimes were committed on a vast scale and attended by all conceivable—and by some inconceivable—circumstances of cruelty and horror. The bulk and the worst of them came out of Nazi/fascist ideology, not least its own peculiar idea of total war, which justified the neglect of whatever laws, rules, and customs stood in the way of its supreme values, the ascendancy of 'master race and master nation'. War crimes accordingly were committed when and wherever the Nazi directorate thought them to be advantageous. They were for the most part the result of cold and criminal calculation.

The law of war thus entered the theatre of international reconstruction in the forensic form referred to shorthand as 'Nuremberg'. Two consequences of this are to be noticed. First, no distinction was made between the Hague and Geneva sides of the law: the Hague side, dealing largely with methods and means of combat, and the Geneva side, focusing exclusively on the protection of victims. This distinction has been noted already but it demands mention again *en passant* because much was to be made of it through the ensuing years. It served the emotional needs of some interested parties, the professional interests of others, and it had the prima-facie justification that Geneva's concern had never been for anything but the protection of victims and sufferers, whereas the Hague's had been for all aspects of war conduct and consequences. Since Geneva law had its own distinct history since 1864 and its own guardian angel, the ICRC, to take a proprietary interest in it, there were obvious enough reasons why it should become regarded as something apart, only with caution to be spoken of in the same breath as Hague Law, and not to be dealt with at the same conferences.

In most practical respects however the distinction between the two was artificial. The Nuremberg indictment and judgment found no need to observe the distinction in their panoramic review of who had suffered what, and why, during the late war. There must in any case appear to be a certain schizophrenia or cognitive dissonance about a law which, in the doctrine of its extremist exponents, is infinitely willing to pick up the human pieces in war, but disclaims interest in the processes that can make them many or few. The discreet apartness which the ICRC had to observe in its protection and relief activities demanded no parallel discretion in the discussion of the law by other parties. The operations of contemporary warfare, meanwhile, with their insistent tendencies to confuse categories and to spread effects, in fact suggested their association. By the turn of the 1970s, the unity of the whole was being accorded some of the respect it deserved. Geneva happened to be the venue of the Diplomatic Conference at which the next round of legislation was undertaken, and amplification of the Geneva Conventions was its avowed business, but the Additional Protocols which completed it in fact contain Hague law of the purest water. Separation had been tried and it had failed. But it is possible to believe that the interests of humanity did not emerge undamaged from the experience which, beginning with Nuremberg's neglect of certain means and methods of total warfare, was sealed when the same were excluded from consideration at the Diplomatic Conference in 1949. It is difficult not to feel that political and technical matters—above all, those concerning nuclear weaponry—thereafter became too much and too often discussed in unnatural isolation from the ethical and legal considerations at least equally relevant to the questions of acquisition, limitation, and control. To a considerable extent, they still are.

The second 'Nuremberg' effect that needs preliminary notice was (as has just been inferred) the selectivity of the war-crimes trials respecting means and methods of warfare. It was inevitable that the means and methods brought by the victors before their courts (and they were 'their courts', notwithstanding that at the same time they were guided by the lights of international law and were consciously serving the global community) should have been those of their defeated enemies which were dubious or beyond question disgraceful. Of such, there were more than enough to give to uncritical observers the impression that they were witnessing the comprehensive revision of Hague law which had long been needed. The quantity of corrections made during the later 1940s, the war-crimes trials' boom years, certainly seemed sufficient to justify such an impression. And yet that impression was a false one. On some issues, e.g. hostages and reprisals, the new case-law spoke with two voices, and jarred with what was done at Geneva. On other issues, e.g. area- and terror-bombing, it spoke not at all. This would not have mattered, if the role of Nuremberg had not been accidentally boosted beyond its original one, already sufficiently ambitious. To bring to public justice, on behalf of and for the future good of humankind in general, the ruling élites and criminal agents of a great power whose policy proclaimed it to be humankind's deadly enemy, was a magnificent aim, from which none of its incidental human and judicial failures could ever much detract. Reaffirmation and revision of the law of armed conflict was only a by-product of the greater process.

War on Land

The great majority of the war crimes indicted at Nuremberg and Tokyo and in all the other trials of those years were crimes against members of the civilian populations of the countries the Axis powers had invaded and occupied. International law was not at that time copiously explicit about the protection of civilians: partly because (as has already been explained) it was well understood that the conduct of some legitimate war-operations precluded the separation of civilians from their country's posture of belligerence, and partly for the reason that the 'standard of civilization' so far accepted by the lawmaking States had made it seem unnecessary to elaborate legal instruments around so self-evident a principle. The only instrument in question in the war-crimes trials was the fourth Hague Convention and its land war regulations. One section of them, in quantity about one-fifth of the whole, concerned 'Military Authority over the Territory of the Hostile State' while several articles in the section on 'hostilities' set limits to how they should affect non-combatants. Beyond and behind these specific rules was the Martens clause in the preamble, declaring that 'in cases not included in the Regulations . . . , the inhabitants and the belligerents remain under the protection and the rule of the principles of the law of nations, as they result from the usages established among civilized peoples, from the laws of humanity, and the dictates of the public conscience.'

Introducing his exhaustive section on the protection of civilians in the power of the enemy, Schwarzenberger observes that

The relevant rules of the Hague Regulations . . . were never meant to prevent, unaided, the wholesale relapse of civilized nations into barbarism. They were intended as signposts for belligerents who, by and large, were willing to respect the fabric of a common civilisation, but might occasionally be tempted to turn a blind eye to overzealous commanders or spontaneous excesses of their armed forces.[4]

The moral climate of the world had however changed since such comfortable truths could be taken for granted by reasonable men. In some countries in particular it had changed very much for the worse. Acknowledging that the attitudes of Stalin's Soviet Union and militarist Japan towards peoples in their power were very bad in their own distinctive ways, it is surely difficult to deny that there was something singularly bad about Nazi Germany's. Its disregard of the applicability of the Hague principles and rules to non-

---

[4] Schwarzenberger, 211.

German, non-Aryan members of societies with which it chose to go to war justified itself (not that its devotees thought it needed justification) by: (1) racial theory, claiming for Aryan Germans a superiority, allegedly demonstrable by biological science, over all other peoples; (2) nationalism of the extremest kind, exalting the interests of Germany above all other States and conceiving of international society as no more sociable than an overcrowded jungle; (3) a glad embrace of the idea of total war, envisaging the struggling of entire societies with one another and the use of any means, even the most extreme, to secure total victory; (4) in logical consequence therefrom, but also drawing on a long tradition of German military thinking, an exceptionally severe and extensive doctrine of military necessity; and (5), so far as the conduct of operations against the USSR went, denial that the Hague Regulations mattered in a war against a State which had not, so Germany alleged, reaffirmed its obligation to them since its Revolution.

Whatever were the merits of this latter argument, which went arm in arm with the charge that the 1929 POW Convention did not matter in a war against a State by which it had never been ratified, it cut no ice at Nuremberg. As we have seen, the Hague Regulations were judged to have been, in these principled respects, declaratory of international customary law, i.e. binding on all States whether they chose to sign and ratify the instruments or not, and the same was held to be true of the 1929 Geneva Conventions as well. There *was* a certain standard of civilization, below which no State could fall if it wished to remain a member of international society; and this was it.

The 1899 and 1907 Hague Regulations and the Convention containing them therefore provided the yardsticks against which war crimes against civilian populations were measured. They were found in two major respects to need amplification. Their indefiniteness on the matter of military necessity allowed that doctrine more room for manœuvre than some thought ethically tolerable, and their general principles regarding the protection of civilians in wartime needed to be worked out in practical detail as already had been the principles regarding the protection of prisoners of war. The question of military necessity was dealt with in various of the Nuremberg and associated judgments, as shall at once be shown; the state of the law regarding civilians was dealt with (along with other matters) by the Geneva Conventions whose making is described below.

No legal defence could plausibly be put up against the main heads of crime in this part of the Nuremberg indictment: the extermination and mass murder of people; murder and torture of individuals; wanton destruction of private property and of what belonged to the world's cultural heritage; compulsion to slave labour and brutal deportation of people from their own lands to perform it; systematic plunder of even the most elementary and indispensable economic resources; and/or any combination of those atrocities (e.g. deportation and slave labour were integral to the working of the Auschwitz archipelago, with much destruction, murder, terror, and torture along the way). It was sometimes said by particularly bold or ideologically possessed defendants, that what they had done found its justification in some higher law of racial or national life, or simply in the necessities of total war as they believed it had to be waged. Such a point of view was interesting and alarming enough in its own way, but of course was no acceptable defence in a court chartered to restore the rule of international law and the standards of civilization.

At levels lower than the highest, certain more apparently plausible lines of defence were possible for men and women involved in the execution of these lawless plans and policies. Nazi necessity was one thing, beyond the legal pale altogether; but military necessity and superior orders were another, classically within it. The war-crimes tribunals had to devote much attention to considering defence pleas that such-and-such a destruction or slaughter was excused by 'military necessity'. Much attention had also to be given to the plea of 'superior orders'; not because consideration of it demanded the same amount of expert military and legal knowledge, but simply because it was regularly advanced by defendants at every level, from those personally obeying the Führer right down to privates obeying their corporal—a kind of incantation by which persons involved in the commission of crimes and atrocities thought to excuse their individual participations, without necessarily denying that crimes and atrocities had been committed. On both of these pleas, Nuremberg had important things to say.

Military Necessity

What was said about this in the judgments cleared up some but by no means all of the delicate issues which attach to this idea. The Hague legislators touched the heart of the matter when they described the signatories of the Convention containing the land war regulations as being animated 'by the desire to diminish the evils of war, *so far as military requirements* [necessities, in the 1899 version] *permit*' (my emphasis). War admittedly brought evils with it but those that were not indispensable to the conduct of military operations could be done without. This truth had always been maintained by decent military men and (as was shown in Part I) by the end of the nineteenth century it had been embodied in a sizeable body of customary law. Now was the time to embody it in the even more solid body of treaty law. Hence the Regulations which, besides a lot of definitions, guidelines, and general rules, contained certain special prohibitions of acts (e.g. declaring that no quarter would be given, and employing weapons etc. calculated to cause unnecessary suffering) which no claim of military necessity could ever excuse.

In other cases where the claim might still be advanced, room was specially made for it, e.g. in Article 23(g), prohibiting destruction or seizure of enemy property 'unless such destruction or seizure be imperatively demanded by the necessities of war'. There were a few other articles containing weaker versions of the same qualification. For the rest, the implication was clear enough, that where no such qualification was inserted, 'the rule of the principles of the law of nations' was to be followed. That left some but not too much latitude for the practice of severities and infliction of punishments under the plea of military necessity anticipated in the preamble. Only a minority of commentators (chiefly German, as was to be expected of writers within that national military tradition) persisted in maintaining that the 'military necessities' clause in the preamble trumped everything that came after and, contrary to the majority opinion on the plain meaning of the text, enabled any departure from the rules to be justified by appeal to it.

Such appeal was made at some of the post-war trials, and to some effect. Inevitably in the background of virtually all defences against charges of excessive harshness towards civilians, it came to the foreground in two of the cases heard by the American Military Tribunals in Nuremberg after the IMT had finished. Charges of 'wanton destruction of cities, towns or villages, or devastation not justified by military necessity' were brought against a number of German generals in the so-called 'Hostages' and 'High Command' Trials. The best-remembered use of this line of defence was that of General Lothar Rendulic, dealt with at considerable length in Part III.

Superior Orders and Command Responsibility

Superior orders were among the simpler matters dealt with in the war-crimes trials; which is not to say that the question was then set forever to rest. By its very nature it can never be a restful one. Of all social organizations, armed forces are among the most given to demanding instant and unquestioning obedience to orders. As an Argentinian delegate said at the

CDDH: 'the principle of due obedience [is] the corner-stone of the military system of many countries attending [this] Conference.'⁵ If responsibility for a legally or morally questionable order rests with anyone, it is with the person who gives the order, not the person who obeys it. Kings and commanders have taken pride in assuming this responsibility, before God as well as before men: not least because the men under their command might otherwise be less ready to do terrible-seeming things when ordered to do them. '*Theirs* not to reason why' (my emphasis).

This absolutist military ethic has however never been unchallenged, even among the military themselves. The soldier who disobeys his captain's order to shoot his colonel is more likely to receive the latter's commendation than reproof. Sensible soldiers may be able to distinguish between awful-seeming orders that may have a legitimate basis concealed behind them (e.g. to bombard a quiet-looking town, which higher command may know to be sheltering troops, or whose bombardment may be justifiable as reprisal) and orders that cannot possibly have one (e.g. massacring, torturing, raping unmistakable civilians). A Chilean delegate admitted, in one of the CDDH's many debates about the matter, that while some 'national penal legislations [including his own] had sanctioned the principle of . . . absolute obedience', others adopted the principle of '*rational* obedience or again *considered* obedience, which meant that a subordinate could ask his superior to reconsider his order, but would have to obey if the order was confirmed'.⁶ The civilian interest in civilized societies, moreover, whenever it has been able to assert itself against the military, has never been happy with at any rate the peacetime applications of this obedience ethic. The results inevitably were messy. When Hersch Lauterpacht looked into them on behalf of the International Commission for [Post-War] Penal Reconstruction and Development, he noted how differently the problem was handled by England and the USA on the one hand, by Germany on the other.⁷ The former's military manuals enjoined absolute obedience to orders, but their national legal systems found different ways to relieve order-obeying soldiers from the penalties to which their deeds consequently exposed them. 'The German Code of Military Criminal Law . . . provided that the soldier must execute all orders without fear of legal consequences, but added that this does not

---

⁵ Torres Avalos in Committee I, 6 May 1976. For guidance to this and the next extract, I am grateful to Howard S. Levie's 'superior orders' *Supplement* (New York, 1985) to his four-volume *Protection of War Victims: Protocol I . . .* (1979–81).

⁶ Mr Lyon in Committee I, 5 May 1976.

⁷ Lauterpacht's Memorandum, published in the 1944 *BYIL*, is partly reproduced in the UN War Crimes Commission's *History* of itself (London, 1948), 275–7; p. 281 makes the link with the British and American changes referred to in the next para.

apply to orders of which the soldier knew *with certainty* that they aimed at the commission of a crime.'

In some degree consequent upon Lauterpacht's memorandum were the changes made in 1944 to the British and American manuals, and the insertion in the Charters of the IMTs of this Article: 'The fact that the defendant acted pursuant to order of his government or of a superior shall not free him from responsibility but may be considered in mitigation of punishment if the Tribunal determines that justice so requires.' Justice in the event was found to require sympathetic consideration of the 'superior orders' plea when made by underlings in all but the most atrocious cases, but the plea was indignantly dismissed when offered by officers and officials in the higher echelons. 'These men', said the chief US prosecutor of the highest of them in his closing speech at Nuremberg, 'destroyed free government in Germany and now plead to be excused from the responsibility because they became slaves. They are in the position of the fictional boy who murdered his father and mother and then pleaded for leniency because he was an orphan.'[8] That splendid denunciation implicitly dismissed as humbug the German officer caste's age-old claim that it was 'non-political'. But to be 'purely military' was no excuse either for those in the higher levels of the order-transmitting hierarchy: 'Participation in such crimes as these', said the IMT judgment with particular reference to General Jodl, 'has never been required of any soldiers and he cannot now shield himself behind a mythical requirement of soldierly obedience at all costs as his excuse for commission of these crimes.'[9] No element of Nuremberg legislation was more single-mindedly adhered to than this one, the emphatic assertion of individual responsibility. It appeared in the UN's International Law Commission's statement of the Nuremberg Principles in this form: 'The fact that a person acted pursuant to order of his Government or of a superior does not relieve him from responsibility under international law, provided a moral choice was in fact possible to him.'

Command responsibility is bracketed with superior orders for obvious enough reasons. If servicemen are to be brought to trial for carrying out unlawful and atrocious orders, do not logic and equity demand that their superiors must be brought to trial for issuing the same? Logic and equity were appropriately respected at the IMTs and the other major war-crimes trials. Generals and Field Marshals who had initiated lawless doings were brought to book equally with the NCOs and private soldiers who actually

---

[8] Cited by Yoram Dinstein, *The Defence of 'Obedience to Superior Orders' in International Law* (Leiden, 1965), 145.
[9] British edn. of the judgment, 118.

did the dirty work and whose punishment, often, was mitigated on the ground that, being low in the chain of command, 'no moral choice was in fact possible' for them at the time the order was given.[10] Men near the top of the chain pleaded that no 'moral choice' was open to them either, but, as we saw above, the IMT declined to believe them. Commanders should bear full responsibility for what they ordered to be done. But what about what was done under their command without having been expressly ordered?

This was the other aspect of command responsibility, which mattered little in Europe but much in Asia and which has gone on mattering ever since. The causes of this continental contrast are instructive. The armed forces of Germany, the European ones under intensest scrutiny, were of all armed forces in the world the best disciplined and most efficiently administered; what was ordered to be done would be done, and not much would be done that was not ordered to be done; moreover, German culture was not, except where the Nazi virus had taken hold, dissimilar to that of Germany's foes.[11] In the Pacific war, the situation was quite different. Japanese armed forces indeed were formidably disciplined but their administration was by European standards rudimentary, the distances over which they were operating were often so great that communications were unreliable, and there was no cultural affinity at all between, as it seems, most Japanese soldiers and such alien enemies as they might encounter. The consequence was that war crimes and 'ordinary' crimes committed by Japanese and Korean servicemen, although often done under orders from high up, could just as often be spontaneous and self-directed. The question therefore arose, were commanders whose men did these things culpable for not having trained them better and for not having ordered them *not* to commit atrocities?

This other half of the doctrine of command responsibility received its first full airing in the trial in Manila of General Yamashita, under whose crumbling command—or nominal command, according to the point of view—terrible things had been done to the people of the Philippines during the months preceding the Japanese surrender. No evidence appeared to show that Yamashita had ordered those things to be done, and he maintained at his trial that, had he known about them, he would have stopped them and punished the perpetrators. The court however concluded that he

[10] The IMT's authority for allowing the plea of mitigating circumstances was Art. 8 of its Charter. I have insignificantly adapted the wording of the passage cited in the UNWCC's *History* of itself (1948), 287.

[11] The huge exception that must of course be made in respect of Soviet communism does not affect my argument here; what the German armed forces did on their eastern front, they did under orders and according to plan.

ought to have known about them and that he was guilty of a failure to take action to stop them. Doubts about the legitimacy of the court (an American military one, established by order of General MacArthur) and the fairness of the trial were weighty enough to prompt appeals to the Philippines and the US Supreme Courts, but the principle itself was so central to the indictment at the Tokyo IMT that it almost at once acquired an importance equal to that of superior orders. Nineteen of the accused, recorded one of the several judges who went on to become celebrated authorities on international law, were indicted because, 'being by virtue of their respective offices responsible for securing the observance of [the laws and customs of war, they] deliberately and recklessly disregarded their legal duty to take adequate steps to secure the observance and to prevent breaches thereof, and thereby violated the law of war'.[12]

Hostages, Collective Punishments, and Reprisals

These have to be considered together because the first two, notwithstanding the apparent prohibition of collective punishments by Hague Regulations Article 50, were in some measure a common stand-by of all armies occupying enemy territory, and the third, often called on to justify them, was a lawful-seeming way of doing so.[13] Reprisals, it may again be said, is a very important term of legal art, meaning an act illegal in itself but permissible in reasonable proportion and with proper safeguards as a response to illegal acts already committed by the enemy and as a deterrent to their recurrence.

We need not here linger on the terroristic and exterminatory uses made of these practices in the Second World War by German and German-allied forces, e.g. atrocities infamous under such names as Lidice, Oradour, Kalavyrta, and many more even worse ones with Russian names; or excesses such as the killing of all male relations of killers and saboteurs.[14] For such atrocities no legal excuse was conceivable. But for the taking of hostages to

---

[12] Bert V. A. Röling, 'Criminal Responsibility for Violations of the Laws of War', in *Revue belge de droit international*, 12 (1976), 8–26 at 15. While believing that it was important to assert the principle of command responsibility, he admitted that it could be more difficult to determine guilt by omission than guilt by commission, and opined that, had Yamashita been tried in Tokyo well after his alleged offences instead of in Manila so soon after them, he might have been exculpated, as was the perhaps more guilty Admiral Toyoda. The Yamashita case is tersely and well analysed in Philip R. Piccigallo, *The Japanese on Trial* (Austin, Tex., and London, 1979), ch. 4.

[13] That Article read: 'No general penalty, pecuniary or otherwise, shall be inflicted upon the population on account of the acts of individuals for which they can not be regarded as jointly and severally responsible.' Schwarzenberger's discussion of it on pp. 237–8 discloses its ambiguities.

[14] Nuremberg judgment, as in n. 9 above, 49.

ensure obedience by occupied communities and for the infliction of collective punishments in reasonable measure upon communities undoubtedly sponsoring resistance activities, the explanation was always available that persons and communities under military occupation must not overindulge their inclinations to resist. This is not spelled out in any of the relevant instruments—it is hidden there within the combatant–non-combatant distinction—but national military law manuals (those, anyway, of nations whose armies may have to do some occupying) state it as a simple matter of common sense. The current British one, for example:

It is the duty of the inhabitants to behave in a peaceful manner, to carry on their ordinary pursuits as far as possible, to take no part in hostilities, to refrain from any act injurious to the troops of the Occupant or prejudicial to their operations, and to render obedience to the officials of the Occupant. Any violation of this duty is punishable by the Occupant.[15]

Its US counterpart is very similar, differing only in its beginning with a reminder of 'the restrictions imposed by international law' which are no doubt taken for granted in the British one.[16] The 4th GC in 1949 made very clear what those restrictions were, or at any rate what they ought to be; whether in occupation practice they actually *could* be, was a controversial question to which we shall return. (What restrictions should reciprocally be set to their own conduct by occupied populations was a matter wholly ignored.) But no restrictions were unmistakably spelled out by the Hague Regulations—even Article 50's meaning and scope could be argued about—and how occupying authorities would conduct themselves was limited only by their own preferred readings of customary law, their national military cultures, and their ideological persuasions.

Resistance and occupiers' handling of it therefore remained the legally controversial matter it had been since the later eighteenth century. German military-legal doctrine was probably more intolerant of it than most, but no army with experience or prospect of military occupation could bear more than a limited amount of it. Lawful armed resistance had been to some extent permitted by the Hague Regulations: Article 1 legitimized well-organized and professionally conducted partisans, such as Soviet, Polish, Greek, Italian, Yugoslav, and French partisans sometimes were between 1941 and 1945; Article 2, with an eye on the moral impossibility of forbidding an attacked people to lift a finger in its own defence, legitimized spontaneous non-organized resistance provided that arms were carried

[15] *The Law of War on Land, being Part 3 of the Manual of Military Law* (London, HMSO, 1958), sec. 552.
[16] *The Law of Land Warfare*, Field Manual FM27-10 (Dept. of the Army, 1956), para. 492.

openly and the laws and customs of war respected. That was as far as the representatives of the major military powers at the Hague conferences had been prepared to go on paper, and it was further than they found it comfortable to go in practice. Resistance of any sort was difficult to put up with, and the extraordinary term 'war treason' (of old German origin: *Kriegsverath*) was dusted off to intimidate those who were inclined to resist, even by non-violent means, the quasi-sovereign powers implicitly though illegally claimed by the occupier. The taking and killing of hostages, the infliction of collective punishments, and so on, were regularly used to enforce occupiers' rights; and even those who could not bring themselves to describe resistance by such an outlandish term as war treason could nevertheless agree that resistance, if it wished not to be regarded as merely criminal, had to be conducted according to certain rules. It takes two to tango. There was as much need to define how the inhabitants of invaded and occupied territory should conduct themselves *vis-à-vis* military occupiers as to define how military occupiers should conduct themselves vice versa. Were the occupier on the whole to behave decently, popular armed resistance to him could not be lawful, i.e. to use the term popularized by Richard R. Baxter in the early 1950s, it could be no more than 'unprivileged belligerency'—an infringement of the occupier's rules and orders, no doubt, but not a violation of international law.[17]

Such was the Hague Rules' attempt to square this insoluble circle. But what if the occupier did not behave decently? What if he behaved extremely undecently, as the Germans and their allies often had done in the recent war? Did such behaviour break, so to speak, the contract binding the other party? If an occupier did much less than the law required of him, were the occupied entitled to do more than the law allowed them? The contention sounded reasonable. The case was made at some of the trials. Sometimes it was accepted, at others not.[18] On this delicate and tragedy-laden topic, as to which the Hague Regulations gave no guidance at all, Nuremberg understandably came up with no clear answer. All it did come up with was a number of judgments that clarified the meaning of the relevant parts of those Regulations.

The judgments of the IMT and the other trials at Nuremberg did not entirely or unambiguously outlaw the infliction of collective punishments in

---

[17] No writings of that epoch did more to illuminate the issues in this area of IHL than Baxter's articles 'The Duty of Obedience to the Belligerent Occupant' and 'So-Called "Unprivileged Belligerency": Spies, Guerrillas and Saboteurs', in *BYIL* 28 (1950), 235–66 and 28 (1951), 324–45 respectively.

[18] For a convenient sketch of what happened, see Kalshoven's *Belligerent Reprisals* (Leiden, 1971), 328–30.

occupied territories; nor did it outlaw the taking or even, *in extremis*, the proportionate execution of hostages by occupying armies; nor did it rule out the possibility that collective punishment, the taking of hostages, and other severities towards an occupied population might really be justifiable as reprisals. But, with an indignant eye on the freedom with which the possibly legal end of the gamut had been stretched to cover uses merely terroristic and/or exterminatory, or permitted to rest upon an unacceptably generous interpretation of military necessity, the courts insisted that such measures could be taken only when they were appropriate, discriminating, proportionate, and in any case of last resort.[19] Thus hostage-taking and collective punishment could be legitimate as reprisals if the victims were demonstrably integrated with an organization (it could be anything from a partisan group to a government-in-exile) responsible for some illegal act against the occupier. Whether justifiable as reprisals or not, they must stand in some reasonable proportion to the seriousness of the acts they were designed to punish. As for last resort, the court in the 'Hostages' case offered a list of measures that should be taken

to impose peace and tranquillity before the shooting of hostages may be indulged: (1) the registration of the inhabitants, (2) the possession of passes or identification certificates, (3) the establishment of restricted areas, (4) limitations of movements, (5) the adoption of curfew regulations, (6) the prohibition of assembly, (7) the detention of suspected persons, (8) restrictions on communication, (9) the imposition of restrictions on food supplies, (10) the evacuation of troublesome areas, (11) the levying of monetary contributions, (12) compulsory labour to repair damage from sabotage, (13) the destruction of property in proximity to the place of the crime, and any other regulations not prohibited by international law that would in all likelihood contribute to the desired result.[20]

War at Sea

The post-war trials gave little attention to this dimension of the law of war. Sinister motives have been imputed for this neglect, as two in particular of the victor States had heavily engaged in maritime warfare and in most important respects conducted it the same way as had the vanquished. This was admitted at Nuremberg to the extent that those parts of the indictments of Admirals Raeder and Dönitz were not pressed which could equally well have been made against their British and American counterparts. Why they

---

[19] Law-minded commanders have often had to remind their subordinates that 'necessity' means a lot more than mere convenience.

[20] Cited, with valuable commentary, in Kalshoven's *Belligerent Reprisals* (Leiden, 1971), 226.

were in the indictment at all, I cannot make out. Perhaps there was not, until too late a stage of the process, sufficient liaison between legal and naval persons to have warned the prosecution that the compartment of the box it was opening should be labelled 'Danger! Open with Care!' This hypothesis is the more plausible for the fact that the prosecutors avoided walking into the same trap on the air-force side.[21] But it would be equally plausible to suppose that the main explanation of why charges with this boomerang potential were brought in the one case and not in the other was simply that the state and status of much of the international law relative to war at sea was uncertain. This was not because there was not just as much treaty and customary law for sea war as for land war, but because it had taken a beating in the 1914–18 War and been but partially and feebly re-established between the wars. Badly needing complete overhaul (not least because, like air war, its assumptions had been traumatized by science and technology), it had not received it. As a matter of fact, the same might be said of it now. Nuremberg settled nothing; nor has anything of significance been settled since.

As in their very much bigger concern with criminal misconduct of war on land, the post-war trials of naval persons were partly to do with crimes for which no conceivable excuse was possible other than, of course, 'superior orders' or an excessive stretching of 'military necessity'. For example: the leaving or, worse, deliberate casting of the crews of sunken enemy vessels in water far from land without any conceivable military necessity for doing so; in similar circumstances, the gunning in the water of survivors from a ship on its way to the bottom. Such instances of barbarism excited the general public and cultural anthropologists but not the legal experts, who found in them little to argue about.[22]

Much however was to be argued about the uses made of submarines by the German, British, and American navies as they strove to cut off their

---

[21] Telford Taylor, whose fine book came to hand just before this went to press, tells how the Russian prosecutor Rudenko suggested, not long before the trial opened, that the British might like to 'add a charge based on German bombing of England. . . . Elwyn Jones stated that "consideration had been given to entering a charge for V1 and V2 weapons, but that it had been considered inappropriate", as raising an argument which would be outside the range of the trial.' Taylor comments: 'It was only necessary to look out of the windows at bomb-ravaged Berlin to divine what the "argument" would have been', *The Anatomy of the Nuremberg Trials* (New York and London, 1993), 126.

[22] Because only German submariners were put in the dock for alleged atrocities of this order, it must be pointed out that submariners of other nations were quite capable of doing the same sort of thing, or worse. See e.g. p. 240 of Fenrick's article cited in n. 24 below. The tone of servicemen's and relatives' letters rebutting suggestions of a British instance incidentally indicate why governments are so reluctant to inquire into possible war crimes on their own side; see the article 'The Torbay's Bloody Night' in the *Daily Telegraph*, 26 Jan., and the correspondence in the *Sunday Telegraph*, 19 Feb. 1989.

respective enemies from supplies brought by sea. Maritime powers had always had a keen interest in doing this when they were belligerent, and, as has already been shown, their right to do it had long been recognized by international law. It was, in fact, the great root from which the rest of the international law of naval warfare was to grow. That it grew in such complexity and with such singularities as its unique institution of prize-courts was because of the respect belligerents had to pay to the neutral interest. In all wars falling below the level of the twentieth century's world wars, there were always neutral powers determined to use 'the high seas' for continued trading with each other and also, so far as hostile parties could be threatened or cajoled into allowing it, with belligerents themselves. Belligerents, for their part, could see the point of the neutral argument. Wars would come and go, trade went on forever. Today's belligerent was tomorrow's neutral. So there naturally developed, alongside the crystal-lizing of humanitarian custom parallel to that of land warfare, an ever more complicated body of law (largely, through the prize-courts, case-law) about the limits of what belligerents and neutrals respectively could do when a war was going on.

'Contraband' and 'blockade' were the key words. It was early accepted that a neutral could not expect to retain the advantages of neutrality if he insisted on supplying a belligerent with the materials of war, technically called contraband. A compromise was reached. If the neutral was inter-cepted with such materials *en route*, the law required him to forfeit them; if however he got them there without being intercepted, good for him! Such were the rules of the game. Blockade was a rougher business. Blockade meant the complete closure of a port or coast by a belligerent who was in a position actually to enforce it; once 'declared' according to the proper diplomatic forms, neutrals broke or 'ran' the blockade at their peril; not just materials of war but whole cargoes and even the ships themselves were forfeit if stopped, liable to be attacked and captured or sunk if they would not stop.

Such were the main elements of maritime war throughout recent cen-turies. Battles between fleets and duels between ships, however much more dramatic, were subsidiary to it. What seagoing States sought to do to enemies in war was above all to stop their trade. What States dependent on seaborne trade had to do above all else in war was to keep their trade going. It could be, for them, a matter of life and death.

The laws and customs concerning the blockade, contraband, and so on held together fairly well until the First World War. The system gave rise to constant complaints by neutrals that the big maritime powers presumed too much and strove to press their rights even further than the law allowed. It survived because there was always (except during certain interludes of the Napoleonic Wars) a neutral interest strong enough to make itself respected, because there were technical limits to what the navies of those years could actually do, and because the maintenance of the international commercial system was felt by all progressive States to be good in itself, not lightly to be damaged or upset in a world aspiring to economic development all over and for ever.

1914–1918 however saw this system crumble like a house of cards. Multiple developments in nautical and communications technology— mines, submarines, and wireless telegraphy—meant that there were now few limits to what navies could do, provided the politicians or war-lords would let them. In the atmosphere of total war between industrial mass societies, war-lords and politicians were increasingly inclined to oblige. And by 1917 there was no longer any major neutral interest to restrain them. Only competition for American sympathy, on top of a certain balancing of economic self-interest, held the European antagonists for so long from seeking to enforce their wills on each other by the greatest degree of mastery of the seas they could enforce and by ruthlessness in the use of it. For the British, and later the Americans, this meant extension of the contraband list until it included food supplies, and extension of blockade by minefields as well as guard-ships until it sealed off the whole of the North Sea. For the Germans, this meant above all the use of submarines to throttle the UK's sea links with its sources of food and war materials; by 1917, 'unrestricted submarine warfare' was putting *all* shipping, neutral or otherwise, at mortal risk on approaching the British Isles. The legal rights and wrongs of this maritime *guerre à outrance* were bitterly contested, not least because of their splendid propaganda value: 'piratical U-boats' versus 'starvation blockade', and so on. Once patriotic passions had cooled down, legal commentators in all countries were more or less able to agree that it had been very much a question of 'six on one side, half a dozen on the other'. Analysis of the whole episode, and in particular attempts to identify the first clear breach of the law, was impenetrably clouded by the inadequacy of pre-war law to tame the monsters bred by military technology out of total war. In limited war, they might have been susceptible to taming; in total war, of the kind the 1914–18 conflict soon became, they finally could not be.

The 1939–45 conflict being even more total, that same body of law proved even more inadequate. Far from being updated between the wars, it had only been restated. The several shots at improvement had issued by 1936 in no more than the so-called London Protocol's vigorous reassertion of those very same rules for submarine dealings with merchant vessels which had already proved unworkable.[23] The IMT reasserted them again, but no part of its judgment was less convincing or, one might add, less helpful to those who have subsequently argued that the Nuremberg IMT was at its best on its 'war-crimes' side. Its conclusion that Admiral Dönitz's orders proved him 'guilty of a violation of the Protocol' had to be followed at once by an oblique admission that British and US submarines had been similarly guilty. There being, of course, no question of prosecuting them as well, that part of the charge against Dönitz was dropped. But the authority of the London Protocol was reaffirmed to the evident perplexity and confusion of most who have since then written on the post-Nuremberg phase of the law of maritime warfare.[24]

War in the Air

For reasons obvious enough, there was no international law on aerial warfare before the turn of our century. The Hague Conferences gingerly laid a few foundations. The most significant and the only lasting one aimed to protect civilians against indiscriminate or wanton bombardment from the air as from the ground (Article 25 of the Hague Regulations), but the terms used were soon discovered to be archaic, and vital questions had been begged. Civilians in besieged or attacked places had never been effectively protectable against artillery bombardment, any more than the economic resources of the States had been secure against attack whenever enemies could get at them (which as a matter of fact was not often). But now, from quite early in the 1914–18 War, it was discovered that those resources, even far behind the formal battle zone, could be got at by what became known as strategic bombing. If the morale and fighting spirit of the civilian population was counted as a resource as well, that also could be got at, if not by deliberate bombing, which was too clearly terroristic for generally decent folk to confess to liking, then perhaps by the accidental fall-out from lawful attempts to bomb military targets, which it was only sensible in an age of industrialized warfare to construe as including economic ones. The

---

[23] This document is reproduced, with an appraisal whose cagey inconclusiveness speaks volumes, in Roberts and Guelff, 147–51.

[24] No clearer-headed legal expert than W. J. Fenrick has tackled the subject, but even he has to give up the London Protocol and the IMT's use of it as a bad job in 'Legal Aspects of Targeting in the Law of Naval Warfare', in *Canadian Yearbook of International Law* 29 (1991), 238–81 at 248–53. A somewhat different range of evidence supports the same conclusion in Jane Gilliland, 'Submarines and Targets', in *Georgetown Law Journal* 73 (1985), 975–1005 *passim*.

bombing of the latter so often involved also the bombing of civilians (to the unconcealed gratification, it must be said, of so many total-war enthusiasts) that by the time the war ended, it was commonly assumed, even more perhaps outside the armed services than within them, that 'city bombing' was sure to figure in wars for all time to come. Few who devoted any serious thought to the matter liked this prospect but it seemed almost inescapable.

The part of their activities that *avoidably* killed civilians could however never make sense to persons steeped in the traditions and ethos of the law of war. Legal, military, and humanitarian writers between the wars joined anxious representatives of the general public to keep alive the idea of prohibitions and restraints in this new dimension of warfare as in the older ones. Their concern did not achieve much. Legal experts assembled at The Hague in the winter of 1922–3 produced some draft rules which represented, perhaps, the most plausible compromise that could at that date be made between ethical and legal principle on the one side, military realism on the other. Many air forces took them seriously enough to incorporate them, or bits of them, in their operational manuals, but no State ever ratified them. Statesmen however understood well enough what were the principles which respectable air-warfare rules would have to go by. The classic British statement of them will fairly serve as representative of what all national leaders were willing to say, whether they sincerely meant it or not, on the eve of the Second World War:

In the first place, it is against international law to bomb civilians as such and to make deliberate attacks upon civilian populations. That is undoubtedly a violation of international law. In the second place, targets which are aimed at from the air must be legitimate military objectives and must be capable of identification. In the third place, reasonable care must be taken in attacking those military objectives so that by carelessness a civilian population in the neighbourhood is not bombed.[25]

In view of that authoritative pronouncement, all the more extraordinary is the observation of Britain's longest-serving and most active Bomber Commander, in the course of defending his record very soon after the war, that: 'International law can always be argued pro and con, but in this matter of the use of aircraft in war, there is, it so happens, no international law at all.'[26]

---

[25] The prime minister in the House of Commons, 21 June 1938, in *Hansard* 5th series, Commons 1937–8, vol. 337, col. 937.

[26] Arthur Harris, *Bomber Offensive* (London, 1947), 177. This much-quoted remark about *law* comes in the course of a lengthy and not insensitive passage, one of several such in his book, about the *ethics* of what he had been causing to be done. The ethico-legal case against Harris is not that he had no ethical feelings, but that the feelings which moved him most were those of inter-service rivalry and strategic irrationality, from which the dark 'Dresden' side of his doings resulted.

But he would not have gone too far if he had restricted himself to saying that there was not much of it, and that what there was lay mostly in the realm of principles, as to whose practical application in circumstances of desperate total war against an exceptionally nasty enemy there was bound to be much controversy. At the heart of it was the question, the same question that had been raised by the First World War and had haunted the economically advanced world's dreams ever since: to what extent, if any, could a belligerent lawfully rain death and destruction upon an enemy's economic and administrative infrastructure with the mixed purpose of reducing his armed forces' ability to go on fighting and of reducing his civilian population's will to let the fighting go on?

This great debate began early in the war and, among all the larger sections of public discussion of the legal and ethical aspects of the war, was singular in this respect: it was more a discussion by Britons and Americans among themselves than a slanging-match between them and their enemies. There *was* some of the latter. A much-prized part of the German military tradition, which the Japanese readily shared, cherished the idea that the sufferings and risks of the nation's wars were to be borne by its soldiers at a protective distance from the cities and countryside where its civilians lived; the soldiers willingly suffering for their families' sakes, although in a last tragic resort, families might have to suffer too. This nicely blended one of the more attractive elements of the warrior ethic with the strongest aspiration of humanitarian law. German and (referring particularly to the Doolittle raid on Tokyo in 1942) Japanese moral indignation at British and American city bombing was therefore not wholly factitious and hypocritical. Even in the last winter of the war there were trace elements of self-righteousness in Hitler's justifications of the undiscriminating V-weapons and Goebbels's appeals to Switzerland and Sweden for sympathy over the destruction of Dresden. But so much German and Japanese bombing in earlier days had itself been unprincipled that (even leaving aside other more certainly atrocious aspects of their war-conduct) their wartime criticisms of that for which the allies repaid them tenfold could not be taken seriously. Much more interesting in themselves and significant for the future were the criticisms being made by parts of the British and American publics of what their bombers were up to, so far as official secrecy, misinformation, and disinformation enabled them to understand it. Was this, they asked, the way we should be fighting, despite our enemies having given us provocations and pretexts for doing so?

The history of strategic bombing in the Second World War has been so much, and sometimes so well, written about that there is no need here to do more than sort out the legal elements of it which by the end of the war cried out for clarification.

(*a*) *Civilians.* How could they be defined in this context? Total-war doctrinaires were fecund in reasons why the classic definition should be narrowed. The home front in modern mass-society warfare, they said, invited attack no less than the fighting front; nations at war were organic and/or psychological wholes, and it made just as much sense to lower the morale of the civilian as the military part; sophisticated industrial economies were scarcely susceptible of division into war-sustaining and non-war-sustaining parts; the waterworks which supplied the home supplied also the barracks; if workers in munitions factories (just as likely to be female as male) were at risk while they were there, why were they exempt from risk when they were not? Workers in war-sustaining businesses were so essential to the making of modern war that they invited classification as 'quasi-combatants', and so on. States' attempts, moreover, to evacuate from cities their economically dispensable inhabitants (children, mothers, and old folk: a new species of *bouches inutiles*) implicitly admitted that the answer to the humanitarian problem lay not in banning city bombing but in getting civilians out of cities; it was as much the defender's responsibility to try to move them out of harm's way as the attacker's to try not to harm them. So many plausible arguments could be made, at least for 'dehousing' and making wretched the working population of a modern State at war, that adherents of the fundamental classic principle of discrimination had to go on to the counter-attack to show good cause why it should, and how it could, still be observed.

(*b*) *Collateral damage.* A First World War concept which was found to be immensely useful in the Second World War. It was invented to describe damage done in the vicinity of military targets. Except in the case of besieged cities and blockaded ports, when indiscriminate bombardment of the population was as often done as it was complained about, such damage incidental to artillery bombardments of military targets had on the whole been regretted both for its waste of ammunition and for the death and damage it inflicted on victims. But now, bombardment from the air put such damage into a new light. For one thing, there was such a lot of it; bombing by its very nature was very inaccurate. For another thing, it was likely to be damage which total-war doctrinaires applauded. Collateral damage was a useful, ambiguous way of describing it: a technical-sounding term of art, suggestive of value-free science; but at the same time speaking plainly to those who were willing to get the message that this damage was not useless.

And since it really might be unavoidable, even when military targets in cities were faithfully aimed at, who could tell whether such targets had been bona fide targeted or not? Motives could be as mixed as results. Bombing of civilians, i.e. 'terror bombing' strictly defined, could thus be accomplished under the cover of 'collateral damage'. Knowing for certain that some was so, we may feel sure that there was much more which escapes (as it was meant to escape) documentation.

(c) *Area bombing.* A Second World War concept invented by the British air force in 1941–2 to describe and explain its heavy bombers' main style of operations, more frankly accepted the destruction of non-military areas of cities as a by-product of the legitimate destruction of military targets. Compared with the 'collateral damage' line of justification, this one began from different operational assumptions and had to be challenged (by such persons as wished to resist the pull towards total-war lawlessness) on different grounds. The former began with the assumption that if you set your bomb-sights on military targets, there was at least a fair-to-middling chance of hitting them. The latter, to express it in the terms forced on the British Bomber Command by its admission that aiming at military targets was generally futile (chiefly because heavy bombing could only be done without unbearable losses by night), was that military targets could only be hit if, by aiming at some central point(s), you bombed the whole area within which they were situated.

Challenge to the 'collateral damage' argument had to begin with insisting that, below a certain level of probability of hitting the target, what was claimed to be bona fide strategic bombing was not what it seemed. Challenge to the area-bombing argument rested, first, on enquiry whether there was no other, more discriminating, way in which legitimate bombing purposes could bearably be accomplished, and, second, on insisting that a method so intrinsically, so avowedly undiscriminating could only find justification in the rule of proportionality. If military objectives were big enough, and if the attacker really had no other way to get at them, big damage to civilian surroundings could be excused. (It might be called 'collateral damage' but that was, and remains, a confusion of the issue.)

(d) *Reprisals.* These may be quickly dealt with. This argument was freely used by Britain and Germany in the Second World War to justify departures from straight legality in air as in sea warfare. The argument of reprisals is always thus used. One of the earliest lessons that the student of the law of war has to learn is to be on his guard when he hears the word. Deeper hypocrisy and duplicity attach to it than to any other term of the art. It is not the same thing as retaliation, if only because it has a legal basis as one of the few recognized means of enforcement (i.e. *my reprisal* against *your breach of the law* makes *you* return to law-abidingness); nor is it the same thing as that wilder motivation, revenge. Because it sounds more respectable to legally motivated ears than retaliation (and, *a fortiori*, revenge or merely wanton violence) it is the first of the fingers the international lawyer puts in the hole in the dyke when respect for restraint begins to collapse. There may, or there may not, be something to it, according to circumstances. There was not much to it in the Second World War, when Britain and Germany both used it to help justify bombings they were strongly inclined to do anyway.

(e) *The atom bomb*, as it was then called, came so late in the war (its first use preceded by eight days the Japanese announcement of intention to surrender) that it was only in the post-war *post mortem* that the differences between it and other types of bomb could begin to be well enough understood for it to be considered, along with them, in constructive legal debate, which had to include, of course, the possibility that the advent of the nuclear age revolutionized the law of war just as it might revolutionize war itself.

The aspects of bombing sketched in the immediately preceding paragraphs provided a list of legal issues that urgently needed to be authoritatively settled once the war was over. No 'law-of-war' issues (considering them separately from 'crimes-against-humanity' issues) were of more momentous significance for the future of humankind. The IMT and the other Nuremberg trials however, as has already been observed, passed over strategic bombing in silence, for reasons all too obvious. Whatever the Germans and Italians had done in this line, the Atlantic allies had outdone. Just like the issue of unrestricted submarine warfare, it was one which invited a defence of *tu quoque*. Unlike submarine warfare, it didn't get it, because the charge was never made. A door to it had been opened by the closing phrases of the War Crimes section of the IMT's Charter: 'wanton destruction of cities, towns and villages, or devastation not justified by military necessity'. The prosecution seemed poised to go through that door when, taking its cue from well-established wartime tradition, it singled out the *Luftwaffe*'s highly destructive bombings of Warsaw, Rotterdam, and Belgrade. Not all as wholly 'tactical' as *Luftwaffe* apologists have liked to make out, the first and third at any rate included clear elements of the terroristic. But at that point the prosecution, and after it the judgment, stopped short. London, which could well have been added to the list had there been a wish to move beyond the arguably 'tactical' to the unmistakably 'strategic', was never mentioned; nor were Coventry, Plymouth, Birmingham, and so on. The only mentions in the trials of Lübeck,

Hamburg, Darmstadt, Dresden, and so on were made at their peril (for the courts' instructions forbade them to accept *tu quoque* defences) by defendants seeking to show that not they alone had slaughtered civilians. Nothing appeared in the judgments that could take the law regarding aerial bombardment an inch further than where it had been on the day the war started.

All in all, the war-crimes trials did not have as much of an effect on the international law of war as might have been expected. Noting *en passant* the existence of a certain confusion as to whether the IMTs, under their respective Charters, were making new law as well as clarifying and enforcing old, it may be argued that they did not much develop international law in any of its branches. The branch closest to the hearts of Nuremberg's principal sponsors, the Americans and, after them, the Russians—crimes against peace—was in fact less satisfactorily handled at the IMT than in the UN. It was the Charter of the UN which placed it upon a really firm footing. About the Pact of Paris and other pre-war matters upon which the IMT indictments had to be founded, there could be endless and, for some countries, embarrassing argument. About the UN Charter, none would be possible. Those parts of the Nuremberg and Tokyo indictments that sought to pin on to German and Japanese high dignitaries the crimes of planning aggressive war, war in violation of treaties, and 'a common plan or conspiracy' for the same, have always been the most vulnerable to historical criticism and the first to be jettisoned by persons desirous to found the vindication of the IMTs on their most defensible aspects.

Crimes against humanity, for all their formal novelty, were much less open to destructive analysis. Their crystallization, together with the sharp definition of one group of them in the UN's 1948 Genocide Convention, gave some support to the human rights movement's parallel development of its branch of international law, whose first giant step was the General Assembly's simultaneous passage of the UDHR. Since however most of those newly identified crimes against humanity were also war crimes or just plain crimes by any standard, they cannot be considered to have substantively added much.

As for the war crimes proper, most of those prosecuted at the IMTs and at the thousands of trials that accompanied them were for offences committed under 'old' law, most of it comprised in the Hague Conventions. The main Nuremberg novelty, if novelty it can be called, was to bring closer to clarification the giant issues of superior orders and proportionality which turned up in one form or another whenever there was a prima-facie possibility that an action was not irredeemably illegal, as it might not be if it concerned hostages, executions, destructions, and what were claimed to be reprisals. But, as we shall see, neither issue was sufficiently clarified to move it beyond reach of continued legal or military questioning. The only unmistakable innovations, duly given pride of place in the Nuremberg Principles, was the assertion of personal responsibility, even of heads of States and high government officials, for crimes under international law, and the exclusion of the plea of 'superior orders' as any more than a mitigation. The list of war crimes in the ILC's formulation was unchanged from the IMT's Charter. Issues arising thereunder that had not been settled by the IMT's judgments remained unsettled. Issues that had not been raised in that Charter or the trials still had to be raised. Since those issues comprised the most destructively menacing aspects of modern warfare, it can be understood that much remained to be done. Whether and to what extent the law could be operative in total war as the twentieth century had come to know it—a question that had been waiting for an answer since 1918—awaited an answer still. Not merely in respect of strategic bombing (its most dramatic expression) and naval blockade did it need to be answered. For a few more years it lay concealed inside the land-war question, which the trials had only touched on, of the legitimacy of partisan and popular national resistance to alien or colonial domination. 'People's wars' were not quite yet familiar in the vocabulary of contemporary warfare.

Entr'acte

How the Development of International Society Differed from the Legislators' Expectations

The purpose of Part III of this book is to examine and to evaluate the workings since about 1950 of the arrangements for the legal restraint of warfare which, as described in Part II, by then were seemingly completed. Those arrangements have not worked well. The best that can be said for them is that they have intermittently and patchily worked to some extent, and that the record of their observance in our own times may, after all, not be worse than it has often been in the past. What has gone wrong? This Entr'acte offers some explanations.[1] The arrangements hopefully made between 1945 and 1950 have had to struggle for survival in circumstances of extraordinary difficulty, and (as has been indicated) they entered the world bearing a variety of birth defects. But that is not the sum of their misfortunes and difficulties. Like much else that had its launching just after the Second World War, the reconstructed laws of war were born under a fateful star. Their genes were adapted to another world than that in which they had to make their way.

The genetic image is the more appropriate in that, beneath all the other troubles that came their way, those laws were in major respects regressive. Promoted as making possible the better restraint of warfare, they were founded in assumptions about war as it had been rather than war as it was about to be. There were two sets of assumptions: the one legal, the other political.

Little need now be added to what has already been said about the former. The legal assumptions, unsurprisingly, came straight from the international law of war as it had developed and hardened over the previous three centuries. It took for granted that what that body of law was most likely to be able to control was war between States; States, the very bodies for whom modern international law (as hitherto viewed) exclusively existed, and by whom exclusively it was made. To this major assumption the post-war reconstruction added two minor amendments. The exclusive tendencies of the old term 'war' were replaced by the open-ended implications of a new term 'armed conflicts', and the door was opened to the application of the

[1] This essay is meant mainly for readers who do not already know their way around the history of peace and war in the world since 1945. Readers who *do* know their way might go straight to Part III.

law's fundamental humanitarian principles to armed conflicts taking place, not between States, but within them. This indeed was not at all regressive. It was progressive, and has been of much significance. As an amendment and addition, Common Article 3 was both little and much. It was little for those troubled souls who had been pressing for it in the International Red Cross movement since at least 1912. Yet it marked a notable break with the Statist tradition and, without calling attention to the fact, it staked a claim for recognition of kinship between the principles of the old international law of war and the new international law of human rights. Whether much or little would be made of these progressive potentials, time would show.

The political assumptions underlying the post-war reconstruction were as a matter of course the same optimistic ones which brought into existence the United Nations Organization and the other intergovernmental institutions (World Bank, IMF, ICJ, etc.) from its beginning associated with it as elements of an improved world order, professedly more generous, more just, and above all more peaceful. The years 1945–6 in retrospect invite interpretation as an eye-of-the-storm interlude between the global troubles which preceded and generated it, and those which all too soon succeeded it and which, with disconcerting changes of emphasis, continue still. Such a reading requires a sympathetic suspension of disbelief. Looking back on that extraordinary episode with the knowledge of hindsight, it is impossible now not to see that much in the world even then was palpably unpeaceful and many harbingers of troubles to come must have been evident to those with insight to anticipate. The optimism which launched the UN can be difficult to understand; difficult in particular to understand with regard to the normally hard-headed statesmen, politicians, and diplomats who bore leading and decisive parts in the great enterprise. It is clear from some of the things they then said, and from much of what they subsequently wrote, that their feelings at the time about what they were trying to do were mixed. Their professional habits of caution and scepticism were by no means anaesthetized. But it seems to be clear also that even among those experienced ruling élites of the species, there was enough hope for a while mingled with the experience, enough enterprise with the resignation, and enough idealism and enthusiasm with the 'realism' and cynicism, for so grand a better-world plan to be worth pursuing.[2]

[2] H. G. Nicholas touches on this matter rather effectively in the last paragraph of the chapter on the making of the Charter in his well-known book, *The United Nations as a Political Institution* (4th edn., Oxford, 1971, 40). Noting the variety of (sometimes conflicting) interests and attitudes which sought recognition in it, he writes: 'The Charter embodies, after all, more even than the diversity of mankind; it embodies the contradictions that inhere in each of us as members of the human race.'

'If hopes were dupes, fears might be liars.' Entwined with the hopes and fears could in any case be sensed a vision, not the less persuasive for being to some degree fanciful, of the UN as representing 'humanity's prayer to be saved from itself'.[3] Lessons, after all, could be learned from the previous plan's failures. The UN could reasonably be hoped to do better than the League, which in some ways had not done all that badly. Besides, it was not foolish to suppose, as was then not impossible to do, that the radical changes in human habits upon which success of this revised plan must ultimately depend might receive a boost from the unprecedentedly ghastly and traumatic experiences of the World War just over.

That unprecedented mood and spirit did not last long. Through 1947 and early 1948 it faded into the light of common day, in whose often unkindly glare now had to survive the institutions founded in a 'glad confident morning' gone for ever. A passing fancy of non-historical speculation may be indulged in. One wonders: what if the United Nations, as the winning alliance in the war were calling themselves from 1942, had waited until the war was completely over before setting about the establishment of (as in effect it was) a League of Nations Mark II? What sort of organization could have been framed if the public business (the Dumbarton Oaks and Bretton Woods stages) had been begun even only a year later than it actually was? Make that two years, and the thing is inconceivable. But the material world which history gives us to inhabit as best we can is made of what happened, not of what might or might not have happened. Only Utopians can afford to dispense with the actual. The rest of us have to accept and explain it, before enquiring how it might be improved. All who consider that the world with the UN we have actually got is probably a better world than the one we might imagine without it, will be prepared to make allowances for the legacies of its star-crossed conception. The later leanings of international organizations no less than those of human beings are determined by the experiences of infancy as well as by blood groups and genes. Much of the business that the UN and its cognate bodies (among which I class, for present purposes and probably to its own distaste, the International Red Cross) immediately got going in that post-war interlude would wither in the early frosts that followed, or become curiously embalmed in the business of the UN until they could be given peaceful burials.[4] But some of it had enough early momentum and unideological weight to bear fruit before the bad weather set in.

[3] Conor Cruise O'Brien, *The United Nations: Sacred Drama* (London, 1968), 19.
[4] e.g. the project of controlling nuclear weaponry and the ideas of defining aggression and the right and duties of States.

Among those original ventures was the international legal reconstruction already described in Part II. Its three main limbs were all moving strongly forward through 1947. The grandest war-crimes trials in Europe were already over, and their Pacific counterparts were in progress. The Human Rights Commission was well into its drafting of what was to become the Universal Declaration. The revision and updating of the Geneva Conventions had been solidly started by the Government Experts convened by the ICRC. History hit them in the same way it hits everything. None of them was able to develop as far or exactly in the way their initiators had expected or hoped. The idea of convicting and punishing criminal enemies lost most of its attraction when enemies became allies. Universal human rights took on a less engaging colour when they had to be advanced from rhetoric to reality and to seek implementation as well as applause. The changes in the laws of war which legal and military experts could agree to recommend in 1947 would not be the same as diplomats would be instructed to agree to in 1949. But the combined achievement was none the less substantial. International humanitarian law, as it would soon be hopefully called, was evidently missing in some vital parts and backward-looking in some others, but it was in better shape by 1950 than it had been in 1945. What our warring world would do with it, and how its healing ministrations would be received, has now to be looked at.

The UN and its Charter being the frame and fabric of the umbrella beneath which these questions were going to be settled, it might first of all be noted that according to the pristine theory of the Charter, such questions were hardly supposed to arise at all. The maintenance of peace and security was the Organization's primary purpose. The member States, whatever their actual characters and actions, quickly slipped into the style of habitually describing themselves as 'peace-loving'. All the improvements which its programme envisaged for humankind were predicated on a state of peace, the same state of peace which 'Western' political and legal theory posited as the civilized norm. When it was suggested to the International Law Commission that it might follow up its cagey confirmation of the Nuremberg Principles with an expert revision of the law of war at large, one of its grounds for declining was that to do so would have the effect of making people wonder whether the UN's language about peace was seriously meant. Such prudence was otiose. People would approach that conclusion without the ILC's nudging. Whether the member States meant what they said or not (even friends of the UN, among whom I count myself, cannot deny that the debit side of its effects on international affairs includes the inflation of public mendacity and hypocrisy), peace has in practice been less of a mark of the era of the UN than war.

So much, indeed, has war marked our era and distressed its survivors that social science has striven to quantify it, to calculate its costs and damages, and to classify its various forms. The results of these efforts differ according to the definitions and parameters used, the perceptions of the users, and above all the difficulty of classifying, as either one thing or another, things that were in real life mixed and confused. Hardly any of the armed conflicts which seem to have been purely 'international' (not a numerous list) have been clear of some element of internal strife, and hardly any of the apparently 'non-international' armed conflicts have been free of one or other of the many available forms of outside interference. Whatever may be the significance of the quantifiers' and classifiers' findings in other contexts, they are of limited value here, where the social scientists' tables relate just as obliquely and partially as the humanitarian lawyers' texts to the actual experiences and predicaments of armed-conflict warriors and victims. Readers who have not had to ask themselves what might be the approximate dimensions of the contemporary war-victims' tragedy may however like to know that, by a recent reputable and cautious synthesizer, there were between 1945 and 1989 'at least eighty wars, resulting [between them] in the deaths of between fifteen and thirty million people' and making refugees of about thirty million more.[5]

What follows is a character sketch of all this armed conflict: its types and styles, its sentiments and motivations. I make no pretence at scientific elegance or scholarship sublime. So much of the scene is so troubled, messy, and dark that methodical categorization is beyond my powers. (In fact I believe it is beyond anyone's.) Streams which spring clear and sparkling from their sources run into bogs, marshes, and muddy deltas. Wars well up within wars just as wheels turn within wheels. Nevertheless, some sources and contours are evident enough.

Let us begin with the biggest. The two types of war that were most expected and most feared in 1945–50 never happened: great wars between great powers—as it might be, wars about Germany and Japan all over again—and nuclear war between the USA and the USSR, the superpowers, as they would now become known. The very fact of these non-events is of significance to any discussion about the uses of law for the restraint of war. That such major wars did not happen was not because of the prescriptions

---

[5] Patrick Brogan, *World Conflicts* (London, 1989), vii.

and proscriptions contained in the Charter of the UN and the textbooks of international law, but because of the strength of military alliances and their calculations about deterrence and risk, reciprocity and retaliation. Invocations of law cannot be written off as nothing but window-dressing, but they evidently come from a secondary level of concern, convenient rather than causative. If major reference to the *jus in bello* was thus avoided, it was in some part because prior reference had been made to the principles of the old *jus ad bellum*. Embarking on war which cannot in any acceptable sense of the word be won is banned by the *jus ad bellum* as well as by common sense—which is not surprising, both of them being founded in reason.

That avoidance of what were feared (perhaps mistakenly) as the worst of all possible wars was however not such a virtuous achievement as some of its self-congratulatory beneficiaries have liked to think. Great powers and superpowers have not fought one another front-to-front, but they have found other ways, most of them less directly painful, to indulge their animosities, sublimating some of them in the competitiveness of finance and commerce, and so far as fighting had to be done (which was very often), getting surrogates and substitutes to do it at a safe distance.

The classic term 'imperialism' remains useful in description of some of these great-power activities. Two empires of the classic 'red-on-the-map' kind have in fact survived, for all their patriots' indignant denials and self-deceptions. The most obvious, from 1945 until 1989, was the Russian Soviet empire. A writer at the turn of the 1990s, observing that empire's dissolution, has to note as a fact of history that, by every non-Muscovite perception, the USSR continued in the tracks of the old Russian empire and maintained its authority and security over vassals and satellites by the same old means (in the last resort, military) as well as some new ones. The United States' case is not quite so obvious. Colours on the map have mattered much less to a financial megapower operating (as also the UK did until 1914) largely through economic hegemony and political leverage over apparently independent States. But whatever US ideologues have liked to believe, the perception from other points of view has always been that Washington's instinctive attitude to its hemispheric and Pacific Ocean neighbours is imperial, enforced in the last resort by force of US arms but at earlier stages by the arms of subordinate regimes.

Lesser imperial continuities show elsewhere on the globe than in the spheres of influence of the Soviet Union and the USA. France has managed to preserve something of an imperial relationship with most of its sub-Saharan African former colonies. China's neighbours and subject peoples perceive and feel China as the same hemispheric imperial presence it has intermittently been for them time out of mind; much of the explanation of its feud with Vietnam is that Vietnam was once an empire too, and a serious challenge to China on its south-eastern fronts. Ethiopia is another revolutionized ancient empire which, until the early 1990s, maintained ancient imperial habits, to the vexation of Eritreans, Tigrayans, Somalis, and other neighbours and subjects. Iranians, who since 1979 have impinged on the consciousness of other countries mostly as revolutionaries and as Muslims, may themselves be more conscious that they were, some hundreds of years ago, the imperial power of their region. Iraq's recent remarkable will to war rests in part on its dictator's evocation of the far more remote glories of the empires of Sargon and Nebuchadnezzar.

Neo-imperialism, with its sibling neocolonialism, is the term found more useful by many observers to describe the way the massive economic power of the wealthiest 'developed' States asserts itself at the expense of the merely 'developing'; which is to say, the way the economic order of the world, essentially unchanged by twenty years' endeavours in the UN to promote development, works more to the advantage of the First World States which constructed it than to that of the Third World States which didn't. The rich and established always do better out of free markets than the poor and struggling. The latter find themselves forced willy-nilly into a relationship of dependency. 'Dollar imperialism', like 'sterling imperialism' before it, is obviously much of this character; but so also are the powers of the yen, the franc, and the mark, which have not grown out of the barrels of guns in the same way. The argument (concerning whose disputed merits I take no position) is that the workings of this system, by bending the economies of poorer countries to the service of richer, not only keeps the developing in a state of dependence, probably in a more backward and socially distressed state than might otherwise be theirs, but also breeds violence and oppression (not to mention waste of resources) by encouraging otherwise needless military forces whose main business becomes enforcement of the system's demands and crushing its critics. To the grindings and graspings of neo-imperialism are thus attributed the poverty and suffering which partly explain civil strife and justify revolutionary wars.

Ideology, revolution, and counter-revolution together make one of the most potent causes of armed conflict since the Second World War. To label it simply 'revolution' hardly does justice to the contemporary complexity of its texture. The modern ideologies which largely promote it are similar in ambition and function to traditional religions (potent cause of so many armed conflicts in the past and, for that matter, part cause of many still) but the revolutionary enthusiasms which they engender are very different from the democratic parliamentary faith which generally guided national liberators and revolutionaries from 1776 to 1917–19. That older creed has by no means faded away. Our century's revolutionary tradition is directly descended from it. But since the October Revolution it has had to compete with the self-styled 'scientific' ones of Marx, Lenin, and, since 1949, Mao Zedong. This ideology, for simplicity's sake here called simply communism, has become mightily mixed up in contemporary armed conflicts in an extraordinary variety of ways, the most significant of which in the present context are that while communism which in one or another of its dogmatic forms has inspired many revolutionary and civil wars, an equally intense anti-communist dogma and prejudice has fuelled and fed them from the opposite direction. Any well-devised index to a contemporary-history book ought to contain the entry: 'Revolution: see also Counter-Revolution'.

And for communism, in the present context, see also capitalism. World history from the later 1940s into the 1980s, boiled down to its basic political essential, can be simply summed up as the contest of communism with capitalism: the Cold War. Preponderant as the issue in many conflicts, it coloured or shadowed most of the rest. Within three years of the foundation of the UN, the superpowers were locked into an antagonistic relationship and were content to describe it in these simple and simplistic terms. From the USSR and then also (with interesting variations) from China came waves of hostility to capitalism and all that was believed to go with it; trumpet-calls of assurance to its enemies and underminers all around the globe that their revolutionary cause would surely triumph, and diplomatic, economic, and military support—'underground' as well as open—to help it do so. From the USA above all came waves of counter-hostility to communism and all that was believed to go with it; diplomatic economic and military efforts ('covert' as well as admitted) to 'contain' it, to 'roll it back' and 'save' countries from it, and to subvert and 'destabilize' countries where it could not otherwise be got at, plus quantities of private initiatives (often, business-backed) which tended especially to embody the 'crusade' dimension which gave many anti-communists added relish for the Cold War.

Cold it may have been called and relatively cold it may have felt in the countries which conducted it, but it was usually too hot for comfort in the countries where it was actually fought. These were *par excellence* those remote-controlled wars already referred to in connection with neo-imperialism, wars fought, with no matter what mixtures of local motives and compulsions, mainly by surrogates for the ideological principals, to the scale of whose assistance and egging-on the longevity and ferocity of those wars may credibly be attributed. Only in three of them did those principals allow their own armed forces to become directly and substantially engaged: in Korea, 1950–3 (US and other UN members on the one side, China on the other); in Vietnam, 1960–73 (US on one side); and in Afghanistan (USSR ditto). Direct engagement did not go beyond the despatch of 'military advisers', training intelligence and supply officers, and heaven knows how many 'covert' operatives in the other of the cold war's surrogate campaigns, e.g. in Central America and the Caribbean, in Ethiopia, Somalia, and the Yemens, in Angola and Mozambique, in Indonesia and the Philippines.

National and ethnic sentiment—prominent in some of those wars and dominant in others, absent (we may safely say) from none—is another of the teeming sources of contemporary armed conflict, perhaps the most common and widespread of all. No surprise can be occasioned by this. Nationalism after all evidently remains the most familiar and inflammatory of mass political principles. Like the international law which evolved *pari passu* with it, nationalism is one of the European political inventions which (for better or worse) became a world possession. Under the title of national self-determination, in the course of the nineteenth century, it had come to enjoy selective acceptance and admiration as a proper ground for white peoples' resort to armed struggle to achieve national independence or to maintain what had been already achieved, notwithstanding recurrent embarrassments about the question: what constitutes a nation, and what does not? Most of Europe's wars since 1789 had been national wars, and nationalism in various of its forms (including the perverted one of fascism) was pre-eminent in bringing about both of the world wars from which, in 1945, the world was understood to need deliverance. The makers of the UN might reasonably suppose (and surely hope) that the passions of nationalism and the desire for self-determination would cause less trouble in the future than they had done in the past. At that historical juncture, it was possible to believe that recent strong experience must at last have taught the peoples whom they said they represented and who were conventionally said to be peace-loving, the superior virtues of internationalism. For the one area where self-determination could be expected to bring difficulties with it—the movement of colonial and mandated/trust territories towards self-government and perhaps even independence—the Charter made elaborate provision in no less than three of its fifteen chapters.

These plans and hopes were to be quickly dashed. National sentiment and its racial and religious blood-brothers at once began to assert themselves in ways as unpacific as ever before. In Palestine/Israel, across the length and breadth of India/Pakistan, in Indonesia, Indo-China and Malaya, Egypt and Algeria, the shape of violent nationalist things to come was apparent in the shape of violent nationalist things already occurring. The imperial powers at first showed little inclination to study the UN blueprint, and by far the biggest of their 'decolonizations', the establishment of the independent States of India and Pakistan, was quite independent of it. By 1950, the only perceptible movements in its direction were those of the United Kingdom, in its withdrawals from India, Burma, and Palestine, and the Netherlands in its reluctant leave-taking of what had been its 'East Indies'. Within the UN, the moderate provisions of the Charter were soon circumvented by the States determined to speed the break-up of the empires and the liberation of their colonial peoples. National self-determination became their watchword. It was not in the Charter itself. The nearest and sole approach to it in the Charter was the affirmation that the purposes of the UN included the development of 'friendly relations among nations based on respect for the principle of equal rights and self-determination of peoples'. But it soon ballooned into one of the General Assembly's most constant and passionate preoccupations. From being a 'principle', it was advanced to the status of a 'right'; and not just one right among many, but the right of rights, conspicuously heading the list of all others in the two 1966 International Human Rights Covenants.[6] From being a peace-strengthening cause which the UN would peacefully assist, it became a contentious cause which could legitimately be struggled for by every means short of violence, besides being (for an increasing number of States) a cause in pursuit of which the use of violence was legitimate. The global scene and vocabulary of armed conflict were thus enriched by the concept and title of a fighting force that has been constantly on stage ever since: the national liberation movement, fighting (as it was popularly named) a war of national liberation.

These titles and names were most heard of from the later 1950s through the early 1970s, from the Algerian War (1954–61) which first popularized them, until the achievements of independence by Angola and Mozambique (1974–5) and Rhodesia/Zimbabwe (1980). The conclusion of those southern African struggles left for settlement, of the whole list of 'armed conflicts against colonial domination and alien occupation and against racist regimes' which had acquired the UN's certificate of respectability and magnetized centre and left opinion the whole world over throughout the 1960s and 1970s, only those of the Namibians against South Africa, the non-whites against the apartheid system in South Africa, and the Palestinians against Israel. (For political reasons, reflected in UN

---

[6] In both of those Covenants, respectively on economic, social, and cultural rights and on civil and political rights, the first paragraph of the first Article reads: 'All peoples have the right of self-determination. By virtue of that right they freely determine their political status and freely pursue their economic, social and cultural development.'

usage and law, that residue does not include the would-be liberators of East Timor, the Western Sahara, Kurdistan, Azerbaijan, Eritrea, and so on.) What was not settled in any sense was the internal state and the domestic tranquillity of the countries thus nominally self-determining, whether they had got there by armed struggle or, as for example in the cases of most of the British Commonwealth countries, by more or less peaceful succession. Achievement of sovereign independence has not generally brought an end to fighting in the lands where it has occurred. In many cases it has actually increased it.

To what extent this is (as some argue) mainly because of the weight of the ex-colonial millstones left hanging round their necks, the artificiality of most of their boundaries, and the deforming pressures of neo-imperialism, or more (as others argue) because of follies and crimes of rulers and revolutionary 'vanguard parties', ineptitudes and weakness of administrations and generalized political inexperience and incapacity, need not here be gone into. Whatever the causes, the regrettable fact is that few of the new 'nation-States' which revolutionized the map of the world and the General Assembly of the UN have not, subsequent to their independence, experienced some form or other of internal violence, sinking sometimes into primordial anarchy. The world has become familiar with, for instance, military *coups d'état* following civil strife and often in turn provoking more of it; rebellions and civil wars sustained by armed groups resistant to the new set-up, sometimes supported by external interests and commonly with a basis in the immemorial jealousies and antipathies of races and religions and (especially in Africa and SE Asia) tribes and clans; and wars of secession, like those in Nigeria and Pakistan at the end of the 1960s, Ethiopia since the 1970s, and Sudan from the 1980s. Add to that catalogue of woes in new States a corresponding duplicate account of the collapses of social order that have similarly afflicted older States—revolutions and counter-revolutions, military *coups* and regimes all over Latin America, hypernationalist terrorisms and insurgencies like those in Northern Ireland and the Basque provinces of Spain, seemingly unstoppable civil wars like those in Colombia, Peru, Guatemala (where it attains positively genocidal pitch), the Philippines, and Afghanistan, and most recently the terrible violence accompanying the dissolution of Yugoslavia—and this summary sketch of the major types and styles of armed conflict in our world is nearly complete. Nearly, but not quite.

There remain to be brought into the account four facets of contemporary conflict which seem to constitute categories of their own, and are unprecedentedly of our own post-Second World War time.

First, the easy availability of weapons, not just any old weapons, but sophisticated (though not necessarily expensive) modern weapons like assault rifles and high explosives and landmines. Well-run, efficiently policed, socially cohesive, and geographically compact States contrive more or less successfully to keep this deadly flood at bay, but others less blessed by history or nature are beaten by it. There are, for example, reckoned to be at least fifty million Kalashnikov rifles around and about in the world. The suggestion has been made, that no conceivable measure of international aid or intervention could at a stroke contribute more to the pacification of, for example, Africa than an offer by, e.g. a UN-based commission, of something like fifty US dollars (a sum that would be derisory in Missouri could be irresistible in Mozambique) for each Kalashnikov handed in. I found it significant that, when I was drafting the first version of this paragraph in early 1990, within the space of one week I noticed no less than four references in newspaper and television news to outbreaks of this deadly epidemic: in South Africa, Liberia, Panama, and Colombia. Only a few weeks later a colleague who knows much more about Asia than I do told me that the anthem of the Kashmir independence fighters was actually titled 'The Kalashnikov'. Gun lobbies never cease to tell us that mere possession of a gun may not make a man or (as contemporary experience compels us to add) boy into a killer, but it cannot be doubted that where the inclination to kill is for so many reasons so commonplace, easy acquisition of guns can only multiply killings.

Second, terror and terrorism have undoubtedly added a nasty serrated edge to contemporary conflict. But exactly what that addition consists of is not easy to identify. The words are much misunderstood and misused. The cry of 'terrorism!' in itself may mean much or little. The reaction to it of a reasonable man, not to mention an eminent lawyer, was admirably expressed by Frits Kalshoven at the 1985 meeting of the American Society of International Lawyers, when he said: 'I am acquainted with use of the term in the media or by the police and even in legal writings, and often I can make a fairly shrewd guess what impression the user wishes to convey. But this is a far cry from saying I would be able to connect the term with a specific legal notion.'[7] The fact is that 'terrorist!' like 'atrocity!' has become a standardized response, readily exploited by popular leaders and manipulators, to deeds of violence done by unseen enemies or by 'the other side' (never by one's own!) and the pity of it is that this one-sidedness of use and indiscriminateness of application befog the making of a distinction between

---

[7] The 1985 *Proceedings of the American Society for International Law*, 114–18 at 117.

what objectively might be universally recognized as terrorism, and what it is merely tempting or convenient to stigmatize as such.

The one-sidedness moreover has this political twist to it: when internal conflicts are under discussion, the contemporary ear is more accustomed to hear the word applied to persons in conflict with governments than to persons doing governments' bidding. The explanation of this imbalance is purely historical. It comes from the ages when most political theory liked to deny that governments could do wrong, and when governments rejoiced to hear it do so. In the age of the Charter of the UN and the international instruments of human rights, to look no further, that contention is evidently untenable. In the age of Lenin and Mussolini, Stalin and Hitler, of Mao Zedong and Pol Pot, and of very many recent and, alas!, current regimes too notorious to need naming in Latin America, Africa, South-Eastern Europe, and Asia, it is very evident that terror, enforced by methods that may properly be called terroristic (detention without trial, torture, victimization of families, 'disappearances', and so on) can be a principal and permanent instrument of State power. Only custom and habit keep it from being more commonly recognized for what it is. Such however is the force of that habit that most of the ensuing discussion, so far as internal conflicts are concerned, will be in terms of the sorts of terrorism of which anti-State resisters and insurgents are customarily accused.

How, then, is this aspect of contemporary armed conflict to be defined, and how are we to identify that essence of terrorism which most of us, like Professor Kalshoven, believe we 'know when we meet it'? So many writers have had a shot at it, I believe that another shot is worth trying. Essential terrorism, it is suggested, can be detected by three linked characteristics. First, it signals that it may be something other than common crime because its doers—the assassins, bombers, kidnappers, extortioners, or whatever—profess a political purpose which may not be self-evidently unreasonable. Second, its victims and their political representatives on the other hand insist that it *is* common crime—or, more likely, *un*common crime—because it goes beyond the limits of their codes for the conduct of politics and legitimate (i.e. politically justifiable) armed conflict. Third, which follows from the second, its doers are elusive and covert, and by definition beyond the bounds of the prevalent political process, they have to stay hidden. But that admittedly suspicious circumstance does not of itself mean that they have to be universally condemned, or that everything they do must be of indistinguishable equal badness. Terrorist acts may be crimes-plus, but they share with ordinary crimes the characteristic that some are worse than others. To blow up a general in his own bedroom—an act which may in certain political circumstances be wicked—is not so exceedingly wicked as in any circumstances to blow up his tiny daughter in hers, though there will always be some terrorists bad or mad enough to justify even that. Literally universal condemnation is simply unattainable (for reasons further explored in the next paragraph). But I share Professor Kalshoven's feeling (quoted above) that one knows what is meant when one hears the word used and that there is usually something about the criticized act which ought to evoke universal condemnation. What is it?

The all-but-universally agreed essence of terrorism is when the victims (little matter whether they are victims by intention or by accident) are persons distant or even totally detached from the making and conduct of the policy which the doers of the violence dislike. That is a pompous and heavy-handed way of putting it but, although I am prepared to be apologetic, there are good reasons for not resorting to the usual definitions of 'innocents', 'non-combatants', and 'neutrals'. Those words unfortunately do not mean the same to everybody. It has to be remarked that to the furious or frozen mind of the absolute terrorist, unless he or she is simply an unreflective pathological killer, there actually may be a sort of manic rationality according to which almost anyone can be made out to be a limb of the perceived enemy. Some creeds are so solipsistic and unaccommodating as to be beyond the powers of even the most ecumenical of pluralisms to contain them. Extremist communists and anarchists, for example, join extremist anti-communists in telling themselves that all members of the class perceived as enemy are *ipso facto* and indiscriminately involved in its (as they see it) guilt; politically active existentialists in the immediate post-1945 years made fashionable the nihilistic concept, 'we are *all* guilty'; obsessively race-, tribe-, and creed-conscious fighters have often given themselves plausible reason for slaughtering the women and children of their enemies, and so on. These are among the reasons why the definition of terrorism within so confused and mixed an international society will forever evade universality. But they do not constitute a good reason for such a relaxation of the standards of civilization as lets terrorism slip through its net.

Such dehumanized exercises of undiscriminating logic are incompatible with two of the fundamental principles of civilization enshrined in IHL and in the Charter of the UN, the UDHR, and its more realistic subsidiary instruments: first, the idea that international and internal armed conflicts, if they have to happen at all, should be conducted so far as possible with restraint and discrimination; and second, the idea that so long as democratic and equitable processes offer reasonable space and safety for the management of internal differences and disputes, disputants should stick to them.

The essence of terrorism lies in summary rejection of the civilized norms for conflict resolution: within States and in peaceful times, the norms of representative government and the rule of law; in unpeaceful times and when States or other organized parties are in armed conflict with one another, the norms of IHL. Both of these norm-sets posit the limitation rather than the spread of violence and discrimination between opponents' degrees of relevance and responsibility. The laws and rules of armed conflict are dead at the heart if they give up the attempt to distinguish the more from the less involved, the wholly involved from the not-at-all so.

To sum up a summary treatment of an enormously difficult and unavoidably emotive topic. Persons stigmatized as terrorists may be more or less criminal according to criteria and circumstances. In typical contemporary confusions of criteria and circumstances, it is often impossible to be as precise about them as one would wish. Those so-called 'international terrorists' who, virtually unknown to all earlier history, have become an unmistakable though shadowy feature on the edges of the conflicts of our own time, find their origins and explanation in that peculiar characteristic of contemporary armed conflict, that so much of it is indirect, underground, vicarious, and remote-controlled; revolutionary, rebel and resistance fighters from a variety of countries forming from time to time what looks like a mutually supportive network of assassins and bombers, with shadowy support from certain States and autocrats. To return to the reason for devoting so much space to them here: what is beyond doubt, and is all too easy to understand, is that persons and parties thus named by their victims and enemies do figure to an unprecedented degree in contemporary conflicts and that some of them deserve universally to be thus named; diversifying the violence of those conflicts with the bombings, assassinations (often meretriciously dignified as 'executions'), intimidations, kidnappings, and (so far as there is any difference) hostage-takings and so on which are the stock-in-trade of this dark dimension of armed struggle. To which it remains only to add that this list is matched item by item by the familiar operations of State terrorism: destructions, killings (especially within the past fifteen years or so and in Latin America) by 'death-squads', torture, and 'disappearances'.

Third, refugees. Refugees constitute another unprecedented complication in the contemporary experience of armed conflict. It may be noted *en passant* that the unprecedented scale and persistence of the refugee problem makes it one of the most tragically extraordinary features of our time. The masses of refugees who leave homes, cross frontiers, and crowd camps, in a sort of symbiosis with the humanitarian IGOs and NGOs which exist to relieve them, are by no means all driven by armed violence: nature causes disasters as well as man. But some large proportion is thus driven. In most cases, refugees are simply endeavouring to get away from the violence and from its hunger-causing consequences. It is however also possible that they are on the move because a party to a conflict sees advantage in shifting them—and the consequences so far as the law of war goes can be more varied than meets the eye.

Refugee camps can be important pieces on the board of the military game as many nationalist and revolutionary insurgents have learned to play it. Contrary to what that misleading will-o'-the-wisp, common sense, might lead one to expect, life in such camps has in some instances created and forged militant nations in ways that 'ordinary' existence could never have done. This began very early, in the camps (supplied and furnished by one of the UN's first major relief agencies, UNWRA) of the Palestinians who had fled from or been driven out by the new State of Israel in and since 1948. Whatever diffusion of Palestinian national consciousness may in earlier times have resulted from the centuries of Ottoman rule, and notwith-standing the confusing cross-currents of pan-Arab nationalism, a power-fully distinct nationalism quickly developed thereafter when so many Palestinians were perforce resident outside their homeland or, after 1967, subjected to alien rule within it. Some of their 'refugee camps' in Jordan and Lebanon became in due course also military camps and even, as the Israelis discovered in 1982, fortresses.

Refugee-camp forgings and strengthenings of sturdy national conscious-ness have happened also in varying measures to Algerians (in Tunisia), Polisarians (in the Western Sahara), Cambodians (in Thailand), Namibians (in Angola), Salvadoreans (in Honduras), and Guatemalans (in Mexico). Such camps, when close enough to less than perfectly controlled frontiers and when their own perimeters are porous, have also sometimes had a certain military value for insurgents related to the refugees. In them, ac-cording to circumstance, may be found facilities for rest and healing; from them may be drawn recruits, especially as children develop into teenagers; through them may be filtered military and medical supplies, which the internationally accredited relief authorities may not know about, which they may know about but are unable to prevent, or to which they willingly turn a blind eye. There are many sides to the contemporary refugee business, and some of them provide evidence to support the argument that humani-tarian relief for victims of armed conflicts is rarely as separable from military support as the more ingenuous of its promoters, and the more worldly-wise of its beneficiaries, like to maintain.

Fourth, another unprecedented feature of the world's experience of armed conflicts since 1945 is the way in which certain of them—conflicts which in earlier times might have been settled one way or the other by classic assertions of superior force—have been locked by the law, the politics, and the ethos of the era into long-standing hostile relationships ranging from the frozen to the volcanically hot. Korea is an example of one which, after its three-year eruption from 1950 to 1953, has been more or less frozen ever since, the country split along the middle. Cyprus concluded twenty years of minor troubles by becoming split in 1974. (Not that troubles then ceased!) Vietnam, to begin with and for similar post-war reasons split like Korea, only ceased to be a vortex of violence after twenty-five years of awful conflict. The troubles in Northern Ireland, for all their deep historical roots, only became institutionalized when that province was politically split off from the rest of the island in 1923. Lebanon from the 1960s progressively crumbled into conditions of division and anarchy from which salvation came to seem infinitely remote, a main cause of its seemingly terminal tragedy being the contagion it has inescapably suffered from the most notorious of these peculiar and, as one might call them, *chronic* conflicts—the many-sided and many-levelled conflict, unique in all aspects, resulting from the establishment of the State of Israel in 1948.

The question will for ever be debated, whether this extraordinary standing item on the world's political agenda since 1945—the violent relations between Israel and its neighbours, and all the troubles, near and far, that have followed therefrom—might not have been avoided if the UN had been able in classic realist style to enforce Israel's establishment and to secure the originally modest borders assigned to it.[8] The speculation is not entirely fanciful. Such forceful action was one of the options in 1947–8, and would have been lawful within the terms of the Charter if the weightier States in the UN had determined to make it so. But the politics of the UN did not permit, and the ethos of the age did not press. Relations between Israel and its Arab neighbours got off to a thoroughly bad start, recovery from which has ever since been impeded by the influence upon their relations of virtually all the conflict-exacerbating elements listed above. The superpowers have taken sides, helping their protégés to become armed to the teeth, and more often than not failing to restrain them from desperate actions. One of the hottest episodes of war between Israel and its neighbours, the Yom Kippur War in 1973, brought the superpowers them-

[8] It must be noted that the term 'the UN', here as on every occasion when forcible action is involved, means in effect action taken on its behalf by (some of) its more powerful members.

selves to the brink of armed confrontation, the only known parallel to the Cuban missiles crisis. The military occupation of the West Bank and Gaza Strip which has gone on ever since 1967 and which constitutes a war-consequence without parallel or precedent, has made Israel look like a permanent bender of international law. It has been represented by its enemies as a colonial intrusion of the imperialist USA into the Arab region and, because of Zionism, as a racist State, the only parallel, however debatable a one, to apartheid-based South Africa. Pan-Arab nationalism has received a fillip and permanent fuelling otherwise unimaginable. The mutual hatreds of the irreconcilable parties have worked themselves out through numberless unseen channels, the whole world over, e.g. terrorism by Arabs and their revolutionary sympathizers, supplies of arms and counter-insurgency expertise by Israel to some of the world's most repressive and disreputable regimes. If there really was an opportunity in 1947–8 to enforce a viable sharing of territory in Palestine, a terrible price has been paid, not only by the people who live there but by our whole world, for its being missed.

In conclusion of this scene-setting sketch of the types, styles, and motivations of contemporary armed conflict, there has to be brought into account a certain cluster of feelings which often appears to permeate the others in a distinctively late twentieth-century way. Explanations of armed conflict are normally deemed satisfactory without going beyond the classic (and overlapping) headings to which allusion has already been made: nation, ethnic group, empire, profit and loss, ideology, race, religion, tribe and clan, with their taken-for-granted superstructures of such familiar human stuff as fear, ignorance, folly, anger, pride, greed, desperation, and so on. Nothing new about any of these! But what does seem to be new in the world since the end of the Second World War is the near-universality of a profound feeling among the have-nots (their spokesmen and articulate members, anyway) that they need not be forever as badly off as they are and that not only should something be done about it but that something could forthwith be done.

The novelty lies not in the feeling itself, nor even in the terms of its expression, but in the scale and seriousness of its frame of reference. Nothing is or ever has been in human terms more natural than that poverty should resent riches and the slave detest the master. Prevention and suppression of popular riot, revolt, and revolution, and relief or diversion by one means or another of the pressures that produce them, have at all times and in all societies been a common concern of rulers and élites and of the religions in their tow. These are age-old, fundamental constants of human history. Much less ancient but also with a well-worn look from a later twentieth-century perspective, are the corresponding Marxist and Leninist diagnoses and prescriptions. Whatever date historical professionals might wish to fix as 'the beginning of modern times', popular consensus would probably settle for 1917. Following the traumatic events in Russia, it began to be possible to look further afield and to work hopefully and without evident absurdity for world revolution. Communist expectations of riding to triumph on the crest of this wave appear, at the turn of the 1990s and following another series of Russian shocks, to have been at last decisively dashed. So far as the main lines of contemporary world history have been dominated (as from some angles it has plausibly appeared to be) by the struggle of communism with capitalism for the leadership of the cause of universal improvement, communism appears to have lost.

But capitalism cannot as surely be said to have won. Those age-old constants of social and political conflict persist on a planet where poverty and riches, servitude and overlordship, 'losers' and 'winners' are in many respects as starkly juxtaposed as ever they have been, with (thus we return to the point of this conclusion) two crucial differences. First, because of the way that the progress of commerce, mass communications, and international organization has created a sense of (to use the popular and UN-promoted term for it), One World, the 'losers' are more aware of themselves, of the relative extents of their deprivation, and of the great debate on what to do about it than they can ever before have been. The title of an early formulation of their situation which quickly became a classic, *Les Damnés de la terre* (The Wretched of the Earth) (by the Martinique-born, French-educated, Algerian-revolutionary Frantz Fanon, 1961) has been ceaselessly paraphrased and echoed ever since. Not One World, but Three or even Four appear through the humanitarian telescope. Not 'capitalism v. communism', but 'North v. South' or richer v. poorer is the short title of this (since the 1960s) new and contemporary ground-plan of tension and struggle.

The second aspect of this novel situation works to compound its turbulence. Novelty lies not only in what the contemporary eye may see but also in how that eye sees it. The richer side, the 'haves', gave hostages to fortune and the 'have-nots' in this great debate when it was only just beginning by affirming the existence of universal human rights. This necessarily implied an acknowledgement that the worst inequalities and inequities suffered within (another fashionable phrase of the epoch) 'the Human Family' are not forever to be borne, and that they must be put right, however painful and difficult may be the process and however reluctant most of the 'haves' to assist it. Thus has the idea of human rights come to warm the feelings and shape the language of, it seems no exaggeration to say, all the armed conflicts that happen in the contemporary world. Not one of the conflict-categories listed above is incapable of taking on this coloration. The language of human rights has, in fact, become the lingua franca in which the causes and pretexts of violent conflicts are most often expressed. This adds to them an element of moral indignation and ideal purpose which many of them (given that they already have adequate traditional causes) would otherwise lack. Whether or not this novelty makes restraint in them more or less likely, is a question that will be touched on hereafter.

Such was the maelstrom of armed conflicts into which international humanitarian law was expected to bring its healing measures of protection and relief. In such stressful circumstances it was surprising, neither that the mild post-Second World War modifications already described in Part II prove to have done little to prepare it to meet such challenges, nor that the painful experience of trying to do so should beget more radical reconsiderations. Such challenges and responses of course were common experience also for other branches of international law; every one of them, in fact, which had to encounter within the arenas of the UN the arguments of ideology and the pressures of political blocs. New law was proposed or even actually made (there is endless argument about the legal authority of General Assembly Resolutions: how much the weightier of them may indicate of State practice, and what they might cumulatively contribute to customary law) which was based on principles unheard of before 1945. Old law was interpreted in similar novel ways. A common man's summary of these shifts in the conceptual foundations of the international law of war, peace, and neutrality is now offered as a helpful preliminary to the critical scrutiny of the contemporary workings of IHL which fills the remainder of the book.

The centrepiece is, as it for so long had been, the State. The State as it was invented or, some would say, reinvented in early modern Europe is no longer the only 'subject' or 'actor' (to use the technical terms of the science) in the field. For obvious reasons it remains by far the principal one, but not exclusively and unchallengedly so. To some extent this marks a return to the premodern idea that the higher forms of law—divine law, natural law, the *jus gentium*—had as their purpose the determination of the relations towards each other of *all* human beings and their collective institutions.

Human rights law especially, regarding the individual as subject no less than the State, finds origins in those earlier times. But besides the individual, who now stands fairly secure in the middle of the field, there have materialized around its edges institutions with plausible claims to be given some, so to speak, official status among the unquestioned principal actors. The United Nations, to the extent that it is more than the sum of its State parts, is obviously the chief of these, bringing in its wake the assorted lesser bodies of its special agencies. The UN and its agencies and the regional organizations count as Inter-Governmental Organizations, the IGOs. Next come the NGOs, the (International) Non-Governmental Organizations, some of which, like e.g. Save the Children Fund, Amnesty International, Médecins sans Frontières, and above all the International Committee of the Red Cross, have acquired a status and position in the higher strata of international affairs which make the latters' conduct, especially in their grimmer aspects, unthinkable and incomplete without them.[9]

Certain politico-military bodies also have broken to various extents into the States' exclusive circle. In the course of the thirty years' campaign for decolonization, which occupied so much of the General Assembly's time from the later 1950s, it early became apparent to the supporters of the hypothesized States-to-be that political and propaganda advantage could follow the treatment of them, whenever and wherever possible, as actual States-in-waiting. Algeria's was the first of the national liberation movements to be given such acceptance, by the States of the Soviet bloc and the Non-Aligned Movement. The tendency can be regarded as having reached its apogee in the early 1970s, when the Declaration on Friendly Relations among States of 1970 included a sanctification of self-determination struggles and, four years later, the Palestine Liberation Organization was given permanent observer status at the UN. In 1974 also the same campaign took a controversial leap forward when it succeeded in launching its equation of wars of national liberation with *international* armed conflicts towards ultimate acceptance by the 1974–7 Diplomatic Conference to improve IHL.

In no area of international law is the status of an 'actor' more important to establish than that of the law of war. With status and recognition go rights and responsibilities: what law-of-war observances may be expected of the party or group in question, and what it may itself expect. But—to take up again the point made in the last section of my Introduction—establishing

---

[9] The ICRC, not surprisingly in view of its unique legal status and its special relationship with governments, considers itself to be an NGO-plus, and surely deserves to be so considered.

the status of parties etc. is itself, according to the letter of international law, dependent on the status of armed conflicts, and their status is often, in the contemporary world, mixed or unclear. States have naturally found it their interest to keep the letter of the law in this respect restrictive and limiting. Its spirit nevertheless has often been taken much further. The actual workings of 'humanitarian law' cannot be properly described by writing, as legal experts normally write, about law alone. Humanitarian practitioners do not live by law alone.

The makers of Common Article 3 cannot in 1949 have imagined that State practice and ICRC pragmatism would soon converge to partially implement the article even though States would be inhibited from acknowledging its applicability by their embarrassed or haughty reluctance to admit that 'an Article 3 conflict' was going on in their territory. Nor can they in 1949 have foreseen how many sorts and conditions of armed groups (e.g. revolutionary guerrillas in Latin America, 'militias' in Lebanon) would from time to time and according to circumstances be brought by the ingenuity of the ICRC under the Conventions' simple designation of 'parties'. Whatever may be the resourcefulness of the ICRC in implementing the spirit of the law, within or (as is much more often the case, especially when State authority fades away) without the formal cover of the Conventions, its all-important commitment to the letter keeps it, at least in public, from making distinctions between one kind of 'party' and another. How such distinctions might be made is suggested by Amnesty International's definitions of the non-State political actors it is prepared to deal with as either quasi-governmental entities ('possessing some of the attributes of governments') or non-governmental entities: 'armed opposition groups which lack the attributes of a government but nevertheless may be held accountable by AI for certain human rights abuses'.[10] To sum up: however restricted may be the range of parties other than the State recognized by the written instruments of international law, the range included in the practice of humanitarian and human rights law is more confused and generous.

War, peace, and neutrality, the other fundamental concepts of immediate relevance, have likewise lost their earlier, clearer meanings. The eighteenth- and nineteenth-century constructors of modern international law shared the common understanding of their culture that war and peace were contrasted conditions of existence, that peace was morally the more desirable, and that civilization meant a preponderance of peace over war. War, in this view of things, was sometimes unavoidable and even necessary, but in the long run

---

[10] The journal Amnesty, Aug.–Sept. 1990, 22.

exceptional. For civilized States, peace was the norm. The system of international law which those States evolved for themselves therefore made a sharp distinction between the times of war and peace. It produced different sets of rules of behaviour appropriate for each, and alongside them a body of law to regulate the behaviour towards each other of States which were at war and States which were not; another of the assumptions of pre-twentieth century civilization being that, whatever respect might need to be paid to the rights of belligerents, the rights of neutrals had to be remembered too. Declarations of war rarely in practice marked the start of hostilities like shots from a starter's gun, but until the Second World War they remained highly important as public announcements that one international legal regime had given way to another, and that enemy aliens and neutrals accordingly should know what to expect.

These simplicities did not long survive the establishment of the United Nations and the onset of all the armed conflicts sketched above. Not only did the quantity and variety of conflicts become such as to defy clear legal description, the terms of the Charter itself, which States were reluctant to seem to violate, induced States to adopt a terminology which, to all but the UN-initiated, could only appear artificial and devious. There were to be no more old-style formal declarations of war after the Soviet Union's against Japan on 8 August 1945. Article 2(4) of the Charter required members of the UN to 'refrain . . . from the threat or use of force against the territorial integrity or political independence of any State'. The very word 'war' was officially to be avoided—the USA was never 'at war' with North Vietnam, nor Iraq with Iran, nor the UK with Argentina. The word 'aggression', necessarily much used in the proceedings of the International Military Tribunals, was avoided in the Charter because of the difficulties the League of Nations had run into over its definition. Work was however begun at once on defining it, and a consensual definition (i.e. one without any precise meaning) was at last arrived at in 1974.[11] The result of all this was that, although henceforth States' international actions might substantively be aggressive, they had to find some way of describing them which would pretend they were not so—a legerdemain most conveniently done by bringing almost every act of armed force under the description of the 'individual or collective self-defence' permitted (under certain conditions) by Article 51.

The only legitimate exception to this new understanding of international law was armed struggle initiated and carried on by a national liberation

[11] Some confusions have resulted from the French text's translation of 'armed attack' in the UN Charter's Art. 51 as *aggression armée*.

movement defined as the majority of UN members chose to define it. Acts of assistance to an NLM, such as allowing its members 'sanctuary' in one's territory and permitting the supply of arms to it across one's border, were by the same token not counted as the acts of hostility (let alone aggression) they might be in any other circumstances. NLMs in the UN's restrictive definition of them were admittedly a special case. They were also of diminishing importance as their number shrank from its mid-1960s peak to the late 1980s rump of PLO and ANC. What more significantly illustrates the general melt-down of legal definitions (the image is from candles, not Chernobyl) is the way that States became able to engage in proxy wars against one another and to fuel opposite sides in wars both civil and international without it being found necessary to determine whether they were 'at war' or 'at peace' with one another, or whether their respective allies were 'neutral'.

Wars used to be expected to give way to returned peace with the signing of a peace treaty, but peace treaties have become less familiar closures of armed conflicts in our own times than cessations of hostilities, cease-fires, armistices, truces, accords, and agreements, with or without benefit of UN peace-keeping forces. The old trichotomy of war/neutrality/peace belonged to a different world from that of the armed conflicts, for example, which have rattled on for years in Vietnam, Angola, Cambodia/Kampuchea, and, since 1979, Afghanistan, a short list to which the relations between Israel and its neighbours are not added only because they are something else. Another ancient pillar of the law, smartly renovated in Article 2(7) of the Charter, has similarly become little more than a politico-legal stalking-horse, although an exceptionally sensitive and lively one: the principle of 'non-intervention' in States' domestic jurisdictions. So many, momentous, and multiform have interferences by stronger States in weaker States' internal affairs actually become that 'intervention' is by now an established subject of international legal and political study.

Whatever may be the contribution of these circumlocutions and ambiguities to the confusion of persons who wish to know what is actually going on in the world, it can be argued that they are of limited consequence for the practice of IHL. There are no grounds for thinking that the problems and difficulties of securing even its partial observance would be less if the language of the law were to correspond more closely, as it did in former times, to political and military fact. Humanitarian organizations, the ICRC in this field at their head, still find their way to the doors of the authorities, wherever and whatever they are, whose permission is usually an indispensable preliminary to their operations. How helpful law may be beyond that point of entry seems to depend very much on circumstances and personalities. There can be no question but that the ICRC's unique ability to deal directly with governments and to put awkward questions to them rests on its uniquely law-given status. Nor is there any doubting the forensic and exemplary value of legal rules, and of historical practice based upon them or related to them. Representatives of Red Cross and human rights organizations alike have learned that although 'the law' in its entirety may not be respected and that harping on it may even be counter-productive, bits of it can be respected and observed, and that officers and officials may respond to personal approaches and appeals as they will not to presumed legal authority. The actual point of humanitarian contact—'the sharp end', as soldiers put it—will feel remote, and may for all intents and purposes be remote, from lawyers' arguments and diplomats' protestations about the proper classification of the armed conflict in progress and the respective statuses of the parties directing it, the armed persons doing the fighting, and the varieties of its victims. With an eye equally on how strategists, fighters, and victims experience 'the sharp end' and on how politicians, lawyers, and political scientists write about it, the remainder of this book will examine how the major elements of international humanitarian law work out in practice.

PART III

Law and Armed Conflict since 1950

7 | Humanitarian Practice and the Laws of War

The Supposed Equality of Belligerents and Impartiality of Humanitarian Relief

Weapons and how they are used in armed conflict cannot properly be considered in isolation from the question, how far the choice and use of weapons in armed conflict is shaped and determined by things that have happened—decisions made, thoughts thought—before armed conflict begins. This seemingly logical procedure ought to surprise no one. But modern IHL writers have not usually followed it. The usual thing through the past two centuries has been to leave the part of the law which deals with the causes and pretexts of war, the old *jus ad bellum*, to fend for itself and to focus exclusively on the *jus in bello*.

Good reasons for concentration on the *jus in bello* are not lacking. The most persuasive one has become embodied in the law itself. Traditional *jus ad bellum* lost its charm for those pragmatic, moderate-minded men of the seventeenth and eighteenth centuries whose observations taught them that, extravagantly interpreted, it could actually obstruct the restraint and (as the most optimistic of them came to describe it) the humanization of war. The pursuit of justice in this connection as in most others could run to extremes as well as to the moderate middle. The more persuaded men were of the absolute rightness and divine authority of their cause—the nearer they got to interpreting 'just war' as 'holy war'—the more difficult seemed they to find it to exercise restraint and show compassion. To the minds of diplomatic practitioners and men of affairs of early modernizing Europe, moreover, there was a further flaw in the received theory. Inherited just-war theory assumed that, even if 'right' was not wholly and exclusively on one side, more of it must be found on one side than the other, which, in strict logic, was very likely to be the case. But realist political theory and positivist legal theory were waltzing away from such evaluations, preferring not to pronounce judgment on the rights and wrongs of sovereign States in conflict until they knew what the outcome was. The only right that mattered to them was, to put it crudely, whatever was recognized as such and was enforceable within the society of States.

But this was not necessarily the naked rule of might. To represent it as such is to do less than justice to the amount of rights-consciousness that could be present in the decision-making process, not to mention the haunting fact that right without might to protect it is right at risk. Right did not evaporate from international society with the spread of élite readiness to keep the question of what was proper in war apart from that of what was proper in peace. Experience showed (or appeared to show—historians are still unclear as to whether it really did or not) that belligerents' self-restraining senses of common interests and shared civilized concerns were more likely to flourish and fructify if they forgot about the causes of their fighting one another and concentrated on keeping the fighting clean. Humanitarianism, it was clear, might be better served by breaking the ties between the law's two branches and improving the *jus in bello*'s chances of observation by assuming the moral equivalence of belligerents, which meant, in practical terms, positing the irrelevance of *jus ad bellum* to *jus in bello*.

Thus was born the doctrine known as that of 'belligerent equality' or 'equal application'. An acceptable summary of it is given near the beginning of the US air force's 1976 manual.

The law of armed conflict [it says] applies equally to all parties to an armed conflict, whether or not the international community regards any participant as the 'aggressor' or 'victim'. . . . This principle is vitally necessary. Events since the Second World War have demonstrated that it is frequently impossible to obtain international consensus on the reasons for a particular conflict. Obtaining agreement on who is the aggressor and who is the victim is even more difficult. . . . The individual victims of conflict, notably civilians, POWs, and wounded, sick and shipwrecked are the beneficiaries of much of the law of armed conflict. Indeed all military members of nations involved in armed conflict benefit from the law. It is unacceptable to make their legal protection contingent upon an international consensus on the causes of the conflict.[1]

The immediate humanitarian advantages of this doctrine are nowhere more evident than in the value which the ICRC places on it. Indeed, the doctrine's centrality to contemporary IHL may have something to do with the fact that the ICRC, as it has become embedded in IHL's brickwork, has found it could do little without it, nor could the Red Cross and Red Crescent movement do so much. The fundamental principles of the Red Cross and Red Crescent—humanity, impartiality, neutrality, and

---

[1] AFP 110–11 pt. 1–2. d(3). No corresponding passage appears in the US Army's manual, FM 27-10 (1956). I wonder why? Perhaps because the doctrine had never mattered much to the US armed forces until the North Vietnam and Chinese Governments provocatively rejected it in their polemics of the 1960s and at the CDDH.

independence—rely upon it.[2] *Independence* simply means that National Societies ought to be free enough from the power and influence of the States they inhabit to pursue their humanitarian vocation without regard to its political interests. *Humanity* is the ark of the movement's covenant: the Red Cross's calling and duty (even, so far as the letter of the law regarding the ICRC goes, its right) to succour, assist, and, so far as law allows it, protect war's victims and sufferers. The other two principles explain the grounds for expecting the movement's practice of humanity to be universally acceptable. *Impartiality* guarantees that 'it makes no discrimination as to nationality, race, religious beliefs, class or political opinions' and gives priority in treatment only 'to the most urgent cases of distress'. The definition of *neutrality* drops anchor in the equal-application doctrine: 'In order to continue to enjoy the confidence of all, the Red Cross may not take sides in hostilities or engage at any time in controversies of a political, racial, religious or ideological nature.' Whether, therefore, warring parties are great or tiny, 'good' or 'bad', State-supporting or revolutionary, the Swiss-ly neutral ICRC expects to be able to interpose its humanitarian operations without affecting any party's legal or political position. If there is such a thing as pure and disinterested humanitarianism, equally and impartially on offer to all in need, surely this should be it: a *jus in bello* gain well worth divorce from the *jus ad bellum*.

The gains are indisputable, and, whenever the Red Cross and all the other humanitarian organizations who have walked in its wake bring light into dark scenes of wartime suffering, those gains are obvious for all to see.[3] And yet there have been losses too, rather less obvious. The original *jus ad bellum = jus in bello* marriage had offspring, whom the divorce has not served well. Two losses in particular demand scrutiny; both come from the fact that the separation of the one *jus* from the other, no matter how good-hearted the causes for which it was engineered, laid eggs of unreality, whose chicks now awkwardly come home to roost.

Unreality resides, first, in the confusion of meanings which have within the present generation become attached to the idea of 'humanitarian' and the uses to which it has consequently been put. Official IHL theory, dependent upon the equal-application doctrine for opportunity to practise

---

[2] The movement likes to associate with those four principles, these other three: voluntary service, unity, and universality; but they are more of internal than external relevance.

[3] My reference to 'its wake' is not to deny the weight or disparage the value of other organizations, nor to question the independence of their origins. It does however seem undeniable that claims to be undertaking impartial and politically neutral humanitarian relief work, and to be allowed to do so free of political interference, derive their plausibility from analogy with the ethico-legal claim historically pioneered by the Red Cross.

in conflictual situations, is that 'humanitarian relief' is non-political and of no military value—irrelevant therefore to the issues of the conflict and to the means of its resolution, something that no belligerent can reasonably object to. Indeed humanitarian relief can be so, and sometimes is so. This is convenient for parties whose interest it is to argue that it always must be so. But the fact is that the word 'humanitarian' has come to carry a slippery mixture of meanings and applications which facilitate ambiguous and manipulative uses. Relief carried beneath its banner can be, and in our own time often is, politically partial and militarily helpful, of a kind, in fact, which the belligerent on the other side would be entitled to object to and to prevent, did the 'humanitarian relief' argument not make it appear legally questionable and morally mean for him to do so.

This consolidation under the one single heading 'humanitarian' of an actually very wide span of human needs and social situations has developed in parallel with the similar consolidation of a similar great variety of types and situations under the heading of 'civilians'. The two developments are indeed historically and conceptually twinned, as has become unmistakably clear since the opening in the 1950s of the chapters of world history respectively titled 'Decolonization' and 'The Third World'. The humane passion to relieve other countries' war-victims that had been stirred on behalf of the civilian populations of Belgium during the First World War and of Greece and Holland during the Second, and suffering populations all over eastern and central Europe after both wars, found now stimulus chiefly in the disasters and disruptions characteristic of our contemporary era: national liberation struggles against the old empires, and the civil wars and anarchies that accompanied or followed so many of them; revolutionary wars, sometimes indistinguishable from the former; and the unique unclassifiable forty-years' hostility between Israel and its Arab neighbours.

Humanitarian relief, distributed within this confused and disorderly context, was often rather difficult to apply equally. It would have been so, even where the will bona fide existed so to apply it. But such will scarcely existed, nor were the circumstances such as to evoke it. The States and regimes confronted by the first waves of national liberation and revolution-ary movements—France, UK, USA, the Netherlands, Portugal, Belgium, Spain, and then (in hemispherically adjusted terms) almost all the Latin American States too—had no cause to solicit humanitarian aid from exter-nal sources. It was the movements they were confronting which had that cause. Those movements and the struggles they were conducting had com-mon characteristics: 'underdog' beginnings from positions of great material disadvantage, democratic rhetoric, the backing of a majority of members of the UN, appearances (it is unsafe to put it more positively than that) of popular support, and painful evidence of loss and suffering among the various groups of people whom they claimed to represent and among whom they did their fighting. As the law regarding intervention softened to facilitate military aid to NLMs, and as UN practice regarding refugees stretched to succour whole populations fleeing from hostilities, so in sympathy spread the effective meaning of 'humanitarian aid' to include support of those NLMs' people (often encamped beyond borders) whether they were all bona fide 'civilian' or not, and supply of things which, while they might not be military in the strictest sense (e.g. weapons), were practically indispensable to sustained military operations (e.g. transport, communications, and medical supplies). In the prevailing atmosphere of the time, the actually political and engaged effects of such aid, not to mention the purposes which often lay behind them, could hardly become a cause of its prohibition. Legal fiction saved the situation. Aid and areas that were 'humanitarian' must by definition be 'neutral'!

A lively and, to my mind, rather persuasive survey of this phenomenon was published in 1986 by J.-C. Rufin under the title *Le Piège. Quand l'aide humanitaire remplace la guerre* (which may be translated as 'The Snare. How Humanitarian Aid Substitutes for War').[4] Landmarks in its contemporary history, by his account of it, were the success of the Algerian FLN in winning humanitarian legitimization of its sanctuaries across the Tunisian border; the popularization of romantic guerrilla operations by Fidel Castro, Che Guevara, and Regis Debray, and above all the 'Biafran' episode at the end of the 1960s. This latter, I agree, is of exemplary interest in no less than four respects: (1) It showed more than any other episode how the humanitarian impulse can be manipulated and exploited by clever propaganda and professional PR, 'Biafra' having succeeded in persuading most potential aiders that Nigeria's blockade constituted a 'genocidal' strategy of mass starvation, and in blinding them to the fact that the secessionist body's own policy was part of the problem.[5] (2) It is a particularly striking example of how legal and moral confusion can be made into a cover for the pursuit of political purposes, ranging from the French government's unconcealed old-fashioned *realpolitik* to the enthusiastic

[4] Paris, Éditions Lattes, 1986.
[5] That summary of the matter, and the grounds for my other characterizations of the Nigerian civil war, rest principally on my readings of Thierry Hentsch, *Face au blocus: La Croix-Rouge internationale dans le Nigéria en guerre* (Geneva, 1973); John J. Stremlau, *The International Politics of the Nigerian Civil War* (Princeton, NJ, 1977); Rex Niven, *The War of Nigerian Unity* (London, 1970); John de St Jorre, *The Nigerian Civil War* (London, 1972); and Morris Davis (ed.), *Civil Wars and the Politics of International Relief* (New York, 1975).

voluntarist support given to the cause of Biafran secession by religious, political, and humanitarian bodies all over the 'Western' world.[6] (3) Not merely things incidentally useful to military operations were taken to Biafra along with and under the protective cover of the food, medicines, etc. that could be considered simply humanitarian, but things essential to them— guns etc.—were taken too, sometimes even in the same aeroplanes. (4) The question was for the first time raised in a big way, whether lavish supply of 'humanitarian aid' might not actually serve to prolong certain armed conflicts and thus also, necessarily, the human sufferings inseparable from them.[7]

The distinction between humanitarian and other sorts of aid, more militarily valuable, continues to figure crucially in legal appraisals of situations and in the calculations of statesmen and politicians as to how far they will let their States appear to take sides in other countries' disputes. This has been especially evident in the USA, where the distinction between military and humanitarian aid has been a fruitful battleground in many a foreign-policy tussle between President and Congress, and where the war waged independently against Nicaragua by President Reagan and his executive contributed to confuse the distinction to an extraordinary extent. For example, Oxfam-America's consignments of agricultural equipment aid were banned in the 1980s on the ground that they were 'trade with the enemy'; the guerrilla Contras whom Washington supported with humanitarian aid announced that they would regard foreign aid officials as enemy targets; the Nicaraguan Government announced that it regarded the 'humanitarian aid' given to the Contras as 'military logistics'.[8]

From the rather miniature Nicaraguan instance, the gamut of politicized humanitarian relief can be traced through every situation where the situations and vicissitudes of 'civilians' are of interest to belligerent bodies. Not just classic decolonizing NLMs of the 1960s and 1970s, the ANC, SWAPO, MPLA, and so on, but less readily classifiable and longer-living bodies like the PLO, the Eritrean and Tigrayan peoples' fronts, the FMLN in El Salvador, the Mujahedeen of Afghanistan, and (following their expulsion from Phnom Penh) the Khmer Rouge, cannot possibly be imagined to have

---

[6] Because French humanitarians allowed themselves to become as committed in *their* way to the 'Biafran' cause as President de Gaulle was in *his*, it has retained sacred status for them, with Médecins sans Frontières as its living and thriving memorial.

[7] I have found this possibility noticed in various contexts by writers as different as William Shawcross, Raymond Aron, Keith Suter, Sydney Bailey, and Michael Walzer.

[8] Digested from the *Guardian*, 15 May 1985, and *The Times*, 22 Sept. 1986. At the time of first-drafting this paragraph that classic Washington tussle recurred, apropos of Israel's request for ten billion dollars' credit guarantees for 'humanitarian' purposes; purposes which included the building of fortified settlements for armed settlers in the occupied territories.

held together as well as they did without the sometimes enormous quantities of 'humanitarian' support coming under a variety of flags and banners from the world outside to their camps and bases, bases which of necessity tended to lie close to the border beyond which the fighting went on.[9] From the political and military points of view, none of this need seem surprising. Only from the legal point of view may it be surprising to anyone who takes at face value the humanitarian neutrality authorized by the doctrine of equal application.

Military Necessity's Moral Anchor in the *jus ad bellum*

The other significant effect of *jus in bello*'s formal separation from *jus ad bellum* is more difficult to identify, but arguably more serious. Just as a whole can be greater than the sum of its parts, so can parts of a whole, set loose from it, shrink from lack of what that wholeness gave them. Something of this sort seems to have happened when the war-regarding part of *jus gentium* split into two. Early modern European minds that were moved by any part of it—and how many or few at any one time they were, we can only guess; the point concerns quality, not numbers—could hardly have avoided being aware of the whole in which it was embedded. The same ethic, the same sense of religious obligation ran from one end to the other of that body of principles and prohibitions. Conscience was called upon to be active before war began, and it was not necessarily expected to go dormant until war stopped. The conscience duly satisfied that the cause for which its possessor was ready to kill was a just one (a matter earnestly debated for more than a millennium before Henry V and his soldiers argued about it on the eve of Agincourt) might then have to answer for how it did the killing. Even if the fighting had been conducted according to approved custom, it was in earlier centuries nevertheless regarded by directors of conscience as occasion for penitence and penance.[10] European Christians who were in a position to share their culture's intellectuals' thoughts about war might not before the sixteenth century have been readily able to distinguish their pre-war religious/moral duties from the duties which bound them after a war's beginning.

The modern conceptual separation of 'before' from 'after' cannot of course have meant that virtuous men would inevitably make such a dis-

---

[9] Glimpses of every part of this giant phenomenon may be had in the excellent book edited by Gil Loescher and Laila Monahan, *Refugees and International Relations* (Oxford, 1989).

[10] See e.g. Frederick H. Russell, *The Just War in the Middle Ages* (Cambridge, 1975), pages on 'penance' and 'penitential literature'.

tinction. Compartmentalization of the *jus in bello* into a distinct domain for practical legal purposes did not *ipso facto* reduce the significance of *jus ad bellum* and its moral claims. Writers concerned to explain the distinction insisted that morality's claims were still respected. All that had happened was a long-term recasting of the context in which those claims had to be considered, and a spreading acceptance of the idea that the morality of war-fighters was, in some particulars, simply different from that of ordinary persons in ordinary times. The moralist's problem was what it always had been: to justify, in certain exceptional circumstances starting at a certain time, the permission of deeds which until that moment had been impermissible—killing and so on. In wars which satisfied the moralist's criteria of justice, legitimacy, or whatever, killing was no murder, and enemies were enemies only for the time being. By the time this refined explanation of the exceptional had developed into the nineteenth-century realist's relish for describing war as a state in which peacetime's values were simply inverted, the gap between the two sides of the law of war had perhaps become rather difficult to traverse without tripping. For the coarser-minded, adages like the immemorial 'all's fair in love and war' continued to banish moral unease. For the more discerning, Napoleon better expressed the modern politico-military understanding of the demands made by the *jus in bello*, now that it stood on its own: 'My great maxim has always been, in politics and war alike, that every injury done to the enemy, even though permitted by the rules [i.e. customary law], is excusable only so far as it is absolutely necessary; everything beyond that is criminal.'[11]

That sounds all right; humane and conscientious, besides showing such awareness as an honourable commander should show of the possibilities of restraint, and of readiness to seize them *so long as 'absolute necessity' did not prevent him.* Could more be asked? Most of the rest of this book being in one way or another about the problem of distinguishing what is 'absolutely necessary' in war from what is not, we may here stick closely to the one aspect of the problem which nowhere else in the book is expressly considered, namely, whether the idea of the necessary may not be affected by the split between the two *jura*, and in what direction it may be pushed? My contention is that, given the formal separation of the *jus in bello* from

[11] My translation of the French cited by Max Huber in 'Die kriegsrechtlichen Verträge und die Kriegsraison', in *Zeitschrift für Völkerrecht*, 7 (1913), 351–74 at 353. I have not thought it necessary to check the accuracy of the alleged quotation; it is exactly consistent with everything one knows about Napoleon, and in any case it is of equal interest that Huber himself (who was to become the leading light of the ICRC) got it from Jacob Burckhardt's *Weltgeschichtliche Betrachtungen* (1905), 246.

the other, the understanding of necessity can indeed be affected, almost certainly for the worse.

This very significant possibility is worth a book on its own. A good book about it would not be easy to write. The procurement of adequate evidence to support its argument would require a wide-ranging knowledge of war history, the way of the argument itself is hazardous with minefields and booby traps, and moreover it cannot be entered except by way of that complicated category 'civilian–military relations' and that most explosive one, 'the military mind'—explosive, because even the most accessible sort of military men, when one manages to talk with them about it, tend to deny that it exists. They reasonably remind one of the enormous differences between the mentalities characteristic of the several armed services (not to mention the awkward great fact of inter-service rivalry) and of the great variety of attitudes, skills, etc. required by the various departments within each of them. Especially within an army like the British one, where regimental peculiarities are positively cultivated, the idea of a common mentality is bound to seem absurd. And yet, from the civilian standpoint, the military mind certainly does exist. The solidarity which rival British regiments can muster in defence of their regimental system is at one end of the same scale which, at the other, sees the military interest, all the world over, rally against what it perceives as inferior civilian values and cleave instead to its distinctive alternatives, of which notions like honour, obedience, courage, death-defiance, loyalty, etc. are regular features.

Therein lie the realities of the military mind, and my grounds for believing that one may reasonably talk about it. But I prefer to say too little rather than too much. It is too simple to say, with representatives of the West's left-liberal anti-militarist tradition, that when civilians lose control of war and soldiers gain it, things get worse. The overworked adage about war being too serious a matter to be left to the generals has some truth in it but perhaps no more than if, instead of generals, it specified politicians. Generals can be stupid and soldiers can be vicious, but so can politicians and civilians be both of those things. More material than the difference between generals and politicians are such differences as those between sensible and virtuous generals and politicians on the one side, stupid or vicious generals and politicians on the other, and (most important of all, though least observed) between the cultures in which the respective mentalities and behaviours of generals and politicians are formed. The old anti-militarist concept of brass-hatted 'militarism' has been seriously unusable at least since Alfred Vagts published his *History of Militarism,*

Civilian and Military two generations ago.[12] So far as that concept of raw militarism related to the belief that soldiers generally were a savage species, that too is incredible for persons whose reading of campaign history and military biography has shown them, on the one hand, how much moral responsibility, practical kindliness, etc. can mark the military professional, and whose experience of non-military affairs, on the other, may have made them aware how capable are civilians of hatred, cruelty, and murderous feelings. The old reach-me-down characterizations crack under the lightest critical pressure.

They crack again if one goes down another familiar road. History seems to offer plenty of examples of military commanders whose pride, single-mindedness, and sense of honour have driven them to pursue 'victory', the supremest goal they can conceive, in ways that pass beyond all reason: victory measured in military terms as the stark and sole antipodes from defeat, victory gained at whatever cost it demands and (in the nature of the case stated) not likely to contain much of the moderation and longer-term peace-planning posited in the pure doctrine of the *jus ad bellum*. Military victory in unmistakable terms is what the military mind often most clearly understands and aims for; but the civilian and the political mind can be attracted by it too. German public opinion liked to hear of French sufferings in the wars of 1870–1 and 1914–18. French public opinion would not have objected to an even more punitive peace treaty in 1919. More recently, such all-out victory-seekers as Arthur Harris, Curtis Le May, and Douglas MacArthur had hosts of political/civilian supporters (Harris actually had the British prime minister until the penultimate moment). To track responsibility for what happened in Vietnam is to get into tangled thickets of diplomatic, political, and military decisions and devices. As many examples could be produced of generals (ground-army generals, that is; perhaps not so many air-force ones) preferring a more measured policy than their political masters pressed on them, as of generals going for the enemy more roughly than their political masters wished.

The conclusion seems inescapable that whatever spin may be given to the conduct of war by *jus in bello*'s separation from *jus ad bellum*, decisive responsibility for it can be pinned on neither side of the civil–military relationship. But that is not to say that the separation leaves war-conduct unspun. Those who unreflectingly repeat the adage that the end justifies the means forget that some means can alter ends and some means even can make the end unattainable. Unless the two laws, the pre-war and the in-war,

---

[12] New York, 1937. A generation later, the same point was remade by I. L. Horowitz, *The War Game: Studies of the new Civilian Militarists* (New York, 1963).

move in close harmony with one another, the apparent exigencies of in-war law will tend to trump pre-war law as soon as the going gets rough; as Bishop George Bell so well put it when opening a debate on British bombing policy in early 1944, 'It is common experience in the history of warfare that not only wars but actions taken in war as military necessities are often supported at the time by a class of arguments which, after the war is over, people find are arguments to which they never should have listened.'[13] Under the wartime hammer of necessity *to win*—or at least and at all costs, not to be defeated!—the calm assessment of war aims (supposing they were there in the first place) inevitably loses its attractions, and pre-war principles of war-conduct have to bend accordingly. There is no need to cite examples of what is so familiar. Only three international conflicts since 1945 (and one of them, only a 'war' by courtesy) spring to mind as examples of wars whose histories do not to a greater or lesser extent map such lines of pressure: the uniquely situated, uniquely restrained war between Britain and Argentina in 1982, the UN-authorized operation to expel Iraq from Kuwait in early 1991, and the bloodless intermittent 'fish war' between Iceland and Britain (and to lesser extent, West Germany) in 1972–6.

Another facet of the two-laws relationship may helpfully be brought to mind before we return to the methods and means by which *jus* is observed or not observed *in bello*, a two-sided facet in fact, for it is embedded in another, more material relationship: that between how a State (or other properly belligerent party) is prepared for war, and how war will actually be fought. Time and technology have moved war-planning and war-fighting far from the simplicities of ages when what mattered more than anything else were the weather and the seasons, when most warriors' weapons came ready to hand, and when combatants—on land, anyway—could usually see exactly what they were doing to one another. How wars are fought in our much more complicated age is determined, so far as its material side goes, by decisions made and with hardware acquired months or, more often, years before the event. Exactly what the event will bring, and what wars will actually have to be fought, is however rather difficult to determine in advance! States often become involved in wars they had not expected and planned for. Wars that have been planned for may never happen. What *does* happen is that methods and means may be used—may *have* to be used, say their apologists—which are scarcely suitable and which actually would not have been in the pre-war plan, could there possibly have been one.

---

[13] 9 Feb. 1944, speech in the House of Lords. This is so wonderfully perceptive a remark, I make no apology for having deployed it before, among the epigraphs to my *Humanity in Warfare*.

The USA built giant B-52 bombers in order to be able to bomb the Soviet Union, but the only times it has used them in anger were against North Vietnam, eastern Cambodia, and (as part of the UN-authorized campaign in early 1991) the Iraqi forces invading Kuwait. The merits of what was thus done to North Vietnam and Cambodia having been much debated, it is possible to wonder whether those bombers were used more because they were available and because news of their use would raise morale and spirits than because they offered an ideal means to do either what the *jus in bello* permitted or what the *jus ad bellum* (had it been systematically brought into consideration) preferred. Similar questions have been debated for half a century in the larger-scale debates provoked by much of the bombing done in the Second World War and in the Korean War soon after it. Indeed, there seems to be something in the very nature of aerial-bombardment capability which places it bang in the heart of this matter, something produced by its mix of costly and impressive equipment which clamours to be used; élite personnel who clamour to use it; extraordinary destructive power which through most of its history has been impossible to aim accurately; a unique accompaniment of dramatic sights and sounds and of exaggerated expectations and apparent effects, exciting to combatants and civilians alike; and, to top it all, that peculiarly unformed and elastic relationship with the law of war which has already been noted. No other area of war practice shows such extreme examples of how far uncontrolled, unreflective or unprincipled commanders can stretch bits of the *jus in bello* to excuse extreme departures from anything the *jus ad bellum* could conceivably recommend.

Law comes into this unhappy connection more as cover than cause. The causes why military operations sometimes spiral out of rational relationship with legitimate war aims are latent in the very natures of war and battle. They are part of the critical military historian's bread and butter. For example, John Keegan, in the preliminaries to his *Mask of Command*, remarks on the modern, post-Clausewitzian phenomenon that 'pupil officers' in Euro-American academies study books which 'preach a form of warfare that makes no room for political or diplomatic calculations at all'.[14] A reviewer of Andrew D. Lambert's *Crimean War* observes that 'when massive armies are locked in prolonged combat . . . the battle itself becomes the issue; resources and prestige are committed to a point which may be disproportionate to the strategic value of the particular theatre of war'.[15] The historian of the law of war has only to add the observation that,

---

[14] Penguin Books edn., 1988, p. 7.
[15] 'J.U.' in the *Times Literary Supplement* of 11 Oct. 1991, p. 32.

whatever law's difficulties in putting a brake upon such processes once they are under way, those difficulties must be the greater in proportion with the exclusion of legal and ethical considerations from debate about the purposes for which war is being fought. It is not only 'the other side' which is at risk when an embattled commander-in-chief insists that his only object is *to win*.

The Spirit of Humanitarianism and the Letter of Law

Contemporary law of war has become in some respects very complicated, but its innermost functional elements are the same as they always have been: to limit the cruelties and damages inflicted in armed conflict against specified opponents and to protect 'innocent' victims, and to do this by drawing lines between forms of attack that are permitted and forms that are not, between weapons that may be used and weapons that may not. The qualification 'against specified opponents' is worth noting. These essential restraints and prohibitions, which are the easier to miss for having generally been unwritten and unspoken, seem always to have varied in relation to the opponent in view and the calculated consequences of conflict with him. The ground rules for internal war might differ from those for external, those for conflicts within one's own culture, religion, or class from those for outside; ruses and perfidies permissible (even, laudable) against foreigners would be frowned on if practised against compatriots; and so on.

In its contemporary embodiment, this ancient, diffused, and infinitely adaptable idea of law in war has taken an odd turn. At the same time as it has become rather complicated in some of its upper-level compartments and entered into that enriching alliance with human rights law which has already been noticed, overall and by way of contrast it has become extremely simplified in two major respects. It has been universalized, regardless of regional, national, and other 'vertical' differences, and it has been 'horizontally' standardized. This standardization may be observed on three levels of application. Its peaks and high plateaux are the well-known and weighty body of law designed to apply to armed conflicts between States, a level at which human rights law is of little relevance. Lower down, on the slopes surrounding those heights, is the slighter but still clearly identifiable body of law (some of it, human rights law) designed to apply to the more serious sorts of violent conflicts within States. In the valleys lower still, dark and clouded for the most part, is the extensive but disjointed and much-argued-about body of law (much of it, human rights law) supposed to apply to all other, supposedly lesser internal violences.

Whether this stratification has helped or hindered the observance of humanitarian law, is perhaps open to question. It may be that legal gain (as the legal profession would deem it to be) has involved humanitarian loss. But the community of humankind has to do the best it can with what it has got. These developments have happened. They are historically explicable, as elements of the continually evolving international society of States. And they constitute the structure within which all serious exposition of the law and discussion of its implementations has to take place. A gap has opened therefore between the areas on which the law-minded like to linger and the areas which the humanitarian-minded find disturbing. For the law-minded, with the professional legal experts at their head, the most challenging and rewarding area is where the law looks most highly developed and elaborate: the high peaks of the Conventions and Protocols and their High Contracting Parties. That accordingly is what the bulk of IHL literature is about. The dirty work going on down the slopes and in the valleys figures less in the perspectives of lawyers and the books they write. For one thing, the amount of IHL which is, strictly speaking, applicable therein is so much smaller and more disputable; for another, it coexists there with human rights law, plentiful in quantity and presumed applicability but, compared with IHL, an inexperienced newcomer on the humanitarian stage of as yet unproved practical worth.

Turn however to the area of practical humanitarian endeavour, and things look very different, rather as the change of filters on a camera can give the same landscape warm or chilly aspects. The 'official' divisions between 'international' and 'non-international' fields of application, so firm and important on paper, on the ground look incomplete and perforated. Arguments about whether a war is of one sort or the other or a bit of both, and about whether particular non-international armed conflicts qualify for legal recognition as such, seem relatively immaterial. As examples elsewhere in this book copiously demonstrate, humanitarian observances are just as likely to occur where the legal expert is not prepared for them as they are likely not to occur where he is. War-fighting parties on the middle legal slopes can agree to borrow provisions from the top level, as the middle level's charter, Common Article 3 of the 1949 Conventions, expressly invites them to do: 'The Parties to the conflict should further endeavour to bring into force, by means of special agreements, all or part of the other provisions of the present Convention.' But parties on the bottom level, even if the conflict they are engaged in may not attain the distinction of 'Article 3 status', are by no means barred from doing the same, should they wish earnestly enough to do so and provided a generally acceptable neutral intermediary is ready to help them. In any case, belligerent parties don't have to study IHL books before they can experience humanitarian urges. The ICRC, which inevitably is the neutral intermediary most likely to serve, has long experience of arranging for the satisfaction of those urges wherever and whenever they occur. The modest 'right of initiative' which entitles it to offer its services in *any* painful circumstances seems neither more nor less likely to facilitate its usefulness on the slopes and in the valleys than when the Geneva Conventions grandly empower it to intervene on the heights. The ICRC's remarkable record shows it to be capable of fulfilling its mission at all levels of conflict, from the formal/straightforward to the irregular/ anarchic, but at no level, not even the highest, can it be sure of a reliable welcome.

Because humanitarian observances may occur at any of the levels by which IHL experts classify conflicts and because the observances that occur lower down are often explicitly in emulation of what goes on higher up, the discussion of 'methods and means' which follows disregards their conventional classification and assumes that they are applicable all over. My method here is simply to set out in material detail the logical implications of the several 'unofficial' miniature versions of the essentials of IHL which have recently been produced with the aim of encouraging and facilitating the adoption in lower-level conflicts of higher-level manners, methods, and means. The most ambitious and elaborate of them, published in the May–June 1991 issue of the *IRRC* and *AmJIL* 85 (1991) is a draft 'Declaration of Minimum Humanitarian Standards', promulgation of which by the UN is believed by its promoters to be the best way to spread its gospel.[16] The briefest is the first of them, 'Fundamental Rules of International Humanitarian Law Applicable in Armed Conflicts', which the Red Cross produced in 1978 and which fills less than one page in Roberts and Guelff; its principle is evidently that it can do all the good of which it is capable as a self-evidently 'unofficial' thumbnail sketch.

The fact that presentation of the latter, so excellent in its miniature way, has to be accompanied by heavy underlining of its 'informal and unofficial character' emphasizes the disadvantages accompanying high-level IHL's separate distinctness, and the wrong impressions given by it.[17] If some statements of law are formal and official, how seriously are informal and unofficial statements of it to be taken? The shaping of the answer to that question must be a matter of judgment, but in the 1990s

---

[16] A view not shared by everyone. A veteran Canadian expert, L. C. Green, opines that it 'would probably command even less respect than does the UDHR'. See *Columbia Journal of Transnational Law* 28 (1991), 852.   [17] Roberts and Guelff, 469.

it is likely to be more sympathetic and undogmatic than it would have been eighty, even only fifty years ago. No longer is it taken for granted almost universally that the only international law which matters is that which States have formalized by committing themselves to it in treaties made between themselves and in the decisions of their courts. One has to add the qualification 'almost universally' because the memory of international law's ancient universalist source never entirely faded. Thoughtful persons could sense its presence in the law of war, and it famously came out from the closet into the preamble to the fourth Hague Convention (1907): the so-called Martens clause with its reference to 'the principles of the law of nations as they result from the usages established among civilized peoples, from the laws of humanity, and the dictates of the public conscience'.

The Martens clause was, to begin with, not much more than a swallow announcing a summer still some way off. Much more attention has been paid to it in the second half-century of its life than was paid in the first. It attracted no significant attention until the public conscience of the victorious civilized peoples, establishing on ground as firm as possible the post-war trials of notoriously uncivilized enemies, found the idea of 'laws of humanity' peculiarly interesting and useful. In particular it added persuasiveness to the Nuremberg tribunals' judgment that the fourth Hague Convention was to be regarded as *customary* international law and to the movement of opinion which has gathered momentum since then, thus also to regard basic common parts of the Geneva Conventions.[18] The parallel and simultaneous crystallization of human rights law contributed to the impression, which has marked IHL literature ever since, that the Martens clause was an exceptional early statement of an idea whose time had now come.

With the ever-growing importance of the customary elements of IHL and their counterparts on the human rights side has come also a new interest in the potentially supportive content of a layer of law more fundamental still, variously described by those who are most closely concerned to elucidate it as 'peremptory norms of general international law' (alias *jus cogens*) and 'fundamental (or basic) human rights', from which emerge encouraging references to 'elementary [dictates or] considerations of humanity, even

---

[18] Thus the ICJ in the *Nicaragua* case, 1986. The most that can be made of this is made by Rosemary Abi-Saab, 'The "Geneva Principles" of International Law according to the ICJ', in *IRRC* 259 (1987), 367–75. Meron in *AmJIL* 81 (1987), 348–70 rather powerfully argues that the court went further than evidence permitted. Kalshoven's Farewell Address at Leiden, 3 Feb. 1989, incidentally shows him to share the same opinion. See also pp. 8–9, above.

more exacting in peace than in war'.[19] This then is the fertile soil in which 'informal and unofficial' statements of IHL may be received with more enthusiastic respect and serious intent than their prudent and (almost inevitably) 'officially' situated framers dare claim for them. Allowing the concept of 'the public conscience' to have some reality, one may certainly attribute to it the belief that 'the *core* of humanitarian law should be the same for all types of large-scale politically motivated violence'.[20]

Groups engaged in violent struggles within States sometimes try to observe humanitarian norms and more often criticize opponents for disregarding the same. Statesmen, commenting on other States' internal troubles, freely criticize governments and insurgents alike for using unacceptably odious (read, 'unlawful') methods and means. The public conscience was affronted when the Nicaraguan dictator's aeroplanes bombed residential parts of Matagalpa in 1979 and when Yugoslav/Serbian armed forces bombarded residential parts of Dubrovnik in 1991. The Iraqi despot's use of poison gas in 1988 against his own dissident subjects was denounced even more than his use of it against foreign enemies. Israel exchanges 'prisoners of war' (at extraordinarily unfavourable rates) with States which do not recognize its existence and with organizations it absolutely will not recognize. When the Provisional IRA kills British civilians, it sometimes excuses the killings as a mistake, 'the sort of thing that happens in war'; when it plants a large bomb under the military wing of a Belfast hospital, causing predictable damage to its civilian parts as well, a local politician voices the universal reaction by describing the deed as one 'that would be a war crime in any war'.[21] International law only knows refugees when they have crossed State frontiers, but the UN's humanitarian agencies deal equally with those who have not. 'Relief' is popularly expected to be allowed to reach 'civilians' in internal wars as well as international ones, and the bargaining, posturing, and manœuvring that accordingly goes on is the same in both cases. So long as the conduct of internal armed conflicts and violent social disturbances is sometimes accompanied by emphatic marks of respect for IHL norms and procedures, the humanitarian will leave it to the technical legal experts to worry over the question whether such-and-such a method or means, in such-and-such a situation, is 'legal' or

[19] For this line of argument as a whole, see the last ten years' writings of Theodor Meron; esp. relevant at this point is 'On a hierarchy of international human rights', in *AmJIL* 80 (1986), 1–23.

[20] These words are borrowed from the US's leading law-of-war academician of the last generation, Richard Baxter. They are reported by Meron in *AmJIL* 77 (1983) at 603.

[21] John Hume of the anti-unionist SDLP, on the BBC Radio 4 'Today' programme, 4 Nov. 1991. Full report in the *Independent*, 4 Nov. 1991, p. 3.

not. The rough-and-ready answer of the pragmatic humanitarian might be that, even if it is not 'legal', much is gained by behaving as if it were; and in any case, the fact that something is by every conceivable test 'illegal' does not, in the real world, mean that those responsible are likely to be brought to justice and to receive their just deserts.

8 | Methods and Means

Combatants, Non-Combatants, and Civilians

Restraint in the conduct of armed conflict being the purpose of laws and customs of war, wherever and whenever they are found, it follows as surely as night follows day that their basic principle must be the banning of methods and means which, if used, would negate that aim. War being the violent and inherently escalating thing that it is, the total absence of restraint can only lead to degrees of mutual slaughter and destruction which civilized societies have, on the whole, wished to avoid.[1] The adage, 'all's fair in love and war', gives as egoistic and unbalanced an idea of relations between the sexes as of relations between States and other politically purposive warring parties. Reckoning precisely what is fair and what is not fair has, indeed, often been a problem; the more so for having as its Siamese twin the problem of reckoning what to do if fair fighting promises defeat. Such however are among the problems which would-be fair fighters and their consciences have always had to live with. Laws and customs of war developed none the less, and in the earliest years of their codification bred this ungainly first statement of their fundamental principle: 'The right of belligerents to adopt means of injuring the enemy is not unlimited.'[2]

In that and in all its subsequent appearances, statement of the principle is immediately followed by short lists of deeds and devices singled out for particular prohibition, perhaps giving to the uninitiated the impression that it is to those methods and means alone, or (at any event) to them above all others, that this fundamental principle of limitation applies. The historic fact is very much otherwise. The statement of that fundamental principle concerning what violence could be done to 'the enemy' came long, long

---

[1] Such use of the word 'civilized' begs questions and raises hackles but I see no way to avoid it, nor do I see how to avoid the risk of offending readers content to describe as civilized, societies which believe it proper to fight wars of extermination.

[2] Article 22 of the 1907 Hague Regulations, which in Article 35 of AP1, 1977, becomes, 'In any armed conflict, the right of the Parties to the conflict to choose methods or means of warfare is not unlimited.' Its first appearance as an independent article appears to have been in the 1874 Brussels Project of an International Declaration concerning the Laws and Customs of War: 'Art. 12. The laws of war do not recognize in belligerents an unlimited power in the adoption of means of injuring the enemy.' This seminal document is printed in Schindler and Toman, 25–34.

after the achievement of a preliminary fundamental limitation: a consensus agreement among civilized States to restrict combat to combatants and to distinguish them, whom we still call combatants, from non-combatants, whom we now call civilians.

Legislation for what is ambitiously called the protection of civilians in wartime has gone very far since that fundamental distinction gained general acceptance. We saw in the middle part of the book how to the existing three Geneva Conventions was added a new fourth one for the protection of civilian persons under enemy occupation etc. Because the other great cause of civilian suffering which the Second World War had notably displayed—bombardment—was at that time hardly touched upon, it therefore joined weapons of mass (i.e. indiscriminate) destruction at the top of humanitarian lawyers' list of methods and means still to be dealt with. The business of the 1949 Diplomatic Conference had hardly been concluded before the ICRC took the first of the many steps it was to take over the next two decades 'for the Limitation of the Dangers Incurred by the Civilian Population in Time of War' (title of the Draft Rules it promulgated in the later 1950s).

It may be questioned whether that first step dated 5 April 1950 was a prudent one, and whether the ICRC was wise thereafter to become increasingly involved with what had hitherto been exclusively 'Hague law' matters. Its 1950 appeal to HCPs to the Geneva Conventions to hurry to reach agreement on the banning of atomic and other indiscriminate weapons was not an absolutely new departure—the Second World War had seen the ICRC confidentially begging governments to stop area- and terror-bombing—but in the international political atmosphere of that year it was bound to be taken up by the USSR-orchestrated 'peace campaign' and to cause the Committee to appear to be taking sides in the cold war.[3] Because of that suspicion, because the US and British governments (and presumably their NATO allies also) believed that the ICRC was involving itself with matters beyond its proper remit and competence, and because the uses and control of nuclear energy constituted an unprecedentedly awkward complex of new questions which, it was reasonable to argue, should be handled in new ways, the 1956 Draft Rules, approved by the 1957 International Red Cross Conference, made no headway among the governments intended to be impressed by them. Within the Red Cross movement and the legal circles connected to it, however, those Draft Rules remained a

---

[3] A high official in the foreign-operations department of the American Red Cross, the collective thinking of which usually ran close to that of the State Department, told a colleague, 'It looks to me like a Swiss Government-International Committee plea for better relations between themselves and the Soviet Union.' AM RC archives, RG4, 101.11 G Cs 1949, no. 4; W. de St Aubin to Gaile Galub, 9 May 1950.

document to conjure with. No vision of IHL can more powerfully have moved the minds of those who, through the 1960s, pressed ever more strongly for its authoritative updating to match the demands of ever more distressing varieties of wars and war techniques. Those pressures, which made themselves felt also along the human rights channels of the UN, received their reward in the series of UN and ICRC conferences and reports which culminated in the two Additional Protocols in 1977 and the Convention on Conventional (*sic*) Weapons three years later.

The first Additional Protocol (which, let it not be forgotten, is nominally designed for application only in international armed conflicts) carries to its logical conclusion the concern to protect civilians in wartime which has headed the IHL agenda since the Second World War. It perfects the classic combatant—civilian distinction by paring down to a minimum the combatant category and at the same time maximizing the civilian one. Everybody who is not a combatant is declared to be a civilian, every object which is not military is declared to be civilian; in cases of doubt, the latter protected status is generally to be assumed. Civilians are advised that they will retain their protected status 'unless and for such time as they take a direct part in hostilities', i.e. in the event of their so taking part in guerrilla warfare and living to tell the tale, they can go back to being civilians afterwards. Combatants are warned not to pretend to be civilians (e.g. in order to escape enemy notice) unless they feel they absolutely have to, in which event they must not expect, if captured, to enjoy all the advantages of prisoner-of-war status.[4]

An attentive reading of the text supported by an informed reading between its lines will indeed reveal that civilians cannot expect war to leave them inviolate and that they may be as much at risk from their own side (should it, e.g. place them close to military targets) as from the enemy's. The casual and uninstructed reader however may pick up a different impression from such headings as 'General Protection against Effects of Hostilities' (Part IV, sect. 1) and such sentences as 'The civilian population and individual civilians shall enjoy general protection against dangers arising from military operations' (start of Article 51). The popularization of humanitarian law has brought with it risks as well as benefits, all the more so for its being a body of law in which, as this part of the book amply demonstrates, the hard and the soft have become inseparable and to the lay

[4] That is my summary way of extracting the gist from Art. 44's notorious ambiguities and confusions. Readers wishing to check up on me and to make sense of it for themselves, after taking the obvious first step of studying the relevant pages in the two authoritative commentaries, will appreciate Aldrich's exegesis in *AmJIL* 75 (1981), 764–83 at 773–4, and Greenwood's remarks in *Israel Yearbook on Human Rights*, 19 (1989), 187–207 at 203.

mind indistinguishable. The description 'international humanitarian law', which the Red Cross and Crescent movement successfully inserted into popular usage, sounds less grim and paradoxical than the traditional law of war which it has replaced. This was no doubt its intended effect. One may however wonder whether it has been an unmixed blessing.

Widened knowledge and appreciation of IHL has brought with it the risk that words, which mean one thing to the (presumably) war-seasoned lawyers whose stock-in-trade they are, will mean another thing to humanitarian enthusiasts and sections of the general public who may not well understand the realities of contemporary war and warfare. What can members of the public do but attach to words their plain and ordinary meanings? Chapter headings in Conventions and Protocol, for example, which announce the 'repression' of breaches, abuses, and infractions and describe in great detail how this is to be done must give the impression that breaches, abuses, and infractions are actually likely to be repressed, whereas the fact is that while the vast majority of such breaches etc. are never even investigated, the very few which are brought to light and more or less properly punished are dealt with under national military auspices, not obviously Geneva ones. And the same, it is suggested, must be true of what is said in the Conventions and Protocol about 'protection' of civilians.

'Protection' is in fact a term of legal art. It is the ICRC's golden word describing the work the Geneva Conventions authorize it to do for the better protection of the interests of specified categories of persons menaced or victimized by armed conflict. The same word is used in relation to wounded, sick, and shipwrecked combatants and to combatants who have been taken prisoner, and in those connections makes good enough sense, as it does also in respect of enemy (or 'occupied') civilians who have been interned. In those contexts it is realistically achievable and it has a moral integrity which is not so apparent in its other uses. But civilians at large, civilians in general: how far they can actually enjoy the protection it promises must largely depend, as it always has done, on circumstances, politics, personalities, accident, luck, and so on; things which the soldier never forgets, but which the civilian hardly ever remembers. (The Red Cross's programme of 'dissemination' of IHL does *not* include 'war studies'.) Civilians, in AP1's blanket definition of them, cannot in most wars be protected in the plain and ordinary sense of the word. What the legal instruments offer in real terms is no more than a reminder of the ideal aimed at, the hope that circumstances may exceptionally allow of its achievement, and a helpful broad array of principles, rules, and practical advices as to how that may be made more likely. 'Protection' must therefore be understood in relative terms. Part of the business of the remainder of this chapter is to explain why.

The endeavour to distinguish combatants from civilians and thus to improve the latters' chances of protection in wartime has become the driving concern of contemporary IHL development. The line of distinction has been drawn sharper than ever before, but the difficulties of observing it remain as marked as ever. They may even have become worse. The official legal definition of civilian has itself become so awkwardly questionable that the case for permanently parenthesizing the word retains a certain force. Consideration for the reader urges adoption of the simpler usage; the reader is however requested to remember that the question remains an open one.

It will be well to begin this gloomy and (so the writer fears) unpopular scan of the emotive heart of the subject with a brief recapitulation of what was dealt with more fully in Part I. To call it the heart of the subject is no misnomer. This is its affecting and compassionate side, called into existence along with the recognition by those on its prudential and self-interested side that there were categories of nominally 'enemy' human beings whom it was possible and desirable not to hurt, persons whose degree of non-involvement in the struggle or whose irrelevance to it commonly led to their characterization as 'innocent'. So many of them clearly could be 'innocent' or utterly unthreatening—infants, disabled, ancients in all circumstances; women, children, and old folk in many—that it has always been a matter of genuine regret for warriors working within the standards of civilization that the entire exclusion of civilians from wartime hurt and hardship could be guaranteed only in exceptional circumstances, when for example campaigns took place in howling deserts or desolate mountain ranges, or on islands inhabited principally by penguins and sheep.

But civilians' remoteness from land- or sea-battles might not save them from involvement in those battles' preliminaries and aftermaths. It is a relatively recent development in the history of warfare that the armies of some countries have become able to transport and feed themselves instead of doing so at the expense of local populations. When armies are not fighting formal battles (which must be for much of the time) they are likely to be moving through enemy territory or forcefully occupying it. When navies are not battling at sea (which means for most of the time, perhaps for all of it) they are likely to be intercepting commerce and blockading coastlines and probably doing some bombardment as well. On such occasions, so familiar in the histories of land and sea warfare alike, the lives and properties of civilians were almost inevitably at risk, and, to the extent that the enemy's wealth and war-making capacity was embodied in them, intentionally so.

Blockades of enemy ports and sieges of his defended places have therefore figured considerably in the legal history of war precisely because, to an exceptional extent, they could offer opportunities for humanitarian discrimination. Civilians penned up alongside the soldiers in such places, especially if they were of no economic significance, invited humanitarian sympathy. Should they be allowed release from the dangers of bombardment and starvation or should they not? The question was one on which views might differ within the walls as well as without. Soldiers can be just as reluctant to admit that the civilians on their own side do not wholeheartedly support what is professed to be done on those civilians' behalf, as they can be quick to suppose that civilians on the other side actually do support it. In relation to the sieges, blockades, and bombardments of Genoa in 1800, for example, of Atlanta in 1864, Paris six years later, Le Havre in 1944, Vukovar and Dubrovnik in 1991, the same points were at issue. Could the respective commanders have allowed civilians to escape without seriously limiting their military options, and, in the event that they could have, were they criminally culpable for not having done so?

The inhabitants of blockaded or besieged places apart, the civilians so far imagined for the purpose of argument have been persons of wholly 'innocent' kind, incapable of hostile or resistant activity, unfortunates finding themselves in areas of armed conflict without their knowledge and against their will, unrecognizable as 'enemies' except through the distorting lenses of barbarous or fanaticized mentalities. With this core of the current definition, there should be no room for quarrel. Around the core however can be seen a variety of civilians who are not so evidently innocent in the same sense and who may more or less effectively be 'enemies', whose moral entitlement to exclusion from attack or the risks of attack is not so clear. Their inclusion in the current blanket definition is the outcome of two centuries of professional self-respect, humanitarian endeavour, and politico-legislative response to it: the principal landmarks along the road to 1977 being (as was amply shown in Part I) Rousseau's striking assertion in the 1760s of an unbridgeable conceptual divide between non-combatants and combatants, and the St Petersburg Declaration's restrictive definition, a hundred years later, of a belligerent's war capability. Thus was the idea of the non-combatant shifted from that of a person who formed no part of an enemy country's armed strength and made no contribution to it, towards that of an enemy person not dressed in a markedly military way and not enlisted in a designated military organization. Thus also was it established that no *legal* distinction existed between, for example, the peasant in the forest-clearing and the industrial engineer in the suburban villa, or between the politically impotent civilian population of a pre-industrial society and the democratically empowered civilian population of a highly developed one.

It seems to me that this legal development is not without moral and political difficulties. It has produced rules of law which may not correspond with the moral and political realities of societies in armed conflict. It marks as much of a going-beyond common-sense reasonableness in one direction as the ancient undifferentiating perceptions of enemy populations were a falling-short of it in the other. Civilian subjects of enemy States were in former times and places commonly viewed as falling entirely into the disposal of the victor in war, to be massacred, enslaved, and uprooted at his discretion. We have seen in Part I how those primitive severities came to be reckoned undesirable and condemned as inhumane. Distinction was made between the active and the passive enemy and was found to be reasonable when read as a distinction between those who, whether in military uniform or not (as was especially the case with the guerrilla and the privateer), actively promoted or engaged in hostilities and those who (normally not in uniform) did not. Notwithstanding the embarrassments and disgraces accompanying the rough requirements of campaigning in enemy territory and the severities and scandals so often inseparable from blockades and sieges, the great distinction was considered sufficiently observable by eighteenth- and nineteenth-century professional armies (when they were simply fighting one another, which was how the ruling élites preferred land war to be conducted) for the distinction to be placed at the law-of-war's centre, where it remains still. What happened at sea was of less significance; the professional activities of the very few navies capable of conducting effective blockades attracted, by comparison, little attention and in any case were, before 1914, unimaginable on the scale they were to achieve even only two years later.

The very same years that saw the canonization of that distinction saw also, however, the multiplication of problems in its observance. Difficulties and complications have crowded in upon it, as already noted: mass enthusiasms for war-making and the accompanying difficulty of reckoning how far they are spontaneous, how far contrived; the mobilization of whole societies and economies for war and the industrialization of warfare which made it necessary; and alongside them, paradoxically or (one might consider) contradictorily, the spread of humanitarian sentiment, its establishment as an accepted element in democratic political programming, and its use by those who could claim the title of civilian to claim the widening web of protections that went along with it.

For men entrusted with the serious task of fighting and winning wars, and above all for those who took seriously their traditional concern to spare non-combatants, these developments brought perplexing difficulties. On the one hand, the tendency of the law and the aspirations of the parties most vocally interested in it were towards the maximization of non-combatant protection, for which moreover there was the good objective ground that war's new weapons of mass destruction and means of delivering them made it horribly easy to maximize non-combatant *non*-protection. On the other hand, the non-combatant or, as he was increasingly being known, the civilian, was in some ways less easy to recognize than in the past. Mass politics and industrialization were creating so many new ways for the civilian to relate constructively to the making of war that the concept of an undifferentiated civilian, towards which the 'progressive development' of IHL was tending, found itself teetering on the edge of a credibility gap.

The entirely and indelibly 'innocent' (as defined above) remained as innocent as ever; but what about adults who shared in the political and psychological encouragement and support of war? Was it reasonable, was it right that they should be spared all but accidental ill-effects of a war for which they did not conceal their support or for which, as was usually the case, their support was credibly claimed by their ruling representatives? That was the credibility gap in its political aspect. On its more economic side there was the fact that civilians could be closely, even vitally involved on modern war's supply side; involved above all in the invention, manufacture, and distribution of all the material stuff necessary to the conduct of hostilities and the maintenance of all the plant necessary to the functioning of modern organizations. Was it reasonable, was it right that such persons should share the same protections and be entitled to the same immunities as the indisputably 'innocent' ones? The apparent unreasonableness and injustice of it so much struck some writers between the wars that they suggested the introduction of an intermediate category of 'quasi-civilians'.[5]

There were, there are, no neat answers to this question. The only way the indelibly 'innocent' can be protected from the risks attaching to the

---

[5] This episode is noticed and criticized with his customary acuteness by Henri Meyrowitz in 'Le bombardement stratégique d'après le Protocole additionel aux Conventions de Genève', in *Zeitchrift für ausländisches öffentliches Recht und Völkerrecht*, 41 (1981), 1–68 at 21–4. He points the finger particularly at Spaight. That the idea got nowhere was perhaps less because it was unappealing than because it seemed otiose, the need it purported to address being to some extent manageable by exercise of the principle of proportionality, and (if bombardment was involved) under cover of the excuse of 'unavoidable collateral damage'.

arguably less so is by complete physical separation. This is not as fanciful as it may sound. History shows non-combatants now and then being evacuated from defended places in advance of expected attacks, and criticism of attackers who have heartlessly forced them to return. In some European countries in the Second World War attempts were made to evacuate all children and many of their mothers from cities and neighbourhoods that were likely to be attacked. The ICRC has repeatedly put forward proposals for, and the Geneva Conventions contain articles framed to facilitate, the formation of well-marked demilitarized or 'neutral' zones, civilian reservations as it were, to which civilians could be moved by belligerent parties' agreement. Prospective belligerents have never so far agreed in advance to the designation of such major zones, but the ICRC has quite often succeeded in arranging during armed conflicts for the establishment of minor ones *ad hoc* when local situations have permitted it.

This zeal for the protective segregation of the most 'innocent' sort of civilians, which marks one extremity of the range of opinions about the problem of civilians in wartime, is matched at the other extremity by several levels of inability or unwillingness to see that a problem exists. Parties possessed by collective ideologies and passions may find it difficult or simply impossible to discriminate between categories of individuals within the undifferentiated alien group towards which they feel hostility. What Nazi Germany did towards the extermination of Europe's Jews and gypsies was only a peculiarly businesslike, intense, and subsequently well-publicized implementation of an idea which has recurrently appeared throughout world history, not least in those chapters of it dealing with the establishment of the European empires and the United States of America.[6] Not biological but religious or political ideology can prompt scarcely less total approaches to the extermination of fellow nationals categorized as class enemies, heretics, or irredeemable 'subversives' by ruthless regimes, conspicuously, communist ones (Lenin's and Stalin's USSR, Pol Pot's Kampuchea), but recent episodes in the histories of Iran, Iraq, Syria, Pakistan, Indonesia, Guatemala, El Salvador, Yugoslavia, and Sudan remind us that regimes of other complexions can have similar ideas. In some of these latter cases, the characteristics of clan and tribe can be seen to contribute to the indiscriminately exterminatory process. They appear to form an essential part of it in the aggravated African circumstances thus described by Alex de Waal.

---

[6] 'The Germans probably exterminated more intensively, and the Anglo-Saxons more extensively than other peoples,' concluded Martin Wight in his valuable section on this humbling subject in ch. 4 of his *International Theory: The Three Traditions* (1991) at p. 62.

Violent clashes over resources such as wells, pastures and farmland are all familiar from African history . . . The advent of modern automatic weapons . . . has introduced an element of inflation into the established principles of reciprocal limited homicide. It is now possible, and not uncommon, for one group to engage in neighbourly genocide. Traders who need to protect monopolies in shrinking markets make new strategic alliances with rural communities, inflaming the cycle of violence. . . . Wars are fought against the economic base of the populace . . . Civilians, including women and children, are equally targets of attack as are [sic] armed men.[7]

Thus, in some of the most impoverished of countries, is all-out war found to be practised against civilians in the manner of some of the richest.

The current law regarding civilian protection must therefore appear less than wholly satisfactory to enquirers with such matters as natural justice and political realism on their minds (let alone guerrilla warfare, which presents awful problems of another sort, to be dealt with in due course). Some war-making mentalities perceive no civilians to be protected; the law's distinction between civilian and combatant is unreal to them. Others perceive some so-called civilians who ought not to be protected; the more imaginative of them might go on to argue that, by the same token, some so-called combatants better deserve protection. All can agree that the nature of war is such that even civilians who undoubtedly deserve protection cannot in fact be guaranteed it.

What, then, are we provisionally to think about this giant branch of IHL before we go on to see how it works in practice and selective detail? First, its imperfections are more easily understood when we remember that, in common with the entire IHL tree, it is a product, not of lucid logic or consultant expertise, but of history and politics; rough history, one might add, and (especially in the 1968–77 phase) tough politics. Second, although the absoluteness of its blanket distinction between combatants and civilians is open to all sorts of objections, a straight line has as much to be said in its favour as a fuzzy one, and what is oversimplified may be a better humanitarian working-tool than what has become endlessly complicated. Prohibitions so absolute, and in some particular respects unreasonable, will sometimes be broken, but at least the fact of the breach will be clear and its causes exposed to investigation. The fuzzier the line and the further the spread of small print around it, the more opportunities must it offer to the risk-taker and the limit-stretcher, and the greater the risks that fog will hamper the investigator. The dilemma in any case is a common one.

---

[7] From a review article in the *Times Literary Supplement*, 13 Sept. 1991, p. 5.

Ordinary peacetime criminal investigators, faced with a dead body, have no initial quarrel with the blanket definition 'homicide' although they know that it must subsequently be refined into something more specific. They are called to the scene because there is evidence of 'killing', not of a *crime passionel* class 3c'.

Defining 'the civilian' is one thing; protecting civilians in war, is another. My initial sketch of the current definition was prudently glossed by an intimation that the protections highlighted in that 1977 instrument have to be read in context with the less conspicuous specifications indicating, more by implication than otherwise, what the civilian must do or *not* do if he is to retain his protected status; likewise, and more directly, what belligerents must do, and must *not* do, if civilians are to enjoy the protections the law lays down for them.

Whatever may be civilians' understanding of their position and personal inclinations regarding it, their options are likely to be limited once armed conflict has begun to rage around them. The time for adult civilians to consider war's bearings upon them and to make their opinions about it felt is before war has begun. Even at that safer stage, freedom of choice may be limited. Female civilians' freedom of choice almost always seems to have been minimal, and in most cultures still evidently is so. But it may be a mistake to suppose that male civilians are necessarily better placed. The international dimension of politics is notoriously less susceptible to popular understanding and control than the domestic. The political alliances and connections which largely determine involvement in external troubles may theoretically be open to the influence of democratic political processes, where they exist, but even in the most authentic-seeming democracies the making of decisions which crucially determine the directions and characters of future wars—decisions for instance about weapons procurement, military training, strategic planning, and targeting criteria—are well known to contain reserved and secret areas guarded by military authorities and by their established political protectors on grounds respectively of professional autonomy and national security. Nations moreover, whatever may be their preparations for war or expectations of it, do not always get the war they want; nations that do not want war or expect it, may nevertheless find it coming upon them. The programmes of IHL instruction pursued (under their name for it, 'dissemination') by the International Red Cross and Red Crescent organizations make the beginnings of a base for the better appreciation by civilians of the range of possibilities open to them, which only needs the addition of some elementary education in political science to make it realistically useful. War, when it happens, is always rich in shocks and bungles, even for the political and military planners who are supposed to understand the most about it. Persons who think instructedly ahead from the civilian point of view cannot expect immunity from shocks and bungles, but they will nevertheless perhaps have been able to apply their lever to the unrolling of events and they may certainly be saved from surprise by them.

IHL's principal instruction to civilians is that, so far as their chances of protection turn on their own inclinations (rather than on the inclinations of the combatants, let alone the hazards and accidents of war), they must strive to make sure that the distinction between themselves and the combatants is maintained. When we review the instructions given by IHL to combatants, we shall find this clearly spelled out. Civilians will not find it spelled out to them in the same way. The explanation is partly historical, partly ideological.

Historically, it has to be said that civilians were a minor consideration for the men at the centre of the business of making the law of land warfare through most of its formative centuries. (Maritime warfare was quite different, but the differences need not be explored here.) The modern humanitarian eye delights to notice how religious, philosophical, and humanist concerns combined to clarify the concept of the non-combatant and to get it included in statements of war's laws and customs. The main determinants of the law's development however were the practices observed by professional combatants towards each other, and the readiness of political élites to back them. It was of crucial importance to those combatants to know who they were and how they were to behave. They relied on identifying one another by uniform and bearing, and each side had some confidence that the other would fight by the mutually understood rules. Their image of war and their idea of its laws and customs were understandably self-concerned. Civilians appeared only around the edges of this frame. Prudent civilians who had any choice in the matter would scramble out of the frame altogether. Only imprudent, impulsive, and uninformed ones would deliberately scramble into it. Defence of cottage and field, wife and daughters, village and township made the classic occasions for confusion of roles. Patriotism began at the garden-gate. After the event, which all too often ended in tragedy, there might be debate as to whether civilians who had thus taken up arms might be called fortunate, because they got away with it, or foolhardy, because they didn't. Nothing was more likely to dehumanize the conduct of soldiers than to find themselves being shot at by persons who, by the standards of their professional culture, had no right to do it. Professionals did not readily understand that non-professionals might think they had rights too, and very easily failed to see how such rights might be respected in wartime circumstances. Resistance-fighters, guerrillas, hostile populations, and local heroes made difficulties for the law of war which it never found ways fully to resolve. They were the topics which most regularly brought international conferences on IHL to irreconcilable points of view or shaky compromises, and they still are.

In ideological terms, IHL's present inability to give civilians any more directly constructive advice than an assurance that they are more clearly defined then ever before invites explanation as the dead-centre product of the co-existence of the two opposite war-philosophies which it has to accommodate. On the one hand there is the polished professional military philosophy sketched in the preceding paragraph, within which combatant and civilian were clearly differentiated and civilians needed to be given no more than an intimation that, so long as they kept out of the firing line, combatants would not seek to bring them into it. On the other hand, there is the revolutionary armed-struggle philosophy formalized by Leninism and Maoism out of universal popular and peasant experience, according to which the distinction between civilians and combatants is flexible, dispensable, and in the last resort reducible to a propaganda ploy. From neither of these philosophies can the protection-seeking civilian derive much joy. The traditionalist professional indeed, if he is true to the better side of his tradition, may respect civilians as civilians whenever he comes personally upon them. But one of his ways of doing that is to move them wholesale out of his field of operations, which can be very unpleasant for them; and in any case he is accustomed to put them at risk whenever his ideas of necessity and proportionality tell him that such-and-such military operations in their locality have to be undertaken.

IHL has no advice to give civilians in such circumstances other than to make sure they do not let themselves be mistaken for combatants, and to keep their heads down. IHL is even less helpful when the civilian's problem is revolutionary and ethnic warfare. In these circumstances, his problem is quite opposite. Instead of having to persuade the military command that he really is not a combatant, he now has to persuade it that he ought not to be made to be one. Revolutionary fighters, even supposing them to be of personally humane disposition, tend to regard some categories of civilians as within the struggle—landowners, bankers, and shopkeepers, for example; public officials like mayors and headmen, priests and teachers; all persons regarded as 'class enemies'—at the same time as their philosophy may instruct them that civilians generally are no less expendable than combatants in service of the great cause to which all are committed together.

The fortunes of the civilian in wartime, then, depend very largely on how he is perceived by combatants and how the law works on combatants' perceptions: whether it sharpens or blurs them, and how its concern for the safety of civilians relates to combatants' dedication to their proper business, the trial of strength with the combatants ranged against them. Civilian protection has become the most widely perceived end of IHL: its means, the guidance and restraint of combatants as to what they may and what they may not do.

Permissions and Prohibitions

The current law on civilian protection is comprehensively laid out in AP1. Its appearance of novelty is deceptive. Most of its substance falls well within the parameters of what has become accepted as customary law. There has been development but there has not been change. The reactions of non-ratifying States to this part of the Protocol are therefore of much less moment than they are in relation to the innovative parts. There is no picking and choosing among the contents of customary law, though lawyers cannot be stopped from arguing about what the contents actually mean.[8] Fundamental principles remain what they were accepted to be when the law of war underwent its big reconstruction in the later 1940s. The spelling out of what those principles mean in practice, the attachment of illustrative detail, and the filling-in of gaps in the existing law is expected to reduce the extent to which the law is misunderstood, evaded, and ignored.

The Protocol's plentiful prohibitions, as might be expected, are mostly to do with attacks on civilians and 'civilian objects'. Its permissions have strictly to do with attacks on combatants and 'military objectives', and are accompanied by an array of provisos and precautions governing how they may be carried out. At the centre of this web of wordings is one of the Protocol's most significant developments, a definition of what a military objective actually is, and how to recognize one when you see it.

Tucked away in the second paragraph of Article 52, and hidden under that Article's title, 'General Protection of Civilian Objects', is this definition: 'In so far as objects are concerned, military objectives are limited to those

---

[8] 'It is a codification of the customary law, which it expands, without detracting from various opinions on the scope of one or other of the rules of customary law', was how the ICRC prudently described it in a Working Document on Relations between Pre-existing Customary Law and Protocol I, presented to the 1983 San Remo Round Table on IHL.

objects which by their nature, location, purpose or use make an effective contribution to military action and whose total or partial destruction, capture or neutralization, in the circumstances ruling at the time, offers a definite military advantage.'

This represents the achievement at last of a need that has been felt with increasing urgency for a long time. The urgency has become more marked in exact correspondence with the destructive capabilities of weapons and explosives, which makes the problem peculiarly a twentieth-century one, but in principle it goes back time out of mind. Military professionals and the moralists and lawyers who seek to guide them have had ideas about objects and persons that may legitimately be attacked for as long as they have had ideas about persons and objects that may not. Because sieges and bombardments by their very nature confused the two categories, there was (as we have seen) recurrent argument about the proper ways to conduct them.[9] But where it was a case of (more or less) precise attack on identifiable targets, there was no confusion or argument. The principle was uncontested, that they could only be legitimately attacked if they were definitely 'military'.

Whether the accepted fact of that general principle was enough to secure the end it had in view, and whether its end might not be better achieved by a sharper definition, became a serious question in the early years of the present century. What made it so seems to have been the conjuncture of improved means of destruction, industrialization of warfare, and heightened sensitivity about civilian suffering. Attempts were made to insert definitions of legitimate military objectives into the legal texts, and two of the earliest (and least ambitious) met with varying modest measures of success.[10] The experiences of the Second World War might have been expected to move the question to the head of the reformers' agenda. The powers of what were now called weapons of mass destruction were terribly obvious. Equally obvious were the consequences of leaving the translation of principle into practice to the untutored judgment (or the unconcerned indifference) of commanders and, where they shared in the selection of targets, politicians. But instead of going to the top of the agenda, the question went to the bottom. Victors had become as much implicated in it

---

[9] It is significant that the British 1914 *Manual*'s chapter on the Laws and Usages of War, para. 125, unblinkingly stuck to the conventional doctrine: 'There is no rule which compels the commander of an investing force to allow all non-combatants, or even women, children, aged, sick and wounded, or subjects of neutral powers, to leave the besieged locality. The fact that non-combatants are besieged together with combatants, and that they have to endure the same hardships, may and often does exercise pressure on the authorities to surrender.'

[10] i.e. the 9th of the 1907 Hague Conventions (Concerning Bombardment by Naval Forces in Time of War) and the 1923 Hague Draft Rules of Aerial Warfare. Both are printed by Roberts and Guelff.

as vanquished. Any move that seemed to equate careless, callous, or blanket targeting with war crime was politically impossible. We have already seen how the matter hardly figured at all in the war-crimes trials discussed in Part II, and attempts to bring it within the scope of the new Geneva Conventions were thwarted.

Had these events of the later 1940s constituted the whole of the difficulty in its way, the question of defining the military objective might have been reopened, as the ICRC anxiously wished it to be, once the new Conventions were in place, and the principal business of the war-crimes trials accomplished. Another difficulty of another kind however at the very same time came to darken the sky. Just when one old sort of war practice had come within measurable distance of condemnation by international consensus as intolerable, another entirely new one appeared which threatened to be a hundred times more so. The atomic bomb had been invented and used, and the onset of the Cold War spoiled the chances (admittedly slight but not unimaginable) of its being put under such international controls as would prevent it from further development. States rich and ambitious enough to acquire this new megaweapon did not dare forgo the opportunity. So long as only one power possessed The Bomb, it was held *in terrorem* over that power's enemies. As soon as the chief of those enemies acquired The Bomb too, the two superpowers held it *in terrorem* over each other. The old doctrine of deterrence had acquired its terrifying contemporary nuclear meaning.

The variety and succession of strategic doctrines by which the possessors explained to themselves, their enemies, and the world at large how they proposed to use The Bomb—or rather, *not* to use it, for use and non-use were curiously equated in this rational–irrational discourse—need not be gone into here. What however must be noticed is that the debate about use or threat of use of the nuclear weapon in the Cold War could not be conducted in terms of the classic law of war. The Bomb's first use in the extraordinary circumstances of mid-1945 and as the culmination of the extraordinary happenings of the previous five years was perhaps (the point continues to be controversial) explicable within those terms. The forms of use that came into discussion by 1950 went entirely beyond them, and have for the most part remained so ever since. Nothing in the long history of the law of war, and most certainly nothing in its modernized appearance as IHL, could helpfully grapple with weapons as massively and indiscriminately (and environmentally) destructive as the first generations of nuclear weapons had to be, or with such explanations of their use as 'mutual assured destruction'.

It was possible to make connection with the *jus ad bellum*. War of such a sort as was envisaged was beyond rational justification, and any measures that stopped it happening, even the most irrational-seeming ones, could be welcomed and tortuously justified. But with the *jus in bello*, there was no connection except the formality of a suggestion that the use of The Bomb in the mutually annihilating scenarios envisaged would be justifiable under the description of 'reprisal'. Respect for civilized proprieties required constant reference to international law but it was to other areas of it than IHL that the international community had to look for resolution of the enormous problems posed by the possession and proliferation of nuclear weapons. Arms control and disarmament became a separate area of conferences, agreements, and treaties focused on the nuclear menace and producing its own responses, in its own specialized terms, to IHL's concerns: strategic arms reduction, mutual balanced force reduction, verification, confidence-building, and so on—terms not to be found in IHL's glossary, but not incapable of seeming to indicate cautious, piecemeal movement towards some of IHL's goals.

The effect of all this on IHL's movement towards the definition of military objectives was to delay and aggravate it. The major military powers found themselves, or allowed themselves to become, wedded to weapons of mass destruction to which, in the earlier and coarser stages of their development, no conventional definition of military objective was relevant. Some of the earlier responses to IHL's challenge included the suggestion that conventional definitions had been made irrelevant by State practice during the Second World War, i.e. that the grim pre-war prophets of city and civilian bombing had been proved right, that weapons of mass destruction were here to stay, and that the armed forces dedicated to their use had nothing to be ashamed of. By no means did all justifiers of the threat of massive and nuclear bombardment take so sanguine a view of the matter. Possession of nuclear weapons was not incompatible with purpose to put them under lock and key whenever that could safely be done. Refinement of weaponry and reconsideration of strategic doctrine made it possible by the later 1960s for the USA so far to rejoin the legal mainstream as to say in 1968, when the programme for IHL's updating was being launched in the UN, that 'There are indeed principles of law relative to the use of weapons; and these principles apply as well to the use of nuclear and similar [read, biological and chemical] weapons.'[11] But the USA was joined by the UK and France in making it a condition of participation in the updating conferences, when

---

[11] From a statement made in the General Assembly, cited in Bothe, Partsch, and Solf, 191.

they got going in the 1970s, that none of the business transacted at them or rules established by them should be relevant to the use of nuclear weapons, which, besides being already subject to 'the present principles of international law', were 'the subject of separate negotiations and agreements'.[12]

Whether a State could accept 'principles' and decline to accept 'rules' deduced from them was only one of the many aspects of this business which enraged anti-nuclear enthusiasts and provided much happy mileage for legal controversialists.[13] For pro-nuclear parties, the distinction made sense enough, given the strange situation that actually had to be dealt with; and the distinction seems to matter less after the passage of fifteen years and the successful conclusion of several of those 'separate negotiations and agreements' which, in 1977, could only be sensed beyond the horizon. The question, whether the Protocol's rules regarding military objectives and the management of attacks on them apply to the use of conventional weapons only or to nuclear and other 'unconventional' weapons as well, will not be further explored. The rules themselves however reward all the exploration there is time for.

The definition of military objectives lies at the centre of a web of rules designed to regulate attacks, to prohibit those which are pointless or merely vicious, and to limit the damages done by those which are ill-conceived or ill-executed. The Protocol lightens the scene of its rules with the statement of a few principles but allows no glimpse of the philosophy which sustains and explains the whole. No more than the Geneva Conventions to which it is additional does the Protocol explain the point of the rules. It is a legal instrument, and in its finished form it reads like the work of lawyers writing for lawyers. The fact that theirs was only one of several professions participating in the formative process does not alter the fact that everyone knew that the ultimate test of every sentence was its ability to 'stand up in court'. Some of the rules are expressed in such contorted language, and others are so closely tied to a concealed context, that their point cannot be understood without such guidance as international lawyers take for granted: the *travaux préparatoires*, the 'negotiating history', and the official commentary. They cannot be expected to become intelligible to the

---

[12] From the understanding expressed at the consensus adoption of the Protocol, cited Bothe, Partsch, and Solf, 189.

[13] The relation between principles and rules is of course of interest throughout the whole law-of-war field. One anonymous, and evidently expert and experienced, reader of my typescript observed, apropos of the principles–rules distinction in general, that significant differences probably resulted from whether commanders thought in terms of *principles* or *rules*—and whether they had lots of legal advisers around them, to make them think primarily in terms of the latter!

other most interested parties—armed forces at various levels, politicians, diplomats, bureaucrats, humanitarian IGOs, and NGOs—and to be, so to speak, internalized by them, except by translation into their own non-legal terms.

Let us therefore preface examination of these rules with a reminder of the philosophy to which they owe their being. In that philosophy, the importance of avoiding civilians is twofold. There is the simply humanitarian ground that it is *good*, i.e. ethically admirable, humanly worthy, and, to the minds of the law makers, 'natural', not to hurt fellow human beings unless you absolutely have to, and, with the same qualification, good also to avoid damaging civilian property, especially if it is of cultural interest. And there is the utilitarian ground ('artificial' by comparison with the other) that hurting civilians and their property is *pointless*; civilians being theoretically of no consequence in a military contest between armed forces, which is IHL's rock-bottom understanding of what armed conflict is.

It is worth remarking, *en passant*, that this philosophy has become so deeply embedded in the unspoken assumptions of IHL that the treaty texts nowhere state it. It has not appeared in any such text since the 1860s. Its absence may be thought regrettable. How are civilians, without it, to understand the rationale of their separate status and their required exclusion from participation in hostilities? The nearest (but still oblique) approaches to it seem to be made by national military manuals like the (1956) USA's FM 27-10's paragraph on Basic Principles—belligerents are 'to refrain from employing any kind or degree of violence which is not actually necessary for military purposes'—and by such a commentary as Jean Pictet's *Development and Principles of IHL* (1985), where 'the Principle of Humanitarian Law' is thus defined: 'Belligerents shall not inflict harm on their adversaries out of proportion with the object of warfare, which is to destroy or weaken the military strength of the enemy.' The current (1958) British manual presents an interestingly disillusioned contrast. No soothing syrup for the civilian in *this* manual! Seeking in its old-fashioned way to explain why the rules are as they are—it actually includes in its para. 13 an explicit rebuttal of the Rousseau maxim!—and several times giving clear notice that civilians cannot escape unpleasant involvement, the first of its basic principles as stated in para. 3 is that 'a belligerent is justified in applying compulsion and force of any kind, to the extent necessary for the realization of the purpose of the war, that is, the complete submission of the enemy at the earliest possible moment with the least possible expenditure of men, resources and money.'

Experience has shown that armed forces in action do not always seriously try to restrict their attacks to military objectives, and sometimes do not try at all. Modern history has shown how frightful can be the consequences for civilians, the non-military places they are likely to inhabit, and the buildings of cultural value that may be there. To that short list of prohibited targets, contemporary history has added the environment. Civilized reason can discover no justification for attacking such persons and objects and has become increasingly loath to let its wartime self (NB: I do not say 'its armed forces' because civilian war-planners and war-encouragers are equally committed) be callous or careless regarding them. The scandal and danger were already bad enough to justify action by the time the First World War ended. By the end of the Second World War, the scandal and danger were so very much worse that (as was mentioned above) it was possible for some to argue that the time for action had gone, that it was too late; an argument to which the cult of nuclear weapons, equally beyond justification and suppression, for a while gave fortuitous backing. The nuclear Third World War which would have proved them right was however averted or, as some would prefer to put it, diverted. The anomalies of its nuclear aspect were not allowed forever to delay the completion of this so-long-unfinished business of defining the permissible, prohibiting the pointless and the punitive.

Permissions: Military Objectives

The definition of 'military objective' owes its undoubted success (success being defined as acceptability to all parties and relatively easy passage through the 1974–7 conference) to its combination of exactness with elasticity. Plastic might be a better adjective than elastic, as suggesting an object whose mass and texture remain constant, no matter how it is shaped and what it is used for. The fixed point of the definition lies not in a description or listing of objects, after the manner of the most prestigious of previous definitions, the 1923 Hague Draft Rules, but in the exactness of its inquiry about their relation to the enemy's war effort. The object may be anything or anywhere *provided that*, at the time it is dealt with (and the attacker is reminded that he may have other choices than 'total destruction'), it is 'contribut[ing] effectively' to the other side's 'military action' *and* that dealing with it offers 'a definite military advantage'. What has been simplified on the one hand has been complicated on the other. The definition of a military objective has been relativized. In place of the traditional Hague-law idea of it as a distinct, particular, and describable kind of place—fort, barracks, naval dockyard, ammunition-dump, munitions factory, military transportation facilities—we have the idea of objects, some of which surely will be military objectives all the time (like the old Hague sort) while others perhaps may be military objectives this week but not next week. This refined application of the principle of discrimination, taken together with the various prohibitions examined in the next section, is meant to prevent the massively destructive practices demonstrated during the Second World War and subsequently, practices which implied the legitimacy of destroying anything that might be of military usefulness at any future date, at the same time as they extended the concept of military usefulness unacceptably far into the civilian sector.

The purpose commands admiration, and the standards set are not unattainable. US experts participating in the preparation of AP1 were the better able to support the definition (as an acceptable codification of customary law) for their conviction that their country's aerial bombardments of North Vietnam in the winter of 1972–3 had already conformed to those standards.[14] The UN-authorized coalition's bombings of Iraq in early 1991 for the most part observed them too; only the collapse of inner Iraq's urban water-supply systems, *if* it was deliberately intended (which is not clear) cannot readily be thought to have 'offered a definite military advantage . . . in the circumstances ruling at the time'.[15] The standards are however exacting ones. Not many of the decisions reached with them in mind can be expected to be made at such high levels and with as much high-grade information as those just mentioned. Quality of information is half the heart of this matter. Commanders have to make do with the best they can get, and may have very little time to decide what exactly they will do on the basis of it. The UK no doubt expressed the sentiments of many other parties when it added to its signature of the Protocol this 'understanding' of Article 52 and its neighbours from 51 through 58: 'that military commanders and others responsible for planning, deciding upon or executing attacks necessarily have to reach decisions on the basis of their assessment of the information from all sources which is available to them at the relevant time.'[16]

[14] This point has been powerfully made by W. Hays Parks, 'Linebacker and the Law of War', in *Air University Review*, 34 (1983), 2–30 and, together with a wealth of references to subsequent operations, in his monumental 'Air War and the Law of War', in *Air Force Law Review*, 32 (1990), 1–225, esp. at 143–56.

[15] The other attack which has been much criticized, the attack on the building in Baghdad which bore marks of military use but which also had an air-raid shelter in it, seems to have been an unfortunate accident for whose causation both sides had some responsibility. This incident receives lengthier scrutiny in the section on 'Precautions and Proportionality', below.

[16] Jacques Freymond's scathing comments on this in *AmJIL* 67 (1973) at 685 invited the rejoinder that armed forces like the UK's, accustomed to real fighting, must be expected to be more sensitive about their legal position than those for whom real fighting is only a fantasy.

Even in the event that information is plentiful and trustworthy, however, the commander still has to handle the other half of the matter, and in the last resort he has to use his own judgment. ('He' may of course be 'she' or collective.) He has to make up his mind about 'effective contribution to military action' and 'definite military advantage', etc., and he may not find them as restrictive as some of their framers meant them to be. Bothe, Partsch, and Solf point out that nothing in the definition would have illegitimized the attacks on German military targets in the Pas-de-Calais area which were part of the Allies' grandly deceptive design for their invasion landings, landings not in the Pas-de-Calais but in Normandy.[17] Parks stretches the definition closer to breaking-point, or perhaps beyond it, when he argues that the word 'military' has to be interpreted with enough latitude to include strategic, psychological, and political advantages, and that the word 'definite' cannot be taken so literally as to exclude the 'hoped-for' when consideration is given to 'the fog of war and the speculative nature of many decisions made in war'.[18]

Parks's argument is powerful, but less than perfectly persuasive. Some of his examples work better for him than others. The strongest of them has already been referred to: the Linebacker II bombings of North Vietnam in the winter of 1972–3. Not much fog or speculation there! Their purpose may certainly be called 'political', but it was so in such a tight, clear, and calculated relationship with military reasoning that whether they are called political or military is little more than a matter of personal preference. Moreover, the bombings themselves were as precisely targeted on military objects as was feasible, a fact to which American writers, Parks himself among them, have proudly pointed as evidence of their country's respect for customary restraints. The least persuasive of his examples is his country's surprise bombing of 'terrorist-related targets in Libya' in mid-April 1986. Surely this deed has no proper place in the debate about the laws of war? In so far as it can be justified, it has to be as an act of counter-terrorist vigilantism, explicable not in terms of law but of the inadequacies of law; and not the law of armed conflict either, since it took place in plain peacetime.

More complicated is the case of the Doolittle raid on Tokyo by a cour- ageous handful of carrier-launched US bombers in April 1942. The bomb- ing and (admittedly, injudicious) machine-gunning, no more inaccurate than had to be expected, by no means justified the Japanese authorities'

[17] Bothe, Partsch, and Solf, 325.   [18] His 1990 article, p. 142.

outrage. In so far as there was some element of calculation that the raid would worry and distract the Japanese military, it was subsequently found to have done so. But the governing calculation at the time, and the justification upon which Parks most relies, is that it 'provided a tremendous boost to the morale of the American people after the string of defeats US forces had suffered in the preceding five months', i.e. in his own terms, the military advantage was a psychological one, and not because it would upset the enemy but because it would cheer up the folks back home. This seems to be a dangerous line of argument. It moves the standard of judgment from the purportedly rational and objective towards the probably irrational and admittedly subjective.

The theory of decisions made in light of the law of war is that they are likely to be rational because, first, the persons making them are instructed in the subject and (with luck!) have time to consider what they are about. Secondly, the law itself comes to us soaked in several sorts of reason: the reason of the classical-cum-Christian natural law which originally gave life to the *jus gentium*, the reason of the Enlightenment which made international law a necessary element of civilized international relations, the reason of European military science which was pleased to find compatibility between the law and its own purposes.[19] Educated statesmen, strategists, and soldiers who knowingly stray from those paths of reason and objectivity have scant excuse for doing so. Mass opinion on the other hand, whether it be that of fighting men at the front or the civilians they left behind them, has many excuses for not knowing much about IHL and for not understanding the reason within it. Governments and commanders may find themselves facing an awkward choice when ill-informed and inflamed popular opinion demands actions they know to be questionable. The great monastery of Monte Cassino was only the most famous of many defended places in the Second World War which Allied infantry were reluctant to attack until it had been bombarded into ruins, notwithstanding the fact that the Germans were apt to survive such bombardments and found ruins no more difficult to defend—indeed, sometimes easier to defend—than buildings. What was important for the infantry was the subjective psychological boost of seeing the buildings being spectacularly destroyed. Restraint and rationality will not be promoted by bringing the appeasement of one's own side's psychological needs within the definition of a military objective.

[19] e.g. the maxim, of which I have heard versions from the lips of experienced British and US military men, that 'IHL can be summed up as the doctrine of minimal force plus a bit of something else'.

Prohibitions

Terror, Indiscriminate Bombardment, Starvation

AP1's definition of attackable military objectives is complemented by a mixed array of precautions and prohibitions: precautions that must be taken in contemplating and planning attacks, and prohibitions regarding what must absolutely not be attacked. The critical reader may perhaps wonder whether this is not over-egging the pudding. Can the prohibitions be anything other than the permissions looked at from the other side? Logically considered, they are not much more than that. But viewed in the lights of history and politics, they speak volumes. These prohibitions were of methods and means which experience of armed conflict had caused to appear particularly revolting and unacceptable, and which it was not Utopian to hope that civilized belligerents might be able to dispense with.

Perhaps the furthest-reaching of all the prohibitions was that of deliberate terrorization. The word appears in only one sentence of one article—'Acts or threats of violence the primary purpose of which is to spread terror among the civilian population are prohibited', in para. 2 of Article 51—but the potential reach of the ban is vast and varied. The word 'primary' must be noted. This is not about incidental terror. That civilians are likely to be terrified when military operations are being conducted close to them has to be taken for granted. Nothing much can be done about it, unless it be their evacuation from places likely to be attacked or the giving of advance warning by commanders about to make attacks; precautionary measures which are in some circumstances feasible, and which the Protocol expressly suggests.[20] The attempt by some African and Arab States to bring under the ban also methods and means whose secondary and incidental effect could be terrifying has to be seen as evidence either of frivolity in their approach to the CDDH or of the strength of their will to use it for sectional (to be precise: anti-American and anti-Israeli) purposes.[21] But even without that fantastic extension, the ban on deliberate terror went enormously far. It struck at the heart of one of the most vulnerable points of the civilian in modern wartime and put an end to one of the most odious usages of modern warfare.

Civilians, it is scarcely necessary to repeat, have rarely been wholly immune from the effects of the military operations of their country's

---

[20] For the former, see AP1 Articles 58 and 51(7); for the latter, Article 57(2)c.
[21] Bothe, Partsch, and Solf, 300–1 nn.

enemies. Besides such sufferings as may have been incidental and un-avoidable, civilians have in certain circumstances been made the object of deliberate exercises of armed force, e.g. when they have been enclosed within besieged places, when they have been dependent on vulnerable land- or sea-lines of communication, when an invading or occupying force has been able to lord it over them. Within the tangled history of siege and blockade, raid and seizure, invasion and occupation, it is possible to make out the pursuit of two distinguishable purposes: the economic-warfare purpose, and the popular-pressure purpose. The former willingly hurt enemy civilians who served to maintain their country's economic system or whom it was thought proper to cause to experience its collapse. The latter purpose was willing to hurt enemy civilians whom it believed to be politically influential, implicated in the making of decisions to begin, con-tinue, or conclude war. Civilians being, after all, in a different category from combatants and supposed to be spared from combatants' bodily risks, law-minded belligerents would attempt to moderate the degree of hurt applied to civilians. They had to be able to show that it was something different from that applied to combatants, and something less. But the march of time made this more difficult to do, and less rewarding. Industrialization and democratization magnified the war-making importance of economic systems and invited belief in the war-waging responsibility of civilian populations. Destruction of the systems and demoralization of the popu-lations offered alternative ways to win wars, ways whose attractiveness was much enhanced after 1918 by their promise to win without further Western-front-style mass slaughters.

That these new ways might merely transfer slaughter from combatants, who had always been expected to face it, to civilians, who hadn't, was not clearly foreseen by all the innovators, and was not desired by many of them. But that is more or less what happened. By the time the most industrially advanced and law-minded belligerents had, in the course of the Second World War, learned how to take to the technical extreme the practices of economic warfare and strategic bombardment, little credibility remained in the classic claim that enemy civilians should be spared the combatants' experience of the full force of war. Terror became a commonplace part of civilian experience in wartime, and some of it was deliberate.

Distinguishing the deliberate from the incidental is not at all simple, for these reasons. First, the Second World War victims, from whom of course the bulk of the complaints about it came, were ill-placed to judge whether it was the one or the other. German civilian sufferers under the visitations of British bombers came to know them indiscriminately as *Terrorflieger*, but whether they merited the title or not can only be established by close enquiry into what they were up to on each particular raid, and how they conducted it. Secondly, as we have already noted, the attackers might be pleased to do both at once, or to conceal the (disreputable) one under the (permitted) cloak of the other: conjoined states of mind familiar to bombing theorists in all the major air powers when they got to work in the 1920s, and enmeshed in the practice and theory of the area- and 'carpet'-bombing which caused so much of the death and destruction of the earlier 1940s. And thirdly, there had been added to the two more or less permissible civilian-pressuring purposes described above, and mixed in with them to extents which can be impossible to measure, a third purpose for which no legitimacy at all could be claimed—the purely terroristic.

'Terror' is not always easy to identify, because belligerents employing it, especially if they feel obliged to present an acceptable face to neutral observation, will confuse the issue with reasonable-sounding explanations which may have a toe-hold in truth. Distinguishing occasions of lawless terror may be more a matter of proportion and psychoanalysis—in short, a matter of judgment—than of straightforward identification. Guernica *was* a road-junction and river-crossing of a certain military significance. Rotterdam *was* a defended place at the start of the day which saw its heart demolished. Dresden, one of the major cities close to the Germans' *Ostfront, did* have a strategically useful railway running through it, and the Western allies *had* promised Stalin to do something to help the Russians' advance. Each of these notorious bombings can be reckoned criminal, but only after painstaking historical scrutiny of particular circumstances. To turn from bombing to other uses of terror, there *was* a problem of popular patriotic resistance with which the Axis invader-occupiers had to cope, and the law-minded historian will do ill to discount it. But equally will he do ill if he fails to remark that there were other ways of coping with it than massacres like those of Lidice and Oradour, the hundred(s)-for-one reprisal killings and the *Nacht und Nebel* 'disappearances'.

The word 'terrorism' has so far not been used as it might have been. This is because popular usage, following the nineteenth-century's original application of the word terrorist to underground assassins and bombers, has given it a rather particular meaning—murder of the priest and the politician, torture of the detainee, bombs in the railway station and under the car, etc.—which at first sight scarcely fit into the context of ordinary acts of major armed conflict with which Article 51, like the whole of its section of AP1, is overtly concerned. Yet the word terrorism ought to be freely usable, because what Article 51(2) prohibits is just as much those particular acts of terror as any others. There is, of course, the usual qualification to be attached, that AP1 applies only to international armed conflicts and that the way to its application (in whole or part) to other situations is prickly with juridical problems. But to that qualification has to be attached, as usual, the rider that the way to its application to less than international armed conflicts is not, given favourable political circumstances, impassable. It has also to be borne in mind that AP2, which at most of the points where it parallels AP1 rather feebly reflects its big brother, on this matter repeats (in its Article 13(2)) the other's language word for word.

Prohibited acts of terror therefore, whenever IHL in its entirety is applicable or the conflicting parties are disposed to apply it, must be understood to mean what is done on the ground and from underground as well as what falls down to the ground from the air above it. The most obvious deliberate spreadings of terror among civilian populations in the present generation are by governments and armed forces seriously at odds with their own peoples or with other peoples under their power, and by insurgents representing (or, purporting to represent) those peoples. Assassinations and 'disappearances', kidnappings and bombings, rapes, tortures, intimidations, and so on and the threat of the same—some items of this dreadfully familiar list are more the speciality of counter-insurgent/revolutionary operations, some more of insurgent and revolutionary ones, but common features are the purpose of terrorizing civilians into submission and the fact that they are prohibited by identically worded articles in both Protocols, irrespective of whether the items in question are unlawful under other Articles and parts of IHL, as in fact many are.

Indiscriminate attacks and the prohibition thereof take up many lines in the civilian-protecting part of AP1. This was to deal with a problem and scandal which, already acute by the end of the Second World War, had become even more so since then in proportion with the ceaseless development of means of destruction and the inclination of possessor-States to use them. What made this a complicated matter, and by no means a simply terroristic one, was that it had come to feature as a familiar element of certain accepted war practices. Indiscriminateness that was accidental or incidental was, everyone knew, sometimes unavoidable; nothing could be done about that other than to keep the amount of it as small as possible. But to one dramatic modern war-practice was attached the claim that it could legitimately include a deliberately indiscriminate element. This was strategic bombing, the history of which is a classic illustration of what happens to ethics and law when science and technology present belligerents with an attractive new weapon whose uses cannot be kept within established limits.

We have looked at it before in other contexts. Now we have to look at it once again.

The trouble with strategic bombardment was that it was found to be extremely difficult to do accurately, with discrimination. Its purpose might be absolutely legitimate, but how could it be achieved legitimately? It was over the question whether its incidental destruction, for which the bombers' favoured description was 'collateral damage', was justifiable or not that controversy raged, and has raged ever since. Were those effects merely 'side-effects', incidental to the primary legitimate purpose and as such excusable? Or had they to be judged inexcusable because the collateral damage was disproportionately great, or (which would bring them into the terror category) because their primary purpose actually *was*, or at any rate included, the destruction of civilian areas?[22]

What AP1 painstakingly says about indiscriminate attacks ought to have put the question as much to rest as it can ever be. Article 51's para. 5 puts an end to Second World War-style area-bombardments by adding to the general prohibitions of para. 4, particular descriptions of two 'types of attacks [which] are to be considered as indiscriminate'. One of these focuses on the material character of a classic area-bombardment: 'treat[ing] as a single military objective a number of clearly separated and distinct military objectives located in [an] area containing a similar concentration of civilians or civilian objects'. The other, focusing on the style of argument most often used for the justification of such attacks, bans them if they 'may be expected to cause incidental' civilian suffering and damage 'which would be excessive in relation to the concrete and direct military advantage anticipated'. Obviously this invocation of the principle of proportionality, offering like all such invocations a rich field of opportunity for ethical enthusiasts and legal advisers, does not of itself ban civilian-endangering attacks which, in the attacker's judgment, are nevertheless justifiable on strong military grounds. Estimates of likely civilian damage and of military advantage will never wholly transcend the subjective. But this appears to be one of those matters of which the same can be said as is said of that necessary but ghostly presence, the illegal order: that although it may be tricky and embarrassing to define in advance, the reasonable man or woman knows one when he

---

[22] This has long been a controversial matter for other than juridical reasons. I am one of many whose studies of it have convinced them that, for (parts of the) British, German, and American air forces alike, the civilian-hitting part was often as important as the other, and was sometimes the principal purpose. Another factor that has helped keep controversy going is the philosophical idea of 'double effect'. This has perhaps raised the tone of the debate and given it an air of religious seriousness, but for my part I cannot see that it has brought the debate any nearer a conclusion.

receives one. The line must be able to be drawn somewhere, and on the plainly illegal other side of it henceforth lie the kind of attacks which sacrifice any number of civilians for even small and dubious military advantages, and which when they happen are likely to signify the restlessness of materially well-endowed belligerents given to believing that (to use the too familiar phrase) 'anything is permissible which saves the life of one of our men'.

'Starvation of civilians as a method of warfare is prohibited.' Thus reads the first paragraph of Article 54, the whole of which is devoted to 'Protection of objects indispensable to the survival of the civilian population'. Para. 2 lists the most obvious of such objects that must not be 'attacked, destroyed, removed or rendered useless': 'foodstuffs, agricultural areas for the production of foodstuffs, crops, livestock, drinking-water installations and supplies and irrigation works'. It also extends the scope of the prohibition. To the simple and obvious purpose of 'starving out civilians' are added those of 'causing them to move away' or, indeed, of causing them to run short of anything else they need to keep body and soul together. Behind these clauses may be perceived (besides, incidentally, the passive victims of blockades and other war-induced hardships) the tens of thousands of country-folk who year by year since the 1960s have been driven from their homes and lands and seen their homes, lands, and crops destroyed by the deliberate actions of, above all, counter-insurgency fighters, the latters' motives and methods often including denial of the means of subsistence to insurgents, clearing the way for free-fire zones and sometimes, no doubt, an element of genocidal hatred.

Such are the kind of war practices which brought about this notable legal innovation. Customary law contained nothing precisely to this effect. Deliberate and 'second-effect' starvation of civilians, as for example in besieged places and because of blockades or eviction from their homelands, had (as we have seen) often attracted humanitarian comment but it had never hitherto been expressly banned. Perhaps that was because most of the peoples who experienced it through most of history carried little weight with the major lawmaking powers who, in fact, were apt to use such methods themselves in the course of their imperial and territorial expansions. The original inhabitants of the Americas, the Hereros of (what is now) Namibia and the Zulus of Natal, Australian Aborigines, Algerian Arabs, Siberian Turkmen and Kazakhs were not on the list of those present at The Hague in 1907. But, forty years later, their successors and sympathizers would increasingly be present in the UN, and they were present in force at Geneva in the 1970s. Article 54 was one of several which most directly addressed their point of view.

Colonial and imperial powers—the USA counting, in this context, as one of the latter—as they strove through the post-war decolonization decades to retain their overseas possessions and to contain communism, found it convenient to isolate their insurgent opponents by depriving them of the foodstuffs they shared with the populations among which they moved. (And not only foodstuffs, but shelter, porterage, and intelligence as well. But it was not with them that Article 54 was expressly concerned.) What consequently befell the 'civilians' after the destruction of their crops, cottages, storehouses, wells, and watercourses would depend on the policy of the government or generals who did it. That they would have to move was sure. Perhaps their fate was simply to become refugees, so to swell the slum populations of towns and cities or the numbers on the rolls of agency-run refugee camps. In countries where rulers felt unable to deal so ruthlessly with them or sought perhaps to engage in the struggle for the people's hearts and minds, the displaced inhabitants would be herded ('relocated') into army-organized 'fortified villages', 'strategic hamlets', or whatever they were called, where they could be kept under surveillance. Such was the complex of counter-insurgency procedures which principally prompted the making of Article 54. It concentrated on the indefensible core of them, the causing of starvation or its imminent likelihood, and banned it. The 'strategic hamlets' part of them, however dislikable on other grounds and in certain circumstances comparable to cultural genocide, could scarcely be viewed as contrary to IHL, since it aimed to protect the lives of 'civilians' otherwise much endangered.

The incident which most Western readers may suppose to have been at the forefront of the legislators' minds, the supposed starvation-blockade of would-be Biafra during the Nigerian Civil War of 1967–70, was not in fact what most of them were concerned with. That war had been of much more concern to the West than it had to the rest of the world. The Biafran cause had been supported by only a small minority of African States and never became a 'Third-World issue' of the same order as, say, decolonization, development, and non-discrimination. A regional secessionist rebellion, which from a distance looked uncomfortably like that of Katanga against Zaïre, was in the nature of things unlikely to attract the sympathies of élites in any but the most secure and self-confident of States. More likely than the sufferings of the population of Biafra to catch attention in the Third World was the moderation and reasonableness of the Nigerian federal government. It was willing to let relief supplies through the net of its blockade provided that it would be given satisfactory assurance, first, that none of the supplies went to the Biafran armed forces and, second, that the transports taking them carried no contraband, conditions which the secessionists remained unwilling to meet.

The legal status of blockades remained unaffected by Article 54, as did the general area of war-making in which they are most likely to happen, naval warfare. The word blockade, it must be remarked, occurs nowhere in the Geneva Conventions or their Additional Protocols. 'Blockade' is one of the porcupine concepts which humanitarian lawyers handle with thick gloves and long tongs. In strictly legal terms it is a belligerent right, and—as Articles 40 and 41 of the UN Charter painstakingly make clear—many steps of economic and diplomatic pressure can be taken before getting to blockade proper. It was interesting to observe how much reluctance there was to call a blockade a blockade when the Security Council moved towards imposing one on Iraq, in consequence of Iraq's invasion of Kuwait on 2 August 1990. 'Economic sanctions' and 'embargoes' were the preferred terms, presumably because they sounded less warlike than blockade, which appears in the Charter (Article 42) in connection with 'action by air, sea and land forces'. Of course belligerents who can enforce a blockade will do so. To propose a blanket ban on blockades would be as futile as it was, between the wars, to try altogether to ban the military use of aeroplanes. Of course blockades, efficiently carried out, impose hardships sooner or later on the civilian populations in the places blockaded, and perhaps that, in part, is what they are meant to do. But blockades may not deserve their dubious reputation. Arrangements can always be made, if the parties are willing, for humanitarian relief supplies to pass through them, as, in the case of Iraq, was provided for in paras. 3(c) and 4 of Security Council Resolution 661. And it may surely be argued that, if civilian populations are to be subjected to the pressures of war, blockade is more humane than bombardment. The suddenness and unpredictabilities of bombardment make its effects much less avoidable than those of blockade. The slow steady workings of blockade give governments time to take avoiding action, e.g. civilian priority in food-distribution, arrangements for relief supplies, or, in the last resort, surrender, *if they are willing to do so*. The trouble is, they hardly ever are. Élites and armed forces are normally the last to go hungry when food is short, the passions of pride and sovereignty run high, and the PR battle for third-party sympathy can be strung out indefinitely.

Cultural property and the environment

The casualties of armed conflicts, when estimates of them are made, normally place people first and property second. One kind of property which may not stand out from the grim gross figures—houses destroyed, miles of track unusable and acres flooded, factories out of action, and so on—has nevertheless been considered to have such special and far-reaching interest and value that IHL has singled it out for special mention in both of the 1977 Protocols: Articles 53 in AP1 and 16 in AP2. This is, to use the title of the 1954 Hague Convention devoted to it, 'cultural property'. Banal it may sound, but some single term had to be found to cover the wide span of fine things which are listed with extraordinary thoroughness in paragraph 1(*a*):

movable or immovable property of great importance to the cultural heritage of every people, such as monuments of architecture, art or history, whether religious or secular; archaeological sites; groups of buildings which, as a whole, are of historic or artistic interest; works of art; manuscripts, books and other objects of artistic, historical or archaeological interest; as well as scientific collections and important collections of books or archives or of reproductions of the property defined above [and in sub-para. (*b*)] museums, large libraries and depositories of archives.

This admirable UNESCO-inspired Convention brought together two long-running rivers of concern: the one originally more national in character; the other, international and universal, both of them bearing human rights silt towards our contemporary delta. The former, first visible in the 1874 Brussels 'Project', appeared twice in the 1899 and 1907 Hague Regulations. Article 27, one of the several focused on sieges and bombardments, desiderated the taking of pains to spare 'buildings dedicated to religion, art, science, or charitable purposes, historical monuments, hospitals', etc. provided (the usual qualification!) 'they are not being used at the time for military purposes'. Article 56 gave the same places the protection which that age deemed appropriate in case of military occupation; they were to be respected as 'private property', and damage or theft would be 'made the subject of legal proceedings' when the war was over. (Typical of that generation's optimism about international law was the unguarded assumption that victor no less than loser would, if charged, go to court and, if found guilty, pay up.) The conceptual context was the ordinary one of the inviolability of private and non-military public property, and the frame of reference was, as in that age it had to be, national. Nevertheless, these early articles embody the germ of the supranational idea, summed up in the preamble to the 1954 Hague Convention, that 'damage to cultural property belonging to any people whatsoever means damage to the cultural heritage of all mankind, since each people makes its contribution to the culture of the world'.

Two antithetical ideas are locked in combat here, and it remains to be seen in what contexts the supranational and universalistic one will prevail over the national and ethnic. Perhaps no area of IHL more discloses the moral chasm which divides the internationally minded élites who write the modern law of war and who on the whole want to avoid fighting from, on the other side and hardly hearing them, the nationally or ethnically minded types who may have no wish to avoid fighting and who in any case generally do the greater share of it. The ethnic conflicts which at the time of writing are racking Yugoslavia and southern areas of the former USSR show all too plainly how the solipsistically ethnic mentality perceives the enemy's most prized cultural possessions and (if he is of different religion) places of worship as primary targets.

But supposedly larger-minded peoples have even recently behaved little better. Looting the enemy's cultural treasures and religious shrines has been a regular feature of aggressive and imperial war time out of mind; it still was so for the war-lords of Germany in the Second World War. Bombarders devoted to cracking enemy civilian morale may believe, almost certainly mistakenly, that wrecking his treasures and shrines is a good way to go about it. One of the first things the Germans did on seizing Warsaw at the end of September 1939 was to destroy the Poles' most beloved national monument, the one to Chopin. Their 'Baedeker raids' (thus nicknamed by the British) on certain cathedral cities in 1942 were planned as responses for British raids on cities of mainly historic and cultural interest such as Lübeck. The Dresden climax of Bomber Command's offensive has acquired its peculiarly bad reputation because, in addition to being of little military importance, it was uniquely destructive of cultural treasures. By the time of the Second World War, however, the countervailing tendency was well in evidence. Oxford and Heidelberg were not bombed, Rome and Paris did not burn, Kyoto was struck off the short list of targets for the first nuclear bomb, and an interesting schizophrenia caused the American and British armies, as they liberated much of Europe, to have in their company certain 'Monuments, Fine Arts, and Archives Officers' whose task it was to provide first aid to such cultural treasures as their gun-slinging colleagues had left standing.[23] The post-war stocktaking included a strong and wholesomely self-critical sense of regret at the cultural damage which Europe had suffered, a concern which the newly founded UNESCO took up and, as was intimated at the start of this section, helped to expand into the global scope of the 1954 Convention.

---

[23] Henry La Farge, *Lost Treasures of Europe* (London, 1946), Introd. There is a widespread belief among *cognoscenti* that Oxford and Heidelberg benefited from a gentlemen's understanding among Rhodes Scholars and such, but none of the suitably placed survivors from that time whom I have asked has been able to substantiate it.

Totally new in contemporary IHL is specific reference to environmental damage, which includes what many would prefer to call ecological damage. Damage of these descriptions has of course often been caused in wars (e.g. forests and orchards felled, farm-lands and watercourses destroyed, lowlands flooded by breakage of dams and dykes), and many years have sometimes had to pass before their repair. Sometimes excused by the argument of military necessity, they have otherwise often appeared to have transgressed the principles and (from 1899 and 1907) rules forbidding the causing of 'unnecessary suffering' and determining the limits of what might lawfully be done to civilian objects and to enemy property. Reparations and recompense for unlawful excesses have therefore subsequently been exacted by victors, as they were by Germany's Western conquerors after the First World War and by its Eastern ones after the Second World War. Soon after 1945, however, it began to appear that the nature and degree of the damage that technically advanced and/or ruthless war-makers were now capable of causing to the environment went beyond the ordinary meanings of civilian objects and private property. The testing of nuclear weapons of ever-increasing size and atmospheric fall-out made their environmental effects, as they gradually became understood, a matter of mounting public concern from the later 1950s, concern which presumably had some share in bringing about the 1963 Treaty banning Nuclear Weapons Tests in the Atmosphere, in Outer Space and Under Water. To those terrors in face of imprudent uses of nuclear energy, the spectacle of Vietnam in the 1960s added further fears about what could result from excessive and imprudent applications of chemistry and biology (defoliation of jungles, herbicidal sterilization of land, and contamination of water) and of mere machinery: the tearing up of farm-land and irrigation-systems by giant ploughs. There were also rumours, believed by Richard Falk to have had some basis in fact, of attempts to achieve the hitherto science-fictional goal of altering weather-patterns.[24] The 1970s therefore not surprisingly witnessed the arrival upon the IHL agenda of the prevention of environmental megadamage, with results as follows.

General prohibitions appeared in two places: AP1 and in the 1977 Convention on the Prohibition of Military or any other Hostile Use of Environmental Modification Techniques, commonly known as the ENMOD Convention. Both employ the same set of key words in defining the environmental damage they aim to prevent—widespread, long-lasting, severe—but with different purposes and conjoined in significantly different

[24] See his ch. in Glen Plant (ed.), *Environmental Protection and the Law of War* (London, 1992), 78–95 at 90.

ways. As Adam Roberts admirably puts it, what the Protocol is concerned with is 'damage *to* the environment, whatever the weapons used' whereas the ENMOD Convention's concern is 'the manipulation of the forces of the environment as weapons'.[25] The Convention carries all the weight attaching to any single-issue commitment and demands from its signatories quite serious undertakings, but the key words 'widespread, long-lasting, *or* severe' [my italics] have quite restrictive 'understandings' attached to them and, as must always be the case with agreements to prohibit particular weapons, the powers which have opted to become parties to it can only have done so after deciding that, all things considered, weapons of this description are of little prospective use to them. The Protocol's prohibitions, in Articles 35(3) and 55, are of 'methods or means of warfare which are intended, or may be expected, to cause widespread, long-term *and* severe damage to the natural environment . . . and thereby to prejudice the health or survival of the population'.[26] This obviously sets quite a high threshold— the damage must be *all* of those things, not just one or other of them—and so it would not appear, for example, to oppose much of a barrier to selective and measured uses of such environment-affecting methods as were used in Vietnam.

To those general prohibitions of doing dangerous things with and to the environment, contemporary IHL has added two particular ones dealing with dangers of particularly nasty kinds. The more significant of these is AP1's Article 56. The 'dangerous forces' figuring in the heading of this labyrinthine Article are those likely to be unloosed by attacks on 'dams, dykes and nuclear electrical generating stations', and the Article itself is a valiant attempt to minimize the likelihood of there being compelling justifications for attacking such objects. The length of the Article and the density of its argumentation result naturally from the mixture of history and myth which prompted it and the difficulty of the problem it seeks to resolve. British bombings in May 1943 of two German dams, the Mohne and Eder (always referred to in tandem, like Hiroshima and Nagasaki), have, like those two more famous bombings of August 1945, never ceased to invite the making of distinctions between them and to excite argument among connoisseurs of wartime ethics. American bombings of dams and dykes in North Korea and North Vietnam were among the most persistently controversial and, to some extent, misrepresented episodes of air-war history since then.[27]

---

[25] Roberts and Guelff, 378.   [26] My emphasis and conflation of the two articles.
[27] On the question of misrepresentation, I follow Parks at pp. 205, 209–18 of his 1990 book-length article already referred to.

The dangers lurking in nuclear power stations are too well known to need emphasis. Explosive release of such dangerous forces is no doubt especially to be deprecated, and responsibility for averting and avoiding it rests partly on the defender, who is asking for trouble if he locates military objectives near such installations or builds such installations close to populous places. And yet this Article may be thought to fall short of its aim. Being the product of reasonable legislators dedicated to accommodating the demands of military necessity to those of humanity and, in this matter, environment, Article 56 implicitly recognizes that these kinds of installations may on certain occasions be of much, perhaps of crucial, value to a belligerent. Stopping short therefore of an absolute prohibition of attacks on them, it details in its para. 2 the strict and demanding conditions upon which alone attacks would be legitimate. The case against these conditions—that not only are they unreasonably strict but also that the quantity and quality of intelligence they expect of the would-be attacker may be unrealistic—has been strongly put, along with criticisms of other aspects of the Article, by one of the Pentagon's senior law experts.[28]

The other particular prohibition comes in the 1981 UN Convention, its (third) Protocol on Incendiary Weapons. It does not amount to much. In its Article 2(4), the familiar military necessity reservation more or less neutralizes the effect of the first half's prohibition of making 'forests or other kinds of plant cover the objects of attack by incendiary weapons'. Falk's summary cannot be bettered: 'What results is a prohibition on frivolous, punitive and vindictive tactics, but no intrusion challenging the logic of warfare itself.'[29]

Perfidy

The uncommon word 'perfidy' and the somewhat old-fashioned word 'treachery' are used in IHL to describe deceptions and tricks which are to varying extents illegitimate. Deceptions and tricks which are legitimate and of which the variety is vast, come under the heading of 'Ruses of War' or, retaining the old French title for this term of military art, *ruses de guerre*. Between perfidious or treacherous acts on the one hand and *ruses de guerre* on the other, the line can be obscure and perplexing. This is a difficult and wobbly area of IHL, as legal experts who write about it freely admit. But it

[28] Parks, *Air War and the Law of War*, 207–18.
[29] In Plant, *Environmental Protection*, 89.

is an area of enormous significance, because perfidy points a dagger at the heart of the whole IHL enterprise.[30]

Perfidy's appearances in the legal instruments and in the authoritative commentaries handle the question less than satisfactorily, because they have to present perfidy as a crime within a frame of law. This is unsatisfactory, except for narrowly conceived legal purposes, because perfidy in its essence is just as much an offence within the frames of religion and ethics. It must never be forgotten that the law of war, wherever it began at all, began mainly as a matter of religion and ethics, and only became also a matter of law as part of the processes of social development and political sophistication. It began in ethics and it has kept one foot in ethics ever since.[31] IHL's frequent appearances in public debate are directly due more often to people's interest in ethics and the applications thereof than to interests in politics or military affairs. Armed forces may like to retain links with it. National military manuals, for example, sometimes include the historic concepts of honour and chivalry in their surveys of fundamental principles; which however is not of itself to be taken to mean much, warriors being known to follow their ideas of honour in beastly as well as in benevolent directions.[32] From the instruments of IHL, however, overt trace of those ethical anchors has disappeared.

Of course, it does not require much imagination for persons involved with IHL to understand its ethical reality and to feel the ethical dimension calling from its nearby lodging in the principles and values of the international organizations to which IHL is wedded. The fundamental principles of the International Red Cross and Red Crescent and the movement's universal secular humanitarian ideal have been embedded in IHL by the special status given in the Geneva Conventions to the ICRC and its affiliated National Societies. The UDHR and its extended family, the 1966 Covenants etc., offer a comprehensive spread of ethical principles and applications from which IHL has become less and less separable. They flesh out in considerable detail the ways the international community expect human beings to think of one another and, when they meet, to behave towards one

---

[30] Readers with special interest in moral conundrums of this sort could not do better than begin with ch. 9, 'Strategems and Ruses', in the current British *Manual of Military Law*, Pt. III: 'The Law of War on Land', which goes into the matter with much refinement and many helpful illustrations and which is honest enough to admit that the distinction is at some points unclear.

[31] Henceforth I abbreviate religion and ethics into ethics *tout court*; not least because I have never been able to feel much difference between them.

[32] See e.g. the British *Manual of Military Law* (1958), Pt. III: 'The Law of War on Land ch. 1, sect. 3; the US Army's Field Manual (1956), *The Law of Land Warfare*, ch. 1, sect. 1. 3(a); and the discussion in my *Honour among Men and Nations* (Toronto, 1982).

another, not just within the communities closest to them but wherever they walk on the surface of the globe. The 'Universal' of the title of the 1948 Declaration means what it says, and is not to be minced into meaninglessness by cultural relativism. International law has rediscovered those of its roots which its *jus gentium* precursor had in the idea of a world-wide humankind to whose members the sense of universal brother- and sisterhood would not seem alien, and among whom mutual respect and goodwill should be observable. IHL and human rights law are the areas of international law where this ethical foundation is most evidently needed and relied on, where it is therefore most important—and where it is incidentally most precarious.

The heart of the matter is plainly stated in the second sentence of AP1's Article 37(1). 'Acts inviting the confidence of an adversary to lead him to believe that he is entitled to, or is obliged to accord, protection under the rules of [IHL], with intent to betray that confidence, shall constitute perfidy.' Examples follow: deceptive use of flags of truce or surrender, feigning incapacitation by wounds or sickness, feigning civilian, non-combatant status, feigning the protected status of membership of the UN or a neutral State, and (as is added in the 'grave breaches' Article 85) abusing or, so far as it means anything different, misusing any of IHL's distinctive protective emblems, principally, of course, those of the Red Cross and Red Crescent.

The tenor of these examples is clear and crucial, so crucial as to justify renewed reference to the fundamentals of the philosophy of IHL. This is a matter not just of restraint but of respect as well. No principles are more inseparable from the practice of IHL. The warrior is required to refrain from doing such-and-such a thing to his opponent in time of armed conflict because of the fundamental principle that, after all, that opponent is a fellow human-being with whom certain fundamental interests and values are shared, and towards whom therefore there should be no wish to behave more hurtfully than last-resort recourse to violence has required. Because of this residual fellow-feeling and common humanity, decent human beings are presumed to be willing to submit even in wartime to the restraints suggested by conscience and imposed by law, restraints doubly binding at the point where those residual ties pull hardest.

Merely to cite these theoretical fundamentals of IHL is to invite the comment that they are ideals, for most of the time far removed from armed-conflict actuality. The comment is just. But such comment can surprise none of us. Honest writing about IHL can never pretend that it is ever observed perfectly, even where circumstances are most favourable to its being so, and must always admit that the usual levels of observance range between the indifferent and the lamentable. This is because circumstances are rarely favourable, because, like most other things in war, the law of war rarely works out according to plan, and because in any case the whole IHL enterprise is objectively paradoxical and (considering the unreliable materials from which it is constructed) far-fetched: war on the one hand, human nature on the other. Yet the enterprise is not abandoned. The self-respect of civilization dare not let it be. And just as some life and credibility is kept in it at one end of the scale by the purposeful prudence which works with calculations of reciprocity and consequences, so at the other end does it depend on the potentially imprudent principles of humanity and honour which decline to believe in the total, unrecognizable alienness, the non-humanity of the enemy, and which accordingly will not resort to perfidy in fighting him.

The distinction between perfidy and *ruses de guerre* is therefore as important as it is in some respects delicate, and misjudgments of it are easily made. The Protocol balances its specimen examples of acts of perfidy by instancing a few examples of the *ruses* that have always been accepted as legitimate: 'the use of camouflage, decoys, mock operations and mis-information'. The deceptions, tricks, and subterfuges which come under this heading have always been accepted, with varying degrees of glee and resignation, as inescapable aspects of warfare, but the practice of them appears not to have been regarded in modern times as a military activity particularly honourable to those engaged in it, and the borderline between it and the positively dishonourable has many unmarked stretches. Camouflage may in some situations legitimately mean enemy uniform, in others not. Is disinformation different from misinformation, and is it closer to perfidy? The spy remains in his curious legal limbo; whether his work is honourable or dishonourable, none can tell. Maritime warriors jealously insist on retaining their age-old permission to use false flags up to the moment of opening hostile action. Q-ships were considered lawful *ruses* by the UK in the First World War, perfidious by Germany. Readers will make differing judgments about the 'word of honour' incident cited in Part I. There is no denying that the areas where the categories intersect are over-hung with much low cloud, but there is no mistaking the clarity with which the main features of the landscape stand out. The *ruse*–perfidy divide rests to a peculiar degree on that distinction fundamental to Geneva law and the humanitarian parts of Hague law (and, one might add, human rights law too): the distinction between 'the man' and 'the fighter'. Consistent with Geneva law's recognition that the enemy, once rendered helpless by wounds, sickness, or surrender, is no longer the enemy he was, it is supposed that he is not such a fellow as will betray a brother's confidence when their family reputation for fair dealing is uniquely at stake.

A few examples to illustrate the point. It is not perfidy for fighting men disguised in the enemy's uniform to try to get past an enemy sentry, because the sentry ought to be careful about that sort of thing and he *can* be, but it is perfidy to try to get past him in the guise of Red Cross personnel because the Red Cross can only do its impartial work of universal mercy if it can be trusted to be mixing it with nothing else. It is not perfidy to refuse to receive an emissary bearing a white flag, but it is perfidy to encourage him to approach and then to shoot him, because that special symbol loses all its life-saving, peace-facilitating usefulness if men cannot be trusted to observe it.

Perfidy, the breach of personal honour, destroys men's last ties with one another when almost all other ties have already been destroyed by their inability to live at peace together. It is, if one may dare to borrow a valuable Christian idea, IHL's 'sin against the Holy Spirit'.[33] It is also a sin which does not cease to be committed: cease-fires broken, white flags and protective emblems ignored or used to deceive, surrenders feigned or deceitfully accepted, humanitarian relief supplies malverted or distorted, and so on. At the same time, it is all too easy to misjudge. Perfidy may be hastily adduced to explain enemy acts for which the better explanations are muddle, bad weather, bad eyesight, ignorance, imprudence, and ordinary human weaknesses. Two examples from recent wars illustrate the point. One is—as alleged 'perfidy' incidents so often are—a 'white flag' incident. On 28 May 1982, in course of the battle of Goose Green in the Falklands/Malvinas Islands,

it appeared that a white flag was raised from the Argentine detachment in the schoolhouse. A platoon commander and two NCOs went forward to arrange a surrender, but discovered this was not the defenders' intention. As they returned, another British position, some distance away, directed machine-gun fire on to the defenders. In response the three British soldiers were fired on in the open, and killed. The rest of the platoon overran the building and killed all the occupants.[34]

The second example comes from the UN-authorized war to liberate Iraq. On 29 January 1991, according to the Pentagon's *Final Report*:

---

[33] This para. and the preceding one incorporate a few sentences from the couple of pages I wrote about perfidy in the afterthoughts attached to my book *Honour among Men and Nations*. I hoped to stimulate interest in so important a subject but, twelve years or so later, I am not aware of having done so.

[34] Lawrence Freedman and Virginia Gamba-Stonehouse, *Signals of War* (London 1990), 374. Thus is the incident summarized by the coolest-headed of subsequent analysts. Inevitably the heated British troops believed that dirty work was afoot, and—less excusably, but no less predictably, a Briton regretfully has to say—the popular press encouraged the same belief.

Iraqi tanks entered Ras Al-Khfji with their turrets reversed, turning their guns forward only at the moment action began. . . . While there was some media speculation that this was an act of perfidy, it was not; a reversed turret is not a recognized indication of surrender *per se*. Some tactical confusion may have occurred, since Coalition ground forces were operating under a defensive posture at that time, and were to engage Iraqi forces only upon clear indication of hostile intent, or some hostile act.[35]

To return to perfidy proper, and to resume the image offered above: we here cross IHL's worrying fault-line. This line is where the IHL enterprise is at its most daring. The idea of humankind upon which it is founded is, after all, an even bolder one than that of human rights law, its twin in this matter. IHL and human rights law, proclaiming the same truth, sing from different scores. The human rights score, on the sunnier side, proclaims that humankind, for all its admitted subspecies diversity and notwithstanding the red herrings of cultural relativism, is one moral community and that its individual members, from whatever part of it they come, can respond to that community's demands and normally wish to do so. The IHL score in more sombre tones, perceiving that the groups composing that community continue to get into deadly quarrels with one another, prudently prescribes rules for their conduct and punishments for breaking them. The evident disparity between the two scores does not surprise experts in international legal and political affairs, accustomed as they are to distinguishing the law's more 'positive' parts and phases from its more 'normative' ones and to eating 'hard' and 'soft' law off the same plate. Given that law's functions are generally understood to include the educational, this accommodation of logical opposites is reasonable enough, and through much of the practice of IHL it is of little account. Shortfalls from the standards set, so commonly accidental or inevitable, cause no great surprise and need do no mortal damage to the standing of the law itself. But perfidy is something else. It is *not* accidental, it is the worst sort of (in football language) 'professional foul', and it is especially damaging to the law's standing because, more than any other illegal or immoral act of war, it spits in the face of the law's rock-bottom assumption of universal kinship.

Prohibited weapons

Prohibited weapons are an ancient and enduring element of the law of war. From its earliest recorded germinations and prototypes, a tendency has appeared among its adherents to denounce the use of weapons (and tactics) other than those to which they were accustomed. Leaving aside the

[35] US Dept. of Defense, *Conduct of the Persian Gulf War. Final Report to Congress*, Apr. 1992, Apps. A-S, o–21.

complexities of a question whose investigation must test the combined energies of the anthropologist, the sociologist, and the historian, the motives behind this attitude may be summed up as a mixture of self-interest (the self-interest characteristically of a certain superior class or caste) and selective humanitarianism. Broadened and universalized into elements of contemporary IHL, these time-honoured attitudes now take pride of place among its basic rules. One of them appears, under that description, in AP1. Following its affirmation of the most basic rule of all ('in any armed conflict, the right of the Parties to the conflict to choose methods or means of warfare is not unlimited'), Article 35(2) says: 'It is prohibited to employ weapons, projectiles and material and methods of warfare of a nature to cause superfluous injury or unnecessary suffering.' The other weaponry rule on which immemorial custom has conferred a basic character is to be found in the Hague Regulations of 1907, by whose Article 23(*a*) it is 'especially forbidden to employ poison or poisoned weapons'.

Between basic rules and their particular applications can lie labyrinths of definition and interpretation. CBW is a notable case in point. 'Poison' seems a simple enough concept, and no doubt had clear and simple enough a meaning in most of the situations where it was employed before the present century. Modern science and technology however have produced so many varieties of what may be called poisonous and so many ways of applying them that the identification of 'poisoned weapons', and the distinction of them from other weapons (perhaps prohibited, perhaps not) has become a complicated business. The weapon popularly known as 'poison gas', for instance, is introduced in Edward Spiers's book, *Chemical Warfare* (London, 1986), under the headings: 'irritating or harassing agents, often disseminated as smokes', 'incapacitating agents', 'choking and vesicant agents', 'blood gases', 'nerve gases', and, overlapping the biological border, 'toxins'. Not many who have heard of experimentation with 'biological weapons' and of allegations of their use on a few occasions within the past half century will realize that the reference specifically must be to about two hundred different 'pathogenic micro-organisms', classifiable under the four headings: viruses, rickettsiae, bacteria, and fungi.[36]

Not less perplexing, in an entirely non-technical vein, is how to understand the famous expression 'superfluous injury and unnecessary suffering'.[37] No believer in IHL can wish to cause superfluous injury or

---

[36] See Nicholas Sims, *The Diplomacy of Biological Disarmament* (London, 1988), 11, borrowing—as everyone who handles the topic of CBW sooner or later must gratefully borrow—from Julian Perry Robinson.

[37] 'Famous' not just because the concept goes back so far but also, among *cognoscenti*, for the mileage which commentators have got out of reading significance into the differences

unnecessary suffering. The inclination not to invent, let alone use weapons likely to do those things, may be assumed to be universal within the IHL community. But there is a problem. War cannot be fought without weapons, and warriors cannot and will not forgo the most effective weapons they can lay hands on in any but rather unusual circumstances, e.g. when their military advantage is so great that they can afford to indulge their softer feelings and accept a possible handicap. Since, in all other circumstances, their opponents will have been laying hands on the most effective defences against those weapons (besides keeping their own weapons up to scratch), the parties are therefore committed to an arms-and-armour competition which can be traced back time out of mind and is nowadays best known in the form of 'the arms race'. The criterion primarily applied to weapons by the men who have to use them is not 'Will they cause more injury than they need do?' but 'Will they cause enough of an injury to do what they are asked to do?'

There is virtue in the modest definition offered in the IHL manual scheduled to have come into use for all German armed forces by the end of 1992: ' "Superfluous injury" and "unnecessary suffering" is caused by the use of means and methods of combat whose presumable harm would definitely be excessive in relation to the lawful military advantage intended.'[38] Whatever is likely to cause less than enough harm is no good. The risk of more than enough harm cannot be avoided. Injuries beyond the minimum necessary to put targeted persons *hors de combat* (the abstract ideal held by the philosophy of IHL) have always occurred in war and have to be reckoned among its inescapably ugly accompaniments. The sufferings that can result from the use of 'ordinary' traditional weapons which no one dreams of banning can be as awful as the sufferings predictable from extraordinary new weapons as yet unused—not to mention the sufferings known to result from extraordinary new weapons already in use. Reason and logic however have to share this debate with custom, convenience,

---

between its English and French versions. The English translations of the authentic French text of the 1899 and 1907 Hague Regulations' Article 23(*f*), which neatly forbade the use of weapons etc. *'propres à causer des maux superflus'* were respectively 'of a nature to cause superfluous injury' and 'calculated to cause unnecessary suffering'. Kalshoven, who must have had to sit through much anglophone pedantry concerning these differences, remarks that 'it is a particularly felicitous solution that both terms have now been included on an equal footing in the (this time also authentic) English version.' *Arms, Armaments and International Law*, in the Hague Academy, *Recueil des Cours*, 191 (1985-II), 183–341 at 244.

[38] I am indebted to Dr Dieter Fleck, on the occasion of a seminar at the British Institute of International and Comparative Law, for a glimpse of the English translation of this admirable book.

myth, passion, and prejudice. The case made between the wars for chemical warfare included what might seem to have been quite convincing demonstrations that its ways of injuring and killing combatants were on the whole *less* nasty than those of weapons, old and new, the use of which did not arouse similar hostility. Such an argument fell on deaf ears. The movement to ban the use of gas, advancing from the legal bridgehead of the 1899 Hague Declaration on 'asphyxiating or deleterious gases', after the First World War began to gather an irresistible momentum which soon received satisfaction in the 1925 Geneva Protocol for the Prohibition of the Use in War of Asphyxiating, Poisonous or Other Gases, and of Bacteriological Methods of Warfare—not quite the first multilateral prohibition of a new science-based weapon, but by far the most prestigious, and still so to be judged, until and unless the 1993 Chemical Weapons Convention displays superior worth.

To the problems of definition and interpretation just noticed, the commentator on prohibited weapons has to add the further problem that the public debate about them is bedevilled by popular confusion between the nature of weapons and the way they are used. The ways weapons are used and their targets chosen may have more relevance to the question whether they should be used or not than is readily understood by those who, seeing appalling consequences of the use of a weapon, attribute them directly to the weapon itself.

Napalm, the most conspicuous of the post-war generation's inventory of incendiary weapons, is a notable case in point. More often heard of as an 'area' weapon than as a 'precise' one, its properties are that it enables even only one aerial delivery to cover a sizeable area with instant fierce flame which, for objects and persons hit by it, is as difficult to extinguish (because petroleum-based) as to escape from (because adhesive). Napalm's first uses in the later months of the Second World War, disturbing though they might be to those who knew about them, attracted little attention by comparison with the grander horrors of the same period. The word moved into general circulation with the lavish use made of it by the US air force in Korea and its employments also by the French in Indo-China and Algeria, the Portuguese in Angola and Mozambique. In the first of those instances, it was only one of the many practices which made the USA's allies in the so-called UN Command wonder whether their common cause was in safe hands. 'I do not like this napalm bombing at all,' Churchill told the Ministry of Defence in August 1952; 'no one [at the time of its invention] ever thought of splashing it about all over the civilian population.'[39] The British government, which to begin with had met parliamentary questions with reach-me-down answers from American stock, became worried enough to solicit the views of the RAF's man on the spot. His reply pointed out that napalm was attended by the same difficulty as were other aerially delivered weapons: it was 'inaccurate except at pointblank range' (ideally, 50–100 feet), which was much lower than pilots were willing to go against defended targets.[40]

But it was napalm's use in Vietnam through the mid- and later 1960s that made it a humanitarian sensation. Whether what was done by napalm in Vietnam was objectively worse than what had already happened or was actually happening elsewhere is of no importance beside the fact that everything done in Vietnam was to an unprecedented degree photographed, filmed, and reported. It did not matter that the reporting was sometimes tendentious or mendacious. Even painstakingly truthful reporting made it clear to the world that napalm was being used in massive and indiscriminate ways that produced drastic and horrible effects upon persons and places subjected to it—persons and places which were very often, in the terminology of the topic, civilian.

The prohibition of napalm understandably moved to the upper level of the reformers' agenda, and was repeatedly demanded whenever IHL was under discussion in UN or Red Cross and Red Crescent milieux. When the legislative conferences of the 1970s closed, however, napalm was still in the military inventory, and for this reason: the military men of major military States of every ideological complexion said they could not do without it. They insisted that it was a valuable and legitimate weapon so long as it was properly (i.e. discriminatingly) used. Provided it were so used, and unless the military concurred in its being made the subject of a universal prohibition like dumdums and CBW, the question of *maux superflus* was neither here nor there: its uniquely sinister reputation came from a mixture of indiscriminate and excessive *mis*uses, which could perhaps in future be avoided, and the usual sort of mishaps and bungles, which probably could not. The prohibitionists, in whose leadership Mexico, Syria, and Sweden were prominent, in the end achieved very little. The third of the three

[39] Personal Minute of 22 Aug. The American explanation that civilians were given warnings and time to get out was, he thought, 'not worth much. If people have to go to their work every day and live in their homes, they have not much choice of dwelling.' PRO/FO 371/99602, FK 1091/90.

[40] Air Vice-Marshal Bourchier's report of 11 Sept. 1952, in ibid. For the earlier reliance on the American explanations, see letters of Eden and Nutting in 371/99598, FK 1091/5 and 6.

Protocols attached to the 1981 UN Convention on Certain Conventional Weapons was to do with incendiary weapons, napalm not being specifically mentioned.[41] Its prohibitions taken along with its precautions and exceptions, the Protocol goes hardly at all beyond the civilian-protecting lines already laid down in AP1. Its only step beyond them is, in the view of some experts, Article 2(2)'s prohibition '*in all circumstances*' (my italics) of making 'any military objective located within a concentration of civilians the object of attack by air-delivered incendiary weapons'.[42] From that particular risk of collateral incineration, at any rate, the unfortunately situated civilian may be a bit better protected. The Birnam Wood side of the environment, for its part, does not seem likely to benefit much from Article 2(2)'s prohibition of making 'forests or other kinds of plant cover the object of attack by incendiary weapons except when such natural elements are used to cover, conceal or camouflage combatants or other military objectives, or are themselves military objectives'.

The 1981 Convention has two other Protocols, the first of little more than token, the second of tremendous significance. Protocol I must be the shortest protocol on record: one sentence merely, prohibiting the use of any weapon, 'the primary effect of which is to injure by fragments which in the human body escape detection by X-rays'. The idea cannot be faulted. Such a weapon, being also in effect an instrument of torture, would offend every humanitarian principle, and the very idea of it moved the legislators to take the unusual step of protecting combatants as well as civilians from the effects of so remarkably vile an invention. That it was, in its pure form, more of an idea than an invention, was not so unusual an aspect of the event. As Kalshoven remarks, the modern history of IHL shows other instances of the prohibition of methods and means which are 'conceivable but not really existing'.[43] In what may be described as an impure form, however, it certainly does exist: the form of the plastic mines dealt with in the next paragraph. What a metal detector cannot pick out when it is whole, X-rays may not pick out when it is fragmented. But the legal purist will plausibly argue that the causing of such injuries is not those mines' '*primary* effect'. Were he not able to do so, presumably, the

[41] Its full title is: 'Convention on Prohibitions of Certain Conventional Weapons which may be deemed to be Excessively Injurious or to have Indiscriminate Effects'.

[42] Kalshoven maintains that this rules out what might otherwise be a permissibly 'discriminate' attack under Protocol I's Article 51(5)(a); see p. 258 of his book cited in n. 37 above. For a more guarded reading, see Parks in *IRRC* 279 (1990), 535–50 at 548. Its definition of 'concentration of civilians' is: 'any concentration of civilians, be it permanent or temporary, such as in inhabited parts of cities, or inhabited towns or villages, or as in camps or columns of refugees or evacuees, or groups of nomads'.

[43] *Arms, Armaments and International Law*, 252.

Protocol would not have been accepted, as in fact it was, more or less on the nod.

Different in every conceivable respect is Protocol II, on Prohibitions or Restrictions on the Use [on Land] of Mines, Booby Traps and Other Devices. Leaving aside (and by no means underestimating the effects of) conventional bullets and bombs, it may be said that mines became for the 1970s and 1980s what napalm had been for the 1950s and 1960s; the weapon whose careless and indiscriminate uses have inflicted the most cruel and extensive injuries on civilians. Why were they slow to acquire the same sensational notoriety as napalm? In part perhaps because they have been ideologically less exciting, having been misused as much by forces of the Left as by forces of the Right. In part also no doubt because images of women on crutches and small children lacking limbs and eyes, typical products of unrestricted mine warfare, although tragic to behold seem not to shock and terrify like pictures of napalm bursts and burns. But in scale and persistence, mines make up a giant problem and scandal. For example, up to four million mines laid, something like 35,000 amputees recorded, and about 250–300 mine injuries happening each month in Cambodia, by reckonings in 1991;[44] 'more than one and a half million . . . believed [by the Minorities Rights Group] to have been planted in northern Somalia', 'more than 20,000 people crippled' in Angola according to Africa Watch;[45] in El Salvador in 1986, 'the military injury rate from mines runs from about 64 to 125 a month, while the civilian rate is between 19 and 25 a month'.[46] And so on.

Mines are weapons the military will absolutely not do without. They are cheap, adaptable, handy, and effective. Science and technology have within the past few decades utterly transformed them from their historic forms and roles. The 'springing' of a mine was through several centuries a great event of siege and trench warfare, the culmination of weeks, perhaps months, of underground labour and accumulations of gunpowder. By the First World War, the single big mine (biggest of all was the 500 tons of explosive

[44] *Independent*, Cambodia Trust letter in issue of 25 June and reports from Phnom Penh by Teresa Poole in those of 13 and 23 Nov. 1991. In the latter Poole strikingly remarks, 'Laying them has been a way of life in Cambodia for more than a decade.'

[45] Caroline Moorehead summarizing the state of the question as of later 1991 in the *Independent*, 26 Aug. The ICRC's 1992 *Panorama* review, p. 19, says 'about 8,500 people have been fitted with artificial limbs since 1979, tens of thousands of amputees await treatment.'

[46] Americas Watch Report, *Land Mines in El Salvador and Nicaragua: The Civilian Victims* (New York and Washington, Dec. 1986), 22. And so on. An excellent up-to-date survey of the whole horrid field is Gerald C. Canderay, 'Anti-Personnel Mines', in *IRRC* 295 (1993), 273–87.

exploded under Messines Ridge after more than a year's tunnelling) had been joined by the minefield, adapting an already well-established naval defensive technique to make stretches of land deadly to foot-soldiers. By the end of the Second World War, sea- and land-mines both had gone into ascending spirals of sophistication which may not yet have reached their end-stop. To the classic minefield of solid fixtures have been added varieties of small or tiny mines that can be placed (and hidden) anywhere or simply scattered (by drops from aircraft or by shell- and bomb-bursts) over surfaces as extensive as you like to imagine. From conventional military points of view, an indisputable great utility of mines used in this mode is instant 'interdiction', the making of strategic tracts of land so hazardous and terrifying to enemy foot-soldiers that it is effectively barred to them until and unless ways are cleared through it, which may indeed be done, but never quickly.

Whether clearance of mines, when attempted at all, is complete or not, must depend on numberless factors: whose land it is, who is likely to be using it, who can be persuaded, paid or made to do the job, what sort of mines are to be cleared, whether there are maps of them or not, and so on. Ideal circumstances for the existence of maps are when mines are of the solider sort, laid at leisure in firm ground and on the layer's own territory. It will easily be understood that such circumstances do not often occur. Injuries and deaths from unremoved mines (not to mention unexploded shells, bombs, etc.) are a familiar part of the aftermaths of wars even between technically efficient and morally respectable opponents. French and Belgian communities continued for years after the First World War to suffer in the areas where that war had been fought, and Poles especially still suffer from the aftermath of the Second World War; the Libyan desert has remained hazardous for users and travellers, large tracts of the East Falklands are out of bounds for anyone who can read the warning-signs, and it remains to be seen how efficient will have been the performance of the contractors who have undertaken the clearance of mines from Kuwait, and who have themselves predictably suffered losses in doing so.

Such are among the accompaniments of mine-warfare on its more decent side. The accompaniments of its less decent side are far worse. By decency is meant, here as elsewhere in this context, a certain degree of understanding of the demands of IHL and an inclination to respond to them even though they may be formally inapplicable—in short, the will to recognize what is due to the human beings likely to suffer in consequence of your actions. These decencies rarely appear in the kind of armed conflicts where the modernly invented mini-mines (my word for them) are most used, such mines as appear in the 1980 edition of *Brassey's Infantry Weapons of the Armies of Africa, the Orient and Latin America*: the USSR's 90-grams DMK-40, 4 by 7 cm. in size, a 'tiny nuisance-value mine', and its 1.8-kg. DM general purpose mine, 13 by 15 by 15, 'a booby-trap in itself as, once armed, it cannot be neutralized'; and, in the 1979 edition of *Brassey's Infantry Weapons of the NATO Armies*, Belgium's 183-gram PRB-M409 plastic mine, 2.8 by 8.2 cm., whose 'clearance presents serious problems since only about 1.5–3 mm. displacement of the pressure membrane will trigger an explosion'.[47] Italian products do not appear in those particular pages, but Italy has for many years been notorious for mass production of undetectable plastic mines. One Italian company is said to have delivered 19 million mines to Iraq between 1982 and 1985.[48] Words that spell notional caution to students in military colleges, trepidation and worse to foot-soldiers forced to traverse paths and areas where these things have been hidden or strewn, spell terror, death, and maiming to the rural populations of those places, against whom deliberately the mines may in fact be directed by parties to whom the terms 'civilian' and 'non-combatant' mean nothing, unless they mean the enemy in one of his many guises.[49] Children appear to suffer even more than adults from this discriminating indiscriminateness; children walk the paths and work in the fields too, and are congenitally prone to pick up unusual objects and play with them—all the more readily when they appear to be toys, as booby-trap mines are sometimes made to do.

Not until the 1981 UN Convention (its second Protocol) has IHL dealt directly with this ghastly aspect of contemporary land warfare. Its dealings before then had been by ways of implication and analogy. The way of implication was clear and unmistakable. 'The Martens clause' had as much bearing on this as upon any other method or means not expressly included in the Hague Regulations. A weapon whose methods of use became of such sinister menace to civilians could not by any stretch of imagination be derived from 'the usages established among civilized peoples' and must

---

[47] The dead-pan technical tone of these pages somewhat appalled me. I wonder whether the manufacturer's advertising would be even more appalling?

[48] My source for those figures is the far from first-hand one of *Exile*, the newsletter of the [British] Refugee Council, Oct. 1992, p. 3. But I am not disinclined to believe it, having heard tell of this Italian speciality from participants in the CDDH and the other legislative conferences of the 1970s.

[49] e.g. the Khmer Rouge in the Kompong Spoe province of Kampuchea in 1990, as reported by Catherine Geach in the *Tablet*, 17 Aug. 1991, pp. 990–1; mines in the rice-fields while villagers were working there, mines in the parts of the jungle where they went in search of food when rice ran out, and mines even in the grounds of the hospital where still-living mine-victims were cared for.

have been considered offensive to 'the laws of humanity and the dictates of the public conscience'. Beyond that and more specifically, there was no lack of law aiming at the protection of civilians and (in the words of the Geneva Conventions' Common Article 3) 'persons taking no active part in hostilities' and to prevent their terrorization. The more law-minded of minelayers might for example, and especially if 'the winning of hearts and minds' was on their agenda, attempt to tell local inhabitants what they were doing; provided that surprise and uncertainty were not of the essence, they might mark or even fence the mined zone.[50]

IHL's handling of the great mines question by way of analogy involved reference to the very specific law formulated before 1914 to regulate the use of mines in war at sea. The advantageous possibilities offered by contact mines were perceived by admirals earlier than by generals, and the dangers they incidentally brought with them were early brought into public debate by anxiously observant spokesmen of the neutral and non-combatant interests. In so far as their use could be presented as the continuation by new means of old and accepted practices of enforcing blockade and arresting contraband, it was difficult to contest. What could be contested were extensions of the sweep of those practices beyond what seemed reasonable and indiscriminate consequences of them. It was therefore demanded that the laying of minefields should be notified to non-belligerents, that they should be swept up when they ceased to have military purpose, and that they should be fitted with devices to disarm them if they broke loose from their moorings or (in the case of unanchored mines) failed within a reasonable fixed time to achieve their intended task. Hague Convention VIII of 1907, Relative to the Laying of Automatic Submarine Contact Mines, did much to meet these demands, besides pioneering two ideas, the interest of which has only grown with time: that parties should respect the stipulated technical standards by making sure their weapons met them, and that the state of the question should be reviewed in seven years, it being clearly understood that the methods of using mines and torpedoes were likely to be revolutionized by ever-busy science and technology.

For the history of the use of mines at sea, the reader must go to the

---

[50] Communication of warnings to inhabitants in alien battle zones has always been an uncertain business. When communication by word of mouth was impractical, leaflets dropped from the air might be less alarming than that other technique dating from colonial-policing days, megaphones from low-flying planes or helicopters. On these benevolent occasions, as on punitive ones when peasants were given warnings of e.g. what was going to be done to their village in thirty minutes' time, it was difficult to be sure that they understood the message, or that, even if they did, they could do much about it.

specialists.[51] Their uses on land have been sketched above. On the credit side must appear the insistence of military authorities (guerrillas of course included) on being able to make tracts and stretches of land impassable to their foes except at nerve-tearing personal risk or unless assisted by costly special equipment. Mines, it must be repeated, are a weapon which land armies may find exceedingly useful, with a usefulness of the sort that cannot be forgone unless there is an iron-clad guarantee that the foe will not use them either. On the debit side appear the damages done to civilians, never more appropriately called 'innocent' than in this context; civilians damaged either deliberately, because they are hated or not perceived as distinct from combatants, or collaterally because, as an apologist might say, they unfortunately got mixed up with the mines, or 'accidentally', the result perhaps of theft from the stores of box-loads of the hateful things, or their use by sentries to save them having to stay awake at night. The few instances of attempts bona fide to adapt the 1907 Convention's guidelines are far outweighed by contemptuous rejection of them, while technology's most conspicuous contribution has been the mass production of mini-mines which, being made of plastic or cardboard, are virtually impossible to detect and, lacking anything in the way of timed self-destructing devices, may lie around indefinitely. It goes without saying that the powers of politics and profit have so far obstructed attempts to activate in this context the international community's other main means of limiting the spread and restraining the misuse of weapons: multilateral agreements of arms control and regulations of arms transfers, with concomitant obligations to police manufacturers. The nature of the weapon in question—on the 'popular' side of its range, so small and cheap—is indeed such as to suggest that measures to control it may leak like sieves. The point nevertheless cannot be made too often that IHL does not stand alone between humankind and the worst that wars can bring, and that other branches of international law may get to parts of the problem that IHL cannot reach. (As also, of course, vice versa.)

By the second Protocol of the 1981 UN Convention, at last, the use of mines and booby traps in land war was subjected to certain positive restrictions. Article 6's prohibition of 'certain booby traps' is unusually absolute; use of the listed ones is prohibited *in all circumstances*, thus protecting combatants as well as everyone else. The list itself has added interest as an

---

[51] e.g. F. H. Swayze, 'Traditional Principles of Blockade in Modern Practice: United States Mining of Internal and Territorial Waters of North Vietnam', in *JAG Journal*, 29 (1977), 143–73; A. G. Y. Thorpe, 'Mine Warfare at Sea: Some Legal Aspects for the Future', in *Ocean Development and International Law* 18 (1987), 255–78; and Myron Nordquist and Margaret Wachenfeld, 'Legal Aspects of Reflagging Kuwaiti Tankers and Laying of Mines in the Persian Gulf', in *German Yearbook of International Law*, 31 (1988), 138–63.

indication of the range of ethical concerns upon which contemporary IHL has come to rest. Some of the booby traps described would qualify in terms of AP1's Articles 37–9 as perfidious, others are there because the hazards they pose are especially menacing to children, medical- and health-care, religion and culture; one even touches the edge of animal welfare. The rest of this 1981 Protocol is less extraordinary, reiterating as it does the more fundamental of the civilian-protecting prohibitions and precautions prescribed in 1977 for the use of weapons overall, and elaborating their application to the weaponry specifically in view. Article 4(2) aims to limit the use of hand-positioned mines in populous places to occasions when combat is actually taking place or at any rate imminent. Article 5 allows the 'remote delivery' of mines (i.e. from aircraft or rockets, shells, etc.) 'only within an area which is itself a military objective or which contains military objectives' and provided that (*a*) their location can be recorded in the style stipulated for *all* minefields, (*b*) they are fitted with neutralizing or self-destructing mechanisms. Articles 7, 8, and 9 elaborate on the necessity of keeping accurate records and maps to facilitate the work of UN peace-keeping forces and missions and, of course, to improve the chances of removing mines after hostilities have ceased.

How effective is this Protocol likely to be? As with regard to IHL as a whole and to every part of it individually, the questions of application and effect cannot be answered in terms of the legal text alone. First of all it has to be established whether a belligerent knows about the text and whether it means much to him. These careful conditions for the regulation of mine-warfare were completed and published to the world in 1981; it must be of some interest that children's-toy booby-trap mines were reported from Afghanistan in the mid-1980s. Enquiry into the likely efficacy of the law has to begin with such questions as: Has this belligerent any serious interest in respecting IHL? If he has, but supposing him not to have signed the Protocol(s) or to be qualified to sign them, does he nevertheless acknowledge any legal or moral weight in them? Supposing these preliminary questions to be answerable on the positive side, the way to the text itself is clearer; and the text of this Protocol suggests that its efficacy will turn largely on how the tension is resolved between the parts which do indeed offer the civilian much-needed protection and those which protect the interests of the military: the same tension which runs through the law of war like the place-name through a stick of Blackpool rock, but which here is unusually apparent, as my two concluding examples will show. Article 3's recapitulation of the 1977 protections against indiscriminate and disproportionate use ends in this bushy piece of hedging: 'All feasible precautions shall be taken to protect civilians from the effects of weapons to which this Protocol applies. Feasible precautions are those precautions which are practicable or practically possible taking into account all circumstances ruling at the time, including humanitarian and military considerations.' A shorter way to the same convenient end is shown in para. 2 of Article 5: 'Effective advance warning shall be given of any delivery or dropping of remotely delivered mines which may affect the civilian population, *unless circumstances do not permit*' (my emphasis).

The 1981 UN Convention and its three Protocols on non-detectable fragments, mines and booby-traps, and incendiary weapons respectively, represent the greater part of the outcome of the broad-based movement against weapons believed to be atrocious and abominable (in IHL terms, to cause superfluous injury and unnecessary suffering), and therefore to cry out for prohibition. To those who had long agitated for strong action in this field, the 1981 Convention seemed a disappointing outcome: no anathema against napalm, no reference to fuel-air incendiaries or fragmentation bombs, no conclusive results from many years of allegations and experiments concerning the effects of high-velocity bullets—in brief, negligible inroads into the colossal armoury available to powers with the money to buy the deadly stuff or with friends to buy it for them. No doubt arms manufacturers and traffickers were pleased at this outcome, for which traditional-minded anti-arms-trade activists suspected those 'merchants of death' to be responsible. But the explanation is really quite simple and rather less arcane. There are two sides to it. On the legal side, it was persuasively argued that in the ultimate humanitarian reckoning, the weapon itself mattered less than the way it was used. Argument might properly rage around the question whether some weapons were of such characters that they absolutely could not be used accurately or discriminately. Eveything that was apprehended about biological weapons, and much that was known about chemical ones, suggested that they indeed came under that description. Nuclear weapons were widely understood to do so too. But as for those so-called conventional weapons on the prohibitionists' list, the appalling harm they had been known to inflict on non-combatants was to be attributed mainly to misuse, which a more faithful observance of the rules (rules greatly clarified and improved in the 1977 and 1981 statutes) and a more feeling regard for the principles underlying them could for the future avoid.

This was not an argument easily to be dismissed. The most obvious hole in it—its implication that armed forces which have not much respected prereformed law will respect a reformed version better—can perhaps be patched by intensifying the awareness of IHL as is globally attempted by the ICRC and as is actually worked into everyday training by a few exemplary armed forces. Helpful backing may come from public pressures on States to shoulder the responsibilities which IHL and human rights law place upon them. Such responsibilities would include (according to AP1's Article 36) the obligation of HCPs not to develop, acquire, or adopt new weapons without determining their compatibility with *any* rule of international law, and a maximal, instead of the prevailing minimal, understanding of the obligation given in Common Article 1 of the Geneva Conventions, 'in all circumstances . . . to ensure respect' for them.

Such is the legal side of the explanation why the list of prohibited weapons has been so little enlarged. The other side is a simply military one. Decent law-abiding military men do not insist on retaining the option of using weapons whose impact can be horrible because they are impressed by the horror.[52] They do so because they are impressed by the impact. The more effective a weapon can be for a lawful military purpose, the more the military will want to have it. In the event that there is at least the risk of horrors accompanying its use, that will be a matter of regret, but two reflections make it bearable. Both derive from the principle of reciprocity, which here as elsewhere exercises its powerful persuasions—as it always will, when the relationship between opponents is more or less symmetrical. The first user of a new weapon will reflect that sooner or later he may find it being used on him. He may further reflect that even if the weapon is of the kind which military men do *not* wish to have used against them and which has therefore been made the subject of a legal ban, he would be a fool not to have it in reserve, ready for reprisal use in case the opponent nevertheless decides to break the ban and use it.

This is exactly the case with chemical warfare. The ban has been there since 1925, and poison gas was not used against one another by the biggest belligerents in the biggest war that has been waged since then: not because those belligerents did not possess stocks of it or fail to prepare troops for the use of it but largely because of calculation that, if they initiated its use, the enemy, who was believed or known to have stocks of it too, would respond in kind. The war referred to is of course the Second World War, and 'largely' in that sentence must be taken to mean, 'to some immeasurable but, in the opinions of historians who have closely enquired into the matter,

---

[52] The sadists and bullies who must be found in all armed forces no doubt may relish the idea of horrible effects but one may assume that they will normally be outnumbered by the decent human beings. The numerous popular-priced periodicals devoted to war, weaponry, and 'combat' certainly tend to be bloodthirsty and conscienceless, but the consumers whose fantasies they feed are obviously civilian.

preponderant extent'. The belligerents' calculations covered many aspects and included the reactions of domestic and foreign opinion, the relative utility of alternative methods and means, and—as for example in the minds of UK and US planners in the closing phases of the Second World War, when victory was only a matter of time and tactics—whether time was pressing or not. Realist cynics go too far when they allege that the non-use of gas by more or less symmetrically matched belligerents has been *entirely* due to *realpolitik*. It would have been militarily 'safe' and technically simple to have used gas against Germany and Japan in the last stages of their resistance, but nevertheless it was not used. The legal and the moral serious-ness of the ban certainly carried weight, but how to separate that from all the other elements in the shifting mixture of the Second World War and how then to measure it, is beyond the resources of social science.

Three lesser international cases are worth consideration in which gas certainly *was* used.[53] Whether the ban carried any weight at all with the Italians who planned their extensive use of gas against Abyssinia, the Japanese who made some use of it against China, and the Iraqis who in the 1980s increasingly made tactical defensive uses of it against Iran, can only be imagined. It signifies something that each of those gas-users sought to conceal and/or deny the fact, for which moral scruples seem unlikely to be the explanation, given the character of their conduct in other respects. In the first two cases, there was technical asymmetry; Italy could be confident that there would be no reprisal, Japan that if there was any, it would not amount to much. Iraq and Iran to begin with were quite evenly matched, and Iraq had to reckon with the possibility that Iran would respond in kind, as in fact it did, tardily and to no great effect. Iraq's respect for IHL during its war with Iran was in other respects lamentable, and its defiantly repeated use of the most prohibited of all prohibited weapons has to be classed among the most serious challenges the law has suffered since the Second World War.[54]

The Iraqi justification which can be dimly made out through the mists of its repeated denials was that *anything* is justified to preserve national existence at desperate moments of struggle against unscrupulous enemies. This line of argument is familiar from ancient history as well as modern, and from nearer the author's home than Baghdad. It was the line that would have been used by the UK had Germany invaded it in 1940 and had the

[53] I see no need to get entangled in the endless arguments about *alleged* chemical warfare—'yellow rain' etc.—in Laos, Kampuchea, and Thailand. They are tersely and intelligibly dis-cussed in Spiers, *Chemical Warfare*, 104–19.

[54] NB the reference is solely to what happened in the international war between Iran and Iraq, not to Iraq's use of gas in its non-international armed conflict with the Kurds, which was even more shocking, but within a different frame of reference.

persuasions of Britain's pro-gas defence planners prevailed over those of the anti-gas ones.[55] It comes naturally to the mind and easily to the rhetoric of persons fixated on the interests of their own ethnic, national, or religious groups, and in the Baghdad instance it only mirrored what was thought and said in Tehran. Whether what is naturally thought and easily said by inflamed belligerents actually issues in deliberate action is another matter; but in any case this is not a line of argument which upholders of international law can accept. IHL however, wedded as it is to the principle of belligerent equality and traditionally deferential to sovereign States, is not the branch of international law best equipped to handle it. The handling has to be done by branches less reluctant to distinguish between the merits of belligerents, and able to back with irresistible power their affirmation that one element in the system has no right to save itself at the expense of the other elements or (an even more intolerable stretch of national egoism) to pull the others down with it in a common ruin. Action towards this end being by definition too late if it is not taken until a disaster-threatening conflict is in progress, it must happen before such conflicts begin; which means it belongs to the parts of international law concerned with disarmament and arms control, and that it must succeed in its dealing with what has always been their principal problem: verification.

Legal prohibitions of weapons, unless they are of weapons of such a nature that no country is likely ever to possess them, are mere ploughings of the sand unless they are accompanied by convincing measures of verification. The move towards convincement has hardly begun when verification goes no further than to check that a State possesses no more of such-and-such a weapon than it admits to possessing. The important thing is to prevent acquisition. Verification only becomes more convincing when its function is to check the truthfulness of a State's assertion that it has not the means to make and to store such-and-such a weapon. (Verification moreover cannot become wholly convincing until the associated business of arms transfers is so controlled as to guarantee that States and other arms-using parties cannot acquire from elsewhere weapons they cannot make for themselves.) The only ground on which a military-minded State can prudently forgo possession of a prohibited weapon is convincing evidence that no other States possess it except those with which armed conflict is inconceivable. That is the heart of the explanation why the 1925 Gas Protocol has not proved more satisfactory.[56] It was no more than an

---

[55] See e.g. Spiers, *Chemical Warfare*, 67–9.
[56] There were also ambiguities in its wording which facilitated wriggling out of its stricter obligations. See Roberts and Guelff, 137–9 for a good summary of them and the Protocol's other shortcomings.

undertaking by HCPs not to use the specified weapon. Optimistic readers of the Protocol might suppose that grateful HCPs therefore would be spared the expense of acquiring it; but how could States bear not to have it, without certainty that their prospective possible enemies did not have it either? Not to mention the fact that every signatory power of any military significance accompanied its adherence/accession with a reservation to the effect that its observance of the prohibition was conditional on enemies' observance too. Without prohibition of development, production, and stockpiling, and without convincing means of verification thereof, mere prohibition of use by sovereign nation-States was vanity of vanities.

The contemporary movement to replace the 1925 Protocol (which, it must be remembered, banned use of both chemical and biological weapons) with a more effective and universal instrument dates, as does the IHL-reform movement in general, from the later 1960s; it has however moved in different company, having been perceived as primarily a matter for settlement by the international community's organs for promoting disarmament and arms control. A modest success was registered early with the General Assembly's approval in December 1971 of a Biological Weapons Convention which had been only three years in the drafting. It acquired 'a certain éclat' as 'the first genuine disarmament measure' and included valuable arrangements for periodical review, but it made no arrangements for verification and the measure of its modesty is the fact that the three review conferences to date have spent most of their time discussing how verification, the absolute necessity for which is by now beyond dispute, may be made politically acceptable and scientifically reliable.[57]

Chemical warfare has taken much longer to do anything about; not least because of the spread among non-nuclear powers (including those not *admittedly* nuclear) of the notion that it was 'the poor State's nuclear bomb'. The argument, at its most respectable, ran thus: that so long as nuclear weapons remained the monopoly of only a few of the richer States, and so long as those States made no great progress towards general reductions in nuclear weapons promised in the Nuclear Proliferation Treaty, it was not unreasonable for poorer States to protect themselves against nuclear threat by acquiring and holding in reserve for potential reprisals weapons no more illegal than nuclear ones were generally held to be. Such an argument, besides its attractions for States with less presentable purposes, healthily reminded the nuclear powers of the immoral aspects of their own situation.

---

[57] The quotations are from Nicholas Sims's excellent book *The Diplomacy of Biological Disarmament* (London, 1988), 94 and 163 respectively. It was hailed as the first real disarmament measure because it didn't just limit weapons or their use like arms control and it didn't just proclaim a ban on them like the 1925 Gas Protocol; it actually ensured (in principle) that they were not, and would never be, available.

It understandably found sympathizers in the Third World gratified to see the poor standing up to the rich, and also in that part of the Arab world obsessed with Israel, whose denials of nuclear capability were not believed. It complicated and slowed down the work towards a Convention on Chemical Weapons which split off early from its biological twin and has only now, in the early 1990s, come to a conclusion. Verification as usual has been the prickliest problem. Plant needed for the production of essential elements of chemical weapons can be very small, and the elements themselves may be capable of peaceful uses. Transfers have to be controlled as well as production. States and private companies are inevitably reluctant to admit inspection on site and without warning, the only sort of inspection that is totally convincing: States because, especially, of pride of sovereignty and concern for security, companies not least because of concern to protect patents and the risk of industrial espionage. And behind the technology of inspection lurks the political question: *Quis inspectabit ipsos inspectores?*

Despite such difficulties, however, negotiations continued in a variety of forums. From the most important and active of them, the UN's standing Conference on Disarmament, emerged at last in January 1993 a remarkably comprehensive Convention on the Prohibition, Production, Stockpiling and Use of Chemical Weapons and on their Destruction which prohibits 'not only the chemical agents as such, but also their means of delivery and any device designed for the use of chemical weapons' and which proposes to achieve this end by a close-knit system of verification procedures under the direction of a specialist new international body, the Organization for the Prohibition of Chemical Weapons based in The Hague. The verification procedures go well beyond anything so far seen in any other field; they include the concept of 'challenge inspections' and not of 'declared facilities' only, but also of undeclared ones. Just how quickly and smoothly so unprecedentedly thoroughgoing a disarmament regime can be established, remains to be seen. The Swedish ambassador who had very much to do with it has thus summed up the prospects: 'The Convention will enter into force 180 days after the date of the deposit of the 65th instrument of ratification, but in no case earlier than two years after its opening for signature.' Nineteen ninety-five is his best guess. 'There is, however,' he notes, 'a risk that linkages will be made between the real or perceived possession of nuclear weapons by certain States and the preparedness on the part of others to renounce the chemical weapons option. Such linkages are likely to complicate the process.'[58]

[58] Citations here are from contributions to the UN's periodic review *Disarmament*, 16 (1993) by Gerard Errera, at p. 25, and Carl-Magnus Hyltenius, at p. 12.

Reprisals

AP1 repeatedly prohibits reprisals.[59] Proper understanding of this insistence requires reference to its associated prohibitions of, e.g. collective punishments and the taking of hostages, and to the particular meaning of the word 'reprisals' in international law. Reprisal is one of a closely bunched group of 're-' words which have unusual resonance in IHL and which must be distinguished from one another. Reciprocity is the least conspicuous but not the least important of them. IHL texts scarcely admit it, yet without reciprocity in practice those texts may be of little avail, for not all belligerents will be so saintly as to observe restraints and to honour humanitarian obligations in face of an enemy's persistent refusal to do so.[60] Revenge is not to be thought of where IHL is taken seriously; the desire to avenge defeats, humiliations, insults, etc. has to be assumed to be part of the mentality of the ordinary human being and fighter, but it is too subjective in nature, too wild in exercise to be bearable in law-abiding company. Retaliation and retortion, words less emotively loaded, represent what may in certain circumstances be reasonable and lawful responses to an enemy's unreasonable but not unlawful excesses, but they have not entered the legal vocabulary in the same way as has the word 'reprisal'.[61] A reprisal is a measured, purposeful, unlawful act in response to an unlawful act of the enemy's; illegal though the reprisal may be, its justification is that nothing less will serve to stop the other in his lawless tracks. The purpose of reprisals is supposed to be simply deterrent and admonitory. Reprisals have long been accepted by authorities on the subject as the law of war's ultimate means of law-enforcement, without denying their risky aspects, and for lack of anything better.

Such is the theory of reprisals. In practice they have served more to justify or camouflage excesses than to check them. Reprisals as theory paints them require amounts of information, self-restraint, goodwill, and (while facts are being established and communications with the enemy kept open) time which are rarely available in real-war conditions. The most acceptable

---

[59] Articles 20, 51(6), 52(1), 53(c), 54(4), 55(2), 56(4).

[60] This point is worth making, because the law of war used not to disguise its partial dependence on reciprocity, implied in Article 2 of the 4th Hague Convention of 1907. Geneva law however, as it differentiated itself from the other, expected unconditional observance 'in all circumstances'; words which first appeared in the 1929 Geneva Conventions (Articles 25 and 82) and are repeated in Common Article 1 of the 1949 ones and in Article 1 of AP1 (but not AP2!). These words are taken by commentators to signify unconditional commitment.

[61] 'Retortion is the technical term for retaliation for discourteous, or unkind and inequitable acts by acts of the same or a similar kind', Oppenheim, pp. 134–5. As such it figures in Pictet's *Commentary*, iv. 227–9.

reprisals, it has been argued, are those which remain no more than threats.[62] Reprisals as modern history best knows them have gone far beyond that stage. They fall into two groups. First, it was as reprisals that Britain and Germany in both world wars justified or excused the tit-for-tat escalation of excesses in the war at sea and, in the Second World War, the escalation of city-bombing—the escalation which culminated in Germany's use of its inescapably indiscriminate V weapons—the V standing not for some victory-like word, as simple Britons were wont to suppose, but for *Vergeltung*, reprisal. The tendency for reprisals and counter-reprisals to spiral beyond control recurs on almost every occasion when they are invoked, and constitutes one of the main arguments aginst them.

The other group of incidents which gave reprisals a bad name came before the public during the post-war period of the war-crimes trials. It was under the general description of reprisals that Germany sought to justify or excuse the standard tactic of its response to acts of sabotage and attacks on its soldiers by the resistance movements of occupied Europe: mass executions of 'hostages' taken from among the local inhabitants on a scale varying from time to time and place to place but rarely less than ten locals for one German and rising on the more awful occasions to several hundreds for one. These 'collective punishments' (to give a respectable name to what could be simply acts of terror) were so notable a feature of German military-occupation policy and figured in so many war-crimes trials that one of the most important of these latter, the official title of which is USA *v*. Wilhelm List *et al.*, has always popularly been known as the Hostages Case. The issues at stake in these trials and judgments were of intense interest to military and legal observers, and have remained so, because, as defence lawyers did not fail to point out, armies of occupation of whatever nationality tend to react heavily to acts of popular resistance and, as military manuals of the victors themselves indicated, it was not the German army alone which in those circumstances considered it proper to take hostages and inflict collective punishments. But the evidence of what had just happened throughout occupied Europe (at their worst in its eastern swathe) left no room for doubt; not even for judges so conventionally minded as to concur with the German generals' perception of 'partisan bands' as 'not lawful belligerents ... but guerrillas liable to be shot on capture'.[63]

The scale on which hostages had sometimes been killed and collective

[62] Bothe, Partsch, and Solf, 315.
[63] I quote from pp. 76–7 of the UN War Crimes Commission's 'Notes on the Case', in its *Law Reports on Trials of War Criminals*, viii (1949).

punishments inflicted was judged to have been excessive, intimidating, and terroristic; some would have added, quasi-genocidal. The acts picked out for censure were not reprisals in the proper understanding of the term, they were retaliations going beyond legal limits of reasonable proportion and just discrimination. The judges in USA *v.* List *et al.* condemned them but less forcefully than they might have done had the relevant law not been so inexplicit and ambiguous. It was not by the court but by the Geneva Conventions of 1949 that IHL was brought to deal expressly with the problem, shown in the Second World War to be even more scandalous than had appeared in the First, of the abuse of the legal conception of reprisals. The first, second, and third Conventions banned reprisals with regard to the categories of war-victims which were respectively their particular concerns. The fourth Convention's wide spread of protections for civilians in occupied territory included specific prohibitions of hostage-taking, pillage, 'collective punishments and likewise all measures of intimidation or of terrorism', and (separately, as if to emphasize that those measures were not to be confused with the real thing) 'reprisals against protected persons and their property'.[64]

Such uncompromising corrections of law's previous flabbiness might have been thought to settle the matter. These prohibitions of 1949 however mark not the end of controversies about reprisals but the opening of a new chapter of them. They left untouched the question whether or not reprisals could be taken, e.g. by bombardment, against civilians *not* in occupied territory but on enemy territory. And they could be thought to protect the civilian in occupied territory more than was reasonable. Occupiers after all had rights too. Wars about land and wars conducted on land by their very nature produce invasions and military occupations. IHL therefore has to try to regulate them, but the regulation of them has proved to be endlessly difficult. The post-war attempt to legitimize patriotic resistance and at the same time protect civilians in occupied territory would have more clearly been seen as the attempt to square the circle it actually was if its measures to legitimize resistance had not been so unrealistic; unrealistic above all in supposing (as in effect it did) that armed resistance might successfully operate in total separation from a civilian population. One of the contemporaries who was not deceived was the eminent Dutch lawyer B. V. A. Roling. Emphatically no friend to occupation-minded military powers, he was moved to the famous (and much quoted) comment on the 1949 changes that 'the road to hell seems paved with "good"

[64] Articles 34 and 33.

Conventions'.[65] Was it possible for an occupying power to maintain itself against the predictable hostility of the population by 'police' measures alone?—such being the only measures available, if the more forceful military ones loosely known as reprisals were outlawed. To men like Roling who tried to think dispassionately about it, the ambiguities of the judgments in the 'Hostages' and 'High Command' cases made sense. What the arch-occupiers of the Second World War had done to put down resistance was criminal, not because they did it at all but because of the excesses in their way of doing it and the ideology which prompted them. What resistance movements had done, however courageous and patriotically valuable it might have been, was sure to provoke strong reactions and, somewhat like spying (which also could be courageous and patriotically valuable), to go beyond where the law of war could greatly help it.

The event (an endlessly protracted one, as it turned out) which brought the post-war's settlement of this question to the test began with Israel's victory in the Six Day War of early June 1967. There had of course already been plenty of insurgency and counter-insurgency warfare which, being fought by much the same 'guerrilla' means as armed resistance against enemy occupation, raised similar humanitarian issues. The parallel seemed close indeed to the person who, about this time, described Latin America as 'a continent occupied by its armies'. The idea moreover had received wide acceptance throughout the anti-colonial and decolonizing parts of the international community that national liberation struggles against colonial powers were to be read as wars of lawful resistance against illegal occupation, an idea which by 1967 was well on the road to its incorporation into IHL. Until that happened in 1977 there remained room for disagreement about the formal legal position of the powers *in situ*, but about Israel's situation after its extraordinary victory, there appeared to be no room for doubt. Must not the fourth Geneva Convention, which Israel had signed along with the first, second, and third at the original signatures ceremony and which it had ratified only eighteen months later, be instantly applicable? Was this not a military occupation pure and simple?

But little is pure and nothing is simple in the relationship between Israel and its Arab neighbours. Its uniquely troublesome character has already been indicated in the Entr'acte following Part II. The complications were now added that weighty forces in Israeli politics insisted on perceiving the end of hostilities not as the beginning of an occupation of alien territory but as the recovery of lands which (on ancient historical and religious grounds,

[65] *The Law of War and National Jurisdiction since 1945*, in the Hague Academy series 'Recueil des Cours' 100(II), 1960, 323–455 at 445. See again, below, p. 391.

the merits of which need not be gone into here) properly belonged to Israel anyway, in signification of which they describe what the rest of the world calls 'the West Bank' [of the Jordan] as the Jewish provinces of Judaea and Samaria. On modern historical and political grounds, moreover, Israeli governments insisted that the territories it now commanded were not 'occupied' but 'administered', a term with no recognized standing in IHL but helpful to Israel's public stance of denying the legal, the *de jure* applicability of the fourth Convention while undertaking to apply its 'humanitarian provisions' *de facto*—accepting, as it were, the spirit though not the letter of fourth Convention law. Nor is this the only exceptional feature of what almost every other member of the international community has nevertheless regarded as a military occupation to which the fourth Convention *de jure* applies, which is the view I adopt here. The occupation has for instance gone on for very much longer than was anticipated when the law was made, thus opening the door for *ad hoc* measures and expedients which could only be judged by their moral compatibility with the spirit of IHL in any case (and also, of course, basic human rights law). Sovereign rights are supposed not to be determined until the conclusion of a formal peace treaty, but official Israeli maps indicate 'absolutely no distinction between what is often called Israel proper (i.e. Israel in its pre-1967 boundaries) and the occupied territories'.[66] There have actually been two territorial annexations (East Jerusalem in 1967, and the Golan Heights in 1980), and Israel's control of the West Bank looked sufficiently like *de facto* annexation by the early 1980s for a distinguished elder of American Jewry to describe it as such.[67] Another extraordinary feature, justified like the annexation of the Golan Heights as necessary for credible national defence, has been the progressive implanting of Jewish defended settlements in the occupied territories at the expense every time of their Palestinian inhabitants and with no apparent justification in any part of international law.

There is no doubt that this military occupation, *qua* military occupation, has been exceptional and unique, and in its relation to international law confusingly complex. The analyst must attempt to separate as best he can the elements which are explicable in terms of would-be lawful occupation policy from those elements—as e.g. economic exploitation and implantation of settlements—which relate rather to unlawful ideas of annexation or original title. The attempt is not foredoomed to failure. No matter how much that has gone on in the course of it can scarcely be appraised by

---

[66] Roberts *et al.*, *Academic Freedom under Israeli Military Occupation* (London and Geneva, 1984), 21.
[67] Arthur Hertzberg in *Foreign Affairs*, 61 (1983), 1064–77.

reference to the principles and rules of IHL, much else can be so appraised, and Israel itself shows the way. Whatever reservations may be discerned behind the Israeli Government's refusal to recognize the *de jure* applicability of the fourth Geneva Convention, it has at least acknowledged 'the relevance of international legal standards' as for instance have not, in comparable circumstances, the USSR in Hungary, Czechoslovakia, and Afghanistan, the Republic of South Africa in Namibia, and, one might add, Indonesia in East Timor. Israel's military authorities have allowed the ICRC considerable freedom of access to the occupied territories and its Supreme Court has affirmed the applicability of the Hague Regulations.[68] It is relevant to remark also that the Israel Defence Forces' commitment to the three other Geneva Conventions has never been in doubt, and that Israel has permitted an almost unexampled latitude of comment, from within its armed forces as well as from without, on the compatibility of their operations with their legal and ethical obligations.

The experience since 1967 of Israelis as occupiers and Palestinians as occupied alike suggest one or both of two things: that the norms of 1949 are inadequate to meet the reasonable demands of *both* parties, and/or that there is simply no satisfactory way legally to regulate the relations between an occupying party determined to enforce his will and an occupied party determined to resist him. The military occupation part of the Civilians' Convention, with or without AP1's supplements to it, may simply be an exercise in wishful thinking. But it must be admitted that the West Bank and Gaza Strip have not constituted a fair test for the new law. The makers of the Civilians Convention can never have envisaged a military occupation as unprecedentedly prolonged as this, or circumstances as uniquely intractable as those which tangle together the new State of Israel, the neighbouring Arab States (most of them in some sense new too), and the dispossessed Palestinian people bearing the aspect of a State-in-waiting. The story of the 4th Convention's vicissitudes in this extraordinary situation cannot be taken as other than a provisional judgment on the Convention's merits. It is however a discouraging story, the story of a military occupation maintaining itself over a long period of time by means which would scarcely have been different if the legislation of 1949 had never happened.

Curfews, closures, and arrests have been in the occupier's repertoire, time out of mind. Measures corresponding to those which Germany took in the

---

[68] I here cite from and roughly summarize pp. 62–4 of Adam Roberts's 'Prolonged Military Occupation: the Israeli-Occupied Territories since 1967', in *AmJIL* 84 (1990), 44–103. For the context of the ICRC's access, see Forsythe, in Fox and Meyer (eds.), *Effecting Compliance* (London, 1993), 88–103.

Second World War are taken still, and are still called reprisals, though their less murderous scale and aim sometimes permit explanation in terms of proportionality and discrimination which can sound reasonable. Other old words of evil repute continue to be used with contrasting and conflicting meanings. Arab parties take hostages and admit readily to doing so, the 'administrative detainees' held by Israel seem sometimes to serve a hostage-like purpose. Terrorism has been for so long and so carelessly alleged by each side against the other that it requires a special effort of will to remember that some acts thus branded can be more discriminating, proportionate, and in certain circumstances justifiable than others. Whether the reprisals that Israel has regularly taken against what it has called crimes or acts of terror have been as excessive, intimidatory, terroristic, etc. as their victims have claimed is a matter as to which there is no agreement. Explaining its raids (mostly aerial) on alleged terrorist bases beyond its own borders, it has argued that the incidental deaths of civilians in them result from the terrorists' failure to separate civilians from fighters. Explaining its demolitions of the properties of alleged terrorists' families and close neighbours, Israel has argued that collective punishments make good sense in a culture characterized by clannishness, the ethic of familial obligation, and distrust of government—one of the many reminders in these pages that the ideas of society, human nature, and the rule of law which guided the ICRC and the majority of the 1949 legislators may have been too open and individualistic to fit cultures and experiences so different.

The 1949 Conventions, taken necessarily in conjunction with the Hague Rules, mark the end of the reprisals line so far as Israel is concerned, for Israel has not signed, and presumably never will sign the 1977 Protocols, whose prohibition of reprisals is even more extensive.[69] The 1977 addition to what was there already is twofold. It includes the Protocol's protected objects in the fields of religion and culture, the environment and the means of subsistence also; and by 'civilians and civilian objects' it means not just those in enemy-occupied territory (as was mainly the case in 1949) but emphatically also those in enemy territory. Reprisal bombing or blockading of civilians is therefore ruled out, and the second half of the great Nuremberg gap thereby formally closed. No room is left for the lawful use of reprisals except against military personnel and objectives.

Whether this offers enough space for reprisals to do any good is a question that was much debated at the CDDH and has continued to be debated since. Without disputing the wisdom of the Kalshoven doctrine that

---

[69] The ban recurs also in the Mines-and-Booby-Traps Protocol of the 1981 UN Convention, Art. 3(2). Reprisals however appear not at all in AP2.

reprisals threatened are preferable to reprisals taken, it seems for instance improbable that the pressures of mass politics would permit an embattled government to stay its reprisal-dealing hand in face of repeated attacks on its own people. Aspiration to protect civilians from every danger in wartime may have gone as much too far in 1977 as it went in 1949 with restricted regard to civilians in occupied territory. Law which makes it impossible for a belligerent power decently to maintain a military occupation does not necessarily make life better for the occupied, it may simply set the signals for making it worse. The 4th Geneva Convention is, after all, somewhat one-sided. An ideal code for the humanitarian management of a military occupation would contain rules as comprehensive for the conduct of the occupied as for the occupier. Adam Roberts sums up the matter very well, near the close of his monumental 1990 article (already referred to), when he deplores the General Assembly's use of the law on occupations as 'a stick with which to beat occupants . . . rather than a serious means of seeking to reconcile the conflicting interests of the parties'. IHL will indeed have attained a fine state of sophistication and acceptance when members of the international community find that they can manage military occupations without any recourse to reprisals at all.[70]

Safety zones

Further indications of the seriousness with which contemporary IHL holds the civilian's interests at heart come in AP1's articles protecting safety zones (Articles 59 and 60 on 'Non-Defended Localities' and 'Demilitarized Zones' respectively, to be precise) and civil defence organizations (Articles 61–7). Civil defence constitutes a new item in the range of civilian protections, but safety zones or, as the ICRC prefers to call them, protected areas have a long history. Their earliest sources lie in the religious institution of sanctuary. They are related to the time-honoured practice of declaring undefended populous places to be open cities, as was more or less done to Rome, Florence, Paris, and other cities in the course of the Second World War, a confused business, which R. J. Jennings did his best to sort out in the 1945 *BYIL*. Protected areas' special role in IHL emerges with the eighteenth and early nineteenth centuries' growing practice of using predetermined flags and emblems to indicate and so, it was intended, to protect persons and activities engaged in collecting and tending the wounded and sick. Formalized and built into IHL's treaty foundations from 1864, the effective-

---

[70] One of the best and most accessible reviews of this latest stage of the great reprisals question is Françoise Hampson, 'Belligerent Reprisals and the 1977 Protocols . . .', in *ICLQ* 37 (1988), 818–43.

ness of the protective emblem was found by bona fide HCPs far to outweigh its failures. Some hospital localities had shells and bombs fall in them, but many didn't. Hospital ships, their exact functional parallel at sea, more often than not reached their destinations safely. Conspicuously indicated by Red Crosses (or Crescents or whatever), placed preferably at a safe distance from anything that could be regarded as a military objective, and their locations made known to the enemy through somebody's good offices (probably the ICRC's), protected areas of this medical kind became regular features of supposedly law-respecting wars.

The ICRC has long striven to extend the usefulness of the protected-area principle. The innovations made in 1949 have already been noticed. It has sought to persuade belligerents to use it not just for the protection of medical activities but for the protection also of all kinds of persons taking no active part in hostilities, and it has even sought to persuade potential belligerents to establish the location of such areas in advance of the hostilities which would make them necessary. This second idea, which appears in Article 23 of the first Convention and Article 14 of the fourth, never got anywhere. It did not seem quite so extraordinary at the time of its launching as it appears in retrospect. What most of all prompted it in the 1930s and 1940s (and kept some life in it through the Cold War decades) was the use, or threat of use, of 'weapons of mass destruction' against urban areas. While States which feared being at the receiving end of such weapons were planning mass evacuations of civilians from endangered areas to safe ones, there was nothing unreasonable about proposing a legal formalization of the practice which, in the ICRC's view, would make safe areas safer. The relevant article in the fourth Convention mentioned exactly the kinds of non-combatants with which government evacuation programmes were most concerned: 'wounded, sick and aged persons, children under 15, expectant mothers and mothers of children under seven'. Moreover, it served the ICRC's never wholly hidden agenda of calling the attention of high-tech military powers to the logical implications of their 'defence' policies. Governments of such powers however were not keen to have those implications brought to the attentions of their civilian populations. The idea also failed to attract their defence chiefs. Was there any part of their country they could undertake in advance to leave absolutely free of military involvement? And—the verification difficulty, again!—could they believe an enemy's word that the corresponding part of his country really was so? They were reluctant to believe it.

With the other part of its protected-area programme, the ICRC has been more successful. To the traditional sort of hospital zones and localities there have been, since the Second World War, two notable additions. One happened on the high seas, during the war occasioned by Argentina's invasion of the Falkland Islands in 1982.

At Britain's suggestion, and without any special agreement in writing, the Parties . . . established a neutral zone at sea . . . called 'the Red Cross Box' . . . located on the high seas to the north of the islands. Without hampering military operations, it enabled hospital ships to hold position . . . and exchange British and Argentine wounded.[71]

The other innovation is seen in the variety of neutralized zones and protected areas set up primarily for the benefit of civilians; e.g. in Dhaka in 1971, Nicosia 1974, Saigon and Phnom Pen in 1975, 'and in the major cities of Nicaragua in 1979'.[72] How many times the ICRC's efforts in this direction have been successful compared with times when its efforts have failed, there is no means of knowing. The hazards to which such refuges are exposed are innumerable, and the task of establishing them is evidently a delicate and complicated one. 'Parties to the conflict' have to consent to it, and they may be more than two in number; in the ICRC's film about its work in the Lebanon civil war in the later 1970s, its chief delegate describes the vast labour of having to magic simultaneous consent out of *sixteen* separate warring groups.[73] The record of a protected area's existence is very incomplete without facts about its size and duration; a 'neutralized zone' which the ICRC at last managed to set up in northern Afghanistan in April 1990 seems not to have existed for longer than the duration of a 12-hour truce.[74] Its value as a precedent and example may however have been by far the most important thing about it, in a milieu where political neutrality and humanitarian impartiality were obviously not natural moral tastes but acquired ones. Where distinctions between civilian and combatant are not clearly made, and where wounded enemies are commonly killed rather than cared for, the protection of even a few for even a limited period can be worth its weight in gold.

The ICRC's unique capability of opening umbrellas of neutrality of course means that it is the usual agent in the establishment of protected areas and their like, but it is not the only one. The Geneva Conventions leave several doors open for action by 'other humanitarian organizations';

[71] Sylvie-Stoyanka Junod, *Protection of the Victims of Armed Conflict Falkland-Malvinas Islands 1982* (ICRC Geneva, 1984), 26.
[72] Examples given in the ICRC *Bulletin*, 175, Aug. 1990.
[73] The film is 'The Delegates', the delegate is Jean Hoefliger (subsequently, Director of the Institut Henry-Dunant) and the negotiation was for exchange of prisoners, but it might just as well have been for a Protected Area.
[74] ICRC *Bulletin*, 172, May 1990, p. 2.

action for which in any case many of them scarcely need formal legal sanction, or for which legal sanction is readily found elsewhere; in human rights law, for instance, or among the UN's many-branched refugee activities. The Holy See was instrumental in the establishment of a 'sanctuary zone' in the Dominican Republic in 1965, and UNICEF has several times succeeded in the not wholly dissimilar enterprise of persuading warring parties to cease fire for long enough to allow local vaccination programmes to be carried out.[75] The UN itself made an ambiguous and confusing entry into the business when, in April 1991, it moved to take some of the steam out of the affair of Iraq's post-war handling of its Kurdish people by establishing what the Secretary-General called 'reception centres' (a term straight from the refugee realm) but what the British prime minister, who seems to have been the prime mover in the European Community's acceptance of the idea, called 'safe havens' (a term much closer to IHL's protected areas).

'Operation Haven' along Iraq's border with Turkey lasted from mid-April until mid-July 1991, and whether the experience of it will in the end be seen to have helped or hindered the cause of humanitarian neutrality, none can yet say. That the UN might convincingly stand in a neutral or detached posture *vis-à-vis* any particular armed conflict is of course undeniable, and there is perhaps no end to the amount of protection it could in such a case offer to victims and sufferers. But a strong pair of rose-tinted spectacles was required for seeing the UN in such a light *vis-à-vis* Iraq in 1991, and too many ambiguities had to be given the desired interpretation. The war to expel Iraq from Kuwait and to punish Iraq for its misdoings may not have been 'a UN war', as the Secretary-General stoutly insisted, but it was certainly in some sense a UN-authorized one.[76]

The more than 20,000 troops of the 'multilateral coalition' supervising 'Operation Haven' came from thirteen nations; some of them had not been involved in the recent fighting, but American, British, and French troops predominated and 'overall co-ordination' was provided by the USA.[77] Security Council Resolution 688 of 5 April 1991, condemning Iraq's repression of its civilian (and especially its Kurdish) population as a threat to international peace and security may turn out to have been the landmark in international law which the human rights movement has hailed it.

[75] Sydney Bailey, 'Non-official Mediation in Disputes: Reflections on Quaker Experience', in *International Affairs*, (1985), 221; V. Brittain in the *Guardian*, 30 Mar. 1989, p. 1.

[76] S-G's speech to the European Parliament, 18 Apr. 1991.

[77] Quotations and figures from article in the *Sunday Times*, 4 Aug. 1991, by one of its senior British officers, Maj.-Gen. Robin Ross, who evidently understood it to be part of a continuing process of disciplining the regrettably surviving dictator.

Some years will have to pass, however, before it sheds its appearance as one of the string of Security Council Resolutions enforcing the law of the Charter on one extravagantly lawless member of the international community, and as prompted by the embarrassments of the UN's executive coalition in face of the troublesome turn unexpectedly taken by the Kurdish question.[78]

(Circumstances compel me to pass over the UN's further ventures into this humanitarian protective field in the former Yugoslavia. They began after I drafted this section and they are still going on as I prepare its finalized version for the press. By the time the book comes out, we shall know a great deal about the strengths and weaknesses, the potentials for success and failure of UN-proclaimed safe havens and protected areas.)

As for the associated subject of civil defence, it reminds the student of contemporary IHL that there is no necessary relation between the permanent importance of things and the space they occupy in its instruments. The seven articles, a whole chapter, of AP1 given to civil defence are a case in point. This subject was a special interest of a relatively small number of countries, Sweden, West Germany, and the Soviet bloc prominent among them, whose fears at the time of drafting included being bombed, fought over, and/or occupied, and who had the wealth and the administrative talent to take elaborate precautions accordingly. For such countries, this chapter provided an ideal model of the very best they could expect in very bad circumstances; from their point of view, civil defence was worth taking very seriously. It is a measure of the contradictions and gambles in which nuclear weapons could enmesh States possessing them that the UK, whose civilian population's prospects in a nuclear war were singularly bad, has never since the Second World War taken civil defence with comparable and convincing seriousness, and that it contributed little to the work on these articles.[79]

The governing assumption in the civil defence chapter of AP1 is that a well-organized law-abiding State will have, or at any rate should have, a civil defence organization 'to protect the civilian populations against the dangers, and to help it to recover from the immediate effects, of hostilities or disasters and also to provide the conditions necessary for its survival'.

---

[78] This difficult question is subjected to a searching review by Philip Alston, 'The Security Council and Human Rights: Lessons to be Learned from the Iraq–Kuwait Crisis and its Aftermath', in *Australian Yearbook of International Law*, 13 (1993), 107–76.

[79] Adam Roberts has some discreetly strong words on this aspect of the matter in his contribution to Michael A. Meyer (ed.), *Armed Conflict and the New Law* (BIICL, London, 1989), 175–207. Less discreet, in the same sense, is Michael Howard, *The Causes of War* (London, 1983), 113–14.

The governing principle is, in the words of the commentators, that 'civil defence forms part of civilian life'.[80] The governing purpose of the chapter is to make sure that this organization, under its very own distinctive sign of 'an equilateral blue triangle on an orange ground' is not mistaken by an invading or occupying power for part of its enemy's forces or war effort. How tightrope-walking and temper-testing an effort this might prove to be, appears in the long Article 65 on Cessation of Protection. The invader/occupier may interfere with the civil defence members' maintenance of the fabric of their civil society only if they commit, 'outside their proper tasks, acts harmful to the enemy', and then 'only after a warning has been given setting, whenever appropriate, a reasonable time-limit, and after such warning has remained unheeded'. The article goes on to list acts that shall not be considered harmful to the enemy. They include 'that civil defence tasks are carried out under the direction or control of military authorities', 'that civilian civil defence personnel bear light individual weapons', and that their organization shall be 'along military lines'. It might be thought that these are rather unrealistic provisions. The vindicator of this area of contemporary IHL would have to admit that, however firmly this latest version of it in many important respects has its feet on the ground, its head here has gone heavenwards.

Precautions and Proportionality

Among the most valuable provisions of the first Additional Protocol are the two Articles 57 and 58 about precautions expected to be taken by attackers and defenders alike, in the interests of protecting civilians and civilian objects from avoidable harm. Nothing like this had ever before appeared in the treaty texts; and yet the idea is as old as the idea of restraint itself. It is as fundamental as the idea of distinction. But whereas the principle of distinction was early recognized as such and given the place it merited in those texts, the principle of proportionality took much longer to solidify; not because the idea of it was unknown or the force of it unadmitted, but (presumably) because it was thought to be too slippery and in its potential implications embarrassing to commit to a set form of words. Only after 1945 did it come out of the closet. The judges of the war-crimes tribunals repeatedly had to assess the merits of legal arguments about the lack of precautionary care evident in wilful or negligent conduct of operations, the contempt for moral principle contained in severities to varying degrees

[80] Bothe, Partsch, and Solf, 401.

disproportionate. From then on, the word 'proportionality' became increasingly familiar in IHL discourse, as concerned persons agonized over the armed conflicts of the age and debated the causes of their awfulness.[81]

With familiarity came controversy. There were two ways of looking at the matter. To representatives of the people and places which were thought to have suffered excessively and needlessly from culpable shellings and bombings, almost any measure of incidental civilian death and damage looked like too much. To shrug it off as 'collateral' damage, they felt, was too comfortable an evasion of responsibility; methodically to debate the pros and cons of it under the title of proportionality was to dignify it with a respectability it did not deserve. Nor was this an argument merely about what had happened in the Second World War. The parties who took this line about proportionality were less interested in recalling bombings of the past than they were in calling attention to bombings of the present. In so doing they called attention also to the fact that the parties chiefly concerned to establish rules of proportionality were the industrially advanced military powers, for only they had the wealth and equipment that issued in possibly disproportionate attacks and, in their predilection for using machinery rather than men, the motivation for undertaking them. Looked at in this perspective, the proportionality question thus interlocked with the broader-based contention of certain socialist and anti-colonialist circles in the 1960s and 1970s, that IHL's rules of combat were in effect rigged against the Third World, and needed to be revolutionized rather than just revised.

Looked at with more traditionalist eyes, however, the most that needed to be done with the proportionality principle—and in fact the most that realistically could be done—was to bring it firmly into the open, to clarify it in a form that all parties could be persuaded to accept, and to build it into the improved version of IHL that would come out of the CDDH. This was how the ICRC approached the matter. The ICRC's responsibilities through the years of conference preparations and then the four years of the conference itself included, besides the promotion of its own point of view, the accommodation of conflicting points of view held by others. The law provided the ostensible issues that were argued about, but the motives and mainsprings for argument were often political; some of the CDDH's

---

[81] I recall a senior army legal officer, not long retired, telling me in the early 1980s that he had never heard the word until ten years or so earlier; though he may have been exaggerating for the sake of effect, as professionals sometimes do when discussing their work with laymen. Besides being rather a new word, proportionality is certainly an awkward word. It is a pity that such indispensable and noble words as proportionality and humanitarian(-ism) are in themselves so lumbering, unattractive and inexpressive. But doubtless the time is long past when there was any possibility of finding alternatives.

goings-on were too much like those of the General Assembly for the comfort of the genuinely neutral-minded. If an improved and universally acceptable IHL was to come out of the conference, it was essential that Third World difficulties about the existing law should be overcome. On many matters, the ICRC was rather sympathetic to Third World and/or socialist-bloc opinion; so much so that American writers in the Reagan years found fault with it as for being anti-American.[82] But when it came to proportionality, there was no doubt where the ICRC stood. The Draft Rules for the Limitation of the Dangers Incurred by the Civilian Population in Time of War, which acquired the character of holy writ within the Red Cross movement following their promulgation in 1956, included a long chapter on Precautions in Attacks on Military Objectives, and from that the draft text of AP1's Articles 57 and 58 obviously derived.

These articles, like so many other of IHL's rules and prescriptions, are attempting to find safe ways across the quicksands between, on the one side, urgent desire completely to protect civilians from danger in wartime and, on the other, tragic awareness that the nature of war makes complete protection unlikely. If emphatic and repeated prohibition of attacks directly on civilians could suffice to protect them, their safety would by now be secure; the prohibition theme recurs in IHL's instruments *ad nauseam*. But civilians are not thereby made secure; not even when further supported by the dramatic clarification of what *may* be attacked in AP1's definition of military objectives, already scrutinized. Accidents will happen. The best-laid schemes go wrong. The best-aimed bombs and bullets cannot be guaranteed to hit nothing but their targets. But the risks can be reduced. The taking of reasonable precautions can perhaps avoid certain dangers to civilians; dangers that cannot be avoided may be minimized. And so these articles spell out the kinds of precautions that may reasonably be expected to be taken by 'those who plan, decide upon' and/or 'decide to launch any attack'; taking 'attack' to mean *any* 'acts of violence against an adversary, whether in offence or defence'.[83]

Proportionality as such is not mentioned but that is what must guide the commander as he and his advisers (who will, in unusually law-minded

[82] See e.g. Parks, 'Air War and the Law of War', 79 n. and 105 n.

[83] Bothe, Partsch, and Solf, 366. Their exegesis of this point is far from perspicuous. The ICRC *Commentary*'s p. 603 is better, remarking *inter alia* that 'attack' in this context really means nothing other than 'combat action'. To the lay mind, 'action' would seem to have said it all, and to have been less open to misunderstanding. The definition matters not least because of the *offensive* connotation which the word 'attack' has in most ears. Clearly it is of the utmost importance to prevent it being thought that only aggressors (supposing the possibility of agreeing upon their identity, which is another question) are obliged to take these precautions seriously.

armed forces, include legal ones) weigh against one another (1) the 'concrete and direct' military advantages anticipated from a possible action, (2) the 'incidental loss of civilian life, injury to civilians, damage to civilian objects or a combination thereof' which might accompany it, and (3) what precautions are 'feasible'. Let us briefly consider each of these in turn.

(1) recalls the emphases in Article 52(2)'s definition of military objectives. That sought to add to the idea of an unmistakable military objective an element of the demonstrable and immediate; the legitimately attackable was not anything that might at some future date be of military advantage to the enemy but something that effectively and definitely contributed to his military capability as of *now*.[84] To 'effective' and 'definite' are now added 'concrete and direct'.

(2) This is the core of the moral reactor. That there will almost certainly be incidental loss of civilian life has to be taken for granted. The big question is, how much may be risked? How much would be 'excessive'? 'Excessive' is the key word. In paras. 2(a)(iii) and 2(b) the commander is required to make up his mind whether an attack is likely to cause 'incidental loss' etc., as cited above, 'which would be excessive in relation to the concrete and direct military advantage anticipated'. Some of the more interesting aspects of the problem of calculating this relationship will be examined below.

(3) 'Feasible's' principal role here as elsewhere is to reassure warriors that they are not being asked to do the objectively impossible or to do what is possible only by forgoing military advantage. So those who plan or decide upon an attack must 'do everything feasible to verify that the objectives to be attacked are neither civilians nor civilian objects', etc., *and* choose 'means and methods of attack with a view to avoiding, and in any event to minimizing, incidental loss of civilian life', etc. There was much argument at CDDH about what word to use, and then, after 'feasible' had been fixed on, about what precisely it was to be understood to mean. The UK's understanding, shared probably by more others than openly said so, is this seemingly permissive one: 'feasible' means 'that which is practicable or practically possible, taking into account all circumstances at the time including those relevant to the success of military operations'. Italy's 'statement of interpretation' is similar but even vaguer, inasmuch as the circumstances to be taken account of include 'humanitarian' as well as military considerations.[85] Whether such verbiage amounts to anything significant, the reader must decide.

---

[84] That interpretation of 'in the circumstances ruling at the time' appears to be authorized by Bothe, Partsch, and Solf, 326.   [85] Roberts and Guelff, 467, 465.

Decision-making commanders are unlikely to lose sleep over 'feasible' but they have to wrestle seriously with 'concrete and direct' and with 'excessive'. How well placed is a commander for making such a judgment? The lower his level within an operational field, the greater may be the difficulty. Second lieutenants and sergeants are not normally privy to the grand designs of staff officers and generals. The incidental loss likely to be suffered by an inhabited village may look excessive to the platoon commander ordered to fight his way through it but may look minimal in the larger perspective of the divisional planners. Hence the reservation entered by Switzerland (with the support of many other States) that these provisions 'did not create obligations except for commanding officers at battalion or unit level upwards and at higher echelons'.[86] The lower-level commander in free-moving combat may still have plenty of opportunities to make independent moral decisions but it is well understood that, like the soldiers immediately under him, in the context of larger operations he has to trust the judgment of his superiors. The question with which this paragraph began nevertheless besets them in another form. They may be highly enough placed in the chain of command but their decisions can only be as good as the information put before them. Again and again Article 57 has to assume the adequacy and accuracy of the information fed into the calculations as to what may be 'excessive', but in the heat and haste of battle reliable information may be as hard to get as cool calculation will be hard to undertake.

Even in less hot and hurried circumstances, sources of information may be defective. A recent celebrated case of defective information with an arguably 'excessive' loss of civilian life as a result, was the bombing on 13 February 1991 of the bunker in Baghdad which, built during the Iraq–Iran War as an air-raid shelter, now doubled as some sort of command-and-control centre, which the attack planners knew about, and as a night-time air-raid shelter, which they didn't. Notwithstanding that the bunker was in the midst of a civilian district, the bombing itself satisfied the highest legal standards, with little or no reported collateral/incidental damage. But a large number of the civilians sheltering there were inevitably killed. The matter at once became a *cause célèbre*. While uncertainty about the facts kept the American targeters from giving a confidently satisfactory explanation, Iraq's denial that it was anything other than a shelter and presentation of the event as an example of civilian-killing lawlessness was swallowed by media reporters and instant commentators who knew nothing of Iraq's practice of mingling civilian with military objectives, drew no conclusions from the bunker's external trimmings of barbed-wire and camouflage, and

---

[86] The wording varies insignificantly from State to State. See ibid. 467.

understood not at all the relations of these things to legality. Only when the fighting was over could the other side of the story be filled in.[87] What the targeters would or should have done had they found out about the bunker's confusing secondary function as an air-raid shelter before the attack was ordered, is the sort of question that IHL seminars love to mull over. Paragraph 2(c)'s injunction to issue 'effective advance warning . . . unless circumstances do not permit' would have been no help, because advance warning would simply have enabled the Iraqi authorities to move their military users of the bunker out of harm's way. Calculations about what might constitute excessive civilian loss would have had to take into account the military value of the command-and-control functions of the bunker, so far as it was understood, within the full context of the Iraqi war machine, so far as it was known. AP1 has usefully brought the principle of proportionality into the open and made it easier to understand, but it cannot make the practice of it easy.

Another case which usefully illustrates the potential complexity of proportionality's equation between quality of information, 'concrete and direct' military advantage, and incidental civilian losses, is the Second World War case of the German general Lothar Rendulic. He was one of the defendants in 'USA v. List et al.', already referred to. He was not the most famous of the generals in the dock on that occasion but part of the judgment which was delivered in his case has turned out to be of exceptional significance because of its relevance to the question of proportionality and the guidance it gives to military commanders for the handling of it. Rendulic was indicted for a variety of crimes committed in the Balkans and—at the urgent request of Norway—for having excessively laid waste the northernmost districts of Norway, the county of Finnmark, and the northern half of the county of Tromsö, while commanding the German retreat during the winter of 1944–5.[88] He was found guilty of the former offences (which constituted by far the greater share of his indictment) but not guilty of the latter. It is with the latter alone that we need be concerned. The American court found that his devastations, although admittedly extreme and, indeed, as total as they could be, were excusable because, although the Russians

---

[87] I follow, finding no cause to disbelieve, pp. 14–16 of Appendix O, 'The Role of the Law of War' of the US Defense Department's *Final Report to Congress on Conduct of the Persian Gulf War* (Apr. 1992). It must be emphasized that although this report often refers to AP1, the USA has not ratified it; its contents are referred to because the USA has no quarrel with those parts of AP1 which are deemed to embody customary international law.

[88] The British reader must not think of counties in terms of the UK. From the Director of the Finnmark Reconstruction Office, D. H. Lund's article in *Geographical Journal*, 109 (1947), 185–97 it appears that the county of Finnmark covered a larger area than the whole of Denmark.

were, in fact, *not* in hot pursuit of him, he could not be sure that they were not. The legitimacy of devastation to impede pursuit was not contested.[89] The information at his disposal, it was pleaded on Rendulic's behalf, was limited and imperfect, but it was the best he could get; therefore he was entitled to act upon what might now be called the 'worst-case hypothesis'. Northernmost Norway, whose population inevitably underwent much suffering during its forced evacuation, took years to recover.

Recovery was still far from complete when news of the judgment reached Norway early in 1948. It was received with outraged indignation. In the Norwegian parliament's debates, the tone of which was, considering the circumstances, remarkably calm and intellectually elevated, the justice of Rendulic's acquittal was most convincingly contested on the following grounds. (1) He may indeed have been unable to be sure that the Russians were not close behind him, and his initial devastation of eastern Finnmark (all of it except the very easternmost bit around Kirkenes, which the Russians had seized before winter set in) was excusable in terms of military necessity, but the excuse wore thinner in proportion as the months passed, the German withdrawal continued, and still the Russians did not appear. (2) He pleaded that he was under pressure to act quickly, but plans for such a devastation had been laid well beforehand, and demolition explosives placed in all the predictable places. (3) Uncertainty about Russian intentions was not the only driving idea in his mind. The ruthless and intimidatory way the evacuation was ordered and executed, the frightful totality of the destruction, were of a piece with German policy in general—and, we might add, with the conduct in the Balkans for which he was found guilty. This particular example of it had been ordered well before the event by *Oberkommando Wehrmacht*, and had formed (a small) part of the indictment of General Alfred Jodl before the IMT.[90] Rendulic, a fanatically anticommunist Austrian who, though not apparently a party member, rejoiced in obedience to his Führer, was not one of those easier-going German generals who took risks to moderate the effects of the Führer's extremer orders. Similar devastation had been done during the retreat through Finnish Lapland in later 1944, when the purpose could scarcely have been

[89] James F. Gebhardt's study of *The Petsamo-Kirkenes Operation: Soviet Breakthrough and Pursuit in the Arctic, October 1944* (Fort Leavenworth, Kans., 1990) shows on p. 125 how difficult military movements in that region already were, without the additional difficulty made for them by 'scorched earth' or whatever.

[90] Eugene Davidson, *The Trial of the Germans* (New York, 1966), 355 thus summarizes Jodl's response: he 'had not been consulted but had only drafted and distributed the order and had done his best to hold the demolitions to a minimum'. Like so many Axis acts of war, when awkward questions were asked about it afterwards it turned out to be something which nobody at the time had liked or wanted, but which was done just the same.

to impede dangerous pursuers, so unlikely were the Finnish troops (made to change sides by the Russians) to advance beyond their own frontier.[91] Far from acting with the understandable temporary wildness of a frightened man in the dark, Rendulic was methodically executing in daylight a preplanned policy of vindictive desertification.[92]

The Norwegians failed in their attempt to secure a rehearing of their case against Rendulic. The general was not taken to Norway for retrial, nor would the American commander of the American-occupied zone contemplate hearing it on appeal. After serving less than ten of his twenty years sentence, Rendulic was released, to finish writing his memoirs and to be metamorphosed into the patron saint of commanders who plead ignorance or error for doing more 'incidental' harm to civilians than others may think necessary.[93] Readers may share the author's wonder whether the apparent strength of the Norwegian arguments against his beatification are not such as to make the American court's judgment in 1948 a shaky pillar to lean on.

AP1's Article 58, concerning Precautions against the Effects of Attacks, may be much more quickly dealt with. No new or unfamiliar principle is here; what is new is its appearance in treaty print.[94] This Article spells out the implications of what has always been the logical extension of the principle of distinction: the attacker's obligation not deliberately to attack civilians and civilian objects must be accompanied by the defender's obligation not deliberately to cause them to be attacked. This has long been customary in principle. Forcing non-combatants to serve as shields or decoys has always been reckoned dishonourable and indecent; refusal to let them escape from places under fire has always been controversial. If those directing the fire were indifferent as to whether it hit non-combatants or not, that was controversial too; but if the fire happened to be directed at military objectives and non-combatants happened to live close to them, the firer did not have to feel that he was to blame; the deliberate placing of non-combatants (or prisoners) in or on military objectives was one of the

[91] For this glimpse of a little-known theatre of war, I am indebted to a conference paper by Malcolm Mackintosh, 'The Western Allies, the Soviet Union and Finnmark 1944–45', pp. 14–15, pointed out to me by Dr Mats Berdal.
[92] For copies of the relevant Norwegian parliamentary debates on 4 Mar. and 22 Nov. 1948, and for translation of the most relevant passages in them, I am gratefully indebted respectively to Professor Olaf Riste and to Dr Berdal.
[93] For a good broad sketch of those trials and their aftermath, see Frank M. Buscher, *The US War Crimes Trial Program in Germany, 1946–1955* (New York, 1989).
[94] The five scraps of pre-existing law cited by Bothe, Partsch, and Solf, p. 370, do not amount to much. Three of them come in the 4th GC, and apply only to its particular category of protected persons. The other two, from 1907, concern cultural property and anticipate the 1954 Hague Convention.

things that, in the eighteenth and nineteenth centuries, excited the same sort of indignation as do war crimes in the twentieth.

This shady corner of the law remained formless until disclosure of the nature of war as waged by modern industrial and urbanized societies brought it into the spotlight. The 1930s' adage 'the bomber will always get through' achieved its notorious popularity *after* experience had shown that some bombers always did get through. Even when civilians were not deliberately bombed, bombardment was now more dramatically hurtful of civilians than it had been before. Along with the argument that more care should be taken to avoid them came the counter-argument that States should be more careful to keep them out of the way. In States with densely populated industrial areas, this was easier said than done. As Hays Parks put it ten years ago: 'aerial warfare is not a gentlemen's game of horseshoes in which each side obligingly identifies its military targets and sets them apart from the civilian population.'[95] The extent to which States could reasonably be expected to create a physical divide between military targets (even supposing agreement as to what those were) and civilian populations was disputable. The case for not making it narrower than it had to be was however unanswerable. The ICRC's Draft Rules recognized this and actually gave proportionately more space and force to it than AP1. Article 58 enjoins belligerents 'to the maximum extent feasible' (the Draft Rules simply said, 'so far as possible') 'to remove the civilian population [etc.] under their control from the vicinity of military objectives', to 'avoid locating military objectives within or near densely populated areas' and to 'take the other necessary precautions to protect [civilians etc.] against the dangers resulting from military operations' which, so far as it points to anything precise, points towards the promotion of civil defence. Article 51(7), the substance of which might just as well have figured in Article 58, completes the picture. Picking up the long-standing disgust at the use of non-combatants as shields, it expressly prohibits such 'attempts to shield military objective from attacks or to shield, favour or impede military operations'.[96]

Recent events illustrate the wisdom of these rules. Instances of their neglect may be found in several of the most-studied armed conflicts of the present generation. (1) Bach Mai Hospital was a very big hospital nearly two miles from the middle of Hanoi but about half a mile from the airfield

[95] 'Conventional Aerial Bombing and the Law of War', in *Proceedings of the US Naval Institute*, 108 (1982), 98–117 at 107.
[96] But what about camouflaging a giant aircraft factory in California as a 'civilian residential area'? The writer of the caption of the illustration to p. 111 of Parks's article calls it a 'legitimate ruse', but that seems questionable.

of the same name which contained the North Vietnamese command-and-control headquarters; 'it frequently housed antiaircraft positions'.[97] (2) The London *Sunday Times* on 8 August 1982 reported: 'The Israelis explain the bombing of [Beirut] by saying that their only aim is to drive out the PLO, who are deliberately using civilian buildings to protect their gun emplacements and their ammunition dumps. That justification is becoming harder to sustain.' From that account and many others cited by 'the MacBride Report', *Israel in Lebanon* (London 1983), let alone other reports on the same tangled affair, it is evident that the PLO indeed did thus make military use of civilian places. To what extent this was by deliberate choice or enforced by circumstances, was one of the questions that had to be asked— a question to which the answer given depended very much on the answerer's political preferences. Another was whether the Israel defence forces were justified in killing and injuring so many (neutral) civilians in the process of attempting to kill or injure their enemies—a question to which most (neutral) observers gave an answer decidedly in the negative. (3) In early 1991,

Iraqi military helicopters were dispersed into residential areas; and military supplies were stored in mosques, schools, and hospitals in Iraq and Kuwait. . . . The Government of Iraq elected not to take routine air-raid precautions to protect its civilian population. Civilians were not evacuated in any significant numbers from Baghdad, nor were they removed from proximity to legitimate military targets. There were air-raid shelters for less than 1 per cent of the civilian population of Baghdad. The Government of Iraq chose instead to use its civilians to shield legitimate military targets from attack, exploiting civilian casualites and damage to civilian objects in its disinformation campaign to erode international and US domestic support for the Coalition effort to liberate Kuwait.[98]

The last point is well worth emphasizing, as an example of the contemporary phenomenon already several times noted: the exploitation of apparent excesses and illegalities, and even the deliberate manufacture of them, as part of the propaganda and PR war which in contemporary circumstances always accompanies the fighting war and which can have great effects on its conduct and its consequences. (4) From an armed conflict even more tangled and brutal than Israel's in Lebanon, the London *Independent*'s reporter Marc Champion on 1 August 1992 reported from Kostajnica, Yugoslavia: 'Mr Mujocevic and numerous eyewitnesses have told how the Serbian militia entered the town in two trucks using 40 Croats as a human shield.' What happened next was very awful, and, like that use of unarmed 'enemies' as a shield, the sort of thing that is unlikely to happen in modern wars between high-tech professionals; 'When three Croatian policemen surrendered rather than fire, they were stripped and shot.'

Combatants and Prisoners

Inseparable from one another in the history and practice of IHL are its very important categories: combatants and prisoners. They are inseparable because the law regarding prisoners of war, which for many war-involved persons has long been and perhaps still is the part of IHL that most moves them, could only develop and harden on the basis of a clear understanding as to which persons were entitled to its privileges and protections, and which were *not*. The matter was put on its modern footing by the 4th Hague Convention (1907). Articles 4 to 20 of its annexed Regulations established the legal regime for POWs which ruled unchanged through the First World War and, complemented by Geneva law from 1929, the Second World War as well; Geneva law's take-over in 1949 further elaborated the details but left the framework essentially unchanged. Articles 1 to 3 of the Hague Regulations made it clear that the benefits of this regime were restricted to the personnel of armies and to members of 'militia and volunteer corps'. The attributes of 'armies' were so well and universally understood in that age that nothing more needed to be said about them but 'militia and volunteer corps' were a mixed bag whose admission to equal status under 'the laws, rights and duties of war' was made conditional on their being either integrated into their States' proper armies or so organized and trained that they would behave in properly army-like ways. These ways were thus defined: '1. To be commanded by a person responsible for his subordinates; 2. to have a fixed distinctive emblem recognizable at a distance; 3. to carry arms openly, and 4. to conduct their operations in accordance with the laws and customs of war.'

These conditions and qualifications were not settled until after much debate, some of it, passionate. The debate had in fact been going on ever since the mighty wars of the 1860s for the first time made the laws and customs of war a matter of international public interest and discussion. Two great principles were pitted against one another. It was an article of nationalist (and, so far as it was any different, republican) political faith that men should be proud to take up arms in defence of their land, in its professionally led armed forces, if such were available, but otherwise in any way that offered. And it was an article of professional military (and, so far as it was any different, aristocratic) belief that popular military enterprise, besides being politically dangerous in time of peace, tended to be lawless and wasteful in time of war. Professional soldiers of the major military powers after 1870 no longer needed to look back to Napoleon's armies' experiences in Spain and Russia for illustrations of the nuisance and nastiness that accompanied popular armed resistance to the invader and the occupier. In the second, post-Sedan, *franc-tireur* phase of the war of 1870–1 they had an up-to-date case-study, which for German military publicists became something of an obsession. But to spokesmen of the smaller nations, the matter looked quite different. They ardently maintained the right of peoples to take up arms against invaders and occupiers. Minimizing the nuisance the *francs-tireurs* had been to their own compatriots, they tended to exaggerate the nuisance they had been to the enemy. But small and not-so-rich countries had to do what they could with such means as were at their disposal.

Small and modest countries could never match the major powers in mass of personnel and weapons. The best they could do was to rely on their patriots to mobilize against invaders and, if foreign occupation became their fate none the less, to make life difficult for the occupier. Why should men who fought to defend their nations in perhaps unprofessional style be held in lower esteem than men who sought in fullest professional style to invade and occupy, and possibly to annex, them? And, to fix on the point about the proposed new Hague Rules for the protection of prisoners of war, why should not the valiant patriot benefit from them, instead of being strung up or shot as a criminal or a 'war-traitor'?[99]

Thus ran the argument through the later nineteenth century, and thus has it run again through the later twentieth. Technology and ideology have upped the ante but in essentials the issues and the problems are the same as they were when the modern definition of the combatant crystallized in 1899 and 1907, notwithstanding the slight modification of 1949 and the more ambitious one of 1977. It is difficult for fighters in guerrilla or people's-war mode to meet the conditions for prisoner-of-war protection (the 1949 way of putting it) or for 'combatant and prisoner-of-war status' (the 1977 way) even if they sincerely wish to. A run through those conditions will show where the difficulties lie.

The requirement to be an 'organized group under responsible command' cannot be viewed as a difficulty. This requirement figures, with insignificant differences of wording, in 1907, 1949, and both of the 1977 APs. The point

---

[99] 'The outmoded and academic concepts of war treason and war rebellion', as he describes them, were readably examined by Richard R. Baxter, 'The Duty of Obedience to the Belligerent Occupant', in the *BYIL* 27 (1950), 235–66.

of it is eminently reasonable. No armed force can be trusted to comply with the relevant IHL principles and rules and to enter into the implied relationship of reciprocity towards its opponent(s) unless it is cohesive and disciplined; opponents and third parties (of whose legitimate interest IHL is never unmindful) need to know who is in command, and to be assured that he or she really *is* in command. Commanders and groups who find this condition objectionable are in fact lining up with bandits, freebooters, and criminals. This requirement has ever been basic to this part of IHL precisely because bandits, freebooters, and criminals inevitably make hay in times of disorder and anarchy, sometimes trying to pass themselves off as respectable guerrillas or forging *ad hoc* alliances with the same. Whether the 'war-lords' (as reporters on the spot describe them) and lesser chieftains of the Serbian, Croatian, and Bosnian popular fighters who at the latest moment of writing (spring, 1993) continue to ravage the former Yugoslavia are best described in the same terms, remains for history (and perhaps for certain courts of law) to judge. Their lawless goings-on have amply vindicated the legislators' wisdom, for time and again the peace-making and humanitarian efforts of the UN, its agencies, and the ICRC have been thwarted by the inability of (nominally) superior authorities to make (supposedly) lower-level commanders obey the terms of agreements signed in their name.

The requirement to 'carry arms openly', which figured unambiguously in 1907 and 1949, thereafter proved so difficult to observe in all circumstances that it was much modified in 1977; the requirement to be 'distinctively recognizable at a distance' was actually scrapped. The difficulties with both requirements were found to become insuperable on occasions when guerrilla operations, self-contained though they might be in mountains, marshes, and forests, moved close to civilian populations or mingled with them. Here we hit upon the heart of the matter referred to so often throughout this book. The 'regular' armies for whom and indeed, until our contemporary epoch, by whose representatives exclusively the law of war was made, were conscious of the distinction between themselves and civilian populations and sought to maintain it; their professional ethic taught them to spare civilians, they liked their appearance and behaviour to differ as much as possible from that of civilians, and they preferred to get their fighting done, though not necessarily their campaigning, in places where there were no civilians to get in the way. But the guerrilla and resistance fighter (supposing him to be the respectable and not the criminal sort) saw the civilian the other way round. Far from being conscious of distance and difference, he was more likely to feel closeness and affinity; he was, perhaps literally, 'one of them'. Far from setting out to look unlike a civilian, 'the guerrilla was often safer when he looked like one. He often had to move in among civilians, and he might have to fight there too.

The discussion so far has followed the usual pattern of contemporary IHL texts, treating guerrillas as if they were straightforwardly identifiable with 'combatants' and treating 'civilians' as if they were, whatever the nature of the armed conflict, the same the whole world over. Simplicity of legal classification is in this respect, however, no helpful preparation for handling the complexities of social reality. It was helpful to the argument, a few lines above, to sketch how different might be the guerrilla's perception of the civilian from that of the regular soldier, but the fact is, that in many armed conflicts and among many embattled peoples and groups, the guerrilla might have no perception at all of the civilian as he is known within Geneva's beneficent empire. This book's aim being not simply to describe contemporary IHL but rather to explain it, not to assume that it functions adequately but to enquire whether it functions adequately or not, this point about the identification of the civilian in wars of insurgency is so important as to merit a page or two of further exploration. My exploration will proceed along the lines of a comparison between the actual situations of civilians in the two types of wars which are customarily distinguished from one another in discussions of this sort: wars of insurgency/counter-insurgency, and so-called conventional wars.

Let us begin with conventional wars. The distinction between civilian/non-combatant and combatant has appeared in these pages so far as something which has developed in course of wars fought by so-called conventional armed forces and *pari passu* in association with the idea that wars were properly fought by them alone, and preferably at some distance from their civilian populations. We have seen how the law adapted in face of the facts that, especially in the modern industrial State, some civilians were bound to be less wholly civilian than others, and that maintaining distance from the civilian population—distance that might be physical or figurative or both—became, for most societies, more and more difficult. Theory had to accommodate the fact that Law demanded more than War could deliver. Whether and to what extent enemy civilians ought in their own person to share the damages and sufferings consequent upon their State's military efforts, was a matter upon which theologians' and philosophers' opinions were more mixed and complex than those of the legislators. IHL's position by the 1950s was fixed and simple. It was taken for granted that many civilians were directly helpful, often indeed indispensable, to their nation's military efforts. But, haunted by the holy-grail concept of civilian immunity and urged by humanitarian and peace-movement opinion to pursue it, IHL allowed no other means of bringing pressure to bear on those civilians than (what it could in any case not prevent) the indirect or incidental violences of blockade and bombardment, direct and deliberate acts of violence being authorized only against military persons and objectives.

With regard to wars of insurgency, the law of 1907 and 1949 observed a different standard. Its rules for privileged/lawful combatant status—i.e. qualification for POW status—made the intermingling of guerrilla fighters with civilians so difficult that one may fairly say that civilians' necessary involvement in their society's military effort was *not* taken for granted. This conclusion is easy enough to understand. The armed conflicts in which guerrillas usually appeared were internal ones with which *international* law was not primarily concerned. They were sometimes wars of revolution or secession, which State authorities detested and other States were supposed not to get mixed up in. The humanitarian impulse of course was not deterred by such legal and political considerations from showing sympathy for the victims of these internal struggles and concern about the standards of conduct displayed in them. It received a helpful boost from the foundation of the League of Nations and the post-1918 boom in relief activities, but none of this affected international law's pre-1939 position on the rights or, as some preferred to call them, privileges of combatants in the only sorts of wars the law of war recognized: international wars. Even the pressures brought to bear by the experiences of 1939–45 resistance did not, as we have seen, force much of a change.

Only in 1977 did IHL make a move in the direction indicated by logic and equity: recognizing at last that internal wars might have causes no less good (or bad) than international ones, that the ways they had to be fought required realistic regulation too, and that this meant questioning the old-established inhibitions against acknowledgement of the fact of civilian participation in military activity. Proper, that is, to the same extent and by the same criteria as had long implicitly governed legislation for international wars. The modes of participation ran in parallel; necessarily they differed in kind, but functionally their roles were identical. For example, while civilian members of societies involved in 'conventional' armed conflicts maintained the roads and tracks, drove the trucks and trains and so on that kept materials moving into arms factories and weapons moving out of them, civilian members of societies involved in insurgencies built and maintained the tracks that led to where the fighting was and carried most of the war materials themselves. While the former kept a sharp look-out for spies and staffed the telephone exchanges and printing presses that formed part of their society's intelligence and information network, the latter kept a sharp look-out for hostile troop movements and took the information as they travelled from place to place to those who could make military use of it.

This parallel is instructive in another way too. In both situations, civilians could be at odds with the authority purporting to fight on their behalf. Authoritarian and (so far as the distinction is a real one) totalitarian States approach the position of plausibly denying the existence of dissidence by massive efforts of PR, propaganda, policing, and repression. For democratic States, the difficulty cannot so conveniently be got rid of. The French and the US military authorities in turn learned this to their cost. First over Indo-China, then over Algeria, the French army felt itself betrayed by anti-war movements at home. The American military establishment continues to be haunted by memories of the anti-Vietnam-War movement. American armed forces will never again happily undertake substantial overseas commitments unless they feel confident that, however badly things may go, the folk back home will not let them down. How much overt anti-war feeling and activism, how much mere indifference an endangered democracy can live with, has not yet been tested; the principle of conscientious objection to military service may itself be queried on conscientious grounds, and the current endeavour to add it to the ever-lengthening list of human rights is not unopposed. But no matter how hard may sometimes be the lot of conscientious and other objectors in democratic States and no matter how hard they must usually find life in police States, they are unlikely to be worse off than their conflict-opposing counterparts in places where insurgents hold a whip hand. The quantities and kinds of violence used against persons who are less than wholeheartedly supportive of an insurgency are often atrocious, so much so, as to lend colour to the argument that the hazards of life under almost any form of fixed government must be preferable to the hazards of life during almost any insurgency against it.

The parallelism of the two situations is not yet exhausted. The wartime lot of civilians under fixed governments can be atrocious too. The international community in 1945 began to equip itself theoretically with powers to intervene when governments treated civilians very badly; the end of the Cold War encouraged it to try to use them. Iraq from later 1990 felt them being used, and if reactions in 1992 to events in what used to be Yugoslavia are any guide, those same powers are now understood by some to justify intervention on behalf of civilian sufferers from the atrocious misdoings of insurgent bands. As with intervention, so with judgment. If States' grounds for taking up arms can be judged good or bad by the international community, so in principle can those of insurgents. Such principle became practice in the era of decolonization when criteria were evolved to facilitate the identification of acceptable NLMs, implying that movements which did not meet those criteria (like e.g. the Provisional IRA) were not so acceptable. From such applications of the law of the Charter of the UN, the law of human rights which goes with it, and the law made or laid down by resolutions of Security Council and General Assembly (to specify the areas of law which this paragraph has so far had in mind), it is only a little move further to the body of law with which this book is primarily concerned. If the conduct of States' armed forces is something the international community seriously cares about, so must be that of insurgents who themselves aspire to share or to take over the responsibilities of statehood. We have seen how unreasonable it was that IHL should forever avert its eye from the possibility that parties engaged in civil/internal wars might have as good a title to be regarded as privileged/lawful combatants as any regular soldiers in conventional wars. It is now time to see how IHL has got round this awkward corner.

The answer can with some difficulty be dug out of AP1. The definition of a privileged/lawful combatant is no longer marked (as it was in Article 1 of the Hague Regulations and Article 4 of the Prisoners Convention) so as to be clearly recognizable from a distance, but the definition is there nevertheless, mixed up with all the repetitive stuff about protection of civilians; which is actually quite fitting, the essence of the problem being to find ways for guerrillas and resistance fighters to do what they have to do without entirely sacrificing the fundamental combatant/civilian distinction. This attempt had to be made. It cannot be considered entirely unsuccessful, but the extent to which in practice it may work depends, to a greater extent than is usual in the realm of IHL, on the moral culture and the good faith of belligerents. At heart and strictly speaking, of course, the problem is insoluble. The attempt to solve it can go no further than offer a choice of grim options under grey skies. Our parallel between the characters of conventional wars and wars of insurgency here at last breaks down. There is no way that civilians in wars of insurgency can be sure of the same sort and level of protection that may be within their reach in wars of the old-fashioned conventional kind.

That these parts of AP1 are in their native state rather difficult to make sense of—difficult, that is, for others than the few thousands of legal experts in the world specially trained to do it—is partly because the attention of the CDDH was focused more on the requirements of NLMs and guerrilla warfare than on those of regular armed forces, partly because the ethos of the humanitarian community prefers that talk of fighting should be in the prohibitive rather than the permissive vein. There is plenty of the permissive and, more, the mandatory in the parts of AP1 dealing not with fighting but with the effects of fighting, with relief and rescue work and with protection (in the Red Cross's technical sense) of prisoners and detainees and of wounded, sick, and shipwrecked. But the fighter who wishes to know how he is actually permitted to conduct guerrilla/insurgent fighting has to wrestle with much opacity and indirectness, unless, of course, the authority to which he answers provides him with an appropriately boiled-down version. He will however correctly gather, if he puts together what is said with what is *not* said, that he is permitted to live, move, and fight in much closer proximity to civilians than was formerly the case. He may in fact live like a civilian and look like a civilian for most of his non-operative time. Provided he is a proper member of 'the armed forces of a party to the conflict' possessing 'an internal disciplinary system which, *inter alia*, shall enforce compliance with the rules of international law applicable in armed conflict', the basic rule is that he only has to distinguish himself from the civilian population 'while engaged in an attack or in a military operation preparatory to an attack'.[100] Exactly how the guerrilla is to distinguish himself is not indicated, although it may be inferred from what follows in the next sentence that 'carrying his arms openly' must be the main thing, and it may be supposed that his own organization's convenience and *amour propre* will cause him to wear the conventional distinctive sign.

Nor does AP1 offer any guidance (such as is so carefully given in respect of military objectives) as to what might be the parameters of that 'military operation'. Bothe, Partsch, and Solf, whose opinion has to be taken seriously, opine that 'such military operations as recruiting, training, general administration, law enforcement, aid to underground political authorities, collection of contributions and dissemination of propaganda' cannot be construed as 'preparatory to an attack', but that the new rule must be 'construed broadly enough to include [preparatory] administrative and logistic activities'.[101] Evidently there is plenty of room for argument here. What however cannot be argued about is that, so far as concerns the purpose and conduct of attacks and of military operations leading to them, the guerrilla and resistance fighter is as much bound as any 'regular'

---

[100] Respectively from Articles 43(1) and the first sentence of 44(3). On the face of it, this puts him in a very different position from the troops of the 'regular' armed forces against whom he may be presumed to be fighting. To them is addressed in afterthought manner Art. 44's para. 7: 'This Article is not intended to change the generally accepted practice of States with respect to the wearing of the uniform by combatants assigned to the regular, uniformed armed units of a Party to the conflict.' Yet AP1's homogenization of all combatants within one single category, criticized earlier as an unhappy development, inescapably brings with it the conclusion that 'regulars' cannot be doing anything unlawful if they fight in the same manner as guerrillas in a lawful struggle. [101] Bothe, Partsch, and Solf, 252.

by the 'rules of international law applicable in armed conflict' which include, of course, the civilian-protecting rules found elsewhere in the Protocol. Thus, to look no further than Article 51, neither the civilian population nor individual civilians may be attacked; they may not be the object of 'acts or threats of violence the primary purpose of which is to spread terror' among them; they must not be indiscriminately attacked; and, perhaps most important of all, they 'shall not be used to render certain points or areas immune from military operations, in particular in attempts to shield military objectives from attacks or to shield, favour or impede military operations'. It is in these reiterations of existing rules and codifications of customary ones, which contrast surprisingly with its relaxed references to combatants' weapons and appearances, that AP1 holds the line for the protection of civilians when armed conflicts rage around them. It prohibits most of the civilian-oppressing forms of behaviour which seem inseparable from much guerrilla and insurgency existence. It insists that guerrillas no less than their more regular opponents must try to avoid involving in the violent consequences of their military operations the people whose interests they claim to represent, which means, among many other things, that they must not do what so often causes the nastiest incidents of insurgency/counter-insurgency warfare: launch attacks from places where civilians are, or shelter in those places from attacks upon themselves.

The Legislators of the 1970s: The Additional Protocols

Much more could be said about AP1's Article 44 on Combatants and Prisoners of War which, together with its flanking Articles 43, Armed Forces and 45, Protection of Persons who have taken part in Hostilities, constituted the outcome of the most hard-fought battles of the CDDH. The extent of that battle, and of how much more could be said, may be judged from the fact that our examination of it has so far scarcely gone beyond the meaning of Article 44(3)'s first sentence. The second sentence is where the difficulties really begin. They inevitably result from the legislators' desperate pursuit of formulae to square the circle of their endeavour to authorize the sort of secretive and surprising military operations which NLMs and resistance groups *in extremis* may adopt, at the same time as to protect them from being treated, if taken alive by their opponents, as mere terrorists and criminals. There is, within the limits of this book, no need to get involved in this controversial legal maze. The reader who wishes to enter it will find plenty of expert guides.[102] The last word about it here, before we move on to the less complicated matters of political explanation and practical application, may be given to one of them:

> There is no doubt that the new definition . . . will remedy a defective law. It was unsatisfactory to have a lack of symmetry, for example, between the concept 'prisoner of war' and 'combatant': . . . On the other hand, the criteria of a combatant are still vague and difficult to apply in practice. . . . There is still confusion as to who is a combatant and who is a civilian due to the lack of stringent criteria for qualification as a combatant.[103]

And the civilian, for whose qualification (in a practical social sense) criteria may differ from culture to culture, remains unfortunately in the middle of the mess.

That difficulties should remain even after so many months of conference wranglings and consensual expedients may be taken to indicate the intrinsic and intractable difficulty of this part of the CDDH's agenda. A porous compromise relying rather heavily on goodwill was as satisfactory a conclusion as could have reached in any circumstances, even the most favourable. But certain circumstances were by no means favourable to making the best of this indifferent job. We must now turn to the political side of its story.

All law-making is at some level a political process. That this is not more obviously and often apparent is because the *idea* of law blessedly includes so many elements that are not overtly and in the ordinary sense of the word political, e.g. justice, right, humanity, equity, and because those elements are the ones which legal authorities and expositors naturally emphasize. The most satisfactory systems (in the sense of proving satisfactory to the users) are those whose politics can, in the ordinary course of events, be forgotten about; something the more easily done if politics appeared never to have loomed large in the first place.

Geneva law as it evolved within the European and American system of States carried little evident political baggage and proved satisfactory to most

---

[102] Lengthy scrutinies are given in the two main commentaries: Bothe, Partsch, and Solf at 241–58, and the ICRC one at 519–42. Ingrid Detter de Lupis offers a sensible summary in *The Law of War* (Cambridge, 1987) at 112–17. Almost every IHL expert has had his or her crack at it somewhere or other. The most balanced I know are those of (unenthusiastic) Christopher Greenwood, 'Terrorism and Humanitarian Law: The Debate over API', in *Israel Yearbook on Human Rights*, 19 (1989), 187–207 at 201–5, and (sympathetic) George H. Aldrich, 'New Life for the Laws of War', in *AmJIL* 75 (1981), 764–83 at 770–5. Acutely critical is F. R. Ribeiro, 'International Humanitarian Law: Advancing Progressively Backwards', in *South African Law Journal*, 97 (1980), 42—64; dismissively so, Guy B. Roberts, 'The New Rules for Waging War', in *Virginia Journal of International Law*, 26 (1985), 109–70. Aldrich's response follows in the same volume (but 1986), 692–720.

[103] De Lupis, *Law of War*, 117.

of its users until the years with which this book is primarily concerned. Hague law and its modern history were not so universally admired, but of its two least satisfied users, Germany of course had no share in the reconstructions following its defeats in 1918 and 1945, while revolutionary Russia, although infinitely more influential after 1945 than it had been after 1918, was still a minority presence, unable, as was shown in Part II, to derail the post-1945 legislative process from the lines on which its more satisfied co-victors wished to proceed.

Radical change however was on the way. What made it inescapable was the movement to dissolve the overseas empires and to develop the multitude of new States which filled the maps of, above all, Africa and Asia in their place. As their number grew, the new States and their sympathizers among the old ones more and more dominated the business of the General Assembly which was, inevitably, the main arena of their campaigning. By the early 1970s the greater part of it was becoming focused on the creation of a New International Economic Order and the modification accordingly of what were perceived to be the world's unfair trade and money systems. Through the 1960s however, while these economic and material aspirations were still taking shape, the most consistently exciting focus of debate was decolonization. Nothing more inflamed Third World opinion against the existing legal order than what were perceived to be the difficulties it unfairly placed in the way of independence and, as they now became generally known, national liberation movements. Even when imperial powers were inclined to let subject territories become independent without bloodshed, they would not concur in the new political doctrine that imperial possession had been morally wrong in the first place and that independence forthwith was an absolute right. And when blood did flow, as directly after the war it began to do in the Dutch East Indies, French Indo-China, North Africa, and British India, the imperial powers and their Cold-War allies would not concur in the emerging view that wars of national liberation were 'just wars' and that they ought to be fought by the same rules as international wars, so as to give freedom-fighters, in case of capture, the legal protection they deserved. Year in, year out in the debates of the General Assembly, its committees and special events and in the other regular forums of the Third World (e.g. meetings of the non-aligned movement), this was the bit of IHL which mattered most to the States which had not participated in its post-1945 reconstruction or which had then been in a minority. No wonder that it was what was at the forefront of their minds when they arrived at Geneva for the opening of the CDDH on 20 February 1974, and what they were determined above all else to achieve.

What happened at the CDDH puzzled and upset apolitical humanitarians and unreflecting conservatives, whose characteristic complaint was that it represented the irruption of politics where politics had no cause to be. Indeed there are grounds for believing that some of the work of the CDDH would have been done to the better benefit of humankind at large had the atmosphere been less politicized. But just as it was fantasy for members of the humanitarian community to believe that politics had never mattered in the work of its previous conferences, so was it naïve for them or for anyone else alive in the early 1970s to doubt that politics would rush into this one.

The year 1974 happened to come at just about the climax of a sustained crescendo of liberationist agitation by the Third World and its First and Second World sympathizers. This crescendo and climax are a context essential to the understanding of what happened at the CDDH. Its main events may be simply listed: 1960, the Declaration on Granting Independence to Colonial Peoples; 1964, UNCTAD 1 and the 2nd, Cairo, meeting of the Non-Aligned Movement; 1965, the Resolution on the right to use force in wars of national liberation; 1966, priority given to Economic, Social and Cultural Rights over Civil and Political Rights in the two UN Covenants, and pride of place given in both to the assertion, 'All peoples have the right of self-determination'; 1968, 'International Human Rights Year' and the dead-set against Israel at the Human Rights conference in Tehran; 1970, the 3rd Non-Aligned Conference at Lusaka and the Declaration on Principles of International Law concerning Friendly Relations and Co-operation among States in accordance with the Charter of the UN, wherein the GA proclaimed self-determination an international law right; 1972, UNCTAD 3 and the Resolution delegating to regional organizations [read, the OAU and the Arab League] the selection of legitimate NLMs; 1973, the 4th Non-Aligned Conference at Algiers, the Resolution on the 'basic principles of the legal status of the combatants struggling against colonial and alien domination and racist regimes', and (following the Yom Kippur War) the beginning of the Gulf States' attempt to use what was popularly called the oil weapon against Israel's backers; and so to 1974, when UNCTAD turned from the topic of trade in general to North–South relations in particular, two GA special sessions launched the NIEO, the PLO was given permanent observer status at the UN—and the CDDH opened for business.

For how long the conference would have to continue, no one could tell, but it is certain that none of those who first assembled in February 1974 believed that they would have to sit through four successive annual sessions and only conclude the business (and even then, only by dint of last-minute rushes to pack it all in) in mid-1977. Its unexpected longevity was partly because hardly anything was accomplished in its first session beyond elucidation of the political fact that the price of the conference's achieving anything at all was going to be the identification of 'armed conflicts in which peoples are fighting against colonial domination and alien occupation and against racist regimes' as *international* armed conflicts, thus giving their combatants the completest POW protection.[104]

The politically driven movement just described had some aims in common with that part of the humanitarian community which for many years had been anxious to extend IHL's usefulness with regard to 'armed conflict not of an international character'. The door in that direction had been opened by the GCs' Common Article 3 and the ICRC had cautiously squeezed through as best it could, but sovereignty-sensitive States could never be comfortable with it and, of course, the States to which it should most have applied—States with such armed conflicts unmistakably going on within their borders—were the very ones least likely to admit its applicability. As internal wars of one sort or another multiplied through the 1950s and 1960s and their characteristic horrors became widely known, the case became yearly stronger for replacing or supplementing Article 3 by something more substantial and formal. The international Red Cross movement favoured the projection of Geneva-style legal protections into the field of non-international conflicts. An alternative approach appeared among human rights lawyers and activists, many of whom were as sympathetic towards 'freedom-fighters' as towards civilian sufferers, and whose programme for extending the protection of human rights in armed conflicts in 1968 prodded the UN into a fruitful burst of activity.[105]

As to the best way forward, there was an interesting variety of opinion. Once it had become apparent that whatever was going to be done, was going to be done under Swiss and ICRC rather than UN auspices, the Geneva Conventions were bound to be the foundation of the work. No new Convention, but Protocols additional to the existing Conventions became the guiding concept. To some IHL experts, it seemed best to retain the

---

[104] Sticklers for precision are advised that that sentence telescopes four years of history and several sentences of the legal instruments. Those incantatory words come from APi's Art. 1(4) which does not actually include the word 'international' but is referred, *via* Art. 1(3), to Common Art. 2 of the Geneva Conventions; which does not itself include the word 'international' either, but was unquestioningly understood to mean it.

[105] Indispensable for evaluation of this short-lived UN-based intervention to which Red Cross-based writers tend to pay insufficient attention is Keith Suter's excellent monograph, *An International Law of Guerrilla Warfare: The Global Politics of Law-Making* (London, 1984).

traditional distinction between international and non-international, and therefore to aim at equally solid Protocols for both. To others, it appeared preferable to sink the distinction and to aim at one single solid Protocol which would cover every sort of armed conflict, whether international or not.[106] But to none of them, except to the extent that their judgment was swayed by the *tiers-mondiste* anti-Americanism sketched in the preceding paragraph, could it seem to the advantage of IHL to build into its new model a privileged place for the combatants in exclusively one sort of non-international armed conflict—and a historically specific sort at that, which had recently loomed large in the world but which, by the end of the CDDH, would amount to little more than the still unresolved situations in Palestine and Southern Africa.

This however is what happened, and the fall-out from the drive to achieve it went further still. Not only were those few remaining NLMs exceptionally classified as belligerents in *international* armed conflicts, with the appropriate privileges and advantages of POW-status etc., but much less was consequently done than might otherwise have been done to extend the regime of IHL over *non-international* ones. Adding to the number of newly sovereign States which might swell the currently prevailing majority in the GA was one thing; adding to the difficulties of possibly insecure governments in States new or old by strengthening the claims of insurgents, rebels, or secessionists to humanitarian respect was another. Having conferred dignity on their own preferred group of insurgents, the anti-Western majority of States at the CDDH lost interest in projects for improving the situation of any others. They were not attracted by the project to produce, for non-international armed conflicts, a Protocol as solid as that for international ones, not least, because of the door into their own internal affairs that might thereby be opened to the international community and the ICRC. The brief but sturdy generalities of Common Article 3, they had to live with; to its expansion into the comprehensive and explicit instrument hoped for by the conference planners, they would not agree.

AP2 therefore, as finally and hastily passed, has what the experts correctly call a high threshold. Explicitly inapplicable to 'situations of internal disturbances and tensions, such as riots, isolated and sporadic acts of violence', etc., it applies only to armed conflicts 'which take place in the territory of an HCP between its armed forces and dissident armed forces or other organized armed groups which, under responsible command, exercise such control over a part of its territory as to enable them to carry out sus-

---

[106] Bothe, Partsch, and Solf, 605, admirably summarize these different projects and their subdivisions.

tained and concerted military operations and to implement this Protocol'. Insurgent armed forces etc. must already have progressed quite far in their struggles to satisfy such a stringent territorial-control requirement, a requirement which, be it observed, includes by its reference to 'implementing the Protocol' the capabilities (as well as the will) to care properly for the wounded and sick and to treat prisoners decently. The FMLN in El Salvador by the mid-1980s seemed to come about as close to meeting the requirements as any well-established insurgency could.[107] Observe also that AP2 cannot, *stricto sensu*, be applied at all except where it has been ratified or acceded to by an HCP, which by the time of signing meant that, since the chances of South Africa or Israel signing it were zero, it would never be applied by the States at which it was most directly aimed. And, to return to the point with which this section started, AP2 keeps well away from the combatant–POW relationship which was so crucial to the making of AP1. It approaches no nearer to mentioning (let alone to defining) combatants than in the implication of its protective glance towards 'persons who do not take a direct part or who have ceased to take part in hostilities'. Its nearest approach to the highly charged expression POW is no more than to bring 'persons deprived of their liberty for reasons related to the armed conflict' into its general category of 'persons whose liberty has been restricted', for whose humane handling its Articles 4 and 5 make many excellent recommendations.

Prisoners, Detainees, and the ICRC

What was it about the POW that made his identification and definition a matter so emotive and important? In Part II, I said something of the socio-pyschological aspects of the POW's rise to centrality in the humanitarian perspective. By the end of the Second World War he was the most sharply silhouetted of IHL's *dramatis personae*. Among the peoples which had had most to do with the development of IHL, the POW was typically (imagined as) a valiant patriotic fighter who through no fault of his own, and possibly because he was wounded as well, fell into the hands of the enemy. Desirous to protect him in that exposed and perhaps protracted situation, the international community made unique and remarkable arrangements in its

---

[107] The State of El Salvador was remarkable for having ratified *both* APs as early as Nov. 1978. The FMLN signified readiness to observe the AP2 rules three years or so later. For a good survey of the legal issues and their practical outcomes, which were less than satisfactory but perhaps as good as could realistically be expected, see esp. Robert K. Goldman, 'International Humanitarian Law and the Armed Conflicts in El Salvador and Nicaragua', in *American University Journal of International Law and Policy*, 2 (1987), 539–78.

response to the intensity of national communities' feelings about their absent loved-ones. Not all national communities, it must be noted, felt the same way or (one cannot be quite sure whether this was not the case) were allowed to show the same sort of feelings. Japan, for example, knew nothing of the compassionate cult of the POW. Japanese fighting men who willy-nilly fell into enemy hands suffered from shame and self-contempt, and no warm welcome awaited them if ever they returned to their homeland. The Soviet Union in the Second World War more or less washed its hands of the (very many) soldiers who surrendered to the enemy, and treated brutally those (by no means so many) who returned, or who were returned, to the USSR when the war was over. Yet those harsh attitudes, not disavowed by other communist regimes in the post-war period, proved to be compatible with the keenest of interests in the political and propaganda uses of the POW parts of IHL. There are grounds for wondering how widely in the world POWs are thought of in the same way as they were by the majority makers of the 1949 GCs. This is one of the areas of IHL where humanitarian professions may cover, or coexist with, the pursuit of other purposes, and where the standards which guide IHL can most benefit from the support of those founded in human rights.

The POW, then, may not on every public appearance be the simple figure enshrined in the POW Convention; politics and ideology can find him too useful to allow him to play so straight a role. And that is not the only risk he runs. The road to the theatre itself is hazardous. Certain risks, rooted in the sociologies of armed forces and in the actualities of armed conflict, have to be surmounted before a combatant can become a POW at all.

About the principle of giving quarter, the law is and has long been unambiguous. The Hague Regulations Article 23(c) simply said: 'it is especially forbidden . . . to kill or wound an enemy who, having laid down his arms, or having no longer means of defence, has surrendered at dis-cretion.' AP1's more complicated and resourceful formulation in its Articles 40 and 41 intimates that things might not be quite so simple. 'It is prohib-ited to order that there shall be no survivors' is followed by the prohibition of attacks on persons *hors de combat*: a person *hors de combat* being thus defined:

(a) he is in the power of an adverse Party; (b) he clearly expresses an intention to surrender; or (c) he has been rendered unconscious or is otherwise incapacitated by wounds or sickness, and therefore is incapable of defending himself; provided that in any of these cases he abstains from any hostile act and does not attempt to escape.

This is an improvement inasmuch as it takes account of the variety of sources from which risks to the potential POW arise. The first prohibition kills two vicious birds with one stone: the impatient, ruthless, or brutal commander, and (less obviously) the tough-talking bravado of training-camp and barrack-room, where military-macho pride may relish the reputation of taking no prisoners. It is not unreasonable to conclude that such were among the explanations of the 'summary executions' of captured soldiers deplored by the ICRC early in the war between Iraq and Iran: 'these executions were sometimes acts of individuals involving a few soldiers fallen into enemy hands, sometimes systematic actions against entire enemy units, on orders to give no quarter.'[108] Clause (b) and the first part of clause (c) remind the prisoner-taker that beside the bona fide, hands-held-high, weapon-thrown-down surrenderers there may be many kinds of involuntary and accidental ones. The second part of clause (c) valuably reminds the would-be prisoner that becoming one is a two-way transaction for whose success he too has some responsibility.

Many of the situations which cause surrenderers not to be taken alive are thus admirably foreseen and dealt with. But some remain, for which no legislation seems likely ever to be adequate. There are limits to the amount of humanitarian observance that desperately fighting flesh and blood can actually stand. A typically unpredictable situation is when a well-protected machine-gunner, defending his safely-retreating compatriots, succeeds in killing a great many of his attackers before at the last moment emerging (if he is *very* unwise, with a confident smile) to surrender to their surviving mates.[109] Nearly as unpredictable and possibly tragic may be the situation when hard-pressed troops in continuing action find themselves with prisoners on their hands whom they have no means to conduct under guard to safety away from the combat zone. Max Hastings tells how a sergeant of the *Luftwaffe* parachute division in Normandy in mid-1944, 'embarrassed by the burden of 34 prisoners, had them locked in a nearby barn, and left them there when his squad pulled out: "In Russia [he said later], we would have shot them." '[110] Hastings concludes from his searching enquiry into

---

[108] Leonard Doyle citing the ICRC in a report on the UN's parallel concerns, in the *Independent*, 23 Jan. 1991. Not mere brutality and barrack-room bravado may work to this effect, but also religious fanaticism. The *Independent* on 29 Mar. 1989 carried from its man in Islamabad news of the 'Saudi-backed Wahhabi guerrilla groups . . . previously kept away from the war, but allowed in by the Pakistanis to boost the standing of the more extremist Islamic Afghan groups. They are under oath not to take prisoners.'

[109] In principle, this is a 20th-c. counterpart to the situation which often occurred in earlier centuries: a fortress refusing to surrender even when its walls had been breached, so that the besiegers had to go through the often hideous business of an assault. Customary law for long entitled the besiegers, once they were inside, to put the garrison to the sword, not to mention what by custom they usually did to the civilian inhabitants.

[110] *Overlord. D-Day and the Battle for Normandy* (London, Book Club Associates edn. 1984), 11-12.

battlefield behaviour in this campaign (which was in fact a relatively gentle-manly one, by Second World War and subsequent standards) that 'overall it seem doubtful whether [the murdering of captives] was done on a greater scale by one side or the other'.[111]

That POWs have been at the centre of a series of IHL rows since 1950 cannot seriously be attributed to defects in the Prisoners Convention. The minority of States which found it not entirely to their liking were dissatisfied because it went too far rather than because it did not go far enough. They resented its opening of their gates to the ICRC, they felt it was soft on (those whom they might regard as) war criminals, and they reckoned it set standards of care for POWs which were unnecessarily, even unreasonably, high. Those issues apart, the POW-specific articles of the Convention were relatively uncontroversial, and their net effect was comprehensive, covering every conceivable aspect of the prisoner's life and welfare from the moment of capture until the order of release. Its articles and annexes fill more pages of the ICRC's standard edition than the 4th Convention and more than the 1st and 2nd GCs together. Scarcely anything was done to it at the CDDH except, in response to the demands of the States which felt that things would have been done differently in 1949 if their interests had been represented then, to change the rules about eligibility for POW status: certain popular categories of guerrilla fighter were made eligible, and one most unpopular category of fighter, the mercenary, was made ineligible.[112]

And yet this area of IHL has rarely been out of the limelight. Parties to armed conflicts have repeatedly exploited the weaknesses of the POW regime and the vulnerability of its objects in order to serve their own political interests. No element of IHL has more readily lent itself to deploy-ment in the PR-war which nowadays accompanies every fighting one. The account given in Part II of the troubled background to the repatriation articles of the Prisoners Convention will have given a hint of the kind of difficulties which might accompany its implementation. The first—and, as it turned out, worst ever—burst of them was not long in coming.

The Korean War began on 25 June 1950, when North Korean armies drove across the border by which the Cold War had divided the Democratic

---

[111] Ibid. 212. See also pp. 105, 209–13 *passim*, and (for respect for the Red Cross emblem) 223. Another thoughtful expert on soldiers' behaviour, John Keegan, touches on this painful subject in *The Face of Battle* (London, 1976), 49–52.

[112] Article 47 of AP1 contains a six-point definition which approximates as nearly as conference politics permitted to the idea of the (white) mercenary figure who had, not without reason, become a primary object of anti-colonial and post-colonial African revulsion since the early 1960s. It includes neither foreign advisers (so long as they keep out of actual combat) nor foreign volunteer fighters of ideological or religious motivation.

People's Republic of Korea (backed by the USSR and, as soon as it was established, the People's Republic of China) from the Republic of Korea, backed by the USA whose troops were present in large numbers in nearby Japan and whose warships protected the rump Nationalist-China administration in Formosa/Taiwan. Korea had been in political turmoil since its liberation by Soviet and American armed forces in later 1945. Its *de facto* division, like that which developed at about the same time between West and East Germany, was supposed to be only temporary, and each of the rival superpowers claimed to look forward to leading Korea back into unity. But what happened on 25 June came as a universal surprise. North Korea had not been thought likely to attempt unification by force. The UN's reaction to this act of aggression, as non-communists understood it to be, was the more prompt and forceful for the USA's dominance in the UN at that time, coupled with the extraordinary chance of the USSR's (self-imposed) absence from the Security Council when it most mattered. The armed force rapidly mustered to rescue South Korea from the military disaster which initially menaced it was officially a UN one but it was mainly American in composition. It could not have existed without enthusiastic American support, and its American C-in-Cs (successively MacArthur, Ridgway, and Clark) managed it with a high American hand. At the same time, whatever might have been the UN's idea of the war's purpose was swamped by its absorption into the USA's global strategy of containing communism. When the newly established and neighbouring Red China entered the war to rescue North Korea from the disaster which menaced it in turn after MacArthur's successful counter-attack, the ideological character of the war was perfected.

In every other repect, its character was far from perfect. 'An unparalleled degree of destruction was visited on the peninsula in the course of what the West called a "limited war"', writes one of its best historians. The northern parts of Korea especially were devastated: physically wrecked, depopulated by death—reasonable estimates vary between twelve and fifteen per cent—and departure; simply starvation rather than political preference was the reason why legions of refugees moved southwards.[113] Hostilities were conducted in ways as violent and unmeasured as could be. Proportionality and precision were at a discount; opportunities for destruction seemed always to be taken to maximal extents, epecially by the US air force, whose principal purpose (for neither the first nor the last time) was inter-service rivalry, to show that air power was what won wars. There was little of the fellow-

---

[113] Callum MacDonald, *Korea: The War before Vietnam* (London, 1986), 258–9.

feeling between belligerents which sometimes serves to maintain decent standards, and very much of the self-righteousness which helps to erode them. The non-Asian majority of soldiers in the so-called UN Command tended to feel racially detached from their Korean allies as well as their Korean and Chinese opponents. The implacably hostile North and South Korean Governments were not likely to handle enemies from without less roughly than they were already accustomed to handle enemies within. The Chinese, when they joined the fray from October 1950, came from the regime which would soon impress upon the world its detachment from prevailing norms of international behaviour.

Prisoners of war, in such circumstances, and setting aside the unnumbered who might have been taken prisoner but were killed instead, were doomed to have a bad time, though none could have foreseen the strange form the badness would latterly take.[114] The ICRC at once busied itself to persuade the belligerents to observe the rules and standards of the 1949 Convention which some had signed but none had yet had time to ratify.[115] All of them sooner or later (China not until mid-1952) expressed themselves as willing to observe the principles of the Convention, but how far North Korea and China actually did so in practice, it was impossible for the ICRC to ascertain, because both States persistently refused to have anything directly to do with it.[116] They did after a while, during the first phase of cease-fire negotiations, and as a preliminary to the release of prisoners, produce lists of them (not quite 12,000) to match those (about 132,000) of the UN Command.[117] Neither side believed the other's explanations of why these lists were smaller than had been expected, and already by early 1952 the lines were becoming clear on which the next and most lamentable stage of the POWs' process would be fought.

The beginning of Article 118 of the brand-new POW Convention appeared to be straightforward and unambiguous enough: 'Prisoners of war shall be released and repatriated without delay after the cessation of active hostilities.' The Northern side insisted that repatriation simply meant what it said: prisoners were to be sent back to their homeland. The Southern side

[114] For specific evidence about killing of prisoners, see the references in Julian G. Verplaetse, 'The Jus in Bello and Military Operations in Korea 1950–1953', in *Zeitschrift für ausländisches öffentliches Recht und Völkerrecht*, 23 (1963), 679–738 at 725.

[115] In any case the Convention could not begin to come into force until after the first two States had ratified, which happened to work out at 21 Oct. 1950. For details relevant to this complicated matter, see Pictet's *Commentary*, 3 (1960), 643–4.

[116] The relative qualities of prison camps North and South of the 38th parallel are well summed up by Forsythe in his 1977 book, 134–5.

[117] There are many sources for these figures, each different. Mine are those used by Tae-Hoo Yoo, *The Korean War and the UN* (Louvain, 1965), 89.

insisted that, although this might be the general rule and desirable norm, it could not mean compelling prisoners to go back who did not wish to do so. Had these differing readings represented the whole substance of the dispute, they might have yielded to resolution through some acceptable mediator's good offices. But they were far from the whole. They were no more than the pretexts for pursuing agendas of national, political, and ideological purposes which kept the war going for fifteen months longer than it need have done.[118]

Each side wanted to show that its prisoners did *not* wish to go home, and each side had means of persuading them not to do so. North Korea and South Korea competitively claimed to represent the real Korea, and it was not prima-facie improbable that some Korean prisoners would take their captor's side. China and North Korea, like the USSR after the Second World War, refused to believe (or pretended to refuse to believe) that any of their men could *not* wish to go home; if a communist prisoner was reported by his captors to be so disposed, it could only be because his duties and interests had not been properly explained to him. On the other hand, it was delightful to the communist authorities of those countries to be able to report that non-communist prisoners, exposed by their captivity to Marxism-Leninism as it really was, had become converts to the true faith; all the more delightful if they were Americans.

The Americans and South Koreans for their part saw things through the Cold-War looking-glass, holding the same attitudes the other way round. Their particular pain was to hear of Americans converted to communism or to sympathy with it, which they could only explain as the outcome of 'brainwashing' or moral deficiency. Their special delight was the conversion of communist Chinese to the cause of Chiang Kai-shek's 'Nationalist China'. The admission to their camps of that regime's representatives to assist with the 'explanations' which were part of the procedures supposed to ensure that no prisoner was involuntarily repatriated was only one of the many ways in which those procedures became nightmarish parodies of fair dealing, unrecognizably remote from what the makers of the POW Convention had in mind. Violence and subtler sorts of pressures were used both to bring prisoners to the 'right' conclusion and to prevent them coming to the 'wrong' one, and it was not from outside the camps alone that violence and pressures came. The internal management of camps on the Southern side was, by custom and convenience as well as in rough conformity with the Convention, largely in the hands of the prisoners them-

---

[118] MacCallum adds that the cost to the USA of the war's protraction was 2,500 American casualties a month: *Korea, the War before Vietnam*, 253.

selves. The consequence was that, as soon as repatriation procedures had become a political issue, some camps became dominated by communist gangs and others by anti-communist ones, whose zeal for promoting their respective party lines sometimes ran to murder, riot, and, in the later stages, mass refusal to attend 'explanation' sessions.

In such strange and scandalous circumstances, it was more than usually difficult for the armistice negotiators at Panmunjom to locate the kind of neutral intermediary presence which alone might have a chance of cajoling the jinn of repatriation back into his bottle. The professionally neutral ICRC, usually the front runner for jobs of this kind, was out of the running because of communist distrust. The UN, which can in certain circumstances appear in an impartial posture, never looked less impartial than here. But in the end a serviceable performance of neutrality was provided by India. The newly independent giant of South Asia, wanting no part of the Cold War, was accustomed to communicating, on its own and others' behalf, with Beijing. It was ready now to sit with Sweden, Switzerland, Poland, and Czechoslovakia on a so-called Neutral Nations' Repatriation Commission and to do the military donkey-work of maintaining custody over the remaining 22,600 POWs until the last phase of formalities had been gone through. The Armistice Agreement was at last signed on 27 July 1953. The Repatriation Commission's attempts to do what it was supposed to do—to give the prisoners a fairly informed free choice between going back where they came from or opting for South Korea or Formosa—bent before the determination of the USA and its satellites to show the world that subjects of communist regimes, given the opportunity to escape from them, did so. Only about 3,000 ever had the choice properly explained to them, and only 440 Chinese and 188 North Koreans chose repatriation.[119]

The Korean episode was an ominous trial run for 1949's improved version of the POW part of IHL. Those who preferred to look on the bright side of things could say that the shortcomings in the treatment of prisoners, sometimes very bad on the Northern side, and the scandals attendant on the process of release from Southern camps were explicable in terms of the inexperience of some belligerents, the inexplicitness of their obligations, and the overall complexities of the political situation. But difficulties like these or even worse were to recur. A string of subsequent experiences has shown that, for all the ICRC's repeated reminders and tireless endeavours, 'release

---

[119] Figures from ibid. 252. The trouble with the NNRC was that in those early years of the cold war, neutrals found it difficult not to be neutral on either one side or the other. For its agitated history, see Shiv Dayal, *India's Role in the Korean Question. A Study in the Settlement of International Disputes under the UN* (Delhi, 1959).

and repatriation without delay after the cessation of active hostilities' rarely happens. Severely wounded and sick prisoners have indeed often been repatriated while hostilities are still going on. The ICRC is well used to arranging exchanges of POWs who are in such bad shape that, humanitarian considerations apart, their return to active military service is inconceivable. But the relatively undamaged are obviously held by belligerents to be a different matter.[120]

On occasions when detaining powers find it convenient or advantageous to let POWs go straight home, the Convention maps out a fast track. On one occasion at least since 1950—the little South Atlantic War of April–June 1982—the circumstances were so exceptional that the Convention was able to operate almost perfectly. For Argentina, political and diplomatic advantage dictated getting off its hands without delay the few Britons captured at the very outset of the affair; they were rushed to Montevideo and handed over to neutral Uruguay for repatriation even before the ICRC could get into the act. The ICRC then assisted with three repatriations, of over 1,200 men in all, via Montevideo while the war was still going on— a most unusual occurrence. (Whether Britain would have been so ready for their immediate release had it had anywhere to retain them other than desolate moorland or overcrowded shipping is a nice question.) For Britain, winter weather and logistic difficulties dictated repatriating as soon as possible the more than 10,000 prisoners who suddenly became its responsibility when the commander of the Argentinian forces in the Falkland Islands surrendered on 14 June 1982. The ICRC's celebratory booklet on this war makes no mention of the political difficulties which for a little while threatened to delay the process.[121] Were hostilities at an end or not? London supposed that they must be; in Buenos Aires, however, mortified pride joined lingering hope of diplomatic advantage to refuse publicly to admit as much. 'At first, the Argentines failed to respond to reports on the condition of the prisoners. Also, at one point, Argentina refused to guarantee the British safe passage in Argentine waters in order to

---

[120] Articles 109–117 of the 4th Convention provide an elaborate legal framework not just for repatriation of the disabled but also for internment of special categories of able-bodied in neutral countries, e.g. those who have been inside for excessively long terms. The ICRC of course is free to make whatever simpler arrangements it can persuade belligerents to agree to, which is what it does in any case whenever the GCs are not obviously applicable.

[121] S.-S. Junod, *Protection of the Victims of Armed Conflict: Falkland-Malvinas Islands, 1982* (Geneva, IRRC, 1984), 31. Mme Junod's handsomely produced booklet could not be more lucid or readable, and since it admittedly does not pretend to tell the whole story (see the author's note on p. 7), must not be criticized for not doing so. From less committed standpoints, however, it inevitably reads like the story of the war with most of its harsh realities left out.

return them.'[122] The one British POW held in Argentina was not released until 10 July. Repatriation proceeded nevertheless by agreement between competent authorities and with ICRC assistance and was completed by the 14th; the British Foreign Office having concluded that 'active hostilities [were] at an end', even though Argentina would not admit it.[123]

Even in the unique circumstances of the South Atlantic War of 1982, therefore, the implementation of IHL was not entirely trouble-free. But it must have been by far the most nearly trouble-free the ICRC has ever had to help with. A few examples will show what has been the more common experience even in more or less straight international armed conflicts. The nine years' war between Iraq and Iran offered a grim exhibition of breaches of almost every important humanitarian rule, including the most persistent attempts at 'brainwashing' since North Korea's, this time by Iran and with Islamic fundamentalist purposes rather than secular political ones. The exhibition did not close with the cease-fire on 20 August 1988. Active hostilities were over but neither side showed any sign of readiness to release the prisoners it held (the ICRC with difficulty had managed to register over 50,000 Iraqis in Iran and 19,000 Iranians in Iraq, but knew not how many more it had been prevented from seeing) until a peace settlement was agreed, and to the haggling over that there seemed no end. Even the repatriation of sick and wounded prisoners which the ICRC was most anxious to get on with, hobbled painfully.[124] This most unsatisfactory situation came abruptly to an end with Iraq's invasion of Kuwait at the beginning of August 1990. Iraq was now of course desperate at all costs to keep Iran out of it. The ICRC now could not move fast enough to suit Baghdad's convenience. Obstacles miraculously vanished, and by 21 August the ICRC was reporting extraordinary progress: 'Both governments wish to speed up daily rhythm of repatriations to 5,000 POWs by road and 3,000 by air', etc.[125]

[122] I am indebted for these significant details to a paper done in 1982–3 by a graduate student at the American University, Jane Burgess, which she kindly presented to me when she visited Sussex in April 1983. Her evidence, carefully documented, came mainly from the *New York Times* and *Washington Post* war reports. The British statement cited just below is attributed to the latter's issue of 13 July 1982.

[123] Apart from the works of Junod and Burgess already referred to, I have drawn mainly (but not uncritically) on Freedman and Gamba-Stonehouse, *Signals of War* (London, 1990) and on the British Foreign and Commonwealth Office's Sept. 1982 Background Brief, 'The Falkland Islands Conflict: Some Humanitarian Aspects'.

[124] Digested from ICRC's *Bulletin* for Sept. 1988 and its *Annual Report* for that year, pp. 77–9.

[125] Telex circular TB5516 of that date, as received by the British Red Cross Society. Nor did obstacles appear a year later when 'about 13,000 Iraqi prisoners' refused to go home, preferring to stay as refugees in Saudi Arabia after the UN's coalition's expulsion of Iraq from Kuwait. Reported from 'the Red Cross' in Bahrain, the *Independent*, 13 Sept. 1991.

The two weeks' war between India and Pakistan in December 1971 was followed by another such manhandling of the POW Convention's rules for release and repatriation. The law and politics of the affair were this time much more complicated. While Pakistan was determined to present it simply as an international war, India was determined to present it also as Bangladesh's war of independence; East Pakistan might have had no chance to become Bangladesh at all had not India intervened to take on the Pakistani forces engaged in repressing the (from the Pakistani point of view) secessionist rebellion going on there. Whether you chose to look at it as an international armed conflict or as a Common Article 3 one, or as both at once, was a question on which the theory and practice of politics had as much to say as humanitarian principle. While Pakistan (what was left of it, westwards) wanted to get back the tens of thousands of its soldiers who had been taken prisoner in (what India now regarded as) Bangladesh but had been moved into camps in India, Bangladesh wanted to get back the tens of thousands of Bengali civilians and former soldiers who were stuck in Pakistan. Additional major complications were Bangladesh's desire (power-fully encouraged by India and the international humanitarian legal com-munity) to bring to trial nearly 200 Pakistani servicemen credibly accused of war crimes, and India's desire to sponsor Bangladesh for membership of the UN. Pakistan, fortified by the backing of Washington *and* Beijing (seated at last in the UN, and famously befriended by President Nixon early in 1972) was of course determined to thwart them. In such a maelstrom of conflicting interests, the ICRC's simple suggestion fell on deaf ears, that India should simply do what Article 118 of the POW Convention apparently obliged it to do. The conclusion of the matter was not reached until 1974. No war-crimes trials were held, Pakistan got its soldiers back, and Bangladesh was admitted to the UN.[126]

What more need be said about the business of release and repatriation? There must almost always be difficulties. 'The cessation of active hostilities' has not proved to be as reassuringly definitive an event as the framers of Article 118 perhaps supposed. Truces, cease-fires, armistices, and so on are

[126] The sources at my disposal carry no indication of what moral pressures, if any, the ICRC was applying to Pakistan at the same time as it was applying them to India. Even Forsythe, the only authoritative writer to take an interest in such things, refers (*Humanitarian Politics*, 2–3) only to the Indian side of the affair. My paragraph represents a digestion of matter mostly from Paust and Blaustein, 'War Crimes Jurisdiction and Due Process: The Bangladesh Experience', in *Vanderbilt Journal of Transnational Law*, 11 (1978), 1–38; T. W. Oliver, *The UN in Bangladesh* (Princeton, NJ, 1978); K. P. Misra, *The Role of the UN in the Indo-Pakistan Conflict* (Delhi, 1973); *Official Records of the Security Council*, 1972; *International Legal Materials*, Sept. 1973 and May 1974; *Yearbooks of the International Commission of Jurists*, 1972–3 and 1973–4; and ICRC *Annual Report* for 1972.

not the same thing as treaties of peace. Governments as well as armed forces will use them, if they can, for restoring their positions and preparing to do better next time. The wheels of diplomacy and politics, propaganda, and PR are in perpetual motion. Moreover, while there remains a chance that hostilities may be resumed, a detaining power must be forgiven for pondering the risks of returning to an enemy men who might be used again against him, the fairness of requiring a quid pro quo or at least a guarantee of some sort. Instead of simply acting publicly as the technical arranger and manager of returns and exchanges, the ICRC can hardly avoid finding itself privately pressed to participate in the negotiations and bargainings which must usually accompany them. Such negotiations will in any case be the basis of the operation when an armed conflict is of that indeterminate description which lies beyond the boundaries of the 1949 Conventions.[127]

Negotiations can rarely be more difficult than they have been in connection with the long conflict between Israel and its neighbours, especially following Israel's victory in the Six Day War of 1967 and its subsequent military occupations of the West Bank and Gaza Strip. The application of IHL in that area is a perpetual puzzle. Every normal definition is disputed. 'War' between Israel and those neighbour States never so much began or ended as it recurrently flared up and down. What had been Israel's most stable neighbour, Lebanon, virtually dissolved through civil strife in the later 1970s to become a sort of Tom Tiddler's ground for the conduct of hostilities by sub-State surrogates. The most persistent of Israel's antagonists since the early 1970s has been the PLO which since 1988 has stood before the world as the (absent) government of a Palestinian State which Israel especially does not recognize. Its modes of attacking Israel have mostly been terroristic; to the Israeli mind, wholly so. At the only time when something like an IHL-defined 'armed conflict' was fought (characteristically, in Lebanon!) between Palestinian and Israeli armed forces, Israel would not recognize that captured or detained Palestinians were entitled to be treated as POWs proper; it did however give them what a competent authority called 'treatment equivalent to POW treatment'.[128]

---

[127] What the ICRC actually does in relation to particular negotiations is ordinarily impossible for an outsider to find out. Diplomacy is a confidential business, there are many modes of it, and the ICRC's grounds for maintaining its reputation for neutrality and impartiality command respect. Outsiders may nevertheless estimate that its input into such negotiations must sometimes be significant and even crucial. Inevitably its situation can become such that it is prompted to remark, e.g. apropos of two tricky El Salvador episodes: 'It should be noted that the ICRC took no part in the actual negotiation', and 'This was done . . . at the request of the parties involved and as a strictly neutral intermediary', ICRC *Annual Reports* respectively for 1985, p. 37 and 1988, p. 45.

[128] W. V. O'Brien, 'The PLO in International Law', in *Boston University International Law Journal*, 2 (1984), 349–413 at 405. It must be said that O'Brien is a good deal given to espousing the Israeli view of things.

With less justification, and as already mentioned, Israel has refused to admit that its post-1967 occupations come under the rule of the 4th GC. The list of juridical anomalies and political peculiarities could be continued indefinitely, but the only question here is: What in *these* circumstances has been done with regard to the release and repatriation of prisoners and (as Israel more often describes the persons it puts inside) detainees? Some hint of what must happen on lesser occasions may be gained from the story of the spectacular release and exchange of 24 November 1983—several thousands of Palestinians and Lebanese in return for six PLO-held Israeli soldiers—to which the ICRC was an essential party: 'months of negotiations conducted by the ICRC with Israel, on the one hand, and with the PLO on the other'; the operation itself 'carried out in stages, [with] the full support of the parties concerned and of the Algerian, Egyptian and French Governments'.[129]

The word hostages has not so far been mentioned but every reader who knows what has been going on in the world through the past twenty-five years or so will have realized that by now we have entered hostage country; which is kidnap country too. The word hostage, often enough encountered in the parts of national military-law manuals which dealt with the control of occupied enemy territory, did not appear in the earlier international law-of-war texts. No need was felt for it before the Second World War showed how the practice of hostage-taking could be atrociously abused. The post-war judgments made criminal the killing of hostages; Articles 34 and 147 of the Civilians Convention did the same for the mere taking of them. The POW Convention says nothing about hostages in relation to its primary aim, the regulation of international conflict. The awkward possibility that prisoners might be held as hostages was circumvented by the demand that they should be promptly released and repatriated. It was only in the Conventions' Common Article aiming to regulate non-international conflict that the taking of prisoners (and others) as hostages was expressly banned, the matter presenting itself to the legislators' minds as one which needed to be noticed only in the context of conflicts where standards of conduct were believed to be lower.

It is no doubt true that kidnapping and hostage-taking have continued to

[129] O'Brien, 'PLO in International Law', 407, is so concerned to emphasize Israel's diplomatic purity that he gives a wrong impression of the operational complexity when he describes this as 'a PLO/Israeli agreement negotiated directly between the parties without any Israeli formal recognition of the PLO'. He goes on to say (without wholly accepting the logic of their position) that 'The Israelis consider agreements of this kind to be comparable to agreements that governments made with criminals holding hostages.' This perhaps explains a shabby feature of the affair for which one must turn to the ICRC's account of it: Israel's failure in the end to produce over 200 of the prisoners promised, and subsequent refusal to let the ICRC visit them. See its *Annual Report* for 1983, pp. 62–3.

happen more in internal conflicts and 'situations' than in international ones. Opportunity for them is more plentiful and the case for their usefulness more plausible. Lebanon and Colombia come at once to mind as countries torn by civil strife and lawlessness where both practices have become painfully familiar.[130] If foreigners are present and if the seizure of them seems to offer advantages (as it has done so conspicuously in Lebanon), then of course they will become involved too. But it is not just as an overflow from domestic disasters that kidnapping and hostage-taking have come to afflict the international community. Most of the politically motivated aircraft hijackings which were such a remarkable phenomenon of the years 1968–73—there were about ninety in the worst year—were related to the Arab–Israel antagonism. The ICRC, writes Forsythe, became involved (or, as better describes what sometimes happened, entangled) in some of the worst of them because it was already by then 'rather well known to most Middle Eastern parties through its protection and assistance roles . . . The release of the hostages was achieved on a number of occasions.'[131]

It may not be fanciful to see in these events and the mostly less spectacular kidnapping and hostage-taking practices which still continue (and which, if they come within the scope of APs 1 and 2, would fall under the ban of their respective Articles 75(2)[c] and 4(2)[c]) a low-level extension of the meaning of the world 'hostage' to match its more pretentious use in popular renderings of nuclear strategy. There, it describes the situation of civilian city populations of nuclear-armed powers: in effect held hostage to secure each other's abstention from use of nuclear weapons, and at risk of extinction if their governments' system of mutual deterrence were to break down. Reciprocity, here as in so many areas, may roughly back humanitarian principle, whether humanitarians of principle ask it to or not.[132]

The same has to be said of the other parts of IHL dealing with prisoners and detainees as of those parts intended to secure speedy release and repatriation: none of them works as well as it should. This is not because of imprecision or incompleteness. Quite the contrary! The Prisoners Convention, as has admiringly been remarked already, is exceptionally complete and comprehensive, and the Civilians Convention's sections regulating the

[130] In the *Independent*, 7 Oct. 1991, Robert Fisk reported the calm explanation of Lebanon's present kidnapping habits ('a kind of routine') given by the Hezbollah leader, Sheikh Abbas Moussawi. He dated their current phase from when the civil war started in 1975.
[131] Forsythe, *Humanitarian Politics*, 88–97, followed by a few pages on kidnapping pure and simple, provides the best available scan of these tumours on the body of IHL.
[132] The ICRC *Commentary* on the APs, p. 874, remarks that 'During recent years the term "hostages" has acquired different meanings', but understandably does not notice the nuclear-warfare usage mentioned here.

treatment of internees are scarcely less so, which is not surprising, the POW Convention having been in this respect its model. Neither Convention leaves any room for doubt regarding the duties of Detaining Powers and the rights of Protecting Powers and the ICRC which may on many occasions act in their stead. But the ICRC, untiring and persistent though it certainly is, every year has to record no more than partial success in performance of its statutory tasks of protecting the interests and welfare of prisoners and detainees, from the time they pass into the hands of the captor right up to the time of their return home.

Just as this partial failure is no more attributable to any fault of the ICRC than to any incompleteness of the parts of IHL it stands for, neither can it be related to that peculiarity which pops up throughout these pages: IHL's sliding scale of applicability. From the maximal degree of observance stipulated in respect of identifiably international armed conflicts, that scale descends through a middle region of applicability of Common Article 3 in supposedly identifiable non-international armed conflicts down to the shady zone of 'internal strife' where it may be difficult to identify exactly what is going on but possible to agree that what is going on is bad enough to demand the observance of fundamental humanitarian principles. In fact and in experience, it must again be said, there is no correlation between degrees of legal applicability and actual observance. The law respecting POWs can be as ill-observed when there is no excuse for not observing it, as it can be decently observed when there are plenty of excuses for its not being so. The ICRC, whose authority and practice encourage it to try to protect prisoners and detainees wherever they are so because of public violence, may find itself as welcome in situations beyond the obvious borders of the Conventions as unwelcome within them.

A few examples will suffice to show what can happen. An international war as plainly international as can be was that between Iraq and Iran from 22 September 1980, the day when Iraq invaded Iranian territory, to 18 July 1988, when Iran accepted, twelve months after it was first made, the Security Council's demand for a cease-fire in its Resolution 598, 20 July 1987. Both belligerents were parties to the Geneva Conventions and both regularly appealed to IHL in their PR warfare against one another, but their treatments of POWs—such surrendered and/or disabled enemies, that is, as survived the initial phases of capture—broke most of the rules. The listing and registration of prisoners, essential preliminary to all the good works the ICRC is authorized to do and to arrange for national agencies to do for the protection and relief of POWs, was often long delayed (which allowed captors plenty of time to do the torturing which seems to have happened very often) and far from complete. Once in camps and properly registered, prisoners' material circumstances appear to have been adequate, but there was an unusual amount of ideological pressure. Writing in thankfully free and secular circumstances, I wonder whether compulsory exposure to Radio Baghdad's political broadcasts would be more or less bearable than urgent proselytizing by Iran's revolutionary version of Shiite Islam. Consequent faction-fighting among Iraqi prisoners led to riots and killings, the worst of which, in October 1983, began while ICRC delegates were visiting the Gorgan camp and issued in their being blamed for it and in their expulsion, yet again, from Iran. It was above all the recurrent inability to do their statutory visiting duties that moved the ICRC twice in 1984 to the very unusual step of appealing to the whole array of signatory States to use what influence they could to persuade both Gulf War belligerents to take IHL seriously.[133]

The impression given by the Iraq–Iran War that Saddam Hussein's Iraq had as little respect for IHL as for other branches of international law was seriously confirmed by events which followed fast on that war's heels: his seizure of Kuwait in August 1990, his defeat at the hands of the UN-authorized coalition early in 1991, and his handling of Kurdish and Shiite insurgents and resisters subsequently. Whereas between 1980 and 1988 *most* of IHL's principles and rules were ignored by Iraq, in 1990 and 1991 they *all* were. I quit this horrible episode with the recollection of something unforgettable seen on British television in early or middle 1992: a covertly taken video film of 'Saddam Hussein and his generals' (it was impossible to tell if he was really there, because they all looked alike) with a few prisoners taken in the campaign to recover control of the southern Iraq marshlands; one of those senior officers having hit a helpless prisoner, the others at once hastened to follow suit.

Indo-China 1960–73 (henceforth, following common usage, 'Vietnam'), El Salvador 1980–91, and Israel since 1967 provide illustrations of the sort of things that can happen to prisoners and detainees in armed conflicts of less than unmistakably international character. Identifying the character of the conflict is something which matters differently to the different parties involved in negotiations about prisoners. The ICRC, which in strict law need not be, but in practice almost always *is*, the only neutral agent representing prisoners' interests, of course seeks to clarify the legal basis of its claims on their behalf: can it demand full recognition of the 3rd Conven-

---

[133] This summary account is digested from a broad spectrum of sources: Red Cross ones (ICRC press releases, monthly *Bulletins*, and *Annual Reports*), UN reports, newspaper and periodical articles, and ten years' occasional attendance at IHL meetings and conferences.

tion, is it a Common Article 3 affair, or must the ICRC, as so often happens, simply do the best it can by virtue of its moral authority ('the humanitarian mandate conferred on it by the international community' etc.) and by means of its confidential diplomacy?

In Vietnam, the armed conflict had developed to such an extent by the mid-1960s that the ICRC put it to the four parties most directly concerned—the Republic of Vietnam (= South Vietnam), the Democratic Republic of Vietnam (= North Vietnam), the latter's protégé in South Vietnam, the National Liberation Front (= the Vietcong), and South Vietnam's external prop and ally the USA—that the Geneva Conventions in their entirety had become applicable. The USA and South Vietnam accepted this, in respect not only of soldiers from North Vietnam captured in the South, which was to be expected, but also of Vietcong fighters, which was more remarkable, considering the variety of ways they might fall below the POW Convention's definition of a protectable combatant. The ICRC was thus enabled to visit camps holding those categories of combatants, something like 40,000 of them, from beginning to end.[134] With regard to civilian detainees, however, the situation was not so good. South Vietnam parted company from the USA by insisting that the very large number of civilians it detained on security and political grounds were beyond the GCs' scope; it refused to accept the ICRC's contention that, if those persons were not protected by the 3rd Convention, they must be protected by Article 5 of the 4th. The best the ICRC could do on behalf of those persons, some of whom it supposed to be wrongly labelled POWs and many of whom it suspected of simply being disliked by the government, was to press its claims as their protector under Common Article 3 and/or because of the ICRC's customary entitlement to try to protect political prisoners. So many difficulties, humiliations, and wrangles resulted from these attempts that in the end the ICRC gave them up as a bad job.[135]

Its dealings with the Vietcong and with North Vietnam were much simpler. They refused to have anything to do with it, so far as POWs were concerned. The manner of their refusal was remarkable for its rejection not merely of what they regarded as 'bourgeois' and 'Western' law but also of

[134] The number is taken from Forsythe's exemplary survey of this difficult stretch of Red Cross history; *Humanitarian Politics*, 152–67.
[135] The ICRC from the outset distrusted this bit of the Civilians Convention, discussed in Part II. Pictet's *Commentary* (1958, p. 52–8) characterizes it as 'an important and regrettable concession to State expediency'. It presciently concludes thus: 'What is most to be feared is that widespread application of the Article may eventually lead to a category of civilian internees who do not receive the normal treatment laid down by the Convention but are detained under conditions which are almost impossible to check.' See above p. 125.

the ways in which every other party reasoned about it. The Vietcong maintained that the GCs were of no concern to it because they did not speak to its constitution and because it had not participated in the making of them; it is relevant to recall that the Algerian FLN, a not dissimilar body in a not dissimilar situation, had not participated either, but it had embraced the GCs nevertheless and accepted (even if mainly for PR purposes) the orthodox doctrine on non-State parties' obligations and entitlements.[136] North Vietnam's readiness to complain about its opponents' neglect of IHL contrasted strangely with its insistence on handling Article 85 of the POW Convention differently even from how the Soviet bloc handled it, which was itself already different enough from, so to speak, the NATO way.[137] In consequence of these ideologically motivated objections, the ICRC never got to see how North Vietnam treated its prisoners and to do its proper works of communication and relief on their behalf; nor, *a fortiori*, had it ever an opportunity to see what the Vietcong did with its handfuls of captives.

In armed conflicts with less obviously international characteristics than that of Vietnam, States may be able to snub the ICRC with less risk of censure. The questions, how much the ICRC is to be allowed to see of the dark realm of detention centres, prisons, and camps, and whether it is to be allowed to see anything at all, in practice become (although they need not become, and ought *not* to become) entangled in arguments about the legal status of the conflict. What ought to be a straight run for the ICRC often turns out to be a torment of hurdles and handicaps.

The Israel area is of course the one where such arguments are at their most endless and inventive. A glance at a recent issue of the ICRC's series of *Annual Reports* (I have lighted on the one for 1985) will suggest how much protection of POWs and so on nevertheless remains possible. In the Lebanon section, under the heading 'Persons Arrested': 'Throughout the year, the ICRC visited or tried to visit the persons arrested in connection with the Lebanese conflict and the Israeli occupation of the south of the country': thirteen visits to Ansar camp, 2,192 civilian internees seen and registered; thirty visits to detainees under interrogation under an 'agreement (obtained after numerous negotiations conducted since the start of the

---

[136] A fine exposition of this doctrine may be found in pp. 169–73 of Henri Meyrowitz, 'Le droit de la guerre dans le conflit vietnamien', in *Annuaire français du droit international* (1967), 153–201.

[137] For a good brief review of this odd business, see Forsythe, *Humanitarian Politics*, 155–7. The question was not how to read the text of Art. 85 but how to read the reservation which the Soviet bloc and its friends attached to it. For a searching introduction to the matter, see the Pictet *Commentary* (1960) iii. 413–16, 423–5.

Israeli occupation in June 1982)' which in its latest form stipulates notification within 15 days of arrest, the first visit within 20 days, and visits every 14 days thereafter; no access to the Khiyam prison, 'despite repeated requests to the Israeli authorities and the South Lebanon Army'; 'forty-seven visits to 481 persons detained by several militias'; continued enquiries about 'persons missing'; and no more to do with 'hostages' than is dictated by 'the interest of the victims and the wish to help them'. Of Israel and the occupied territories, the subsections record: interviews without witness of 1,405 'detainees under interrogation' in nine places on the West Bank and in the Gaza Strip; 4,000 'persons convicted or awaiting trial' visited in thirty different places; 'visits to 133 administrative detainees', i.e. 'preventive arrest' in breach of the 4th GC; and well over 1,000 Palestinians and Lebanese 'arrested in southern Lebanon' and taken to the Atlit camps in Israel in violation again of the 4th GC. Such a summary speaks volumes about the complexity of the ICRC's task in attempting to do what IHL expects of it in respect of POWs and their sadly numerous extended family of relations.

El Salvador, by contrast, presents a legal situation which is as simple and straightforward as can be. The armed conflict which has torn that unhappy country and killed over 80,000 of its people since 1979 is a clear case of a Common Article 3 'non-international armed conflict', and seems to have been universally recognized as such; even, so far as may reasonably be expected, by the government of El Salvador itself. The case of El Salvador is unusual because although the world has since the 1950s been full of armed conflicts of that description, most governments within whose territories such conflicts rage deny that they are so. Armed conflicts as persistent and terrible as those in, e.g. El Salvador, Sri Lanka, Ethiopia, Mozambique, Angola, and Uganda, have as surely been Article 3 ones, as probably have been lesser ones like those, e.g., in Northern Ireland (the Provisional IRA), Turkey (the Kurds), and India (the Sikhs). But whether their case is arguable or beyond sensible dispute, governments hardly ever acknowledge that Common Article 3 applies. Touchy about their sovereignty and nervous about security, they feel such acknowledgement to be *infra dig.* and moreover they know that in practice (despite the Article's closing sentence's assurance to the contrary) it raises the status and reputation of their opponents.[138]

The case of El Salvador is unusual in two respects. First, in that its government let itself so nearly acknowledge the applicability of Article 3

---

[138] The closing sentence reads: 'The application of the preceding provisions shall not affect the legal status of the Parties to the conflict.'

and AP2 as not expressly to deny it when the ICRC publicly came to the conclusion that it could be taken for granted. In this area, where so much has to be read between lines and where the nearest you may get to an affirmative is the absence of a negative, there is a significant difference between the first sentences of the El Salvador sections of the ICRC's *Annual Reports* for 1982: 'For the third consecutive year, the ICRC pursued its protection and assistance activities on behalf of victims of the internal armed conflict which is tearing the country apart', and for 1983: 'In accordance with the provisions of the GCs covering such conflicts (Article 3 . . . and AP2 . . .) the ICRC has for the fourth successive year', etc. as before.[139] The case of El Salvador is also unusual as the closest thing the world has yet seen to an armed conflict in terms of AP2. As the ICRC's just-quoted reference to it might have led one to suppose, El Salvador ratified AP2 in November 1978 and the 'dissident armed forces or other organized armed groups', i.e. the FMLN, appeared by 1983 or thereabouts to satisfy the Protocol's requirements that such forces or groups be 'under responsible command [and] exercise such control over a part of [the] territory as to enable them to carry out sustained and concerted military operations and to implement this Protocol'. To the objection that the FMLN in fact failed to implement the Protocol, in so far as some of its ways of fighting breached IHL, it seems not unreasonable to rejoin that some of the State's armed forces' ways breached it too.

An eminent expert on human rights and IHL has thus summed up this unusual situation.

Although Article 3 automatically applies when a situation of internal armed conflict objectively exists [writes Robert K. Goldman] the ICRC is not legally empowered to compel the warring parties to acknowledge the article's applicability. Thus, despite the fact that both the Salvadorean and Nicaraguan governments have permitted the ICRC to establish permanent delegations in their territory, neither government has publicly recognized the existence of an internal armed conflict as defined in Article 3. The fact that both governments allow the ICRC access to captured dissidents and to engage in civilian relief operations in combat zones, where ICRC delegates have come into contact with dissident forces, however, suggests that both governments tacitly acknowledge the existence of another internal party to these conflicts.

He goes on to point out that, by the same token, AP2 is applicable too, although the Salvadorean Government has (not surprisingly) been 'reluctant to officially recognize' the fact.[140]

To the common-sense enquiry, what signs and degrees of recognition are

---

[139] That form of wording remained in use at least until 1988.
[140] Goldman, 'International Humanitarian Law', at 544–5 and 549–50.

similarly expected to be made by the insurgents, the reply has to be that neither Common Article 3 nor AP2 invites any (whereas AP1 pointedly and repeatedly refers to both 'the HCPs' *and* 'the Parties to the conflict'). Legal doctrine holds that their assent and acceptance are taken for granted following the signatures of the States from which they are seeking to secede or whose governments they are seeking to overthrow. On the face of it, this has an absurd aspect, but in practice two advantages follow. First, the ICRC and humanitarian agencies generally can approach insurgents with the presumption that they are of humanitarian disposition until proved not to be so.[141] Second, the way is open for them to affirm such a disposition by declaring their will and fitness to observe IHL's basic principles and rules. Many NLMs and other insurgent parties have in fact done so since the Algerian FLN boldly blazed the trail; but whether they have thereafter greatly observed them, and to what extent their intentions have in each case been more humanitarian or political, are matters for inquiry and debate.[142]

Here, then, is an armed conflict to which the GCs (through the simplified medium of Common Article 3) and AP2 are said by the ICRC to apply, and which the international community is presumed to believe them to apply to. The ICRC has acted accordingly. How have its labours in protection of POWs and so on fared? Its *Annual Reports* from 1979 present a picture of humanitarian pertinacity in face of many obstacles and complications. Visits and, more important, 'regular visits' to 'persons detained in connection with the events' (also referred to as 'the situation' and 'the conflict') are recorded from early on. In 1982, for example, there were 1,296 visits to 171 'places of detention' controlled by a variety of military, police and civil authorities; in 1984, 1,866 visits 'to 254 places of detention and five hospitals', both in San Salvador and in the provinces; the delegates' findings being 'regularly brought to the attention of the authorities' and (to continue

[141] Michael Bothe however shrewdly notes the *dis*advantage that since AP2 applies only to 'relations between a government and dissidents' it cannot in El Salvador apply to relations between the latter and 'non-governmental armed groups of the Right'. See his 'Article 3 and Protocol II: Case Studies of Nigeria and El Salvador', in *American University Law Review*, 31 (1982), 899–909 at 906.

[142] It is also matter for debate, when and how the El Salvador insurgents' humanitarian commitment was registered. Goldman's authority for his statement 'that the FMLN has pledged to respect IHL' ('International Humanitarian Law', 550 n. 37) is the ICRC's 1983 *Annual Report*, 29; but the ICRC does *not* there say anything of the sort. The Americas Watch Study, 'Violation of Fair Trial Guarantees by the FMLN's *Ad Hoc* Courts' (May 1990), 9 n. 12 relies on Goldman, but its opening assertion that 'the Salvadorean rebels are directly bound' by Common Article 3 and AP2 is based not on any alleged statement of theirs but, following legal orthodoxy, on the ICRC's 'express recognition' and on presumed recognition by the Salvadorean government 'or at least important sectors' of it. The earliest explicit FMLN recognition cited in that Study, p. 9, is dated Oct. 1988.

with words from 1983) 'raised in several meetings with the President of the Republic and the Minister of Defence'.

So far, it might seem, so good. But three dark shadows hang over these modest achievements. Two categories of detainees were tragically notable by their absence. First, there were those thousands of civilians (as most of them must be considered to have been) who could not be visited because they had been 'disappeared' and assassinated. The ICRC said in 1983 that it had 'again and again strongly censured such practices, which violate the most fundamental principles of humanitarian law'. Second, there were those thousands of detainees whom the ICRC was not told about and to whom it could not get until many days after their capture or arrest, i.e. after they would have been subjected to the torture and other maltreatment which, if they were going to happen at all (and El Salvador was one of the many countries in which they did happen), always happened within the first hours or days. By 1985, its task facilitated by having as many as thirty delegates at work in so small a country, the ICRC sounded not dissatisfied with the progress it had made in this respect: 'in accordance with the procedures agreed upon with the Salvadorean authorities, [it] was usually informed [fairly promptly] of arrests and granted subsequent access to the detainees.'

The third shadow, particularly troubling to the ICRC because of its urgent need to show impartiality and because it was bound to take seriously IHL's above-mentioned assumptions about insurgents, was the difficulties it encountered in carrying its protective work into the insurgents' hide-outs and, in their 'controlled zones', bases. The *Annual Reports* intimate that contacts were made with the FMLN in (or by) 1981 and that 'protective action started on 8 August 1982, the ICRC having obtained [no doubt, from both sides] the guarantees necessary to go into the fighting-areas'. Nine visits to four groups of prisoners resulted in the release of 244 government soldiers, whom the ICRC 'escorted to their barracks'. An intermittent trickle of visits, releases, and exchanges went on until the fighting ended in 1991–2. But the ICRC never succeeded in seeing everyone it asked to see, and in 1985 complained that it 'did not always receive replies—for the purpose of reassuring their families—to its enquiries into the whereabouts of persons reported missing and presumed to be in the hands of the FMLN'.

That the ICRC should voice such a complaint suggests that its relations with the insurgents were good enough for it to expect rather a lot of them. One reason why the FMLN, especially early on, did not deliver as much as might have been expected was its fear that unscrupulous officers on the government side, knowing where ICRC delegates were going to meet insurgent representatives, would use the knowledge to launch attacks directly after the meeting was over. Although relations between the ICRC and the FMLN evidently had their ups and downs, they seem to have been closer and more productive than in most of the internal conflicts into which the ICRC managed to interpose itself. (A regular sad feature of the *Annual Reports* is their naming of States which would not admit the ICRC at all, and of insurgent parties which would not meet it.) Among its more extra-ordinary achievements in El Salvador were its joint programme with the national Red Cross over several years to feed and nourish tens of thousands of 'displaced persons, needy residents and, systematically, families with children suffering from malnutrition [in] regions totally or partially affected by the fighting, where no other agency could penetrate'; and, in the same year 1985, its action at the request of both government and FMLN, to facilitate and manage the amazing simultaneous release and exchange on 24 October of, from the one side, the President's daughter, a lady friend of hers, and '23 mayors and municipal officials', and from the other, 'some 20 security detainees . . . as well as the evacuation to other countries, for adequate treatment, of about 100 seriously wounded FMLN fighters'.

9 | Application, Implementation, and Enforcement

For the legal specialist approaching any IHL issue, the beginning of wisdom lies in the answers to the questions: What law is applicable in this particular situation? Is it treaty law, applicable because the State or States concerned signed and ratified such-and-such a treaty when it was made, or acceded to it later? Or is it, in whole or in part, customary law, which is applicable to all States, no matter whether or not they would have wished to accede to it if the choice had been open to them?[1] Application may therefore be broad or narrow, dubious or certain, according to the mixture of elements in each particular case: the nature of the situation which makes application of IHL a possibility, and the extent to which the State or States in the case are involved, either by their treaty undertakings or by customary obligation. Always a State or States will appear in the front line, because public international law has until quite recently been very reluctant to recognize any but States as its (to use its own language) subjects, persons, or actors.

The question of the application and applicability of IHL has a different aspect for humanitarian persons and organizations striving actually to make it useful in given situations. The fact is that it may practically be applied where it is not, in strictly legal terms, applicable. Examples in this book have shown how States sometimes dismiss their legal obligations as mere scraps of paper or pick and choose among them which they will observe and which they won't. On the other hand we see that IHL can make its way into situations where its legal applicability is by no means clear. To the bulk of the persons and organizations dedicated to its service, this mismatch between the letter and the spirit of the law is of no importance except to the extent that unfriendly States, resting on its letter and on their lawyers' ingenuity in making the most of it, may use their legal rights to obstructive effect.

To speak of the application of IHL as a practical matter is to speak of what many people would call its implementation. For the whole of the

---

[1] Those are only the starters for the big meal of questions about the applicability of IHL and human rights law which exercise the skills of juridical experts. The human rights side is thoroughly covered in recent articles by one of the most eminent of those experts, Theodor Meron; 'On a Hierarchy of International Human Rights', in *AmJIL* 80 (1986), 1–23, and 'The Geneva Conventions as Customary Law', in ibid. 81 (1987), 348–70.

humanitarian community, from the legal experts at one end to the perhaps unlettered medical personnel and relief workers at the other, it is a matter of high importance that IHL should not just be admired in the shop window but should actually come into service and do the good work for which the international community designed it. And, as the preceding pages have amply shown, good work can certainly be done. But it is often done in ways and by means other than those prefigured in the treaties.

The most remarkable evidence of this phenomenon is the nearly total uselessness, to date, of the agent to which supervision of the implementation of the Geneva Conventions was primarily entrusted: the Protecting Power. The PP was a classic international-law device developed over several centuries by States which, having come into conflict with one another but being conscious of continuing membership of the same society, wished to remain (even if indirectly) in communication with their temporary enemy and not wholly to abandon whatever interests they might have within his territory. Neutral States, acting on behalf of belligerents and mutually acceptable on both sides, would protect those interests themselves; hence, the description of such neutrals as Protecting Powers. As IHL developed, it too relied on them. Prisoners of war, especially if they were wounded or sick, and civilian detainees could not but be its main concern in this connection. PPs were not actually mentioned in the POW part of the Hague Regulations, but they became intensively used during the First World War (American representatives until April 1917 visited camps in the UK and France, Spanish reps visited them in Germany, and so on) in parallel with the work already being done by the ICRC (which was not mentioned either) and its national 'relief societies', to promote the flow of letters between prisoners and their families, to convey relief parcels safely to them, and to negotiate their repatriation in the event that they were seriously sick or badly wounded. By 1929 the PP was out of the chrysalis. The POW Convention of that year called on it repeatedly, and experience of the working of the institution during the Second World War, although mixed, was not so bad that the 1949 Convention would not build upon it.[2]

[2] There was of course in the Second World War some difficulty, acute towards the end, in finding neutrals which were both willing and capable enough to become PPs. Pictet's *Commentary*, iii. 95 n. 2, says that 'At one time Switzerland alone was PP for no fewer than thirty-five belligerent countries'. It also interestingly says, on pp. 95–6, that PPs increasingly 'found themselves responsible for representing the respective interests of two opposing Parties at one and the same time. This gave them additional authority, and incidentally altered their role'; a PP thus situated becoming 'not so much the special representative of each of them, as the common agent of both, or a kind of umpire. This enabled it to bring directly into play that powerful instrument, the argument of reciprocity.'

372 Law and Armed Conflict since 1950

Protecting Powers are placed in the forefront of the protective battle in all four GCs, but it is of course the POW and Civilians Conventions which give them the most to do. Those parts of their texts which define the rights of POWs and lawfully detained civilians and which lay down standards and procedures for where they are held and how they are handled, rely on the PPs to take the lead in making sure that the Conventions are implemented. So far is the existence and role of PPs taken for granted, that the Conventions needed to say nothing about the mode of their appointment. Common Article 8/8/8/9, where the PP is cued to make its entry, simply says: 'The present Convention shall be applied with the co-operation and under the scrutiny of the Protecting Powers whose duty it is to safeguard the interests of the Parties to the conflict.' The language is peremptory and confident, but the two Common Articles which follow show that the legislators doubted whether things would work out so simply. What if the PP were after all to miss its cue, to be indisposed, or to have an accident on the way to the theatre? Elaborate arrangements were therefore made for stand-ins and understudies, which boiled down to letting the ICRC act as a substitute. What remains after sweating off the politic verbiage of Common Articles 9 and 10 is the clearing of a path for the ICRC 'to assume the humanitarian functions performed under the present Convention by a Protecting Power designated by the Parties to a conflict'.[3]

That path by now is worn broad and smooth. Only on four known occasions since 1950 are Protecting Powers known to have been appointed at all: 'in the Suez conflict in 1956, in Goa in 1961, in the Indo-Pakistan war in 1970/1 [and] in the Falkland/Malvinas conflict'; 'the designation' [in the two latter cases] being 'limited to the traditional diplomatic functions'.[4] Otherwise, the ICRC will probably in some measure have been performing its nominal substitute role, which most States are in any case happy for it to do. Conspicuous exceptions have been the States of the former Soviet bloc and the People's Republic of China, which entered reservations of objection to the Detaining Power's right, under Article 10/10/10/11, to proceed to the engagement of a substitute regardless of the preferences of 'the Power of which the protected persons are nationals'. Thus did they signalize their

---

[3] NB. Strictly speaking these are Common Articles 9/9/9/10 and 10/10/10/11. 'Humanitarian functions' are specified because no HCP will normally wish the substitute to assume the PP's potential diplomatic and political functions, which in any case are the sort of things the ICRC does not wish to become involved with.

[4] *Encyclopedia of Public International Law*, iv (1982), 318. API's complex Article 5, the rationale of which is well explained in that article, purports to make the appointment of a PP or its substitute more inescapable, but it is no bolder than the GCs in face of the ultimate barrier, the necessity of States' consent.

unwillingness to allow the ICRC (or any other body or neutral State which might take a Detaining Power's fancy) to have access to such of their nationals as were detained by their enemy. Their congenital suspiciousness and siege-mentality had no doubt been fortified by the non-repatriation of some thousands of their soldiers after the Second World War and, as we have seen, the war in Korea. But the ICRC at any rate may get there just the same if, instead of going through the stately motions of being constituted a PP-substitute in the terms of the GCs or AP1, it simply acts as best it can in the circumstances of the place and time, relying on its aura of authority and its unique standing within the international community. The ICRC may further refer questioners to the antepenultimate sentence of Common Article 3 of the GCs, which empowers it to 'offer its services to the Parties' and the Common Article which emphatically protects 'the ICRC or any other impartial humanitarian organization' in whatever activities they may, with the Parties' consent, 'undertake for the protection of prisoners of war and for their relief'.[5]

The ICRC's authority and standing are remarkable and important enough to warrant particular comment. Both as ideas and institutions, IHL and the ICRC have become inseparable from one another, and although friends of the ICRC may argue that since about 1950 they have become entangled to a greater extent than is actually for the good of the ICRC and the humanitarian activity it alone can undertake, it remains impossible to imagine any future for IHL that does not have the ICRC and the National Red Cross and Red Crescent Societies conspicuous in it. What above all else makes the ICRC and its associated bodies so useful and, it is not too much to say, indispensable to the working of IHL is their unique quality of humanitarian neutrality. This is different from the political neutrality which is inseparable from considerations of war and peace, and which is so well known to be subject to degrees of bias and preference that there is no longer much humour in the apocryphical non-belligerent's ingenuous question, 'Which side are we neutral on?' Within the Red Cross and Red Crescent movement, however, such a question could only be answered one way, and *is* so answered whenever the movement's principles come into discussion. The movement's key principles of neutrality and impartiality, if they bend at all, bend simply on the side of (the first in its list of principles) humanity, which in the IHL context means the prevention and alleviation of human suffering in time of armed conflict, the protection of life and health, and

---

[5] Article 3 of course relates only to 'non-international armed conflicts'. The other Article referred to is 9/9/9/10.

commitment to respect for human beings without regard to their nationality, race, religious beliefs, class, or political opinions, and without taking sides in hostilities or controversies connected with them.[6]

Neutrality and, what goes so naturally with it, impartiality have a special central place in the context of IHL. It is not too much to say that, shorn of their leavening presence, IHL itself could not survive. That presence has in some simple form been in the idea of IHL from its very beginnings. The humanitarian instinct or principle without which our laws of war could never have developed at all was, after all, the assertion of values different from those of the warrior—different, but in their way no less appealing. Demanding the suspension in time of war of the hatreds and cruelties which were its usual concomitants, those values transformed the stricken enemy into an enemy no longer. This aspect of the evolving laws and customs of war was not, to the best of my knowledge, overtly identified as having anything to do with neutrality until the early 1860s, when the connection was perceived by the newborn Red Cross movement. Its founding body, the Geneva International Conference of October 1863, concluded by recommending

that in time of war the belligerent nations should proclaim the neutrality of ambulances and military hospitals, and that neutrality should likewise be recognized, fully and absolutely, in respect of official medical personnel, voluntary medical personnel [and] inhabitants of the country who go to the relief of the wounded, and the wounded themselves.

This recommendation was generously taken up in the first Geneva Convention of August 1864; four of its ten articles actually use the word 'neutral(ity)' and the idea is discernible in most of the others. The word itself was ousted from the Conventions which followed. Generals and international lawyers, making their influence felt in a business which by the turn of the twentieth century was booming, appear to have considered its use improper and confusing. The idea however has found a fixed and permanent lodging in the principles and practice of the ICRC, which could not function without it.

The fundamental importance of the idea of neutrality to the whole scheme of IHL goes far beyond its particular importance for the ICRC, but

---

[6] The clumsiness of that sentence is because I have sought to use the very language of the movement's guiding principles (which apply equally to its roles in peace and war and have to satisfy all sectors of a varied constituency) in expressing their particular application to IHL. The latest statement of the principles, hardly at all changed from the previous, 1965 version, fills the preamble to the Statutes of the IRCRC Movement, adopted at its 15th International Conference, in Geneva 1986.

that is where it matters most. In order efficiently to execute the international community's instruction to play the lead part in the implementation of IHL, the ICRC has to be able to appear equally acceptable and unthreatening to *all* warring parties—its agents (delegates from Geneva headquarters and authorized officers of the associated National Societies) have to be able to work safely in situations otherwise characterized by danger, tension, and suspicion—and the places and vehicles necessary for their work have to be inviolable. Hence the special significance of 'the distinctive emblem', the Red Cross or Red Crescent and the odd variants forced upon the movement by the exigencies of international politics.[7] The distinctive emblem or sign is the only thing that protects the Red Cross protectors who must by definition be themselves unarmed.[8]

The GCs and their commentaries understandably make much of the distinction between the emblem as a 'protective sign' used in international wartime with the authority of the GCs to protect the wounded and sick and the personnel authorized by belligerents to tend them, and its uses on all other occasions of war and peace as a sign merely 'indicatory' of membership of the Red Cross and Red Crescent in any of its branches and of connection with any of their works. The former are the uses of the distinctive emblem upon which the implementation of IHL absolutely depends at some of its most vulnerable points, and the national legislation by which HCPs are expected to incorporate the law of the GCs is expected at the same time to prevent such misuses of the sign as may lead persons to become uncertain, when in situations of conflict they see the sign, whether it is being used in its 'protective' capacity or not.[9] For if its use *is* 'protective', the humanitarian neutrality and impartiality of the users and their purposes can be taken for granted and, indeed, according to the law *must* be taken for granted. Persons who take advantage of that generous assumption to use it as a cover for party purposes are criminals and their crime may be that most heinous and IHL-wrecking one, perfidy. The maintenance in all circumstances of such a clear distinction between the emblem's protective and

---

[7] Iran, unaccountably allowed to use the Red Lion and Sun in 1924, reverted to the Muslim countries' preferred Red Crescent at the time of its Islamic Revolution in 1980. Israel's Red Shield of David has been recognized *de facto* since the rows about it in 1948 and 1949. No need to linger on the plagiarizing emblems of self-constituted relief societies, which are a study in themselves.

[8] Not surprisingly, there are permissions for medical personnel in dangerous situations to carry 'light individual weapons' for self-defence and the defence of their patients.

[9] I have here striven to digest into two sentences (admittedly long ones) more than forty pages (some of them dense and tortuous) of Pictet's *Commentary* on GC1, where the matter is exhaustively dealt with. Readers to whom it is important to get it exactly right must study those pages themselves, and see also François Bugnion, *The Emblem of the Red Cross: A Brief History* (Geneva, 1977).

indicatory uses can scarcely be guaranteed, but within a humanitarian perspective that should not matter much; the Red Cross and Crescent movement in all its parts is committed by its guiding principles to maintain neutrality and impartiality in relation to *all* situations of conflict. The distinctive emblem's moral significance remains the same, no matter which of its law-distinguished senses is to the fore, or whether it is blazoned large or small on the garments, vehicles, and buildings of its users.

Notwithstanding these statutory protections and the movement's endeavours to make its principles better appreciated, and no matter that subscribers to IHL ought to have no difficulty in perceiving that the neutrality and impartiality of the ICRC is integral to its implementation, the ICRC is not everywhere trusted as it should be and the distinctive emblem is not everywhere respected as it should be. This matter being so very important, the causes of these weak spots in IHL's structure are worth identifying.

First, the ICRC. So far as they are anything to do with the ICRC, these weak spots can hardly be said to be of the ICRC's *making*, but it is difficult not to see them as an unavoidable consequence of its *being*. Its emphatic Swiss-ness (to which has to be added its private-society status) no longer constitutes the same self-evident proof of neutrality that it used to do in politically simpler times and in the years of Europe's ascendancy. Neutrality as understood by the international lawyer and the diplomat does not *ipso facto* impress a modern person with the North–South map of the world in his head and the interests of international finance and trade on his mind. Especially will it not impress if that mind has Marxism-Leninism in it too. Neutrality simply seems impossible, a delusion and fantasy, to those for whom international society is divided between revolutionary and counter-revolutionary States; in such a reductionist scheme of things, Switzerland's place can hardly be in doubt. Nor does the ICRC's insistence upon its entire separateness from the Swiss Federal Government convince sophisticated observers, although the evident sympathy, mutual helpfulness, and personal connections between the two may not worry them much either.

To recognize that the ICRC is to some extent enmeshed in the affairs of the country of which it is so distinguished an ornament and in the politics of the international community where it cuts such a striking figure is not to say that that involvement is unnatural or unreasonable. Nor, more important, is it to say that such involvement necessarily damages or biases the service which the organization renders to humanity by means above all of the neutrality and impartiality which it is committed to show in delivery of that service. A few States, at periods when they were high on Marxism-Leninism or its Maoist variant, have alleged a supposedly damaging deliberate bourgeois bias, but that is not an opinion shared by respectable analysts and commentators who have scrutinized the ICRC most closely. Errors of judgment, clumsiness, and bungles indeed there have been, but not always or solely because of the ineptitude of individuals. White Europeans such as fill the ranks of the ICRC can unwittingly arouse resentment and suspicion in countries and continents sensitive about colour and style, and the ICRC cannot always win the delicate games of diplomacy and PR which it some-times has to play against wily parties seeking to outmanœuvre it. But to notice these political involvements and the embarrassments which some-times accompany them is no more than to recognize that the implemen-tation of IHL in political situations (as armed conflicts to some degree always are) cannot always and at all levels be done without political awareness and capability. They do not mean that the political part of the job has to spill over into the humanitarian part where it practically matters most—in the field.

That much said about the capacity of humanitarian neutrality and im-partiality to weather the gusts and gales of politics which sometimes blow around them, more real and serious dangers have to be noted elsewhere. The worst of these dangers is simply stated: the ideas of neutrality and impar-tiality are unintelligible to some types of fighting person and in some situations of conflict and war. At no point of any survey of IHL as it functions in our world do the factors of cultural difference and historical discontinuity weigh more heavily. The old law of war has been developed into modern IHL with a degree of apparent continuity which tends to mask the tensions which can be created by the cultural climates in which it has to function. We saw in Part I how an extraordinary conjuncture of circum-stances made it possible for the rulers and ruling classes of early modern Europe to learn that wars could be 'just' on both sides, that enemies did not have to be hated, that limited wars were preferable to total ones, and that the leaders of States could bear in mind the superior interests of their international society even while now and then resorting to armed force to establish the pecking-order within it.[10] Modern IHL thus took shape in a historical time and place when men could say, with some sincerity, that 'men who take up arms against one another in public war do not cease on this account to be moral beings, responsible to one another and to God',

---

[10] Similarly indicative of the same interest in restraining public violence were, through the same years, the evolution of constitutional and representative government in parts of Europe and North America, teaching parallel lessons in limited government and in political compromise.

and 'the ultimate object of all modern war is a renewed state of peace'.[11] Within such an overarching idea of social and political relations, there was room for neutral and impartial reminders of values higher than the exclusively national and better than the exclusively warring. They were rightly considered indispensable to the implementation of IHL by all its early codifiers and they have been so considered by all who since then have reaffirmed and developed it.

Indispensable, but difficult. To what extent warring parties willingly admitted the possibility of third parties being neutral and impartial with regard to their quarrels or, at the battlefield level, paid to the distinctive emblem the respect it deserved, are questions that only the historian can answer. In any case, one does not have to be a historian or any other sort of scholar to be able to list the factors that might, within the circumstances of any given case, cause a belligerent to demand sympathy or self-servingly to violate the emblem. Limited war is not a concept that makes sense in cultures where consciousness of enemies is obsessive and hatred of enemies obligatory. That justice should be found on both sides of a deadly quarrel must be as improbable an idea to the average political believer as, to the average religious believer, the idea that salvation should be possible outside one's own faith. To go no further than the religion with which I am familiar, it is sadly clear that not 'blessed are the peacemakers' or 'love your enemies', but 'he who is not with me is against me' has usually been the more popular text for believers engaged in a war thought to be just. In face of such distractions, it is perhaps more remarkable that Red Cross neutrality and impartiality have been so largely accepted and respected in the wars of modern times than that they have now and then been rejected and abused.

That neutrality and impartiality in relation to the armed conflicts of our own times have become less accepted and respected than they used to be seems undeniable, perhaps mainly because so many of the worst of those conflicts are internal ones. The ICRC, which ought to know, has increasingly experienced rebuffs, some of which are mentioned in its monthly *Bulletin* along with evidences of the distinctive emblem being repeatedly ignored or misused. The ICRC's *Annual Reports* offer a less colourful but more systematic survey. Another of its publications, *Dissemination*, whose main purpose is to inform and encourage those who strive to diffuse

---

[11] The statements within quotation marks come straight from Lieber's Instructions, Articles 15 and 29. He was a representative man, doing his best to summarize the relevant wisdom of his age, and conscious of no great difference between it and the wisdom of a hundred years before. The extent to which the pioneer law-of-war codifications of the succeeding fifty years stood directly in his debt shows how well he did his job; they appear as documents 2 and 3 in Schindler and Toman.

understanding of IHL, gave in its April 1992 issue (pp. 14–16) an admirable sketch of the situation in which would-be neutral and impartial bearers of the Red Cross and Red Crescent emblems increasingly find themselves. After noting the difficulties which National Societies—related as they somehow must be to political structures perhaps dominating or unsympathetic—may encounter in observing the movement's principles, it goes on:

The next difficulty is the fact that the parties to the conflict often take a dim view of neutral behaviour. In countries where an internal conflict is taking place, the armed forces fail to understand why the National Society does not condemn the activities of those they regard as 'bandits', much less why it wants to provide assistance to any of their number no longer able to fight. As for the opposition, they are critical of the Society's connections with the authorities.

Anyone trying to work on both sides to help non-combatants is considered at best naïve, at worst a traitor. The extremely polarized nature of many struggles is such that not taking a stand is a hostile act in itself. . . . [A]nother problem is that the National Society is judged not only by its public statements but also by its every act, the underlying humanitarian motivation of which is not always understood. Thus, bringing food to displaced, destitute people assembled by the government in camps can be construed as support for a policy of emptying a territory of its civilians the better to crush the combatants. Giving cooking utensils to peasants whose dwellings have been burned down by a guerrilla movement is sometimes considered by the movement as tantamount to supporting people who, to its way of thinking, received the punishment they deserved for collaborating with the authorities. Treating wounded individuals who come to the National Society in the mistaken belief that they will benefit from some form of immunity can give rise to mistrust on the part of those looking for them, who will feel that the National Society, in agreeing to care for them, has demonstrated where its sympathies lie.

The suspicions which the ICRC itself encounters in seeking to 'conduct its assistance and protection activities in conformity with operational ethics based on impartiality, independence and neutrality' are for the most part similar or analogous.[12] There is however this additional problem, that its diplomatic propriety and the confidentiality it guarantees in its dealings with governments sometimes shroud difficult dealings in such obscurity that anti-government parties can find cause to wonder whether the ICRC is actually being as neutral and impartial as it claims to be. Against such suspicions, the ICRC has no other defence than to point to its record, to invite sympathetic understanding of its problems in dealing with devious and obstructive governments, and in the last resort simply to ask to be

[12] The words cited are those, no doubt very carefully chosen, of its President in the ICRC's pamphlet *Respect for International Humanitarian Law*, his gloomy review of the years 1987–91, 15.

believed when it says it is doing as much good as circumstances permit. Its ability to attract trust is not universally enhanced by the facts that it always goes in the first instance to governments, and that it has in the last resort no power to overcome law-flouting governments' refusals. All it can do is to 'go public' with its criticisms (a confidentiality-breaching extremity to which it is loath to go) or to beg law-abiding HCPs to exercise private pressure on IHL's behalf, which was tried with scant success during the Iran–Iraq War. The respect thus always paid (at least initially) to established State authorities and the primacy always given to neutrality/impartiality (even when it means giving aid etc. to parties that do not need it to match what is given to those that do) have caused some humanitarian activists to despair of the ICRC's ever reaching some very deserving candidates for relief and protection, and to launch alternative approaches. For a well-rounded presentation of the ICRC's position and a fair appraisal of the strengths and limitations of its 'operational ethics', the reader cannot do better than consult various of the works of David Forsythe.[13]

Most prominent of the alternative approaches just mentioned is that of certain French-originated organizations, the best known of which are Médecins sans Frontières and Médecins du Monde. Impatience with the limitations set to humanitarian activity by the ICRC's understanding of what is demanded by its fundamental principles of independence and neutrality has led these francophone activists to promote a rival understanding of what is demanded by fundamental principles of human rights. The rights of sovereignty, they argue, cannot include a right to stand in the way of urgently needed humanitarian relief; the Geneva side of IHL strongly suggests this, and human rights law unmistakably implies it. Where such need is acute enough, so the argument continues, persons with the will and the means to relieve it are morally entitled to go ahead and do so without waiting for governments' permission, as, for example, MSF and its allies very notably did on behalf of the anti-Kabul, anti-Russian resistance movement in Afghanistan, becoming incidentally one of the few sources of fresh information about conditions on that side of the conflict. From asserting this moral right to intervene, *le droit d'ingérence*, the movement's theorists have gone on to claim that it is not just a right which individuals and

---

[13] He is the most scholarly and experienced of all who have written about the ICRC 'from outside'. By that I mean no more than that an American political scientist is in a position to view the ICRC with a degree of detachment which I believe to be beyond the reach of anyone on its payroll or of Swiss nationality. See esp. the conclusion to his *Humanitarian Politics*, his article 'Human Rights and the ICRC', in *Human Rights Quarterly*, 12 (1990), 265–89, and his chapter in Hazel Fox and Michael A. Meyer (eds.), *Effecting Compliance* (London, 1993), 83–103.

organizations may exercise but a duty, *un devoir*, to which the international community ought to give explicit legal recognition.

Whether or not this is a good idea has become the subject of much interesting debate.[14] It has been given more serious attention than it would have received even only ten years ago, because the idea of humanitarian intervention itself has, in the early 1990s, rather suddenly acquired a weight and respectability in international legal and political circles long sought by its disciples but never so far able to prevail against the principle of sovereignty, to which, of course, it was abhorrent, and by which, accordingly, interventions by one State in another's affairs which bore a humanitarian appearance (e.g. India in East Pakistan on behalf of the Bangladeshis, Tanzania in Uganda to hasten the end of Idi Amin's grim rule) had to be officially explained in other ways.[15] Security Council actions since 1991 with regard to Iraq, Yugoslavia, and Somalia have caused the question to be raised again in a perhaps more substantial form.

The francophones' idea would seem to fit in with this movement to do something positive about human rights standards which have so far lain on the storeroom shelf, but impatient zeal to implement them will surely damage the principles of independence and neutrality that have so far lain at the moral heart of IHL. Such is the nature of most contemporary armed conflict that what is claimed to be humanitarian activity on behalf of one side to a conflict must be seen as hostile activity by the other. Humanitarian activists who protest that this should not be so are either simple-minded or disingenuous. It is difficult to know how, in this context, to assess MSF and its progeny, other than to observe that their origins lie in their nation's frankly partisan support for Nigeria's Biafran secessionists in the late 1960s, their impatience at that time with the ICRC's attempt to maintain the neutral and impartial line, and their subsequent readiness to adopt partisan attitudes whenever, since then, impartial ones have become impossible. It is difficult not to conclude that although ICRC practice sometimes amounts indirectly to helping one side more than or rather than another, MSF's practice more often and more readily does so. The very possibility of humanitarian neutrality and impartiality must thus be made to appear so much the more doubtful, and the bearers of its distinctive emblem the more exposed to danger.

[14] For an exhaustive survey of the whole area, see Olivier Corten and Pierre Klein's articles 'Droit d'ingérence ou obligation de réaction non-armée?' and 'Devoir d'ingérence ou droit de réaction armée?', in *Revue belge de droit international*, 23 (1990), 368–440 and 24 (1991), 46–131 respectively.

[15] A convenient résumé of these and other instances is Michael Akehurst's chapter in Hedley Bull (ed.), *Intervention in World Politics* (Oxford, 1984), 95–118.

Beyond such immediate damage to this most familiar vein of practical humanitarian activity, there is the damage that may be done to the less obvious uses of these principles in the implementation of IHL and for the civilized purpose that stands behind it, the general restraint of war. Neutrality and impartiality matter in other connections than the ICRC and the world-wide movement associated with it. They did not become essential because they were in the Red Cross's principles, the Red Cross built them into its principles because they were already essential. They represent universal values and interests which quickly succumb in times of war and yet which are necessary to the 'humanization' of war and the bringing of it to better rather than worse ends: preference for peaceful rather than conflictual relations between peoples, respect for the equal integrity and dignity of all human beings, and (perhaps above all) respect for objective truth. To many people, whether they are at war or not, it is painful to observe how fellow human beings are demonized or 'dehumanized' by those who perceive them as enemies. The independent and impartial mind sees this as one of the greatest shames of war and a major cause of IHL's breakdowns, exceedingly difficult to correct and counteract. Another major cause which however can be more responsive to correction is the fog of lies, rumours, myths, and misunderstandings which darkens the thinking of peoples at war, civilian populations and armed forces alike, and prompts them to do things they *might* not do (human nature in wartime being what it is, one cannot put it more positively than that) if more correctly informed.

We are here concerned with only one dimension of a giant problem. Truth, it has often been remarked, is the first casualty in time of war. Leaders of States and the managers of their public opinion can find it difficult enough to tell truth in time of peace. When war is upon them, the difficulties mount and, it has to be admitted, excuses and extenuations for not telling it can become more persuasive. There is a great grey area here where casuists may play forever. But they will not find it easy to persuade upholders of IHL to join them. Nothing is calculated more rapidly to erode observance of the rules of IHL than false notions of what the other side has done *and*, it has to be added, of what one's own side has done.[16]

---

[16] e.g. British and American strategic bombing practices might not have become so gross towards the close of the Second World War if the British and American publics (which, unlike the German public, were somewhat able to influence war policy) had been allowed to know more exactly what had been going on. Noble Frankland courageously touched on this possibility in his 1963 Lees Knowles Lectures, *The Bombing Offensive against Germany: Outlines and Perspectives* (1965), 100. In fact, *every* formerly belligerent society might come to think differently about its behaviour in the next war if it could be brought to an honest understanding of how it behaved in the last one.

This important matter is best gone into by distinguishing, in the first instance, the areas and time-scales within which the establishment of truth may support the implementation and enforcement of IHL. They lie along a spectrum running from where the prompt dispelling of untruth may avert imminent horrors, through a broad middle area where the disclosure of truth may serve to bring about longer-term changes for the better, to the 'business' end where evidence may be assembled to support the bringing of criminal charges.

In the first of those areas, truth usually arrives too late. The speed and scope of modern media have made it possible for civilian masses to share the rush of vengeful rage which easily overwhelms fighting men told by rumour, myth, or manipulative mendacity that their enemy is fighting dirty. Stories about the enemy refusing quarter, mutilating bodies, firing dumdums, serrating bayonet-edges, etc. turn up in all wars, and promptly produce talk about retaliation in kind. It is impossible not to believe that such tales are sometimes true but it is even more impossible not to believe that more often they are false, in which case nothing less than a quick convincing rebuttal by some independent impartial authority can have a chance to interpose before the dread spiral of retaliation and counter-retaliation begins to spin. Independent activities of enterprising war correspondents and journalists, special categories of civilians to whom IHL has hopefully extended a protective hand, might incidentally conduce to the restoration of reasonableness; on the other hand, one can very easily think of combinations of circumstances which would cause them to do just the opposite.[17]

More reliably truth-telling, at least because their announced purposes are impartial and their credentials transparent, are those private human rights-monitoring organizations which have so generously read their responsibilities as to pursue their enquiries into live conflict situations, and which, because they are of modest stature and travel light, have been able to operate and to publish their findings quickly. Conspicuously useful, and to the best of my knowledge unique in this respect has been the work of the 1981-started, regionally concerned Committees grouped under the general heading of the New York- and Washington-based organization, Human Rights Watch. Its executive director Aryeh Neier described in a 1990 issue of its modest magazine how it impartially 'monitored violations of the laws of war in internal military conflicts'.

As the laws of war—known as international humanitarian law—apply equally to both sides [he continues], we monitor guerrilla abuses as well as abuses by govern-

---

[17] IHL's interest appears in Article 4 (A, 4) of the POW Convention and Article 79 of AP1.

ment forces. We report on deliberate and indiscriminate attacks on civilians by bombings, strafings, shellings, the use of landmines and booby traps and in ground sweeps. We report on forced displacement; on starvation as a means of warfare, and on the denial of medical supplies to civilians in combat regions; on forced labour in the service of the armed forces and rebel groups; on abusive conscription practices; and on abuses by paramilitary units.[18]

The director went on to list the conflicts thus covered: El Salvador, Nicaragua, and Peru covered by Americas Watch; Somalia, Sudan, Liberia, Ethiopia, and Mozambique by Africa Watch; Afghanistan, Burma, Cambodia, and the Philippines by Asia Watch; the Kurdish regions of Turkey and Iraq by Helsinki Watch and Middle East Watch respectively. He mentioned also that the last-named committee had just issued a report on 'violations of the laws of war in the international conflict that began with Iraq's invasion of Kuwait', a bold extension from the organization's previous concentration on internal conflicts which may be thought regrettable, at least inasmuch as what it had been doing before (and doing very well) was done by hardly anyone else, whereas international wars suffer from no lack of attention.[19]

Good examples of what these Human Rights Watch Committees do and how quickly they can do it are three recent Americas Watch Reports, whose titles tell their own story: 'Carnage Again: Preliminary Report on Violations of the Laws of War by Both Sides in the November 1989 Offensive in El Salvador' (duplicated and stapled, dated 24 November 1989); 'Update on El Salvador: the Human Rights Crisis Continues in the Wake of the FMLN Offensive' (ditto, dated 16 December 1989); and, a less instant but unusually searching report, 'Violation of Fair Trial Guarantees by the FMLN's *Ad Hoc* Courts', dated May 1990. Impartiality in IHL reportage, which is what this genre of Human Rights monitoring amounts to, could scarcely go further.

It should be explained, *en passant*, why the best-known and most publicized human rights organization, Amnesty International, has not so far been of anything like comparable relevance. For many years from its foundation in 1961 it intersected hardly at all with IHL because of its intense concentration on politically identified 'prisoners of conscience', and

---

[18] *Human Rights Watch*, 3 (Summer, 1990).

[19] Its report on 'Humanitarian Law Issues and the Persian Gulf Conflict' which duly appeared under the name of deputy director Kenneth Roth, although admirably impartial in tone, purpose, and method, suffers from a certain armchair legalism and some unfamiliarity with the necessary characteristics of modern major warfare. It was among the papers discussed at the 1991 meeting of the (annual) San Remo Round Table on Current Problems of IHL, to one of whose participants I am indebted for a sight of it.

its publicized censure of their oppressors who, by AI's criteria, were to be found only on the State side of internal struggles.[20] In any case, AI kept well away from IHL involvement; along with the International Commission of Jurists it declined to participate in the ICRC's 1971–3 preparations for the CDDH.[21] More recently however an enlarged understanding of the responsibilities of 'the human rights community' and a confessed commitment to publicize abuses of human rights by *both* sides to internal struggles have opened the prospect that AI's admirably prompt reports may become reliably impartial enough to promote improved observance of those areas of IHL which attract its attention.[22]

Where speed (not the media's but that of military action) is not too pressingly of the essence, a mutually trustable neutral and impartial body like the ICRC should, in principle, be able to ascertain the facts about suddenly contentious events, but experience suggests that such ascertainment may be precisely what some belligerents least desire. The ICRC, in this area of IHL as in so many others, has to be on its guard against manipulation for propaganda purposes and political exploitation. Nazi Germany, normally concerned to veil its more infamous activities from Genevan eyes (and generally successful in doing so), was quick in 1943 to invite the ICRC to inspect the remains of the Polish officers it accused the USSR of having massacred at Katyn; the ICRC would not act without Moscow's agreement, which of course was never given. When North Korea and China in early 1952 accused the UN Command (read, the USA) of practising 'germ warfare', the ICRC agreed to the American request to conduct an investigation, but China and North Korea refused to admit it. Cuba for many years refused to forgive the ICRC for its readiness to help implement the Secretary-General's delicate plan for defusing 'the Cuban Missiles Crisis' in October 1962 without, so Fidel Castro maintained, Cuba having been adequately consulted about it. Such are a few of the many painful experiences which have taught the ICRC that the reputation for independence, neutrality, and impartiality which is indispensable to its humanitarian undertakings is no protection against loss of rudder in political storms, which, should it become involved in them, can damage its humanitarian usefulness.

---

[20] An article by Alexander Cockburn in the *London Review of Books*, 9 May 1991, polemical though it may be, shows how unimpartial (in the sense required for IHL implementation) AI and like-minded organizations could be. Notable in this one-sided respect was AI's otherwise informative report on Colombia in Sept. 1989.

[21] Jacques Freymond in B. G. Ramcharan (ed.), *Human Rights: Thirty Years after the Universal Declaration* (The Hague, 1979), 67–81 at 72–3.

[22] A good review of the debate about that community's responsibilities appeared in the editorial section of the *Human Rights International Reporter*, 11/4 (1986), 3–6.

Truth has a better chance of coming out when there is no rush for it to do so, or when it simply cannot be ascertained in a hurry, not to mention when the truth-discovering party is willing to risk upsetting the party about whom awkward truth is discovered. The ICRC, as has been shown, is normally reluctant to tell all that it knows, and with good enough reason. It has however gone along with the wholesome 1980s trend (presumably at least in part a product of the 1970s upsurge of concern for the improvement of IHL and its observance) of assisting implementation and, should it go so far, enforcement by publishing the guidelines for how far it is prepared to commit itself 'in the event of breaches of IHL'.[23] Affirming that confidentiality will remain its preferred style, the ICRC says it

> reserves the right to make public statements ... if the following conditions are observed: the violations are major and repeated; the steps taken confidentially have not succeeded in putting an end to the violations; such publicity is in the interest of the persons or populations affected or threatened; the ICRC delegates have witnessed the violations with their own eyes, or the existence and extent of those breaches were established by reliable and verifiable sources.

These conditions are evidently so restrictive as to discourage expectation of any significant change of policy. The small number of public statements about violations and abuses which the ICRC has made since publishing those guidelines are not of such a character as to promise to bring it into the front-line of truth-telling and of the new legal business that AP1 has introduced under the description of fact-finding.[24]

The ICRC has had much to do with the promotion of the International Fact-Finding Commission delineated in Article 90 of AP1, and materialized in March 1992 after the accession of Canada in November 1990 had brought to twenty, the stipulated minimum, the number of States willing to accept its competence. As a conventionally stately intergovernmental body, made up of 'fifteen members of high moral standing and acknowledged impartiality' (it goes without saying that the persons elected by the HCPs are almost all lawyers) and entirely dependent for the undertaking of its cumbersome operations on the consent of the parties to any dispute in question, its contributions to the winnowing of wartime truth from error seem sure to be of the kind that

---

[23] See the *IRRC* 221 (Mar.–Apr. 1981), 81–3.
[24] Those statements, or the more important of them, are listed by J. Ashley Roach in n. 11 to his article 'The International Fact-finding Commission', in the *IRRC* 281 (Mar.–Apr. 1991), 167–89 at 184.

comes long after the events in question and are thus useful mainly to the historian.[25]

The United Nations Organization and the major regional organizations have also responded to this new mood of the 1980s by undertaking a variety of inquiries into alleged violations and abuses of IHL and/or of human rights in armed conflicts, most of them, but not all, internal ones. The UN's Human Rights Commission has, over the years, sent special rapporteurs, alias 'envoys' or 'representatives', to such distressful countries as Chile, Sri Lanka, El Salvador, Guatemala, Afghanistan, and (at the time of writing) most recently the former Yugoslavia. It has also instituted particular inquiries into such horrid accompaniments of internal struggles (though not of those alone) as 'Torture' and 'Disappearances'.[26] The UN's Human Rights Committee, the annually meeting body set up by the 1966 International Covenant on Civil and Political Rights, has frequently received reports on what has been going on in countries experiencing various levels of 'public emergency'.[27] The Secretary-General has caused reports to be made on the treatment of POWs and on the use of chemical weapons in the war between Iran and Iraq, and perhaps— only time will tell—most significant of all, the Security Council in its Resolution 780 of 6 October 1992 has instituted a Yugoslavia War Crimes Commission.[28] The OAS's Inter-American Commission on Human Rights since the 1960s has inquired into many aspects of member States' handling of their internal conflicts and national emergencies.[29] The EC's Council of Ministers and the CSCE have felt obliged to follow suit in respect of Serbia, Croatia, and Bosnia, the countries of Europe which have reminded their mother-continent that even it can produce social

[25] 'Consent' of course does not mean just the *ad hoc* consent of parties on particular occasion but also includes the acceptances of those HCPs to AP1 which have supported the Commission's existence.

[26] The quality of the rapporteurs' work appears to be uneven, varying according to the terms of access agreed by the States visited and the visitors' relations with their hosts. The British lawyer who did the Guatemala report (UN document A/38/43 dated 4 Nov. 1983) has been especially criticized; see Tom Farer in Roberts and Kingsbury (eds.), *United Nations, Divided World* (1st edn., Oxford, 1989), 137 and n. 95.

[27] Only States Parties to the Covenant are obliged thus to report. By the end of 1991 there were as many as one hundred of them. Article 4 indicates how far States may go—and beyond what limits they may *not* go: 'In time of public emergency which threatens the life of the nation and the existence of which is officially proclaimed', which of course covers many of the situations to which IHL is applicable.

[28] The S-G's reports between 1984 and 1988 are conveniently listed in n. 9 of the Roach article cited above. This War Crimes Commission is of such significance because the Security Council is uniquely situated to do something about such matters.

[29] Besides its occasional very detailed reports on 'the situation of human rights' in particular States, it digests copious summaries of its work into the Annual Reports published by its General Secretariat in Washington, DC.

hatreds and murderousness just as terrible as those of any other part of the world.[30]

Also concerned to discover the truth about dark lawless deeds but in a class of their own on account of their location, cause, and purpose are the *Nunca Mas*/'Never Again' reports on the means used by the armed forces of Brazil, Argentina, Chile, and Uruguay in their campaigns, mostly during the 1960s and 1970s, against the groups and persons they regarded as 'enemies within'. So deep were the social divisions produced by those terrible events and so irreconcilably have persons engaged in debate about them tended to stay on one side or the other of the argument, that a distant and sheltered observer ventures to generalize about them only with some diffidence. But these unique reports cannot be properly understood without a historical introduction, even if only a sketchy one. What happened was that the armed forces of Latin America, most of them no strangers to political involvement, came to feel themselves and what they believed they stood for ('the nation', 'national honour', 'national security', 'Western/ Christian civilization', etc.) threatened as never before by hosts of 'subversives'—the significantly all-embracing term under which their imaginations lumped together the actual or potential deployers of violence against the regime and the various non-violent socialists, liberals, and democrats who, whatever political company they chose to keep, certainly did not keep it with the conservative, authoritarian, militarist, and fascistic Right.

It cannot be denied that they of the Right had cause for concern. The Cuban Revolution sought followers from its earliest days, and was hospitable to as many Latin Americans as liked to visit it. Che Guevara inspired young persons with a mind for change. The overthrow of Chile's brief venture into revolution by parliamentary means left the field to Marxism-based theoreticians and publicists of every stripe, 'scientifically' diagnosing the myriad defects of the existing regime and preaching the gospel that structures so awful could not stand up to a good revolutionary push. Bank raids, barrack-bombings, urban kidnappings, and so on, advertised as 'urban guerrilla warfare' by its *aficionados* and sometimes justly denounced as terrorism by its victims, became the hallmarks of the most active pushers, with crime and banditry, as always, not far behind them. But all that their

---

[30] The EC report, made apparently in some secrecy to ascertain whether stories of the systematic rape of Bosnian Muslim women by Bosnian Serbian 'fighters', was summarized in the *Independent*, 6 Jan. 1993. Secrecy ceased with the public hearing at the European Parliament in Brussels, 18 Feb. 1993. The CSCE's mission 'to inspect places of detention' did so between 29 Aug. and 4 Sept. 1992. A British FCO 'Background Brief' dated Oct. 1992 says it 'had only limited access to the centres'.

confident revolutionism and political romanticism achieved (in the short-term, anyway) was to provoke the forces of the existing regimes to counter-revolutionary action of terrible efficacy and extraordinary illegality. Its hallmarks were indiscriminate attacks on everyone labelled 'subversive', detention without trial, torture, murder, and—giving a grim new word to the language—'disappearances', which all too often included the other three as well.[31]

There were variations of method and emphasis from country to country, from Mexico all the way down to the point of the southern cone. It seems however to be generally agreed that the most concentrated display of these methods is to be seen in the 'dirty war' waged by Argentina's armed forces from 1976 to about 1980. They were lawless by every re-levant international standard. (By national constitutional standards too, of course, but that is not our present business.) Human rights law allows seriously harassed governments temporarily to suspend many ordinary protections of civil and political liberty. It does not permit the more or less permanent suspension of the basic processes of justice and, as need hardly be said, it certainly does not authorize systematized torture, ab-duction, and assassination. The explanations and excuses offered for these excesses—so far as any have been offered; their perpetrators have on the whole been unembarrassed about them—have been of the kind which could be predicted of military men formed in the fashions of their con-tinent who found themselves facing unpalatable and, to them, immeasur-able dangers. Necessity was invoked to justify everything and anything that could win what was frankly conceived by the military men fighting it as a *war* for national survival; and which indeed was, like many similar Latin American internal disorders, self-evidently serious enough to come under the GCs' Common Article 3. But, leaving aside the ethical and political questions raised by armed forces' claims to a unique understanding of their nations' best interests, not to mention the historical and psycho-logical questions of how these particular armed forces actually per-ceived the persons and the political movements they were fighting, it has to be said that IHL offers no cover for the excesses to which the Argentinian military (and, necessarily, their civilian collaborators) devoted themselves. They showed contempt for every rule of Common Article 3 and for IHL's guiding principles of discrimination and proportionality. And they sought to conceal their doings and to protect themselves by secrecy and untruths

---

[31] It was a regional adaptation of Nazi Germany's *Nacht und Nebel* technique of terrorizing occupied populations in the Second World War.

while the 'dirty war' was going on, by amnesties and impunity after its conclusion.

⁻ Such are the peculiar circumstances from which the 'Never Again' reports were born. In the political context, they are part of the process by which is sought a return to constitutional practices (to the extent that they formerly existed) and the strengthening of their foundations by revealing what dreadful things resulted from their neglect. In the context of human rights and IHL, these carefully documented reports are the best that can be done to vindicate the principles of justice and decency, given the impenetrable armour of impunity in which the lawbreakers have protected themselves. The whole many-sided subject is currently being studied by Alexandra de Brito, from whose overview of it these sentences may, to conclude this brief sketch of it, be cited.

This 'truth-telling' exercise combined elements of political retribution, moral cleansing of society and assertion of the dignity of the victims. . . . All four projects aimed to reveal the truth about military-led State terrorism in Brazil, Argentina, Uruguay and Chile, and they showed a remarkable similarity in aims and structure [for all that two of them were democratically originated while the other two were done by independent NGOs]. They differed from all other contemporary accounts of repression in their claims to scope, impartiality and identification only with the cause of democracy and the sufferings of the victims. . . . It is in this pure 'truth-telling' capacity that the reports were most successful. These are reports of hidden and terrible facts. . . . The problem remains ultimately that, while their release was to some degree cathartic, the reports could never match up to the hopes and desires of the victims and relatives for compensation. . . . For these people and a great proportion of the population in all four countries . . . the books became surrogates for legal justice.[32]

Similar substitute satisfaction seems likely to be the most that can be expected by the survivors of El Salvador's long civil war, even though the report in March 1993 of the Truth Commission (established by the UN as part of the 'peace process' it engineered in 1990–1) identifies a large number of guilty and otherwise undesirable individuals.

The Latin American case is unusual in that its armed conflicts almost all take place *within* States; but the issues of fact-finding, truth-telling, and finally judicial decision are the same from one end of IHL to the other. Can victims of lawless war-conduct ever hope for anything more than the *Nunca Mas* projects' 'surrogacy for legal justice'? This is the heart of the matter to be considered in the next section, on enforcement.

[32] Alexandra de Brito is a research student at St Antony's College, Oxford. I am grateful for her advice and permission to cite at such length from her article 'Recording the Past: The *Never Again* Reports on Human Rights Violations' in *Oxford International Review* (Summer 1992), 16–18.

It would ordinarily be expected that a body (or system or regime, call it what you will) of law, elaborate and detailed after centuries of growth, must be, in the plain sense of the word, enforceable; but IHL is not like that. As I close my survey of it with a summary of such means of enforcement as it does have—not just its powers of persuading persons to observe it out of virtue, benevolence, prudence, self-interest, or common sense, but how it may actually be *enforced* on those who find no cause to observe it—it seems apposite to recapitulate what was said at the book's beginning: IHL is part of public international law, and public international law is, in that ultimate sense, scarcely enforceable either.

This fact and its implications for IHL has never been better expressed than by the eminent Dutch judge and jurist Bert Röling, already cited on account of his service on the bench of the Tokyo IMT. His views are the more valuable for his notable part in the drama of IHL since 1945. Not, it must be said, what one might call an official part. He was not one of the types of person who fill most of the seats of the national delegations to the international conferences which figure so largely in this story. He was very much his own man, as early appeared in his independent-minded partial dissent from the Tokyo majority judgments, and his whole career from then on shows him to have been, by the ordinary standards of his profession, something of a maverick. He was early alerted to the justice of some of the new third-world States' complaints about the principles and rules of the Western-made international law they were expected to espouse.[33] No narrow-viewed single-subject humanitarian, his lively interest in the larger context of IHL led him to help found and direct the Polemologish Instituut (read, Conflict Studies) at Groningen. But unlike some humanitarians and peace-seekers, he was a realist about war and the limits of law's capacity to control what was done in it. It was Röling who coined the oft-repeated epigram (which I do not hesitate to repeat again here) about the unrealistic aspects of the Geneva Conventions: 'The way to international hell seems paved with "good" conventions.'[34] Unrealistic bits of the Additional Protocols later drew from him reminders that 'laws of war are not intended to alter power relations, and if they do they will not be observed!' and 'one should take care not to prohibit what will foreseeably occur'.[35]

---

[33] See esp. his *International Law in an Expanded World* (Amsterdam, 1960).

[34] *The Law of War and National Jurisdiction since 1945*, in the Hague Academy series Recueil des Cours, 1960, Pt. 2, 445. The powerful passage from which this sentence came is given in my *Humanity in Warfare*, 296.

[35] 'Criminal Responsibility for Violations of the Laws of War', in *Revue belge de droit international*, 12 (1976), 8–26 at 25 and 26.

Those reminders came near the close of a remarkable article about enforcement, whose opening sentences I will cite because the matter could not be put better:

> International law is a body of law characteristic of an undeveloped legal community, lacking a central power which is able to enforce the law.... Another feature of its underdevelopment is the absence of a central court which can decide upon conflicts concerning the interpretation of the law. Because such a court with compulsory powers does not exist, international law is compelled to recognize the right of each party to interpret the law as it chooses. States, and other subjects of international law, are bound by international law, but their right of autointerpretation of that law is also recognized.... It is in connection with the laws of war that the impossibility of enforcing the law is most striking. The lack of a central authoritative power leaves the enforcement to the parties themselves.[36]

Röling proceeds, as all legally instructed writers do, to say that, things being as they are, the primary means of enforcement is the unpleasant one of reprisals. Reprisals have been mentioned so often already in this book that there is no need to say much more about them. Difficult to distinguish in their promptings, purposes and practice from retaliation, retorsion, and revenge, and easily misused as a cover for those and worse malpractices, they perforce retain a respectable aspect as the only apparent means by which an opponent can, perhaps, be dissuaded from continuing to do unlawful things. Unlawfulness itself often being disputable, and experience having shown that generally the effect of reprisals, far from being the diminution of lawless behaviour, is more often its aggravation through a vicious spiral of purported reprisals and counter-reprisals, recourse to reprisals by common consent ranks high among the many regrettable 'necessities' to which belligerents may claim to be driven. Reprisals are indeed so regrettable that an authority as eminent as Frits Kalshoven has argued that they do so much more harm than good that States seriously desirous of supporting the ideals of IHL should cease to use them and should concur to ban their use.[37] And indeed their use, so far as it might affect civilians and virtually anyone except active combatants, *was* banned by AP1 in 1977, but without putting at rest the question which continued

---

[36] 'Criminal Responsibility for Violations of the Laws of War', 8.

[37] Kalshoven's case is made out with a wealth of supporting evidence in *Belligerent Reprisals* (Leyden, 1971); updated with interesting modifications in 'Belligerent Reprisals Revisited', *Netherlands Yearbook of International Law*, 21 (1990), 43–80. For differing views, see the uneasiness expressed even by such proponents of the APs as Stanislaw E. Nahlik, 'From Reprisals to Individual Penal Responsibility', in A. Delissen and G. Tanja (eds.), *Kalshoven Festschrift* (Dordrecht etc., 1991), 165–76 and Françoise J. Hampson, 'Belligerent Reprisals and the 1977 Protocols', in *ICLQ*, 37 (1988), 818–43.

to be debated after the more modest bannings of 1949: Did not protective enthusiasm here run riskily ahead of armed-conflict practicality?

Would-be banners of reprisals will have no persuasive answer to that question until the international community devises reliable means of doing at least these four things: (1) generally succeeds in dealing with serious disputes before they turn into armed conflicts; (2) reduces the volume of arms-trading and regulates international arms transfers to such an extent that vast quantities of arms and ease of acquiring them cease to figure among the causes of armed conflicts; (3) brings the production and possession of ABC weapons and their materials under such effectively verified control that armed conflicts will not be caused by possession or fear of them; and (4) in the event that armed conflicts nevertheless occur, is able to guarantee that violators of IHL will be brought to trial and, if convicted, appropriately punished. Of those four conditions, only the last falls within the scope of this book. The other three are mentioned in order to keep the reader from day-dreaming that IHL could do the job on its own. IHL after all is only part, and perhaps not the most important part, of the international system of law, organization, persistent policing, painstaking politics, and eternal vigilance by which peace actually is, and might more largely be, secured.

Law enforcement which is to be acceptable as well as effective rests not only upon courts whose decisions will be respected and upon a policing system which can be relied on to bring accused persons into court in the first place, but also upon a clear view of the kinds of offences which will cause them to be brought there. These latter, at any rate, together with a few indications of the jurisdictions within which they should be tried, are already well defined. Offences that are already set to be punished may loosely be listed thus:

1. War Crimes pronounced in the 6th of the Nuremberg Principles to be 'punishable as crimes under international law':

Violations of the laws or customs of war which include, but are not limited to, murder, ill-treatment or deportation to slave-labour or for any other purpose of civilian population of or in occupied territory, murder or ill-treatment of prisoners of war, of persons on the seas, killing of hostages, plunder of public or private property, wanton destruction of cities, towns or villages, or devastation not justified by military necessity.

2. Crimes against Humanity, described in the same place as:

Murder, extermination, enslavement, deportation and other inhuman acts done against any civilian population, or persecutions on political, racial or religious grounds, when such acts are done or such persecutions are carried on in execution of or in connection with any crime against peace or any war crime.

As was noted in Part II, there is so much limitation here and so much overlap with other crimes, that its practical usefulness is not very obvious. The same may be said of genocide, defined as an international crime *sui generis* in the UN Convention of December 1948. The Genocide Convention's capacity for usefulness is most of all limited by the fact that, failing the action of an international penal tribunal like the IMTs, the only courts able to enforce it are those of the State committing the genocide, which is no doubt partly why Georg Schwarzenberger was led to remark, 'The Genocide Convention is unnecessary when applicable and inapplicable when necessary.'[38]

　　3. Grave Breaches of the four Geneva Conventions, as defined in their respective Articles 50, 51, 130, and 147. The Articles' lists differ from one another, because the acts they thus classify are to be read as such only (to cite a phrase which occurs in all of them) 'if committed against persons or property protected by the Convention'. The Civilians Convention's list is the longest and, since it incidentally includes almost everything that is in the others, may serve to represent them all:

Wilful killing, torture or inhuman treatment, including biological experiments, wilfully causing great suffering or serious injury to body or health, unlawful deportation or transfer or unlawful confinement of a protected person, compelling a protected person to serve in the forces of a hostile Power, or wilfully depriving a protected person of the rights of fair and regular trial prescribed in the present Convention, taking of hostages and extensive destruction and appropriation of property, not justified by military necessity and carried out unlawfully and wantonly.

　　4. Other Grave Breaches, added to the above lists by Articles 85 and (in its specialized way) 11 of AP1. Article 85 is one of the IHL minefields which should not be gone through without good legal guidance; what is said here must not be taken as more than an allusive introduction. There is however no mistaking its two principal purposes. The first was to widen the Grave Breaches category to include certain Hague-law matters as well as its original Geneva-law ones. The widening and sharpening was not, in the event, nearly as extensive as the ICRC and various other participants in the CDDH desired, but this list was agreed on:

making the civilian population or individual civilians the object of attack; launching an indiscriminate attack affecting the civilian population or civilian objects in the knowledge that such attack will cause excessive loss of life, [injury and damage] . . . ;

[38] Schwarzenberger, 143.

launching an attack against works or installations containing dangerous forces in the knowledge [etc.] . . . ; making non-defended localities and demilitarized zones the objects of attack; making a person the object of attack in the knowledge that he is *hors de combat*; the perfidious use . . . of the distinctive emblem of the red cross [etc.] of or other [recognized] protective signs.

The other main purpose was to bring under the Geneva-law heading matters which particularly bothered certain parties represented at the CDDH and which for one reason or another could muster majority support there: transfers by occupying powers of their own people into occupied territory or deportations of citizens of it; 'unjustifiable delay' in repatriations; 'practices of *apartheid*' etc.; attacks on places recognized to be of special significance in 'the cultural and spiritual heritage of peoples'; and denial to IHL-protected persons of 'the rights of fair and regular trial'.[39]

5. Breaches of the Geneva Conventions not therein classified as 'grave breaches'. That violations of IHL should include breaches of the GCs which are not so grave as well as those singled out as grave, might seem so obvious as not to be worth mentioning. But the difference is in fact of huge legal significance. For not so grave breaches, the procedures of trial and punishment are commonplace. So far as a belligerent's own subjects/citizens and military personnel are concerned, they will be dealt with in the appropriate national courts. If persons of enemy nationality are in question, and they are of military/combatant character, they will have to be dealt with as the POW Convention prescribes; if they are not military, they must be 'protected persons' as defined in Article 4 of the Civilians Convention and be dealt with as *that* Convention prescribes.[40]

6. For completeness' sake, it is necessary to recall that all armed forces have their own codes of military justice and war conduct, into which much or little IHL may be incorporated, according to political and cultural taste. In the British case, for example, *every* relevant treaty and convention is printed *in extenso* in the army's manual, and reference is repeatedly made in the text to international legal obligations. The US army's field manual's very first page, its foreword, sets the international legal framework within which the book is to be read; the very first sentence of its text announces that its

[39] The first batch of Grave Breaches comes in Article 85(3) and is prefaced by the requirement that they must have been committed wilfully and actually caused deaths or serious injury; the second batch comes in 85(4). Article 11's preoccupation is (to cite Bothe, Partsch, and Solf, 111) 'the detailed regulation of the taking of tissue (including blood) and organs' from protected persons in the course of the medical care to which they are entitled.

[40] 'Persons protected by the Convention are those who, at a given moment and in any manner whatsoever, find themselves, in case of a conflict or occupation, in the hands of a Party to the conflict or Occupying Power of which they are not nationals.' I leave out of consideration whatever small differences might have to be noted in respect of States parties to AP1.

purpose 'is to provide authoritative guidance to military personnel on the customary and treaty law applicable to the conduct of warfare on land and to relationships between belligerents and neutral States'. It may be doubted whether many countries go so far to spell out the IHL limits within which they are committed to operate. But whether they do or do not, those national military manuals and codes constitute the context within which the persons responsible for the conduct of the nation's armed forces determine what are to be regarded as criminal offences, and—quite another matter!— may choose to prosecute as such.

We may conclude that there is virtually no violation of IHL—certainly no serious violation of IHL—which could slip through so many identifying screens. The question regarding enforcement therefore is not: Is such-and-such an act punishable or not? but: Who is going to do anything about it?

The Geneva Conventions, when they came before the world in the summer of 1949, appeared to ensure that grave breaches of them would be punished. They contained a Common Article (49/50/129/146), the second paragraph of which says:

Each HCP shall be under the obligation to search for person alleged to have committed [the listed] grave breaches, and shall bring such persons, regardless of their nationality, before its own courts. It may also, if it prefers, and in accordance with the provisions of its own legislation, hand such persons over for trial to another HCP concerned, provided such HCP has made out a prima-facie case.

This establishment of a universal jurisdiction was revolutionary. Its excellent theory was that no alleged grave breach would go uninvestigated, because if a State holding an accused person had no interest itself in undertaking the task, it would hand that person over to a State which did; thus meeting the demand of the classic Roman maxim, always cited in discussions of this matter, *aut punire aut dedire*: 'either punish the criminal yourself or let someone else do it'.

In practice however this noble innovation has achieved nothing, for reasons both obvious and obscure. The obvious reasons are that States which find it difficult (as all States in fact do find it) to charge their own military personnel with war crimes (which is what politicians and public opinion will call them, whether they are grave breaches or not) find it even more difficult to hand them over to another and possibly unfriendly State to be charged there. The obscurer reasons lie hidden behind the simple-seeming clauses 'in accordance with the provisions of its own legislation' (cited above) and, in the opening paragraph of the Article: 'The HCPs undertake to enact any legislation necessary to provide effective penal sanctions for persons committing, or ordering to be committed' grave breaches. Handing over someone who does not wish to go is extradition, a politically delicate business which States normally undertake only according to the rules of cautiously framed bilateral extradition treaties. And the enactment of appropriate legislation, in countries where there are parliaments to go through and anything like a free press to face, has generally run into many domestic difficulties; more of them, no doubt, in countries whose armed forces are likely to have to fight against foreign enemies than in countries where IHL responsibilities might weigh less heavily.[41]

None of this is to say that committers of grave breaches and other violators of IHL have not now and then been brought to justice.[42] Even as I write these last pages, trials more or less of that description are reported by the most enterprising and courageous of Britain's IHL experts to be taking place in what used to be Yugoslavia. But her story is hardly one to encourage confidence in the virtue of national tribunals. Proceedings against persons of the same nationality are scarcely to be met with; the few which have happened seem mainly to be exercises in PR. Proceedings against persons from 'the other side' are predictably more numerous. They serve valuable propaganda purposes and, within that horrid climate of ethnic hatreds, are unrestrained by the prudence which has usually held such affairs in abeyance until the conflict is over. Political and prudential considerations apart, these early trials appear to have been marked by inconsistencies and confusion. Françoise Hampson's conclusion is that, 'overall, there have been very few trials, given the number of allegations of serious violations of [IHL]. This is hardly surprising in the case of continuing conflicts or where there are difficulties in obtaining custody of an accused. It is nevertheless a reflection of a serious problem in relying exclusively upon national jurisdictions to enforce the law of armed conflicts.'[43]

A few cases, because they have evoked memories of the Holocaust or because they have been connected with political *causes célèbres*, have commanded international attention. How many unnoticed others there have been, and what they amount to as a proportion of those there ought to have been, defies calculation. But the indictments of such persons, to the best of my knowledge, have as a matter of course been expressed explicitly in terms of national law, with the nationally flattering implication that sovereign

[41] To these obscure but still discernible explanations has to be added the possibility that States are not uniformly or wholly 'serious' when they undertake humanitarian commitments.

[42] I set aside the diminishing trickle of questionable prosecutions of ageing late-discovered Second World War criminals.

[43] Françoise Hampson, 'Violation of Fundamental Rights in the former Yugoslavia', Occasional Paper No. 3 of the David Davies Memorial Institute (London, Feb. 1993), esp. p. 9.

States initiate legal action of their own volition, not because of external obligation. Something of this appeared even in the extraordinary case of Adolf Eichmann, a leftover from Nuremberg if ever there was one. The State of Israel, having kidnapped Eichmann from Argentina, and for all that it (Israel) had not existed at the time of Eichmann's crimes, claimed that 'pursuant to the principle of universal jurisdiction' it was 'acting in the capacity of guardian of international law and agent for its enforcement'; the Nuremberg Principles and the principle of the Genocide Convention being brought to bear through the medium of Israel's Nazi and Nazi Collaborators (Punishment) Law of 1950.

Much more ordinary was the other most publicized 'war-crimes' case of our period, the 1971 prosecution of the lowly US army officer William Calley for his leading share, three years previously, in the slaughter of between four and five hundred South Vietnamese persons—many of them of unmistakable civilian description—at the place known in Vietnam as Tinh Khe but to Anglo-Americans as My Lai (or, from its locality, Son My).[44] Lt. Calley was charged with offences against his country's Uniform Code of Military Justice, as were all the other members of the US armed forces whose bad conduct in Vietnam resulted in their being disciplined. Opinions differ as to whether that code and the way it was used matched up to the requirements of the IHL it was supposed to embody and enforce.[45] One respect in which it short-changed the GCs was pointed out in a major-general's contribution to a symposium on *Law and Responsibility in Warfare: The Vietnam Experience.*[46]

The Geneva Conventions of 1949 [wrote Robert G. Gard Jun.], which, after all, have the force of law in the United States, provide that each HCP is obligated to search for persons alleged to have committed grave breaches and to bring such persons before its own courts. Now, thus far, this country has limited such trials to persons who are still members of the armed services. The United States has ignored its responsibility to apply the law to those who are protected by having been discharged.

Enforcement of IHL in respect of their own nationals by national courts is, for obvious reasons, unlikely to be zealous or comprehensive, in the event that it happens at all. The military chieftains responsible for conducting the 'dirty wars' of Latin America have within the past decade shown the surest

[44] Lewy, *America in Vietnam* (New York, 1978), 326 says 400 dead; Martin Woollacott, after visiting the place, credits the Vietnamese figure of 500 in the *Guardian*, 27 May 1980.
[45] Lewy, *America in Vietnam*, painstakingly describes its employment with regard to violations of IHL. Opinions vary as to its efficacy. For moderate scepticism, see e.g. Gary D. Solis, *Marines and Military Law in Vietnam: Trial by Fire* (Washington, DC, 1989), 241–4.
[46] Book of that title: Peter D. Trooboff (ed.), (Chapel Hill, NC, 1975), 229.

way to make sure that it never does happen to them or to the men and women who have obeyed their orders: they have secured the passage of (superficially constitutional) amnesty laws before making way for the return of non-military government. The wars in question were, admittedly, civil ones, but the precedent has more extensive relevance. If powerful wrong-doers can award themselves impunity in respect of internal armed conflicts, could they not manage to do the same in respect of international ones? And, moving our focus from conflicts to courts, the question is bound to come to mind: Would an international court or tribunal be better able to deal with such obstructions and evasions than any national one?

And so finally we come to the prospect of enforcement which can never be far from minds in which bells are set ringing by the words, Nuremberg and Tokyo. Those precedents for *ad hoc* IMTs exist. Can they not be followed? Those original tribunals disbanded when their work was accomplished, but could their torch not be taken up by a permanent international criminal court? The idea of the latter has enjoyed a pathetic sort of half-life ever since the General Assembly's request, in 1947, that it should be added to the ILC's lengthening agenda.[47] Demands for 'a Nuremberg trial' have been voiced on many occasions and with varying motives by many parties, and at the time of writing an IMT 'for the prosecution of persons responsible for serious violations of IHL in the former Yugoslavia' has actually been launched by Security Council resolution 808 of 22 February 1993.[48] What will come of this bold move, and indeed whether anything will come of it, remains to be seen. I believe however that its prospects, along with those of the international criminal court project, can be put into reasonable perspective by considering what must be the characteristics of *any* such tribunal if it is to merit the noble name of a court of justice.

A permanent and proper international criminal court must, I suggest, have these characteristics: (1) its bench will be truly cosmopolitan and supranational, in the sense that judges in particular cases will be drawn not only from States directly concerned in them; (2) it will take at face value the 3rd Nuremberg Principle: 'The fact that a person who committed an act which constitutes a crime under international law acted as Head of State or responsible Government official does not relieve him from responsibility'; (3) it will be backed and assisted by authority and power so universally effective and irresistible that no national or regional interest will be able to

---

[47] Its history and entanglements since then are handily summarized by Sydney Bailey in *War and Conscience in the Nuclear Age* (London, 1987), 59–62.

[48] This follows SC resolution 780 of 6 Oct. 1992 which resulted in the establishment of a Yugoslavia War Crimes Commission under the presidency of Frits Kalshoven.

thwart its orders; it will thus (4) be able to haul before it every person duly indicted, and the world will hold no safe havens for persons seeking to evade its grasp; (5) the international community will have become morally and politically homogenized at least to the extent that the principles of the law administered by the court and the way the court works will be universally accepted and its sentences will not excite outrage; and (6) its sentences will be enforced.

To sketch this character is *ipso facto* to suggest that it is unattainable. Whether the next best thing, the flawed and faulty sort of tribunal that has been attained and remains attainable (perhaps modestly improvable too) is better than nothing, is a question that can only be decided in the light of calculations about consequences and of the values ascribed to prudence and compromise. The Nuremberg IMT was not a truly cosmopolitan court, but that did not stop it doing much good work, along with some less good work, on behalf of the international community. It was a victors' court, administering victors' justice in so far as it turned a deaf ear to the force and relevance of the *tu quoque* argument. But *something* had to be done to record and adequately to stigmatize the more horrific deeds of Nazi Germany, and Nuremberg did it. Moreover, it made the gigantic innovation (as did not quite its Tokyo twin) of pinning responsibility upon even the most highly placed givers of unlawful orders as well as upon the underlings who executed them.

It must however be borne in mind that the IMTs were able to do these good and striking things only because of the extraordinary historical situation in which they were placed. Germany and Japan were so totally and comprehensively defeated that they were in no position to bargain about peace terms or to object to whatever the victors—which is to say, virtually the whole of international society, by then calling itself the United Nations—decided to do to them. Morally and politically, those losers were friendless in the world of 1945. Such circumstances perhaps were historically unique. More usual, and predictably the common stuff of peacemakings for the future as it has been throughout the past, are circumstances in which demands for the vindication of international law and the punishment of its violators have to be accommodated to such facts as that vanquished governments still exist and have to be negotiated with, that they have items to bargain with (prisoners still in their hand, for example), and that the members of international society are by no means of one mind about the merits of the case. Bringing a scattering of criminal small fry to trial, which seems likeliest to happen, does indeed assert the vital principle and perhaps serve usefully as warning and example, but it is a far cry from the great cathartic and cleansing achievement which proponents of the idea of an international criminal court have in mind. Perhaps the way ahead lies somewhere between the national (which happens but cannot be relied on to act impartially) and the international (which might so be relied on, but rarely happens). The idea of a *regional* war crimes tribunal has come into the debate about former Yugoslavia, and no better test-bed for it could be provided.

| Epilogue

Having at last completed this study of IHL's place and functions in international affairs, I take the opportunity to return, in more adventurous spirit, to the question with which Part III has been largely concerned: Why is so much of today's IHL so badly observed? Part III's answer, as will have emerged plainly enough from its pages, is mainly that much of it is unsuited to the circumstances in which it has to operate, and unable in any case to operate whenever a warring party has no interest in helping it to do so, which unhappily often happens. That answer, so far as it goes, may be thought sufficient. But I wonder whether it goes far enough. It seems to me that beyond the first question lies a second one. If some of the law is virtually inoperable, and if some parties have little interest in observing it, why have the nations of the world joined to construct and to applaud an extensive, portentous, and peremptorily worded apparatus of humanitarian law which some parts of their decision-making collective minds must tell them they cannot or will not observe? If all this law is in some measure no more than aspirational, 'normative' standard-setting—if it is what is called *soft* law— can it be a good idea that so much of it should claim to be *hard*? Does it weigh upon the States parties to it any more heavily than human rights law, the instruments of which many States evidently sign or accede to with no serious intention or expectation of having to do anything about them? In what sense can the States subscribing to it be said to be *serious* about it?

I find it difficult to escape the conclusion that in some sense they are *not*. The evidence available to support this depressing conclusion tends however to be of a different order from what has served as evidence in support of argument so far. Some of it is circumstantial evidence and some is not evidence in the forensic or scholarly sense at all but is simply reasonable speculation, informed guesswork. However, I don't see why that should block the investigation of significant matters which would otherwise escape comment. I believe my hypotheses are reasonable—they certainly seem to explain things that cannot be explained otherwise—but I cannot prove them, I cannot produce the quantity of annotated evidence which scholars rightly demand, and I therefore give this part of the book the modest description of an essay and present it as an Epilogue. Readers may nevertheless consider it worth while to remember that I have been living with this subject and practitioners of it for twenty years, and to give my swan-song a fair hearing.

My thoughts about humanitarian law have changed a good deal since I first began to study it. Impressed at the outset by the moral and religious seriousness of its underlying ideas; believing with the ICRC experts whose place in its practice was pre-eminent that its contemporary development was truly (in the UN-bred phrase they adopted) progressive; and assuming, with the enthusiasm of a novice, that whatever was moral and humanitarian must be above the political *mêlée*, I took the law and its practice as I found them, and when in the later 1970s I became a zealous helper with the Red Cross's 'dissemination' programme, I thought it satisfactory to tell awkward questioners that nothing was wrong with the law that a better understanding of it by all parties (military and civilian alike) and some more 'progressive development' would not put right.

The awkward questions that sometimes came from audience and class however began to pale beside the awkward questions I began to frame for myself. The *idea* of restraint in warfare, I have ever regarded as admirable; one of civilization's greater achievements. That the variety of religions, cultures, and ideologies which distinguishes our community of humankind is no insuperable barrier to transnational observance of such restraint, I continue to believe. But facts must be faced. The degree of observance at present remains lamentably low. Instances of neglect, disregard, carelessness, selectivity, ignorance, misunderstanding, contempt, bad faith, and cynical manipulation abound. A great gulf yawns between, on the one side, the host of legal specialists who write and (sometimes in company with counterparts from governments and armed forces) confer about IHL and, on the other, the amount of respect actually paid to IHL, the actual observance of it, in the armed conflicts which loom so large in the contemporary history of our world. How much of that gulf, I have asked myself, comes from failure in execution—familiar effects of 'the friction of war' and human frailty—and how much from flaws at the more fundamental level of design and construction? Does the structure expect more than well-intentioned subscribers can give and than ill-intentioned subscribers will give? Is so precious a balm safe in such a leaky vessel?

My few attempts to discuss these questions with some of the people who shared in the making of the vessel got hardly anywhere. Somewhat to my surprise, I discovered that my interdisciplinary commitments were really not at all helpful. Interdisciplinarity may seem well suited to the pursuit of inquiries spreading beyond academic departmental borders and the diffusion of their findings beyond academic circles, but it can evoke surprise, anxiety, and suspicion among scholars accustomed to the neatness and security of work within departmental confines. For example, I once gave a lecture on 'Ethics and International Relations' to the IR students at an Ivy League college, and at the end of it my genial host exclaimed something like: 'Wonderful! here's a realist who is also an idealist!' He was right, and not just in the way he intended, which presumably was to help his students place me in relation to the political-science categories familiar to them. I am a realist—in the commonplace sense of accepting the use of force (armed force, if need be) in international relations as in the protection of civil society, and of facing the fact that this can mean much unpleasantness; I am an idealist—in my belief that legitimate force need not turn nearly as often as it does into illegitimate violence, and that respect for the military must be balanced by rejection of militarism.

It might be thought that readiness to try to understand and accommodate both sides of this great debate (a debate which, moreover, parallels the law-of-war's classic tension between military necessity on one side, the imperatives of humanity on the other) would make my project bilaterally attractive, but the longer I have gone on with it, the more have I become aware that it can also make it bilaterally suspect. Dedicated partisans of this or that organization or school of thought have not necessarily esteemed me more highly for my seeming to be now on the one side, now on the other, and their suspicion therefore that anything revealed to me might end up being used against them. This has shown, not in discourtesy or rebuffs but typically in affable uncommunicativeness whenever my pursuit of subtext, hidden agenda, and second thoughts drove me to advance from 'What do you think?' to 'Yes, but what do you *really* think?', an advance demanded if I were to explain the otherwise somewhat inexplicable.[1]

The somewhat inexplicable is at its thickest in the conduct and achievements of the 1974–7 CDDH, at which (as has been amply shown above) the history of the law of war took such an extraordinary turn and the law itself became such a peculiar mixture of hard and soft. 'What do you *really* think?' has not got me very far in my attempt to make sense of it. Members of the four main classes of participants in that conference are for various reasons unreliable witnesses. I summarize thus their respective approaches:

1. Diplomats are used to putting a smooth face on rough things and in any case are professional experts in keeping quiet about their countries' hidden political agendas.

---

[1] Only twice in twenty years have I met any roughness of response. A veteran USAF general privately took against my summary of the sources of the 1944–5 area-bombings (in which he had played a leading part), and a gallant old British general blew up when I detected excessive and insular professional self-satisfaction in what he had written.

2. International lawyers, to the extent that they are serving in their own professional capacities and not as political hired hands, belong to an international guild whose bread and butter comes from expounding, and forever arguing about, what the law at any given moment actually is rather than what it ought to be or could have been.

3. Red Cross representatives are used to making the best of a bad job (one fairly senior man, when I asked him if he really believed a particularly dubious enactment would do any good, stoutly replied, 'We have to believe it!') and in any case are trained to be as diplomatic as the diplomats.

4. Real military men, however openly they may speak when closeted among their own kind or in a confidential *tête-à-tête*, are famous for keeping their own counsel when confronted by civilians in general, by politicians and writers in particular; and are as well able as any close professional community to present a common front when considerations of honour and loyalty, or even merely interest, powerfully move them to do so. By 'real military men', I must explain, no rudeness is meant towards any kind of officer; I choose the phrase simply to express the differences of attitude and perception there must be between the professional fighting kind of officer and the officer better characterized as a lawyer-in-uniform, to whom representation of the military interest at the conferences of the 1970s was by some States entrusted. The fact of a difference somewhat of this description became public and momentous in the case of the USA, and formed part of the explanation why, after some seeming military experts had said they could live with the Additional Protocols, the Pentagon after all advised against them.[2]

Whatever the thoughts of the participants about the way it was going, the CDDH would go on for as long as governments reckoned its continuation to be worth while and a signable final document to be attainable. The first, 1974 session, besides departing from precedent in the nakedness of its political pursuits and the grossness of its General Assembly-style conduct, must have seemed so fruitless as to make some Western delegations wonder whether any good would come out of it at all. The rush with which business was brought to a close in the fourth year was due to general weariness and agreement that enough was enough—not to mention the inabilities of their hosts to go on paying poor States' delegates' expenses *ad infinitum*. One hundred and nine States stuck it out to the end and all but (inimitably) Israel

---

[2] Again I follow W. Hays Parks (incidentally, a fighting man before he became an IHL expert) in his mammoth article, already several times referred to, in *Air Force Law Review*, 32 (1990), 1–225, esp. nn. 76–7, and 86–103.

found enough that was acceptable in the final document to enable them to sign it.[3]

The Additional Protocols were the best that could be produced in the circumstances, compromise texts containing something for everyone and nothing that could not be accepted subject to the usual public declarations and reservations (apart from whatever further unadmitted reservations, qualifications, and equivocations might lie beyond the horizon). As humanitarian instruments (the technical legal term for them), they are like that exemplary glass which is either half full or half empty, according to how you choose to regard it. Whether dedication to the humanitarian cause and appreciation of the good points excuse freedom of comment on the bad ones is a matter on which the committed practitioner may understandably hold a different opinion from the detached historian.

What in any case remains indisputable is that humanitarian multilateral treaties, however else they may be regarded, are political products. The motives that cause States to construct them and to engage to take them seriously are as usual mixed in measures varying from State to State and in line with individual States' perceptions of their interests and styles of politics.[4] Some States, inevitably, are more interested in one part of the law than another. The parts relating to prisoners of war for instance are of very much more acute concern to the USA than the parts relating to military occupation. Pursuit of special interests in multilateral treaty-making is nothing unusual. Total lack of interest however is very difficult to conceive of. It is impossible to think of any State to which the legal protection in wartime of *some* element(s) of its own armed forces or civilian population would not appear desirable. It is almost impossible to imagine that even a State governed by solipsistic ideology (e.g. Hoxha's Albania, Pol Pot's Kampuchea) could not recognize, beyond its own borders, limited categories of war-victims for whom legal protection is proper. From societies permeated by more universalist ideologies, sympathy may go out to the conven-

---

[3] 'One hundred and nine' comes from Schindler and Toman, 538. It comes near the start of an illuminating five-page tabulation of States and other bodies represented there, and which session they attended.

[4] Direct experience of war does not necessarily correlate with public agitation about law's relation to it. Discounting the stage-managed demonstration of public concern characteristic of single-party States, it appeared e.g. that pacific States like Norway and the Netherlands had bigger domestic humanitarian constituencies in the 1970s than the UK, whose armed forces have seen action somewhere or other in the world every year since 1945, while Sweden, whose armed forces have for more than a hundred years been no closer to danger than border-guarding and UN peace-keeping, looked as if it had the most active public opinion of all. Nor can promptness of ratification be taken to signify much: the first ten ratifications of AP1 came (in this order) from Ghana, Libya, El Salvador, Ecuador, Jordan, Botswana, Cyprus, Niger, Yugoslavia, and Tunisia.

tional categories of war-victims world-wide, sympathy such as is articulated and channelled above all by the Red Cross/Red Crescent movement. Individual, social, sub-, and non-governmental expressions of humanitarian commitment may often be disinterested and bona fide. Yet none the less they can make a mark on treaties only through the channels of govern-mental involvement and State interest, and this is where bonae fides become suspect. States' expressions of humanitarian concern are just as likely to be insincere as not, and it is not difficult to understand why.

This measure of insincerity comes into the process and the product at the stage where the single purposes of philanthropic private individuals and humanitarian NGOs (in this respect, the ICRC should be regarded as an NGO-plus) mix with the State interests and skills which alone open the gates to international legislation. The pure humanitarianism which I assume to be substantially present in the earlier stages becomes politicized and adulterated. No doubt some process of this sort is inevitable, and in so far as it is the price to be paid for effective implementation, it is a price the humanitarian well-wisher ought ungrudgingly to pay. But dedicated parties ought to be aware of what goes on. I only linger on it here because I do not think it is helpful to the humanitarian cause to talk, as some earnest spokesmen do, as if it doesn't happen.

There appear to be three ways in which this politicization is to be explained: (1) the ordinary workings of multilateral politics; (2) response to and manipulation of humanitarian public opinion; and (3) the peculiar politics of the 1974–7 CDDH.

Multilateral Politics

Considering what happened in course of the multilateral gatherings at which IHL underwent its major modern changes, one may wonder whether the accompanying adulteration was anything other than what must often happen on such occasions: 'idealists' have to accommodate to 'realists', and may end up as 'realists' themselves. Military experts and major-power diplomats who had never thought of themselves as idealists anyway, smugly observed an education of this sort taking place at the 1947–9 and 1971–7 conferences. No doubt this happened, but it did not mean that the humani-tarian substance emerged undamaged. To say with those military men and diplomats that what began as impractical idealism was turned into practi-cable realism is to imply the positive gain that the product, although admittedly simplified and coarsened, can at least be implemented. But that is where the difference comes. The so-called realistic product is no more sure to be implemented than the so-called idealistic project was. The gain held out as fair exchange is illusory. 'Realism' has in the event meant no more than that frowns at the *force majeure* of politics have turned into smiles.

Beyond that, one is bound to ask whether what happened to IHL as it went through those multilateral mills was any different from the common fate of every cause subjected to the same. Does not every species of representative politics, national and international alike, demand the same tributes of bargaining, compromise, and humbug? Indeed they do. The international gatherings which contrive the great revisions and updatings of IHL are in their compositions and workings no different from countless others engaged in similar legislative business. The behaviours and events which made the 1974–7 CDDH so strange and, to the unpolitically minded, distasteful came as no surprise to those familiar with what went on at United Nations assemblies; all that had happened was that a majority of States (plus their NLM protégés) were behaving not as if the matter in question was something special but as if it were something ordinary.

But that is where the difference comes. The matter in question *is* something special. It is not a new matter (new, that is, as an item on the international legislative agenda) like destruction of natural resources, environmental pollution, atomic energy, space, and Aids, but an ancient one; and it anciently became one because the question, whether men who couldn't avoid fighting one another could nevertheless minimize the damage done to one another, was such an extraordinary question that it could only be answered in religious terms. The history of the law of war began in the temple and the church. Restraint in the conduct of hostilities has always been most effective when grounded in religion and ethics; nothing else has the same power to move warriors to place the interests of other and enemy persons above their own. Enlargement, codification, and 'progressive development' of the law of war have brought benefits with them but, as was observed earlier on, also a clouding of the religious and ethical elements of the law and a weakening of the immediacy with which they speak to the human spirit. Multilateral politics bleached the great ideas of honour and chivalry out of its legal instruments along with 'the Supreme Being' (see Part II). Those ideas are still there but (*a*) in the less magnetic form of listed prohibited acts of perfidy and treachery and (*b*) in any case inconspicuous among textual thickets contrived principally, one is tempted to think, by lawyers for lawyers, with the guiding professional thought in mind that their highest purpose is to be argued about in court.[5]

Humanitarian Public Opinion

To humanitarian public opinion must be ascribed cheapening effects as well as good ones. Humanitarian sentiment—to be distinguished from deeper-based humanitarian *principle*—has become so universal and articulate that it is something governments cannot readily afford to ignore. Response to its pressures can move in either of two directions: inward or outward. The inward one is the more obvious but also the more demanding. A government sensitively responsive to public opinion may find it advisable to make changes in this or that part of its own national apparatus, to admit shortcomings and errors or at any rate to institute enquiries into whether there have been any. The outward response is easier and cheaper. Expressions of humanitarian and human-rights concern trip easily off the lips of popularity-minded statesmen and politicians, not to mention those influential persons, 'celebrities'. Criticisms of humanitarian and human-rights violations are standard stock-in-trade on the superficial side of foreign relations. They cost nothing, they sound serious, and they may be slightly effective. Most States appear to be sensitive to credible allegations of breaches of human rights and humanitarian law, at least to the extent that their usual and prompt response is to take the heat off by denying them and/or making counter-allegations.

It is not quite true to say that *no* State likes to be held up as a notorious violator of universally valid behavioural norms. Saddam Hussein's Iraq was unusual in showing no embarrassment when it comprehensively violated the entire span of them (plus novel assaults on the environment) for a few months in late 1990 and early 1991. The despot presumably reckoned that he would soon achieve a victory so terrific that criticisms could be shrugged off for ever. More usual are excuses and counter-attacks like China's insistence (in the awkward months after the Tiananmen Square massacre), first, that it hadn't happened, and second, that in any case it was no business of any other country; or like Khomeini's Iran through the 1980s, insisting that it cared just as much about human rights as any other country, but that its ideas of human rights were different (and of course superior). States more

---

[5] 'Chivalry' still explicitly has a prominent lodging in national military manuals e.g. the UK's *Law of War on Land* (1958), ch. 1, para. 2, and the USAF's *International Law: The Conduct of Armed Conflict and Air Operations* (1976), ch. 1, sec. 3. The US Navy and Marine Corps' *Commander's Handbook on the Law of Naval Operations* (1989), ch. 5, para. 2 says: 'Dishonorable (treacherous) means, dishonorable expedients, and dishonorable conduct during armed conflict are forbidden.'

steadily acculturated to the international community than China (uncommonly self-sufficient in values) and Iran (in its most Islamic revolutionary years) cannot do much other than deny, riposte, and perhaps try to avoid repetition.

Human rights law and IHL, although alike in the facility with which they lend themselves to use in the exchange of public anxieties, insults, and criticisms, are different in the respect that humanitarian law can be much the more arousing. Opportunities for its invocation are fewer, but when they come they are—especially if they involve POWs—reliably inflammatory. Breaches of human rights law happen so much and so regularly in some countries as almost to seem like facts of nature; and, moreover, they lie for the foreign critic tantalizingly beyond the sovereignty divide, except on the occasions when liberal-principled governments experiment with making human rights a consideration in foreign policy. Breaches of IHL, besides being publicized less often, in their most stirring instances affect the critic's own kith and kin, and in these post-Nuremberg years have carried with them the exciting suggestion that they might be punishable. (Witness quite recently the rash talk, led by the then British prime minister Margaret Thatcher, about 'bringing Saddam Hussein to trial' during and just after the Gulf War.)

From the contemporary public's readiness to respond to humanitarian stimuli and to undergo the bombardment of charges and countercharges that accompanies it, mixed consequences follow for IHL. One must be beneficial to its cause. It can hardly be doubted that more people, in more countries, now know something about the law of war than ever before, and to some extent share serious concerns about it too, i.e. do not just indulge in instant responses to its polemical and propaganda promptings. Failures to understand its basic points, let alone its nuances, during the Gulf War marred some of even the highest-quality British media reportage and commentary. On the other hand, some of the staff of the same newspapers and programmes produced very well-informed work, to which were sometimes added bought-in contributions from academic experts. Those experts moreover were not only from faculties of law and political science. Such was the public—even, popular—interest in measuring the morality of the war that (at any rate in the UK and the USA) faculties of philosophy and divinity were also called upon to help evaluate it by just-war and cognate criteria.

This serious sort of 'Western' public interest has been growing by fits and starts since the late 1950s and early 1960s when, according to my sense of it, the world outside France came to share the ethico-legal concerns which the Algerian War had already aroused in France itself, and concerns about what was happening in Vietnam began to stir in the USA. It was the Vietnam War and its argumentative aftermath to which is principally due the familiarization with the law and ethics of war of so large a part of the populations of the USA and the countries culturally allied to it, along with which inevitably came politicians' awareness of the propaganda and PR uses of law-founded arguments and accusations. The USA's backward-looking military intervention in Grenada in 1983 was unhappily code-named 'Urgent Fury', but its 1989 intervention in Panama bore the prudent and diplomatic title of 'Just Cause'. When it came to the Gulf War against the aggressiveness of Iraq, unprecedented pains were taken, first of all in the preparatory stages to explain the legitimacy of applying UN-authorized force against Iraq, and then, when the fighting resumed with a vengeance in early 1991, to justify in legal terms what was being done. There appears to be no room for doubt but that Western publics at any rate (I know so little about others that I say nothing of them) have become knowledgeable enough about IHL, and impressed enough with a sense of its importance, to impress upon their governments the need for care in presenting to the world the legal justifications of their goings to war and their conduct of military operations.

So far, so good. Nothing unserious about the revival of just-war debate and bringing the democratic principle of executive accountability to bear upon even the weightiest items of foreign relations! But this popularization of the IHL idea has less attractive correlations. Not many States know accountability of that high order, and even governments of those that do can find coarser uses for humanitarian law. I return to those propaganda and PR uses mentioned above. So common nowadays is casual acquaint-anceship with prominent patches of IHL that all States and warring parties can rely on sympathetic responses to charges that their opponents are breaking the law. So important to belligerents have become the sympathy and support of third parties that a propaganda and PR battle goes on all the time alongside the battle of bullets and bombers. Readers whose instant reaction is to consider that statement extravagant are invited to reflect on the role of PR in shaping perceptions *and in conditioning outcomes* of the armed conflicts in Algeria, Vietnam, Nigeria, the Palestinian territories occupied by Israel, Afghanistan, and Nicaragua to name a prominent few. In these cases, PR was—and in respect of the occupied Palestinian territories conspicuously still is—war carried on by other means. Allegations and stories of human rights abuses and IHL breaches are among the weapons most used in that parallel battle for the hearts and minds of onlookers and, through them, the attitudes of their governments. Truthfulness matters less than effect. Lies may be corrected after the event, but for each person who registers the correction, how many are there who don't?[6]

Such are among the *un*attractive consequences of contemporary responsiveness to IHL issues, to be borne in mind along with the more attractive ones. What at one end of the spectrum becomes an editorial in the *New York Times* becomes at the other a headline in the *Sun*. Behind the ambulance comes the garbage-truck. The head of humanitarian steam, so easily fomented, can work bad engines as well as good. The immemorial wartime descant of 'atrocity stories' has been enriched by a new vein of material tagged as breaches of IHL. No atrocity stories can have come more copiously from the wars of the twentieth century than those of the bombing or shelling of places marked with the Red Cross, and of attacks on 'civilians'. By such stories, publics are manipulated in the old familiar way; what seems to me new is that smatterings of IHL knowledge open new opportunities for emotionally sensitive publics to let themselves be manipulated.

One aspect of this manipulation has a sinister quality that demands special notice. The appearance of respect for IHL having become a valuable asset in the PR battle for hearts and minds, States aim to score in the field of reputation by so managing their relations with the ICRC as to make it appear that their observance of IHL is better than it actually is. The ICRC, for its part, is of course well aware that attempts are made to use it in this way. One cannot doubt that it does what it can to prevent it, but even elementary knowledge of the conditions in which the ICRC has to operate shows how very difficult it is to prevent.

The ICRC starts from a morally advantageous position. Not many States are bold enough to be seen to keep the ICRC out when there is a prima-facie case for its being allowed in. But not many States are virtuous and clean-handed enough to give the ICRC *carte blanche* to go wherever it wishes and to be admitted on demand to whatever institution, to visit whomsoever it pleases. Because of the ICRC's understandable secrecy about its relations with governments, the true facts of its episodic relations with them are impossible to establish. What however is believed to happen whenever outbreaks of armed conflict or civil disturbance authorize the ICRC confidently to ask to be allowed to fulfil its mandate or modestly to 'offer its services', is that a bargaining process begins. States, unless they are extraordinarily virtuous, will have a double aim. On the one hand they will wish

---

[6] One-party States and personal despotisms have of course led the way in the use of misinformation and 'disinformation', as media fibs are now often known, but 'free States', which ought to know better, can do it too.

to discover, with how little access to prisons and prisoners (the ICRC's biggest concern) the ICRC can be fobbed off. On the other hand—given the power of public opinion and the seriousness of the PR war—they will probably wish to appear desirous to honour their IHL obligations and will therefore not wish to push or press the ICRC too far. Beyond a certain extreme point, it will not let them go.

Even the patience of the ICRC can be exhausted. When unscrupulous States publish selectively favourable quotations from its confidential reports, the ICRC responds with publications of complete texts. In the direst cases it can (unless it is thrown out first!) withdraw. It will then have the nice question to decide, whether or not to make public the grounds for its withdrawal. It may find that the threat of withdrawal carries with it enough potential embarrassment to cause a disagreeable government to change its policy. But it is in the nature of things that its relations with States can rarely be easy; plenty of evidence appeared in the pages above to show why. When relations with a State actually are easy, it is likely to be because of a State's calculation that advantage can come of it. That the ICRC may at the same time calculate that some at least of its humanitarian mission will have been fulfilled does not alter the fact that very unsavoury States can thus appear to be given certificates of moral health. Those disposed to be critical of the ICRC dislike this happening, but it really is not easy to see how the ICRC can act otherwise. The true stories of each episode of its difficult diplomacy can never be told. States cannot tell it, unless—a rare case!—they have no humanitarian shortcomings to conceal; the ICRC will not tell it, because for an NGO—even such an exceptional one as this—to expose a State's shortcomings is to ensure that its doors will never be opened again.

The CDDH, 1974–1977

The final area in which a certain insincerity has latterly infiltrated IHL is more closely defined than the two so far displayed. Those were of a general character, belonging to the nature of politics itself (the politics in which the making and implementation of IHL is embedded) and to the very history of the age; in bold mood, I might even call it 'the Zeitgeist'. This third area is located rather specifically in the mid-1970s, in the nature and proceedings of the 1974–7 CDDH to which, along with the two APs that issued from it, so much reference has already been made.

Debate about the merits of the APs continues at the time of writing. Inevitably the debate focuses upon the texts: exactly what they say and how they are to be interpreted. Since parts of the texts are found by some of the most significant parties to be in varying degrees imperfect, obscure, or objectionable, their interpretation is a matter of enormous importance. Interpretation means going in the first place to what international law experts call 'the negotiating history' and to the authoritative commentaries which are themselves based to a large extent upon it. The two great commentaries are respectively of 746 and 1625 pages in length. The authoritative negotiating history is contained in the seventeen volumes of *Official Reports*; reports, that is, of the business actually done there and of that proportion of the debates and discussions which was to go on public record.

To mention no more than these three front-line guides to interpretation is sufficiently to indicate that a great deal of interpretation stands to be done. This need surprise no one who understands the variety of purposes being pursued at the conference and the complexity of the issues caught up in their cross-currents. The contrast between this four-year (on and off) conference in the mid-1970s and the four-month one in 1949 with which, on account of its professed object, it is naturally compared, could hardly be greater.[7]

The difference between 1949 and 1974–7 is not, as some anguished complainants about the latter alleged, that humanitarian legislation had become politicized. Indeed the proceedings were in some ways highly political but, as Georges Abi-Saab was quick to point out in their explanation, that was nothing new. The making of international law of war always had been political. The States which were in a position to make it made it to suit primarily their own convenience. Until the 1940s, this meant exclusively Western convenience, and in 1949, as has already been shown, hardly meant anything beyond. The law's political dimension had only not been more commented on because States and parties whose convenience it did *not* suit lacked a forum in which to make the point. By the 1960s however their situation had changed. An increasing number of Third World forums became available to them. Above all there was the UN. As was shown in Part III, a new look at IHL became an additional item on the agenda which the Third World, the new States, and their sympathizers were promoting throughout the UN's organizational empire. What from one angle could be presented as 'the reaffirmation and development of IHL', from another angle had more attractiveness as a project to de-Westernize the law of war.

The 1974–7 CDDH then was, to an extent probably greater than is usual in multilateral conferences, a political event as well as a legal and humani-

---

[7] I have it on good authority that some Swiss government and ICRC dignitaries were quite taken aback when they found the proceedings so unlike what their memories of 1949 and their perception of IHL as an unideological subject had prepared them for.

tarian one. Every State which was a party to the Geneva Conventions was invited to the conference, besides some non-State parties which were not. The ICRC, whose recent endeavours to operate in Vietnam and Nigeria had brought it under fire from the Second and Third Worlds for being snobby, bourgeois, and white, found it highly desirable to meet the demand that Third World States should be brought into the debate and that the conference should generate texts in the making of which every political and racial region of the world could be said to have had a hand.

That Third World interests should be satisfied was just as important as that IHL itself should be improved. A tendency therefore appeared in those members of the conference who represented Third World States and States sympathetic to them, to equate the Third World demands with legal improvements. Opinions within the Western bloc as to whether appeasement of the Third World was so desirable varied, of course, in the wake of their electoral politics, but Western States by that time were accustomed to being on the minority side in General Assembly debates on North–South issues, and to facing therefore the choice, when it came to voting, of either standing out in an awkward minority or of going along with the irresistible majority on terms moulded to be as comprehensive as possible. 'Consensus' being the great moulding machine which enabled many divisive debates in the UN to achieve this happy end of *nem. con.* agreement, it accordingly and unsurprisingly now became indispensable to the conduct of the CDDH.

Procedure by way of consensus has much to be said in its favour. Issues debated within communities are not always so clear-cut that simple Yes or No votes are satisfactory ways of deciding them, nor do they always have to be settled with that degree of speed which a majority decision alone can make possible. Communities cherishing ideas of right and of rights moreover cannot safely give absolute power to majorities, not even to the most democratic of majorities. It is no wonder that the virtues of consensus were increasingly discovered within the UN, whose members were forever touchy about their sovereign rights, whose permanent majority (from the 1960s) of developing States could get nowhere by divisive voting against its minority of highly developed ones, and where the gradual implementation of global agreements like GATT depended on devolution and discretion. By the 1970s, consensus was to members of the UN so familiar a way of getting over and around difficulties—one might colloquially describe it as 'keeping the show on the road'—that its use on many occasions within the CDDH seemed a natural and good thing. Michel Veuthey, for example, a high official of the ICRC, gives it as his (personal) judgment that 'Almost all the Articles of Protocol I were adopted by consensus; even on those few occasions when consensus was lacking, the number of negative votes was so often so small that the rules of this first Protocol reflect universal *opinio juris*, rules of positive law governing all international armed conflicts.'[8]

Without claiming as much for the results as that, and taking (as was proper to his position) a more national viewpoint, the head of the US delegation wrote in the conclusions to his official report that the USA and other major military powers would not have got the results they most wanted had the Conference not 'worked by a modified form of consensus', 'quasi-consensus procedure', and all the making of compromises and bargains that went with it, although consensus could on occasion, so he recalled a few years later, be so close to genuine unanimity as to be defined as 'everybody except the Romanians'.[9]

Not all definitions of consensus in 1974-7 were as benign as those of Ambassador Aldrich. Where he saw reasonable compromises, others saw fudge and flannel. Opponents of AP2, recorded the political scientist David Forsythe, insisted that its adoption by consensus 'did not represent a consensus on the substantive desire to develop the law, but rather was only a consensus on the procedural desire not to block what *others* might accept'.[10] Eyeing that same use of the procedure, the jurist Luigi Condorelli expressed himself in these strong terms: 'the practice of seeking consensus, so frequently followed in all international milieus, now and then [as in this instance] reveals its true aspect as the enemy of international legal development.'[11] It is true that other international law authorities take a more optimistic view of the place of consensus in legal development. Rosalyn Higgins for example writes of it as subsuming 'consent' and 'custom' and, although 'often tacit and sometimes unenthusiastic', as constituting in fact the very 'basis of international law'.[12] The history of the making of AP2 especially seems expressly designed to disappoint optimism such as hers. What sort of basis for sound development can an instrument be, whose text was hastily emasculated in order to be acceptable by consensus in the last days of an over-long conference, especially when its subject is the very part

[8] My translation from page xx of the 'Postface' to the 2nd edn. (1983) of his celebrated 1976 book, *Guérilla et Droit Humanitaire* (Geneva).

[9] *Report of the United States Delegation [to the CDDH]* ('the Aldrich Report'), 4th session, p. 29; 'Panel on the Additional Protocols', 18 Apr. 1980, in *PASIL* 74 (1980), 191-212 at 207.

[10] 'Legal Management of Internal War: The 1977 Protocol on Non-International Armed Conflicts', in *AmJIL* 72 (1978), 171-95 at 282.

[11] In A. Cassese (ed.), *The New Humanitarian Law of Armed Conflicts* (Naples, 1979-80), 390.

[12] Her contribution to W. M. Reisman and B. H. Weston (eds.), *Towards World Order and Human Dignity* (New York, 1976), 79-94 at 87.

of humanitarian law, the part to do with internal armed conflicts, which most States are most reluctant to observe?

Prevalence of consensus was not the only feature of the 1974–7 proceedings to make one wonder about the extent to which States were (and are, in the event that they have ratified their signatures) serious-minded about the Protocols that issued from them. Acceptance of the texts was made conditional, by many States, on the attachment of specific 'reservations', 'declarations', and 'interpretative statements', over and above such qualifications and expressions of doubt as were voiced in the debates, and such as were only voiced out of them or subsequently. (It would be interesting to know whether the quantity of these public reservations etc. was greater than is usual on comparable occasions— if there are comparable occasions.) Not even the protagonists of the Protocols have denied that the meanings of some crucial Articles in them—but especially in AP1—are ambiguous and subject to differing interpretations.[13]

This would matter less if the Protocols and the Geneva Conventions to which they are additional were 'soft' law of the declaratory standard-setting sort in which the UN has been so productive. But parts of IHL are, and are meant to be, 'hard'! In particular there are those Articles in the GCs, reaffirmed and further hardened in AP1, defining what 'grave breaches' of the law shall be considered criminal and how they shall be brought to justice. It might appear to be an odd reaffirmation and development of IHL which cannot withhold from States a measure of subjective judgment in the definition of the crimes for which they are empowered to bring alleged war-criminals to trial, conviction, and punishment. Whether or not States will avail themselves of that entitlement is another matter. Prudence and self-interest may whisper to them that it would be very unwise; the satisfaction of publicly pronouncing enemy airmen guilty of war crimes, for example, might not be thought worth the risk of having one's capital city bombed to bits. And the ubiquitous three Rs—reciprocity, reprisal, retaliation—will affect their thinking in this context as in all others: 'you bring my men into court, I'll bring yours'. But this way out of the problem is no more attractive than the way in. There still seems to be something wrong with a body of law, the public defects of which can only be corrected by private diplomacy and threats.

---

[13] George Aldrich, the sturdiest defender of his delegation's performance at the CDDH and the most persuasive American proponent of ratification, maintains that this was inevitable and would be, in practice, insignificant. See esp. his 'Prospects for US Ratification of AP1', in *AmJIL* 85 (1991), 1–19 at 17–18.

To conclude with a return from the particular to the general, and a confession of faith: I care too much for the observance of restraint in warfare to take pleasure in pointing out the weaknesses of contemporary IHL and the correlative insincerities of the States (and, nowadays, non-State entities) which profess to respect it. But a scholar in pursuit of truth has to follow it even along mean streets, and I do believe that the humanitarian cause is ill served by looking (as is the way with writers committed to 'selling the product') only on the bright side. There is a dark side too, and by my reckoning it is getting darker. IHL has become overinflated. This has happened at the same time as it has become underimplemented, and there may be a connection between the two things. More is not always and necessarily better.[14] The Geneva Conventions are perhaps bulkier than ideally they ought to be; some of the regulatory detail in the POW and Civilians Conventions would look better in appendices. The first Additional Protocol is bulkier and messier than it ought to be; it is an overstuffed miscellany in which golden items of crucial and permanent value are mixed with items merely trivial and transitory, and many items of both qualities are overdressed. No wonder the past few years have witnessed so many proposals for distilled and concentrated versions of the main points of humanitarian law, from which persons with neither legal expertise nor time on their hands (which, after all, means most of humankind) could get the gist of it in a few minutes!

Reference to those summaries and digests, whenever it is made by IHL experts or in legal *milieux*, is commonly accompanied by reminders that, no matter what their substantive excellence and practical utility, they are not substitutes for the international legal instruments and cannot have the same force of law as them. Without lingering on the question whether they must not have the same legal authority as the customary law whose principles they are largely engaged in reproducing, I observe that the force of IHL is easily overrated and misunderstood. The ways in which it actually can be and sometimes is enforced, i.e. made effective in the field, are not those specified in the texts. The ways of the texts are not inviting. I have already displayed the continuing debility of the Protecting-Power system, historically the basic means of bringing the law into effect. Its revivification is doubtless much to be desired. Developments relative to former Yugoslavia

---

[14] Of course there are areas in which the law cannot avoid elaboration, e.g. the complication brought by science and technology to the means of killing people has to be matched by complication in the means of saving lives; see e.g. what was said in Part II about the attempt to identify and to protect Red Cross ships and aircraft among the instant hazards of the electronic battlefield.

will show whether the threat of judicial proceedings will be as empty in the future as it has been in the past; even if some judicial proceedings do take place, the awkward question will remain to be settled, whether those proceedings will be perceived as morally satisfactory. Trials of (ex-)enemy persons for 'grave breaches' or other war crimes are unknown outside the unique category created by the Second World War. On the few occasions when a country's own nationals have been brought to trial for those kinds of offences, they have been tried for offences against national rather than, explicitly, international law. Actions against foreigners for gross breaches of international human rights law have begun to take place but are not yet proven to be able to overcome national political obstacles. An international criminal court tough and impregnable enough to punish every national breach of IHL has been talked about for decades but remains an idealist's chimera. The ICRC, as has repeatedly been mentioned, succeeds in securing a good deal of humanitarian observance from time to time and place to place, but much of that is 'extralegal', *ad hoc*, and informal. States and other warring parties like the FMLN and PLO do some of what the ICRC requests or suggests or begs, not because they are obliged to do so (in the sense that they will surely be punished if they don't) but because they choose to do what is perceived to be prudent, respectable, useful, and even, in circles where it matters to them, popular.

The most effective actual working engine of IHL observance, far from being established or even mentioned in the Geneva Conventions and their Additional Protocols, works in fact in apparent defiance of them. Reciprocity is its name, and it has uses both negative and positive. The negative uses are to stop bad things happening. Just as no State at war can afford to let an enemy unlawfully gain advantages or inflict damages which could be stopped by response in kind, so will a State only forbear from using unlawful means to gain advantages and inflict damages if it knows the other side can and will do the same, or worse, back to them. But reciprocity has a more positive aspect too. Good deeds by one side are likely to be reciprocated by the other. In such matters as releases and exchanges of prisoners, they very often are, and the ICRC pre-eminently is accustomed to be their benevolent godfather and go-between. What IHL expects States to do, and what they would do if they voluntarily obeyed the law, will usually only get done if some experienced neutral body like the ICRC succeeds in assuring each side that the other won't cheat. Given the suspicions which each side will usually entertain about the other—with anarchic situations like Lebanon's, it would be truer to say, all the others—arrangements of mutual advantage are almost impossible to set up unless a reliable intermediary is willing to go to the (probably enormous) trouble of making them. But whether or not such truth-telling and fair-play-seeing help is at hand to smooth the way, reciprocity has to be respected. Canada's leading IHL expert sums it up thus: 'The practical effectiveness of the law of war in a particular conflict is conditional upon, among other factors, a crude reciprocity and a rough equivalence of benefits.'[15]

The prospects for IHL, then, are by no means wholly dark. Warring parties which positively wish to observe it can do so, with credit and advantage to themselves and other members of their society; they will find it observable in almost all circumstances, and there are ready-made means of resolving disputes about alleged violations. Warring parties which feel no positive attraction to IHL may yet observe much of it for reasons of self-interest: the head is quite capable of valuing an up-to-date body of rules of conflict-behaviour, even if the heart is not committed. The ICRC and such other transnational organizations as choose to emulate its ideals of neutral and impartial humanitarian service will offer their services, perform such good works as lie within their means, and may sometimes penetrate to areas of wartime suffering which more partisan organizations cannot reach. And yet the surrounding darkness persists. Some warring parties pay no serious attention to IHL, perhaps because they know little about it or find much of it incomprehensible, perhaps because they consider it alien and frustrating. It is evident that warring parties can know plenty about it and yet regard it chiefly as an intrusive institution, to be manipulated to gain advantages and to win points.

Readers who have accompanied me thus far will of course understand why I have referred merely to 'warring parties'. The stately terminology of international law and international relations scarcely matches the war scene today: a disorderly range of warring parties from secure and proper States at one end to a confusion of 'war-lords', national, ethnic, and religious groups, terrorists, and criminals at the other; all of them, armed to the teeth.

It is my submission that IHL unfortunately has little to offer towards lightening the darker side of the scene. Over there, its ethical principles cannot be relied on to moderate ill-feelings. Its prudential content is not self-evidently persuasive. Its supposed means of enforcement are illusory. Persons who care for IHL must therefore recognize that care for it on its own is not enough; they must care no less for other and neighbouring branches of international standards and security.

---

[15] Fenrick in the *Kalshoven Festschrift* at 434. It would be interesting to know Col. Fenrick's estimation of those 'other factors'. The biggest of them, to my mind, would be the PR and propaganda factor to which I have referred so often.

The great ethical offering of IHL has always been, and still is, that it makes war less terrible than war would be without it. A danger seems to me to have arisen that because this offer is so attractive and because there is by now so much IHL, we who believe in it or want to believe in it have insufficiently noted its limitations and have neglected to make enough of the (more demanding) institutions which from other directions approach the same end: the avoidance of war and, if that is impossible, the moderation of its conduct. Those parts of international and, especially, regional law and organization must be strengthened which can prevent armed conflicts happening in the first place. Their gentler way is the strong-minded control of the traffics and attitudes which make armed conflict likelier, and prompt pro-action towards potentially peace-breaking conflicts (something for which the last two Secretaries-General of the UN have realistically pleaded). Their tougher way is the rapid and irresistible uses of power to stop self-centredly unreasonable warring parties in their tracks. It is no good for those of us who want the results that IHL promises to shrink from the alternative means of achieving them. If the failure to moderate war marks the vanishing-point of IHL, the persistence of immoderate war could mark the vanishing-point of civilization.

Suggestions for Further Reading

English-language books (and one small French one) for readers who wish to read around the subject. Those who wish to go further into its expressly legal aspects will obtain excellent guidance from the bibliography appended to Roberts and Guelff's easily obtainable book of documents.

Bailey, Sydney D., *War and Conscience in the Nuclear Age* (London, 1987). Succinct survey of and commentary on international legislation, arms control, and disarmament as well as IHL, with the UN very much to the fore.

Best, Geoffrey, *Humanity in Warfare: The Modern History of the International Law of Armed Conflicts* (London, revd edn., 1983). Pioneer work which remains useful chiefly for its wealth of historical examples from mid-eighteenth century to the end of the Second World War.

Bull, Hedley, *The Anarchical Society. A Study of Order in World Politics* (London, 1977). A famous and influential book, the second of whose three main sections examines why international law is made and what are the conditions of its efficacy.

Cassese, Antonio, *International Law in a Divided World* (English trans., Oxford, 1986). Includes a lively chapter on 'international legal regulation of armed conflict' as one of the 'crucial issues of today'.

Clark, Ian, *Waging War: A Philosophical Introduction* (Oxford, 1988). An excellent brief analysis of the war phenomenon; from which all else proceeds.

Donelan, Michael, *Elements of International Political Theory* (Oxford, 1990). Thoughtful introduction to main lines of thought about the relations to one another of States in peace and war, with the ethics and laws of the latter often in view.

Draper, G. I. A. D., *The Red Cross Conventions* (London, 1958). Strictly speaking, one of the technical works not supposed to be included, but it is a surprisingly readable exegesis and wise commentary by the UK's leading professional expert of the post-war period.

Falk, Richard, Kolko, G., and Lifton, R. J., *Crimes of War* (New York, 1971). Handy source-book of documents on principles and laws, together with contemporary material on the US involvement in Vietnam.

Forsythe, David, *Humanitarian Politics: the International Committee of the Red Cross* (Baltimore, Md., 1977). Unique study of how the ICRC actually works within the international community, providing much illustrative matter on the years since 1945.

Howard, Michael, *Restraints on War: Studies in the Limitation of Armed Conflict* (Oxford, 1979); also *War and the Liberal Conscience* (London 1978 and a revd edn., New Brunswick, NJ, 1986). *Restraints* gave IHL one of its earliest British exposures to the non-specialist public. The other book is a searching scrutiny of the ills proceeding from muddle-headedness about the place of armed force in the relations of States.

Howard, Michael, Andreopoulos, George J., and Shulman, Mark R. (eds), *The Laws of War: Constraints on Warfare in the Western World* (New Haven and London, 1994). Twelve good essays, from ancient Greece to national liberation movements, plus useful suggestions for further reading.

Human Rights Watch, *Landmines: A Deadly Legacy* (New York, 1993). Fills in much about this most notorious scourge that was too inconclusively dealt with in the pages above.

Johnson, James Turner, *Ideology, Reason and the Limitation of War. Religious and Secular Concepts, 1200–1740* (Princeton, NJ, 1975). Also *Just War Tradition and the Restraint of War: A Moral and Historical Inquiry* (Princeton, NJ, 1981). Good books about the ethical aspects of IHL by a historically minded specialist in religious studies.

Kalshoven, Frits, *Arms, Armaments and International Law*, in The Hague Academy 'Recueil des Cours' series, vol. 191 (1985-II); also *Constraints on the Waging of War* (ICRC, Geneva, 1987). From the non-specialist point of view, Kalshoven is the most helpful of the IHL experts; what he writes is as intelligible to the ordinary reader as it is professionally impeccable. A pity therefore that both books must be, for most enquirers, rather difficult to locate.

Karsten, Peter, *Law, Soldiers and Combat* (Westport, Conn., 1978). Readable enquiry by a historian into the factors making for and against observance of IHL, based mainly on Vietnam experiences.

Keegan, John, *A History of Warfare* (London, 1993). Because this excellent book considers war as a total cultural, not a merely military phenomenon, it naturally includes a good deal about the religious and ethical principles which peoples have brought to their warmaking through the ages, and to the laws and customs consequent upon them.

Miller, Richard I. (ed.), *The Law of War* (Lexington, Mass., 1975). Unusual book, unprecedented in its investigation of how the observance of IHL is conditioned by national and regional cultures; limited however to those of the USA's antagonists in the Cold War.

O'Brien, William V., *The Conduct of Just and Limited War* (New York, 1981). Remarkable systematic application of legal criteria to contemporary wars, by conservative Catholic expert.

O'Connell, Daniel, *The Influence of Law on Sea Power* (Manchester, 1975). Uniquely informative, by an eminent international law professor who was also a naval officer.

Palwankar, Umesh (ed.), *Symposium on Humanitarian Action and Peace-Keeping Operations* (Geneva, ICRC, 1994). Usefully complements Roberts's 1995 article on problems of implementation.

Paskins, Barrie, and Dockrill, Michael, *The Ethics of War* (London, 1979). Unusual combined operation by a moral philosopher and a modern historian; the examples they use and the questions they debate are not explicitly in legal terms but IHL implications are clear enough.

Piccigallo, Philip R., *The Japanese on Trial. Allied War Crimes Operations in the East, 1945–1951* (Austin, Tex., 1979). Fair-minded, brisk survey of the whole field, not just (as is the case with most relevant books) the Tokyo IMT.

Roberts, Adam, and Guelff, Richard (eds.), *Documents on the Laws of War* (2nd edn., Oxford, 1989). Indispensable for the documents (and the bibliography, mentioned above) but valuable also in its provision of terse exegesis of the texts and critical commentary on them.

Roberts, Adam, 'The Laws of War: Problems of Implementation in Contemporary Conflicts'. Exceptionally useful, not least for what it says about trials for war crimes and crimes against humanity, with regard to which much has happened since this book first went to press. It is available in two places: Vol. 1, pp. 13–82 of *Law in Humanitarian Crises*, a two-volume collection published by the European Commission in Luxembourg in 1995; and *Duke Journal of Comparative and International Law* (Durham, NC) Vol. 6, No. 1, Fall 1995, pp. 11–78.

Taylor, Telford, *The Anatomy of the Nuremberg Trials* (New York and London, 1993). The best heavyweight book about the IMT and what happened at it, and a useful introduction to the legal issues. Probably the best of the more popular books is *Nuremberg* by Airey Neave (London, 1978) who, like Taylor, had participated in the great event.

Torrelli, Maurice, *Le droit international humanitaire* (Paris, 1985; no. 2211 in the Presses Universitaires de France series, 'Que sais-je?'). A fine little expository survey for the general reader, in plain French, by a professor of law at the University of Nice.

Walzer, Michael, *Just and Unjust Wars. A Moral Argument with Historical Illustrations* (New York, 2nd edn., 1992). Justly famous book (1st edn., 1978) by a moral philosopher, testing the ethical quality of IHL in a well-studied variety of tough war situations from ancient Athens to the present.

Index

Printed in the United Kingdom
by Lightning Source UK Ltd.
102070UKS00001B/14